FIRST CANADIAN EDITION

# Strategic Management

## Competitiveness and Globalization

# CONCEPTS

**Michael A. Hitt**
Arizona State University

**R. Duane Ireland**
University of Richmond

**Robert E. Hoskisson**
The University of Oklahoma

**W. Glenn Rowe**
The University of Western Ontario

**Jerry P. Sheppard**
Simon Fraser University

**NELSON**

★

TM

**THOMSON LEARNING**

Australia • Canada • Mexico • Singapore • Spain • United Kingdom • United States

**NELSON**

™

**THOMSON LEARNING**

**Strategic Management:**
**Competitiveness and Globalization—Concepts**
**First Canadian Edition**

by Michael A. Hitt, R. Duane Ireland,
Robert E. Hoskisson, W. Glenn Rowe, and
Jerry P. Sheppard

**Editorial Director and Publisher:**
Evelyn Veitch

**Acquisitions Editor:**
Edward Ikeda

**Marketing Manager:**
Anthony Rezek

**Senior Project Editor:**
Karina Ten Veldhuis

**Managing Production Editor:**
Susan Calvert

**Production Coordinator:**
Hedy Sellers

**Copy Editor/Proofreader:**
Karen Rolfe

**Art Director:**
Angela Cluer

**Interior Design:**
Katherine Strain

**Cover Design:**
Fizzz Design

**Senior Composition Analyst:**
Tammy Gay

**Indexer:**
Andrew Little

**Printer:**
Transcontinental Printing Inc.

**National Library of Canada
Cataloguing in Publication Data**

Main entry under title:

Strategic management:
competitiveness and globalization:
concepts

1st Canadian ed.
Includes bibliographical references
and index.
ISBN 0-17-616864-8

1. Strategic planning. 2. Industrial
management. I. Hitt, Michael A.

HD30.28.S728 2001      658.4'012
C2001-902776-1

Michael A. Hitt—
To Frankie. I love you. We share everything.

R. Duane Ireland—
To my wife Mary Ann and our children, Rebecca and Scott. I love each of you deeply and look forward to the excitement and challenges of our new journeys. Truly, these are our Glory Days – the best of our lives.

Robert E. Hoskisson—
To my father, Claude W. Hoskisson, who taught me to be honest and dedicated in my work, and in memory of my mother, Carol B. Hoskisson, who provided my life with a foundation of love.

W. Glenn Rowe—
To Fay and Gillian. I love you both very deeply. Thank you for being who you are and for the support you both give me.

Jerry P. Sheppard—
To my family: I love you. To Marnie, my bright light in this cloudy place; I could not have done this without your time, loving support and drive. To Jesse and Benjamin, yes, we can do that now. To my parents, Rocky and Rose, whose loving encouragement helped me along the way.

# CONTENTS IN BRIEF

# TABLE OF CONTENTS

## PART TWO

## CHAPTER 5

## CHAPTER 10
## Cooperative Strategy . . . . . . . . . . . . . . . . . . . . . . . . . . . . . . . . .360

## PART THREE

### CHAPTER 11

## CHAPTER 13

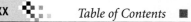

# ABOUT THIS BOOK

The First Canadian Edition of *Strategic Management: Competitiveness and Globalization* continues the tradition from previous U.S. editions of integrating cutting edge research with an engaging writing style. As such, the many features and careful revisions enhance the value of this market-leading textbook.

## FEATURES

- Chapter Opening Cases and Strategic Focus segments feature Canadian organizations.
- Many Canadian company-specific examples are integrated with each chapter's topic.
- A chapter on performance is included—the only undergraduate strategy textbook with this feature.
- Substantial emphasis on the use of the Internet and e-commerce is integrated throughout the book.
- Coverage of strategic issues in the 21st-century competitive landscape, including a strong emphasis on the competition created through e-commerce ventures and startups.
- Global coverage with more emphasis on the international context.
- Current research is integrated throughout the chapters' conceptual presentations.
- Review Questions, Discussion Questions, and Ethics Questions at the end of each chapter include issues suggested by the e-commerce phenomenon.
- Internet Exercises at the end of each chapter encourage readers to use the Internet as an information source and problem-solving tool.
- An updated and expanded case analysis guide.

These new features provide a unique competitive advantage to this book. With 14 new Opening Cases and 41 new Strategic Focus segments, we offer 55 major case examples in the chapters. In addition, more than 75 percent of the shorter examples used throughout each chapter are completely new. Many of these examples are Canadian.

This First Canadian Edition also emphasizes a global advantage with comprehensive coverage of international concepts and issues. In addition to comprehensive coverage of international strategies in Chapter 9, references to and discussions of the international context and issues are included in every chapter. The Opening Cases, Strategic Focus segments, and individual examples in each chapter cover numerous global issues and markets.

Importantly, this First Canadian Edition solidifies a research advantage for our book. For example, each chapter has more than 100 references. Drawn from the business literature and academic research, these materials are used to present current and accurate descriptions of how firms use the strategic management process. Our goal while preparing this First Canadian Edition has been to present you, our readers, with a complete, accurate, and up-to-date explanation of the strategic management process as it is used in the Canadian context and the global economy.

# THE BOOK'S FOCUS

The strategic management process is the focus of our textbook. Described in Chapter 1, organizations (both for-profit companies and not-for-profit agencies) use the strategic management process to understand competitive forces and to develop competitive advantages. The magnitude of this challenge is greater today than it has been historically. A new competitive landscape is developing in the 21st century as a result of the technological revolution (especially in e-commerce) and increasing globalization. The technological revolution has placed greater importance on product innovation and the ability to rapidly introduce new goods and services to the marketplace. The global economy, one in which goods and services flow relatively more freely among nations, continuously pressures firms to become more competitive. By offering either valued goods or services to customers, competitive firms increase the probability of earning above-average returns. Thus, the strategic management process helps organizations identify what they intend to achieve and how they will do it.

In addition, we also use a wide range of company-specific examples to discuss e-commerce applications of the strategic management process. E-commerce examples are presented in each chapter to show the pervasive effect of the Internet and e-commerce on competition in the global economy. Through these examples, our text is clearly differentiated from others regarding e-commerce applications of the strategic management process.

This book is intended for use primarily in strategic management and business policy courses. The materials presented in the 14 chapters have been researched thoroughly. Both the academic, scholarly literature and the business, practitioner literature were studied and then integrated to prepare this edition. The academic literature provides the foundation to develop an accurate, yet meaningful description of the strategic management process. The business practitioner literature yields a rich base of current domestic and global examples to show how the strategic management process's concepts, tools, and techniques are applied in different organizations.

## THE STRATEGIC MANAGEMENT PROCESS

Our discussion of the strategic management process is both traditional and contemporary. In maintaining tradition, we examine important materials that have historically been a part of understanding strategic management. For example, we thoroughly examine how to analyze a firm's external environment and internal environment.

*Contemporary Treatment:* To explain the aforementioned important activities, we try to keep our treatments contemporary. In Chapter 4, for example, we emphasize the importance of identifying and determining the value-creating potential of a firm's resources, capabilities, and core competencies. The strategic actions taken as a result of understanding a firm's resources, capabilities, and core competencies have a direct link with the company's ability to establish a competitive advantage, achieve strategic competitiveness, and earn above-average returns.

Our contemporary treatment is also shown in the chapters on the dynamics of strategic change in the complex global economy. In Chapter 6, for example, we discuss how the dynamics of competition between firms, dynamics that are often "hypercompetitive," affect strategic outcomes. Chapter 6's discussion suggests that in most industries, a firm's strategic actions are influenced by its competitors' actions and reactions. Thus, competition in the global economy is fluid, dynamic, and fast-paced. Similarly, in Chapter 8, we explain the dynamics of strategic change at the corporate level, specifically addressing the motivation and consequences of mergers, acquisitions, and restructuring (e.g., divestitures) in the global economy.

We also emphasize that the set of strategic actions known as strategy formulation and strategy implementation (see Figure 1.1) must be integrated carefully if a firm is to achieve strategic competitiveness and earn above-average returns. Thus, this book shows that competitive success occurs when firms use implementation tools and actions that are consistent with the previously chosen business-level (Chapter 5), corporate-level (Chapter 7), acquisition (Chapter 8), international (Chapter 9), and cooperative (Chapter 10) strategies.

*Contemporary Concepts:* Contemporary topics and concepts are the foundation for our in-depth analysis of strategic actions firms take to implement strategies. In Chapter 11, for example, we describe how different corporate governance mechanisms (e.g., boards of directors, institutional owners, executive compensation, etc.) affect strategy implementation. Chapter 12 explains how firms gain a competitive advantage by effectively using organizational structures that are

matched properly to different strategies. The vital contributions of strategic leaders are examined in Chapter 13. Chapter 14 addresses the important topic of corporate entrepreneurship and innovation through internal corporate venturing, strategic alliances, and external acquisition or venture capital investments.

## KEY FEATURES OF THIS TEXT

To increase our book's value for you, several features are included.

*Learning Objectives:* Each chapter begins with clearly stated learning objectives. Their purpose is to emphasize key points you will want to master while studying each chapter. To both facilitate and verify learning, you can revisit individual learning objectives while preparing answers to the Review Questions appearing at the end of each chapter.

*Opening Cases:* An Opening Case follows the learning objectives in each chapter. The cases describe current strategic issues in modern companies such as Nortel, Abitibi-Consolidated, Microsoft, and Fishery Products International, among others. The purpose of the Opening Cases is to demonstrate how specific firms apply individual chapter's strategic management concepts. Thus, the Opening Cases serve as a direct and often distinctive link between the theory and application of strategic management.

*Key Terms:* Key terms that are critical to understanding the strategic management process are boldfaced throughout the book. Definitions of these key terms appear in chapter margins as well as in the text. Other terms and concepts throughout the text are italicized, signifying their importance.

*Strategic Focus Segments:* Two to four Strategic Focus segments are presented in each chapter. As with the Opening Cases, the Strategic Focus segments highlight a variety of high-profile organizations, situations, and concepts. Each segment describes issues that can be addressed by applying a chapter's strategy-related concepts.

*End-of-Chapter Summaries:* Closing each chapter is a summary that revisits the concepts outlined in the learning objectives. The summaries are presented in a bulleted format to highlight a chapter's concepts, tools, and techniques.

*Review Questions:* Review Questions are pointedly tied to the learning objectives, prompting readers to reexamine the most important concepts in each chapter.

*Discussion Questions:* These questions challenge readers to directly apply the part of the strategic management process highlighted in that chapter. The questions are designed to stimulate thoughtful classroom discussions and to help readers develop critical thinking skills.

*Ethics Questions:* At the end of each chapter, readers are challenged by questions about ethical issues requiring careful thought and analysis. Preparing answers to these questions helps readers recognize and confront ongoing ethical issues facing management teams. Discussing these difficult issues in class heightens awareness of the ethical challenges encountered in today's global organizations and markets.

*Internet Exercises:* The Internet is an invaluable source for exchanging information worldwide. Each exercise is designed to help readers develop an ability to recognize information sources that can aid in problem solution.

*Examples:* In addition to the Opening Cases and Strategic Focus segments, each chapter is filled with real-world examples of companies in action. These examples illustrate key strategic management concepts and provide realistic applications of strategic management.

*Indexes:* Besides the traditional end of book Subject and Name indexes, we offer a Company index as well. This index includes the names of all organizations discussed in the text for easier accessibility.

## THE STRATEGIC ADVANTAGE

The strategic management process is critical to organizational success. As described in Chapter 1, strategic competitiveness is achieved when a firm develops and exploits a sustained competitive advantage. Attaining such an advantage results in the earning of above-average returns; that is, returns that exceed those investors could expect from other investments with similar amounts of risk. For example, Intel has developed and sustained a competitive advantage over time because of its significant emphasis on innovation even though it operates largely in highly competitive ever-changing high technology industries.

## THE COMPETITIVE ADVANTAGE

Success in the 21st-century competitive landscape requires specific capabilities, including the abilities to (1) use scarce resources wisely to maintain the lowest possible costs, (2) constantly anticipate frequent changes in customers' preferences, (3) adapt to rapid technological changes, (4) identify, emphasize, and effectively manage what a firm does better than its competitors, (5) continuously structure a firm's operations so objectives can be achieved more efficiently, and (6) successfully manage and gain commitments from a culturally diverse workforce.

# THE GLOBAL ADVANTAGE

Critical to the approach used in this text is the fact that all firms face increasing global competition. Firms no longer operate in relatively safe domestic markets as many Canadian firms, such as Eaton's, have discovered. In the past many companies, including most in Canada, produced large quantities of standardized products. Today, firms typically compete in a global economy that is complex, highly uncertain, and unpredictable. To a greater degree than in a primarily domestic economy, the global economy rewards effective performers, whereas poor performers are forced to restructure significantly to enhance their strategic competitiveness. As noted earlier, increasing globalization and the technological revolution have produced a new competitive landscape in the 21st century. This landscape presents a challenging and complex environment for firms, but one that also has opportunities. The importance of developing and using these capabilities in the 21st century should not be underestimated.

*Strategic Management: Competitiveness and Globalization—Cases* (ISBN 0-17-616898-2) is the casebook to accompany the "Concepts" textbook. The 32 cases speak to many different strategic issues. As shown by the cases, strategic issues surface for firms competing in e-commerce, manufacturing, service, consumer goods, and industrial goods industries. Importantly, given the 21st-century competitive landscape and the global economy, many of these cases represent international business concerns (e.g., ABB in China: 1998, Alcoholes de Centroamerica, S.A. de C.V.). Also, we offer cases dealing with the Internet (e.g., Advanced Book Exchange Inc. and Maritime Trading Company), entertainment (e.g., Asiasports), and service firms (e.g., Amazon.com, Starbucks, and Outback Goes International). Some of the cases focus specifically on issues at larger firms (e.g., Bombardier and The United Colours of Benneton), while others emphasize strategic issues of entrepreneurial or small- and medium-sized firms (e.g., Jan and Dave Bailey's Big Decision and The Puzzle Store). We have also included some cases on non-profit organizations that are facing strategic issues (e.g., The Hagwilget Band cases). Finally, a large number of the cases deal specifically with Canadian firms and the issues they face. These can include dealing with moving into the U.S. (e.g., E.D. Smith), international issues (e.g., Fishery Products International Ltd.) or deal with simply running a business well at home (e.g., Investment Opportunities Unlimited).

Selected personally by the text authors, this unique case selection has been reviewed carefully. Our goal has been to choose cases that are well written and deal with important strategic management issues. The comprehensive set of strategic management issues included in the cases yields a rich set of learning experiences for those performing case analyses.

Consistent with the nature of strategic issues, the cases included are multidimensional in nature. Because of this, and for readers' convenience, a matrix listing all cases and the dimensions/characteristics of each one is provided following the table of contents. Furthermore, the matrix lists each text chapter that provides the best fit for teaching that particular case. While many of the cases are concerned with well-known national and international companies, several examine the strategic challenges experienced in smaller and entrepreneurial firms. Given the current challenge within the global economy, over 50 percent of the cases include an international perspective.

## SUPPORT MATERIAL

We offer one of the most comprehensive and quality learning packages available for teaching strategic management. Each part of the supplement package is integrated carefully and effectively with the text's materials.

### For the Instructor

*Instructor's Resource Manual and Instructor's Case Notes.* A comprehensive Instructor's Manual provides teaching notes, suggestions for presentation, and chapter summaries. The teaching notes include discussion summaries or highlights of each Opening Case, Strategic Focus segment, table, and figure appearing in the text. The suggestions for presentation provide the instructor with a choice of strategies for integrating various text features into a lecture format. The Instructor's Case Notes provide details about each case within the framework of case analysis. The structure of these case notes allows instructors to organize case discussions along common themes and concepts. For example, each Case Note details a firm's capabilities and resources, its industry and competitive environment, and key factors for success in the industry. In addition, the case notes feature aspects of the cases that make them unique. Thus, a common analytical framework—one that is tied to materials in the book's 14 chapters—yields multiple opportunities to apply the strategic management process in different organizational settings.

*Test Bank.* The Test Bank contains more than 1,200 multiple choice, true/false, and essay questions. Each question has been coded according to Bloom's taxonomy, a widely known testing and measurement device that is used to classify questions according to level (easy, medium, or hard) and type (application, recall, or comprehension).

*Computerized Test Bank.* This test-generating software supplement allows instructors to create, edit, store, and print exams quickly and efficiently using the questions taken from the Test Bank.

*PowerPoint® Presentation Files.* Jerry Sheppard and Marnie Young, Simon Fraser University, and David Williams, The University of Oklahoma, redefined and improved a comprehensive set of PowerPoint® Presentation Files. Now with over 350 slides, the PowerPoint® files feature figures from the text, lecture outlines, and innovative adaptations to enhance classroom presentation. Sheppard and Williams lend their academic media expertise in offering a unique and colourful set of presentations through which learning is guided and facilitated.

*U.S. Supplements.* Also available for instructors are Videos I & II from the U.S. edition. This unique two-volume package features 15 minute segments on such companies as Mercedes-Benz, Ben & Jerry's, and Yahoo! During the segments, questions are posed and viewers are asked to analyze different evolving strategic management situations.

## For the Student and Instructor

Web Site: (http://hitt.nelson.com) This continually updated site offers students and instructors access to case updates, definitions of strategy terms, important strategy URLs, and a section on how to write a case analysis. In addition, all Strategic Focus segments from the first three U.S. editions are offered for students and instructors to use as strategy examples. These are indexed by broad subject categories. All Internet exercises from the Third and Fourth U.S. Editions are also available.

*U.S. Supplements.* Also available for students from the U.S. edition is *Insights: Readings in Strategic Management.* This comprehensive collection of readings from the academic and popular business press offers an excellent and convenient literary supplement to the text.

## ACKNOWLEDGMENTS

We want to thank those who helped us prepare this First Canadian Edition. The professionalism, guidance, and support provided by the editorial team of Evelyn Veitch, Edward Ikeda, Karina TenVeldhuis, Susan Calvert, and Karen Rolfe are gratefully acknowledged. We appreciate the excellent work of our research assistants: Denise Gibbons, James O'Brien, Tami Hynes, Kelly Monaghan, and Marnie Young. In addition, we owe a debt of gratitude to our colleagues at Arizona State University, University of Richmond, The University of Oklahoma, Memorial University of Newfoundland, The University of Western Ontario, and Simon Fraser University. Finally, we are sincerely grateful to those who took time to read and provide feedback on drafts of this First Canadian Edition. Their insights and evaluations have enhanced this text, and we list them below with our thanks:

Kamal Argheyd, Concordia University
David Barrows, York University
Robert Blunden, Dalhousie University

Barry Boothman, University of New Brunswick
Shamsud Chowdhury, Athabasca University
Christopher Gadsby, British Columbia Institute of Technology
Robert Gephart, University of Alberta
Ann Gregory, Memorial University of Newfoundland
Ike Hall, British Columbia Institute of Technology
Jack Ito, University of Regina
Knud Jensen, Ryerson Polytechnic University
Ian Lee, Carleton University
Lee Maguire, Ryerson Polytechnic University
Alfie Morgan, University of Windsor
Tom Wesson, York University

## FINAL COMMENTS

While e-commerce company stocks have fallen on harder times, the potential of the Internet to change the way we do things is one that cannot be underestimated. The Canadian authors of this text worked on opposite coasts to produce this work. Jerry Sheppard at Simon Fraser University in Vancouver, BC, and Glenn Rowe, who at the time was at Memorial University in St. Johns, NFLD, were literally a continent apart—yet chapters were transmitted instantaneously via email to each other and our editorial team in Toronto, ON. Thus, in spite of downturns in the fortunes of some companies reliant on the Internet revolution, we still see a great deal of promise in these firms.

In general, organizations face exciting and dynamic competitive challenges in the 21st century. These challenges, and effective responses to them, are explored in this First Canadian Edition of *Strategic Management: Competitiveness and Globalization*. The strategic management process conceptualized in this text offers valuable insights and knowledge to those committed to successfully meeting the challenge of dynamic competition. Thinking strategically, as this book challenges you to do, increases the likelihood that you will help your organization achieve strategic success. In addition, continuous practice with strategic thinking and the use of the strategic management process gives you skills and knowledge that will contribute to career advancement and success. Finally, we want to wish you all the best and nothing other than complete success in all of your endeavors.

Michael A. Hitt
R. Duane Ireland
Robert E. Hoskisson
W. Glenn Rowe
Jerry P. Sheppard

# Strategic Management Inputs

# Chapter One

## Strategic Management and Strategic Competitiveness

### LEARNING OBJECTIVES

*After reading this chapter, you should be able to:*

1. Define strategic competitiveness, competitive advantage, and above-average returns.
2. Discuss the challenge of strategic management.
3. Describe the new competitive landscape and how it is being shaped by global and technological changes.
4. Use the industrial organization (I/O) model to explain how firms can earn above-average returns.
5. Use the resource-based model to explain how firms can earn above-average returns.
6. Describe strategic intent and strategic mission and discuss their value to the strategic management process.
7. Define stakeholders and describe the three primary stakeholder groups' ability to influence organizations.
8. Describe the work of strategists.
9. Explain the strategic management process.

## A New World Order in the Telecommunications Industry

The telecommunications industry seems to be changing as fast as the signals it transmits. There are several Canadian illustrations of these changes. For example, Alberta's Telus engaged in over $10 billion in mergers and acquisitions (all figures in Canadian dollars). Telus first merged with BC Tel and then bought a majority stake in QuebecTel in an effort to build a viable national telecommunications company. In addition, Telus bid $6.6 billion for wireless competitor Clearnet, announcing the acquisition on October 20, 2000. In Atlantic Canada, telecom companies Bruncor (in New Brunswick), Island Telecom (in Prince Edward Island), Maritime Telegraph and Telephone Company (in Nova Scotia), and Enterprises Limited (in Newfoundland and Labrador) joined forces to form the Aliant Group. Serving as BCE's strategic partner in Atlantic Canada, the new firm has a market capitalization of $3 billion and revenues of $2 billion. Finally, in order to secure a better competitive stance in broadband telecommunications, Rogers Communications and Quebecor World fought a $6 billion battle for Montreal's Videotron. Whatever is going on, the telecommunications industry will never be the same.

The above mergers are just the tip of the iceberg. Brampton, Ontario's Nortel Networks has expanded its global presence to over 150 countries by acquiring Bay Networks in September 1998. Its combined revenues were over $30 billion, and employees numbered over 60 000. To take advantage of growth in the fibre optics industry and offer customers a one-stop provider for fibre optic network components, Ottawa's JDS Fitel merged with San Jose's Uniphase in a $9 billion deal. To address the growth of international multilevel marketing competitors, such as ACN from the United States, Montreal's Teleglobe merged with Dallas's Excel Communications and created the fourth-largest telecommunications carrier in North America. Even the CN Railroad has extensive telecommunications interests. Along with 11.4 million shares of fibre optic network provider 360networks, CN's merger proposals should provide it with an uninterrupted fibre network between Vancouver, Halifax, and New Orleans.

http://www.aliant.ca

http://www.nortelnetworks.com

http://www.wcom.com

All of this hectic activity in the telecommunications industry is due to the major changes occurring in and predicted for this industry. The changes began with WorldCom's $53 billion acquisition of MCI. This bid is about equivalent to MCI WorldCom's bid for Orange, Britain's third-largest wireless phone company. Yet it was dwarfed by MCI WorldCom's $175 billion acquisition bid for Sprint, which failed.

Firms in the industry are attempting to be more competitive as changes occur. Some predict changes in the telecommunications industry as profound as those in the computer industry with the advent of the microcomputer. Deregulation is a major change in many domestic industries, resulting in increased competition. In Canada, the telecommunications industry was deregulated in October 1998. Canada's deregulation made it one of the first to do so among the countries who were party to a World Trade Organization agreement in which 69 countries pledged to open their telecom markets. To compete in a global market, many telecommunications executives feel that their firms must be large to have the necessary market power.

Spending in the global telecommunications industry is expected to maintain a level of $1 trillion per year through 2005. Moreover, there are new markets opening up. For example, the Chinese market will require massive investments to compete. China alone represents a $1 trillion opportunity. Of course, it is not only the size of the market affecting major investments but also the need to be at the forefront of rapidly advancing technology.

Changes in the industry are clearly not limited to Canadian or U.S. firms. For example, a consortium of European phone companies agreed to merge their international phone networks to create the largest service provider in Europe. PTT Nederland NV of the Netherlands, Telia AB of Sweden, and Swiss Telecom formed the Unisource consortium. Unisource has a joint venture with AT&T that will be aided by Tato, a large Italian firm, which formed a strategic alliance with Deutsche Telecom to bid for Italy's third cellular telephone licence and make a $5 billion move into the fixed-line market. STET, another Italian company, already controls the largest cellular phone network in Europe, after buying into systems in Austria, Serbia, and Spain.

A final example comes from Asia. Northern Telecom, Lucent Technologies, Motorola, and Qualcomm are cooperating to develop a common format of the code division multiple access (CDMA), a digital transmission technology. These four competitors are also cooperating to help Nippon Telephone and Telegraph (NTT) to develop a world CDMA, which will help Asian carriers such as NTT because of the tremendous growth in Asian markets.

These changes are some of the examples of the transformation occurring in the global telecommunications industry. The changes are required to remain competitive in a rapidly developing and dynamic industry.

Sources: http://www.telus.com/clearnet/pressroom/index.html (Retrieved February 9, 2000); Nortel Networks, 2000, *Nortel Networks home page,* http://www.nortel-networks.com (Retrieved June 22); Aliant, 2000, *Aliant Company home page*, http://www.aliant.ca/english/home_frame.htm (Retrieved June 1); K. Leger, 2000, Videotron deal not dead yet, *National Post*, April 26, C4; Canadian Press Newswire, 2000, CNR reports record operating income in first quarter, April 24, CBCA, http://delos.lib.sfu.ca: 8366/cgi-bin/slri/z3950.CGI/209.206.52.205.849165856/? cbca.db (Retrieved June 23); R. Gibbens, 2000, Telus takes aim at Bell with QuebecTel deal, *National Post*, D1; T. Valdmanis, 2000, MCI WorldCom mulls $40b bid for UK firm, *National Post*, April 22, D1, D2; A. Edelson, 1999, Teleglobe set to sell long distance door to door, *Silicon Valley North*, January 10; P. Verburg, 1999, Rebel without a pause, *Canadian Business*, April 9, 74–83; JDS, 1999, JDS-Uniphase merger wins shareholder approval, *National Post*, June 29, C5; P. Elstrom, C. Yang, and J. Flynn, 1997, The new world order, *BusinessWeek*, October 13, 26–33; Europe's Unisource confirms its merger of global networks, 1997, *The Wall Street Journal Interactive Edition*, June 5, http://www.interactive5.wsj.com; Four wireless rivals link up to work for CDMA standards, 1997, *The Wall Street Journal Interactive Edition*, June 4, http://www.interactive5.wsj.com; D. E. Kalish, 1997, WorldCom-MCI deal makes merger history, *Houston Chronicle*, November 11, C1; A. Kupfer, 1997, Transforming Telecom: The big switch, *Fortune*, October 13, 105–16; J. Rossant, 1997, Lean, mean—and state-owned Italian companies, *BusinessWeek*, June 16, http://www.businessweek.com.

Strategic competitiveness is achieved when a firm successfully formulates and implements a value-creating strategy.

A sustainable or sustained competitive advantage occurs when a firm implements a value-creating strategy of which other companies are unable to duplicate the benefits or find it too costly to imitate.

Above-average returns are returns in excess of what an investor expects to earn from other investments with a similar amount of risk.

Risk is an investor's uncertainty about the economic gains or losses that will result from a particular investment.

Average returns are returns equal to those an investor expects to earn from other investments with a similar amount of risk.

The strategic management process is the full set of commitments, decisions, and actions required for a firm to achieve strategic competitiveness and earn above-average returns.

The actions undertaken by firms such as Nortel, JDS Uniphase, WorldCom, PTT Nederland NV, Deutsche Telecom AG, STET, and Nippon Telephone and Telegraph, among others, are designed to help the firms achieve strategic competitiveness and earn above-average returns. **Strategic competitiveness** is achieved when a firm successfully formulates and implements a value-creating strategy. When a firm implements a value-creating strategy of which other companies are unable to duplicate the benefits or find it too costly to imitate,[1] this firm has a **sustained or sustainable competitive advantage** (hereafter called simply a competitive advantage). A firm is assured of a competitive advantage only after others' efforts to duplicate its strategy have ceased or failed.[2] Even if a firm achieves a competitive advantage, it normally can sustain it only for a certain period of time.[3] The speed with which competitors are able to acquire the skills needed to duplicate the benefits of a firm's value-creating strategy determines how long a competitive advantage will last.[4] Understanding how to exploit its competitive advantage is necessary for a firm to earn above-average returns.[5]

By achieving strategic competitiveness and successfully exploiting its competitive advantage, a firm is able to accomplish its objective—the earning of above-average returns. **Above-average returns** are returns in excess of what an investor expects to earn from other investments with a similar amount of risk. **Risk** is an investor's uncertainty about the economic gains or losses that will result from a particular investment.[6] Firms that are without a competitive advantage or that are not competing in an attractive industry earn, at best, only average returns. **Average returns** are returns equal to those an investor expects to earn from other investments with a similar amount of risk. In the long run, an inability to earn at least average returns results in failure. Failure occurs because investors will choose to invest in firms that earn at least average returns and will withdraw their investments from those earning less.

Dynamic in nature, **the strategic management process** (see Figure 1.1) is the full set of commitments, decisions, and actions required for a firm to achieve strategic competitiveness and earn above-average returns.[7] Relevant strategic inputs, from analyses of the internal and external environments, are necessary for effective strategy formulation and strategy implementation actions. In turn, effective strategic actions are a prerequisite to achieving the desired outcomes of strategic competitiveness and above-average returns. Thus, the strategic management process is used to match the conditions of an ever-changing market and competitive structure with a firm's continuously evolving resources, capabilities, and competencies (the sources of strategic inputs). Effective strategic actions that take place in the context of carefully integrated strategy formulation and strategy implementation processes result in desired strategic outcomes.[8]

In the remaining chapters of this book, we use the strategic management process to explain what firms should do to achieve strategic competitiveness and earn above-average returns. Through these explanations, it becomes clear why some firms consistently achieve competitive success and others fail to do so.[9] As you will see, the reality of global competition is a critical part of the strategic management process.[10]

Several topics are discussed in this chapter. First, we define the concept of strategy from different perspectives. Second, we examine the challenge of strategic management. This brief discussion highlights the fact that the strategic actions taken to achieve, and then to maintain, strategic competitiveness demand the best of managers, employees, and their organizations on a continuous basis. Third, we describe the new competitive landscape, created primarily by the emergence of a global economy and rapid techno-

■ ■ **FIGURE 1.1**

*The Strategic Management Process*

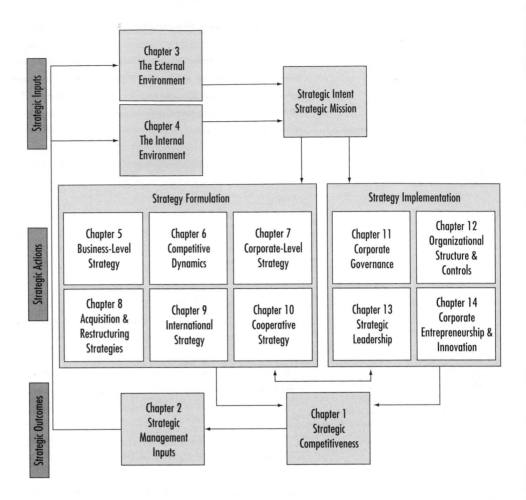

logical change. The new competitive landscape establishes the contextual opportunities and threats within which the strategic management process is used by firms striving to meet the competitive challenge raised by demanding global standards.

We next examine two models that suggest conditions organizations should study in order to gain the strategic knowledge necessary to select strategic actions in the pursuit of strategic competitiveness and above-average returns. However, the emphases of these two models differ. The first model (industrial organization) suggests that the external environment should be the primary determinant of a firm's strategic actions. The key to this model is locating and competing successfully in an attractive (that is, profitable) industry. The second model (resource based) suggests that a firm's unique resources and capabilities are the critical link to strategic competitiveness. Comprehensive explanations of these two models in this first chapter and in Chapters Three and Four demonstrate that, through the combined use of these two models, firms obtain the full set of strategic inputs needed to formulate and implement strategies successfully.

Analyses of its external and internal environments provide a firm with the information it needs to develop its strategic intent and strategic mission (intent and mission are defined later in this chapter). As shown in Figure 1.1, strategic intent and strategic mission influence strategy formulation and implementation actions.

The chapter's discussion then turns to the stakeholders served by organizations. The degree to which the needs of stakeholders can be met increases directly with enhancements in a firm's strategic competitiveness and its ability to earn above-average returns. Closing the chapter are introductions to organizational strategists and the elements of the strategic management process.

## STRATEGY—WHAT IS IT?

Strategy has had different meanings for different people throughout history. Prior to 450 B.C., *strategos* meant a role, such as a general in command of an army. Later, it meant the psychological and behavioural skills with which a general occupied the role, or "the art of the general." In modern times, strategy has also had different meanings. Some of the diversity in the definitions of strategy is presented in Table 1.1.[11]

Mintzberg gives five definitions of strategy: a plan, a ploy, a pattern, a position, and a perspective. By plan, Mintzberg means that the firm is undertaking a conscious and intended course of action to deal with a situation. Strategy as a ploy means that the firm is attempting some kind of "specific 'manoeuvre' intended to outwit an opponent or competitor." Mintzberg also views strategy as a pattern of fairly consistent actions rather than a set of intended courses of actions. Strategy, per Mintzberg's fourth definition, is seen as a position. Under this definition, strategy reflects placing the organization in a particular environment (i.e., a market niche) that puts the organization at a competitive advantage and allows it to produce a greater than normal rate of return. Lastly, according to Mintzberg, strategy reflects a perspective or the organization's "ingrained way of perceiving the world" (i.e., there's the right way, the wrong way, and the way we do it here).[12]

| ■ ■ TABLE 1.1 | Alternative Definitions of Strategy |
| --- | --- |

"The formulation of basic organizational missions, purposes, and objectives; policies and program strategies to achieve them; and the methods needed to assure that strategies are implemented to achieve organizational ends" (Steiner and Miner 1977, 7).

"A unified, comprehensive, and integrated plan designed to ensure that the basic objectives of the enterprise are achieved" (Glueck 1980, 9)

The pattern or plan that integrates an organization's major goals, policies, and action sequences into a cohesive whole. A well formulated strategy helps to marshal and allocate an organization's resources into a unique and viable posture based on its relative internal competencies and shortcomings, anticipated changes in the environment, and contingent moves by intelligent opponents" (Quinn 1980).

"The way to achieve organizational goals" (Hatten and Hatten 1988, 1).

"Strategy is a pattern of resource allocation that enables firms to maintain or improve their performance. A good strategy is a strategy that neutralizes threats and exploits opportunities while capitalizing on strengths and avoiding or fixing weaknesses" (Barney 1997, 17).

Mintzberg makes another important contribution to our understanding of strategy when he differentiates among intended, emergent, and realized strategies (see Figure 1.2).[13] Intended strategies are those plans or conscious courses of actions required to deal with a specific situation that lead to deliberate strategies. Intended strategies are usually top-down from senior management and reflect a hierarchical view of strategy. This hierarchical perspective suggests that corporate senior managers are responsible for the corporate mission and objectives, business unit senior managers are responsible for business unit strategies flowing from corporate missions and objectives, and functional area managers within the division are responsible for tactics/policies that flow from the business unit strategies. Some intended strategies are never implemented—they are "unrealized strategies."

Emergent strategies are patterns of actions that emerge over time in an unintended manner. They are actions and decisions senior managers may not have intended to pursue but that nevertheless emerged. Emergent strategies generally are a by-product of other intended strategies or strategies that emerge bottom up as opposed to top down. They are those strategies that result from the pattern of everyday actions and behaviours of managers and employees almost without conscious thought or planning.

■ ■ **FIGURE 1.2**

*Intended, Emergent, and Realized Strategies*

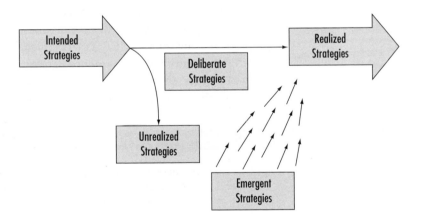

Source: Copyright © 1987, by the Regent of the University of California. Reprinted from the *California Management Review*, 30 (1). By permission of the Regents.

A firm's realized strategies are the combination of deliberate and emergent strategies. What is important about this view of strategy is the awareness that realized strategies are the result of what everyone (senior managers, middle managers, and employees) in an organization does as they go about their daily activities. This means that senior managers must appreciate the need for all members of their organizations to be aware of, understand, embrace, and, on a day-to-day basis, act in accordance with the proposed strategy of the firm and its subordinate business units. In an organization where senior managers do not have a clear mission, clear objectives and, therefore, no clear strategy, what may emerge may destroy shareholder wealth. Even in organizations where senior management has an intended strategy, but it is not clearly communicated or clearly understood by middle managers and employees, patterns of behaviour may emerge that will unintentionally destroy shareholder wealth. We now turn to the challenge of strategic management.

## THE CHALLENGE OF STRATEGIC MANAGEMENT

The goals of achieving strategic competitiveness and earning above-average returns are challenging—not only for firms as large as WorldCom but also for those as small as your local dry cleaners. The performance of some companies, of course, more than meets strategic management's challenge. At the end of a recent year, for example, Microsoft and General Electric had created more wealth (as measured by market value added) than other U.S. firms (approximately $629 billion in the case of Microsoft, roughly $467 billion for GE). The top 10 U.S. wealth creators for 1998, including Microsoft and GE, are shown in Table 1.2. Microsoft moved from 10th in 1994 to first in 1999. More dramatically, AOL America Online exploded from 425th in 1994 to 7th in 1999.[14]

### ■ ■ TABLE 1.2          Top Ten United States Wealth Creators

| 1999 | 1998 | 1994 | Company | Market Value Added (Millions) |
|---|---|---|---|---|
| 1 | 1 | 10 | Microsoft | $629 470 |
| 2 | 1 | 2 | General Electric | 467 510 |
| 3 | 8 | 50 | Cisco Systems | 348 442 |
| 4 | 5 | 3 | Wal-Mart | 282 655 |
| 5 | 3 | 26 | Intel | 253 907 |
| 6 | 9 | n.a. | Lucent Technologies | 200 540 |
| 7 | 23 | 425 | AOL America Online | 187 558 |
| 8 | 41 | 38 | Oracle | 154 263 |
| 9 | 11 | 78 | IBM | 154 219 |
| 10 | 19 | 25 | Home Depot | 148 358 |

Source: The 1999 Stern Stewart United States 1000 MVA Ranking at http://www.stern-stewart.com/content/performance/info/us.pdf

In Canada, Nortel Networks and BCE have created more wealth than any other Canadian firms. Nortel created $169 billion in 1999 while BCE created $18 billion.[15] The top 10 Canadian firms are shown in Table 1.3.

Few large corporations have managed to remain competitive in the face of long-term changes in the environment. The fact that only 2 of the 25 largest U.S. industrial corporations in 1900 are still competitive today attests to the rigors of business competition and the challenge of strategic management. The remaining 23 companies have failed, been merged with other firms, or are no longer of significant size relative to competitors.[16] Moreover, in a recent year, almost 150 000 U.S. businesses either failed or filed for bankruptcy.[17] In Canada close to 10 000 businesses filed for bankruptcy in 1999.[18] Results such as these support the view that competitive success is transient.[19] Thomas J. Watson, Jr., formerly IBM's chairman, once cautioned people to remember that, "cor-

| ■ ■ TABLE 1.3 | | | Top 10 Canadian Wealth Creators | |
|---|---|---|---|---|
| **1999** | **1998** | **1990** | **Company** | **Market Value Added (Millions)** |
| 1 | 1 | 2 | Nortel Networks Corporation | 168 851 |
| 2 | 2 | 184 | BCE | 65 609 |
| 3 | 5 | 14 | Bombardier | 16 142 |
| 4 | 3 | 1 | The Thomson Corporation | 13 467 |
| 5 | 6 | 10 | Toronto-Dominion Bank | 13 273 |
| 6 | 11 | 6 | Rogers Communications | 7 924 |
| 7 | 13 | 5 | Imperial Oil | 7 545 |
| 8 | 4 | 179 | Royal Bank of Canada | 6 552 |
| 9 | 10 | 12 | George Weston Limited | 4 814 |
| 10 | 18 | 161 | Shell Canada | 4 360 |

Source: *National Post*, October 14, 2000, C4; The 1999 Stern Stewart Canadian 300 MVA Ranking at: http://www.sternstewart.com/content/performance/info/canada.pdf

porations are expendable and that success—at best—is an impermanent achievement which can always slip out of hand."[20]

Successful performance may be transient and impermanent; at least as reflected by *Fortune*'s Most Admired Corporation lists. In 1986, IBM held the number-one position on *Fortune*'s list for the fourth consecutive year. By 1995, IBM's position had slipped to number 281. Since then, IBM has recovered. But not all firms are fortunate enough for their problems to be temporary. Eaton's was unable to stay in business, as explained in the Strategic Focus on the impermanence of success.

While Zellers and Honda are making changes to return to their days of success, questions remain about whether their efforts will result in the success they once enjoyed. Both have significant competition. The U.S. market drives Honda, and so it is vital for the firm to re-establish its relationship with the U.S. consumer. Zellers must do the same by offering consumers products that compete effectively with Wal-Mart in Canada. In both cases, Honda's world car and Zellers' new products, the success of these efforts will make the difference in each firm's ability to again achieve strategic competitiveness and to earn above-average returns.[21]

## STRATEGIC FOCUS

### The Impermanence of Success

Zellers is Canada's oldest, and until recently, most dominant discount store chain. It has long positioned itself as "truly Canadian"—being 100 percent owned by the Hudson Bay Company. For years, mass-market retailer Zellers promised customers competitive prices with its catchy slogan "the lowest price is the law." Zellers pioneered retail database marketing and used it to develop its Club Points program to reward customers for repeat spending. In 1994, Zellers faced its most daunting challenge when Wal-Mart came to Canada. Wal-Mart's volume-buying
*continued*

power and inventory management excellence allowed it to offer the lowest prices, thereby undermining Zellers' strategy and toughening the battle for market share in the Canadian retail market. Indeed, with over 2000 retail stores and total sales of approximately one and one-half times the total Canadian department store market, Wal-Mart was a strong new market presence. In 1997, Zellers reported a net loss of $90 million, down from its 1993, pre–Wal-Mart era profit of $256 million. Following a period of sluggish sales growth in the mid-1990s, Zellers repositioned itself in 1998 with its exclusive and slightly upscale Martha Stewart Everyday and Cherokee lines. This allowed Zellers to offer consumers greater value while still remaining price competitive. Sales in 1999 were more than 33 percent higher than in 1994—and more than 18 percent over 1998, suggesting that Zellers is successfully meeting the challenge of the changing Canadian retail market.

Some other retailers have not been as fortunate. Although Zellers survived, Wal-Mart left the catalogue company Consumers Distributing in its wake. In 1999, Eaton's closed its doors and ended a 130-year history as Canada's national retailer. Timothy Eaton, an Irish immigrant, started the company in 1869. Eaton's traditional catalogues had bridged geographical distances and provided Canadians with retail goods from soap to furniture to shoes. The family-owned company discontinued the catalogue in 1976 and operated primarily from downtown and urban retail stores located from Halifax, N.S. to Victoria, B.C. Its main competitors were Sears and The Bay. Unfortunately, in the early 1990s the company was rumoured to have financial difficulties. Sales dropped $500 million a year from 1991 to 1996. It seems that Eaton's failed to remain competitive and sense consumer shifts in retailing. Despite turnaround attempts, Eaton's continued to post losses and began closing stores and was awarded creditor protection in late 1999. On December 29, 1999, Sears Canada bought several of Eaton's stores, its name and other trademarks, and its Web site.

Another retailer with a very long history in Canada is the Hudson's Bay Company. It was established in 1670 as a fur trading company and has been in the department store business since 1913. The Bay's troubles began in the 1980s when the firm posted large losses. Financial performance picked up in the 1990s, but the fall of Eaton's has sent a very clear signal that retailers must compete effectively or they will not survive.

While not as severe as those explained above, Honda also experienced problems and is now making major changes to reassert itself in the global automobile market. A few years ago, Honda redesigned its popular Accord to make it look sportier. However, the car had too little internal space to satisfy North American customers and was not adequately sporty for the Japanese consumers. As a result, Honda began to lose market share in several major markets around the world. This was an awakening for Honda executives, who had become perhaps too complacent with the strong demand for the firm's autos. Honda took drastic action and is now trying to build a "world car." This car has the same basic design but is adapted for consumer tastes in different markets. For example, in 1997 Honda launched two versions of the Accord, one in North America and one in Japan. The North American version is 189 inches long and 70 inches wide to be a midsize competitor of the Ford Taurus. The Accord in Japan is six inches shorter and four inches thinner. The Japanese version is a sporty compact with many high-tech features. In 1998 a European Accord was

*continued*

introduced, which had a short narrow body designed for manoeuvring on narrow streets. Analysts are optimistic, but Honda must fight to maintain its efficiency, as cost is a major factor in global auto sales.

Sources: S. Silcoff, 1998, Boutique Z, *Canadian Business*, May 28, 62–66; http://www.hbc.com.annualrpt98/annual_report.html.asp; J. Chidley and S. Silcoff, 1999, The job from hell, *Canadian Business*, May 8, 39–45; http://www.acmi.canoe.ca/ MoneyGrowthEatons/aug20_eatonsicon.html; K. Naughton, E. Thorton, K. Kerwin, and H. Dawley, 1997, Can Honda build a world car? *BusinessWeek*, September 8, 100–8.

In recognition of strategic management's challenge, Andrew Grove, Intel's CEO, observed that only paranoid companies survive and succeed. Intel is the number-one computer chip manufacturer in the world, with market capitalization greater than the top three U.S. automakers combined. Such firms know that current success does not guarantee future strategic competitiveness and above-average returns. Accordingly, these companies strive continuously to improve so they can remain competitive. To be strategically competitive and earn above-average returns, Nortel, Aliant, Zellers, and Honda must compete differently in a world being shaped increasingly by globalization, technological changes, and the information revolution. For all these companies and others that are competing in the new competitive landscape, Andrew Grove believes that a key challenge is to try to do the impossible—namely, to anticipate the unexpected.[22]

## THE NEW COMPETITIVE LANDSCAPE[23]

The fundamental nature of competition in many of the world's industries is changing.[24] The pace of this change is relentless and increasing. Even determining the boundaries of an industry has become challenging. Consider, for example, how advances in interactive computer networks and telecommunications have blurred the definition of the "television" industry. Because of these advances, the near future will find firms such as ABC, CBC, CBS, NBC, CTV, and HBO competing not only among themselves but also with AT&T, Microsoft, Rogers, Sony, and Telus. An example of this new form of competition occurred in late 1995 when News Corporation, owner of Fox Broadcasting, formed a strategic alliance with Tele-Communications, the largest U.S. cable system. Viewed as a venture that would control a global web of sports TV networks, this alliance was considered to be a major competitor for ESPN and other sources interested in delivering sports events to customers around the world.[25]

Still other characteristics of the new competitive landscape are noteworthy. Conventional sources of competitive advantage such as economies of scale and huge advertising budgets are not as effective in the new competitive landscape. Moreover, the traditional managerial mind-set cannot lead a firm to strategic competitiveness in the new competitive landscape. In its place, managers must adopt a new mind-set—one that values flexibility, speed, innovation, and integration, and one that embraces the challenges that evolve from constantly changing conditions.[26] The conditions of the new competitive landscape result in a perilous business world, one where the investments required to compete on a global scale are enormous and the consequences of failure are severe.[27]

Hypercompetition is a term often used to capture the realities of the new competitive economy. According to Richard A. D'Aveni, hypercompetition

*results from the dynamics of strategic manoeuvring among global and innovative combatants. It is a condition of rapidly escalating competition based on price-quality positioning, competition to create new know-how and establish first-mover advantage, competition to protect or invade established product or geographic markets, and competition based on deep pockets and the creation of even deeper pocketed alliances.*[28]

Several factors have created hypercompetitive environments and the new competitive landscape. As shown in Figure 1.3, the emergence of a global economy and technology, coupled with rapid technological changes, are the two primary drivers.

■ ■ **FIGURE 1.3**

*The New Competitive Landscape*

**Technology and Technological Changes**
- Rapid technological changes
- Rapid technological diffusions
- Dramatic changes in information technologies
- Increasing importance of knowledge

**The Competitive Landscape**

**The Global Economy**
- People, goods, services, and ideas move freely across geographic borders
- Significant opportunities emerge in multiple global markets
- Markets and industries become more internationalized

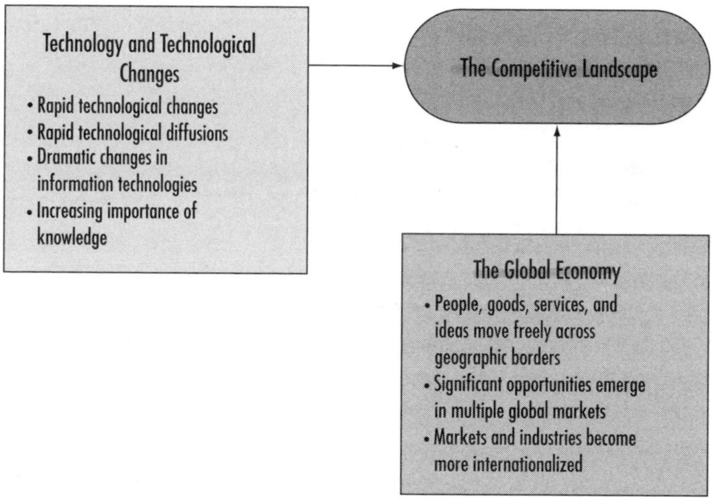

## The Global Economy

A **global economy** is one in which goods, services, people, skills, and ideas move freely across geographic borders.

A **global economy** is one in which goods, services, people, skills, and ideas move freely across geographic borders. Relatively unfettered by artificial constraints, such as tariffs, the global economy significantly expands and complicates a firm's competitive environment.[29]

Interesting opportunities and challenges are associated with the global economy's emergence. For example, Europe, not the United States, is now the world's largest single market. If countries from the former Soviet Union, and other Eastern bloc nations are included, the European market has a gross domestic product (GDP) of $5 trillion with 700 million potential customers.[30] In addition, by 2015 or perhaps sooner, China's total GDP will be greater than Japan's, although its per capita output will be much lower.[31] Some believe that the United States, Japan, and Europe are relatively equal contenders in the battle to be the most competitive nation, or group of nations, in the 21st century. Achieving this status will allow the "winner's citizens to have the highest standard of living."[32] Given that Canada, the United States, and Mexico all adhere to the North American Free Trade Agreement (NAFTA), and that the majority of Canada's exports go to the United States, it is clear that Canada's success will be linked to that of the United States.

To achieve strategic competitiveness in the global economy, a firm must view the world as its marketplace. For example, Procter & Gamble believes that it still has tremendous potential to grow internationally in such countries as China where demand for household products has not yet reached the mature stage.

A commitment to viewing the world as a company's marketplace creates a sense of direction that can serve the firm well. For example, Whirlpool Corporation, the world's largest manufacturer of major home appliances, intends to maintain its global leadership position. With production facilities in 12 countries and through its marketing efforts in 120 nations, the company's sales volume outside its home country, the United States, is now over 40 percent. Recently Whirlpool had investments in three appliance companies in Brazil, one in Canada, a subsidiary in Argentina, and joint ventures in Mexico, India, Taiwan, and China.

Vic Young, CEO of Fishery Products International (FPI) (headquartered in St. John's, Newfoundland and one of the largest fish companies in the world), is convinced that globalization is a key to his firm's growth. Young aggressively led his company into buying fish products in over 30 countries and selling them in over 15 countries. Under Young's aggressive leadership, FPI's portion of sales from the international arena is 85 percent, and it obtains over 85 percent of its fish products from international sources.[33]

## The March of Globalization

Globalization is the spread of economic innovations (innovations pertaining to the development, production, marketing, and use of income and commodities) from one country to another and the political and cultural adjustments that accompany this diffusion. Globalization encourages international integration, which has increased substantially during the last generation. In globalized markets and industries, financial capital might be obtained in one national market and used to buy raw materials in another. Manufacturing equipment bought from a third national market can be used to produce products that are sold in yet a fourth market.[34] Thus, globalization increases the range of opportunities for firms competing in this new competitive landscape. As noted in the Strategic Focus, this is the case for Wal-Mart.

## STRATEGIC FOCUS

### The March of Globalization: Wal-Mart, China, and Beyond

Wal-Mart is the world's largest retailer. The world should beware, however, because Wal-Mart has plans for getting much bigger. It is now moving aggressively into international markets. For example, the firm invested $1.2 billion to buy a controlling interest in Cifra SA, a large Mexican retailer with which it had a six-year joint venture. This move is the first direct investment in one of its foreign partners. While the international division of Wal-Mart is currently small compared to the rest of Wal-Mart's organization, analysts estimate that international sales are still $27 billion (17 percent of Wal-Mart's annual revenues). Currently, other retailers, such as Tengelmann and Aldi from Germany, Ahold from the Netherlands, and Carrefour from France, have higher foreign sales.

Wal-Mart is trying to achieve boundary-less retailing with global pricing, sourcing, and logistics. Wal-Mart is also sensitive to local needs and

*continued*

http://www.walmart.com

seeking out local suppliers. In Canada, Wal-Mart sources 80 percent of its merchandise from Canadian suppliers or distributors. Most of Wal-Mart's international investments have been in Canada and Mexico, with close proximity to the United States. However, Wal-Mart has moved recently into Argentina, Brazil, Indonesia, and China. Supercentre stores in Buenos Aires sell as many as 15 000 items in a day, twice as many as in comparable U.S. superstores.

Wal-Mart plans to export its North American dominance to other regions of the world as well, including China. China is trying to boldly reform its economy, moving toward a more open and entrepreneurial system. The Chinese government plans to sell a majority of its 13 000 large and midsize state-owned enterprises, along with many small firms as well. President Jiang Zemen has stated, "We should encourage mergers of enterprises, standardise bankruptcy procedures, divert laid-off workers, increase efficiency by downsizing staff and encourage re-employment projects." Wal-Mart plans to expand operations in China because its managers estimate that purchasing power in China will equal current levels in North America within seven years. Others are venturing into China as well. These companies range from Motorola's $2 billion fabrication plant to a joint venture between Enron and Singapore Power. This joint venture is designed to develop smaller-scale power projects that are expected to explode in number over the next several years in China.

U.S. companies such as Wal-Mart are spreading throughout the world. Yet globalization also means that foreign firms are moving into the United States. Though we may perceive it as a stronghold of multinationals, the United States is not immune to foreign incursions. For example, a foreign firm, Petroleos de Venezuela, owns the largest gasoline retailer in the country, with 14,054 Citgo gasoline outlets. As well, DaimlerChrysler lists Stuttgart Germany, and Auburn Hills Michigan, as its headquarters. However, DaimlerChrysler's 2000 annual meeting was held in Berlin.

Source: Daimler-Chrysler, 2000, *Daimler-Chrysler home page*, http:// www.daimlerchrysler .com/index_e. htm (Retrieved June 24); A. Kryhul, 1999, The Wal-Mart decade, *Marketing Magazine*, December 20/27, 11–12; S. Faison, 1997, Bold economic reforms proposed at opening of China Congress, *New York Times*, September 13, nytimes.com; M. M. Hamilton, 1997, At gasoline pumps, an urge to merge, *Washington Post*, July 15, washingtonpost.com; L. Lee and J. Millman, 1997, Wal-Mart to invest $1.2 billion for control of Mexican retailer, *Wall Street Journal Interactive Edition*, June 4, http://www.interactive3.wsj.com; *Wall Street Journal*, Singapore Power, Enron units form joint venture in China, June 21, http://www.wsj.com; W. Zellner, L. Shepard, I. Katz and D. Lindorff, 1997, Wal-Mart spoken here, *BusinessWeek*, June 16, http://www.businessweek.com.

The internationalization of markets and industries makes it increasingly difficult to think of some firms as domestic companies. Automaker Magna International (discussed further in Chapter 5) may be headquartered in Aurora, Ontario, but more than 60 percent of its almost 60,000 employees reside outside Canada.[35] Mitel Corporation of Kanata, Ontario, derives about 80 percent of its approximately one billion dollars in revenue from non-Canadian sources. We may think of Honda Motor Company as a Japanese firm, yet in North America Honda employs over 14 000 people and has the production capacity to produce 800000 autos (75 percent of its parts/assemblies are produced in North America). About 20 percent of Honda's North American production is made in

Canada.[36] Similarly, DaimlerChrysler produces minivans in Canada, LeBarons in Mexico, Dodges in the United States, and Mercedes in Europe. Likewise, a few years ago, Japan's Bridgestone Corporation acquired Firestone Corporation, then an American firm. Now, Bridgestone is planning to build a $400 million manufacturing facility in the United States. Bridgestone's intent is to enhance its competitive position in the North American market with its ninth U.S. plant and a $430 million upgrade of existing facilities.[37]

Given their operations, these firms should not be thought of as Japanese, European, American, or Canadian but should be more accurately classified as global companies striving to achieve strategic competitiveness in the new competitive landscape. Some believe that because of its enormous economic benefits, globalization will not be stopped. It has been predicted, for example, that genuine free trade in manufactured goods among NAFTA, Europe, and Japan would add 5 to 10 percent to the triad's annual economic outputs; free trade in the triad's service sector would boost aggregate output by another 15 to 20 percent. Realizing these potential gains in economic output requires a commitment from the industrialized nations to cooperatively stimulate the higher levels of trade necessary for global growth. Eliminating national laws that impede free trade is an important stimulus to increased trading among nations.[38]

Global competition has increased performance standards in many dimensions, including those of quality, cost, productivity, product introduction time, and smooth, flowing operations. Moreover, these standards are not static; they are exacting, requiring continuous improvement from a firm and its employees. As they accept the challenges posed by these increasing standards, companies improve their capabilities and individual workers sharpen their skills. Thus, in the new competitive landscape, competitive success will accrue only to those capable of meeting, if not exceeding, global standards. This challenge exists for large firms as well as small and midsize companies that develop cooperative relationships (e.g., joint ventures) with larger corporations in order to capitalize on international growth opportunities.[39]

The development of newly industrialized countries is changing the global competitive landscape and significantly increasing competition in global markets. The economic development of Asian countries outside Japan is increasing the significance of Asian markets. Firms such as Wal-Mart, Motorola, and Enron are making major investments in Asia. Of course, there are also firms such as Petroleos de Venezuela and Honda that have made major investments in North America. Thus, international investments come from many directions and are targeted for many different regions of the world. There are risks with these investments, however. We discuss a number of these risks in Chapter 9. Some have referred to these risks as the liability of foreignness.[40] Critical to success in international markets is a firm's ability to manage international operations such that it takes advantage of the opportunities presented by operating in these markets and overcomes or avoids most of the challenges that exist in these markets. Moreover, performance may suffer with substantial amounts of globalization. For instance, firms may overdiversify internationally beyond their ability to manage the diversified operations that have been created.[41] The outcome can sometimes be quite painful to firms.[42] Thus, movement into international markets, even for firms with substantial experience in such markets, requires careful planning and selection of the appropriate markets to enter and the most effective strategies to operate successfully in those markets.[43]

# Technology and Technological Changes

There are three categories of technological trends and conditions through which technology is significantly altering the nature of competition.

## Increasing Rate of Technological Change and Diffusion

Both the rate of technology changes and the speed at which new technologies become available and are used have increased substantially over the last 15 to 20 years. "Perpetual innovation" is a term used to describe how rapidly and consistently new, information-intensive technologies replace older ones. The shorter product life cycles resulting from these rapid diffusions of new technologies place a competitive premium on being able to quickly introduce new goods and services into the marketplace. In fact, when products become somewhat indistinguishable because of the widespread and rapid diffusion of technologies, speed to market may be the only source of competitive advantage (see Chapter 6).[44]

There are other indicators of rapid technology diffusion. Some evidence suggests that after only 12 to 18 months, companies likely will have gathered information about their competitors' research and development and product decisions. Often, merely a few weeks pass before a new North American product introduced in North American markets is copied, manufactured, and shipped to North America by one or more companies in Asia.

Once a source of competitive advantage, today's rate of technological diffusion stifles the protection firms possessed previously through their patents. Patents are now thought by many to be an ineffective way of protecting proprietary technology. Many firms competing in the electronics industry often do not apply for patents so as to prevent competitors from gaining access to the technological knowledge included in the patent application.

## The Information Age

Dramatic changes in information technology have occurred in recent years. Personal computers, cellular phones, artificial intelligence, virtual reality, and massive databases are a few examples of how information is used differently as a result of technological developments. Intel's Andrew Grove believes that electronic mail (e-mail) systems are the first manifestation of a revolution in the flow and management of information in companies throughout the world. In Grove's view, "The informed use of e-mail has two simple but startling implications: It turns days into minutes, and allows each person to reach hundreds of co-workers with the same effort it takes to reach just one."[45] An important outcome of these changes is that the ability to gain access to and effectively use information has become an important source of competitive advantage in virtually all industries.

Companies are now being wired to build electronic networks linking them to customers, employees, vendors, and suppliers. IBM has made this a major thrust in its drive to reorient and revive its business. IBM and others refer to these networks as e-business. Both the pace of change in information technology and its diffusion will continue to increase. It is predicted, for example, that the number of personal computers in use will grow from over 150 million today to 278 million in 2010. The declining costs of information technologies and the increased accessibility to them are also evident in the new competitive landscape. The global proliferation of relatively inexpensive computing power and its linkage on a global scale via computer networks combine to increase the speed and diffusion of information technologies. Thus, the competitive potential of information technologies is now available to companies throughout the world rather than only to large firms in Europe, Japan, and North America.[46]

The Internet provides an important electronic pathway through which relatively inexpensive data and information are being distributed. Combined, the Internet and the World Wide Web create an infrastructure that allows the delivery of information to computers in any location. Access to significant quantities of relatively inexpensive information yields strategic opportunities for a range of industries and companies. Retailers, for example, use the Internet to provide abundant shopping privileges to customers in multiple locations. The power of this means of information access and application has resulted in an astonishing array of strategic implications and possibilities.[47]

Anticipating and even creating users' future needs for access to and competitive use of information is challenging. The nature of this complex situation in an emerging industry seems to argue against a firm's long-term competitive success. Microsoft CEO Bill Gates observed that while his firm may be the most dominant force in the personal computer industry today, "The landscape is changing fast enough that the company's continued role is far from guaranteed." This opinion was offered at a time when Microsoft controlled more than 80 percent of the world market for PC operating systems.[48] Thus, even for companies holding dominant positions such as Microsoft, the information age's rapid changes yield an uncertain and ambiguous future.

## Increasing Knowledge Intensity

Knowledge (information, intelligence, and expertise) is the basis of technology and its application. In the new competitive landscape, knowledge is a critical organizational resource and is increasingly a valuable source of competitive advantage. Because of this, many companies now strive to transmute the accumulated knowledge of individual employees into a corporate asset. Some argue that the value of intangible assets, including knowledge, is growing as a proportion of total shareholder value.[49] The probability of achieving strategic competitiveness in the new competitive landscape is enhanced for the firm that realizes that its survival depends on the ability to capture intelligence, transform it into usable knowledge, and diffuse it rapidly throughout the company.[50] Companies that accept this challenge shift their focus from obtaining the information to exploiting the information to gain a competitive advantage over rival firms.[51]

Our discussion of conditions in the new competitive landscape shows that firms must be able to adapt quickly to achieve strategic competitiveness and earn above-average returns. The term **strategic flexibility** describes a firm's ability to do this. Strategic flexibility is a set of capabilities firms use to respond to various demands and opportunities that are a part of dynamic and uncertain competitive environments.[52] Firms should develop strategic flexibility in all areas of their operations. Such capabilities in terms of manufacturing, for example, allow firms to "switch gears—from, for example, rapid product development to low cost—relatively quickly and with minimum resources."[53]

To achieve strategic flexibility, many firms have to develop organizational slack. Slack resources allow the firm some flexibility to respond to environmental changes and may be considered the most critical element in assuring a company's survival.[54] When the changes required are large, firms may have to undergo strategic reorientations,

**Strategic flexibility** is a set of capabilities firms use to respond to various demands and opportunities that are a part of dynamic and uncertain competitive environments.

which can drastically change a firm's competitive strategy.[55] Strategic reorientations are often the result of a firm's poor performance. For example, when a firm earns negative returns, its stakeholders (see discussion later in this chapter) are likely to place pressure on the top executives to make major changes.[56] To achieve continuous strategic flexibility, a firm has to develop the capacity to learn. As such, the learning is continuous and provides the firm with new and current sets of skills. This allows it to adapt to its environment as the environment changes.[57]

Through careful strategic decisions, Coca-Cola Enterprises (CCE) has created strategic flexibility by developing effective distribution of its products. For example, several years ago Coca-Cola developed a subsidiary bottling operation. The company wanted to build an experienced and large bottling network to benefit from economies of scale and have significant capital to invest in distribution systems to enhance sales of Coca-Cola. Today, this small set of anchor bottlers serves as the base for Coca-Cola's global distribution system. Because of its success, CCE is becoming Coca-Cola's primary bottler in Great Britain, France, Belgium, the Netherlands, and Luxembourg. Thus, CCE has the resources and expertise to move into different regions of the world, which only increases its economies of scale.[58]

Next, we describe two models used by firms to generate the strategic inputs needed to successfully formulate and implement strategies and to maintain strategic flexibility in the process of doing so.

## THE I/O MODEL OF ABOVE-AVERAGE RETURNS

From the 1960s through the 1980s, the external environment was thought to be the primary determinant of strategies firms selected to be successful.[59] The I/O (industrial organization) model explains the dominant influence of the external environment on firms' strategic actions. This model specifies that the industry chosen in which to compete has a stronger influence on a firm's performance than do the choices managers make inside their organizations.[60] The model states that firm performance is determined primarily by a range of an industry's properties, including economies of scale, barriers to entry, diversification, product differentiation, and the degree of concentration[61] (these industry characteristics are examined in Chapter 3).

Grounded in the economics discipline, the I/O model has four underlying assumptions. First, the external environment is assumed to impose pressures and constraints that determine the strategies that would result in above-average returns. Second, most firms competing within a particular industry, or within a certain segment of an industry, are assumed to control similar strategically relevant resources and pursue similar strategies in light of those resources. The I/O model's third assumption is that resources used to implement strategies are highly mobile across firms. Because of resource mobility, any resource differences that might develop between firms will be short-lived. Fourth, organizational decision-makers are assumed to be rational and committed to acting in the firm's best interests as shown by their profit-maximizing behaviours.[62]

The I/O model challenges firms to locate the most attractive industry in which to compete. Because most firms are assumed to have similar strategically relevant resources that are mobile across companies, competitiveness generally can be increased only when these firms find the industry with the highest profit potential and learn how to use their resources to implement the strategy required by the structural characteristics in that industry. The five-forces model of competition is an analytical tool used to help firms with this task. This model (explained in detail in Chapter 3) encompasses many variables and tries to capture the complexity of competition.[63]

The five-forces model suggests that an industry's potential profitability (i.e., its rate of return on invested capital relative to its cost of capital) is a function of interactions among five forces (suppliers, buyers, competitive rivalry among firms currently in the industry, product substitutes, and potential entrants to the industry).[64] Using this tool, a firm is challenged to understand an industry's profit potential and the strategy that the company should implement to establish a defensible competitive position, given the industry's structural characteristics. Typically, this model suggests that firms can earn above-average returns by manufacturing standardized products at costs below those of competitors (a cost leadership strategy) or differentiated products for which customers are willing to pay a price premium (a differentiation strategy). Cost leadership and differentiation strategies are described fully in Chapter 5.

As shown in Figure 1.4, the I/O model suggests that above-average returns are earned when firms implement the strategy dictated by the characteristics of the general, industry, and competitive environments. Companies that develop or acquire the internal skills needed to implement strategies required by the external environment are likely to succeed, while those that do not are likely to fail. As such, above-average returns are determined by external characteristics, not by their unique internal resources and capabilities.

Let us consider the bagel industry as an example. It is a high-growth industry with substantial potential to earn above-average returns. U.S. industry sales increased from $1.6 billion in 1995 to $2.3 billion in 1996, more than a 40 percent rise in one year. Industry experts predict this growth trend for global sales as well. Interestingly, the bagel industry is in its infancy and thus has much potential. Evidence of this fact is shown by the growth of The Great Canadian Bagel. It was started in 1993 and, by the summer of 1998, it had 161 bakeries in operation. Other bagel firms are opening operations in Europe and Asia. Clearly it is an attractive industry to enter.[65]

Recent research provides support for the I/O model, showing that approximately 20 percent of firm profitability is explained by industry. In other words, 20 percent of a firm's profitability is determined by the industry or industries in which it chooses to operate. This research also showed, however, that 36 percent of the variance in profitability could be attributed to firm characteristics and actions.[66] The results of this research suggest that both the environment and firm characteristics play a role in determining a firm's specific level of profitability. Thus, there is likely a reciprocal relationship between the environment and firm strategy, and this interrelationship affects firm performance.[67]

As the research results suggest, successful competition in the new competitive landscape mandates that firms build a unique set of resources and capabilities. This should be done, however, within the framework of the dynamics of the industry (or industries) in which a firm competes. In this context, a firm is viewed as a bundle of market activities and a bundle of resources. Market activities are understood through application of the I/O model. The development and effective use of a firm's resources, capabilities, and competencies is understood through application of the resource-based model. Through an effective combination of results gained via both the I/O and resource-based models, firms dramatically increase the probability of achieving strategic competitiveness and earning above-average returns. In summary, we can view the I/O model as looking outside the firm while the resource-based model, which is examined next, can be viewed as looking inside the firm.

■ ■ **FIGURE 1.4**

*The I/O Model of Superior Returns*

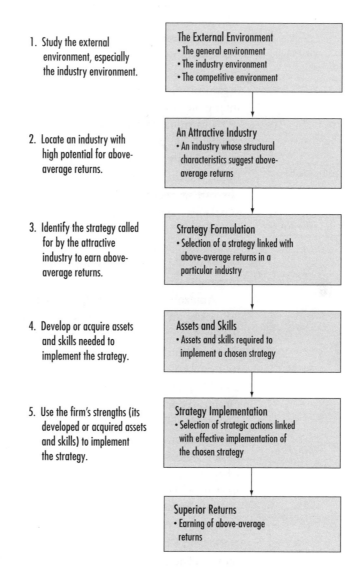

1. Study the external environment, especially the industry environment.

**The External Environment**
- The general environment
- The industry environment
- The competitive environment

2. Locate an industry with high potential for above-average returns.

**An Attractive Industry**
- An industry whose structural characteristics suggest above-average returns

3. Identify the strategy called for by the attractive industry to earn above-average returns.

**Strategy Formulation**
- Selection of a strategy linked with above-average returns in a particular industry

4. Develop or acquire assets and skills needed to implement the strategy.

**Assets and Skills**
- Assets and skills required to implement a chosen strategy

5. Use the firm's strengths (its developed or acquired assets and skills) to implement the strategy.

**Strategy Implementation**
- Selection of strategic actions linked with effective implementation of the chosen strategy

**Superior Returns**
- Earning of above-average returns

# THE RESOURCE-BASED MODEL OF ABOVE-AVERAGE RETURNS

The resource-based model assumes that each organization is a collection of unique resources and capabilities that provides the basis for its strategy and is the primary source of its returns. In the new competitive landscape, this model argues that a firm is a collection of evolving capabilities that is managed dynamically in pursuit of above-average returns.[68] According to this model, differences in firms' performances across time are driven primarily by their unique resources and capabilities rather than by an industry's structural characteristics.[69] This model also assumes that, over time, a firm acquires different resources and develops unique capabilities. As such, all firms competing within a particular industry may not possess the same strategically relevant resources and capabilities. Another assumption of this model is that resources may not

**Resources** are inputs into a firm's production process, such as capital equipment, the skills of individual employees, patents, finance, and talented managers.

A **capability** is the capacity for a set of resources to integratively perform a task or an activity.

be highly mobile across firms. The differences in resources form the basis of competitive advantage.[70]

**Resources** are inputs into a firm's production process, such as capital equipment, the skills of individual employees, patents, finance, and talented managers. In general, a firm's resources can be classified into four categories: physical, human, financial, and organizational capital.[71] Described fully in Chapter 4, resources are both tangible and intangible in nature.

Individual resources alone may not yield a competitive advantage. For example, a sophisticated piece of manufacturing equipment may become a strategically relevant resource only when its use is integrated effectively with other aspects of a firm's operations (such as marketing and the work of employees). In general, it is through the combination and integration of sets of resources that competitive advantages are formed. A **capability** is the capacity for a set of resources to integratively perform a task or an activity.[72] Through continued use, capabilities become stronger and more difficult for competitors to understand and imitate.[73] As a source of competitive advantage, a capability "should be neither so simple that it is highly imitable, nor so complex that it defies internal steering and control."[74]

Amazon.com has taken the retail book market by storm, after being the first firm to sell books on the Internet. As such, Amazon.com has developed important capabilities for marketing and distributing books online. This firm has shown that a large inventory and beautiful facilities are not necessary to sell books. However, Amazon.com's capabilities can be imitated. In fact, large and powerful book companies such as Barnes & Noble and Chapters are imitating them. Chapters opened an online bookshop via Chapters Online, which owns Chapters.ca. (the ".ca" reaffirming their Canadian origins). Chapters Online went public in 1999 and has grown to become Canada's largest online book retailer, partially because it helps customers avoid high exchange rates. According to an Angus Reid/Deloitte and Touche survey, the number of shoppers to the Chapters.ca site during the 1999 Christmas season equalled the number of visitors to the next three largest Canadian e-tailers. In addition, Chapters Online received Internet World Canada's Site of the Year Award for its positive impact on Canadians.[75] Developing Web sites and online order-taking is copied easily, as shown by Barnes & Noble and Chapters. It remains to be seen whether Amazon.com will enjoy many first-mover advantages. (See Chapter 6 for a full discussion of first-mover advantages.)

The resource-based model of competitive advantage is shown in Figure 1.5. In contrast to the I/O model, the resource-based view is grounded in the perspective that a firm's internal environment, in terms of its resources and capabilities, is more critical to the determination of strategic actions than is the external environment. Instead of focusing on the accumulation of resources necessary to implement the strategy dictated by conditions and constraints in the external environment (I/O model), the resource-based view suggests that a firm's unique resources and capabilities provide the basis for a strategy. The strategy chosen should allow the firm to best exploit its core competencies relative to opportunities in the external environment.

Not all of a firm's resources and capabilities have the potential to be the basis for competitive advantage. This potential is realized when resources and capabilities are valuable, rare, costly to imitate, and organized to be exploited.[76] Resources are valuable when they allow a firm to exploit opportunities and/or neutralize threats in its external environment; they are rare when possessed by few, if any, current and potential com-

■ ■ **FIGURE 1.5**

*The Resource-Based Model of Superior Returns*

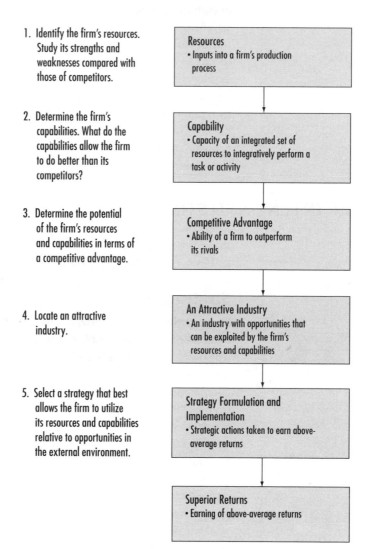

1. Identify the firm's resources. Study its strengths and weaknesses compared with those of competitors.

**Resources**
• Inputs into a firm's production process

2. Determine the firm's capabilities. What do the capabilities allow the firm to do better than its competitors?

**Capability**
• Capacity of an integrated set of resources to integratively perform a task or activity

3. Determine the potential of the firm's resources and capabilities in terms of a competitive advantage.

**Competitive Advantage**
• Ability of a firm to outperform its rivals

4. Locate an attractive industry.

**An Attractive Industry**
• An industry with opportunities that can be exploited by the firm's resources and capabilities

5. Select a strategy that best allows the firm to utilize its resources and capabilities relative to opportunities in the external environment.

**Strategy Formulation and Implementation**
• Strategic actions taken to earn above-average returns

**Superior Returns**
• Earning of above-average returns

petitors; they are costly to imitate (nonduplicable or nonsubstitutable) when other firms either cannot obtain them or are at a cost disadvantage to obtain them compared to the firm that already possesses them; and they are organized to be exploited when they are supported by the appropriate structure, controls, and rewards.[77]

When these four criteria are met, resources and capabilities become core competencies. **Core competencies** are resources and capabilities that serve as a source of sustained competitive advantage for a firm over its rivals.[78] Often related to a firm's functional skills (e.g., the marketing function at Pepsi-Cola has been considered a core competence), the development, nurturing, and application of core competencies throughout a firm may be highly related to strategic competitiveness. Managerial competencies are important in most firms. For example, such competencies have been shown to be critically important to successful entry into foreign markets.[79] Such competencies may include the capability to effectively organize and govern complex, diverse

**Core competencies** are resources and capabilities that serve as a source of sustained competitive advantage for a firm over its rivals.

operations and the capability to create and communicate a strategic vision.[80] Another set of important competencies is product related. Included among these competencies is the capability to develop innovative new products and to reengineer existing products to satisfy changing consumer tastes.[81] Competencies must also be under continuous development to keep them up to date, which requires a systematic program for updating old skills and learning new ones.[82] Dynamic core competencies are especially important in rapidly changing environments such as those that exist in high-technology industries.[83] Thus, the resource-based model argues that core competencies are the basis for a firm's competitive advantage, its strategic competitiveness, and its ability to earn above-average returns.

# STRATEGIC INTENT AND STRATEGIC MISSION

Analyses of a firm's internal and external environments results in information required to form a strategic intent and develop a strategic mission (see Figure 1.1). Both intent and mission are linked with strategic competitiveness.

## Strategic Intent

**Strategic intent** is the leveraging of a firm's internal resources, capabilities, and core competencies to accomplish the firm's goals in the competitive environment.

**Strategic intent** is the leveraging of a firm's internal resources, capabilities, and core competencies to accomplish the firm's goals in the competitive environment.[84] Concerned with winning competitive battles and obtaining global leadership, strategic intent implies a significant stretch of an organization's resources, capabilities, and core competencies. When established effectively, strategic intent can cause people to perform in ways they never imagined would be possible.[85] Strategic intent exists when all employees and levels of a firm are committed to the pursuit of a specific (and significant) performance criterion. Some argue that strategic intent provides employees with the only goal worthy of personal effort and commitment—to unseat the best or remain the best, worldwide.[86] Strategic intent has been formed effectively when people believe fervently in their product and industry and when they are focused totally on their firm's ability to outdo its competitors.[87]

The following examples are expressions of strategic intent. Chapters Online is "Committed to providing a convenient and hassle-free e-commerce experience; Chapters Online offers a secure shopping environment, easy-to-use search tools, and industry leading customer service." Fishery Products International's strategic intent is to continue to be "a Newfoundland-based international seafood enterprise ... dedicated [to building] our global leadership position ... We have long believed in innovation, environmental responsibility, quality assurance and relationship building." Phillips Petroleum seeks "to be the top performer in everything" the company does. Intel intends to become the premier building-block supplier to the computer industry. Microsoft believes that its "Holy Grail" is to provide the Yellow Pages for an electronic marketplace of on-line information systems. Canon desires to "beat Xerox," and Honda strives to become a second Ford (a company it identified as a pioneer in the auto industry). Bombardier's strategic intent is to be a market leader through excellence in its aerospace products, transportation equipment, recreational products, financial services, and other related services and products. At Procter & Gamble, employees participate in a program the CEO calls "combat training" to focus on ways the company can beat the competition. AlliedSignal wants to be known as one of North America's premier profitmakers by achieving 6 percent annual productivity improvements "forever."[88]

Because of its emotional edge, strategic intent may even be described metaphorically. In a recent annual report, Reebok International showed a series of pictures depicting an athlete crossing a high-jump bar. In her own handwriting, the athlete described her commitment to being the best and to winning:

*It's about raising the bar. I can jump higher. I know it. I can see it. I'm stronger, faster; I've learned more. The key is to focus, to concentrate on each basic element that goes into a jump. Jumping is my gift and it's a privilege to improve the gift. When everything works right, when you're focused and relaxed, it's kind of like flying. One thing that keeps you involved in jumping is that you are always trying to clear the next height. Even if you miss, you come away from every jump knowing you can go higher.*[89]

The words of this athlete reflect Reebok's intent to focus and concentrate on every part of its business in order to constantly improve its performance and, by doing so, achieve strategic competitiveness and earn above-average returns.

But it is not enough for a firm to know only its own strategic intent. To achieve high performance demands that we also know our competitors' strategic intent. Only when intentions of others are understood can a firm become aware of the resolve, stamina, and inventiveness (traits linked with effective strategic intents) of those competitors.[90] A firm's success may be grounded in a keen and deep understanding of the strategic intent of customers, suppliers, partners, and competitors.[91]

## Strategic Mission

As our discussion shows, strategic intent is internally focused. It is concerned with identifying the resources, capabilities, and core competencies on which a firm can base its strategic actions. Strategic intent reflects what a firm is capable of doing as a result of its core competencies and the unique ways they can be used to exploit a competitive advantage.

Strategic mission flows from strategic intent. Externally focused, the **strategic mission** is a statement of a firm's unique purpose and the scope of its operations in product and market terms.[92] A strategic mission provides general descriptions of the products a firm intends to produce and the markets it will serve using its internally based core competencies. The interdependent relationship between strategic intent and strategic mission is shown in Figure 1.6.

An effective strategic mission establishes a firm's individuality and is exciting, inspiring, and relevant to all stakeholders.[93] Together, strategic intent and strategic mission yield the insights required to formulate and implement the firm's strategies.

Based partially on a firm's strategic intent and mission, top executives develop a strategic orientation and a predisposition to adopt a certain strategy or strategies over others.[94] Strategic orientation is also affected by the national culture in an executive's home country and the institutional environment where the firm's operations are located.[95] A competitor's strategic orientations can be predicted based on knowledge of its strategic intent and mission, the institutional environment where its home office is located, and the cultural values of the top executives' home country.

The **strategic mission** is a statement of a firm's unique purpose and the scope of its operations in product and market terms.

■ ■ **FIGURE 1.6**

*The Interdependent Relationship between Strategic Intent and Strategic Mission*

When a firm is strategically competitive and earning above-average returns, it has the capacity to satisfy its stakeholders' interests. Stakeholder groups with whom a firm may interact are examined in the next section.

## STAKEHOLDERS

An organization is a system of primary stakeholder groups with whom it establishes and manages relationships.[96] Stakeholders are the individuals and groups who can affect and are affected by the strategic outcomes achieved and who have enforceable claims on a firm's performance.[97] Claims against an organization's performance are enforced through a stakeholder's ability to withhold participation essential to a firm's survival, competitiveness, and profitability.[98] Stakeholders continue to support an organization when its performance meets or exceeds their expectations.

Thus, organizations have dependency relationships with their stakeholders. Firms, however, are not equally dependent on all stakeholders at all times; as a consequence, every stakeholder does not have the same level of influence. The more critical and valued a stakeholder's participation is, the greater a firm's dependency on it. Greater dependence, in turn, results in more potential influence for the stakeholder over a firm's commitments, decisions, and actions. In one sense, the challenge strategists face is to either accommodate or find ways to insulate the organization from the demands of stakeholders who control critical resources.[99]

## STRATEGIC FOCUS

### Stakeholders Are on Both Sides

There are several types of stakeholders, and firms must be sensitive to the needs of all of them to earn above-average returns. General Motors, for example, must deal with the United Auto Workers (UAW) union (product market stakeholder), which represents many of its employees, while at the same time satisfying its shareholders and potential shareholders (capital market stakeholders). This can be challenging. In 1997, GM had the lowest productivity in the auto industry,

*continued*

requiring 47 worker-hours to produce an automobile while Nissan did it in 28 worker-hours. Chrysler and Ford required 38 and 41 worker-hours respectively. This productivity gap costs GM $700 more per car than Nissan. Shareholders and analysts on Wall Street placed significant pressure on GM to improve its productivity. To do so, GM planned to eliminate 50 000 plant jobs over several years. However, the UAW fought GM on this decision and threatened to strike.

Unions have employees, too. For example, the Teamsters Union experienced a threatened strike from its office and professional employees. The employees were dissatisfied with the union's proposal that would require employees to have 33 years service to reach the top pay scale, the introduction of time clocks, and restrictions on the use of flextime. The office and professional employees union forced the dispute to be submitted to a mediator. Not all unions are as tough in their negotiations. The German Chemical Union agreed to a reduction in wages. Because of financial problems in German companies, the union agreed to a 10 percent decrease in wages. The union has been pressured by the federal government in Germany to make concessions because of 11 percent unemployment. The German union negotiator called the agreement a reaction to the changing economy.

Bell Canada, Canada's largest telephone company, must deal with the Communications, Energy and Paperworkers union, which represents many employees, while satisfying its shareholders and potential shareholders. This is challenging to the former monopoly, particularly since deregulation in the telecommunication industry has increased competition. In 1999, Bell attempted to lower costs by selling its operator services to a U.S. company, which could offer the services in Canada at a lower cost. Bell faced labour strife and ultimately a strike by the operators.

Source: S. F. Swoboda, 1997, Teamsters on unusual side in labour tiff, Washington Post, July 16, washingtonpost.com; *Wall Street Journal Interactive Edition*, 1997, German chemical union agrees to let companies cut wages, http://www.interactive5.wsj. com; B. Vlasic, 1997, GM can't afford to budge: To compete on productivity, it risks strikes, *BusinessWeek*, June 16, http://www. businessweek.com; C. Perkel, 1999, Bell workers hit bricks as strike deadline looms, *Canadian Press Newswire*, April 8; M. MacDonald, 1999, Bell's union woes come amid sweeping changes, *Canadian Press Newswire*, April 8.

The discussion in the Strategic Focus regarding stakeholders suggests the potential differences in power among stakeholders. In the case of GM, shareholders and Wall Street were more powerful than the union representing workers. GM and others are willing to accept a strike if necessary in order to achieve the increase in productivity desired by the shareholders. The Strategic Focus also provides examples of several different types of stakeholders, the topic of our next discussion.

## Classification of Stakeholders

The parties involved with a firm's operations can be separated into three groups.[100] As shown in Figure 1.7, these groups are the capital market stakeholders (shareholders and the major suppliers of a firm's capital), the product market stakeholders (the firm's primary customers, suppliers, host communities, and unions representing the workforce), and the organizational stakeholders (all of a firm's employees, including both nonmanagerial and managerial personnel).

Each of these stakeholder groups expects those making strategic decisions in a firm to provide the leadership through which their valued objectives will be accomplished.[101] But these groups' objectives often differ from one another, sometimes placing managers in situations where tradeoffs have to be made.

■ ■ **FIGURE 1.7**

*The Three Stakeholder Groups*

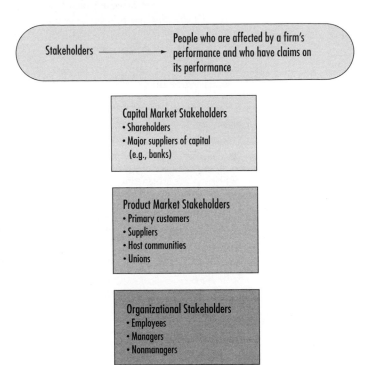

Grounded in laws governing private property and private enterprise, the most obvious stakeholders are shareholders—those who have invested capital in a firm in the expectation of earning at least an average return on their investments. Shareholders want the return on their investment (and, hence, their wealth) to be maximized. This could be accomplished at the expense of investing in a firm's future. Gains achieved by reducing investment in research and development, for example, could be returned to shareholders (thereby increasing the short-term return on their investments). However, a short-term enhancement of shareholders' wealth can negatively affect the firm's future competitive ability. Sophisticated shareholders, with diversified portfolios, may sell their interests if a firm fails to invest in its future. This is exemplified in the Strategic Focus, as GM's shareholders are exerting pressure to increase the firm's productivity. Those making strategic decisions are responsible for a firm's survival in both the short and the long terms. Accordingly, it is in the interests of neither the organizational stakeholders nor the product market stakeholders for investments in the company to be unduly minimized.

In contrast to shareholders, customers prefer that investors receive a minimum return on their investments. As such, customers could have their interests maximized when the quality and reliability of a firm's products are improved without a price increase. High returns to customers might come at the expense of lower returns to capital market shareholders.

Because of potential conflicts, each firm is challenged to manage its stakeholders. First, a firm must carefully identify all stakeholders who are important to it. Second, it must prioritize them in case it cannot satisfy all of them. In doing this, power is the most critical criterion. Other criteria might include the urgency of satisfying each particular stakeholder and the degree of importance to the firm.[102] When earning above-average returns, this challenge is lessened substantially. With the capability and flexibility provided by above-average returns, a firm can more easily satisfy all stakeholders simultaneously.

When earning only average returns, however, a firm may find the management of stakeholders to be more difficult. In these situations, tradeoffs must be made. With average returns, a firm is unlikely to maximize the interests of all stakeholders. The objective becomes one of at least minimally satisfying each stakeholder. Trade-off decisions are made in light of how dependent the firm is on the support of each stakeholder group. An example of how stakeholders can demand satisfaction of their claims on a firm's performance is provided in the next subsection. A firm earning below-average returns does not have the capacity to minimally satisfy all stakeholders. The managerial challenge in this case is to make tradeoffs that minimize the amount of support lost from stakeholders.

Societal values influence the general weightings allocated among the three stakeholder groups. Although firms in at least the major industrialized nations serve all three groups, the priorities in their service vary somewhat because of cultural differences. These differences are shown in the following commentary:

*In [North] America … shareholders have a comparatively big say in the running of the enterprises they own; workers … have much less influence. In many European countries, shareholders have less say and workers more … In Japan … managers have been left alone to run their companies as they see fit—namely for the benefit of employees and of allied companies, as much as for shareholders.[103]*

Thus, it is important that those responsible for managing stakeholder relationships in a country outside their native land use a global mind-set. A **global mind-set** is the "capacity to appreciate the beliefs, values, behaviours, and business practices of individuals and organizations from a variety of regions and cultures."[104] Use of a global mind-set allows managers to better understand the realities and preferences that are part of the world region and culture in which they are working.

In the next three subsections, additional information is presented about the stakeholder groups that firms manage.

## Capital Market Stakeholders

Both shareholders and lenders expect that a firm will preserve and enhance the wealth they have entrusted to it. The returns expected are commensurate with the degree of risk accepted with those investments (i.e., lower returns are expected with low-risk investments; higher returns are expected with high-risk investments).

A **global mind-set** is the capacity to appreciate the beliefs, values, behaviours, and business practices of individuals and organizations from a variety of regions and cultures.

If lenders become dissatisfied, they can impose stricter covenants on subsequent capital borrowing. Shareholders can reflect their dissatisfaction through several means, including the sale of their stock. When aware of potential or actual dissatisfactions among capital market stakeholders, a firm may respond to their concerns. The firm's response to dissatisfied stakeholders is affected by the nature of its dependency relationship with them (which, as noted earlier, is also influenced by a society's values). The greater and more significant the dependency relationship, the more direct and significant a firm's response will be.

The power and influence of capital market stakeholders are exemplified in their effects on New Brunswick's Repap. In 1999, TD Asset Management and Third Avenue Funds announced their concern with the compensation package for Repap's Chairman, Steven Berg. Both institutional investors considered the package excessive given Repap's recent poor performance. Both investors had a significant stake in Repap and considered it their responsibility to cite their concern. Repap ultimately announced that in light of these shareholder concerns five directors had resigned from the board.[105]

Shareholders also had an effect on Rubbermaid. In 1997, investors drove Rubbermaid's stock price down 11 percent after management announced that earnings would be more than 30 percent below expected. When there was a second announcement of bad news, shareholders increased pressure that led many managers to resign. Management then sought new ways to distribute the firm's products by forming an alliance with Amway and tapping specialty stores and the Internet. Thus, shareholders have prompted significant actions on the part of Rubbermaid's top management.[106] At least in the short run, this added support for the capital market stakeholders may come at the expense of returns to other stakeholders.

## Product Market Stakeholders

Initial observation of customers, suppliers, host communities, and unions representing workers might suggest little commonality among their interests. However, close inspection indicates that all four parties can benefit as firms engage in competitive battles. For example, depending on product and industry characteristics, marketplace competition may result in lower product prices being charged to a firm's customers and higher prices paid to its suppliers (the firm might be willing to pay higher supplier prices to ensure delivery of the types of goods and services linked with competitive success). Fishery Products International has this dual problem with its customers and suppliers (see the FPI opening case in Chapter 13), which has impacted its performance in the past decade.

As will be noted in Chapter 5, customers, as stakeholders, demand reliable products at the lowest possible prices. Suppliers seek assured customers willing to pay the highest sustainable prices for the goods and services they receive. Host communities want companies willing to be long-term employers and providers of tax revenues, without placing excessive demands on public support services. Union officials are interested in secure jobs, under ideal working conditions, for employees they represent. Thus, product market stakeholders are generally satisfied when a firm's profit margin yields the lowest acceptable return to capital market stakeholders (i.e., the lowest return lenders and shareholders will accept and still retain their interests in the firm). The relationship between satisfaction of customers' needs and strategic competitiveness is examined in detail in Chapter 5.

## Organizational Stakeholders

Employees, nonmanagerial and managerial, expect a firm to provide a dynamic, stimulating, and rewarding working environment. These stakeholders are usually satisfied working for a company that is growing and developing their skills, especially the skills required to be effective team members and to meet or exceed global work standards. Workers who learn how to productively use rapidly developing knowledge are thought to be critical to organizational success. In a collective sense, the education and skills of a nation's workforce may be its dominant competitive weapon in a global economy.[107]

In the next section, we describe the people responsible for the design and execution of strategic management processes. Various names are given to these people—top-level managers, executives, strategists, the top management team, and general managers. Throughout this book, these names are used interchangeably. But, in all cases, they describe the work of persons responsible for designing and implementing a successful strategic management process.

As is discussed in Chapter 13, top-level managers can be a source of competitive advantage. The decisions and actions these people make to combine resources and create capabilities can also result in a competitive advantage.

# ORGANIZATIONAL STRATEGISTS

Small organizations may have a single strategist. In many cases, this person owns the firm and is deeply involved with its daily operations. At the other extreme, large, diversified firms have many top-level managers. In addition to the CEO and other top-level officials (e.g., chief operating officer, president, and chief financial officer), these firms have managers who are responsible for the performance of individual business units. This is seen in such diverse firms as the Royal Bank of Canada, Nortel Networks, JDS Uniphase, Aliant, and Corel.

Typically, stakeholders have high expectations of top-level managers, particularly the CEO. These expectations place significant pressure on top executives. Because of these pressures and the complexity and challenges of the job, many people do not want to be managers, particularly top-level managers. In the current global economy and new competitive landscape, top managers hold insecure positions. Many middle-management positions have been eliminated through restructuring, placing more stress on the remaining top- and lower-level managers.

Top-level managers play critical roles in firms' efforts to achieve desired strategic outcomes. In fact, some believe that every organizational failure is actually a failure of those who hold the final responsibility for the quality and effectiveness of a firm's decisions and actions.[108]

Decisions for which strategists are responsible include how resources will be developed or acquired, at what price they will be obtained, and how they will be used. Managerial decisions also influence how information flows in a company, the strategies a firm chooses to implement, and the scope of its operations. In making these decisions, managers must assess the risk involved in taking the actions being considered. This risk is then factored into the decision.[109] The firm's strategic intent (discussed earlier) will affect the decisions managers make. Also, managers' strategic orientations, which include their personal values and beliefs, will affect the decisions.[110] Additionally, how strategists complete their work and their patterns of interactions with others significantly influence the way a firm does business and affect its ability to develop a competitive advantage.

How a firm does business is captured by the concept of organizational culture. Critical to strategic leadership practices and the implementation of strategies, **organizational culture** refers to the complex set of ideologies, symbols, and core values shared throughout the firm, which influences the way it conducts business. Thus, culture is the "social energy that drives—or fails to drive—the organization."[111] Accenture's (formerly Andersen Consulting) core values include the requirement that employees attend company-sponsored training classes in professional attire, an expectation of hard work (up to 80 hours per week), and a willingness to work effectively with others in order to accomplish all tasks that are part of the company-wide demanding workload.[112] These core values at Andersen Consulting provide a particular type of social energy that drives this firm's efforts. As we discuss in chapters 13 and 14, organizational culture is a potential source of sustained competitive advantage.[113]

After evaluating available information and alternatives, top-level managers must frequently choose among similarly attractive alternatives. The most effective strategists have the self-confidence necessary to select the best alternatives, allocate the required level of resources to them, and effectively explain to interested parties why certain alternatives were selected.[114]

When choosing among alternatives, strategists are accountable for treating employees, suppliers, customers, and others with fairness and respect. Evidence suggests that trust can be a source of competitive advantage, thereby supporting an organizational commitment to treat stakeholders fairly and with respect.[115] Nonetheless, firms cannot succeed without people who, following careful and sometimes difficult analyses, are willing to make tough decisions—the types of decisions that result in strategic competitiveness and above-average returns.[116]

## The Work of Effective Strategists

Perhaps not surprisingly, hard work, thorough analyses, a willingness to be brutally honest, a penchant for always wanting the firm and its people to accomplish more, and common sense are prerequisites to an individual's success as a strategist.[117] John Sculley, former CEO of Apple Computer, describes the reality of work today, suggesting that sleeping at night is a remnant of agrarian and industrial ages. "People don't live that way anymore," Sculley believes. "It's a 24-hour day, not an 8-to-5 day."[118]

In addition to the characteristics mentioned, effective strategists must be able to think clearly and ask many questions. Their strategic effectiveness increases as they find ways for others also to think and inquire about what a firm is doing and why. But, in particular, top-level managers are challenged to "think seriously and deeply ... about the purposes of the organizations they head or functions they perform, about the strategies, tactics, technologies, systems and people necessary to attain these purposes and about the important questions that always need to be asked."[119] Through this type of thinking, strategists, in concert with others, increase the probability of identifying bold, innovative ideas. When these ideas lead to the development of core competencies—that is, when the ideas result in exploiting resources and capabilities that are valuable, rare, costly to imitate, and organized to be exploited—they become the foundation for taking advantage of environmental opportunities.

**Organizational culture** refers to the complex set of ideologies, symbols, and core values shared throughout the firm, which influences the way it conducts business.

Our discussion highlights the nature of a strategist's work. Instead of simplicity, the work is filled with ambiguous decision situations—situations for which the most effective solutions are not easily determined. Yet the opportunities suggested by this type of work are appealing. These jobs offer exciting chances to dream and to act. The words given as advice by his father to Steven J. Ross (former Time-Warner chair and co-CEO) describe the opportunities in a strategist's work: "There are three categories of people— the person who goes into the office, puts his feet up on his desk, and dreams for 12 hours; the person who arrives at 5 a.m. and works for 16 hours, never once stopping to dream; and the person who puts his feet up, dreams for one hour, then does something about those dreams."[120] The organizational term used for a dream that challenges and energizes a company is "strategic intent."[121]

Strategists have opportunities to dream and to act, and the most effective strategists provide a dream or vision (strategic intent) to effectively elicit the help of others in creating a firm's competitive advantage.

## THE STRATEGIC MANAGEMENT PROCESS

The pursuit of competitiveness is at the heart of strategic management and the choices made when designing and using the strategic management process. Firms compete with each other to gain access to the resources needed to earn above-average returns and to provide superior satisfaction of stakeholders' needs. Effective use of the interdependent parts of the strategic management process results in selecting the direction the firm will pursue and its choices to achieve the desired outcomes of strategic competitiveness and above-average returns.

As suggested by Figure 1.1, the strategic management process is intended to be a rational approach to help firms respond effectively to the challenges of the new competitive landscape. This process calls for a firm to study its external (Chapter 3) and internal (Chapter 4) environments to identify its marketplace opportunities and threats and determine how to use its core competencies in the pursuit of desired strategic outcomes. With this knowledge, the firm forms its strategic intent so it can leverage its resources, capabilities, and core competencies and win battles in the global economy. Flowing from strategic intent, the strategic mission specifies, in writing, the products a firm intends to produce and the markets it will serve when leveraging its resources, capabilities, and competencies.

A firm's strategic inputs provide the foundation for its strategic actions. As strategic actions, both formulation and implementation are critical to achieving strategic competitiveness and earning above-average returns.

As suggested by the horizontal arrow linking the two types of strategic actions (see Figure 1.1), formulation and implementation must be integrated simultaneously. When formulating strategies, thought should be given to implementing them. During implementation, effective strategists seek feedback that allows improvement of the selected strategies. Thus, the separation of strategy formulation from strategy implementation in Figure 1.1 is for discussion purposes only. In reality, these two sets of actions allow the firm to achieve its desired strategic outcomes only when they are carefully integrated.

Figure 1.1 shows the topics we examine to study the interdependent parts of the strategic management process. In Part II of this book, actions related to the formulation of strategies are explained. The first set of actions studied is the formulation of strategies at the business-unit level (Chapter 5). A diversified firm, one competing in multiple product markets and businesses, has a business-level strategy for each distinct product market area. A firm competing in a single product market has but one business-level strategy. In all instances, a business-level strategy describes a firm's actions designed to exploit its competitive advantage over rivals. But, as is explained in Chapter 6, business-level strategies are not formulated and implemented in isolation. Competitors respond to and try to anticipate each other's actions. Thus, the dynamics of competition are an important input to the formulation and implementation of all strategies, but especially to business-level strategies.

For the diversified firm, corporate-level strategy (Chapter 7) is concerned with determining the businesses in which the company intends to compete, how resources are to be allocated among those businesses, and how the different units are to be managed. Other topics vital to strategy formulation, particularly in the diversified firm, include the acquisition of other companies. This means, when appropriate, the restructuring of the firm's portfolio of businesses (Chapter 8). In addition, the selection of an international strategy that is consistent with the firm's resources, capabilities, and core competencies and its external opportunities (Chapter 9) is very important. Chapter 10 examines cooperative strategies. Increasingly important in a global economy, firms use cooperative strategies to gain competitive advantage by forming advantageous relationships with other companies.

To examine more direct actions taken to implement strategies successfully, we consider several topics in Part III of this book. In Chapter 11, we examine the different mechanisms used to govern firms. With demands for improved corporate governance voiced by various stakeholders, organizations are challenged to manage in ways that will result in the satisfaction of stakeholders' interests and the attainment of desired strategic outcomes. The matters of organizational structure and actions needed to control a firm's operations are considered in Chapter 12, the patterns of strategic leadership appropriate for today's firms and competitive environments are discussed in Chapter 13, and the links among corporate entrepreneurship, innovation, and strategic competitiveness are addressed in Chapter 14.

As noted earlier, competition requires firms to make choices to survive and succeed. Some of these choices are strategic in nature, including selecting a firm's strategic intent and strategic mission; determining which strategies to implement to offer a firm's products to customers; choosing an appropriate level of corporate scope; designing governance and organization structures that will properly coordinate a firm's work; and, through strategic leadership, encouraging and nurturing organizational innovation.[122] When made successfully, choices in terms of any one of these sets of actions have the potential to result in a competitive advantage for a firm over its rivals.

Primarily because they are related to how a firm interacts with its stakeholders, the majority of strategic decisions have ethical dimensions.[123] Organizational ethics are revealed by an organization's culture; that is to say, a firm's strategic decisions are a product of the core values that are shared by most or all of a company's managers and employees. Especially in the turbulent and often ambiguous new competitive landscape, those making strategic decisions are challenged to recognize that their decisions do affect capital market, product market, and organizational stakeholders differently and to evaluate the ethical implications of their decisions. Relationships between organizational ethics and particular strategic decisions are described in virtually all of the remaining chapters of this book.

As you will discover, the strategic management process examined in this text calls for disciplined approaches to the development of competitive advantages. These approaches provide the pathway through which firms will be able to achieve strategic competitiveness and earn above-average returns in the 21st century. Mastery of this strategic management process will effectively serve readers and the organizations for which they choose to work.

## SUMMARY

- Through their actions, firms seek strategic competitiveness and above-average returns. Strategic competitiveness is achieved when a firm has developed and learned how to implement a value-creating strategy successfully. Above-average returns—returns in excess of what investors expect to earn from other investments with similar levels of risk—allow a firm to simultaneously satisfy all of its stakeholders.

- A new competitive landscape—one in which the fundamental nature of competition is changing—has emerged. This landscape challenges those responsible for making effective strategic decisions to adopt a new mind-set, one that is global in nature. Through this mind-set, firms learn how to compete in what are highly turbulent and chaotic environments that produce disorder and a great deal of uncertainty. The globalization of industries and their markets and rapid and significant technological changes are the two primary realities that have created the new competitive landscape. Globalization—the spread of economic innovations around the world and the political and cultural adjustments that accompany this diffusion—is likely to continue. Globalization also increases the standards of performance companies must meet or exceed to be strategically competitive in the new competitive landscape. Developing the ability to satisfy these global performance standards also helps firms compete effectively in their critical domestic markets.

- There are two major models of what a firm should do to earn above-average returns. The I/O model argues that the external environment is the primary determinant of the firm's strategies. Above-average returns are earned when the firm locates an attractive industry and successfully implements the strategy dictated by the characteristics of that industry. The resource-based model assumes that each firm is a collection of unique resources and capabilities that determines a firm's strategy. In this model, above-average returns are earned when the firm uses its valuable, rare, costly to imitate, and organized to be exploited resources and capabilities (i.e., core competencies) to establish a competitive advantage over its rivals.

- Strategic intent and strategic mission are formed in light of the information and insights gained from studying a firm's internal and external environments. Strategic intent suggests how resources, capabilities, and core competencies will be leveraged to achieve desired outcomes in the competitive environment. The strategic mission is an application of strategic intent. The mission is used to specify the product markets and customers a firm intends to serve through the leveraging of its resources, capabilities, and competencies.

- Stakeholders are those who can affect and are affected by a firm's strategic outcomes. Because a firm is dependent on the continuing support of stakeholders (shareholders, customers, suppliers, employees, host communities, etc.), they have enforceable claims on the company's performance. When earning above-average returns, a firm can adequately satisfy all stakeholders' interests. However, when earning only average returns, a firm's strategists must carefully manage all stakeholder groups in order to retain their support. A firm earning below-average returns must minimize the amount of support it loses from dissatisfied stakeholders.

- Organizational strategists are responsible for the design and execution of an effective strategic management process. Today, the most effective of these processes are grounded in ethical intentions and conduct. Strategists themselves, people with opportunities to dream and to act, can be a source of competitive advantage. The strategist's work demands decision tradeoffs, often among attractive alternatives. Successful top-level managers work hard, conduct thorough analyses of situations, are brutally and consistently honest, and ask the right questions, of the right people, at the right time.

# REVIEW QUESTIONS

1. What are strategic competitiveness, competitive advantage, and above-average returns? Why are these terms important to those responsible for an organization's performance?
2. What is the challenge of strategic management?
3. What are the two factors that have created the new competitive landscape? What meaning does this competitive landscape have for those interested in starting a business firm in the near future?
4. According to the I/O model, what should a firm do to earn above-average returns?
5. What does the resource-based model suggest a firm should do to achieve strategic competitiveness and earn above-average returns?
6. What are the differences between strategic intent and strategic mission? What is the value of the strategic intent and mission for a firm's strategic management process?
7. What are stakeholders? Why can they influence organizations? Do stakeholders always have the same amount of influence over an organization? Why or why not?
8. How would you describe the work of organizational strategists?
9. What are the parts of the strategic management process? How are these parts interrelated?

# DISCUSSION QUESTIONS

1. As suggested in the opening case, the outcomes in the telecommunications industry are uncertain. Go to your library to study Nortel's current performance. Based on your reading, do you judge Nortel to be a success? Why or why not?
2. Choose several firms in your local community with which you are familiar. Describe the new competitive landscape for them and ask for their feedback about how they anticipate the landscape will affect their operations during the next five years.
3. Select an organization (e.g., school, club, church) that is important to you. Describe the organization's stakeholders and the degree of influence you believe each has over the organization.
4. Are you a stakeholder at your university or college? If so, of what stakeholder group, or groups, are you a part?

5. Think of an industry in which you want to work. In your opinion, which of the three primary stakeholder groups is the most powerful in that industry today? Why?
6. Reject or agree with the following statement: "I think managers have little responsibility for the failure of business firms." Justify your view.
7. Do strategic intent and strategic mission have any meaning in your personal life? If so, describe how. Are strategic intent and strategic mission guiding your current actions? If yes, how? If not, why not?

# ETHICS QUESTIONS

1. Can a firm achieve a competitive advantage and thereby strategic competitiveness without acting ethically? Explain.
2. What are a firm's ethical responsibilities if it earns above-average returns?
3. What are some of the critical ethical challenges to firms competing in the global economy?
4. How should ethical considerations be included in analyses of a firm's internal and external environments?
5. Can ethical issues be integrated into a firm's strategic intent and mission? Explain.
6. What is the relationship between ethics and stakeholders?
7. What is the importance of ethics for organizational strategists?

# INTERNET EXERCISE

The following is a list of Canadian companies:

Aliant: **http://www.aliant.com**
Chapters Online: **http://www.chapters.ca**
Fishery Products International: **http://www.fpil.com**
Bombardier: **http://www.bombardier.com**
Repap: **http://www.repap.com**

Select two of these companies. For each company, use the Internet to collect sufficient information to compile a list of the company's major stakeholders. In what ways are the stakeholders of each company similar and in what ways are they different? In your research, did you find any evidence that the companies you studied are actively managing their stakeholder groups?

# STRATEGIC SURFING

*Strategy & Business* is a publication that prints a variety of thoughtful articles, interviews, and case studies focused on strategic management and general business issues. The online version of this publication can be accessed at the following Web site:

**http://www.strategy-business.com**

# NOTES

1. J. B. Barney, 1994, Commentary: A hierarchy of corporate resources, in P. Shrivastava, A. Huff, and J. Dutton (eds.), *Advances in Strategic Management*, 10A, (Greenwich, Conn.: JAI Press), 119.

2. Ibid.

3. D. J. Collis and C. A. Montgomery, 1995, Competing on resources: Strategy in the 1990s, *Harvard Business Review*, 73 (4): 118–28.

4. R. M. Grant, 1995, *Contemporary Strategy Analysis*, 2nd ed. (Cambridge, Mass.: Blackwell Business), 138–40.

5. R. A. D'Aveni, 1995, Coping with hypercompetition: Utilizing the new 7S's framework, *Academy of Management Executive*, IX (3): 54; D. Schendel, 1994, Introduction to the Summer 1994 special issue—Strategy: Search for new paradigms, *Strategic Management Journal* (Special Summer Issue) 15: 3.

6. P. Shrivastava, 1995, Ecocentric management for a risk society, *Academy of Management Review*, 20: 119.

7. R. P. Rumelt, D. E. Schendel, and D. J. Teece (eds.), 1994, *Fundamental Issues in Strategy* (Boston: Harvard Business School Press), 527–30; A. D. Meyer, 1991, What is strategy's distinctive competence? *Journal of Management*, 17: 821–83.

8. Schendel, Introduction to the Summer 1994 special issue, 1–3.

9. Rumelt, Schendel, and Teece, *Fundamental Issues in Strategy*, 534–47.

10. M. E. Porter, 1994, Toward a dynamic theory of strategy, in R. P. Rumelt, D. E. Schendel, and D. J. Teece (eds.), *Fundamental Issues in Strategy* (Boston: Harvard Business School Press), 423–25.

11. G. A. Steiner and J. B. Miner, 1977, *Management Policy and Strategy: Text, Readings and Cases* (New York: MacMillan), 7; W. F. Glueck, 1980, *Business Policy and Strategic Management* (New York: McGraw-Hill), 9; J. B. Quinn, 1980, *Strategies for Change: Logical Incrementalism* (Homewood, IL: Irwin); K. J. Hatten and M. L. Hatten, 1988, *Effective Strategic Management* (Englewood Cliffs, NJ: Prentice-Hall), 1; J. B. Barney, 1997, *Gaining and Sustaining Competitive Advantage* (Don Mills, ON: Addison Wesley Publishing), 17.

12. H. Mintzberg, 1987, Five Ps for strategy, *California Management Review*, Fall, reprinted in H. Mintzberg and J. B. Quinn, 1996, The Strategy Process: Concepts, Contexts and Cases, (Upper Saddle River, NJ: Prentice-Hall), 10–17.

13. Mintzberg and Quinn, 1996, 12.

14. The Stern Stewart Performance 1000, http://www.sternstewart.com/content/performance/info/us.pdf (Retrieved June 14, 2000).

15. P. Bagnell, 1999, Nortel leads in creating value: Shareholder boost [Market Value Added], *National Post*, July 3, C1, C4.

16. C. J. Loomis, 1993, Dinosaurs, *Fortune*, May 3, 36–42.

17. *The State of Small Business: A Report of the President*, 1994, Washington, D.C., 41–42.

18. Government of Canada, Office of the Superintendent of Bankruptcy, 2000, *Enhanced Statistics*, http://strategis.ic.gc.ca/SSG/br01011e.html (Retrieved June 24).

19. Rumelt, Schendel, and Teece, *Fundamental Issues in Strategy*, 530.

20. Loomis, Dinosaurs, 36.

21. K. Naughton, E. Thorton, K. Kerwin, and H. Dawley, 1997, Can Honda build a world car? *BusinessWeek*, September 8, 100–8.

22. A. Reinhardt, 1997, Paranoia, aggression, and other strengths, *BusinessWeek*, October 13, 14; A. S. Grove, 1995, A high-tech CEO updates his views on managing and careers, *Fortune*, September 18, 229–30; S. Sherman, 1993, The secret to Intel's success, *Fortune*, February 8, 14.

23. This section is based largely on information featured in two sources: M. A. Hitt, B. W. Keats, and S. M. DeMarie, 1998, Navigating in the new competitive landscape: Building competitive advantage and strategic flexibility; in the 21st century, *Academy of Management Executive*, 12(4), 22–42; R. A. Bettis and M. A. Hitt, 1995, The new competitive landscape, *Strategic Management Journal* (Special Summer Issue) 16: 7–19.

24. S. Kotha, 1995, Mass customization: Implementing the emerging paradigm for competitive advantage, *Strategic Management Journal*, 16: 21–42.

25. Associated Press, 1995, Fox-TCI to challenge ESPN, *Dallas Morning News*, November 1, D1, D11.

26. C. K. Prahalad, 1995, Foreword in R. Ashkenas, D. Ulrich, T. Jick, and S. Kerr (eds.), *The Boundaryless Organization: Breaking the Chains of Organizational Structure*, (San Francisco: Jossey-Bass Publishers), xiii–xvii.

27. R. D. Ireland and M. A. Hitt, 1998, Achieving and maintaining strategic competitiveness in the 21st cen-

tury: The role of strategic leadership, *Academy of Management Executive*, 13(1), 43–57.

28  D'Aveni, Coping with hypercompetition, 46.

29  K. Ohmae, 1995, Letter from Japan, *Harvard Business Review*, 73 (3): 154–63; P. Gyllenhammar, 1993, The global economy: Who will lead next? *Journal of Accountancy*, 175: 61–67.

30  J. C. Madonna, 1992, If it's markets you need, look abroad, *New York Times Forum*, January 5, F13.

31  T. A. Stewart, 1993, The new face of American power, *Fortune*, July 26, 70–86.

32  L. C. Thurow, 1992, Who owns the twenty-first century? *Sloan Management Review*, 33 (3): 5–17.

33  Annual Report, 1999, Fishery Products International; Personal conversation, 2000, Paul Kavanagh, Corporate Controller, Fishery Products International, June 15.

34  P. Krugman, 1994, Location and competition: Notes on economic geography, in R. P. Rumelt, D. E. Schendel, and D. J. Teece (eds.), *Fundamental Issues in Strategy*, (Boston: Harvard Business School Press), 463–93; W. W. Lewis and M. Harris, 1992, Why globalization must prevail, *McKinsey Quarterly*, 2: 114–31.

35  Magna International, 2000, *Magna International home page*, http://www.magnaint.com (Retrieved June 23).

36  Honda, 2000, *Honda Company home page*, http://www.Honda.com (Retrieved June 23).

37  R. Narisetti, 1997, Bridgestone plans to build a factory for tires in U.S., *Wall Street Journal*, July 15, B12.

38  Lewis and Harris, Why globalization must prevail, 115.

39  R. M. Kanter, 1995, Thriving locally in the global economy, *Harvard Business Review*, 73 (5): 151–60; M. E. Porter and C. van der Linde, 1995, Green and competitive: Ending the stalemate, *Harvard Business Review*, 73 (5): 120–34.

40  S. Zaheer and E. Mosakowski, 1997, The dynamics of the liability of foreignness: A global study of survival in financial services, *Strategic Management Journal*, 18: 439–64.

41  M. A. Hitt, R. E. Hoskisson, and H. Kim, 1997, International diversification: Effects on innovation and firm performance in product-diversified firms, *Academy of Management Journal*, 40: 767–98.

42  R. W. Moxon and C. Bourassa-Shaw, 1997, The global free-trade dilemma: Can you control the personal gale of creative destruction? *Business*, 18 (Spring): 6–9.

43  W. Hopkins and S. A. Hopkins, 1997, Strategic planning-financial performance relationships in banks: A casual examination, *Strategic Management Journal*, 18: 635–52.

44  *BusinessWeek*, 1997, The rich ecosystem of Silicon Valley, August 25, 202.

45  Grove, A high-tech CEO, 229.

46  A. L. Sprout, 1995, The Internet inside your company, *Fortune*, November 27, 161–68.

47  Liberation, courtesy of the Internet, 1995, *BusinessWeek*, December 4, 136; Sprout, The Internet inside your company, 161–68.

48  A. Goldstein, 1995, Microsoft may not always be king of the hill, Gates says, *Dallas Morning News*, November 24, D4.

49  T. A. Stewart, 1995, Mapping corporate brainpower, *Fortune*, October 30, 209–12; T. A. Stewart, 1995, Trying to grasp the intangible, *Fortune*, October 2, 157–61; T. A. Stewart, 1995, The information wars: What you don't know will hurt you, *Fortune*, June 12, 119–21.

50  C. A. Bartlett and S. Ghoshal, 1995, Changing the role of top management: Beyond systems to people, *Harvard Business Review*, 73 (3): 141.

51  T. A. Stewart, 1995, Getting real about brainpower, *Fortune*, November 27, 201–03.

52  R. Sanchez, 1995, Strategic flexibility in product competition, *Strategic Management Journal* (Special Summer Issue) 16: 135–59.

53  Kotha, Mass customization, 21.

54  J. L. C. Cheng and I. F. Kesner, 1997, Organizational slack and response to environmental shifts: The impact of resource allocation patterns, *Journal of Management*, 23: 1–18; J. P. Sheppard, 1995, A resource dependence approach to failure prediction, *Social Science Research*, 24: 28–62; J. P. Sheppard, 1994, Strategy and bankruptcy: An exploration into organizational death, *Journal of Management*, 20: 795–33.

55  V. L. Barker III and I. M. Duhaime, 1997, Strategic change in the turnaround process: Theory and empirical evidence, *Strategic Management Journal*, 18: 13–38.

56  W. Boeker, 1997, Strategic change: The influence of managerial characteristics and organizational growth, *Academy of Management Journal*, 40: 152–70.

57  N. Rajagopalan and G. M. Spreitzer, 1997, Toward a theory of strategic change: A multi-lens perspective and integrative framework, *Academy of Management Review*, 22: 48–79.

58  N. Deogun, 1997, Coca-Cola Enterprises uncaps a global bottling play, *Wall Street Journal*, October 29, B4.

59  Our discussion of the I/O model is informed by the following works: Barney, *Firm resources*, 99–120; A. A. Lado, N. G. Boyd, and P. Wright, 1992, A competency-based model of sustainable competitive advantage: Toward a conceptual integration, *Journal*

*of Management*, 18: 77–91; R. M. Grant, 1991, The resource-based theory of competitive advantage: Implications for strategy formulation, *California Management Review*, 33 (Spring): 114–35.

60  D. Schendel, 1994, Introduction to competitive organizational behavior: Toward an organizationally based theory of competitive advantage, *Strategic Management Journal*, (Special Winter Issue) 15: 2.

61  A. Seth and H. Thomas, 1994, Theories of the firm: Implications for strategy research, *Journal of Management Studies*, 31: 165–91.

62  Seth and Thomas, Theories of the firm, 169–73.

63  Porter, Toward a dynamic theory of strategy, 428.

64  M. E. Porter, 1985, *Competitive Advantage* (New York: Free Press); M. E. Porter, 1980, *Competitive Strategy* (New York: Free Press).

65  Great Canadian Bagel, 2000, *The Great Canadian Bagel home page*, http://www. greatcanadianbagel.com (Retrieved June 24); C. Mulhern, 1997, Bagel boom: Rising star of food franchising takes the world by storm, *Entrepreneur Magazine Online*, June 3, http://entrepreneurmag.com.

66  A. M. McGahan and M. E. Porter, 1997, How much does industry matter, really? *Strategic Management Journal*, 18 (Summer Special Issue): 15–30.

67  R. Henderson and W. Mitchell, 1997, The interactions of organizational and competitive influences on strategy and performance, *Strategic Management Journal*, 18 (Summer Special Issue): 5–14; C. Oliver, 1997, Sustainable competitive advantage: Combining institutional and resource-based views, *Strategic Management Journal*, 18: 697–713; J. L. Stimpert and I. M. Duhaime, 1997, Seeing the big picture: The influence of industry, diversification, and business strategy on performance, *Academy of Management Journal*, 40: 560–83.

68  J. R. Williams, 1994, Strategy and the search for rents: The evolution of diversity among firms, in R. P. Rumelt, D. E. Schendel, and D. J. Teece (eds.), *Fundamental Issues in Strategy* (Boston: Harvard Business School Press), 229–46.

69  K. Cool and I. Dierickx, 1994, Commentary: Investments in strategic assets: Industry and firm-level perspectives, in P. Shrivastava, A. Huff, and J. Dutton (eds.), *Advances in Strategic Management*, 10A (Greenwich, Conn.: JAI Press), 35–44; Rumelt, Schendel, and Teece, *Fundamental Issues in Strategy*, 553; R. Rumelt, 1991, How much does industry matter? *Strategic Management Journal*, 12: 167–85.

70  Barney, Commentary, 113–25.

71  Barney, Firm resources; Grant, Resource-based theory; Meyer, What is strategy's distinctive competence?

72  Grant, Resource-based theory, 119–20.

73  Rumelt, Schendel, and Teece, *Fundamental Issues in Strategy*, 31.

74  P. J. H. Schoemaker and R. Amit, 1994, Investment in strategic assets: Industry and firm-level perspectives, in P. Shrivastava, A. Huff, and J. Dutton (eds.), *Advances in Strategic Management*, 10A (Greenwich, Conn.: JAI Press), 9.

75  Chapters Online, 2000, *Chapters Online home page*, http:// www.chapters.ca (Retrieved June 24).

76  J. B. Barney, 1995, Looking inside for competitive advantage, *Academy of Management Executive*, IX (4): 56; J. B. Barney, 1997, *Gaining and Sustaining Competitive Advantage*, (Don Mills, Ontario: Addison-Wesley Publishing).

77  Barney, Firm resources; Barney, *Gaining and Sustaining Competitive Advantage*.

78  Lado, Boyd, and Wright, A competency based model; Grant, Resource-based theory; M. A. Hitt and R. D. Ireland, 1986, Relationships among corporate level distinctive competencies, diversification strategy, corporate structure, and performance, *Journal of Management Studies*, 23: 401–16.

79  A. Madhok, 1997, Cost, value and foreign market entry mode: The transaction and the firm, *Strategic Management Journal*, 18: 39–61.

80  A. A. Lado, N. G. Boyd, and S. C. Hanlon, 1997, Competition, cooperation, and the search for economic rents: A syncretic model, *Academy of Management Review*, 22: 110–41.

81  A. Arora and A. Gambardella, 1997, Domestic markets and international competitiveness: Generic and product specific competencies in the engineering sector, *Strategic Management Journal*, 18 (Summer Special Issue): 53–74.

82  D. J. Teece, G. Pisano, and A. Shuen, 1997, Dynamic capabilities and strategic management, *Strategic Management Journal*, 18: 509–33.

83  D Lei, M. A. Hitt, and R. A. Bettis, 1996, Dynamic core competences through meta-learning and strategic context, *Journal of Management*, 22: 547–67.

84  G. Hamel and C. K. Prahalad, 1989, Strategic intent, *Harvard Business Review*, 67 (3): 63–76.

85  S. Sherman, 1995, Stretch goals: The dark side of asking for miracles, *Fortune*, November 13, 231–32; G. Hamel and C. K. Prahalad, 1994, *Competing for the Future* (Boston: Harvard Business School Press), 129–36.

86  Hamel and Prahalad, Strategic intent, 66.

87  S. Sherman, 1993, The secret to Intel's success, 14.

88  Chapters, 2000, About our Company, *Chapters home page*, http:// www.chapters.ca (Retrieved June 24); Fishery Products International, 2000, *FPI home page*, http://www.fpil.com (Retrieved June 24); Phillips Petroleum Company, 1994, *Health,*

*Environmental and Safety Report*, 4; Bombardier, 2000, *Bombardier home page*, http://www.bombardier. com (Retrieved June 24); M. Loeb, 1993, It's time to invest and build, *Fortune*, February 22, 4; S. Sherman, 1993, The new computer revolution, *Fortune*, June 14, 56–84; C. A. Bartlett and S. Ghoshal, 1995, Changing the role of top management: Beyond systems to people, *Harvard Business Review*, 73 (3): 136–37; Z. Schiller, 1992, No more Mr. Nice Guy at P&G, *BusinessWeek*, February 3, 54–56; S. Tully, 1995, So, Mr. Bossidy, we know you can cut, 73; AlliedSignal, 1995, *Value Line*, August 11, 1357.

89  Reebok, 1992, *Annual Report*, 2–12.

90  Hamel and Prahalad, Strategic intent, 64.

91  M. A. Hitt, D. Park, C. Hardee, and B. B. Tyler, 1995, Understanding strategic intent in the global marketplace, *Academy of Management Executive*, IX (2): 12–19.

92  R. D. Ireland and M. A. Hitt, 1992, Mission statements: Importance, challenge, and recommendations for development, *Business Horizons*, 35 (3): 34–42.

93  A. D. DuBrin and R. D. Ireland, 1993, *Management and Organization*, 2nd ed. (Cincinnati, Ohio: Southwestern), 140.

94  N. Rajagopalan, 1992, Strategic orientations, incentive plan adoptions, and firm performance: Evidence from electric utility firms, *Strategic Management Journal*, 18: 761–85.

95  M. A. Geletkanycz, 1997, The salience of culture's consequences: The effects of cultural values on top executive commitment to the status quo, *Strategic Management Journal*, 18: 615–34, M. A. Hitt, M. T. Dacin, B. B. Tyler, and D. Park, 1997, Understanding the differences in Korean and U.S. executives' strategic orientation, *Strategic Management Journal*, 18: 159–67.

96  M. B. E. Clarkson, 1995, A stakeholder framework for analyzing and evaluating corporate social performance, *Academy of Management Review*, 20: 92–117; T. Donaldson and L. E. Preston, 1995, The stakeholder theory of the corporation: Concepts, evidence, and implications, *Academy of Management Review*, 20: 65–91; T. M. Jones, 1995, Instrumental stakeholder theory: A synthesis of ethics and economics, *Academy of Management Review*, 20: 404–37.

97  Clarkson, A stakeholder framework; R. E. Freeman, 1984, *Strategic Management: A Stakeholder Approach* (Boston: Pitman), 53–54.

98  G. Donaldson and J. W. Lorsch, 1983, *Decision Making at the Top: The Shaping of Strategic Direction* (New York: Basic Books), 37–40.

99  Rumelt, Schendel, and Teece, *Fundamental Issues in Strategy*, 33.

100  Donaldson and Lorsch, *Decision Making at the Top*, 37.

101  M. J. Polonsky, 1995, Incorporating the natural environment in corporate strategy: A stakeholder approach, *Journal of Business Strategies*, 12: 151–68.

102  R. K. Mitchell, B. R. Agle, and D. J. Wood, 1997, Toward a theory of stakeholder identification and salience: Defining the principle of who and what really count, *Academy of Management Review*, 22: 853–86.

103  Donaldson and Preston, The stakeholder theory of the corporation, citing a quote from *The Economist*, 1994, Corporate governance special section, September 11, 52–62.

104  Don't be an ugly-American manager, 1995, *Fortune*, October 16, 225.

105  1999, Excessive pay and poor management, *The Globe and Mail* Editorial, June 16; 1999, *Repap, Repap Enterprises, Inc. Media Statement*, http://www.repap.com (Retrieved June 17).

106  T. Aeppel, 1997, Rubbermaid warns 3rd-quarter profit will come in far below expectations, *Wall Street Journal*, September 19, A4.

107  New paths to success, 1995, *Fortune*, June 12, 90–94; T. A. Stewart, 1995, Mapping corporate brainpower, 209–11; S. Lee, 1993, Peter Drucker's fuzzy future, *Fortune*, May 17, 136.

108  J. O. Moller, 1991, The competitiveness of U.S. industry: A view from the outside, *Business Horizons*, 34 (6): 27–34.

109  G. McNamara and P. Bromiley, 1997, Decision making in an organizational setting: Cognitive and organizational influences on risk assessment in commercial lending, *Academy of Management Journal*, 40: 1063–88.

110  L. Markoczy, 1997, Measuring beliefs: Accept no substitutes, *Academy of Management Journal*, 40: 1228–42.

111  M. A. Hitt and R. E. Hoskisson, 1991, Strategic competitiveness, in L. W. Foster (ed.), *Advances in Applied Business Strategy* (Greenwich, Conn.: JAI Press), 1–36.

112  Bartlett and Ghoshal, Changing the role of top management, 139.

113  K. Weigelt and C. Camerer, 1988, Reputation and corporate strategy, *Strategic Management Journal*, 9: 443–54; J. B. Barney, 1986, Organizational culture: Can it be a source of sustained competitive advantage? *Academy of Management Review*, 11: 656–65.

114  R. D. Ireland, M. A. Hitt, and J. C. Williams, 1992, Self-confidence and decisiveness: Prerequisites for effective management in the 1990s, *Business Horizons*, 35 (1): 36–43.

115  R. C. Mayer, J. H. Davis, and F. D. Schoorman, 1995, An integrative model of organizational trust, *Academy of Management Review*, 20: 709–34, J. H. Davis, F. D. Schoorman, and R. C. Mayer, 1995, The trusted general manager and firm performance: Empirical evidence of a strategic advantage, paper presented at the Strategic Management Society conference; J. B. Barney and M. H. Hansen, 1994, Trustworthiness as a source of competitive advantage, *Strategic Management Journal*, 15: 175–90.

116  G. Belis, 1993, Beware the touchy-feely business book, *Fortune*, June 28, 147; A. E. Pearson, 1988, Tough-minded ways to get innovative, *Harvard Business Review*, 66 (3): 99–106.

117  J. S. Harris, 1995, Bill Dodson, *Dallas Morning News*, September 3, H1, H2; Tully, So, Mr. Bossidy, we know you can cut, 70–80; K. W. Chilton, M. E. Warren, and M. L. Weidenbaum (eds.), 1990,

*American Manufacturing in a Global Market* (Boston: Kluwer Academic Publishers), 72.

118  A. Deutschman, 1993, Odd man out, *Fortune*, July 26, 42.

119  T. Leavitt, 1991, *Thinking About Management* (New York: Free Press), 9.

120  M. Loeb, 1993, Steven J. Ross, 1927–1992, *Fortune*, January 25, 4.

121  Hamel and Prahalad, *Competing for the Future*, 129.

122  Rumelt, Schendel, and Teece, *Fundamental Issues in Strategy*, 9–10.

123  Our discussion of ethics and the strategic management process, both here and in other chapters, is informed by materials appearing in J. S. Harrison and C. H. St. John, 1994, *Strategic Management of Organizations and Stakeholders: Theory and Cases* (St. Paul, Minn.: West Publishing Company).

# Chapter Two

## Strategic Management and Firm Performance

## Nortel Leads in Creating Value for Its Shareholders

In recent years, Nortel has been identified as one company that has built value for its shareholders. The Brampton, Ontario–based Nortel outpaced all other companies in the ranking that assesses the "market value added" (MVA) of 300 Canadian firms. In the 2000 MVA rankings, Nortel was credited for adding more market value during its history than any other Canadian firm, including its parent, BCE. Nortel's MVA was $168.9 billion, while BCE was second at $65.6 billion. Research in Motion jumped from 58th to 11th with an increase in MVA from $0.49 billion to $4.28 billion. With the volatility in tech stocks, these stellar performances will, at least, come down to earth. More notable in the 2000 rankings—perhaps because of their consistency of being in the top ranks from the prior year—were the big five banks. The Toronto-Dominion ranked fifth (up from sixth a year earlier) with an MVA of $13.27 billion; the Royal Bank ranked eighth (down from fourth) with an MVA of $6.55 billion; the Bank of Nova Scotia ranked thirteenth (down from eighth) with an MVA of $3.99 billion; the Canadian Imperial Bank of Commerce was 24th with $2.7 billion; and the Bank of Montreal was 29th with an MVA of $2.17 billion, down from $6.0 billion.

What does this MVA measure mean, and why is it becoming so important to shareholders? Market Value Added is the difference between a firm's total market value (equity + debt) and its economic book value (the amount lenders and shareholders have contributed throughout the history of the company to achieve that value). A related concept is Economic Value Added (EVA). EVA is a measure of wealth creation during a particular period of time, generally a year. It is measured as the difference between the return on operating capital minus the cost of capital, multiplied by year-end operating capital. MVA is considered the net present value of the anticipated future EVAs.

Many large Canadian firms are now using the MVA and EVA concepts. On May 31, 1998, Molson Company announced that it had contracted Stern Stewart to put an EVA system in place. According to Dan O'Neill, Molson's chief

http://www.nortelnetworks.com
http://www.bce-inc.com
http://www.teleglobe.com
http://www.molson.com

operating officer: "We are focusing on creating shareholder value, and to do that we must think like owners." Molson's ranked 260th among Canadian companies in 1999 in MVA and wanted to improve this ranking.

Other notable Canadian companies listed on the 2000 MVA rankings are Bombardier and Air Canada. Bombardier, a Montreal-based transportation systems-maker, has been consistently ranked high in the Canadian MVA rankings over the past decade. In 2000, it ranked third with an MVA of $16.1 billion. Air Canada ranked 277th in 1999, at a negative $387 million but improved to 65th in 2000 with an MVA of $473 million. Its 1999 ranking was prior to its acquisition of Canadian Air, which ranked 235th in 1999 with a negative $100 million. Of course, Air Canada suffered from a strike in 1998, which adversely affected its 1999 MVA ranking.

Sources: S. Miles, 2000, Nortel rewrites history in terms of market value, *National Post,* October 14, C4; The 2000 Stern Stewart Canadian 300 MVA Rankings, 2000, *National Post,* October 14, C4; P. Bagnell, 1999, Nortel leads in creating value: Shareholder boost, *National Post,* July 3, C1, C4; The Stern Stewart Performance 1000, 1998, New York: Stern Stewart; The 1999 Stern Stewart Canadian 300 MVA Rankings, 1999, *National Post,* July 3, C4.

In Chapter 1, we stressed the importance of understanding how to exploit competitive advantages to ensure that a firm earns above-average returns. This is consistent with most definitions of strategy since most of these definitions have at least one attribute in common: they focus on the effect of a firm's strategy on performance in the short- and/or long-term. The definition of strategy as the allocation of resources to enable the maintenance or enhancement of performance illustrates this point very well.[1] In addition, this emphasis on performance is explicit in the description of the strategic management process in Chapter 1: The strategic management process is the full set of commitments, decisions, and actions required for a firm to achieve strategic competitiveness and earn above-average returns.[2]

An important question in the study of organizations is: What is performance? In some settings, the notion of performance is very clear. In athletics, the person who throws the javelin the furthest, the person who runs 100 metres the fastest, the person who jumps the highest in a pole vaulting competition—all of these people have outperformed their competition. In sports, the team that wins the Stanley Cup in the National Hockey League playoffs, the team that wins the World Series in baseball, the team that wins the National Basketball Association's league championship—these teams are considered to have outperformed the rest of the teams in their respective sports. However, in many organizations, the definition of performance is more complicated. In this chapter, we present one reasonable approach to defining performance. Then we examine several measures of organizational performance. Finally, we suggest that there is no single measure of performance that is flawless and that using multiple approaches is an appropriate perspective for conducting strategic analyses.[3]

## DEFINING PERFORMANCE CONCEPTUALLY

To understand performance conceptually, it is necessary to define what is meant by an organization. An organization is an association of productive assets (including people) who have voluntarily come together to accomplish a set of goals. In the case of the business organization, this means gaining an economic advantage.[4] For the "coming together" to occur, there must be a point of equilibrium between contributions to the organization and inducements from the organization such that people and owners of other productive assets, such as shareholders and financial lenders, are willing to stay with the organization; in simple terms it must be "worth it" for these people to be involved with the organization.[5] In addition, owners of productive assets must be satisfied with the use of these assets by an organization and, therefore, be willing to permit the organization to retain the assets and continue to exist.[6] Further, the owners of assets will voluntarily make these assets available to an organization if, and only if, they are satisfied with the income they are receiving. They will be satisfied only if the income they are receiving—as adjusted for risk—is at least as high as the next best alternative.[7]

Building on the above insights, strategy researcher Jay Barney developed a conceptual definition of performance that compares the actual value created by an organization using its productive assets with the expected value that the assets' owners anticipated the organization would create.[8] The comparison of actual value created with the value owners expected leads to three levels of performance. These three levels are below-normal, normal, and above-normal performance. Below-normal performance is when an organization's actual value created is less than the value owners expected. Normal performance is when the actual value created is equal to the expected value. Finally, above-normal performance is when the actual value created is greater than the expected value. The positive difference between actual value created and expected value is also known as economic rent. In addition, Barney argues that resources and capabilities that are sources of competitive disadvantage will lead to below-normal performance, while those that are sources of competitive parity will lead to normal performance, and those that are sources of either temporary or sustained competitive advantage will lead to above-normal performance. We will discuss this further in Chapter 4.

Before proceeding further, we will define and briefly discuss the concept of value. One marketing researcher has defined value as what is gotten for what is given. In the context of creating customer value, he argues that customers give money, time, energy or effort, psychological costs, and sensory costs (negative aspects of the setting in which the interaction takes place, such as noise, drafts, or uncomfortable seats). After a transaction the customer will ask, "Did I receive more than I gave?"[9] If the answer is yes, value was created, but if the answer is no, value was destroyed. For shareholders, value creation means getting more from an investment than could have been received from another investment with similar risk. As a student, ask yourself whether you are receiving value for the money, time, and effort invested in buying and reading this textbook. Have shareholders who invested in General Motors over the years received more than they gave, considering the destruction of shareholder value by successive Boards of Directors, CEOs, and senior management teams?

The terms "below-normal," "normal," and "above-normal" performance were derived from microeconomic theory and refer to levels of firm performance achieved under conditions of perfect competition. If a firm uses its resources to create just enough value to fully compensate the owners of all resources (including a rate of return that is risk-adjusted for the suppliers of capital), it is achieving normal performance, and the owners of resources will keep those resources in that firm. These firms are surviving.[10] When firms are achieving below-normal performance, the owners of resources will move them to another firm where it is expected that they will be used to achieve at least normal performance. When this happens to all of a firm's resources, the firm no longer exists economically and eventually may cease to exist legally. Certainly, firms such as Eaton's, Woodward's, and Canadian Airlines no longer exist economically because they created less value than the owners of their resources expected them to create. Firms achieving above-normal performance will retain their current productive resources and will attract even more productive resources. These firms can be said to be prospering.

Building on the above insights and using terminology from Chapter 1, we state that when a firm achieves strategic competitiveness and successfully exploits its competitive advantages, it is able to accomplish its primary objective—achieving above-average returns. **Above-average returns** are those returns in excess of what an investor expects to earn from other investments with a similar amount of risk. Firms that are competing without any competitive advantages will earn, at best, average returns. **Average returns** are those returns equal to what an investor expects to earn given a similar amount of risk. If a firm does not achieve at least average returns, the result is failure. Failure occurs because the owners of productive assets will choose to withdraw their investments from these firms and invest them in firms that are earning at least average returns. This last group of firms is said to be earning below-average returns. **Below-average returns** are those returns that are less than an investor expects given a similar level of risk. Table 2.1 presents the relationships among the expected value of a firm's resources, their actual value, and firm performance.

This conceptual approach to defining performance has several advantages.[11] It is consistent with the perspective from microeconomics, it is consistent with most definitions of performance developed in organization behaviour and organization theory, and it helps in the analysis of the impact of a firm's resources, capabilities, and external environment on its performance. Because this definition of performance is difficult to measure, we present several measures of performance in the next section. It is suggested that those assessing performance use more than one measure of performance.

**Above-average returns** are those returns in excess of what an investor expects to earn from other investments with a similar amount of risk.

**Average returns** are those returns equal to what an investor expects to earn given a similar amount of risk.

**Below-average returns** are those returns that are less than an investor expects given a similar level of risk.

| ■ ■ **TABLE 2.1** | **The Relationships among Expected Value, Actual Value, and Firm Performance** |
|---|---|
| Average Returns | A firm creates with its resources value **equal to** what owners of those resources expected the firm to create given similar levels of risk. |
| Below-average Returns | A firm creates with its resources value **less than** what owners of these resources expected the firm to create given similar levels of risk. |
| Above-average Returns | A firm creates with its resources value **greater than** what owners of these resources expected the firm to create given similar levels of risk. |

Adapted with permission from J. B. Barney, 1997, *Gaining and Sustaining Competitive Advantage*, (Don Mills, Ont.: Addison-Wesley Publishing Company), 33.

# THE MEASUREMENT OF FIRM PERFORMANCE

Firm performance can be measured through a variety of techniques. All have some limitations, and each has its critics and supporters. Because of the limitations associated with each technique, it is advisable that multiple measures of performance be used when conducting a strategic analysis of a firm. Six approaches to measuring firm performance will be described in the following sections. We will also review the strengths and weakness of each approach.

# FIRM SURVIVAL AND PERFORMANCE

One measure of performance is the ability of a firm to survive over an extended period of time. Obviously, if a firm survives for an extended period of time, it is creating at least average returns as defined in Table 2.1. Firms generating less than average returns will not survive in the long term unless they receive some kind of subsidy either from government (as was the case for years for the Canadian National Railroad) or some private benefactor.[12]

## Strengths of Using Firm Survival

This measure of firm performance is relatively easy to use because it does not require detailed information about a firm's economic condition, only whether a firm is still continuing operations. If this is the case, the firm must be generating average returns or, if it were not, the owners of assets would have transferred them elsewhere.[13]

## Weaknesses of Using Firm Survival

Unfortunately, this measure of performance has several major limitations. First, it is sometimes difficult to know when a firm no longer exists. Although determining when some firms no longer exist may be easy—as in the case of smaller firms such as individually owned gas stations, restaurants, and small newspapers. It may be more difficult to determine whether a larger firm has ceased to exist. For example, in 1999, Air Canada legally acquired Canadian Airlines. Arguably, Canadian Airlines now no longer exists. But its assets are relatively intact, it probably serves many of the customers it served prior to being acquired, and competes in many of the same markets. Thus, has Canadian Airlines ceased to exist? When Ontario's Small Fry Snack Foods purchased the trademarks, distribution system, and other key assets of the U.S. Humpty Dumpty corporation in order to continue the brand, did it keep Humpty Dumpty in existence?[14]

In addition, does a firm cease to exist when it declares bankruptcy? Similar to a legal acquisition, many bankrupt firms continue to use the same productive assets, service the same customers, and compete against the same firms. In fact, some firms appear to do better after declaring bankruptcy. There is some evidence that suggests the possibility that strategic bankruptcies—a bankruptcy filed in order to deal with some specific problem[15]— may be a way to maintain or maybe even improve performance. Some firms are declaring bankruptcy to enable restructuring with the intention of being a stronger, better-performing firm in the future. Yet, research shows that circumstances under which a "strategic bankruptcy" may be profitably employed are so limited as to be useless as a strategy.[16]

A second limitation is that the death of a firm can occur over an extended period of time. This is particularly true when a firm has generated above-average returns and therefore acquired many assets that are of value and whose liquidation can extend survival. During times such as this, it is not clear whether the firm is going out of business or facing temporary setbacks. This means that using "survival" as the only definition of performance may lead to ambiguous results. [17]

Even firms that survive for an extended period of time may change themselves in such a way that analyzing them as one firm may be illogical. The Hudson Bay Company is an example of a firm that has survived as a legal entity for more than three centuries. Obviously, the business activities of the Hudson Bay Company in the 1700s (building and maintaining trading posts for the fur trade) are much different than the activities of 2001 (being the owner and operator of large department stores). Focusing solely on survival as one measure of performance would miss the transition that has taken place in the Hudson Bay Company.[18]

A final limitation regarding the use of survival as a performance measure is that it does not provide any information concerning above-average returns. Survival differentiates only between below-average returns and average returns. Some of the firms generating at least average returns may be generating slightly above-average returns or well-above-average returns. In strategic management, we are interested in conditions that enable firms to earn above-average returns. A focus only on survival means that these insights are not available.[19]

This is not to say that financial ratios and other indicators (such as the quality of the board of directors) that are related to survival are not important. Slack financial resources (e.g., high liquidity or low debt to equity ratio) and quality board members (e.g., boards that may have many personal connections with other corporate boards) will aid a firm's condition and chance for survival. In fact, in one piece of classic research, Edward Altman combined several financial measures that were indicative of a firm's likelihood of survival. His measure, known as "Altman's Z" (shown below) uses measures of profitability, liquidity, and solvency to determine a company's likelihood of bankruptcy or default on bondholders (a major stakeholder).[20] Altman's Z scores of below 1.8 represent very high potential for failure, scores between 1.8 and 3.2 represent a grey zone, and scores above 3.2 are likely to survive.

Altman's Z =
$$.012(WC/TA)+.014(RE/TA)+.033(EBIT/TA)+.006(MVE/BVD)+.100(SALE/TA)$$

Where WC    = Company's Working Capital; TA = Firm's Total Assets;
EBIT = Firm's Earnings Before Interest & Taxes; BVD = Firm's Book Value of Debt;
MVE = Firm's Market Value of Equity (Shares Outstanding × Average Market Value);
RE = Firm's Retained Earnings;

However, we must note that the simple act of surviving without considering any indicators related to the likelihood of survival—such as the accounting measures discussed below or Altman's Z noted above, is insufficient to allow a complete picture of the performance of the organization.

Therefore, while survival is an important technique in assessing firm performance, it is only one. Other authors have suggested several reasons for the limited ability of survival as a performance measure. First, it is difficult to apply to new organizations. Second, it gives no guidance to short-term decisionmaking. Third, it is possible that a firm will survive because of the intervention of others, i.e., government, therefore making the measure artificial. Finally, it is possible that focusing solely on survival may cause senior managers to ignore other important goals and objectives that are essential for the firm's long-term well-being.[21] We now turn our attention to accounting measures of performance.

## ACCOUNTING MEASURES AND FIRM PERFORMANCE

Accounting measures of firm performance are the most popular in strategic management.[22] Some would suggest the popularity of accounting measures is due to the data's being easily accessible for publicly traded firms. Others contend that accounting numbers are important both because managers use them when making strategic decisions and because accounting numbers actually provide insights into economic rates of return.[23] However, others have criticized accounting measures of performance because accounting numbers have a built-in short-term bias, are subject to manipulation by managers, and undervalue intangible assets.[24]

In defence of accounting data, it is necessary to understand that the criticisms noted in the last paragraph were developed to defend large U.S. firms in anticompetition or "antitrust" suits against charges that these firms (e.g., IBM) were earning monopoly rents. Thus, it was important to argue that accounting rates of return did not reflect economic rates of return. In addition, some finance scholars note that stock exchanges (e.g., the Toronto Stock Exchange) put great emphasis on the quality of accounting data so that investors may better estimate a firm's future returns.[25] Finally, some researchers have defended the use of accounting measures of performance by arguing that if one assumes that stock market data are indicative of economic profits, then accounting information must also provide insights into economic performance to some degree, particularly if investors consider accounting numbers useful.[26] Thus, while accounting-based measures of performance may present certain problems, there is broad support for their use as a measure of financial performance.

The more common approach to using accounting data to assess firm financial performance is to use ratio analysis. Some of the more important ratios and what they mean with respect to firm performance are listed in Table 2.2. The categories most used are (1) profitability ratios (where some measure of profitability is used as the numerator, and some measure of size is used as the denominator); (2) liquidity ratios (which focus on the ability of a firm to pay its short-term debts); (3) leverage ratios (which measure the amount of a firm's indebtedness); (4) activity ratios (which assess the level of activity in a firm); and (5) miscellaneous ratios (these are ratios that do not fall into one of the previously mentioned categories).

| ■ ■ **TABLE 2.2** | **Key Financial Accounting Ratios, Their Calculation, and What They Mean** | |
|---|---|---|
| **Ratio** | **Calculation** | **What the Ratio Means** |
| Profitability Ratios | | |
| Gross profit margin | $\dfrac{\text{Sales} - \text{Cost of goods sold}}{\text{Sales}}$ | Measures the revenue left to cover operating expenses after taking out the cost of procurement |
| Operating profit margin | $\dfrac{\text{Profit before interest \& taxes}}{\text{Sales}}$ | Assesses firm profitability without regard to interest charges as a result of the capital structure |
| Net profit margin (return on sales) | $\dfrac{\text{Profits after taxes}}{\text{Sales}}$ | After-tax profits per dollar of sales. |
| Return on total assets | $\dfrac{\text{Profits after taxes}}{\text{Total assets}}$ | Measures the return on the total investment in the firm. |
| | $\dfrac{\text{Profits after taxes} + \text{interest}}{\text{Total assets}}$ | It is appropriate to add interest to the numerator to obtain a measure of returns to both classes of investors |
| Return on shareholders' equity | $\dfrac{\text{Profit after taxes (PAT)}}{\text{Total shareholders' equity}}$ | Rate of return to shareholders given their investment in the firm |
| Return on common equity | $\dfrac{\text{PAT—Preferred stock dividends}}{\text{Common shareholders' equity}}$ | Return on investment that common shareholders have made in the firm |
| Earnings per share | $\dfrac{\text{PAT—Preferred stock dividends}}{\text{\# of common shares outstanding}}$ | Earnings available to common shareholders |
| Liquidity ratios | | |
| Current ratio | $\dfrac{\text{Current Assets}}{\text{Current Liabilities}}$ | Measure of ability to cover short-term debt by assets convertible to cash in approximately same period as short-term debt matures |
| Quick ratio (Acid-Test Ratio) | $\dfrac{\text{Current assets} - \text{inventory}}{\text{Current liabilities}}$ | Measure of ability to pay off short-term debt without relying on inventory (the most difficult current asset to convert to cash) |
| Inventory to net working capital | $\dfrac{\text{Inventory}}{\text{Current assets} - \text{current liabilities}}$ | Measure to which firm's working capital is tied up in inventory |
| Leverage Ratios | | |
| Debt-to-assets ratio | $\dfrac{\text{Total debt}}{\text{Total assets}}$ | Measures use of debt to finance operations |
| Debt-to-equity ratio | $\dfrac{\text{Total debt}}{\text{Total shareholders' equity}}$ | Measures use of debt relative to shareholders' investment in firm |

(continued)

| ■ ■ TABLE 2.2 | Key Financial Accounting Ratios, Their Calculation, and What They Mean (continued) | |
|---|---|---|

| Ratio | Calculation | What the Ratio Means |
|---|---|---|
| Long-term debt to equity ratio | $\dfrac{\text{Long-term debt}}{\text{Total shareholders' equity}}$ | Measures balance between debt and equity in long-term capital structure of firm |
| Times interest earned | $\dfrac{\text{Profits before interest and taxes}}{\text{Total interest charges}}$ | Measures how much profits can decline before firm is unable to meet its interest obligations |
| Fixed-charge coverage | $\dfrac{\text{Profits before taxes and interest + lease obligations}}{\text{Interest charges + lease obligations}}$ | A more inclusive measure of ability of firm to handle all of its fixed-charge obligations |
| **Activity Ratios** | | |
| Accounts receivable turnover | $\dfrac{\text{Annual credit sales}}{\text{Accounts receivable}}$ | Measures average time to collect on credit sales |
| Average collection period | $\dfrac{\text{Accounts receivable}}{\text{Total sales/365}}$ | Average time it takes to receive payment for a sale |
| Inventory turnover | $\dfrac{\text{Cost of goods sold}}{\text{Average inventory}}$ | Measures speed with which firm is turning over its inventory. |
| Fixed-assets turnover | Sales/Fixed assets | Measures sales productivity and plant & equipment utilization |
| Total assets turnover | Sales/Total assets | Measures utilization of firm's assets. If below industry average, firm is not generating the volume expected given its investment in assets |
| **Shareholders' return and other ratios** | | |
| Dividend yield on common stock | $\dfrac{\text{Annual dividends per share}}{\text{Current market price per share}}$ | Measures return to common shareholders |
| Price-earning ratio | $\dfrac{\text{Current market price per share}}{\text{After-tax earnings per share}}$ | Indicates market perception of the firm. Usually, faster-growing or less risky firms tend to have higher P/E ratios than more risky or slower-growing firms |
| Dividend payout ratio | $\dfrac{\text{Annual dividends per share}}{\text{After-tax earnings per share}}$ | Indicates dividends paid out as a percentage of profits |
| Cash flow per share | $\dfrac{\text{After-tax profits + depreciation}}{\text{\# of common shares outstanding}}$ | Measures total cash per share available to firm |
| Break-even analysis | $\dfrac{\text{Fixed costs}}{\text{Contribution Margin}}$ where Contribution Margin $= \dfrac{\text{(Selling price/unit)}}{\text{(variable cost/unit)}}$ | Measures the number of units that need to be sold to begin to make a profit on that product or service |

The following sources are available to access Canadian and U.S. industry averages in order to judge a particular firm's ratios relative to its closest competitors in a particular industry:

Corporation Financial Statistics, Statistics Canada http://stcwww.statcan.ca/english/sdds/2508.htm

Market Research Handbook, Statistics Canada http://www.statcan.ca/english/ads/63-224-XPB/intro.htm

Key Business Ratios, Dun & Bradstreet Canada http://www.dnb.ca/prods_svcs/allprods.htm

Dun & Bradstreet, Industry Norms and Key Business Ratios http://www.dnb.conf

Robert Morris Associate Annual Statement Studies http://www.rmasvc.org/

*Troy Almanac of Business and Industrial Financial Ratios* (available in book form)

## The Limitations on Using Accounting Measures

There are three important limitations to using accounting measures to assess firm performance: managerial discretion, short-term bias, and valuing intangible resources and capabilities.[27]

### Managerial Discretion

Managers have some discretion when they choose methods of accounting.[28] Managers decide when to account for revenues and/or costs, how to value inventory, and how to depreciate assets. Consequently, accounting measures of performance may reflect managerial preferences and interests.

### Short-Term Bias

A second limitation is the built-in short-term bias in accounting measures.[29] This short-term bias occurs because longer-term, multiyear investments are generally treated as costs in the year where they do not generate identifiable revenues. This means that investments in research and development, human resource management training and development, and market research may be expensed in the short term rather than viewed as an investment in the long term. If managers' bonuses are based on short-term financial results, the managers may reduce these types of strategic investments to increase their bonuses.

### Valuable Intangible Resources and Capabilities

A third limitation is the valuing of intangible resources.[30] Intangible resources and capabilities are productive assets that have a significant effect on performance but are difficult to observe, describe, and value using accounting measures. Resources such as brand awareness, a sense of affiliation and identity with the firm, trust and friendship among managers and employees, close relationships with suppliers and customers, and close relations with shareholders are difficult to assess and measure but are critical components of firm success.[31]

These limitations do not mean that accounting measures are bad or should be ignored. They do suggest that judgment and care should be used when assessing firm performance using accounting measures. Next, we will examine the multiple stakeholders' view of performance.

# FIRM PERFORMANCE AND THE MULTIPLE STAKEHOLDER APPROACH

The conceptual approach described earlier suggests a stakeholder approach to measuring performance.[32] This means that a firm's performance should be viewed relative to the preferences of those stakeholders who are important to the firm and can impact firm performance. Some stakeholders who may impact firm performance are customers, employees, suppliers, managers, top executives, equity holders, debt holders, communities where plants and offices are located, and governments (local, provincial, and federal). The problem is that different stakeholders may have differential interests in how the firm should be managed. These differential interests may be a result of how much of each resource is being supplied by each stakeholder and the effect that firm decisions will have on each stakeholder.

Different stakeholders will use different criteria to judge firm performance. Consequently, it will be difficult to formulate and implement strategies that will satisfy each. Firms that sell their products at a lower than optimal price may satisfy their customers but may not have the financial resources to satisfy employees with better pay, managers with better furnishings, and governments with higher taxes. While the multiple stakeholder approach to performance is intuitively appealing, it is very difficult to apply in strategic analyses that lead to formulating and implementing appropriate strategies. As one strategy researcher wrote: "Each stakeholding group, and perhaps each individual stakeholder, may define performance in an idiosyncratic way."[33] This means that there may be several varied dimensions firms must assess, causing performance for the few very important stakeholders to deteriorate. Consequently, it may be necessary to adopt those measures that emphasize a few stakeholders over others. These stakeholders need not always be the owners, and in cases where others are more critical to the firm's interest in the short run, their interests may take precedence. For example, XWave Solutions of St. John's has decided to emphasize employee satisfaction as well as customer satisfaction. Senior managers at Xwave consider that this will mean better service for customers and higher shareholder value in the long term. In the field of higher education, universities are becoming more student oriented. This is a major shift from the 1980s, when they were faculty oriented. We would argue that universities must be faculty, staff, student, and alumni oriented if they are to satisfy some of their more important stakeholders. But this is difficult given the differing needs and perceptions of what value means even among this small group of stakeholders.

## STRATEGIC FOCUS

### University Stakeholders: Who Does Maclean's Ask to Rank?

For the last several years, *Maclean's* magazine has published rankings of medical/doctoral, comprehensive, and primarily undergraduate universities in Canada. These rankings illustrate the stakeholder concept by allowing the organization of shareholders for each university. Although not endorsing these rankings as a measure of performance, they are valuable in helping us understand the concept of performance and a multiple-stakeholder approach.

**Students** *Maclean's* asks for the averages of incoming students, and the proportion of students with averages equal to or higher than 75 percent. To assess drawing power, *Maclean's* determines the proportion of students from out of province in the first-year undergraduate class, and for medical-doctoral and comprehensive universities, the percentage of international students at the graduate level. In addition, *Maclean's* measures graduation rates and the percentage of full-time, second-year undergraduate students who graduate from the institution within one year of the expected time of graduation. Further, *Maclean's* measures the success of the student body at winning academic awards at the national level over the past five years. Other measures related to students are: the entire distribution of class sizes at the first- and second-year levels, and the third- and fourth-year levels and the percentage of first-year classes taught by tenured/tenure-track professors, considered a measure of how available top faculty are to new students.

**Faculty** *Maclean's* assesses the number of professors with doctorates and the percentage of faculty members who win national awards. The magazine also measures the success of faculty members in obtaining research grants from national granting agencies such as the Social Sciences and Humanities Research Council of Canada.

**Other Stakeholders** Finally, *Maclean's* measures each university's reputation. To assess reputation, *Maclean's* surveys a broad range of stakeholders. These include graduates as measured by how many times they give in the form of alumni support, heads of national and regional organizations, high school guidance counsellors, university officials, chief executive officers of small and large for-profit organizations, and corporate recruiters from large and small firms.

Obviously, each university cannot satisfy all of the stakeholders implied in the above paragraphs. Robert Birgeneau, the new president of the University of Toronto, the highest-rated university in the medical-doctorate category, has pledged to make U of T a world-class university. He already has a $1.2 billion endowment and plans for raising another $1 billion by 2004. His goals appear to be appropriate for engendering value for students, faculty, and the larger community of Canada. Simon Fraser's past president, Jack Blaney, believes that SFU's recruitment of top-flight faculty members, especially from the United States, has helped it attract top students and to be ranked the top university in the comprehensive category. Mount Allison University's president, Ian Newbould, has focused on wiping out his university's debt, then beautifying the campus and maintaining the university's low student enrollment. His goal is the overall development of students, and he seeks to look after their needs better than any other university. In Newbould's nine years as president, Mount Allison has topped the primarily undergraduate category every year.

Sources: J. Schofield, C. Wood, and J. DeMont, 2000, The Winners: A celebration of academic innovation and excellence, *Maclean's*, November 20, 58–60; A. D. Johnston and M. Dwyer, 2000, Window into the Rankings: How *Maclean's* takes the measure of Canadian universities, *Maclean's*, November 20, 15.

# PRESENT VALUE AND FIRM PERFORMANCE

One measure of performance, grounded in finance theory, is the present value of cash flows.[34] This approach seeks to avoid some of the limitations of other performance measures. It avoids short-term bias by measuring cash flows over time, and it values all resources made available to a firm by using the discount-rate concept. Firms that use present value estimate net cash flows and expected discount rates for several years into the future. This allows them to assess firm performance and individual project performance on a forward-looking basis. Table 2.3 shows the relationship between a firm's net present value and firm performance.

| ■ ■ TABLE 2.3 | The Relationships between Net Present Value and FirmPerformance |
|---|---|
| Net Present Value < 0 | Below-average returns |
| Net Present Value = 0 | Average returns |
| Net Present Value > 0 | Above-average returns |

Adapted with permission from J. B. Barney, 1997, *Gaining and Sustaining Competitive Advantage* (Don Mills, Ont.: Addison-Wesley Publishing Company), 50.

## Strengths and Weaknesses of Present-Value Measures

This way of measuring performance has several strengths. First, there is the close link between present value and the conceptual definition of performance proposed by Jay Barney.[35] In addition, research suggests that firms who apply present-value principles and invest in positive net present-value strategies do maximize the wealth of shareholders. These firms will probably also generate enough cash to satisfy other stakeholders such as employees, managers, customers, suppliers, and governments.

However, there are also several weaknesses that have been highlighted in the literature. The first is the problem of accurately predicting cash flow patterns several years into the future. Misjudging these cash flows on projects worth several billion dollars and lasting several decades may be problematic. Second, measuring the discount rate is problematic. Estimating the discount rate means that one needs to assess the firm's systematic risk (beta). Unfortunately, the measurement of beta may be problematic and may change over time. Finally, many researchers question the adequacy of the economic model (the Capital Asset Pricing Model [CAPM]) on which the estimation of beta is based.[36]

Does this mean we should not use net present-value measures? Of course not. Just as we suggested with other measures, the use of net present value must be done with its limitations in mind. In fact, using this measure may allow for a deeper understanding of firm performance.

# MARKET-BASED MEASURES AND FIRM PERFORMANCE

In recent years, strategy researchers have increasingly relied on market-based measures of firm performance, either alone or in conjunction with accounting-based measures, when assessing a firm's financial performance.[37] This increased use of market-based measures of firm performance may partially be a response to the criticisms of accounting-based measures outlined earlier. The theoretical basis for using market-based performance measures is that they are a more accurate reflection of a firm's economic performance than accounting-based measures. This argument is based on the semi-strong form of the efficient market hypothesis[38] that suggests that all publicly available information is immediately reflected in a firm's stock price. This assumption has led to the use of the Capital Asset Pricing Model (CAPM) to determine systematic (beta) and unsystematic risks and risk-free firm returns (e.g., as measured by Jensen's Alpha, defined below).

Some researchers have argued that while accounting data may be used to measure the effects of a firm's strategies *post hoc*, they are not useful for assessing the economic value of a given strategy or for choosing between strategies that are being evaluated for possible implementation.[39] Another viewpoint suggests that market-based measures are intrinsically different from accounting-based measures because the former focus on the present value of future streams of income, (e. g., on the expected value of future cash flows), whereas the latter focus on past performance.[40] Thus, we will examine several measures of firm performance based on stock market data. However, before we do, we will discuss the manner in which these measures are developed.

## Stock Market Measures

Stock market measures are based on the assumption that capital markets are "semi-strong form efficient." This means that all publicly available information is reflected in the price of a firm's equity and debt. Accepting this assumption allows us to develop measures of risk and performance for a publicly traded firm. To develop these measures, we need prices for the firm's stock over a period of time and values for the market index on which the stock is traded. For example, let's take a hypothetical firm traded on the Toronto Stock Exchange. In our example, we will examine the change in our firm's closing stock price for a period of 250 trading days. We take these closing stock price changes and regress them (in a statistical procedure called linear regression) on the daily change in the closing values of the TSE 300. This is reflected below:

$$S - RFR = a + b(M - RFR) + e$$

where

$S$ = the percentage change in closing stock prices over 250 trading days

$RFR$ = a measure of the risk-free rate of return for each of the 250 trading days

$a$ = Jensen's alpha, the risk-free rate of return for the firm's stock

$b$ = beta, the systematic risk or risk associated with movements in the stock market

$M$ = the percentage change in daily closing value of the stock market index (e.g., TSE 300) for each of the 250 trading days

$e$ = the residual obtained when estimating alpha and beta

Once this regression is conducted, it is possible to obtain measures of risk. The standard deviation of "S" is used as the measure of total risk. Beta is used as the measure of systematic risk, and the standard deviation of "e" is used as the measure of unsystematic risk. Market performance can now be assessed using four different measures: (1) the Sharpe's measure, (2) the Treynor's measure, (3) Jensen's Alpha, and (4) the Appraisal Ratio.[41]

Sharpe's measure is used to assess return per unit of total risk. The formula is:

**Sharpe's = (S − RFR)/Standard Deviation of "S"**

Treynor's measure is used to assess return per unit of systematic risk. The formula is:

**Treynor's = (S − RFR)/Beta**

Jensen's Alpha is used to assess a risk-free return and is measured by "a"

**Jensen's Alpha = a**

The Appraisal Ratio is used to measure the risk-free return per unit of unsystematic risk. The formula is:

**Appraisal Ratio** = Jensen's Alpha/Standard Deviation of "e"

In summary, the Sharpe's measure compares a firm's stock market performance to the firm's total risk. The higher the value of the Sharpe's measure, the better the firm is performing. The Treynor's measure compares a firm's stock market performance to the firm's systematic risk. As with the Sharpe's measure, a higher Treynor's means better firm performance. Jensen's Alpha compares a firm's stock market performance to the firm's risk-adjusted expected performance. A Jensen's Alpha greater than zero (one standard deviation or more above the mean) suggests that the firm is outperforming the market and achieving above-average returns. A Jensen's Alpha equal to zero suggests that the firm is performing as well as the market and achieving average returns. A Jensen's Alpha less than zero (one standard deviation or more below the mean) suggests that the firm is underperforming the market and achieving below-average returns. Table 2.4 summarizes the relationship between Jensen's Alpha and firm performance. The Appraisal Ratio is a measure of the abnormal return per unit of risk that the firm could diversify away by becoming more diversified in the scope of its product markets. The higher the Appraisal Ratio, the better a firm is performing.

| ■ ■ TABLE 2.4 | Relationships between Jensen's Alpha and Firm Performance |
| --- | --- |
| Jensen's Alpha < -1 | Below-average returns |
| Jensen's Alpha = 0 | Average returns |
| Jensen's Alpha > +1 | Above-average returns |

## Limitations of Market Measures

The first limitation of these measures is that they were not originally designed for the measurement of firm performance, but for the assessment of investment portfolio performance. Recently, however, strategy researchers have used them as a measure of firm performance.[42] A related problem is that the Sharpe's and Treynor's measures implicitly use the risk-free rate as the cost of capital. This may not be as much of a problem as it used to be for large publicly traded firms in the United States and Canada. The cost of capital and the rate of return on capital are available for the largest 1000 U.S. firms and the largest 300 Canadian firms from the Stern Stewart 1000 and 300 performance lists, respectively. However, accessing this information is still a problem when assessing smaller firms in both countries.

A second related problem is that the Treynor's measure uses the firm's systematic risk (beta), which assumes that any unsystematic risk is fully diversified away. This may be appropriate for investment portfolios but may not be appropriate for firms. For example, the beta of Fishery Products International (FPI) was found to be approximately 0.70 with only 10 percent of the variance explained by the change in the TSE 300. This suggests that most of the total risk in FPI is composed of unsystematic risk or risk inherent in the firm. This means that FPI has not diversified away all unsystematic risk—an assumption underlying the use of Beta in the Treynor's measure. Finally, some have questioned the use of market indexes such as the TSE300. The TSE300 is frequently criticized as being too heavily influenced by Nortel Networks. The TSE300 weights each stock in the index by the number of shares each firm has outstanding. Critics argue that this gives Nortel's stock an inordinate amount of influence on the index. They argue that weight should be capped at 10 percent, although others argue for the status quo, which reflects the reality of the index.[43]

Although these four measures have limitations, they do provide insight into the ability of a firm to achieve above-average returns, average returns, or below-average returns. Empirically, Sharpe's measure, Treynor's measure, Jensen's Alpha, and the Appraisal Ratio are highly correlated. One study found that the correlations of Sharpe's, Treynor's, and Jensen's Alpha were in the 0.84 to 0.90 range.[44] Another study found that Sharpe's, Treynor's and the Appraisal Ratio had correlations in the same range.[45] However, both studies found that the correlations between the accounting measures described earlier and the market measures were in only the 0.15 to 0.30 range. Though statistically significant, the results suggest that market measures tell us something different about performance than the accounting measures do.

## MARKET VALUE ADDED AND ECONOMIC VALUE ADDED

As we illustrated in the opening case, Market Value Added (MVA) and Economic Value Added (EVA) are measures of performance used by many firms to judge their performance. In this section, we will describe these two concepts and discuss their limitations. These two concepts—developed by Stern Stewart—allow for the appraisal of performance and evaluation. They further suggest that using MVA and EVA will enhance benchmarking, assessing business and financial risk, setting goals, spotting investments, and screening acquisition targets, among others.[46]

### Market Value Added

**MVA** is the difference between the cash investors expect to receive given the current market value of the firm and the amount of cash that debt and equity holders have invested in the firm since its inception.

**MVA** is believed to be a definitive measure of firm performance, with performance being defined as shareholder wealth maximization through the most efficient management and allocation of resources. MVA is the difference between the cash investors expect to receive given the current market value of the firm and the amount of cash that debt and equity holders have invested in the firm since its inception. For example, a firm that has been given $20 billion by its debt holders, $15 billion by its equity holders, and retained $30 billion through its operations, and currently has a total market value of $75 million, has an MVA equal to $10 billion. This $10 billion represents the cumulative amount that the firm has increased shareholder wealth. Of course, a negative MVA would represent the cumulative amount that the firm has reduced shareholder wealth.[47]

Stern Stewart argues that not only is MVA a good measure of shareholder wealth creation or destruction but that it also captures the ability of a firm to manage scarce capital resources. The reasoning behind this argument is that MVA is considered an estimate of the net present value of all the firm's capital projects, both those currently being pursued and those that are being anticipated by investors. Just as a net present-value analysis takes the up-front investment and subtracts it from the present value of the expected cash flows of a future project, MVA takes the capital investment in the firm to date and subtracts it from the firm's current gross market value (the expected present value of the firm's future cash flows). The difference is the firm's net present value. Positive MVAs suggest that firms are maximizing shareholder wealth and that these firms are efficiently allocating the resources flowing to them.[48]

Consequently, MVA shows how much shareholder wealth has been increased and how well the firm's senior leaders are managing the firm's capital. This measurement of firm performance is a better measure of success than rankings that focus on measures of size such as sales, revenue, or market capitalization.

Changes in MVA over a period of time are significant and should be examined closely by a firm's stakeholders. This change may be a more effective measure than absolute MVA at a particular point in time. A positive increase in MVA means that the firm's market value grew more than the amount of any additional funds raised through debt, equity, or retained earnings. This means that the firm's net present value increased and so did the wealth of its shareholders. A decrease in MVA means that the firm's net present value became less and shareholder wealth was destroyed. Stern Stewart argues that a change in MVA could be the result of many factors, including a change in stock market values, changes in expectations for a specific industry, and/or the effectiveness of a firm's senior leaders and the strategic choices that they have made.

An examination of the most recently published MVAs (1999 and 1998 rankings, see Table 2.5) for several prominent Canadian firms demonstrates that some firms increased shareholder wealth from 1998 to 1999 while some others destroyed shareholder wealth. In the first group are Nortel (up from $23.4 billion to a Canadian record of $168.9 billion), BCE Inc (up from $18.0 to $65.6 billion) and Bombardier (up from $4.8 billion to $16.1 billion). In the second group are Hudson's Bay (down $0.44 billion to negative $1.21 billion), Magna International (down $3.7 billion to negative $1.3 billion), and National Bank of Canada (down $1.2 billion to negative $0.8 billion). Table 2.5 shows the MVA, EVA, return on operating capital, and cost of capital for the top 20 and bottom 10 Canadian firms on the 2000 Stern Stewart Canadian 300 MVA Ranking List.

| ■ ■ TABLE 2.5 | | The 1999 Stern Stewart Canadian 300 MVA Ranking | | | | |
|---|---|---|---|---|---|---|
| MVA Rank 1999 | MVA Rank 1998 | Company Name | MVA 1999 | EVA 1999 | Return on Operating Capital 1999 (%) | Cost of Capital 1999 (%) |
| 1 | 1 | Nortel Networks Corporation | 168 588 | (131) | 12.4 | 12.8 |
| 2 | 2 | BCE | 65 609 | (2794) | 2.7 | 10.6 |
| 3 | 5 | Bombardier | 16 142 | 340 | 14.2 | 9.5 |
| 4 | 3 | The Thomson Corporaton | 13 467 | (165) | 7.5 | 8.5 |
| 5 | 6 | Toronto-Dominion Bank | 13 273 | 724 | 19.7 | 12.1 |
| 6 | 11 | Rogers Communications | 7924 | 33 | 9.4 | 8.4 |
| 7 | 13 | Imperial Oil | 7545 | 118 | 9.4 | 7.9 |
| 8 | 4 | Royal Bank of Canada | 6552 | 241 | 12.4 | 10.5 |
| 9 | 10 | George Weston Limited | 4814 | 227 | 10.9 | 7.5 |
| 10 | 18 | Shell Canada | 4360 | 106 | 10.2 | 7.9 |
| 11 | 58 | Research in Motion | 4282 | 7 | 17.9 | 12.0 |
| 12 | 19 | DuPont Canada | 4069 | 183 | 36.4 | 9.1 |
| 13 | 8 | Bank of Nova Scotia | 3991 | 487 | 16.3 | 11.8 |
| 14 | 38 | Telesystme Int'l Wireless | 3782 | (560) | (12.7) | 10.1 |
| 15 | 20 | Suncor Energy | 3500 | (34) | 7.6 | 8.4 |
| 16 | 12 | Barrick Gold Corp. | 3499 | (152) | 8.5 | 10.8 |
| 17 | 284 | Alcan Aluminium | 3483 | (473) | 6.8 | 10.4 |
| 18 | 44 | Clearnet Communications | 3421 | (560) | (36.9) | 9.6 |
| 19 | 40 | Microcell Telecom | 3408 | (394) | (60.3) | 9.8 |
| 20 | 17 | ATI Technologies | 3147 | 199 | 53.4 | 10.7 |
| 291 | 68 | National Bank of Canada | (848) | (44) | 9.1 | 10.2 |
| 292 | 294 | Sherrit Int'l Corp. | (1029) | (19) | 8.0 | 10.5 |
| 293 | 289 | Methanex | (1032) | (351) | (6.0) | 6.9 |
| 294 | 297 | Stelco | (1039) | (84) | 6.2 | 9.3 |
| 295 | 291 | Renaissance Energy | (1059) | (203) | 3.5 | 7.8 |
| 296 | 285 | Cameco | (1116) | (142) | 3.3 | 8.4 |
| 297 | 293 | Hudson's Bay Co. | (1218) | (96) | 4.4 | 6.3 |
| 298 | 288 | Moore | (1267) | (38) | 5.9 | 7.7 |
| 299 | 21 | Magna International | (1287) | (303) | 13.5 | 7.9 |
| 300 | 299 | Canadian Pacific Limited | (1587) | (399) | 6.2 | 8.3 |

Source: *National Post,* October 14, 2000, C4.

# Economic Value Added

**Economic Value Added** (EVA) is an internal measure of a firm's ability to generate MVA in the future. It is the amount of operating capital at the beginning of each year multiplied by the difference between the rate of return on capital and the weighted average cost of the debt and equity capital employed.

**Economic Value Added** (EVA) is an internal measure of a firm's ability to generate MVA in the future. EVA is measured by taking the amount of operating capital at the beginning of each year and multiplying it by the difference between the rate of return on capital and the weighted average cost of the debt and equity capital employed. Measurements are made at the beginning of the year because new capital investments take at least a full year to reach maturity. As mentioned earlier, EVA is linked to MVA in that MVA is the present value of all projected EVAs.

Obviously, there are several things that can be done to create shareholder value; however, all relate to doing one of the following three,[49] all of which will improve EVA:

- Improve return on capital already employed (i.e., generate more profits without employing more capital);
- Invest more capital in strategies that have a greater rate of return than the cost of the capital employed; and
- Withdraw capital from strategies or projects that have a cost of capital greater than their rate of return.

## STRATEGIC FOCUS

### The Pursuit of EVA

In the early 1980s when the late Robert Goizueta took over as CEO of Coca-Cola, he took over a company in which nobody had taken the time to explain what Coke's cost of capital was. In addition, Coke was not reinvesting in itself and was paying out more than 60 percent dividends. Once the cost of capital was understood by Coke's managers, they found the firm was not earning its cost of capital on its business (approximately 16 percent with no debt). Goizueta found the same problem in Coke's wine business. Although EVA was unknown at that time, Goizueta did know that the best way to improve performance was to obtain money at one rate, invest it at a higher rate, and pocket the difference. To achieve this, Goizueta led Coke to make several strategic moves over the next several years.

For example, Coke stopped buying five- and twenty-gallon delivery containers and started delivering in big tank trucks. Coke sold its wine business and boiler-making and desalting plants. Coke's managers and employees worked hard to rediscover who their customer was, and they stopped believing the press that said the soft-drink industry was mature. By 1995, Coke's return on capital was almost 35.5 percent, and its cost of capital had dropped to 10 percent. Coke's EVA (U.S.$1.9 billion versus Merck's second-largest EVA at U.S.$1.1 billion) was the largest of the top four firms in the 1995 Stern Stewart MVA rankings. However, the EVA was based on the smallest operating capital of the top four at $8.5 billion (GE's was largest at U.S.$45.6 billion, Wal-Mart's was U.S.$26.6 billion, and Merck's was U.S.$18.9 billion). Coke's net rate of return of 25.5 percent was the best among the top four that year, and, not surprisingly, its MVA was a record U.S.$60 billion that year. GE was second at U.S.$52 billion.

*continued*

Jack Welch took over General Electric (GE) as CEO at approximately the same time as Goizueta at Coke, the early 1980s. He discovered that some of GE's businesses were comparing themselves only to their direct competitors and not to themselves. If their returns were 9 percent and their competitors' returns were 7, they considered themselves to be doing well. The fact that 15 percent was more appropriate was difficult for managers to comprehend. Welch admits that in those days there was no understanding of MVA and EVA. Yet he concludes that firms such as Coke and GE, which have received a lot from their capital, are demonstrating that using capital efficiently is a driving force behind better performance. Firms that have had difficulties are those that have been using capital but not getting much return from it.

Some Canadian firms that have had an outstanding net rate of return (return on operating capital minus cost of capital) are JDS Uniphase, Geac Computer Corporation, ATI Technologies, and BioChem Pharma. JDS describes itself as the market leader in the design, development, manufacture, and distribution of advanced fibre optic products for the cable and telecommunications industries. Its net rate of return in the 1999 MVA Ranking was 63 percent, with a rate of return of 72.4 percent and a cost of capital of 9.4 percent. Geac Computer describes itself as "among the world's largest suppliers of mission-critical e-Business Enterprise Resource Planning (ERP) software and systems solutions to corporations around the globe." Its net rate of return is 51.2 percent, with a rate of return of 64.8 percent and a cost of capital of 13.6 percent.

ATI Technologies is one of the world's largest suppliers of 3D graphics and multimedia technology. It designs, manufactures, and markets multimedia solutions and graphics for personal computers. ATI supplies 2D/3D graphics accelerators to OEM and retail customers. ATI's net rate of return in 1999 was 47.3 percent, with a rate of return of 57.0 percent and a cost of capital of 9.7 percent. BioChem Pharma is an "international biopharmaceutical company dedicated to the research, development and commercialization of innovative products for the prevention and treatment of human diseases, with a focus in cancer and infectious diseases." Its net rate of return was 25.7 percent, with a rate of return of 39.7 percent and a cost of capital of 14.0 percent.

Sources: *Fortune*, 1995, A conversation with Roberto Goizueta and Jack Welch, *Fortune*, December 11, 96–99; A. B. Fisher, 1995, Creating stockholder wealth, *Fortune*, December 11, 105–16; http://www.jdsunph.com; http://www.geac.com; http://www.ati. com; http://www.bio chempharma.com.

http://www.jdsuniphase.com
http://www.geac.com
http://www.atitechnologies.com
http://www.biochempharma.com

## Limitations of MVA and EVA

Several writers do not agree with the many benefits of MVA/EVA touted by Stern Stewart. One article in *CMA Management* listed seven weaknesses the authors considered were associated with the use of MVA/EVA.[50] First, EVA does not assess economic value or profit. The authors argued that economic value is calculated as a firm's expected cash flows discounted at the firm's cost of capital. Economic profit is the difference in economic value at two different points in time. They suggested that EVA does not measure cash flow but measures accounting net income that has been accrued. In addition, the authors suggested that EVA does not measure future cash flows but past accounting income. Second, the authors argued that there is a lack of consistent definitions for EVA, capital, and net operating profit after taxes. Third, EVA is too complex in that it requires 160 accounting adjustments to the generally accepted accounting principles (GAAP). Fourth, EVA is an inadequate single measure for any decision in that it measures only short-term profitability, which is not appropriate. Fifth, given that EVA is a short-term measure, it may be inappropriate to reward managers based only on EVA. Sixth, EVA is not appropriate for capital budgeting.

Finally, EVA is easy for managers to manipulate. The authors give five ways for managers to manipulate EVA and reduce firm performance:

- EVA requires the capitalization of R&D, which could allow the capitalization of R&D expenditures as assets rather than as expenses when the expenditures have no future value.
- Managers could develop a short-term bias.
- Managers could decide to spend little or no time on quality improvement.
- EVA permits the capitalization of restructuring charges, which could lead to unnecessary restructuring.
- EVA permits the holding back of expenditures in asset accounts. Expenditures with no future value could be recorded as assets.

Brian Schofield of Canadian firm Sustainable Investment Group Ltd (SIGL), argues for the use of EVA and argued against the suggested weaknesses described above.[51] He suggests that an educated approach to using some of the 160 adjustments is necessary. Because SIGL calculates quarterly EVAs for over 125 firms, their calculations are based on explicit decisions regarding each of the 160 accounting adjustments and their applicability on an industry-specific basis. SIGL adds a few adjustments of its own and in total makes less than 20 adjustments—the 20 or so most meaningful to each firm and the industry in which it operates. Schofield's argument is that assessing the future direction of a firm's EVA and understanding its value-creating/destroying capabilities allows SIGL to derive likely scenarios for future stock prices. He concludes that EVA methodology, applied appropriately, is very valuable in unveiling hidden investment opportunities and overvalued projects and strategies.

EVA and MVA methodology are fairly new concepts with many people for, and some against, their use. Although both have been used successfully by large firms such as GE and Coca-Cola, a major limitation is the proprietary nature of the methodology; to have EVA/MVA applied to your firm in accordance with the Stern Stewart philosophy means hiring consultants from Stern Stewart. Of course, as the methodology becomes better known, others will apply their own version of the Stern Stewart MVA/EVA techniques (as SIGL has done), and the current proprietary nature of the techniques will no longer be as much of a problem.

## SUMMARY

- Performance is the comparison of the actual value created by an organization using its productive assets with the value that the assets' owners expected the organization to create. The comparison of actual value created with the value owners of assets expected the organization to create leads to three levels of performance. These three levels are below-normal, normal, and above-normal performance. When an organization's actual value created is less than the value owners of assets expected, it is below-normal performance; when the actual value created is equal to the expected value, it is normal performance; and when the actual value created is greater than the expected value, it is above-normal performance.

- Firm survival is one measurement of firm performance that is easily applied. If a firm survives over an extended period of time, it is creating at least average returns.

- One common approach to measuring firm performance is the use of accounting data. The type of data used are (1) profitability ratios (where some measure of profitability is used as the numerator and some measure of size is used as the denominator), (2) liquidity ratios (these focus on the ability of a firm to pay its short-term debts), (3) leverage ratios (these measure the amount of a firm's indebtedness), (4) activity ratios (these assess the level of activity in a firm), and (5) miscellaneous ratios (these are ratios that do not fall into one of the previously mentioned categories).

- Another method of measuring firm performance is the stakeholder approach. This means that a firm's performance should be viewed relative to the preferences of those stakeholders who are important to the firm and can impact firm performance. Some stakeholders who may impact firm performance are customers, employees, suppliers, managers, top executives, equity holders, debt holders, communities where plants and offices are located, and governments (local, provincial, and federal).

- Net present value is the measurement of future cash flows and discounting of them using an appropriate discount rate and then subtracting the up-front investment. This approach seeks to avoid some of the limitations of other performance measures. It avoids short-term bias by measuring cash flows over time, and it values all resources made available to a firm by using the discount-rate concept. Firms that use present value estimate net cash flows and expected discount rates for several years into the future. This allows them to assess firm performance and individual project performance on a forward-looking basis.

- Market-based measures have been used to measure firm performance in recent years. These measures include Sharpe's measure, Treynor's measure, Jensen's Alpha, and Appraisal Ratio. These measures rely on the assumptions underlying the Capital Asset Pricing Model, especially the semi-strong market efficiency argument, and have been criticized for this reason.

- Market Value Added is the difference between the cash investors expect to receive given the current market value of the firm and the amount of cash that debt and equity holders have invested in the firm since its inception.

- Economic Value Added is an internal measure of a firm's ability to generate MVA in the future. It is measured by taking the amount of operating capital at the beginning of each year and multiplying it by the difference between the rate of return on capital and the weighted average cost of the debt and equity capital employed.

## REVIEW QUESTIONS

1. Discuss the conceptual meaning of performance. Is this a theoretically sound way to think about firm performance? Does this conceptual definition help us focus on the challenge of strategic management? Explain.

2. Briefly describe survival as a performance measure and its strengths and weaknesses.

3. Why are accounting measures of performance so popular? Is their continued use to measure performance justified? Why or why not?

4. Is the stakeholder approach a useful performance measure? Describe how you would use this measure.

5. Net present value is a well-grounded financial performance measure. Discuss this measure conceptually based on your finance textbooks. Do the authors of these textbooks agree or disagree with the limitations discussed in this chapter?

6. Market-based measures have been used recently to measure performance. Borrow an investment textbook from a friend and use material from the

textbooks to conceptually discuss whether market-based measures are appropriate for assessing firm performance.

7. Describe in detail what the measures Market Value Added and Economic Value Added mean. Are they valid measures of firm performance?

# DISCUSSION QUESTIONS

1. Make a list of several firms in your local community. For two or three of these firms, phone one of the members of the senior management team and ask how management measures the firm's performance. For the rest of the firms, find out how long they have been in business. Are they achieving above-average returns? Can you tell from length of time in business alone?

2. Find the Web site for several well-known firms and assess their performance using the accounting ratios in Table 2.2. Take one or two of the firms you surveyed and assess whether they are achieving above-average returns using the accounting data you have collected.

3. Describe the stakeholders who impact and are impacted by decisions made by your university. Describe some dimensions that these different stakeholder groups might have for assessing your university's performance. Based on this assessment, is your university achieving above-average performance?

4. Take a prominent publicly traded firm in your local community and gather its stock prices and the market index of the stock exchange on which it is traded. Using a risk-free rate of 4 percent, calculate the values of Sharpe's measure, Treynor's measure, Jensen's Alpha, and the Appraisal Ratio. Is this firm achieving above-average returns?

5. Locate *National Post*'s summer issue when the Canadian MVA/EVA rankings are published. Take a few of your favourite firms (where you might want to apply for a job) and assess their MVA, EVA, operating capital, return on capital, and cost of capital. Are these firms achieving above-average returns? Would you work for them if one of them you offered a job?

# ETHICS QUESTIONS

1. Take each of the six ways of measuring performance discussed in the chapter and assess its potential for fostering ethical performance measurement. In your answer, discuss what ethical performance measurement means.

2. Discuss some of the conditions required for ethical performance management. Does the firm you want to work for meet these conditions? If not, will you still work there?

3. Discuss the implications of each of these performance measures for the ethical measurement of performance in the long term. Do you think that any of these measures will force ethical performance if the firm currently has a sense of "follow the legal requirements but do only what is necessary and no more?"

4. What is the relationship between ethics and above-average returns?

5. *Saturday Night* magazine (February 17, 2001: 15) noted Howard Stringer's response to the view of one panel at the Dravos World Economic Conference. The magazine noted that "The panel spoke grandly of ever-increasing efficiency, productivity, and adaptability in the corporate workplace. Stringer piped up, 'Doesn't anyone here think this sounds like a version of hell? When will there be time for sex or music or books? Stop the world, I want to get off.'" What Stringer seems to be saying is that economic performance is not all that matters. Comment on his remarks. Now comment knowing that Stringer is the chairman of Sony America, an entertainment company that has a vested interest in supporting the positive value of leisure time.

# INTERNET EXERCISE

The following is a list of Canadian companies:

JDS Uniphase: **http://www.jdsuniphase.com**
Geac Computers: **http://www.geac.com**
Nortel Networks: **http://www.nortelnetworks.com**
Bombardier: **http://www.Bombardier.com**

Select two of these companies. For each company, assess its performance using all six methods discussed in Chapter 2. Are they achieving above-average returns, average returns, or below-average returns? Are they achieving their performance in an ethical manner based on the information you have gathered?

## STRATEGIC SURFING

Performance of Canadian firms can be assessed using many measures of performance. One measure that is available but hard to get is Market Value

Added. this measure along with Economic Value Added is available for 300 Canadian firms at the following Web site:

**http://www.sternstewart.com/content/performance/info/canada.pdf**

# NOTES

1　J. B. Barney, 1997, *Gaining and Sustaining Competitive Advantage,* (Don Mills, ON: Addison-Wesley Publishing Company), 30–64.

2　R. P. Rumelt, D. E. Schendel, and D. J. Teece (eds.), 1994, *Fundamental Issues in Strategy* (Boston: Harvard Business School Press), 527–30; A. D. Meyer, 1991, What is strategy's distinctive competence? *Journal of Management,* 17: 821–33.

3　W. G. Rowe, and J. L. Morrow, Jr. 1999, A note on the dimensionality of the firm financial performance construct using accounting, market and subjective measures, *Canadian Journal of Administrative Sciences,* 16 (1): 58–70.

4　A. Alchian and H. Demsetz, 1972, Production, information costs, and economic organization, *American Economic Review,* 62: 777–95; R. H. Coase, 1937, The nature of the firm, *Economica,* 4: 386–405; R. H. Hall, 1987, *Organizations: Structures, Processes, and Outcomes,* Fourth Edition (Engelwood Cliffs, NJ: Prentice-Hall); M. C. Jensen and W. H. Meckling, 1976, Theory of the firm: Managerial behavior, agency costs, and ownership structure, *Journal of Financial Economics,* 3: 305–60; J. P. Sheppard, 1994, Strategy and bankruptcy: An exploration into organizational death, *Journal of Management,* 20: 795–833; H. A. Simon, 1976, *Administrative Behavior* (3rd Edition), (New York: MacMillan).

5　Barney, *Gaining and Sustaining Competitive Advantage*; Simon, *Administrative Behavior,* 30–33.

6　Barney, *Gaining and Sustaining Competitive Advantage,* 30–33; Coase, The nature of the firm; Jensen and Meckling, Theory of the firm: Managerial behavior, agency costs, and ownership structure.

7　Alchian and Demsetz, Production, information costs, and economic organization; Barney, *Gaining and Sustaining Competitive Advantage,* 30–33.

8　Barney, *Gaining and Sustaining Competitive Advantage,* 30–33.

9　J. G. Barnes, 2001, *Secrets of Customer Relationship Marketing: It's All About How You Make Them Feel,* (Montreal, QC; McGraw-Hill), 81–110.

10　J. P. Sheppard, 1994, Strategy and bankruptcy: An exploration into organizational death, *Journal of Management,* 20: 795–833.

11　Barney, *Gaining and Sustaining Competitive Advantage,* 30–33.

12　Barney, *Gaining and Sustaining Competitive Advantage,* 34–36; H. Demsetz, 1973, Industry structure, market rivalry, and public policy, *Journal of Law and Economics,* 16, 1–9.

13　Barney, *Gaining and Sustaining Competitive Advantage,* 34–36.

14　Small Fry takes big steps into US with Humpty Dumpty assets, *National Post,* January 26, C8.

15　K. J. Delaney, 1992, *Strategic Bankruptcy: How Corporations and Creditors use Chapter 11 to Their Advantage,* (Berkeley, CA: University of California Press); W. N. Moulton and H. Thomas, 1993, Bankruptcy as a deliberate strategy: Theoretical considerations and empirical evidence, *Strategic Management Journal,* 14 (2), 125–35; J. P. Sheppard, 1992, When the going gets tough, the tough go bankrupt: The questionable use of Chapter 11 as a strategy, *Journal of Management Inquiry,* 1 (3), 183–92.

16　J. P. Sheppard, 1993, Corporate Diversification and Survival, *Journal of Financial and Strategic Decisions,* 6 (1), 113–32.

17　Barney, *Gaining and Sustaining Competitive Advantage,* 34–36.

18　Ibid.

19　Barney, *Gaining and Sustaining Competitive Advantage,* 34–36; M. E. Porter, 1980, *Competitive Strategy,* (New York: Free Press); R. P. Rumelt, D. Schendel, and D. Teece, 1991, Strategic management and economics, *Strategic Management Journal,* 12 (Winter Special Issue), 5–29.

20　Altman, E. I., 1968, Financial ratios, discriminant analysis and the prediction of corporate bankruptcy, *The Journal of Finance,* 23(4): 589–609; Altman, E. I., 1982, *Corporate Financial Distress: A Complete Guide to Predicting, Avoiding, and Dealing with Bankruptcy,* (New York: John Wiley and Sons).

21　Barney, *Gaining and Sustaining Competitive Advantage,* 34–36; R. M. Kanter and D. Brinkerhoff, 1981, Organizational performance: Recent developments in measurement, *Annual Review of Sociology,* 7, 321–49.

22　Rowe and Morrow, Jr., A note on the dimensionality of the firm financial performance construct using accounting, market and subjective measures, 58–70; Barney, *Gaining and Sustaining Competitive Advantage,* 36–43.

23　I. Horowitz, 1984, The misuse of accounting rates of return: Comment, *American Economic Review,* 74, 492–493; R. Jacobson, 1987, The validity of ROI as a measure of business performance, *American Economic Review,* 77, 470–78; W. F. Long, and D. J. Ravenscraft, 1984, The misuse of accounting rates of return: Comment, *American Economic Review,* 74, 494–500.

24　G. Bentson, 1982, Accounting numbers and economic values, *Antitrust Bulletin,* Spring, 161–215; F. M. Fisher, and J. J. McGowan, 1983, On the misuse of accounting rates of return to infer monopoly profits, *American Economic Review, 73,* 82–97; R. L. Watts, and J. L. Zimmerman, 1978, Towards a positive theory of the determination of accounting standards, *The Accounting Review, 53,* 112–33; R. L. Watts, and J. L. Zimmerman, 1990, Positive accounting theory: A ten-year perspective, *The Accounting Review, 65,* 131–56.

25  T. E. Copeland and J. F. Weston, 1983, *Financial Theory and Corporate Policy,* (Reading, MA: Addison-Wesley).

26  W. F. Long, and D. J. Ravenscraft, 1984, The misuse of accounting rates of return: Comment, *American Economic Review, 74,* 494–500.

27  Rowe and Morrow, Jr., A note on the dimensionality of the firm financial performance construct using accounting, market and subjective measures, 58–90; Barney, *Gaining and Sustaining Competitive Advantage,* 36–43.

28  R. L. Watts and J. L. Zimmerman, 1978, Towards a positive theory of the determination of accounting standards, *The Accounting Review, 53,* 112–33; R. L. Watts, and J. L. Zimmerman, 1990, Positive accounting theory: A ten-year perspective, *The Accounting Review, 65,* 131–56.

29  Barney, *Gaining and Sustaining Competitive Advantage,* 36–43.

30  H. Itami, 1987, *Mobilizing Invisible Assets,* (Cambridge, MA: Harvard University Press); Barney, *Gaining and Sustaining Competitive Advantage,* 36–43.

31  Barney, *Gaining and Sustaining Competitive Advantage,* 36–43.

32  R. W. Sexty, 1995, *Canadian Business and Society* (Scarborough, ON: Prentice Hall).

33  Barney, *Gaining and Sustaining Competitive Advantage,* 46.

34  S. A. Ross, R. W. Westerfield, B.D. Jordan, and G.S. Roberts, 1996, *Fundamentals of Corporate Finance* (2nd Canadian Edition) (Toronto: Irwin), 136–86; Barney, *Gaining and Sustaining Competitive Advantage,* 46–53.

35  Barney, *Gaining and Sustaining Competitive Advantage,* 46–53.

36  W. F. Sharpe, G. J. Alexander, J. V. Bailey, and D. J. Fowler, 1997, *Investments* (2nd Canadian edition) (Scarborough, ON: Prentice Hall), 234–62; Z. Bodie, A. Kane, A. J. Marcus, S. Perrakis, and P. J. Ryan, 1997, *Investments* (2nd Canadian Edition) (Toronto: McGraw-Hill Ryerson), 288–321.

37  R. E. Hoskisson, M. A. Hitt, R. A. Johnson, and D. D. Moesel, 1993, Construct validity of an objective (entropy) categorical measure of diversification strategy, *Strategic Management Journal, 14,* 215–35; R. E. Hoskisson, R. A. Johnson, and D. D. Moesel, 1994, Corporate divestiture intensity in restructuring

firms: Effects of governance, strategy, and performance, *Academy of Management Journal, 37* (5), 1207–51.

38  Z. Bodie, A. Kane, and A. J. Marcus, 1993, *Investments* (2nd Canadian edition) (Boston, MA: Irwin), 401–04.

39  M. Hergert and D. Morris, 1989, Accounting data for value chain analysis, *Strategic Management Journal,* 10, 175–88.

40  A. Seth, 1990, Value creation in acquisitions: A re-examination of performance issues, *Strategic Management Journal,* 11, 99–115.

41  Z. Bodie, A. Kane, A. J. Marcus, S. Perrakis, and P. J. Ryan, 1997, *Investments* (2nd Canadian edition) (Toronto: McGraw-Hill Ryerson), 450–54.

42  Rowe and Morrow, Jr., A note on the dimensionality of the firm financial performance construct using accounting, market and subjective measures; R. E. Hoskisson, M. A. Hitt, R. A. Johnson, and D. D. Moesel, Construct validity of an objective (entropy) categorical measure of diversification strategy, 215–35; R. E. Hoskisson, R. A. Johnson, and D. D. Moesel, Corporate divestiture intensity in restructuring firms: Effects of governance, strategy, and performance, 1207–51.

43  A. Bell, 1999, Nortel's might skews stock market, *The Globe and Mail,* October 13, B1.

44  R. E. Hoskisson, M. A. Hitt, R. A. Johnson, and D. D. Moesel, Construct validity of an objective (entropy) categorical measure of diversification strategy, 215–35.

45  W. G. Rowe, 1996, *Persistence and Change in CEO Succession Processes,* Texas A&M, unpublished doctoral dissertation.

46  I. Ross, 1998, The 1997 Stern Stewart Performance 1000, *Journal of Applied Corporate Finance,* 10 (4): Winter, 116–20; I. Ross, 1997, The 1996 Stern Stewart Performance 1000, *Journal of Applied Corporate Finance,* 9 (1): Spring; L. Walbert, 1995, The 1994 Stern Stewart Performance 1000, *Journal of Applied Corporate Finance,* 7 (4): 104–18.

47  The Stern Stewart Performance 1000, 1997, (New York: Stern Stewart Management Services), 2–19.

48  Ibid.

49  Ibid.

50  D. Keys, M. Azamhuzjaev, and J. MacKey, 1999, EVA: To boldly go? *CMA Management,* September, 30–33.

51  B. Schofield, 2000, EVA, *CMA Management,* December/ January, 8–9.

# Chapter Three

## The External Environment: Opportunities, Threats, Industry Competition, and Competitor Analysis

### LEARNING OBJECTIVES

*After reading this chapter, you should be able to:*

1. Explain the importance of studying and understanding the external environment.
2. Define the general and industry environments.
3. Discuss the four activities of the external environmental analysis process.
4. Name and describe the six segments of the general environment.
5. Identify the five competitive forces and explain how they determine an industry's profit potential.
6. Define strategic groups and describe how they influence a firm's competitive actions.
7. Describe what firms need to know about their competitors and different methods used to collect competitive intelligence.

## Genesis, Transformation, and Change in Industry Environments

Fewer than a dozen years ago you could not use a Web browser to surf the Net; there weren't any Web browsers. Although there are currently about 40 000 references to the Internet in the Canadian Business and Current Affairs database, in that same database there were virtually no references to the Internet, the World Wide Web, or Netscape prior to 1995.

Humans went to the moon before computers talked to each other. However, the first moon trip in 1969 did signal the dawn of a new era, not because Neil Armstrong walked on the moon but because Leonard Kleinrock connected two computers. For years Kleinrock pursued the idea of connecting computers by short, millisecond-long packets of data over telephone lines. The telecommunications industry saw no promise in the idea. However, the U.S. Department of Defense did, and with Kleinrock, they created ARPANET—the Internet's predecessor. For the next 20 years, universities became almost the sole users of the Net.

This all changed in the early 1990s when the World Wide Web was created, and more graphical user interfaces were developed. The ease of programs such as Netscape made the Net accessible to the average person, which meant huge increases in demand for the telephone companies; the very industry that had scorned the idea of the Internet.

Internet usage increased as modem development improved access speeds and new providers drove down prices. Now cable companies such as Rogers and Shaw, along with phone companies such as BCE and AT&T, offer high-speed connections that allow for high-speed downloads, as well as live audio and video streaming. As the Internet continues to develop, participants in the virtual marketplace will have many diverse core competencies and product offerings. Some will provide access to the Net, others will help build or run the fibre optic infrastructure, and others will sell services and goods via the Net. There are conditions within three general environmental segments driving the changes that will structure the competitive market segments in the industry.

http://www.zeroknowledge.com
http://www.buystream.com

The *political/legal segment* has always had an effect on the industry. The Internet was created at government behest, and governments are investing in the fibre optical backbone of the Internet. Canada's $120 million CA*net-3 was built with $30 million from the federal government. Ottawa's interest is not hard to fathom: the Net presents an economical way to connect remote locations, deliver educational services, and transmit medical images from one place to another for better diagnosis.

Regulators will be asked by Internet providers to allow providers a piece of the market for high-speed Internet access through cable and ADSL phone lines. Yet, in some ways, the CRTC will become irrelevant when users can use their Internet connection as a telephone, videophone, or broadcasting site. Witness the difficulties in controlling iCraveTV.com when it rebroadcast TV signals over the Internet. Stopping iCrave's rebroadcasts took months of legal wrangling.

Conditions in the *technological segment* are at work to foster the changes in the industry. New technologies may offer us the Internet and hundreds of TV channels at the same time. CA*net-3 now transmits over 30 channels simultaneously through one hair-fine optical fibre. Yet the number of channels increases constantly. In theory, eight fibres could carry one petabyte (a million gigabytes) per second—80 million file-drawers full of text. If optical fibre network hardware gets inexpensive enough, it will allow for signal speeds at home that are far faster than anything now available. In such a future, a video from your local store is a one-second download away. Similarly, there are critical implications to companies such as Chapters when just about any book can be downloaded from the Internet in a second.

The Internet is so pervasive that one can find it almost anywhere; it is the ultimate change in the *global segment* of the general environment. Ordering goods from anywhere in the world with the Internet is now easy. What happens to distributors of lightweight, high-value products when the same goods can be purchased over the Internet directly from the manufacturer in China for half price and delivered by air within days? What happens to engineering costs when drafting can be done quickly and correctly in India for far less and with the same turnaround time?

The Internet is attracting phenomenal attention and investment. The AOL and Time Warner merger is the biggest and most obvious example. Although that merger seeks to connect an Internet connection provider (AOL) with a content provider (Time Warner), there are an infinite amount of other moves being made around the Internet. In order to become a global telecommunications player, BCE spent $10 billion to purchase Teleglobe.

Multi-billion dollar deals are not the only interesting action around the Internet. Deals seem to come from every direction—including those that create products that are the exact opposite of others. For example, Ottawa's Buystream.com created a program called "Architect" that allows corporations to determine the effectiveness of their Web sites by developing profiles of visitors. On the other hand, Montreal's Zeroknowledge.com has created a program called "Freedom" that allows Net users to surf without leaving identifying trails of information on the sites they visit—the very information Buystream's "Architect" endeavours to gather!

Source: D. Akin, 1999, Web firm lands biggest equity financing yet, *Financial Post,* December 30, C1; B. Bouw and D. Akin, 2000, Rogers sees Web threat to costly speciality TV, *Financial Post,* March 2, C9; B. Johnson, 1999, Internet turns the big 30 (don't crash the party), *Advertising Age,* August 30, 28; P. Morton, 2000, iCraveTV's Craig set to go with new speciality service, *Financial Post,* March 2, C1; J. Vardy, 2000, Software called 'missing link' of e-commerce, *Financial Post,* March 6, C3; Whatis.Com, 2000, http://www.whatis.com/ petabyte.htm (Retrieved March 6).

Research has shown that the external environment plays a significant role in the growth and profitability of firms.[1] This is vividly demonstrated in the case of significant and constant changes facing firms directly associated with the Internet: telecom firms, fibre optic companies, and Internet providers. Which companies will succeed in these industries will be determined largely by firms' reactions to changes in the environment. This chapter focuses on how firms should analyze and understand their external environment, as shown in Figure 1.1 in Chapter 1.

Many companies now compete in global, rather than domestic, markets. Technological changes and the explosion in information-gathering and processing capabilities, such as those surrounding the Internet, demand more timely and effective competitive actions and responses.[2] Rapid sociological changes occurring in many countries affect labour practices and the nature of products demanded by increasingly diverse consumers. Governmental policies and laws affect where and how firms choose to compete as well as the strategic direction and competitive environment of both foreign and domestic firms. Thus, companies must be aware of and understand the implications of these environmental realities to compete effectively in the global economy.

In high-performing, strategically competitive organizations, managers seek patterns to help them understand their external environment.[3] It is vital for decisionmakers to have a precise and accurate understanding of their company's competitive position. One of the first decisions Louis Gerstner, Jr. made when he became IBM's CEO was to visit with each member of IBM's senior management team. Because he was hired from outside the firm, a key reason for his visits was to learn about each business area's competitive standing in the industry (or industries) in which it competed.[4] Strategic decisionmakers know that understanding their firm's external environment helps to improve a company's competitive position, increase operational efficiency, and win battles in the global economy.[5]

Through a variety of means, firms attempt to understand their external environments by gaining information about competitors, customers, and other stakeholders in the external environment. In particular, firms are attempting to gain information to build their own base of knowledge and capabilities.[6] These firms may attempt to imitate the capabilities of able competitors or even successful firms in other industries, or build new knowledge and capabilities, to develop a competitive advantage. Based on the new information, knowledge, and capabilities, firms may take actions to buffer themselves from environmental effects or to build relationships with stakeholders in that environment.[7]

In this chapter, we discuss the external environment. Through an integrated understanding of the external and the internal environments, firms gain the information needed to understand the present and predict the future.[8] By looking at the environment, firms endeavour to develop a sense of the potential opportunities and threats that may be present in the environment. Ultimately, strategists must match environmental changes to the strengths and weaknesses of the firm. Weaknesses that are exacerbated by a looming threat need to be effectively addressed; e.g., lack of knowledge in information technology when your industry's product or service is increasingly sold through the Internet. Strengths that can exploit change should be effectively developed; e.g., e-commerce knowledge developed in selling products in one industry may be applied in other industries. Note that the same event—in the previous examples, development of e-commerce—can be an opportunity or a threat depending on the strengths or weaknesses of the company.

The **general environment** is composed of elements in the broader society that can influence an industry and the firms within it.

As shown in Figure 3.1, a firm's external environment has three major components: the general, industry, and competitor environments. The **general environment** is composed of elements in the broader society that can influence an industry and the firms within it.[9] These elements range from people-oriented items to the broader world around us. We group these elements into environmental segments called the demographic, sociocultural, political/legal, economic, technological, and global segments. Examples of elements analyzed in these six segments are shown in Table 3.1. Firms cannot directly control these elements. Instead, the strategic challenge is to understand each segment and its implications so that appropriate strategies can be formulated and implemented.

### ■ ■ FIGURE 3.1

*The External Environment*

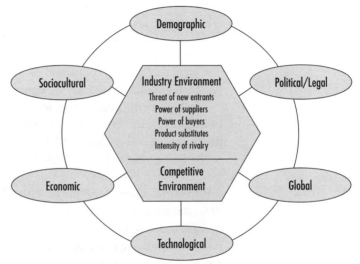

These elements not only impact the industry environment but also other general environment elements. Technological changes such as the Internet have impacts on the economy (most obviously in terms of development of e-commerce and stock market wealth creation—or destruction) and sociocultural (instant messaging and chat rooms that create new ways for people to meet and interact). Another example is environmental concerns. These are of particular interest to the many communities in Canada that depend on natural resource extraction for their well-being. One could even suggest that the concern over the natural environment touches so many of the elements of the general environment that it really could be an additional element to the group of six already mentioned.[10] For example, the environmental movement—as a sociocultural phenomena—creates political action on a global basis. Such action can then create changes in legal standards for timber harvests and promote technologies that increase the efficiency of such harvests.[11]

## GENERAL, INDUSTRY, AND COMPETITOR ENVIRONMENTS

The **industry environment** is the set of factors—the threat of new entrants, suppliers, buyers, product substitutes, and the intensity of rivalry among competitors—that directly influences a firm and its competitive actions and responses. In total, the inter-

The **industry environment** is the set of factors—the threat of new entrants, suppliers, buyers, product substitutes, and the intensity of rivalry among competitors—that directly influences a company and its competitive actions and responses.

actions among these five factors determine an industry's profit potential. The challenge is to locate a position within an industry where a firm can favourably influence these factors or successfully defend against their influence. The greater a firm's capacity to favourably influence its industry environment, the greater the likelihood that it will earn above-average returns.

We also discuss in this chapter how firms gather and interpret information about their competitors. Called competitor analysis, a firm's understanding of its current competitors complements the insights provided by study of the general and industry environments. In combination, the results of these three analyses influence the development of a firm's strategic intent, strategic mission, and strategic actions.

| ■ ■ TABLE 3.1 | The General Environment: Segments and Elements |
|---|---|

**Demographic Segment**

| | |
|---|---|
| Population size | Geographic distribution |
| Income distribution | Age structure |
| Ethnic mix | Immigration |

**Sociocultural Segment**

| | |
|---|---|
| Women in the workforce | Attitudes about quality of work life |
| Workforce diversity | Shifts in work and career preferences |
| Environmental Concerns | Shifts in preferences regarding product and service characteristics |

**Political/Legal Segment**

| | |
|---|---|
| Competition laws | Educational philosophies/policies |
| Labour laws | Regulation/deregulation philosophies |
| Taxation laws | Philosophies regarding government economic involvement/ownership |

**Economic Segment**

| | |
|---|---|
| Inflation and interest rates | Trade deficits or surpluses |
| Personal savings rate | Budget deficits or surpluses |
| Business savings rates | Gross domestic product |

**Technological Segment**

| | |
|---|---|
| Product innovations | Focus of private and government-supported R&D expenditures |
| Process innovations | |
| Applications of knowledge | New communication technologies |
| Global Segment | |
| Important political events | Newly industrialized countries |
| Critical global markets | Different cultural and institutional attributes |

Analysis of the general environment is focused on the future; analysis of the industry environment is focused on understanding the factors and conditions influencing a firm's profitability; and, analysis of competitors is focused on predicting the dynamics of competitors' actions, responses, and intentions. Although each analysis is discussed separately, a firm's performance improves when the insights from analyses of the general environment, the industry environment, and the competitive environment are integrated. The process of external environmental analysis is discussed in the next section.

## EXTERNAL ENVIRONMENTAL ANALYSIS

Most firms face external environments that are growing more turbulent, complex, and global. This makes the environment increasingly difficult to interpret.[12] To cope with often ambiguous and incomplete environmental data and to increase their understanding of the general environment, firms engage in a process called external environmental analysis. This process includes four activities: scanning, monitoring, forecasting, and assessing (see Table 3.2). External environmental analysis should be conducted on a continuous basis.[13]

| ■ ■ TABLE 3.2 | Components of the External Analysis |
|---|---|
| *Scanning* | Identifying early signals of environmental changes and trends. |
| *Monitoring* | Detecting meaning through ongoing observations of environmental change and trends. |
| *Forecasting* | Developing projections of anticipated outcomes based on monitored changes and trends. |
| *Assessing* | Determining the timing and importance of environmental changes and trends for firms' strategies and their management. |

**Opportunities** are conditions in the general environment that may help a company achieve strategic competitiveness.
**Threats** are conditions in the general environment that may hinder a company's efforts to achieve strategic competitiveness.

An important objective of studying the general environment is identification of opportunities and threats. **Opportunities** are conditions in the general environment that may help a company achieve strategic competitiveness. **Threats** are conditions in the general environment that may hinder a company's efforts to achieve strategic competitiveness. In essence, external environmental opportunities represent possibilities, while threats are potential constraints.

To analyze the general environment, several sources are used. Included among these are a wide variety of printed materials (e.g., trade and business publications, newspapers, the results of academic research and of public polls); the content of conversations with suppliers, customers, and employees of other organizations; business-related "rumours" provided by various people; and attendance and participation in trade shows.[14] In fact, for the computer industry, attendance at the annual Comdex Trade Show is so important that the Canadian government has organized press conferences for small Canadian companies to help them make connections with other firms.[15] Additional sources of information and data include individuals in "boundary-spanning" positions who interact with external constituents such as salespeople, purchasing managers, public relations directors, and human resource managers. Decisionmakers should verify the validity and reliability of the sources on which their environmental analyses are based.[16]

## Scanning

While most **scanning** focuses on the external, it should also involve looking within the firm. Internal scanning can provide business insights, identify slack, and improve firm effectiveness. The managerial practice of "management by walking around" is an example of internal scanning.

Scanning entails a study of all segments in the general environment. Through scanning, firms identify early signals of potential changes in the general environment and detect changes that are already under way.[17] When scanning, analysts typically deal with ambiguous, incomplete, and unconnected information. Environmental scanning has been found to be critically important for effective performance in firms that operate in highly volatile environments.[18] Additionally, scanning activity must be aligned with the organizational context; a scanning system designed for a volatile environment is inappropriate for a firm in a stable environment.[19]

Analysts in financial institutions are observing several changes in the general environment. First, some analysts believe a combination of personal savings, private pensions, and Canada Pension Plan income may be insufficient to support baby boomers' (those born between 1947 and 1964) retirement. It has been suggested that financing baby boomers' retirement needs threatens the financial stability of most industrial nations. The first of the baby boomer generation will retire in 2012. These retirements will push the total number of retirees from about four million in 2001 to eight million in 2026.[20] By combining this information with data gleaned from scanning other environmental segments (e.g., the demographic, sociocultural, and political/legal segments), analysts can determine trends to monitor, forecast, and assess. Such analyses might result in an opportunity for financial institutions to effectively serve the baby boomers' retirement needs.

## Monitoring

When monitoring, analysts observe environmental changes to see if an important trend is emerging.[21] Critical to successful monitoring is an ability to detect meaning in different environmental events. For example, an emerging trend in education might be suggested by changes in the amount and type of federal and provincial funding for educational institutions, changes in educational requirements, and changes in school course content.

Take just one area of the educational system: special education. The need for special education in Canadian schools has expanded from 20 special-education students in 1920 to estimates that about 15.5 percent of Canada's school-aged population needs some form of specialized help at school. The resulting increase in provision of special-education services in Canadian schools has surpassed expectations of even its strongest initial supporters. Yet the general trend may be reversing; there are efforts to merge special-education students into regular classes. Monitoring the timing and extent of this trend reversal has important implications for school design, teacher/student ratios, and thus school payrolls and school board budgets.[22] In this instance, analysts should determine whether these different events suggest an educational trend and, if so, whether other information should be studied to monitor it.

## Forecasting

Scanning and monitoring are concerned with events in the general environment at a point in time. When forecasting, analysts develop feasible projections of what might happen, and how quickly, as a result of the changes and trends detected via scanning and monitoring.[23] For example, analysts might forecast the time that will be required for a new technology to reach the marketplace, the length of time before various corporate training procedures are required to deal with anticipated changes in the composition of the workforce, or how much time will elapse before changes in government tax policies will affect consumers' purchasing patterns. Forecasts can have immediate impacts. For example, forecasting an increase in sales will result in an increase in inventories. At Apple Computer, a recent forecast of lower sales and earnings led to a downturn in the firm's stock price.[24] When Europe's biggest computer games company, Eidos (makers of Tomb Raider) announced quarterly shipments were off by 5 percent, markets quickly knocked almost one-third off their share price. Thus, as these examples show, because markets respond so quickly, forecasts can lead to negative outcomes quickly.[25]

## Assessing

The objective of assessing is to determine the timing and significance of the effects of environmental changes and trends on the strategic management of a firm.[26] Through scanning, monitoring, and forecasting, analysts are able to understand the general environment. Going a step further, the intent of assessment is to specify the implications of that understanding for the organization. Without assessment, analysts are left with data that are interesting but of unknown relevance.

For example, there have been increases in the number of small, health-conscious, dual-income families. Faced with these trends, Kitchener, Ontario's J.M. Schneider moved to lowering the fat, salt, and cholesterol in its products. Given the small families' need for convenience it also developed the Lunchmates line of pre-packed children's meals and bought the frozen entrée–maker Michelina's. By combining health and convenience needs, Schneider's introduced Michelina's Lifestyle light entrees.[27] Rubbermaid is an example of a firm that has learned to be careful about scanning, monitoring, forecasting, and assessing its external environment to avoid future problems with customers and losing market share to emerging competitors. Rubbermaid has been ranked at the top of *Fortune*'s most admired companies. Yet more recently, Rubbermaid experienced a number of problems. Besides being confronted by several new competitors, Rubbermaid faced major increases in the cost of resin (a vital raw material in many of its products). The company attempted to pass these costs onto customers through large price increases. Wal-Mart, as a huge Rubbermaid customer, was particularly angered. In response, Wal-Mart refused to stock a number of Rubbermaid products, did not promote some others, and began to feature Rubbermaid competitors in promotional materials. Given that Wal-Mart is Rubbermaid's largest customer, accounting for more than 15 percent of Rubbermaid's household-product sales, the anger from Wal-Mart's executives seems well founded. Rubbermaid suffered from these forecasting errors and miscalculations. Expert competitive assessments in the future will contribute to Rubbermaid's efforts to avoid these types of difficulties.[28]

## SEGMENTS OF THE GENERAL ENVIRONMENT

The general environment is composed of segments that are external to the firm (see Table 3.1). Though the degree of impact varies, these environmental segments affect each industry and its firms. The challenge is to scan, monitor, and assess those elements in each segment that are of the greatest importance to a firm. Results should include recognition of environmental changes, trends, opportunities, and threats. Opportunities are then matched with a firm's core competencies. When these matches are successful, the firm achieves strategic competitiveness and earns above-average returns.

# The Demographic Segment

The **demographic segment** is con-cerned with a population's size, age, structure, geographic distribution, ethnic mix, and income distribution.

The **demographic segment** is concerned with a population's size, age, structure, geographic distribution, ethnic mix, and income distribution.[29] As noted previously, executives must analyze the demographics of the global areas potentially relevant to their firms, rather than only those of the domestic population. In the following materials, each demographic element is discussed briefly.

## Population Size

Observing the demographic changes in populations highlights the importance of this environmental segment. For example, in some advanced nations, there is negative population growth (discounting the effects of immigration). In some countries, including Canada, the United States, and several European nations, couples are averaging fewer than two children. Such a birth rate will produce a loss of population over time (even with the population living longer on average).[30] Population loss requires that a country increase immigration to have an adequate labour pool.

In contrast to Western nations, rapid growth rate in the populations of some developing countries is depleting those nations' natural resources and reducing citizens' living standards. This rapid growth rate in these populations may be a major challenge into the 21st century.

## Age Structure

In some countries, and certainly in Canada, the population's average age is increasing. In Canada, the percentage of the population aged 65 and older is expected to increase from roughly 10 percent in 2000 to approximately 20 percent in 2025.[31] Contributing to this change are declining birth rates and increasing life expectancies. Among other outcomes, these changes create added pressures on health care systems. Beyond this, these trends may suggest numerous opportunities for firms to develop goods and services to meet the needs of an increasingly older population.

## Geographic Distribution

About three-quarters of Canada's population lives in urban areas, and half of all Canadians live in the industrial corridor between Windsor and Quebec City. However, the population distribution is changing. Canadians living east of Ontario declined from almost 40 percent in 1961 to less than 33 percent today. While Saskatchewan and Manitoba suffered a decline from about 10 to 7 percent over the same period, Ontario, Alberta, and British Columbia had big gains.[32]

The geographic distribution of populations throughout the world is being changed by the capabilities resulting from advances in communications technology. For example, through computer technologies, people can remain in their homes and communicate with others in remote locations to complete their work. In these instances, people can live where they prefer while being employed by a firm located in an "unattractive" location. The Internet has meant that people are now, more than ever, able to work from home. In fact, half of all small companies are now based in the owner's home.[33]

Partially because of the advances in communication technology, almost one-third of all Canadian jobs involve contingency work. Contingency work includes part-time, temporary, and contract employment. As a result, these employees are more mobile. It is that the number of contingency workers will continue to grow.[34] This trend of using contingency workers exists in other parts of the world as well, including the United States, Western Europe, Japan, and Latin America. The fastest-growing segment of contingency workers is in the technical and professional area.[35]

## Ethnic and Cultural Mix

The ethnic mix of countries' populations continues to change. About 70 percent of Canadians list some combination of British and French ancestry. Of the remaining number, more than one-third are visible minorities. This is an amount almost double that of the early 1980s.[36] As well, unlike U.S. notions of assimilation, Canada—at least as official policy—tries more for accommodation. This means that cultural differences between groups will not be blended smoothly into a "melting pot" but rather become part of a "cultural mosaic." Thus, the implication for Canadian business is that they must, in a sense, study the pieces of that mosaic. In other words, companies must meet the challenge of being aware of and sensitive to the differences between, and even among, the increasingly diverse collection of peoples with which firms must deal.[37] In addition, a specific market may have high concentrations of one particular ethnic group with the result that companies competing in that market may need to be more culturally sensitive to that group. For example, about 20 percent of Toronto's population, and over 25 percent of Vancouver's population, is of Asian origin.[38] So it is not unusual for banks in many Vancouver neighbourhoods to have signs in English and Cantonese. Through careful study, firms can avoid cultural mistakes and develop and market goods and services intended to satisfy the unique needs and interest of different ethnic groups. Canada's workforce is likely to become far more diverse given the need for immigration due to a declining birth rate. Because a labour force can be critical to competitive success, firms are challenged to work effectively with an increasingly diverse labour force.[39]

However, the increasing ethnic and cultural diversity of the workforce yields exciting challenges and significant opportunities,[40] and effective management of a culturally diverse workforce can produce a competitive advantage.[41] Heterogeneous work teams have been shown to produce more effective strategic analyses, more creativity, innovation, and higher-quality decisions than homogeneous work teams.[42] Because of these potential outcomes, a number of companies promote cultural diversity in their workforce and facilitate effective management of such diversity through specialized management training. Among these companies are Royal Bank, British Petroleum, and American Express.[43] For example, in 1998, 1300 of Royal Bank's key personnel across Canada took part in corporate "Understanding and Implementing Diversity Sessions" to increase employee commitment to diversity. To develop and lead diversity efforts among the disabled, Royal established an Employees with Disabilities Advisory Council in 1998. The council consists of 20 employees from all corporate levels who either have a disability or have a close family member who does. The council developed recommendations to the CEO and vice-chairs that were later implemented by the organization.[44]

## Income Distribution

Understanding how income is distributed within and across populations informs firms of different groups' purchasing power and discretionary income. Study of income distributions suggests that while living standards have improved over time, there are variances within and between nations.[45] Firms are particularly interested in the average incomes of households and individuals, which can yield strategically relevant information. For instance, the increase of dual-career couples has resulted in increased income for these couples, although real income has been going down.

# The Sociocultural Segment

The **sociocultural segment** is concerned with different societies' social attitudes and cultural values. Because attitudes and values are a society's cornerstone, they often drive demographic, economic, political/legal, and technological changes. Firms are challenged to understand the meaning of attitudinal and cultural changes across global societies.

A critically important sociocultural issue is the world's environment. Resource-intensive Canadian industries such as mining and forestry are under increasing pressure to exercise better stewardship over the environment. For example, cries for sustainable forestry practices have resulted in less clear-cutting of forests, and selective removal of trees using small tractors to minimize soil impact and wildlife deaths at logging sites.

As a result of these concerns, forestry firms may end up being reviewed by three separate organizations. The International Standards Organization (ISO) has created a set of environmental standards called ISO 14001. Critics claim ISO 14001 does not ensure the entire supply chain is involved in ecologically sustainable practices. The Canadian Standards Association (CSA) goes beyond ISO standards in having firms develop performance goals for designated forests. However, CSA standards are recognized only domestically. The internationally recognized Mexican-based Forestry Stewardship Council (FSC) sets standards for products based on ecological, social, and economic sustainability throughout the supply chain. Only the FSC issues the commercially recognized and highly sought eco-label (a checkmark with a tree).[46]

> The **sociocultural segment** is concerned with different societies' social attitudes and cultural values.

# The Political/Legal Segment

The **political/legal segment** is the arena in which organizations and interest groups compete for attention and resources and includes the body of laws and regulations guiding these interactions.[47] Essentially, this segment represents how organizations try to influence government and how government entities influence them. Constantly changing, this segment (see Table 3.1) influences the nature of competition. Therefore, firms must analyze carefully a new government's business-related policies and philosophies. Laws regarding equity in employment practices, antitrust, taxation, Crown corporation privatization, industry deregulation, and commitment to educational institutions are areas where government policies can affect the operations and profitability of industries and individual firms.

For example, much has been made of the Canadian "brain drain." The combination of higher taxes, more preferable treatment of stock options and eased cross-border work policies have meant many of Canada's best and brightest university graduates have left to work in the United States. Some argue that real Canadian salaries could be driven toward U.S. levels if government policies lowered taxes on manager's compensation

> The **political/legal segment** is the arena in which organizations and interest groups compete for attention and resources as well as the body of laws and regulations guiding these interactions.

packages, made the business environment more favourable through lower corporate taxes, and thus strengthened the Canadian dollar.[48] Others argue that the actual cost of living in good neighbourhoods and having good health care make real after-tax incomes comparable to salaries in the United States.[49]

Viewpoints regarding government philosophies and policies (federal, provincial, and municipal), the most effective means of competition, and the ideal relationship between government and business can vary substantially. In addition to political perspectives, these viewpoints are affected by the nature of the industry in which a firm competes.

As the third millennium opens, business firms across the globe are confronted by an array of political/legal questions and issues. For example, the debate continues over government involvement in business. In general, industries that were previously government monopolies are becoming occupied by numbers of highly competitive firms. Almost all of Latin America is a proving ground for free-market reform.[50] Guatemala opened its market to full competition in all railroad, radio, electrical utilities, and telecommunications segments. In Africa, Econet Wireless, Zimbabwe's largest company, was founded in a battle to privatize that country's phone system.[51]

The results of such privatization policies can be mixed, however. Witness California's attempt at deregulating electrical utilities. Although the state allowed competition, it also froze prices. At the same time, prices for fuel from power-generating plants and electrical power purchased from out-of-state suppliers on the electrical grid rose in price. The resulting squeeze on profits for California utilities led suppliers to question the credit worthiness of the Californians. Without good credit, suppliers were reluctant to provide California utilities with electricity. When rolling blackouts were needed to ration power, the state government stepped in to give credit guarantees to resolve the situation. The end result was that government became more involved, not less. On the other hand, B.C. Hydro, the British Columbia Crown corporation that supplies power to the vast majority of users in that province, has remained under government control. After earning over $400 million in 2000 from power sales to places such as California, B.C. Hydro estimates the level of such power sales at over $1 billion for 2001.[52] Conversely, the government in Ottawa did not stop privatizing with the Canadian National Railway. There are now only 40 federal Crown corporations (there were 20 percent more just a couple of years ago).[53]

Beyond the simple presence of government as a competitor, serious questions have been raised about the types of government support that are proper for a healthy business climate. Cinar received millions of dollars in tax breaks for the production of scripts supposedly produced by Canadian authors. Instead of promoting Canadian authorship, the government's program of tax credits prompted Cinar to commit tax fraud and put the company at risk of being bought (and, in this free trade era, a U.S. company could potentially buy them). On the one hand, tax credit programs may encourage Canadian business; on the other hand they represent a corporate welfare to which many people object.[54]

## The Economic Segment

The **economic environment** refers to the nature and direction of the economy in which a firm competes or may compete.

Clearly, the health of a nation's economy affects the performance of individual firms and industries. As a result, strategists study the economic environment to identify changes, trends, and their strategic implications. The **economic environment** refers to the nature and direction of the economy in which a firm competes or may compete.[55] As shown in

Table 3.1, indicators of an economy's health include inflation rates, interest rates, trade deficits or surpluses, budget deficits or surpluses, personal and business savings rates, and gross domestic product. However, because of the interconnectedness of the global financial community, analysts often must also scan, monitor, forecast, and assess the health of other countries' economies. For example, the economic status of nations with which Canada exchanges many products, particularly the United States, as well as others such as Japan and Germany, affects the overall health of the Canadian economy.

Agreements to lower or eliminate trade barriers between nations, such as the North American Free Trade Agreement (NAFTA), have significant economic consequences for the nations involved. Such multilateral agreements aim to imitate the regional growth that the European Community has created.[56] Economic issues can also have significant influences on political and legal issues. Witness the protests against the World Trade Organization (WTO). In general, the protestors opposed international trade deals they saw as aiding big business at the expense of small businesses, workers, the planet, and less developed nations. Representatives at the WTO however saw no need to address labour organizing, human rights, or environmental standards. Trade liberalization might help millions in developing countries and aid businesses trading with those nations. Yet fears that such trade will hurt standards in industrialized countries is heard loudly by national government officials who must deal with such trade issues.[57]

## The Technological Segment

The **technological segment** includes the institutions and activities involved with creating new knowledge and translating that knowledge into new outputs, products, processes, and materials.

Pervasive and diverse in scope, technological changes affect many parts of societies. These effects occur primarily through new products, processes, and materials. The **technological segment** includes the institutions and activities involved with creating new knowledge and translating that knowledge into new outputs, products, processes, and materials.

Given the rapid pace of technological change, it is vital that firms carefully study different elements in the technological segment. For example, research shows that early adopters of new technology often achieve higher market shares and earn higher returns. Thus, executives must continuously scan the environment to identify potential substitutes for their firm's technology as well as newly emerging technologies from which their firm could benefit. They also need to identify the speed with which substitute technologies are likely to emerge and the timing of any major technological changes.[58]

For example, BC's PMC-Sierra owes most of its worth to the rise of the Internet. PMC-Sierra's components help address the need for high-speed Internet access. The company recognized early the need for computer chips for network equipment builders and now supplies chips for Nortel, Lucent, and others. The market has recognized this technological need and pushed PMC-Sierra's market capitalization to well over $30 billion—at one time making it one of the top five Canadian firms based on market value.[59]

Microsoft is now changing its strategy not only to provide software for the Internet but also to ensure that a new operating system does not displace its Windows business for PCs when a "Web lifestyle" emerges. As a result, Microsoft is working with phone companies and investing in cable companies. Similarly, Bill Gates has invested in WebTV Networks to obtain technology to deliver a high-speed digital stream that can be viewed on televisions.[60]

## The Global Segment

The **global segment** includes relevant new global markets and existing ones that are changing, important international political events, and critical cultural and institutional characteristics of relevant global markets.

The **global segment** includes relevant new global markets and existing ones that are changing, important international political events, and critical cultural and institutional characteristics of relevant global markets. Although the previous segments should be analyzed in terms of their domestic and global implications, some additional specific global factors should be analyzed as well.

Firms must also attempt to identify critical new global markets and/or those that are changing. It is clear that many global markets are fast becoming borderless and integrated.[61] For example, firms may examine emerging markets such as those in South American countries or markets in newly industrialized countries such as those in Asia (e.g., South Korea, Taiwan) for new opportunities. Firms should also be cognizant of the potential threats from these countries.

Firms must also have a reasonable understanding of the different cultural and institutional attributes of global markets in which they operate or hope to operate. For example, a firm operating in South Korea must understand the value placed on hierarchical order, formality, self-control, and duty rather than rights. Furthermore, Korean ideology places emphasis on communitarianism, a characteristic of many Asian countries. Korea's approach differs from that of Japan and China in its focus on *inhwa* or harmony. *Inhwa* is based on a respect of hierarchical relationships and an obedience to authority. Alternatively, the approach in China is focused on *guanxi* or personal relationships, and in Japan on *wa* or group harmony and social cohesion.[62] The institutional context of Korea suggests a major emphasis on centralized planning by the government. The emphasis placed on growth by many South Korean firms is the result of a government policy to promote economic growth in South Korea.[63]

The cultural and institutional contexts in which firms must operate in global markets can be critical. For example, a nationalist campaign against multinational firms in India led to the closing of a Kentucky Fried Chicken (KFC) restaurant in New Delhi. Although the official statement was that the KFC outlet was closed for health reasons after an inspection, executives of several food companies blamed political posturing related to an upcoming election. Also, those who oppose KFC's opening are often those who lobby against meat eating. KFC was one of the first major fast food giants to open a facility in India. Furthermore, it has been quite successful in Asia, with more than 2200 restaurants operating in that region of the world. Still, even a firm that has been as successful as KFC must carefully and thoroughly analyze the institutional and cultural environments of its global markets.[64]

As explained in the Strategic Focus section on the takeover of Hong Kong, China offers not only potential opportunities but also threats to a number of firms, even more so now that Hong Kong is part of China; Hong Kong's growing economic prowess makes its firms potentially significant competitors, particularly in labour-intensive industries. Thus, firms operating in such industries worldwide must view the development of Chinese entrepreneurial operations as an environmental threat. Alternatively, firms that can invest in China may be able to take advantage of the low-cost labour; China also offers a huge and growing market for products. For example, Inline Fibreglass of Etobicoke, Ontario was approached by Yaohua Glass 1997 to form a joint venture. Yaohua, one of China's largest glassmakers, needed a company to supply it with equipment to make windows and patio doors. Inline investigated Yaohua before agreeing to the joint venture and found found that Yaohua was a long-established firm employing 10 000 people in a number of factories.[65] The two companies formed a firm called Qimhuangdao, Yaohua, Inline Energy Savings Door and Window, a move that allowed each partner to capitalize on its strengths and provided Inline a foot in the door of a huge part of the Asian market.[66]

## STRATEGIC FOCUS

### The Strategic Effect of the Chinese Takeover of Hong Kong

The Chinese takeover of Hong Kong occurred on July 1, 1997. The effects of the environmental policy changes portend to be dramatic. There is now one country with two systems and a new economy for Hong Kong, the capitalist hub of Asia. It's not clear whether Hong Kong will become the cosmopolitan capital of Chinese capitalism or whether Chinese-style bureaucrats will change what has made it special and mire its free market spirit in party politics. The economic environment that evolves will determine the ultimate outcome. Either scenario may be inaccurate because China and Hong Kong are major investors in each other. Top government officials in the Hong Kong territories are determined to be more active than were the British, and use Singapore as an example of the type of policy to be implemented. Although Hong Kong will continue to be a standard setter in real estate and financial services, more importantly, it is likely to be the media and pop culture hub for China. Although Hong Kong will certainly be a financial and fashion hub, if it focuses too much on China, the city may lose its standing as a regional centre for all of Southeast Asia. If it is exposed to too many of the economic upheavals because of China's political and economic difficulties, Hong Kong may jeopardize its current standing.

As the change has been anticipated for some time, "red chip" companies—such as corporations controlled by mainland interests but listed in Hong Kong—are emerging as the new pillars of Hong Kong. They are restructuring the old order of local property developers and bankers who previously dominated the Hong Kong stock market. It is conceivable that many of the red chip companies will swallow major Hong Kong companies just as earlier Hong Kong entrepreneurs acquired British-owned companies in the 1980s. There is a question as to who will regulate the red chip companies. Will China be able to dictate who can list companies on the exchange, or will this be determined solely by free market options?

Hong Kong has another concern. Because it does not have a strong manufacturing base, policy and administrative leaders are wondering if it will lose its central economic role as it competes with other economic coastal centres such as Shanghai. Because housing costs are so high in Hong Kong, some suggest that it will cost half as much to employ an engineer in California as in Hong Kong. Therefore, there is little incentive to invest in R&D and staff training in Hong Kong. Hong Kong firms currently rely on young labourers from China's interior who go home after a few years. These workers lack the technical skills required to manufacture more advanced products. Because costs are so high, manufacturers may simply shop for cheaper labour elsewhere in Asia. Thus, there is no clear evidence that Hong Kong will be able to maintain its financial and service centre role without a strong manufacturing base such as that held by Shanghai.

*continued*

In addition, protecting the rule of law that has been the foundation of Hong Kong's economic success may be difficult if civil liberties erode under the Chinese system. There will be severe temptations by Chinese and/or Hong Kong firms to use their mainland connections to special advantage. This can lead to corruption, which undermines the rule of law and the current economic success of Hong Kong.

Another factor is what overseas Chinese, especially in Southeast Asia, will do with the Hong Kong takeover. Expatriate Chinese have kept their distance from the mainland politics. Their loyalties do not lie with the Chinese nation-state but rather with the returns that can be earned there. They have invested only in special economic zones that are protected and where they are free to move their capital. Many would not be willing to relinquish their foreign passport and go back to China. They will invest in China if that is where money can be earned, but if labour costs increase and productivity levels off, they are just as likely to turn to Vietnam to establish operations, or to other areas such as India or Guatemala. If China attacks Taiwan or crushes the spirit and rule of law of Hong Kong, overseas Chinese will not likely continue to invest in China. Loyalties to China will be overcome by economic pressures and fundamental loyalties to families.

How policy and government changes affect the economy will decide the nature of competition among firms and whether the Hong Kong takeover succeeds or fails. What happens in Hong Kong will influence the strategic environment of the firms in Hong Kong and on the Chinese mainland.

Sources: J. Barnathan, 1997, Hong Kong, *BusinessWeek*, June 9, 45–49; M. Elliott and D. Elliott, 1997, Hong Kong: Why the world watches, *Newsweek*, May 19, 30–35; P. Engardio and J. Barnathan, 1997, Red chips rising, *BusinessWeek*, June 9, 50–51; P. H. Kahn, 1997, Waiting for the shoe to drop in Hong Kong, *Wall Street Journal*, October 7, A18; P. Kwong, 1996, The Chinese Diaspora, *World Business*, 2 (26–31).

A key objective of analyzing the general environment is identification of anticipated significant changes and trends among external elements. With a focus on the future, the analysis of the general environment allows firms to identify opportunities and threats. Also critical to a firm's future operations is an understanding of its industry environment and its competitors, which are considered next.

## INDUSTRY ENVIRONMENT ANALYSIS

An **industry** is a group of firms producing products that are close substitutes.

An **industry** is a group of firms producing products that are close substitutes. In the course of competition, these firms influence one another. Typically, industries include a rich mix of competitive strategies that companies use in pursuing strategic competitiveness and above-average returns.[67]

Compared to the general environment, the industry environment has a more direct effect on strategic competitiveness and above-average returns. The intensity of industry competition and an industry's profit potential (as measured by the long-run return on invested capital) are a function of five competitive forces: the threat of new entrants, suppliers, buyers, product substitutes, and the intensity of rivalry among competitors (see Figure 3.2).

Developed by Michael Porter, the five-forces model of competition expands the arena for competitive analysis. Historically, when studying the competitive environment, firms concentrated on companies with which they competed directly. Competition is now viewed as a grouping of alternative ways for customers to obtain the value they desire, rather than being limited to direct competitors. This is particularly important because in recent years industry boundaries have become blurred. For example, telecommunications companies now compete with broadcasters, and automakers provide financing.[68] In addition to focusing on customers to define markets rather than specific industry boundaries, one should examine geographic boundaries as well. Research has shown that different geographic markets for the same product can have considerable differences in the competitive conditions.[69]

The five-forces model recognizes that suppliers could become a firm's competitor (by integrating forward), as could buyers (by integrating backward). This is illustrated by Corel's moves into the Linux operating system. By writing applications for both the Windows and Linux Operating Systems, Corel is hoping to capture an entirely new group of users who want to escape from Windows. In an effort to make this gamble pay off, Corel has packaged its own, supposedly more user-friendly, version of the Linux operating system. By moving backward from its applications programs and into operating systems (OS) that those applications run on, Corel is also hoping to take away some of the lucrative OS market from Microsoft.[70] Firms choosing to enter a new market and those producing products that are adequate substitutes are competitors for an existing company.

■ ■ **FIGURE 3.2**

*The Five-Forces Model of Competition*

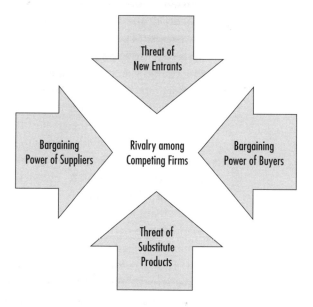

## Threat of New Entrants

New entrants to an industry can threaten existing competitors by bringing additional production capacity. Unless product demand is increasing, additional capacity holds consumers' costs down, resulting in less sales revenue and lower returns for all firms in the industry. Often, new entrants have substantial resources and a keen interest in gaining a large market share the classic case of Wal-Mart's entry to Canada represented such a competitor. Even firms in related industries may become formidable competitors. Ledcor Industries was a privately held engineering and construction firm that occasionally dug trenches for fibre optic cables. The firm saw a future in fibre optic cable and entered that business. Ledcor's fibre optic business became 360Networks—a billion-dollar firm with tens of thousands of miles of fibre optic cable.[71] In this way, new competitors may force existing firms to be more effective and efficient and to learn how to compete on new dimensions (e.g., learning to dig one's own trenches for fibre optical cable if you are a 360Networks competitor). The likelihood that firms will enter an industry is a function of two factors: barriers to entry and the retaliation expected from current industry participants. When firms find entry into a new industry difficult, or when firms are at a competitive disadvantage entering a new industry, entry barriers exist.

## Barriers to Entry

Existing competitors try to develop barriers to market entry. Alternatively, potential entrants seek markets where the entry barriers are relatively insignificant. The absence of entry barriers increases the probability a new entrant can operate profitably in an industry. There are several potentially significant entry barriers.

### Economies of Scale and Scope

As the quantity of a product produced during a given time period increases, the cost of manufacturing each unit declines. In other words, the larger the volume of product processed, the lower the cost. These benefits are referred to as economies of scale. Economies of scope occur when investments have been made and infrastructure developed that can handle additional products. If a company develops the structure for order processing, warehousing, and shipping, there may be little involved in expanding its product line. This is what Amazon.com did when it expanded from book distribution to CDs, and this explains the logic behind Chapters moving into home and garden product distribution. Perhaps the greatest threat posed by the Internet is that it may allow these kinds of transfers of expertise into new fields at very little cost to a competitor.

Scale economies can be gained through most business functions (e.g., marketing, manufacturing, research and development, and purchasing). New entrants face a dilemma when existing competitors have scale economies, because small-scale entry places them at a cost disadvantage. However, large-scale entry, where the new entrant manufactures large volumes of a product to gain scale economies, risks strong reactions from established competitors.

Though still important in some industries (e.g., automobile production), competitive realities of the 21st century may reduce the significance of scale economies as an entry barrier. Many companies now customize their products for large numbers of small customer groups. Customized products are not manufactured in volumes needed to achieve economies of scale. However, mass customization in some industries has occurred because of the introduction of new flexible manufacturing systems that combine advanced computerization with new manufacturing technologies. Mass-customized products can be individualized to the customer in a very short period of time (e.g., within a day). For example, when people popped Sarah McLachlan's *Mirrorball* CD into their computers, they were able to call up a menu linking them to a Web site where, for $5, they could customize a disc of rare and re-mixed versions of her songs. Her record company, Vancouver-based Nettwerk Productions, teamed up with Custom Revolutions in Connecticut to produce the personalized discs via a Web-based business called CustomDisc.com, which allows people to pick songs and even cover art.[72] Mass customization may, in fact, become the norm in manufacturing products generally.[73] Nettwerk CEO Terry McBride notes, "I can definitely see the time when other labels are going to want to do this stuff."[74] Companies manufacturing customized products will thus need to learn how to respond quickly to customers' desires, rather than developing scale economies.

### Product Differentiation

Over time, customers may come to believe that an existing firm's product is unique. This belief can result from service to the customer, effective advertising campaigns, or the firm's being the first to market a particular product. Many firms spend significant amounts of money on advertising to convince potential customers of the distinctiveness of their product. The belief that a firm's product is unique results in loyal customers who have strong brand identification. Typically, new entrants must allocate significant resources over a long period of time to overcome existing customer loyalties. To combat the perception of uniqueness, new entrants may offer their products at lower prices. This can result, however, in lower profitability or even a loss for the new entrant.

### Capital Requirements

Competing in a new industry requires resources to invest. In addition to physical facilities, capital is needed for inventories, marketing activities, and other critical business functions. Although competing in a new industry may appear attractive, the capital required for successful market entry may not be available.

### Switching Costs

Switching costs are the one-time costs customers incur when buying from a different supplier. The costs of buying new ancillary equipment and of retraining employees and even the psychic costs of ending a relationship may be incurred in switching to a new supplier. In some cases, switching costs are low, such as switching soft drink brands. At other times, switching costs are high even for the ultimate consumer; for instance, switching from video tapes to DVDs as a video format. The consumer not only has to buy a DVD player but also incur a higher cost for DVDs than for tapes. If switching costs are high, a new entrant must offer either a substantially lower price or a much better product to attract buyers.

### Access to Distribution Channels

Over time, industry participants can develop effective means of distributing products. Once developed, firms nurture relationships with distributors. Such nurturing creates switching costs for distributors. Access to distribution channels can be a strong entry barrier for potential new entrants, particularly in consumer nondurable goods industries (e.g., in grocery stores, shelf space is limited). Thus, new entrants must persuade distributors to carry their products, either in addition to or in place of existing firms' products. Price breaks and cooperative advertising may be used for this purpose, but their use reduces the new entrant's potential to earn above-average returns.

### Cost Disadvantages Independent of Scale

In some instances, established competitors have cost advantages that new entrants cannot duplicate. Proprietary product technology, favourable access to raw materials, favourable locations, and government subsidies may provide such cost advantages. Successful competition requires new entrants to find ways to reduce the strategic relevance of these factors. For example, the advantage of a favourable location can be reduced by offering direct delivery to the buyer (restaurants with unattractive locations may deliver goods directly to the consumer).

### Government Policy

Through licensing and permit requirements, governments can control entry into an industry. Liquor retailing, banking, and trucking are examples of industries where government decisions and actions affect industry entry. Also, governments restrict entrance into utility industries because of the need to provide quality service to all and the capital requirements necessary to do so. In Canada, it is not just the economic logic of protecting the public from a market failure that prompts the creation and/or subsequent regulation of a monopoly. In many cases, the government may own the monopoly and have a very direct financial interest in restricting competitors in the industry. For example, the Insurance Corporation of British Columbia, a B.C. Crown corporation, is, by law, the only provider of basic auto insurance in that province. The ability of the insurer to coordinate roadway safety improvements and safety programs is, some have argued, the legitimate rationale behind restricting others from entering the industry.[75]

## Expected Retaliation

Decisionmakers will also anticipate existing competitors' reactions to a new entrant. If retaliation is expected to be swift and vigorous, a decision could be reached against entry. Sometimes, a company will publicly announce its intentions. Strong retaliation can be anticipated from firms with a major stake in an industry (e.g., having fixed assets with few, if any, alternative uses), from firms with substantial resources, and when industry growth is slow or constrained.

Firms can avoid entry barriers by searching out market niches not served by the primary competition. Small entrepreneurial firms are generally best suited for searching out and serving these neglected market segments. When Honda first entered the North American market, it discovered a market for small engine motorcycles, a market that firms such as Harley-Davidson did not recognize and thus ignored. By targeting a neglected market segment, Honda avoided competition. Yet, after consolidating its position, Honda used its new strength to attack rivals by introducing larger motorcycles and competing in the broader market.[76] Competitive actions and responses are discussed in more detail in Chapter 6.

## Bargaining Power of Suppliers

Increasing prices and reducing the quality of products sold are potential means through which suppliers can exert power over firms competing within an industry. If unable to recover cost increases through its pricing, a firm's profitability is reduced by the suppliers' actions. A supplier group is powerful when

- it is dominated by a few large firms and is more concentrated than the industry to which it sells;
- satisfactory substitute products are not available to industry firms;
- industry firms are not a significant customer for the supplier group;
- suppliers' goods are critical to buyers' marketplace success;
- the effectiveness of suppliers' products has created high switching costs for industry firms; and
- suppliers are a credible threat to integrate forward into the buyers' industry (e.g., a clothing manufacturer might choose to operate its own retail outlets). Credibility is enhanced when suppliers have substantial resources and provide the industry's firms with a highly differentiated product.

The Strategic Focus case on Dell Computer illustrates how a supplier can use its power and save money for the ultimate consumer. Dell's strategy of selling directly to the corporate market is now being duplicated by others. Dell has reduced its costs relative to other rivals and has increased its power relative to its buyers. Dell is also pursuing the direct consumer market.[77] Gateway sells directly to the consumer market and has decided to pursue the corporate market by moving into larger servers.[78]

## STRATEGIC FOCUS

### Others Want to Imitate Dell. But What Beats a Free Computer?

Dell Computer's approach to selling PCs has focused on direct distribution. Because Dell's business model costs less to produce and distribute, the industry leaders, Compaq, IBM, and Hewlett-Packard (HP), are trying to copy Dell's approach rather than use computer resellers to whom they have outsourced much of their business in this highly competitive industry.

The typical approach to distribution with leading PC manufacturers was based on a forecast of demand from which PC makers would build machines. PCs were then tested and stored before being sent to a reseller's warehouse. Resellers would often unpack the product, remove the computer, load the software, test it, and then re-pack the whole thing—a process that was time consuming and expensive. Often, the average time between production and purchase was six to eight weeks, and the reseller's markup may add up to 9 percent on to the price. Dell cut out the resellers and sped the process.

In a move to copy Dell, Compaq unveiled an optimized-distribution model. Compaq will not build a computer until it receives an order and will customize PCs in its own plants for shipment directly to the reseller. Similarly, HP has sought to reduce inventories and force reseller inventory down to two weeks.

*continued*

One advantage Compaq and HP possess is that they sell half their product overseas. The international consumer base often does not buy computers over the phone or the Internet (as do Dell's customers). At home, however, Dell is forcing the competition to squeeze its resellers so that the product is price competitive for the consumer.

The problem with squeezing resellers' margins is that there is no longer an incentive for resellers to provide the service to the larger producers. For instance, both Compaq and HP have suggested a series of changes in reforming dealer relationships. Rather than shipping finished PCs, they would ship components, which dealers themselves would assemble into a finished unit.

One of the resellers, MicroAge, has dealt with this pressure by transforming itself into an assembler for the likes of IBM, HP, Compaq, and Acer. MicroAge installs software and adds components requested by the customer. Furthermore, the firm collects fees for operating help desks for others and helps manage other firms' computer-buying needs. Thus, MicroAge is searching for creative ways to increase its financial returns.

Except for Dell's approach, buyers' power is increasing relative to sellers'. Dell will battle to maintain a competitive edge as it moves into Gateway 2000's turf, the consumer/home market. Gateway also sells direct and has responded to Dell's actions by seeking to move to the corporate market. Dell is improving its inventory management system and has reduced its parts inventory to less than 12 days—a move that improves Dell's efficiency and power over suppliers.

Yet Dell's move into the consumer market is accompanied by the rise of an aggressive sales technique from resellers: they give away PCs. Such offers last only for a limited time and are not really free. For example, Edmonton-based OA Internet was one firm making the "free" PC offer. OA Internet provided customers a basic Internet-ready PC, but customers were required to pay an up-front fee and monthly Internet connection fees for a three-year period. While a number of companies have had similar promotions, the quality of the PC, quantity of installed software, and monthly fee vary. California-based Free-PC offered a truly free PC with free Internet access. The catch was that the customer needed to disclose extensive personal information, spend a certain amount of time on the PC each month, and endure a quarter of their screen being taken up with advertising, even if the user is not online.

Dell has not slept quietly during the "free" PC battle. Dell's approach though is to package Internet access with the PC for a combined monthly fee. Customers responded positively since they knew the cost up-front and were not subject to onscreen advertising from Dell. While PC promotions—free or otherwise—are likely to keep changing, Dell and others will be certain to keep pricing methods interesting when faced with increasingly demanding buyers.

Finally, Dell is expanding into the network server market. Because of explosive growth in the use of the Internet, the server market is a high-growth sector. Dell hopes to leverage its connections with current customers in order to capture a sizable portion of this market. If successful, those in the computer industry will continue to imitate Dell.

Sources: D. Kirkpatrick, 1997, Now everyone in PCs wants to be like Mike, *Fortune*, September 8, 91–92; A. Zipser, 1997, In search of greener pastures, Gateway moves on Dell's turf, *Barron's*, September 15, 77 (37), 10; L. Zuckerman, 1997, Dell Computer taking aim at consumers, *New York Times on the Web*, http://www.nytimes.com, August 29; T. Gignac, 1999, Canadian computer market on track, *Computer Dealer News*, August 20, 6; P. Lewis, 1999, With a free PC, at least the price is right, *National Post*, August 2, C12; J. M. O'Brien, 1999, High-tech freebies begin to hit Canadian market, *Computer Dealer News*, March 12, 35–36; A. Stirpe, 1999, How will free PCs affect the market? *Computer Reseller News*; August 23, 85, 88; M. Lewis, 2000, Selling Dell, *National Post*, April 8, D1, D8; *About.com*, 2000, Not-so-Free PCs, About.Com, http://contests.about.com/shopping/ contests/ library/weekly/ aa111799.htm? iam=dp&terms= Free+PC.

## Bargaining Power of Buyers

Firms seek to maximize the return on their invested capital. Buyers (customers of the focal industry/firm) prefer to purchase products at the lowest possible price, at which the industry earns the lowest acceptable rate of return on its invested capital. To reduce their costs, buyers bargain for higher quality, greater levels of service, and lower prices as demonstrated in the Strategic Focus on Dell Computer. These outcomes can be achieved by encouraging competitive battles among firms in an industry. Customers (buyer groups) are powerful when

- they purchase a large portion of an industry's total output;
- the product being purchased from an industry accounts for a significant portion of the buyers' costs;
- they could switch to another product at little, if any, cost; and
- the industry's products are undifferentiated or standardized, and buyers pose a credible threat if they were to integrate backward into the sellers' industry.

Relations with customers and the service provided to such customers have assumed significant meaning in recent years. For example, one study showed that a firm's value on the stock market increased with improvements in its customer service.[79] Poor relations with customers can also hurt a firm's performance. Without good relations, retail firms may give less shelf space to its products, similar to the action Wal-Mart took against Rubbermaid that was noted earlier. In addition, Wal-Mart executives openly criticized Rubbermaid. Yet because Wal-Mart is 505 times larger than Rubbermaid, Rubbermaid publicly stated only positive comments about the larger firm.[80]

Another excellent example of a buyer's having significant power over a seller is the relationship between Loblaw and E.D. Smith and Sons. Smith, a Winona, Ontario–based family-owned producer of pie fillings, jams, and sauces had less than $100 million in annual sales. Loblaw, with over $2 billion in sales, was seeking to expand the presence of its "President's Choice" brand from Canada into the United States. To do this, they encouraged Smith to develop operations in the United States, a move E.D. Smith would have otherwise been reluctant to make without the "encouragement" from a very large buyer.[81]

Just as Wal-Mart forced its suppliers into electronic data exchange (EDI), the Internet creates more power for the general consumer. For instance, Amazon.com, the largest Internet bookseller, forced Chapters, Barnes & Noble and others—ready or not—to create Internet sites.[82] The ultimate result of the move to the Web will be a reduction in prices for the buyer because of the enormous volume of sales generated. Thus, the Web could create a buyer- versus seller-centric environment and shift more power to buyers.[83] Rubbermaid is now searching for ways to deal with the power of retailers such as Wal-Mart.[84] Selling to specialty retailers and directly to consumers through direct-seller firms such as Amway and on the Internet is one way the company is trying to solve the problem. It may find, however, that the Internet creates more powerful consumers as well.[85]

## Threat of Substitute Products

Substitute products are different goods or services that can perform similar or the same functions as the focal product (functional substitutes). Capable of satisfying similar customer needs, but with different characteristics, substitute products place an upper limit on the prices firms can charge.

For example, Nutrasweet places an upper limit on the prices sugar manufacturers can charge. Nutrasweet and sugar perform the same service but with different characteristics. Other product substitutes include fax machines instead of e-mail, plastic containers instead of glass jars, paper versus plastic bags, and tea, with its lower caffeine content, as a healthier substitute for coffee.[86]

Generally, the threat of substitute products is strong when customers face few, if any, switching costs and when the substitute product's price is lower and/or its quality and performance capabilities are equal to or greater than the industry's products. To reduce the attractiveness of substitute products, firms are challenged to differentiate their offerings along dimensions that are highly relevant to customers (e.g., price, product quality, service after the sale, and location).

## Intensity of Rivalry among Competitors

In many industries, firms compete actively with one another to achieve strategic competitiveness and earn above-average returns. Competition among rivals is stimulated when one or more firms feel competitive pressure or when one identifies an opportunity to improve its market position. Competition among rivals is often based on price, product innovation, and other actions to achieve product differentiation (such as extensive customer service, unique ad campaigns, and extended product warranties).

Because firms in an industry are mutually dependent, one firm's actions often invite retaliation from competitors. An industry where this pattern of action and reaction (competitive actions and responses) occurs on occasion is Canada's brewing industry. Quick reactions to one firm's price cuts are normal in this industry. Similarly, reactions to the introduction of innovative products, such as ice beer, usually are swift. Labatt's successful "Out of the Blue" ads prompted Molson to reintroduce its "I am Canadian" spots.[87] Thus, in the beer industry, as in many industries, firms often simultaneously apply two or all three of the principal means of competition (price changes, product innovations, and different means of differentiation) used by rivals when trying to gain a favourable marketplace position.[88] The intensity of competitive rivalry among firms is a function of several factors, as described next.

### Numerous or Equally Balanced Competitors

Industries with many participants tend to be characterized by intense rivalry. With many participants, often a few firms believe they can take actions without eliciting a response. However, other firms generally notice these actions and respond, resulting in a pattern of actions and responses, which creates intense rivalry. At the other extreme, industries with only a few firms of equivalent size and power also tend to have high degrees of competitive rivalry because the resource bases of these firms permit vigorous actions and responses. The battles between brewers and newspapers (e.g., *The Globe and Mail* and *National Post*) typify intense rivalry between relatively equivalent competitors.

### Slow Industry Growth

When a market is growing, firms are challenged to use resources effectively to serve an expanding customer base. In this instance, fewer actions may be taken to attract competitors' customers. The situation changes, however, when market growth either slows or stops. Under these conditions, rivalry becomes much more intense; an increase in one firm's market share usually comes at the expense of competitors' shares.

To protect their market shares, firms engage in intense competitive battles. Such battles introduce market instability, often reducing industry profitability. Parts of the fast food industry are characterized by this situation. In contrast to years past, the market for these products is growing more slowly. To expand market share, many of these companies (e.g., McDonald's, Burger King, and Wendy's) are competing aggressively in terms of pricing strategies, product introductions, and product and service differentiation. These firms also search for new international markets to achieve their growth goals.[89]

## High Fixed or Storage Costs

When fixed costs account for a large part of total costs, companies are challenged to utilize most, if not all, of their productive capacity. Operating in this manner allows the costs to be spread across a larger volume of output. Such actions by many firms in an industry can result in excess supply. To reduce inventories, companies typically decrease product prices and offer product rebates as well as other special discounts. These practices often intensify rivalry among competitors. This same phenomenon is observed in industries with high storage costs. Perishable products, for example, lose their value rapidly with the passage of time. When inventories grow, perishable-goods producers often use pricing strategies to sell their products quickly.

## Lack of Differentiation or Low Switching Costs

Differentiated products engender buyer identification, preferences, and loyalty. Industries with large numbers of companies that have successfully differentiated their products have less rivalry. When buyers view products as commodities (i.e., as products with few differentiated features or capabilities), rivalry intensifies. In these instances, buyers' purchasing decisions are based primarily on price and service.

The effect of switching costs is identical to that described for differentiated products. The lower the buyers' switching costs, the easier it is for competitors to attract those buyers through price and service offerings. High switching costs, however, partly insulate firms from rivals' efforts to attract their customers.

## Capacity Augmented in Large Increments

In some industries, the realities of scale economies dictate that production capacity should be added only on a large scale (e.g., in the manufacture of vinyl chloride and chlorine). Additions of substantial capacity can be disruptive to a balance between supply and demand in the industry. Price cutting is often used to bring demand and supply back into balance. Achieving balance in this manner has, however, a negative effect on the firm's profitability.

## Diverse Competitors

Not all companies seek to accomplish the same goals, nor do they operate with identical cultures. These differences make it difficult to identify an industry's competitive rules. Moreover, with greater firm diversity, it becomes increasingly difficult to pinpoint a competing firm's strategic intent. Often, firms engage in various competitive actions, in part to see how their competitors will respond. This type of competitive interaction can reduce industry profitability.

## High Strategic Stakes

Competitive rivalry becomes more intense when attaining success in a particular industry is critical to a large number of firms. For example, diversified firms' successes in one industry may be important to their effectiveness in other industries in which they compete. This is the case when firms follow a corporate strategy of related diversification (where separate businesses are often interdependent). This strategy is explained in detail in Chapter 7.

High strategic stakes can also exist in terms of geographic locations. For example, Japanese car manufacturers are committed to a significant presence in the North American marketplace. Because of the stakes involved, for all manufacturers, rivalry in the automobile industry is quite intense.

## High Exit Barriers

Sometimes companies continue to compete in an industry even though the returns on their invested capital are low or even negative. Firms making this choice face high exit barriers. Exit barriers are economic, strategic, and emotional factors causing companies to remain in an industry even though the profitability of doing so may be in question. For example, Algoma Steel, Canada's third-largest steelmaker, tends to suffer the most when there is an economic downturn in the steel industry. Yet the company seems to hang on because it employs one-third of the people in Sault Ste. Marie, Ontario and is owned by its union. A loss of jobs would be disastrous for both the union and the city and thus represents a significant barrier to exit.[90] Common sources of exit barriers are

- specialized assets (assets with values linked to a particular business or location);
- fixed costs of exit (e.g., labour agreements);
- strategic interrelationships (mutual dependence relationships between one business and other parts of a company's operations, such as shared facilities and access to financial markets);
- emotional barriers (aversion to economically justified business decisions because of fear for one's own career, loyalty to employees, and so forth); and
- government and social restrictions (restrictions often are based on government concerns for job losses and regional economic effects).

# INTERPRETING INDUSTRY ANALYSES

Industry analyses can be challenging and are a product of careful study and interpretation of information and data from multiple sources. A wealth of industry-specific data is available for analyzing an industry. Because of the globalization described in Chapter 1, analysts must include international markets and rivalry in their analyses. In fact, research has shown that international variables are more important than domestic variables in the determination of competitiveness in some industries. Furthermore, because of the development of global markets, industry structures are no longer bounded by a country's borders; industry structures are often global.[91]

In general, the stronger the competitive forces, the lower the profit potential for firms in an industry. An unattractive industry has low entry barriers, suppliers and buyers with strong bargaining positions, strong competitive threats from product substitutes, and intense rivalry among competing firms. These industry attributes make it difficult for firms to achieve strategic competitiveness and earn above-average returns. Conversely, an attractive industry has high entry barriers, suppliers and buyers with little bargaining power, few threats from product substitutes, and relatively moderate rivalry.[92]

A good example of global rivalry is that between Brazil's Embraer and Canada's Bombardier in the regional jet market. The rivalry has not only entangled both companies but also both governments. Numerous moves by the companies and governments—particularly regarding government subsidies and threats of trade sanctions—occur on a continual basis. These moves have created a situation where all the parties have ended up before the World Trade Organization (the WTO) on multiple occasions and will likely continue to do so. While one might be tempted to suggest elimination of government support, that is unlikely. First, the stakes are high. Second, the aircraft industry is expected to be a good-growth, high-tech investment in the future, and thus support for it has some political backing. Finally, the use of government subsidies in the regional jet market shadows the support Boeing and Airbus receive in the commercial jet market.[93]

The five-forces model allows an organization to structure an analysis of its relationships with other organizations. The model also allows the organization to examine the degree to which others firms, which may buy in such volumes as to force oppressive price concessions, possess the power to act opportunistically in the relationship. Through such an examination, the organization can avoid being at a disadvantage relative to these other organizations.

Alternately, the five-forces model allows the organization insight into the degree to which it may use its power relative to others to gain some advantage (e.g., forcing price concessions from suppliers the organization buys from in large quantities). Pressing such an advantage, however, is occurring less frequently. In recent years, the buyer-supplier relationship has undergone dramatic changes. Rather than trying to reduce supplier power, many firms are voluntarily increasing supplier power by forming closer, more collaborative ties with fewer suppliers. In these "partnering" arrangements, suppliers are frequently included on a company's product design team, long-term joint planning is conducted, and proprietary information-sharing becomes common. Interestingly, this ceding of power by the buyer to the supplier often does not reduce the buyer's profitability, but rather increases it by reducing total production costs, improving product quality, and reducing buyer-supplier transaction costs.

# STRATEGIC GROUPS

A **strategic group** is a group of firms in an industry following the same or a similar strategy along the same strategic dimensions.

More than 20 years ago, Michael Hunt studied the home appliance industry. He introduced the term "strategic group" to describe competitive patterns observed in that industry. Although he found differences in characteristics and strategies, Hunt also discovered that many firms were following similar strategies. He chose to label the groups following similar strategies "strategic groups."[94] Formally, a **strategic group** is "a group of firms in an industry following the same or a similar strategy along the [same] strategic dimensions."[95] Examples of strategic dimensions include the extent of technological leadership, the degree of product quality, pricing policies, the choice of distribution channels, and the degree and type of customer service. Thus, membership in a particular strategic group defines the essential characteristics of a firm's strategy.[96] While the strategies of firms within a group are similar, they are different from the strategies being implemented by firms in other strategic groups.

The notion of strategic groups is popular for analyzing an industry's competitive structure.[97] Adding to its popularity is the assertion that strategic group analysis is a basic framework that should be used in diagnosing competition, positioning, and the profitability of firms within an industry.[98] Use of strategic groups for analyzing industry structure requires that dimensions relevant to the firms' performances within an industry (e.g., price and image) be selected. Plotting firms in terms of these dimensions helps to identify groups of firms competing in similar ways. For example, in commercial aircraft, Bombardier, Fairchild, ATI, and Embraer form a strategic group, as do Boeing and Airbus. The products in each of these groups—regional versus jumbo jets—have similar attributes. Within each group, the products or services from one provider become, in the customer's view, substitutes for those of another provider.

Two questions present themselves regarding strategic group analysis. The first is, "What industry (or business) are you in?" Though we discuss this in greater depth in Chapter 5, the answer really depends upon which customer groups are being served, what customer needs are being served, and how those needs are being served.[99] For example, Sleeman's Brewing may consider itself to be in the beverage industry, alcoholic beverage industry, the beer industry, or the microbrewing industry. As a beverage maker trying to address refreshment needs, Sleeman's competes with Coke and Pepsi, as well as other brewers. As an alcoholic beverage provider trying to quench adult thirsts, it competes with wine and cooler makers but not directly with Coke or Pepsi. In the beer industry, Sleeman's fulfills similar needs for adults and competes with Labatt and Molson, but not with wine and cooler makers. As a microbrewer, Sleeman's may also fulfill status needs and compete with a list of micro- and regional brewers from the West Coast to the East Coast, and even to the north, but not directly with Labatt and Molson. [100]

A second question is, "What are the dimensions that are relevant to the firms' performance within an industry?" In other words, "What is important to the customer?" If quality and image are important, the strategic groups may look very different than if price and sales support are the dimensions mapped out. For example, in the brewing industry, beers could be listed along dimensions of beer type—from standard lagers to premium ales—and by brewery size or geographic coverage—from microbreweries to regional breweries to national firms. An example of this kind of strategic map is shown in Figure 3.3.[101] Each circle represents a strategic group. Yet, that map may look very different if price and availability of different-sized containers are the dimensions deemed important.

■ ■ **FIGURE 3.3**

*A Strategic Map for Canadian Brewers' Principle Domestic Brands*

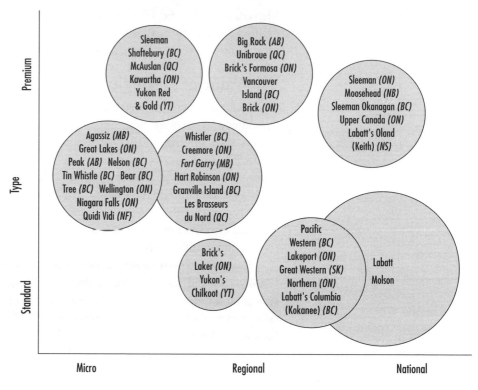

Circle sizes are not scaled to sales volume.

Source: Brewers Association of Canada, 2001, *Brewers Association of Canada home page*, http://www.brewers.ca (Retrieved January 21); RealBeer, 2001, *RealBeer home page*, http://realbeer.com/canada (Retrieved January 21).

Strategic group mapping can also uncover which firms are competing at multiple points. In Figure 3.3, Sleeman's, via its Upper Canada, Okanagan, and Shaftebury operations, competes in a number of groups; as does Labatt through its Columbia and Oland subsidiaries. Both Brick and Yukon compete in the high-end and competitively priced beer markets. In fact, Yukon Gold is a top-rated Canadian golden ale and Yukon Red Ale is an internationally acclaimed amber ale. Yet Yukon also brews Chilkoot Lager—a beer that it claims is "a good old lager beer at a good old lager price."[102]

In summary, there are several implications of strategic groups. First, defining the industry can be problematic—as we saw in the Canadian brewing example. Second, a firm's major competitors are those within its strategic group. Though the dimensions along which to map the industry members may be subjective, those within a group are clearly selling similar products to the same customers. Thus, the competitive rivalry among these firms can be intense. The more intense the rivalry, the greater the threat to each firm's profitability. Third, the strengths of the five competitive forces differ across strategic groups. As a result, firms within the various strategic groups have different pricing policies. Fourth, the closer the strategic groups in terms of strategies followed and dimensions emphasized, the greater the likelihood of competitive rivalry between the groups. For example, Nissan and Pontiac are more likely competitors for Dodge than for

http://www.mcdonalds.com
http://www.burgerking.com
http://www.wendys.com

Mercedes and Porsche. Likewise, in Figure 3.3, Bear or Tin Whistle are more likely competitors for Nelson than are Kokanee or Molson. In contrast, strategic groups that differ significantly in terms of strategic dimensions and strategies do not compete directly.

## The Value of Strategic Group Analysis

Opinions vary about the value of strategic group analysis for understanding industry dynamics and structure. Some argue that there is no convincing evidence that strategic groups exist or that a firm's performance depends on membership in a particular group.[103] Another criticism of strategic groups is that the variances in many firms' product lines make it difficult to capture the nature of a company's outputs through study of a few strategic dimensions. For example, automobile companies manufacture many products with varying attributes. Dodge, for instance, manufactures the family-oriented Caravan minivan, but it also sells the Dodge Viper, a sports car that is expensive and not family oriented.

These criticisms notwithstanding, strategic group analysis yields benefits. It helps in the selection and partial understanding of an industry's structural characteristics, competitive dynamics, evolution, and strategies that historically have allowed companies to be successful within an industry.[104] As is always the case, a tool's strengths and limitations should be known before it is used.

# COMPETITOR ANALYSIS

Along with having an understanding of the general and industry environment, as well as strategic groups, the final activity in the study of the external environment is competitor analysis. Competitor analysis focuses on each company with which a firm competes directly. Though important in all industry settings, competitor analysis is especially critical for firms facing one or a few powerful competitors.[105] Molson and Labatt, for example, are very interested in understanding each other's objectives, strategies, assumptions, and capabilities. Successful firms use the process of competitor analysis to determine

- what drives the competitor as shown by its future objectives;
- what the competitor is doing and can do as revealed by its current strategy;
- what the competitor believes about itself and the industry as shown by its assumptions; and
- what the competitor's capabilities are.[106]

Information on these four issues helps strategists prepare an anticipated response profile for each competitor (see Figure 3.4). Thus, the results of an effective competitor analysis help a firm understand, interpret, and predict its competitors' actions and initiatives.[107]

Critical to effective competitor analysis is the gathering of needed information and data, referred to as competitor intelligence. Analysts are challenged to ethically obtain information and data that inform them about competitors' objectives, strategies, assumptions, and capabilities. Intelligence-gathering techniques commonly considered to be both legal and ethical include (1) obtaining publicly available information (e.g., court records, competitors, help-wanted advertisements, annual reports) and financial reports of publicly held corporations, and (2) attending trade fairs and shows to obtain competitors' brochures, view their exhibits, and listen to discussions about their products.

■ ■ **FIGURE 3.4**

*Competitor Analysis Components*

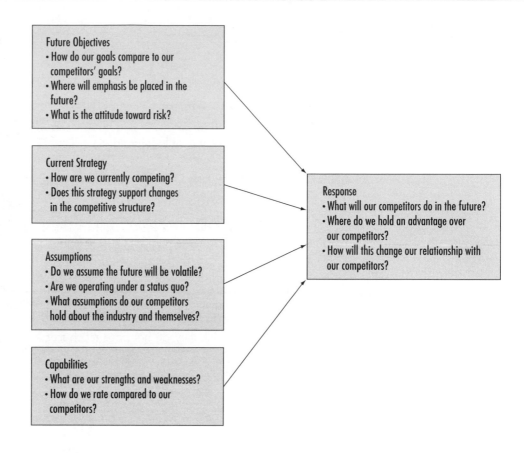

**Future Objectives**
• How do our goals compare to our competitors' goals?
• Where will emphasis be placed in the future?
• What is the attitude toward risk?

**Current Strategy**
• How are we currently competing?
• Does this strategy support changes in the competitive structure?

**Assumptions**
• Do we assume the future will be volatile?
• Are we operating under a status quo?
• What assumptions do our competitors hold about the industry and themselves?

**Capabilities**
• What are our strengths and weaknesses?
• How do we rate compared to our competitors?

**Response**
• What will our competitors do in the future?
• Where do we hold an advantage over our competitors?
• How will this change our relationship with our competitors?

A firm's home country may affect its competitor intelligence. Studies reveal that countries that value information-gathering and have powerful national intelligence services may be more prone to encourage the gathering of information on competitors. Japanese companies go further than North American companies in their efforts to gather information, and Japan even runs a government-sponsored competitor-intelligence school for managers. In fact, for many governments, a great deal of spying is being supported by government agencies that formerly focused on political causes. These actions, called industrial or economic espionage, are becoming more prominent as the main impetus for state-supported intelligence.[108] However, as the Strategic Focus on corporate spying indicates, many firms are not being ethical in the way they pursue competitive intelligence.

A Deloitte & Touche report suggests that 42 percent of major corporations do not have a formal process for gathering and analyzing competitor information—though they may have informal and less systematic means of gathering information. However, 87 percent of these firms obtain information about competitor activities, 82 percent obtain information about changing market structures, and 76 percent felt that they needed better information on competitor activities. As well, 76 percent also felt a need for better information on changing market structures. Nearly all of the firms felt that competitors had used intelligence techniques to gather information on their activities. Thus, firms understand the need for competitor information and gather it, even though in some firms the process may not be systematic.[109]

## STRATEGIC FOCUS

### *Corporate Spying: Mr. Bond Has Left for the Private Sector*

A real-life James Bond might spend most of his time trying to track cybercriminals through the Net. Not as exciting as a car chase but probably more effective at catching the bad guys. For example, if terrorists had sufficient skills, they could not only locate valuable information via the Net but also cause major systems to fail. To illustrate this, the Canadian Security Intelligence Service (CSIS) suggests trying to imagine that the kind of power outages that affected Ontario and Quebec in January 1998 could be brought on by a major cyberattack, instead of an ice storm.

Hacking into a power grid and causing major blackouts is just one scenario. Another is the anti-corporate activist. For example, environmental activists frequently hack into McDonald's information systems to simply sabotage the food chain's operations. However, given the prevalence of industrial espionage, the talents of any good secret agent might be more extensively employed if he or she were busy fighting the release of trade secrets rather than national secrets.

One of the problems noted by security experts is that many Canadian companies think they do not have much to steal. Yet, in the biotechnology, computer, and oil and gas sectors, Canada has sophisticated technologies that other countries would be interested in. Unless they have worked overseas or in high-tech industries, Canadians are generally unaware that they may be targets of wiretaps and other electronic eavesdropping. Such methods, while illegal in North America, may be legal in many other locales. More frightening is that the Internet can allow secrets to be accessed from thousands of kilometres away. Finally, though old-fashioned, a great deal of spying still occurs by having the right people at the right place and listening in on or stealing the right information.

CSIS reports that one Canadian company, trying to secure a profitable contract from another government, allowed the government access to cutting-edge technology that the government later copied. In another case, a scientist working in a biotechnology firm stole laboratory cultures from a Canadian company. As a result, that company lost valuable R&D data and potential earnings. In still another case, executives suspected that their phone conversations to another country were being intercepted. In these conversations, a specific minimum bid was discussed, which was the immediate counteroffer put forward by the host company the following day.

There have been a number of incidents where Canadian companies have become involved in detailed discussions regarding joint ventures with Eastern Europeans only to discover that once the foreign partner had the specifications in hand, the offer disappeared. In another case, two company representatives went to Egypt to meet with a government agency. In a cab, they discussed their negotiating approach. When they arrived, they realized that neither one of them had told the cab driver where they were going—they did not have to because the cab driver turned out to be employed by the government agency.

Many of the above information-gathering actions are excessive. Between the information that companies are required to file with regulatory bodies, Internet and public databases, trade shows, and job fairs, great amounts of information can be gathered. Companies can get a good idea of a compet-

*continued*

itor's products and plans from simplying reviewing the brochures provided at trade shows and analyzing the jobs to be filled. Finally, a simple friendly phone call to a competitor can elicit a great amount of information.

As for protecting company information, counterintelligence secret agents might not be the answer. A great deal can be done if firms take simple precautions: make employees aware of not discussing secure matters outside work, check that representatives of foreign firms work for companies that really exist, and never leave laptops with secure information on the hard drive (or on the floppies inside). As well, companies need to have people dedicated to working on intelligence and security issues. Although only 7 percent of large U.S. companies have competitive intelligence departments, the percentage in Canada is even lower.

Sources: D. Francis, 1999, Cyber threats are all too real: Governments fail to comprehend information warfare, *National Post*, February 20, D3; H. Solomon, 1999, Beware of economic espionage, CSIS warns, *Computing Canada*, July 23, 11, 13; L. Ramsay, 1999, Stealing trade secrets: When the Cold War ended, it didn't end spying, just shifted its focus, *National Post*, October 4, C13; CSIS, 2000, *CSIS home page*, http://www.csis-scrs.gc.ca/eng/operat/es2e.html (Retrieved May 8).

Competitor analysis has grown more important as a new competitive landscape has evolved. The following statements by major firm executives suggest the reality of this new competitive landscape:

*"[Because of the Internet] even the smallest company becomes a global business."*
—John Roth, CEO of Nortel Networks[110]

*"I don't believe in friendly competition. I want to put them out of business."*
—Mitchell Leibovitz, CEO of Pepboys[111]

Therefore, firms need to develop a more systematic means of capturing knowledge about a firm's competitive context. In effect, employees have substantial knowledge about their firms and about external constituencies and stakeholders, but few companies are able to transform this particular knowledge into a company-wide asset. Firms that are able to do so refer to this as structural intellectual capital. Companies such as Monsanto are attempting to link key individuals across the globe to share information they obtain about competitors and other important external stakeholders. Some refer to these as knowledge networks, and linking employees through networks can provide a breadth of knowledge representing a sum of employees' collective experiences and information. Furthermore, the sharing of information helps pass on organizational learning and thus becomes a true organizational asset.[112]

Obtaining competitor information is important, particularly given the statements noted earlier about significant competition and the competitive battlefield. Of course, because of systematic competitor intelligence systems, some firms have trouble maintaining critical secrets about their products, technology, or other operations. Sometimes, competitors steal information by using insiders (employees of the focal company) as illustrated in the Strategic Focus. For example, one study showed that about 75 percent of *Fortune* 1000 companies believed that over a five-year period there was an actual or attempted theft of information they desired to remain secret. Thus, significant pressures can lead to the use of questionable practices to obtain desired information about competitors.[113]

To deal with this situation, some firms communicate misinformation. For instance, Dell Computer set out to secretly produce a monitor for its PCs that was nearly the size of a big-screen TV. The purpose was to allow users to open many work areas on one screen without overlap, thus increasing their productivity. After much research and analysis, it was decided that this type of monitor was inefficient and uneconomical. Researchers decided it would be more economical for users to purchase multiple small monitors and use each as a work area. The top-secret plan was scrapped completely.

As soon as the project was halted, Dell "leaked" the secret in hopes one of its main competitors (e.g., Gateway) would undertake the project. After it heard of Dell's plan, Gateway announced it would build the monitor and would be the first to do so. Without much research or analysis, the monitor was produced and sold. From the start, sales were slow, and half of all units sold were returned for repair. The project was a complete failure, and Gateway realized it had been set up. Dell knew Gateway longed to be a "first mover" and would seize this opportunity. Industry analysts referred to Dell's action as "a corporate headfake." In an intensely competitive industry, the leader may act as if it intends to make a competitive move, when really it is trying only to get the followers to react, wasting time and money.[114]

Certain techniques—eavesdropping, trespassing, blackmail, and the theft of drawings, samples, or documents—are unethical and considered to be illegal.[115] While a number of intelligence-gathering techniques are legal, decisionmakers must determine if their use is ethical. In highly competitive environments, employees may feel greater pressure to rely on these techniques. Interestingly, evidence suggests that most business people believe their competitors use questionable intelligence-gathering techniques far more frequently than they do.[116] Perhaps an appropriate guideline is to use intelligence-gathering techniques that respect the principles of common morality and the right of competitors not to reveal certain information about their products, operations, and strategic intentions.[117]

As with analysis of the general environment, analyses of the industry and competitor environments should result in the identification of opportunities and threats for the focal firm. A procedure for identification of opportunities and threats is explained in the "Introduction to Preparing an Effective Case Analysis."

# SUMMARY

- Firms' external environments are often challenging and complex. Because of their effect on performance, firms must develop the skills required to identify opportunities and threats existing in their external environments.

- The external environment has three major parts: the general environment (elements in the broader society that affect industries and their firms); the industry environment (factors that influence a firm and its competitive actions and responses—threat of entry, suppliers, buyers, product substitutes, and the intensity of rivalry among competitors); and specific analyses of each major competitor.

- Environmental analyses often must assume a nationless and borderless business environment.

- The external environmental analysis process includes four steps: scanning, monitoring, forecasting, and assessing.

- The general environment includes six segments: demographic, economic, political/legal, sociocultural, technological, and global. For each, the objective is to identify and study the strategic relevance of different changes and trends.

- As compared to the general environment, the industry environment has a more direct effect on a firm's efforts to achieve strategic competitiveness and earn above-average returns.
- The five-forces model of competition includes qualities that determine the industry's profit potential. Via study of the five forces, firms select a position in the industry in which they can match their core competencies with an opportunity to attain strategic competitiveness and earn above-average returns.
- Different strategic groups exist within industries (a strategic group is a collection of firms that follow similar strategies). The competition within each strategic group is more intense than is the competition between strategic groups.
- Competitor analysis informs a firm about the objectives, strategies, assumptions, and capabilities of the companies with which it competes.
- Different techniques are available for gathering the intelligence (information and data) needed to understand competitors' actions and intentions. Analysts must determine the appropriate and ethical techniques for use in their firm.

## REVIEW QUESTIONS

1. Why is it important for firms to study and understand the external environment?
2. What are the differences between the general environment and the industry environment? Why are these differences important?
3. What is the environmental analysis process? What do analysts try to learn as they scan, monitor, forecast, and assess?
4. What are the six segments of the general environment? Explain the differences among them.
5. Using information in the chapter, can you justify accepting the following statement: "There are five competitive forces that determine an industry's profit potential"? Explain.
6. What is a strategic group, and what is the value of this concept in choosing a firm's strategy?
7. Why do firms seek information about competitors, and how is that information best collected?

## DISCUSSION QUESTIONS

1. Given the importance of understanding an external environment, why do some managers, and their firms, fail to do so? Provide an example of a firm that understood poorly its external environment and discuss the implications.
2. Select a firm and describe how you characterize the nature of the external environment facing it. As someone who will soon enter the business world, how do you react to these conditions? Why?
3. Describe how it would be possible for one firm to think of a condition in the general environment as an opportunity, whereas a second firm would see that condition as a threat. Provide an example of an environmental characteristic that could be perceived this way.
4. Choose a firm in your local community. Explain the course of action you would follow and the materials you would read to understand its industry environment.
5. Select an industry and describe what firms could do to create barriers to entry in this industry.
6. Is it possible for an industry to exist with only a single strategic group? If so, how? Provide an example of such an industry.

## ETHICS QUESTIONS

1. How can a firm apply its "code of ethics" in the study of its external environment?
2. What ethical issues, if any, may be relevant in a firm's monitoring of its external environment?
3. For each segment of the general environment, cite an ethical issue to which firms should be sensitive.
4. Explain the importance of ethical practices between a firm and its suppliers and distributors.
5. In an intense rivalry, especially one that involves competition in the global marketplace, how can a firm undertake ethical practices and yet maintain its competitiveness? Discuss.
6. While differences in strategies may exist between strategic groups, should commonly accepted ethical values/practices be the same across strategic groups within an industry? Explain.
7. What are the primary ethical issues associated with competitor intelligence practices?

## INTERNET EXERCISE

Go to Bombardier's home page at:
**http://www.bombardier.com**

Familiarize yourself with Bombardier's current products, services, and worldwide operations. Also, using one of the popular search engines such as Yahoo or Excite, search the Internet for other timely information about

Bombardier. After you have completed your search, make a list of the issues affecting Bombardier in its external environment. Organize your list into the different segments of the external environment shown in Figure 3.1.

## STRATEGIC SURFING

There are many online periodicals available that can help firms remain abreast of their external environment. Some examples include:

*BusinessWeek*: **http://www.businessweek.com**
*Financial Post*: **http://www.nationalpost.com**
*Fortune*: **http://pathfinder.com/fortune**

## NOTES

1  J. A. Wagner & R. Z. Gooding, 1997, Equivocal information and attribution: An investigation of patterns of managerial sense-making, *Strategic Management Journal*, 18: 275–86; S. Kotha and A. P. Nair, 1995, Strategy and environment as determinants of performance: Evidence from the Japanese machine tool industry, *Strategic Management Journal*, 16: 497–518.

2  C. M. Grimm & K. G. Smith, 1997, *Strategy As Action: Industry Rivalry and Coordination* (Cincinnati: Southwestern); C. J. Fombrun, 1992, *Turning Point: Creating Strategic Change in Organizations* (New York: McGraw-Hill), 13.

3  K. E. Weick, 1995, *Sensemaking in Organizations* (Thousand Oaks: Sage).

4  Lou Gerstner's first 30 days, 1993, *Fortune*, May 31, 57–62.

5  Fombrun, *Turning Points*, 16–18.

6  M. Farjoun and L. Lei, 1997, Similarity judgments in strategy formulation: Role, process, and implications, *Strategic Management Journal*, 18: 255–73; U. Zander and B. Kogut, 1995, Knowledge and the speed of the transfer and imitation of organizational capabilities: An empirical test, *Organization Science*, 6: 76–92.

7  M. B. Meznar & D. Nigh, 1995, Buffer or bridge? Environmental and organizational determinants of public affairs activities in American firms, *Academy of Management Journal*, 38: 975–96.

8  D. J. Teece, G. Pisano, & A. Shuen, 1997, Dynamic capabilities and strategic management, *Strategic Management Journal*, 18: 509–33.

9  L. Fahey & V. K. Narayanan, 1986, *Macroenvironmental Analysis for Strategic Management* (St. Paul: West Publishing Company), 49–50.

10  One text reviewer made this comment, and we have noted this general sentiment elsewhere. This would also make a very Canadian "group of seven."

11  M. Stark & A. A. Marcus, 2000, Introduction to the special research forum on the management of organ-

izations in the natural environment: A field emerging from multiple paths, with many challenges ahead, *Academy of Management Journal*, 43 (4): 539–47.

12  M. A. Hitt, B. W. Keats, & S. M. DeMarie, 1998, Navigating in the new competitive landscape: Building strategic flexibility and competitive advantage in the 21st century, *Academy of Management Executive*, 12 (4): 22–42.

13  J. F. Preble, 1992, Environmental scanning for strategic control, *Journal of Managerial Issues*, 4: 254–68; K. Gronhaug & J. S. Falkenberg, 1989, Exploring strategy perceptions in changing environments, *Journal of Management Studies*, 26: 349–59.

14  Fombrun, *Turning Points*, 77; Gronhaug & Falkenberg, *Exploring Strategy Perceptions*, 350.

15  D. Akin, 1999, Trying to crack the big time at Comdex: It takes years of hard work to become an overnight success in high tech, *National Post*, November 20, D3.

16  H. Courtney, J. Kirkland, & P. Visuerie, 1997, Strategy under uncertainty, *Harvard Business Review*, 75 (6): 66–79; L. S. Richman, 1993, Why the economic data misleads us, *Fortune*, March 8, 108–14.

17  D. S. Elenkov, 1997, Strategic uncertainty and environmental scanning: The case for institutional influences on scanning behavior, *Strategic Management Journal*, 18: 287–302.

18  I. Goll & A. M. A. Rasheed, 1997, Rational decision-making and firm performance: The moderating role of environment, *Strategic Management Journal*, 18: 583–91; R. L. Priem, A. M. A. Rasheed, & A. G. Kotulic, 1995, Rationality in strategic decision processes, environmental dynamism and firm performance, *Journal of Management*, 21: 913–29.

19  M. Yasai-Ardekani & P. C. Nystrom, 1996, Designs for environmental scanning systems: Tests of contingency theory, *Management Science*, 42: 187–204.

20  Statistics Canada, 2000, Statistics Canada population projections for 2001 and 2026, http://www.statcan.ca/English/ Pgdb/People/ Population/demo23a.htm (Retrieved April 29), http://www.statcan.ca/english/Pgdb/People/ Population/demo23c.htm; R. Dodge, 1997, Summit turns attention to economics of aging, *Dallas Morning News*, June 21, F1, F2; T. Lemay, 1999, Boomers appear complacent about RRSPs, *National Post*, December 17, D4.

21  Fahey & Narayanan, *Macroenvironmental Analysis*, 39.

22  J. Lupart, 1998 Setting right the delusion of inclusion: Implications for Canadian schools. *Canadian Journal of Education*, 23 (3): 251–64.

23  Ibid., 41.

24  I. Mount, 1999, Aggrieved investors slap stocks down, *National Post*, October 14, D3.

25  R. Meares, Not even a superhero could halt the fall in Eidos' share price: reversal of fortunes: Profit warning

knocks Europe's biggest games maker, *National Post*, January 19, C16.

26  T. Aeppel, 1997, Rubbermaid warns 3rd-quarter profits will come in far below expectations, *Wall Street Journal*, September 19, A4; A. B. Fisher, 1996, Corporate reputations, *Fortune*, March 6, 90–93; L. Smith, 1995, Rubbermaid goes thump, *Fortune*, October 2, 90–104.

27  S. Rasula, 1999, Staying the top dog: Schneider's is trying new ways to grow its lead in categories where it's #1. *Marketing Magazine*, March 8: 20–21.

28  Fahey & Narayanan, *Macroenvironmental Analysis*, 58.

29  E. Cornish, 1990, Issues of the '90s, *Fortune*, February 11, 136–41.

30  R. Stodghill II, 1997, The coming job bottleneck, *BusinessWeek*, March 24, 184–85; J. Woodward, 1998, The decline of the Canadian empire: A Statscan report paints a picture of a shrinking nation headed for decrepitude, *British Columbia Report*, July13, 44–46.

31  F. Bula, 2000, Baby boomers: Haves & have nots, *Vancouver Sun*, April 26, A10, A11.

32  G. L. Matthews & R. Morrow, Jr., 1995, *Canada and the World, An Atlas Resource* (2nd Edition), (Scarborough, ON: Prentice Hall); S. Coulombe, 1999, Economic growth and provincial disparity: A new view of an old Canadian problem, *C.D. Howe Institute Commentary*, March, 1–36.

33  J. Jordan, 1999, Professionals head home to work: Worksteaders. Today's home-based workers are highly skilled, well-heeled, *National Post*, October 29, C12.

34  M. Armstrong-Stassen, 1998, Alternative work arrangements: Meeting the challenges. *Canadian Psychology* February/May, 108–23; R. Dodge, 1997, Labor complications, *Dallas Morning News*, September 1, D1, D2; M. N. Martinez, 1995, Contingency workers shed the bad rap, *HR Magazine*, 40 (4): 16–18.

35  Ibid.

36  W. E. Kalbach & M. A. Kalbach, 1999, Becoming a Canadian: problems of an emerging identity, *Canadian Ethnic Studies*, 31 (2) 1999, 1–16.

37  Royal Bank Financial Group, 1998, Living in the Global Village, http://www. royalbank.com/careers/workressurv/ee_report.html (Retrieved January 20, 2001).

38  Statistics Canada, 2000, Population by ethnic origin, 1996 Census, census metropolitan areas http://www. Statcan. ca/english/Pgdb/People/ Population /demo28f.htm (Retrieved May 1, 2001); http://www.statcan.ca/english/Pgdb/People/Population/demo28h.htm.

39  J. R. W. Joplin & C. S. Daus, 1997, Challenges of leading a diverse workforce, *Academy of Management Executive* XI (3): 32–47; G. Robinson & K. Dechant, 1997, Building a business case for diversity, *Academy of Management Executive*, IX, (3): 21–31.

40  J. B. Roesner, 1991, Ways women lead, *Harvard Business Review*, 69 (3): 119–25.

41  F. N. Schwartz, 1992, Women as a business imperative, *Harvard Business Review*, 70 (2): 105–13; C. Torres & M. Bruxelles, 1992, Capitalizing on global diversity, *HR Magazine*, December, 30–33; B. Geber, 1990, Managing diversity, *Training*, July, 23–30.

42  S. Finkelstein & D. C. Hambrick, 1996, *Strategic Leadership: Top Executives and Their Effect on Organizations* (Minneapolis: West); T. Cox & S. Blake, 1991, Managing cultural diversity: Implications for international competitiveness, *Academy of Management Executive*, V (3): 45–46.

43  J. P. Fernandez, 1993, *The Diversity Advantage* (New York: Lexington Books).

44  Royal Bank Financial Group, 1998 Employment Equity Report, http://www. royalbank.com/careers/workressurv/ee_report.html (Retrieved January 20, 2001).

45  J. Landers, 1997, Incomes rising around world, *Dallas Morning News*, September 15, D1, D4.

46  M. Rowan, 1999, Investing in sustainable competitive advantage: Three ways to go with ISO 14001 management standards, *Plant*, June 28, 17; G. Hamilton, 2000, Harvesting a green dream: Eco-certification has taken the B.C. forest industry by storm, *Vancouver Sun*, May 6, E1, E6.

47  Fahey and Narayanan, *Macroenvironmental Analysis*, 13–157.

48  L. Chwialkowska, 2000, Manley admits brain drain, blames taxes, *National Post*, February 16, A1, A10; G. Gherson, 2000, Brain drain vastly underestimated, *National Post*, April 18, A1, A2.

49  R. Steiner, 1999, The brain gain: They were living the Canadian dream: An American degree, an American job, an American salary. So why are they coming back home?, *Financial Post Magazine*, May 18–23.

50  T. Vogel, 1997, Central America goes from war zone to enterprise zone, *Wall Street Journal*, September 25, A18.

51  C. Schuler, 2000, He battled Goliath and won, *National Post*, February 26, A15.

52  G. Middleton, 2001, B.C. Hydro's brokers drive surplus profit, *The Province*, January 19, 2001, A13.

53  R. McQueen, Tellier's next stop: The world? An appropriate corporate strategy for today, *National Post*, December 21, C1, C8; N. Nankivell, 1999, Ottawa must take tougher action on cash-consuming Crowns: there's still more to do in privatization of Crown corps, *National Post*, December 23, C7.

54  B. Bouw, 2000, Cinar close to $10-million tax settlement, *National Post*, February 22, C1, C9.

55  Fahey & Narayanan, *Macroenvironmental Analysis*, 105.

56  S. Clarkson, 1998, Fearful asymmetries: The challenge of analyzing continental systems in a globalizing world, *Canadian-American Public Policy*, 35 (September), 1–66.

57 B. Tieleman, 1999, The wired resistance to global economics: Internet appeals have tapped into deep public concern, *National Post,* December 6, C7.

58 B. L. Dos Santos & K. Peffers, 1995, Rewards to investor in innovative information technology applications: First movers and early followers in ATMs, *Organization Science,* 6: 241–59; S. A. Zahra, S. Nash, & D. J. Bickford, 1995, Transforming technological pioneering into competitive advantage, *Academy of Management Executive,* IX (1): 17–31.

59 D. Hasselback, 2000, PMC-Sierra soars through $20-billion market cap, *National Post,* February 16, C1, C9.

60 D. Bank, 1997, Microsoft's talks with TCI are part of a broader strategy, http://www. interactive.wsj.com (Retrieved October 16); D. Bank, 1997, Microsoft claims digital breakthrough, *Wall Street Journal,* September 16, B14.

61 J. Birkinshaw, A. Morrison, & J. Hulland, 1995, Structural and competitive determinants of a global integration strategy, *Strategic Management Journal,* 16: 637–55.

62 P. Alston, 1989, Wa, guanxi, and inhwa: Managerial principals in Japan, China and Korea, *Business Horizons,* March-April, 26–31.

63 M. A. Hitt, M. T. Dacin, B. B. Tyler, & D. Park, 1997, Understanding the differences in Korean and U.S. executives' strategic orientations, *Strategic Management Journal,* 18: 159–67; S. Yoo & S. M. Lee, 1987, Management style and practice of Korean chaebols, *California Management Review,* 29, Summer: 95–110.

64 K. Singh, 1996, Fried chicken's fearsome foes, *Far Eastern Economic Review,* January 25, 30; M. Jordan, 1995, U.S. food firms head for cover in India, *Wall Street Journal,* November 21, A14.

65 L. Young, 1999, Adventures in joint ventures: the route to expansion, *Canadian Plastics,* November: 12–15.

66 Ibid.

67 S. M. Oster, 1994, *Modern Competitive Analysis,* 2nd edition (New York: Oxford University Press).

68 R. A. Bettis & M. A. Hitt, 1995, The new competitive landscape, *Strategic Management Journal,* 16 (Special Summer Issue): 7–19.

69 G. R. Brooks, 1995, Defining market boundaries, *Strategic Management Journal,* 16: 535–49.

70 A. M. McGahan, 1994, Industry structure and competitive advantage, *Harvard Business Review,* 72 (5): 115–24; R. Laver, 1999, Behind the Linux lunacy. *Maclean's* (Toronto Edition), 112 (51) December 20: 108; Canadian Press, 2000, Corel takes ownership stake in Newlix, *Canadian Press Newswire,* January 12 (via CBCA: Canadian Business and Current Affairs, available at http://delos.lib.sfu.ca:8366/cgi-bin/slri/z3950.CGI/142.58.46.96.533761536/?cbca.db).

71 A. Rose, 2000, The speed of money: Greg Maffei, the much-touted former Microsoft CFO who's heading up Vancouver based 360networks, is betting it travels at the speed of light, *B.C. Business Magazine,* May, 54–60.

72 Factory Logic Web Page, 2001, reprinted from the *Ottawa Citizen* of October 28, 1999, http://www.factorylogic.com/ottawa.asp (Retrieved January 21, 2001).

73 J. H. Gilmore & B. J. Pine, II, 1997, The four faces of mass customization, *Harvard Business Review,* 75 (1): 91–101; S. Kotha, 1995, Mass customization: Implementing the emerging paradigm for competitive advantage, *Strategic Management Journal,* 16 (Special Summer Issue): 21–42; B. Pine, 1993, *Mass Customization* (Boston: Harvard Business School Press); B. Pine, B. Victore, & A. C. Boynton, 1993, Making mass customization work, *Harvard Business Review,* 71 (5): 108–19.

74 Factory Logic Web Page, 2001.

75 B. J. Wise, 1996, *The Automobile Insurance Market in British Columbia: An Examination of the Role of the Insurance Corporation of British Columbia,* Unpublished MBA Project, (Burnaby, B.C. Simon Fraser University).

76 Take on the giants, 1996, *Success,* January/February, 30.

77 L. Zuckerman, 1997, Dell Computer taking aim at consumers, *New York Times on the Web,* http://www. nytimes.com (Retrieved August 29).

78 A. Zipser, 1997, In search of greener pastures, Gateway moves on Dell's turf, *Barron's Online,* http://www.interactive.wsj.com (Retrieved September 15, 2001).

79 P. R. Nayyar, 1995, Stock market reactions to customer service changes, *Strategic Management Journal,* 16: 39–53.

80 Briefing Book, 1997, *Briefing Book,* http://www.interactive.wsj.com (Retrieved November 15, 2000); L. Smith, 1995, Rubbermaid goes thump, *Fortune,* October 2, 90–104.

81 Kenneth F. Harling, 1998, *E. D. Smith and Sons, Ltd.,* Waterloo, Ontario: Wilfrid Laurier University.

82 V. Himmelsbach, 1999, An online battle of the books, *Computer Dealer News;* September 10, 18–19.

83 J. W. Gurley, 1997, Seller, beware: The buyers rule e-commerce, *Fortune,* November 10, 234–36.

84 Aeppel, Rubbermaid warns 3rd-quarter profits will come in far below expectations, A4.

85 Briefing Book, 1997, *Briefing Book,* http://www.interactive.wsj.com (Retrieved November 15, 2000); L. Smith, 1995, Rubbermaid goes thump, *Fortune,* October 2, 90–104.

86 S. Browder, 1997, Tea is bagging a bigger crowd, *BusinessWeek,* August 25, 6.

87 Canadian Press, 1997, Analyst calls beer war stupid. Canadian Press Newswire, June 22 (via CBCA:

Canadian Business and Current Affairs, available at http://delos.lib.sfu.ca:8366/cgi-bin/slri/z3950.CGI/142.58.46.22.536248604/?cbca.db); L. Mills, 1999, As the beer world turns, *Marketing Magazine*, 104 (48): December 20/27, 16; J. Gatehouse, 2000, With glowing hearts we see thee advertise, *National Post*, April 12, A1, A2.

88  R. A. D'Aveni, 1995, Coping with hypercompetition: Utilizing the new 7S's framework, *Academy of Management Executive*, IX (3): 45.

89  R. Gibson, 1997, Burger wars sizzle as McDonald's clones the Whopper, *Wall Street Journal*, September 17, B1.

90  S. Silcoff, 2001, Sault Ste. Marie faces the prospect of becoming a little more than a ghost town should Algoma Steel go under; The whole city would pay the price, *National Post*, January 21: D4. H. J. Moon & K. C. Lee, 1995, Testing the diamond model: Competitiveness of U.S. software firms, *Journal of International Management*, 1: 373–87.

91  Much of the preceding discussion of competitive forces is based on Porter, *Competitive Strategy*.

92  I. Jack, 2001, Brazil fires volley back at Canada in subsidies war, *National Post*, January 21, D9.

94  M. S. Hunt, 1972, *Competition in the major home appliance industry, 1960–1970* (doctoral dissertation, Harvard University).

95  Porter, *Competitive Strategy*, 129.

96  R. K. Reger & A. S. Huff, 1993, Strategic groups: A cognitive perspective, *Strategic Management Journal*, 14: 103–23; J. McGee & H. Thomas, 1986, Strategic groups: A useful linkage between industry structure and strategic management, *Strategic Management Journal*, 7: 141–60.

97  J. B. Barney & R. E. Hoskisson, 1990, Strategic groups: Untested assertions and research proposals, *Managerial and Decision Economics*, 11: 198–208.

98  M. Peteraf & M. Shanley, 1997, Getting to know you: A theory of strategic group identity, *Strategic Management Journal*, 18 (Special Issue), 165–86; R. M. Grant, 1995, *Contemporary Strategy Analysis*, 2nd ed. (Cambridge, MA: Blackwell Publishers), 98.

99  D. F Abell, 1980, *Defining the Business: The Starting Point of Strategic Planning* (Englewood Cliffs, NJ: Prentice Hall).

100  RealBeer, 2001, *RealBeer Home page*, http://realbeer.com/canada (Retrieved January 21). This is an excellent source for province by province detail on breweries, microbreweries, and brewpubs—with a map.

101  This figure is for illustrative purposes only; brewery sizes are approximate; for purposes of comparison the size scale may be considered logarithmic, though the size of each group is not necessarily to scale; evaluation of style may be subject to the opinions of the author developing the figure.

102  Yukon Brewing, 2001, *Yukon Brewing's Brews Page*, http://www.yukonbeer.com/brews/home.htm (Retrieved January 21).

103  D. Nath & T. Gruca, 1997, Covergence across alternatives for forming strategic groups, *Strategic Management Journal*, 18: 745–60; Barney & Hoskisson, Strategic groups, 202.

104  K. G. Smith, C. M. Crimm, & S. Wally, 1997, Strategic groups and rivalrous firm behavior: Towards a reconciliation, *Strategic Management Journal*, 18: 149–57.

105  S. Ghoshal & D. E. Westney, 1991, Organizing competitor analysis systems, *Strategic Management Journal*, 12: 17–31.

106  Porter, *Competitive Strategy*, 49.

107  S. A. Zahra & S. S. Shaples, 1993, Blind spots in competitive analysis, *Academy of Management Executive*, VII (2): 7–28.

108  J. Calor, 1997, For king and country ... and company, *Business Quarterly*, Spring, 32–39; H. Solomon, 1999, Beware of economic espionage, CSIS warns, *Computing Canada*, 25 (28) July 23, 11,13.

109  U.S. companies slow to develop business intelligence, 1995, *Deloitte & Touche Review*, October 16, 1–2.

110  J. Greenwood, 2000, Roth takes Canada to task over Net Business, *National Post*, May 6, D1, D8.

111  D'Aveni, Coping with hypercompetition, 45.

112  T. A. Stewart, 1995, Getting real about brain power, *Fortune*, November 27, 201–03; T. A. Stewart, 1995, Mapping corporate brain power, *Fortune*, October 30, 209–11.

113  M. Geyelin, 1995, Why many businesses can't keep their secrets, *Wall Street Journal*, November 20, B1, B3.

114  A. Zipser, 1997, In search of greener pastures, Gateway moves on Dell's turf, *Barron's Online*, http://www.interactive.wsj.com (Retrieved September 15, 2000).

115  K. A. Rehbeing, S. A. Morris, R. L. Armacost, & J. C. Hosseini, 1992, The CEO's view of questionable competitor intelligence gathering practices, *Journal of Managerial Issues*, 4: 590–03.

116  S. A. Zahra, 1994, Unethical practices in competitive analysis: Patterns, causes, and effects, *Journal of Business Ethics*, 13: 53–62; W. Cohen & H. Czepiec, 1988, The role of ethics in gathering corporate intelligence, *Journal of Business Ethics*, 7: 199–203.

117  J. H. Hallaq & K. Steinhorst, 1994, Business intelligence methods—How ethical?, *Journal of Business Ethics*, 13: 787–94; L. S. Paine, 1991, Corporate police and the ethics of competitor intelligence gathering, *Journal of Business Ethics*, 10: 423–36.

# Chapter Four

## The Internal Environment: Resources, Capabilities, and Core Competencies

### LEARNING OBJECTIVES

*After reading this chapter, you should be able to:*

1. Explain the importance of studying and understanding the internal environment.
2. Define value and discuss its importance.
3. Describe the differences between tangible and intangible resources.
4. Define capabilities and discuss how they are developed.
5. Describe four criteria used to determine if a firm's resources and capabilities are core competencies.
6. Explain how value chain analysis is used to identify and evaluate a firm's resources and capabilities.
7. Define outsourcing and discuss the reasons for its use.
8. Discuss the importance of preventing a firm's core competencies from becoming core rigidities.
9. Explain the relationship between a firm's strategic inputs and its strategic actions.

## People as a Source of Competitive Advantage

In a *Fortune* survey featuring the most admired corporations worldwide, a critical theme emerged. Although no one strength was judged sufficient to place a company on top of the global list of most admired firms, a capability for finding, nurturing, and keeping intelligent and talented employees was most strongly related to a company's overall score. For instance, Disney received the highest score for being the most innovative company. Michael Eisner indicated that "we create a new product—a book, a movie, something—every five minutes and each one has to be superb. Our goal is to do it better every time out. But our real product is managing talent. That's what we really do here, and we never lose sight of that—because without that, what have you got?" Similarly, Jack Welch, GE's CEO, says, "All we can do is bet on the people who we pick. So my whole job is picking the right people." In fact, Welch personally interviews candidates for the top 500 jobs at GE. Most companies in the survey found that the ability to attract and hold talented employees was the single most reliable predictor of excellence.

The Hay Group, which conducted the survey for *Fortune* found seven basic themes contribute to corporate excellence in hiring and career development practices:

- top managers at the most admired companies take their firm's mission statements seriously and expect everyone else to do likewise;
- success attracts the best people, and the best people sustain success;
- top companies know precisely what they're looking for, often through intense psychological testing;
- these companies see career development as an investment, not a chore;
- whenever possible, they promote from within;
- they reward performance; and
- they measure workforce satisfaction.

In essence, the most admired firms in the survey are experts at managing human resources.

http://www.adopt.qc.ca
http://www.disney.com
http://www.ge.com
http://www.microsoft.com
http://www.saic.com

A number of companies take the management of human resources seriously. A small Montreal firm, AD OPT Technologies, has developed scheduling-optimization software that 7 of the 12 largest airlines in North America have spent from $750 000 to $3 million to purchase. The software saves up to 5 percent of aircrew payroll, while allowing pilots and crew to select their own routes and schedules. The airlines are interested in two things; they want to cut costs and increase employee satisfaction. AD OPT has doubled its number of employees to 85, and sales have increased from $2 million in 1994 to $12.5 million in 1999. The president and CEO of AD OPT, Tom Ivaskiv, expects these numbers to explode as AD OPT develops its product line into more labour-intensive, round-the-clock services such as call centres, police forces, and fire departments. Joe Vejvoda, a TD Securities technology analyst, believes that AD OPT differs from a lot of companies that do scheduling and optimization using conventional methods. This means that these firms discount some scenarios because they look more expensive. Vejvoda says that "AD OPT will calculate some scenarios that are not deemed to be more cost-effective because they look at the human side."

Robert Beyster, the chief executive officer and founder of Science Applications International (SAIC), built a scientific consulting firm starting with 12 employees in 1969 to a 25 000 employee high-tech research and engineering firm. SAIC recently bought Bellcore, the former research arm of the Bell operating companies and improved its ranking to the 41st largest private firm in *Forbes's* ranking of the 500 largest private companies. At SAIC, employees own 90 percent of the company, and the other 10 percent is held by consultants or employees who left the company before SAIC required that departing employee owners sell their shares back to the firm. Although Beyster has 1.5 percent of the $3 billion net worth of the firm instead of owning 100 percent, his philosophy has turned employees into committed and motivated stakeholders. The firm has four different employee-ownership programs that are among the most sophisticated in the country. As Narri Cooper indicates, "When I'm making a decision, I don't just make it as an information technology manager, I make it as an owner." Furthermore, 9 employees sit on the 22-person board alongside such luminaries as U.S. Navy Admiral B. R. Inman.

Microsoft views human resources as an organizational capability. The company has sought to make large new product teams work as efficiently as small teams. Although small teams of talented people may be the most desired way to develop new products, this is impossible when the product is complex and short deadlines are required. As a result, firms such as Microsoft find it necessary to manage large teams (perhaps hundreds) of talented engineers to develop new complex software products. Because of this reality, Microsoft has developed innovative ways of managing teams of talented people. These managerial approaches help Microsoft produce innovative products.

In summary, human resources are critical. Developing the ability to hire, manage, motivate, and orchestrate people is an important capability that adds to a firm's core competence. If it can effectively manage this critical capability, the company may become one of the top firms on a most admired corporations' list.

Sources: D. North, 2000, Go ahead, plan my day, *Canadian Business,* March 20, 86; M. A. Cusumano, 1997, How Microsoft makes large teams work like small teams, *Sloan Management Review,* 39 (1): 9–20; A. Fisher, The world's most admired companies, *Fortune,* October 27, 220–40; C. T. Geer, 1997, Turning employees into stakeholders, *Forbes,* December 1, 155–57; C. T. Geer, 1997, Sharing the wealth, capitalist-style, *Forbes,* December 1, 158–60; M. A. Huselid, S. E. Jackson, and R. S. Schuler, 1997, Technical and strategic human resource management effectiveness as determinants of firm performance, *Academy of Management Journal,* 40: 171–88; P. Cappelli and A. Crocker-Hefter, 1996, Distinctive human resources are firms' core competencies, *Organizational Dynamics,* 24 (3): 7–22.

AD OPT, Science Applications International, Disney, GE, and Microsoft have developed capabilities to manage their human resources and create a sustainable competitive advantage. A sustainable competitive advantage is achieved when firms implement a value-creating strategy that is grounded in their own unique resources, capabilities, and core competencies (terms defined in Chapter 1). Firms achieve strategic competitiveness and earn above-average returns when their unique core competencies are leveraged effectively to take advantage of opportunities in the external environment. As the opening case indicates, one way to develop competitive advantage is through people, the firm's employees.[1]

Over time, the benefits of every firm's value-creating strategy can be duplicated. In other words, all competitive advantages have a limited life.[2] The question of duplication is not *if* it will happen, but *when*. During the 1980s, for example, the competitive advantage of brand names began to dissipate. Among the factors causing temporary erosion of the competitive advantage yielded by brand names for some firms was a technological development—the checkout scanner. Studying data available to them from scanners allowed retailers (such as grocery stores) to determine quickly how price promotions on various products affected their sales volume. In the words of one analyst, this new technology "gave retailers tremendous new muscle over the brandmakers, and with all the increased emphasis on discounts and promotions, consumers learned how to bargain."[3]

Effective duplication by competitors may have contributed to Home Depot's performance difficulties. Competitors such as B.C.'s Revy Home Centres have built hangar-size warehouses that offer an array of goods similar to that available from Home Depot. Moreover, competitors' actions have reduced the service gap between them and Home Depot.[4] While Home Depot is taking actions to counteract this duplication, competitors' actions have contributed to reduced financial performance at Home Depot.

In general, the sustainability of a competitive advantage is a function of three factors: (1) the rate of core competence obsolescence due to environmental changes, (2) the availability of substitutes for the core competence, and (3) the imitability of the core competence.[5] The challenge for strategists in all firms—a challenge that can be met through proper use of the strategic management process—is to manage current core competencies effectively while simultaneously developing new ones to use when the competitive advantage derived from application of current ones has been eroded.[6] Only when firms develop a continuous stream of competitive advantages (as explained further in Chapter 6) do they achieve strategic competitiveness, earn above-average returns, and remain ahead of competitors. Nortel, Bank of Montreal, Intel, and Microsoft continuously make investments that are intended to enhance their current sources of competitive advantage and simultaneously spur the creation of new ones.[7] These investments appear to contribute significantly to these firms' ability to achieve and maintain strategic competitiveness.

In Chapter 3, we examined the general environment, the industry environment, and rivalry among competing firms. Armed with knowledge about their firm's environments, managers have a better understanding of the marketplace opportunities and the products necessary to pursue them.

In this chapter, we focus on the firm. Through an analysis of the internal environment, a firm determines what it can do—that is, the actions permitted by its unique resources, capabilities, and core competencies. As discussed in Chapter 1, core competencies are a firm's source of competitive advantage. The magnitude of that competitive advantage is a function primarily of its uniqueness compared to competitors' competencies.[8] The proper matching of what a firm can do with what it might do allows the development of strategic intent, a strategic mission, and the formulation of strategies. When implemented effectively, a value-creating strategy is the pathway to strategic competitiveness and above-average returns. Outcomes resulting from internal and external environmental analyses are shown in Figure 4.1.

▪ ▪ **FIGURE 4.1**

*Outcomes from External and Internal Environmental Analyses*

| By studying the external environment firms identify | By studying the internal environment firms determine |
|---|---|
| • What they *might* choose to do | • What they *can* do |

Several topics are examined in this chapter. First, we review the importance and the challenge of studying a firm's internal environment. We then discuss the roles that resources, capabilities, and core competencies play in the development of sustainable competitive advantage. Included in these discussions are descriptions of the techniques used to identify and evaluate resources and capabilities and the criteria used to select the firm's core competencies from among its resources and capabilities. While studying these materials, it is important to recall that resources, capabilities, and core competencies are not valuable alone; they have value only because they allow the firm to perform certain activities that result in a competitive advantage. To have sustained competitive advantage, these activities must be unique.[9]

As shown in Figure 1.1 in Chapter 1, strategic intent and strategic mission, coupled with insights gained through analyses of the internal and external environments, determine the strategies a firm will select and the actions it will take to implement them successfully. In the final part of the chapter, we describe briefly the relationships among intent, mission, and a firm's strategy formulation and implementation actions.

## THE IMPORTANCE OF INTERNAL ANALYSIS

In the new competitive landscape, traditional conditions and factors, such as labour costs, access to financial resources and raw materials, and protected or regulated markets, can still provide competitive advantage but to a lesser degree now than in the past.[10] A key reason for this decline is that the advantages created by these sources can be overcome through an international strategy (international strategies are discussed in Chapter 9). As a result, overcapacity is the norm in a host of industries, increasing the difficulty of forming competitive advantages. In this challenging competitive environment, few firms are able to make the right strategic decisions on a consistent basis over time. Additionally, less job security for individual employees is an inevitable consequence of operating in this more challenging competitive environment. For example, Canadian Imperial Bank of Commerce laid off 10 000 people in 1999/2000.

The demands of the new competitive landscape make it necessary for top-level managers to rethink the concept of the corporation. Although corporations are difficult to change, earning strategic competitiveness in the 21st century requires development and use of a different managerial mind-set.[11] Most top-level managers recognize the need to change their mind-sets, but many hesitate to do so. In the words of a European CEO of a major U.S. company, "It is more reassuring for all of us to stay as we are, even though we know the result will be certain failure … than to jump into a new way of working when we cannot be sure it will succeed."[12]

Critical to the managerial mind-set required is the view that a firm is a bundle of heterogeneous resources, capabilities, and core competencies that can be used to create an exclusive market position.[13] This view suggests that individual firms possess at least some resources and capabilities that other companies do not have, at least not in the same combination. Resources are the source of capabilities, some of which lead to the development of a firm's core competencies. By using their core competencies, firms are able to perform activities better than competitors or in ways that competitors are unable to duplicate. Essentially, the mind-set required in the new competitive landscape defines its strategy in terms of unique competitive position rather than in terms of operational effectiveness. For instance, Michael Porter argues that quests for productivity, quality, and speed from a number of management techniques (total quality management, benchmarking, time-based competition, reengineering) have resulted in operational efficiency but not strong sustainable strategy.[14]

Increasingly, managers are being evaluated in terms of their ability to identify, nurture, and exploit their firm's unique core competencies.[15] By emphasizing competence acquisition and development, organizations learn how to learn—a skill that is linked with the development of competitive advantage. As a process, learning how to learn requires commitment, time, and the active support of top-level executives. At the U.S. firm Deere & Co., managers have created an "in-house Yellow Pages" to help them find an expert inside or outside the firm.[16] The system is quite inexpensive, about the cost of one engineer to operate it, but it has paid for itself annually, at least six times over, especially when there is a crisis, and an expert is needed to solve it. In the final analysis, a corporate-wide obsession with the development and use of knowledge and core competencies may characterize companies able to compete effectively on a global basis in the 21st century.[17]

By exploiting their core competencies and meeting the demanding standards of global competition, firms create value for their customers. **Value** creation occurs when firms increase revenue by taking advantage of opportunities, reduce costs by neutralizing threats, or do both. Value consists of the performance characteristics and attributes provided by companies in the form of goods or services for which customers are willing to pay. Ultimately, customer value is the source of a firm's potential to earn average or above-average returns. In Chapter 5, we note that value is provided to customers by a product's low cost, by its highly differentiated features, or by a combination of low cost and high differentiation, as compared to competitors' offerings. Core competencies, then, are actually a value-creating system through which a company seeks strategic competitiveness and above-average returns (these relationships are shown in Figure 4.2). In the new competitive landscape, managers need to determine if their firm's core competencies continue to create value for customers.[18]

**Value** creation occurs when firms increase revenue by taking advantage of opportunities, reduce costs by neutralizing threats, or do both.

■ ■ **FIGURE 4.2**

*Components of Internal
Analysis Leading to
Competitive Advantage and
Strategic Competitiveness*

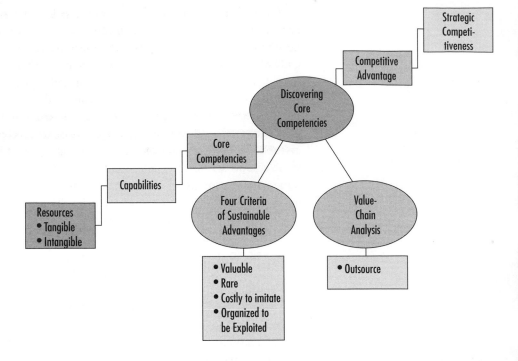

During the last several decades, the strategic management process was concerned most with understanding the characteristics of the industry in which a firm was competing and, in light of those characteristics, determining how the firm should position itself relative to competitors. The emphasis on industry characteristics and competitive strategy may have understated the role of organizational resources and capabilities in developing competitive advantage. A firm's core competencies, in addition to the results of an analysis of its general, industry, and competitive environments, should drive the selection of strategies. In this regard, core competencies, in combination with product-market positions or tactics, are the most important sources of competitive advantage in the new competitive landscape. Emphasizing core competencies when formulating strategies causes companies to learn how to compete primarily on the basis of firm-specific differences rather than seeking competitive advantage solely on the structural characteristics of their industries.[19]

## The Challenge of Internal Analysis

The decisions managers make, in terms of resources, capabilities, and core competencies, have a significant influence on a firm's ability to develop competitive advantages and earn above-average returns.[20] Making these decisions—that is, identifying, developing, protecting, and deploying resources, capabilities, and core competencies—may appear to be relatively easy tasks. In fact, this work is as challenging and difficult as any management task, and it is becoming increasingly internationalized and linked with the firm's success.[21]

Sometimes mistakes are made when conducting an internal analysis. Managers might, for example, select resources and capabilities as a firm's core competencies that do not, in fact, yield a competitive advantage. When this occurs, strategists must have the confidence to admit the mistake and take corrective actions. Firm growth can occur through well-intended errors; indeed, learning generated by making and correcting mistakes can be important to the creation of new competitive advantages.[22]

To manage the development and use of core competencies, managers must have courage, self-confidence, integrity, the capacity to deal with uncertainty and complexity, and a willingness to hold people accountable for their work.[23] Successful strategists also seek to create an organizational environment in which operating units feel empowered to use the identified core competencies to pursue marketplace opportunities.

Difficult managerial decisions concerning resources, capabilities, and core competencies are characterized by three conditions: uncertainty, complexity, and intraorganizational conflicts (see Figure 4.3).

Managers face *uncertainty* in terms of the emergence of new proprietary technologies, rapidly changing economic and political trends, changes in societal values, and shifts in customer demands. Such environmental uncertainty increases the *complexity* and the range of issues managers examine when studying the internal environment. Managerial biases about how to cope with uncertainty affect decisions about the resources and capabilities that will become the foundation of the firm's competitive advantage. Finally, *intraorganizational conflict* surfaces when decisions are made about core competencies that are to be nurtured and about how the nurturing is to take place.

■ ■ **FIGURE 4.3**

*Conditions Affecting Managerial Decisions About Resources, Capabilities, and Core Competencies*

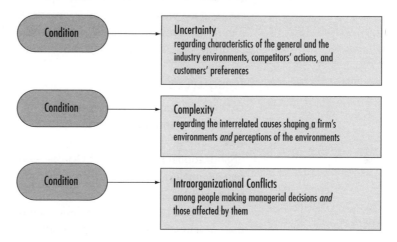

Source: Adapted from R. Amit and P. J. H. Schoemaker, 1993, Strategic assets and organizational rent, *Strategic Management Journal,* 14: 33.

When making decisions affected by these three conditions, managers should use their judgment as opposed to just following rules or standard operating procedures. *Judgment* is a capacity for making successful decisions when no obviously correct model or rule is available or when relevant data are unreliable or incomplete.[24] In this situation, one must be aware of possible cognitive biases. For instance, one must compare internal firm resources and make a judgment as to whether a resource is a strength or a weakness. When exercising judgment, the strategist demonstrates a willingness to take intelligent risks in a timely manner. In the new competitive landscape, executive judgment can be a particularly important source of competitive advantage. One reason judgment can result in a competitive advantage is that over time, effective judgment allows a firm to retain the loyalty of stakeholders whose support is linked to above-average returns.[25]

Significant changes in the value-creating potential of a firm's resources and capabilities can occur in a rapidly changing global economy. Because these changes affect a company's power and social structure, inertia or resistance to change may surface. Firms should not deny the changes needed to assure strategic competitiveness; nonetheless, managers sometimes deny the need for organizational and/or personal change. *Denial* is an unconscious coping mechanism used to block out and not initiate painful changes.[26] Occasionally, an entire industry is accused of being in denial. Some analysts recently cited the automobile manufacturing industry as an example of denial. In light of saturation in some major markets (such as Canada and the United States), automakers have had to increase incentives. The alternative, to reduce production, is a difficult decision.[27] GE's CEO, Jack Welch, believes that top-level executives must demonstrate unflinching candour when making strategic decisions. Part of this candour demands that decision-makers cause their firms and their people to face reality as it is—not as it once was or as they want it to be.[28] Successful strategists have learned that involving many people in decisions about changes reduces denial and intraorganizational conflict.

## RESOURCES, CAPABILITIES, AND CORE COMPETENCIES

Our attention now turns to a description of resources, capabilities, and core competencies—characteristics that are the foundation of competitive advantage. As shown in Figure 4.2, some combination of resources and capabilities can be managed to create core competencies. This subsection defines and provides examples of these internal aspects.

### Resources

Defined in Chapter 1, resources are inputs into a firm's production process such as capital equipment, the skills of individual employees, patents, finance, and talented managers. Broad in scope, resources cover a spectrum of individual, social, and organizational phenomena.[29] On their own, resources do not typically yield a competitive advantage. A professional hockey team may benefit from employing the league's most talented centre, but it is only when the centre integrates his or her play with the offensive and defensive strategies of the rest of the team that a competitive advantage may develop. Similarly, a firm's production technology, if not protected by patents or other constraints, can be purchased or imitated by competitors, but when that production technology is integrated with other resources to form a capability, a core competence may develop that results in competitive advantage. Thus, a competitive advantage can be created through the unique bundling of several resources.[30] Physical assets alone usually cannot provide a firm with sustainable competitive advantages.[31]

**Tangible resources** are assets that can be seen and quantified.
**Intangible resources** range from the intellectual property rights of patents, trademarks, and copyrights to the people-dependent or subjective resources of know-how, networks, organizational culture, and a firm's reputation for its goods or services and the ways it interacts with people (e.g., employees, suppliers, and customers).

Some of a firm's resources are tangible; others are intangible. **Tangible resources** are assets that can be seen and quantified. **Intangible resources** range from the intellectual property rights of patents, trademarks, and copyrights to the people-dependent or subjective resources of know-how, networks, organizational culture, and a firm's reputation for its goods or services and the ways it interacts with people (e.g., employees, suppliers, and customers).[32]

Reputation is viewed as an intangible resource that can endow companies with a competitive advantage. Some equate reputation to "what accountants call goodwill and marketers call brand equity."[33] Among other competitive benefits, a positive reputation allows the firm to charge premium prices for its goods or services and to reduce its marketing costs.[34] Harley-Davidson is a brand that may drive sales on any two-wheeled vehicle. When GT Bicycles licensed the Harley-Davidson brand for a Limited Edition Bicycle, GT sold 1 000 bicycles for $2 500 each. Snapped up by collectors, the bikes have real Harley paint jobs, a fake gas tank, and chrome fenders similar to a Harley soft-tail motorcycle.[35] Similarly, Bombardier used its well-regarded snowmobile name "Skidoo" to promote its jet-ski line, "Seadoo" for water sports.

The four types of tangible resources are financial, physical, human, and organizational (see Table 4.1). The three types of intangible resources (technological and those resulting from the firm's innovation and reputation) are shown in Table 4.2.

| ■ ■ TABLE 4.1 | Tangible Resources |
|---|---|
| Financial Resources | The firm's borrowing capacity<br>The firm's ability to generate internal funds |
| Physical Resources | Sophistication and location of a firm's plant and equipment<br>Access to raw material |
| Human Resources | Training, experience, judgment, intelligence, insights, adaptability, commitment, and loyalty of a firm's individual managers and workers |
| Organizational Resources | The firm's formal reporting structure and its formal planning, controlling, and coordinating systems |

Source: Adapted from J. B. Barney, 1991, Firm resources and sustained competitive advantage, *Journal of Management* 17: 101; R. M. Grant, 1991, *Contemporary Strategy Analysis* (Cambridge, England: Blackwell Business), 100–02.

## Tangible Resources

As tangible resources, a firm's borrowing capacity and the status of its plant and equipment are visible to all. The value of many tangible resources can be established through financial statements, but these statements do not account for the value of all of a firm's assets in that they disregard some intangible resources.[36] As such, sources of a firm's competitive advantage often are not reflected on its financial statements.

Managers are challenged to understand fully the strategic value of their firm's tangible and intangible resources. The strategic value of resources is indicated by the degree to which they can contribute to the development of capabilities and core competencies and, ultimately, a competitive advantage. For example, as a tangible resource, a distribution facility will be assigned a monetary value on the firm's balance sheet. The real value of the facility as a resource, however, is grounded in other factors such as its proximity to raw materials and customers and the manner in which workers integrate their actions internally and with other stakeholders such as suppliers and customers.[37]

| ■ ■ **TABLE 4.2** | **Intangible Resources** |
|---|---|
| Technological Resources | Stock of technology such as patents, trademarks, copyrights, and trade secrets<br>Knowledge required to apply it successfully |
| Resources for Innovation | Technical employees<br>Research facilities |
| Reputation | Reputation with customers<br>Brand name<br>Perceptions of product quality, durability, and reliability<br>Reputation with suppliers<br>For efficient, effective, supportive, and mutually beneficial interactions and relationships |

Sources: Adapted from J. B. Barney, 1991, Firm resources and sustained competitive advantage, *Journal of Management* 17: 101; R. M. Grant, 1991, *Contemporary Strategy Analysis* (Cambridge, England: Blackwell Business), 100–2.

As shown in Figure 4.2, resources are the source of a firm's capabilities. Capabilities are the source of a firm's core competencies, which are the basis of competitive advantages. Intangible resources, as compared to tangible resources, are a superior and more potent source of core competencies.[38] In fact, in today's competitive environment, "... the success of a corporation lies more in its intellectual and systems capabilities than in its physical assets. [Moreover], the capacity to manage human intellect—and to convert it into useful products and services—is fast becoming the critical executive skill of the age."[39] Given its critical importance, human capital needs to be measured. The International Accounting Standards Committee (IASC) has established a movement in this direction, stating that "investment in, and awareness of, the importance of intangible assets have increased significantly in the past two decades," and has published a standard to guide accounting practices for intangible assets. These standards apply to Canadian firms operating in countries following IASC codes and broadly establish a definition of intangible assets.[40]

## Intangible Resources

Because they are less visible and more difficult for competitors to understand, purchase, imitate, or substitute for, managers prefer to use intangible resources as the foundation for a firm's capabilities and core competencies. In fact, it may be that the more unobservable (that is, intangible) a resource is, the more sustainable will be the competitive advantage based on it.[41] As defined earlier, intangible resources range from the intellectual property rights of patents, trademarks, and copyrights to the people-dependent or subjective resources of know-how, networks, organizational culture, and a firm's reputation for its goods or services and the ways it interacts with people (e.g., employees, suppliers, and customers).

Brand names are an intangible resource that help to create a firm's reputation and are recognized widely as an important source of competitive advantage for many companies, especially those manufacturing and selling consumer goods and services.[42] When effective, brand names inform customers of a product's performance characteristics and attributes. When products with strong brand names provide value across time, customers become very loyal by refusing to buy competitors' offerings, including private-label generic products.

When a brand name yields a competitive advantage, companies sometimes strive to find additional ways to exploit it in the marketplace, as the earlier example of Harley-Davidson's using its brand name to sell bicycles demonstrates. Disney has used its brand name to sell clothes representing Disney figures. Currently, Disney is entering the restaurant business through a chain of sport-theme restaurants based on its ESPN cable sports network brand. Disney has also launched ESPN merchandise stores.[43]

Fashion retailer Roots has extended its label to include furniture, housewares, and lodging (as shown in a Chapter 5 Strategic Focus). Copying leading consumer firms such as Disney, Sears has exploited its brand names by opening stores that focus on its powerful Craftsman, Kenmore, and Diehard brands. Sears views these brands as its most valuable assets, its best defence against price competition, and its key to customer loyalty and sustainable competitive advantage. As one top executive stated, "Competitors may be able to copy your features and benefits, but they can't steal your brand."[44]

As a source of capabilities, tangible and intangible resources are a critical part of the pathway to the development of competitive advantage (see Figure 4.2). As discussed previously, resources' strategic value is increased when they are integrated or combined. Defined formally in Chapter 1, a capability is the capacity for a set of resources to integratively perform a task or activity. Capabilities are unique combinations of the firm's information-based tangible resources (see Table 4.1) and/or intangible resources (see Table 4.2) and are what the firm is able to do as a result of teams of resources working together.

## Capabilities

As explained, capabilities represent the firm's capacity to deploy resources that have been purposely integrated to achieve a desired end state. As the glue that binds an organization together, capabilities emerge over time through complex interactions between and among tangible and intangible resources. As explained in the opening case, capabilities are often based on developing, carrying, and exchanging information and knowledge through the firm's human capital. Thus, the firm's knowledge base is embedded in, and reflected by, its capabilities and is a key source of advantage in the new competitive landscape.[45] Because a knowledge base is grounded in organizational actions that may not be understood explicitly by all employees, the firm's capabilities become stronger and more valuable strategically through repetition and practice.

As illustrated in Figure 4.4, the primary base for the firm's capabilities is the skills and knowledge of its employees and, often, their functional expertise. As such, the value of human capital in the development and use of capabilities and, ultimately, core competencies cannot be overstated. Microsoft, for example, believes its best asset is the "intellectual horsepower" of its employees. To assure continued development of this capability and the core competence that follows, the firm strives continuously to hire people who are more talented than the current set of employees.[46] XWave Solutions, headquartered in St. John's, Newfoundland and launched in early 1999, was formed from information technology (IT) companies from St. John's, Newfoundland to Dallas, Texas. In a business where client services are critical, XWave strategists consider that their strength is in their employees. XWave demonstrates their "people" commitment by having an open mind versus just an open-door policy, by trusting and respecting employees, and by creating a climate that balances serious work with a sense of excitement, fun, and pride. In the words of the Vice-President, People, Lloyd Powell, "the better we treat our people, the better work they will do."[47]

■ ■ **FIGURE 4.4**

*Capabilities*

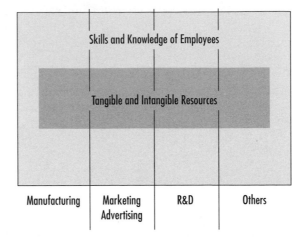

Some believe that the knowledge possessed by the firm's human capital is among the most significant of an organization's capabilities and may ultimately be at the root of all competitive advantages. In the words of one business analyst, "Companies have come to understand that one of the strongest competitive advantages is absolute knowledge."[48] Some even view knowledge as "the sum of everything everybody in [a] company knows that gives [the firm] a competitive edge in the marketplace."[49] Moreover, the rate at which firms acquire new knowledge and develop the skills necessary to apply it in the marketplace is a key source of competitive advantage.[50] To facilitate knowledge acquisition, development, and application, some firms (such as NetPCS in Canada, Coca-Cola, GE, and General Motors) have created a new top management team (this term is discussed in Chapter 13) position—the chief knowledge officer or the chief learning officer (CLO). At Ottawa's NetPCS, Eid Eid was recently hired away from Corel and named chief knowledge officer and executive vice-president.[51] Regardless of the title, the task for these strategists is primarily to help the firm become a learning organization that is open to making the changes required to establish and exploit competitive advantages.

Some evidence suggests that workforces throughout the global economy may lack the skills and knowledge firms require to exploit them as a source of competitive advantage. One manager has noted that "high tech is exploding … And the only thing stopping growth from being even stronger is the lack of qualified high-tech professionals."[52] In particular, this concern, which exists across all types of industries, is directed toward the future. Large firms are not the only ones feeling the shortage of qualified people. In late 1999, Vancouver's Creo Products—a high-technology leader in the computer-to-plate imaging—published a full-page job ad looking for just three managers.[53] David Smith suggests that the number of new faculty members Canadian universities will have to recruit in the next decade is equal to or more than the current total number of faculty members.[54] When confronted with a possible shortage of skilled workers, companies desiring to develop their knowledge as a source of competitive advantage sometimes scan the global economy to find the required labour skills. For example, a number of firms, including Siemens, Motorola, Hewlett-Packard, and Digital Equipment, employed computer engineers from the city of Bangalore, India. The city's thousands of computer engineers have signalled that Bangalore is an important global source of information technology and workforce capabilities.[55]

The international competition for those who have invested in education and have great ability will become more intense. The CEO of Nortel, John Roth, noted that

*when I talk about the brain drain, I'm not talking about commodity engineers. I'm not talking about the average software programmer. I'm talking about the achievers who are going to lead projects. It's those leaders and high-value jobs we're losing and they are a fraction of a percent of the pool. But the impact of their loss on the Canadian economy and on Canadian productivity is major. You lose them and the project teams and career opportunities go with them. That's the brain drain—the real threat to Canada's future in the Internet economy.[56]*

The Canadian information and telecommunications technology industry (ICT) continues to grow, with Canada's IT industry recently contributing $72 billion in revenue to the economy. However, as mentioned above, this growth may be stunted, according to a survey by the Information Technology Association of Canada (ITAC). This survey suggested that Canadian companies are trying to fill vacant positions in the ICT field but that it is becoming more difficult as skilled IT workers are moving to the United States where economic growth is expected to be strong.[57]

The importance of human capital and knowledge to the firm's strategic competitiveness and the need to provide continuous learning opportunities for employees, particularly in light of the forecasted skilled labour force shortages, have been suggested by both business analysts and key government officials. One analyst, for example, believes that in all business organizations (especially those providing services) "… learning and productivity grow from the cumulative decision-making experiences of employees in long-term relationships with customers, vendors and fellow employees."[58] Many top executives believe that the ability to hire and retain good employees is a key part of their job. Jack Welch, CEO of General Electric, states, "All we can do is bet on the people we pick, so my whole job is picking the right people." Evidence of the importance Welch attaches to hiring is seen in the fact that he personally interviews all candidates for the 500 top jobs at GE.[59]

Canada's competitiveness depends very much on its human capital as a resource. In the 1990s, Canada experienced a "Brain Drain" to the United States in many key knowledge-based occupations, according to Statistics Canada 1996 census information. Though the number of workers leaving is small (just 0.1 percent of all tax-paying Canadians), this has been a rising trend, and those leaving were generally better educated and earning more than the average Canadian.[60]

As illustrated in Figure 4.4 and Table 4.3, capabilities are often developed in specific functional areas (e.g., manufacturing, R&D, marketing, etc.) or in a part (e.g., advertising) of a functional area. Research results suggest a relationship between distinctive competencies (or capabilities) developed in particular functional areas and the firm's financial performance at both the corporate and business-unit levels.[61] Thus, firms should develop functional area–distinctive competencies or capabilities in individual business units and at the corporate level (in the case of diversified firms). Table 4.3 shows a grouping of organizational functions and the capabilities certain companies are thought to possess in terms of all or parts of those functions.

| ■ ■ TABLE 4.3 | Examples of Firms' Capabilities | |
|---|---|---|
| **Functional Areas** | **Capabilities** | **Firm Examples** |
| Distribution | Effective use of logistics management techniques | Wal-Mart |
| | Consistent on-time delivery | Mill Creek Trucking |
| Human Resources | Motivating, empowering, and retaining employees | Bank of Montreal |
| MIS | Effective/efficient control of inventories through point-of-purchase data-collection methods | Wal-Mart |
| Marketing | Effective promotion of brand-name products | Sears |
| | Effective customer service | Fishery Products International |
| Management | Effective execution of managerial tasks | Hewlett-Packard |
| Manufacturing | Design and production skills yielding reliable products | Komatsu |
| | Production of technologically sophisticated automobile engines | Mazda |
| Research and Development | Exceptional technological capability | PMC Sierra |
| | Computer-to-plate imaging and laser imaging | Creo Products |

As mentioned in the opening case, AD OPT Technologies, Science Applications International, and Microsoft are respected for their different functional abilities to develop their human resources. In particular, Microsoft has a creative ability to make large new product teams work as efficiently as small teams.[62] Armed with knowledge about resources and capabilities, managers are prepared to identify their firm's core competencies.

## Core Competencies

As the source of competitive advantage for a firm, core competencies distinguish a company competitively and reflect its personality. Core competencies emerge over time through an organizational process of accumulating and learning how to deploy different resources and capabilities. As a capacity to take action, core competencies "... are the essence of what makes an organization unique in its ability to provide value to customers over a long period of time."[63]

By bundling its resources, 3M has developed a strong core competence in product innovation. Its research labs are filled with highly knowledgeable scientists and the latest technologies. Its culture fosters creativity by allowing employees 15 percent free time to tinker around through access to an internal venture capital fund. 3M created a Technical

Forum to encourage the sharing of best practices. Further, it requires that at least 6.5 percent of sales be spent on R&D. Over 30 percent of sales come from products less than four years old. Through its efforts, the company has developed a "perpetual innovation" machine, with nearly 50 000 innovations created since it was founded in 1902.[64]

Not all of a firm's resources and capabilities are strategic assets—that is, assets that have competitive value and the potential to serve as a source of competitive advantage.[65] Some resources and capabilities may result in incompetence because they represent competitive areas in which the firm is weak compared to competitors. Thus, some resources or capabilities may stifle or prevent the development of a core competence. Firms with insufficient financial capital, for example, may be unable to purchase facilities or hire the skilled workers required to manufacture products that yield customer value. In this situation, financial capital (a tangible resource) would be a weakness. Armed with in-depth understandings of their firm's resources and capabilities, strategic managers are challenged to find external environmental opportunities that can be exploited through the firm's capabilities while avoiding competition in areas of weakness.

Additionally, an important question is: How many core competencies are required for the firm to have a competitive advantage? Responses to this question vary. McKinsey & Co. recommends that clients identify three or four competencies around which their strategic actions can be framed.[66] Note the consistency of Rolls-Royce's decisions with this advice to focus on only four competencies. The company has outsourced a number of peripheral activities such as making car bodies and fasteners so it can concentrate "on its core competencies—engines, paint, leather, (and) wood."[67] Trying to support and nurture more than four core competencies may prevent the firm from developing the focus it needs to exploit fully its competencies in the marketplace.

From an impoverished city in southern Italy called Santeramo Del Colle, Pasquale Natuzzi has taken his firm Industrie Natuzzi SpA from selling 100 leather sofas to Macy's in 1982 to having an estimated 25 percent of the U.S. leather furniture market.[68] Because the firm's clients in Italy were pressuring him to send two or three sofas but bill them only for one or two to avoid taxes, he decided to begin selling his furniture overseas. Natuzzi has focused his firm's competencies on design flair, quality leathers, highly skilled craftspeople, each with a computer to maintain efficient operations, and low labour costs with strong worker incentives. Because of Natuzzi's focus on a few critical core competencies, his furniture has maintained attractive designs that meet the needs of this fashion-conscious industry at a price that is 20 percent less than what Macy's paid in 1982.

Not all resources and capabilities are core competencies. The following section discusses two approaches for identifying core competencies.

## BUILDING CORE COMPETENCIES

Two conceptual tools can help to identify and build competencies and the achievement of competitive advantage. First, we discuss four specific criteria to determine which of a firm's resources and capabilities are core competencies. These criteria are known collectively as the VRIO Framework where "V" stands for valuable, "R" means rareness, "I" is costly to imitate, and "O" is organized to be exploited. Because they have satisfied the four criteria of sustainable competitive advantage, the capabilities shown in Table 4.3 are core competencies for the firms possessing them. Following this discussion, we describe value chain analysis for deciding what value-creating competencies should be maintained, upgraded, or developed, and which activities should be outsourced.

## Criteria of Sustainable Competitive Advantage

As shown in Table 4.4, capabilities that are valuable, rare, costly to imitate (nonduplicable and nonsubstitutable), and organized to be exploited are strategic capabilities and a source of sustained competitive advantage.[69] Capabilities failing to satisfy these criteria are not core competencies. Thus, as shown in Figure 4.5, every core competence is a capability, but every capability is not a core competence.

| ■ ■ TABLE 4.4 | Four Criteria for Determining Core Competencies (Strategic Capabilities) | |
|---|---|---|
| Valuable Capabilities | Help a firm to generate revenues by exploiting opportunities and/or to reduce costs by neutralizing threats | |
| Rare Capabilities | Those capabilities possessed by a few firms in a group of competitors | |
| Costly to Imitate Capabilities (Nonduplicable and Nonsubstitutable Capabilities) | Those capabilities that an organization's closest competitors have tried to duplicate or substitute for but have found the cost of doing so greater than the benefits. Three reasons a capability may be costly to imitate are | |
| | • Historical: a unique capability such as a brand name or organizational culture that has developed along a defined historical path | |
| | • Ambiguous cause: the cause of a capability is not clear | |
| | • Social complexity: interpersonal relationships; trust and friendship among managers, employees, suppliers, customers | |
| Organized to Be Exploited | Appropriate structure to support capability | |
| | Appropriate control systems to support capability | |
| | Appropriate reward systems to support capability | |

Source: Adapted from J. B. Barney, 1997, *Gaining and Sustaining Competitive Advantage* (Don Mills, ON: Addison-Wesley Publishing Company), 145–61.

A sustained competitive advantage is achieved only when competitors have tried, without success, to duplicate, or substitute for, the benefits of a firm's strategy or when competitors lack the confidence to attempt imitation. For some period of time, a firm may earn a competitive advantage through the use of capabilities that are, for example, valuable and rare[70] but are imitable. In such an instance, the length of time a firm can expect to retain its competitive advantage is a function of how quickly competitors can successfully imitate a good, service, or process. It is only through the combination of conditions represented by all four criteria that a firm's capabilities have the potential to create a sustained competitive advantage.

■ ■ **FIGURE 4.5**

*Core Competence as a Strategic Capability*

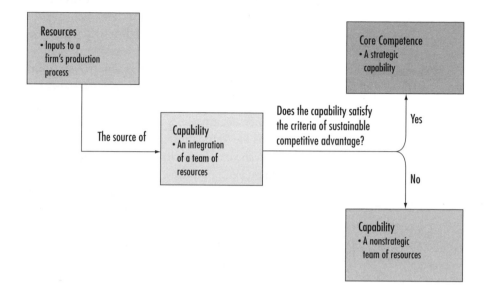

## Valuable

**Valuable capabilities** are those that create value for a firm by exploiting opportunities to generate revenues and/or neutralizing threats to reduce costs.

**Valuable capabilities** are those that create value for a firm by exploiting opportunities to generate revenues and/or neutralizing threats to reduce costs. Valuable capabilities enable a firm to formulate and implement strategies that create value for specific customers. Sony has used its valuable capabilities by dealing with the designing, manufacturing, and selling of miniaturized electronic technology to exploit a range of marketplace opportunities, including those for portable disc players and easy-to-hold 8mm video cameras.[71]

## Rare

**Rare capabilities** are those possessed by few, if any, current or potential competitors. The technical definition is that rare means that the number of competitors having the capability is less than the number of competitors required for perfect competition.

**Rare capabilities** are those possessed by few, if any, current or potential competitors. The technical definition is as follows: "rare" means that the number of competitors having the capability is less than the number of competitors required for perfect competition. A key question managers need answered when evaluating this criterion is "How many rival firms possess these valuable capabilities?" If the answer is less than the number required for perfect competition, the capability is rare. On the other hand, capabilities possessed by many rival firms are unlikely to be a source of competitive advantage for any one of them. Instead, valuable but common (i.e., not rare) resources and capabilities are sources of competitive parity.[72] Firms with valuable and rare resources and capabilities have sources of temporary competitive advantage.

## Costly to Imitate

**Costly to imitate capabilities** are those that other firms cannot duplicate or substitute for easily. Capabilities that are costly to imitate can occur because of one or a combination of three reasons (see Table 4.4).

First, a firm sometimes is able to develop capabilities because of unique historical conditions. "As firms evolve, they pick up skills, abilities, and resources that are unique to them, reflecting their particular path through history."[73] A firm with a valuable, rare, and unique organizational culture that emerged in the early stages of the company's history "... may have an imperfectly imitable advantage over firms founded in another historical period."[74]

A second condition of being costly to imitate occurs when the link between the firm's competencies and its competitive advantage is causally ambiguous.[75] In these instances, competitors are unable to understand clearly how a firm uses its competencies as the foundation for competitive advantage. As a result, competitors are uncertain about the competencies they should develop to duplicate the benefits of a competitor's value-creating strategy. Gordon Forward, CEO of a U.S. firm called Chaparral Steel, allows competitors to tour his firm's facilities. In Forward's words, competitors can be shown almost "... everything and we will be giving away nothing because they can't take it home with them."[76]

Social complexity is the third reason that capabilities can be costly to imitate. Social complexity means that at least some, and frequently many, of the firm's capabilities are the product of complex social phenomena. Examples of socially complex capabilities include interpersonal relationships, trust and friendships among managers, and a firm's reputation with suppliers and customers. Hewlett-Packard's culture is recognized widely as socially complex and as a source of sustained competitive advantage. Socially complex capabilities resulting from this culture include the nurturing of innovation across divisional boundaries and the effective use of cross-functional work teams. Recently this culture provided the capability HP needed to develop work processes through which the firm was able to improve operations dramatically in its North American distribution organization. Designed by a cross-functional work team of 35 people from HP and two other companies, the distribution centre's new work processes reduced the number of days required to deliver products to customers from 26 to 8.[77]

To better link all parts of its supply chain, Nestle Canada decided to redesign its supply chain system. As one of the nations leading food processors, Nestle Canada had traditionally managed product sourcing, manufacturing, and delivery by focusing on satisfying the intermediate parts in the supply chain. To reduce inventory costs, anticipate demand, and better meet customer needs, Nestle linked all supply chain activities—from forecasting demand to the customer's end purchase. Cross-functional groups analyzed the supply chain processes and implemented the radical process improvements in a gradual way. In a presentation to the Institute for International Research in Toronto, Tahira Hassan, a senior vice-president at Nestle Canada, stated, "people strategy has been the crux of this approach ... we believe that our employees are best able to control and contribute to lasting improvements." Significant results attributed to this redesign include a 35 percent reduction in waste and write-offs, a 50 percent drop in stock-keeping units, and a 40 percent drop in goods inventory.[78]

Other firms may find some capabilities very difficult or costly to imitate because they cannot duplicate them or substitute for them. Duplication occurs when a firm can

**Nonsubstitutable capabilities** are those that do not have a strategic equivalent.

develop a very similar capability. **Nonsubstitutable capabilities** are those that do not have strategic equivalents. A nonsubstitutable capability means that: "… there must be no strategically equivalent valuable resources that are themselves either not rare or imitable. Two valuable firm resources (or two bundles of firm resources) are strategically equivalent when they each can be exploited separately to implement the same strategies"[79] In general, the strategic value of capabilities increases the more difficult they are to substitute for or duplicate.[80] The more invisible capabilities are, the more difficult it is for firms to find substitutes and the greater the challenge is for competitors trying to imitate a firm's value-creating strategy. Firm-specific knowledge and trust-based working relationships between managers and nonmanagerial personnel are examples of capabilities that are difficult to identify and for which finding substitutes can be challenging.

## Organized to be Exploited

Being **organized to be exploited** means that firms have the correct structure, control systems, and reward systems to support each source of core competence.

The fourth criteria in our search for core competencies is organized to be exploited. Being **organized to be exploited** means that firms have the correct structure, control systems, and reward systems to support each source of core competence. If a firm is pursuing a product differentiation strategy that is difficult for competitors to imitate, it is important that the structure, controls, and rewards be as follows. Appropriate structural characteristics for product differentiation are cross-functional/cross-divisional linkages, willingness to utilize new structures to take advantage of new opportunities, and willingness to have isolated areas of intense creative efforts. Control systems need to be flexible in the way they control activities, make allowances for creative people, and allow learning from innovative failures. Reward systems should not punish for failure but reward for risk-taking and creative flair, and be qualitative and subjective in measuring performance.[81]

If a firm wanted to pursue a cost leadership strategy that competitors would have difficulty imitating, the structure, control systems, and reward systems should be as follows. Structurally, the firm should have few layers in its reporting system, reporting relationships should be simple, and there should be a disciplined focus on a narrow range of business functions. The control system should be one where there is tight cost control; quantitative cost objectives; closely supervised labour, raw material, inventory, and other costs; and a philosophy of cost leadership. Compensation policies should reward for reducing costs, and there should be incentives for all firm members to be involved in reducing costs.[82] Additionally, it is as critical for sources of competitive parity and temporary competitive advantage to be organized to be exploited as it is for sources of sustained competitive advantage (see Table 4.5).

To summarize, sustained competitive advantages result only through the use of capabilities that are valuable, rare, costly to imitate, and organized to be exploited. Table 4.5 shows the competitive consequences and performance implications resulting from combinations of the four criteria of sustainability. The analysis suggested by the contents of the table helps managers determine the strategic value of the firm's capabilities. Resources and capabilities falling into the first row in the table (that is, resources and capabilities that aren't valuable or rare and that are imitable and for which strategic substitutes exist) are ones the firm should not emphasize to formulate and implement strategies. In fact, organizing to support these capabilities may lead to a sustained competitive disadvantage. Capabilities yielding competitive parity and those yielding either temporary or sustained competitive advantage need to be organized to be exploited.

## ■ TABLE 4.5   Outcomes from Combinations of the Criteria for Sustained Competitive Advantage: The VRIO Framework

**Is the resource or capability ...**

| Valuable? | Rare? | Costly to Imitate? | Organized to be Exploited? | Competitive Consequences | Performance Implications |
|---|---|---|---|---|---|
| No | — | — | No | Competitive Disadvantage | Below-Average Returns |
| Yes | No | — | Yes | Competitive Parity | Average Returns |
| Yes | Yes | No | Yes | Temporary Competitive Advantage | Above-Average Returns |
| Yes | Yes | Yes | Yes | Sustained Competitive Advantage | Above-Average Returns |

Source: Adapted from J. B. Barney, 1997, *Gaining and Sustaining Competitive Advantage* (Don Mills, ON: Addison-Wesley Publishing Company), 167.

Otherwise, the potential performance may not be achieved. Large competitors such as Coca-Cola and PepsiCo may have some capabilities that can yield only competitive parity. In such cases, the firms will organize to exploit and nurture these capabilities while simultaneously organizing to exploit those that can yield either a temporary or sustainable competitive advantage.

What about Toyota's advantage in new product development and production systems in the Strategic Focus? First, Toyota's strategy appears to create value because the firm has been successful selling its designs at a low cost. Its production systems and new product development capabilities are obviously rare. Others have had difficulty reproducing this system even though many competitor executives have visited Toyota plants. Although the techniques may not be causally ambiguous, Toyota's system is socially complex. Furthermore, the firm continues to learn and maintain its early advantage in

## STRATEGIC FOCUS

### Toyota's New Product Development and Production Systems Are Difficult to Imitate

Toyota's secret of competitive success has been its new product development and production systems. Two days a month, more than 50 auto executives and engineers travel to Toyota's large manufacturing complex, in Georgetown, Kentucky. The five-hour tours include an intensive question and answer session for visiting executives of competing car companies. Even though Toyota shows competitors how it makes cars, no other company has bettered Toyota as the most efficient auto company in the world. DaimlerChrysler has sophisticated engineering and

*continued*

excellent styling; Honda has excellent engine technology; but Toyota sets the standard in efficiency, quality, and productivity.

Furthermore, because speed is increasingly important in the 21st century, new CEO Hiroshi Okuda seeks to make Toyota even more efficient. Okuda intends to not only increase Toyota's global market share but also improve its operating margins. In Japan, Toyota has set a 40 percent market share as its goal while its closest rival, Nissan, currently has 22 percent. Toyota currently ranks fourth in unit sales behind the Big Three in the United States with an 8 percent share. Okuda has set a goal of 10 percent market share in the United States. Competitors understand the techniques and practices Toyota uses but cannot reproduce the firm's production system. Although the principles of Toyota's productivity are not complicated, its implementation and coordination require "an incredible amount of detail, planning, discipline, hard work and painstaking attention to detail." Therefore, although the production system is not causally ambiguous, it is highly socially complex. What makes imitation of the production system even more difficult is that Toyota continues to improve its own system.

Some believe that Toyota's exceptional strength lies in its ability to learn. Its employees are always problem conscious and strongly customer oriented, resulting in the company's ability to learn from its mistakes and improve continuously. Although the 1997 Previa was an engineering marvel, it was powered by a small engine, and buyers found it sluggish and too expensive at $44,000. In response, in 1998, Toyota unveiled the Sienna XLE, which may not be an engineering marvel but does have a larger engine, inventive technology, and a $32,000 price tag.

Toyota's new product development is unrivalled in the industry, producing a new car in 18 months. Some U.S. competitors are down to 30 months. Besides its speed at producing a new model, Toyota now develops similar models simultaneously, unlike the industry approach, which is to develop a sedan and then follow sequentially with a coupe or some other variety. Through this method, Toyota has doubled its engineering output over the past four years while increasing its budget by only 20 percent.

Toyota is also excelling as the first automaker to sell a mass-production vehicle with a hybrid engine. A hybrid engine combines gasoline engine technology with an electric motor that receives electricity both from a battery pack and from the car's movement. Using this technology, the Prius gets 66 miles per gallon and generates half the normal amount of carbon dioxide. Toyota hopes to produce 1000 cars a month even though the Prius won't be profitable because it costs twice as much to make as its $17,900 price tag. Toyota has also provided a breakthrough in engine design by designing a 120-horsepower engine for its 1998 Corolla that uses 25 percent fewer parts, making it 10 percent lighter and 10 percent more fuel efficient. This allowed Toyota to slash the price of its 1998 Corolla by $1500 compared to its 1997 model. Toyota realizes that it is also dependent on its suppliers. As such, "it has consciously institutionalized a set of practices for transferring knowledge between itself and the suppliers, so that the whole group learns faster." On average, Toyota's independent suppliers are 59 miles from its assembly plants. By comparison, GM's supplier average is 425 miles from the plants they serve, resulting in a larger inventory for both the supplier and General Motors' plants.

*continued*

Although Toyota is unparalleled in productivity, the firm has had difficulty establishing its systems for production and product development outside Japan. Therefore, Toyota remains Japan-centric. In the long run, this is likely to be a strong hindrance to future growth. In its Georgetown complex, decisions are often referred back to Tokyo, creating a problem of relatively high turnover at the Georgetown complex. Toyota realizes that with the Japanese market quite saturated, growth will have to come in international markets; therefore, the company is pursuing foreign direct investment. As such, production in Japan has dipped from the peak of 4.0 million in 1991 to 3.4 million in 1996. Notwithstanding the difficulties, no one has been able to determine how to duplicate Toyota's product development and production systems.

Sources: A. Taylor III, 1997, How Toyota defies gravity, *Fortune*, December 8, 100–08; A. Pollack, 1997, At Toyota, ten percent share is viewed as a start, http://www.nytimes.com, October 24; M. Krebs, 1997, Toyota ahead of pack on hybrid production, http://www.nytimes.com, July 25; B. Bremner, L. Armstrong, K. Kerwin, and K. Naughton, 1997, Toyota's crusade, *BusinessWeek*, http://www.businessweek.com, April 7.

efficient production systems and new product development. Establishing early advantage and maintaining that advantage will be discussed more fully in Chapter 6. Also, because of the complexity and idiosyncrasy of Toyota's production system, the system is nonsubstitutable. In fact, as we will see in the next Strategic Focus, Toyota has had trouble transferring its production system to other locations such as the Georgetown facility in Kentucky.

The Gap, a specialty retailer, operates more than 1600 company outlets, many of them in Canada, under The Gap, GapKids, Banana Republic, and Old Navy store names. Through the presentation of dressed-down clothes at affordable prices, the firm is thought to have revolutionized the casual-apparel market for women, men, and children. The firm relied on various capabilities to develop competitive advantages in terms of its attention to quality and design and the use of clever advertising slogans and campaigns. To exploit what it saw as an opportunity to serve customers interested in dressed-down clothes but unable to afford The Gap's goods, the firm decided to use its capabilities and competencies to establish Old Navy stores.[83]

What type of advantage, if any, results from the use of some of The Gap's capabilities such as product design and quality, creative advertising, and store design and layout to develop the Old Navy format? It seems that the capabilities being used in this new retailing format are valuable and rare, but at least with respect to The Gap's major competitors, these capabilities can be imitated. For example, The Gap's CEO suggested that "… there are no secrets in retailing. The minute something new—a store or a look—is created in this industry, it is instantly visible, there for all the world to examine and replicate."[84] Strategic equivalents for these capabilities may or may not exist. Thus, an analysis of these capabilities suggests that The Gap has established a temporary competitive advantage with its Old Navy stores (see Table 4.5). In terms of the performance implications, the firm should earn above-average returns until competitors learn how to duplicate the value Old Navy stores creates through exploitation of The Gap's capabilities.

In the next section, we discuss another framework firms use to examine their resources and capabilities to discover core competencies. Value chain analysis allows the firm to understand the parts of its operations (see Figure 4.2) that create value and those that do not. We use the value chain to identify resources and capabilities and then use the VRIO framework to assess the competitive and performance implications of each identified resource and capability. Together, these two frameworks are a powerful tool, and understanding these frameworks is important because the firm earns above-average returns only when the value it creates is greater than the costs incurred to create that value.[85] It is recommended that the two frameworks be used interactively.

## Value Chain Analysis

The value chain is a template that firms use to understand their cost position and to identify the multiple means that might be used to facilitate the implementation of their business-level strategy.[86] As shown in Figure 4.6, a firm's value chain can be segmented into primary and support activities. **Primary activities** comprise a product's physical creation, its sale and distribution to buyers, and its service after the sale. **Support activities** provide the support necessary for the primary activities to take place. The value chain shows how a product moves from the raw material stage to the final customer. For individual firms, the essential idea of the value chain "… is to add as much value as possible as cheaply as possible, and, most important, to capture that value." In a globally competitive economy, " … the most valuable links on the chain tend to belong to people who own knowledge—particularly about customers."[87]

**Primary activities** comprise a product's physical creation, its sale and distribution to buyers, and its service after the sale.
**Support activities** provide the support necessary for the primary activities to take place.

■ ■ **FIGURE 4.6**

*The Basic Value Chain*

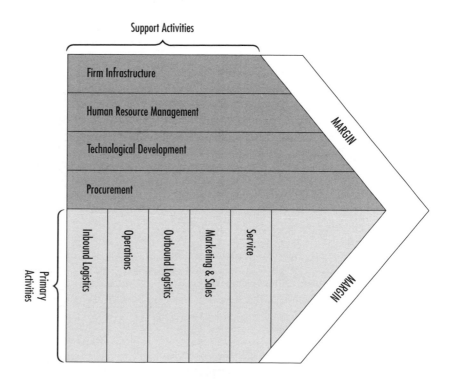

Table 4.6 lists the items to be studied to assess the value-creating potential of primary activities. Table 4.7 shows the items to consider when studying support activities. As with the analysis of primary activities, the intent in examining these items is to determine areas where the firm has potential to create and capture value. Every item in each table should be evaluated with competitors' capabilities in mind. To be a source of competitive advantage, a resource or capability must allow a firm to (1) perform an activity in a manner that is superior to competitors' performances or (2) perform a value-creating activity that competitors cannot complete. Only under these conditions does a firm create value for customers and have opportunities to capture that value. Sometimes, this requires firms to reconfigure or recombine parts of the value chain in unique ways. As shown in Figure 4.7, Federal Express (FedEx) changed the nature of the delivery business by reconfiguring both its outbound logistics (primary activity) and human resource management (support activity) to originate the overnight delivery business, creating value for itself in the process of doing so.

---

### ■ ■ TABLE 4.6 — Examining the Value-Creating Potential of Primary Activities

**Inbound Logistics**

Activities, such as materials handling, warehousing, and inventory control, used to receive, store, and disseminate inputs to a product.

**Operations**

Activities necessary to convert the inputs provided by inbound logistics into final product form. Machining, packaging, assembly, and equipment maintenance are examples of operations activities.

**Outbound Logistics**

Activities involved with collecting, storing, and physically distributing the final product to customers. Examples of these activities include finished-goods warehousing, materials handling, and order processing.

**Marketing and Sales**

Activities completed to provide means through which customers can purchase products after being induced to do so. To effectively market and sell products, firms develop advertising and promotional campaigns, select appropriate distribution channels, and select, develop, and support their sales force.

**Customer Service**

Activities designed to enhance or maintain a product's value. Firms engage in a range of service-related activities, including installation, repair, training, and adjustment.

Each activity should be examined relative to competitors' abilities. This is accomplished by using the VRIO Framework in Table 4.5.

Source: Adapted with the permission of The Free Press, a division of Simon & Schuster from *Competitive Advantage: Creating and Sustaining Superior Performance* by Michael E. Porter, pp. 39–40, Copyright © 1985 by Michael E. Porter.

■ ■ **FIGURE 4.7**

*Increased Value in Human Resource Management and Outbound Logistics Created a Core Competency for Federal Express*

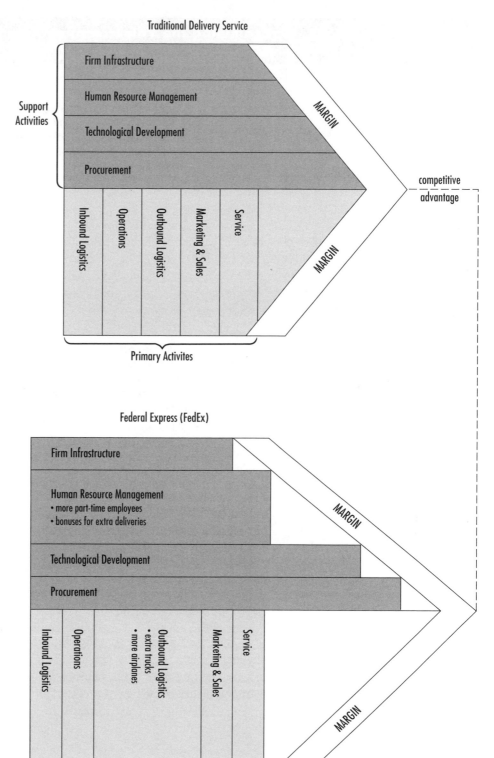

| ■ ■ **TABLE 4.7** | **Examining the Value-creating Potential of Support Activities** |
| --- | --- |

**Procurement**

Activities completed to purchase the inputs needed to produce a firm's products. Purchased inputs include items fully consumed during the manufacture of products (e.g., raw materials and supplies as well as fixed assets—machinery, laboratory equipment, office equipment, and buildings). Are these inputs purchased at a reasonable cost, at a reasonable level of quality, and within an appropriate period of time?

**Technological Development**

Activities completed to improve a firm's product and the processes used to manufacture it. Technology development takes many forms, such as process equipment, design, basic research and product design, and servicing procedures.

**Human Resource Management**

Activities involved with recruiting, hiring, training, developing, and compensating all personnel.

**Firm Infrastructure**

Firm infrastructure includes activities such as general management, planning, finance, accounting, legal support, and governmental relations that are required to support the work of the entire value chain. Through its infrastructure, the firm strives to effectively and consistently identify external opportunities and threats, identify resources and capabilities, and support core competencies.

Each activity should be examined relative to competitors' abilities. This is accomplished by using the VRIO Framework in Table 4.5.

Source: Adapted with the permission of The Free Press, a division of Simon & Schuster from *Competitive Advantage: Creating and Sustaining Superior Performance* by Michael E. Porter, pp. 40–43, Copyright © 1985 by Michael E. Porter.

The opportunity to purchase automobiles through on-line computer networks is an example of firms' efforts to reconfigure the value chain, especially in terms of primary activities. Some companies are using the capabilities of the Internet to sell cars in cyberspace. Companies such as Dell are providing opportunities for customers to buy computers through the Internet and are reconfiguring the value chain in a way that allows these firms to create and capture value.[88]

Rating a firm's capacities to execute the primary and support activities is challenging. Earlier in the chapter, we noted that identifying and assessing the value of a firm's resources and capabilities requires judgment. Judgment is equally necessary when using value chain analysis because there is no obviously correct model or rule available to help in this process. Moreover, most data available for these evaluations are largely anecdotal, sometimes unreliable, or difficult to interpret.

An effective value chain analysis results in the identification of new ways to perform activities to create value. In the Strategic Focus on Costco, we see a firm that has been able to focus on appropriate aspects of the value chain. This concentration has created significant value for customers and shareholders alike. Because the innovations employed at Costco are firm specific—that is, they are grounded in a company's unique way of combining its resources and capabilities—they are difficult for competitors to recognize, understand, and imitate. The greater the time necessary for competitors to understand how a firm is creating and capturing value through its execution of primary and support activities, the more sustainable is the competitive advantage gained by the innovating company.

## STRATEGIC FOCUS

### Costco Companies: The Retail Warehouse Store Revolution

Even in such an unattractive, low-margin business as warehouse retailing, there is room for strong competence and competitive advantage, as evidenced by the Costco approach. A familiar name to Canadians, Costco operates an international chain of Costco and Price Club warehouse membership stores. The company seeks to carry quality brand-name merchandise at substantially lower prices than those found at other conventional warehouse and retail outlets. Although Costco's warehouse approach offers one of the largest product category selections found under a single roof, it has only about 4000 stock-keeping units (SKUs). Comparatively, K-mart and Wal-Mart will carry 40 000 to 60 000. Therefore, Costco's approach focuses on stocking a few branded items in each category such that, in essence, it has done the comparison shopping for its customer. Costco demands the best prices from the vendors and passes these savings on to customers through very low margins. Costco's gross margins were about 10 percent in the early part of 2000. Its closest competitor is Wal-Mart, at about 20 percent.

Costco's approach also entails competitively pricing of expensive items and trying to create repeat business. Furthermore, its vendors largely finance Costco's inventory. For instance, Costco's accounts payable is 80 percent of its inventory, while at Wal-Mart the ratio is 48 percent. Thus, relative to Wal-Mart, Costco requires little working capital.

In addition to well-regarded brand-name items, Costco stocks over 200 private-label items that account for 11 percent of sales. It also sells top-quality products using its Kirkland signature brand. Costco also seeks to build customer trust through its Signature label. For instance, the firm sells a superior Procter & Gamble paper towel because the private-label brand was an inferior product. Costco does not offer extended service warranties or service contracts on appliances because "In our view, those programs are a rip-off." In addition, as James D. Sinegal, the current CEO, indicates, they also try to give before they get. "One way or another, the vendor is going to cheat you if you take too much out of his hide." Therefore, Costco managers try to cooperate with vendors to help them reduce margins and offer valuable suggestions for increasing product value and reducing manufacturing cost.

Costco also promotes from within. Sinegal is an example, having started in the warehouse working under Sol Price, who founded the Price Club chain in 1976. There are very few formal meetings and virtually no bureaucracy. For

*continued*

instance, there is no press or investor relations' staff. Virtually all of the firm's energy is dedicated to the value chain activities of buying and merchandising products. Costco also has a line of periphery stores that provides pharmaceutical, optical, automotive, and business services, which compete with Kinko's in some areas.

As a result of Costco's strategic approach, even with very low margins, it earned about 11 percent return on capital, which is near Wal-Mart's 13 percent. Costco's membership renewal rate is 97 percent among active small businesses. That type of loyalty is more than the average patient's loyalty to physicians. Costco also seeks to screen members (a support activity) to reduce bad cheques and shrinkage (loss to pilferage), which is only 2 percent of sales. This level is one-tenth of that of many supermarkets and is a significant way to hold down overhead costs. Costco can drive down margins so low relative to its competitors that it creates significant and cascading amounts of value for its customers.

Sources: Costco, 2000, *Costco Wholesale* home page, http://www.costco.com (Retrieved June 29); Hoovers, 2000, Form 10Q for Costco Wholesale Corp., filed June 14, 2000, Hoovers Online, http://www.hoovers.com/cgi-bin/offsite? (Retrieved June 29); http://www.edgar-online.com/brand/hoovers/search/?cik=0000909832; T.W. Ferguson, 1997, A revolution that has a long way to go, Forbes, August 11, 106–12; Costco, 1997, *Costco Companies home page*, http://www.pricecostco.com, (Retrieved December 5); Costco companies on the Forbes 500, 1997, http://www.forbes.com, (Retrieved December 11).

What should a firm do with respect to primary and support activities in which its resources and capabilities are not a source of competence and competitive advantage? For instance, if Costco moves too far from its competencies with its periphery stores, it may consider using subcontractors. In these instances, as discussed next, firms should study the possibility of outsourcing the work associated with primary and support activities in which they cannot create and capture value.

## OUTSOURCING

**Outsourcing** is the purchase of a value-creating activity from an external supplier.

**Outsourcing** is the purchase of a value-creating activity from an external supplier. In the view of one consultant, "outsourcing is a strategic concept—a way to add value to the business that converts an in-house cost centre into a customer-focused service operation."[89] Sometimes, virtually all firms within an industry seek the strategic value that can be captured through effective outsourcing. The automobile manufacturing industry is an example of this. Based on an observation of the outsourcing trend in this industry, an analyst concluded that the "whole strategy worldwide now in the auto industry is to get down to your core vehicle-producing operations … That means shedding everything but stamping, powertrains and final assembly … and getting rid of everything that doesn't contribute to those areas."[90]

Several statistics demonstrate the increasing scope of outsourcing. A GR2 Research study indicated in 1997 that Canadian companies spent $442 million outsourcing customer service. This trend is mirrored in the United States where a Dun & Bradstreet report indicated that customer service outsourcing was increasing by 26 percent per year and that firms that outsourced were financially stronger. The Outsourcing Institute, an international organization studying strategic outsourcing, states that "of the US$164 billion estimated to be spent on outsourcing services in 1998, almost US$7 billion will be attributable to customer service functions … and this number is expected to more than double by 2001 to almost US$15 billion."[91] For example, Dun & Bradstreet estimated that global outsourcing would increase to $180 billion in 1998; a 23 percent increase from $146 billion in 1997. Approximately two-thirds of this amount was to come from North American companies.[92] Outsourcing has been one of the trends that has increased the importance of cooperative strategy (e.g., the more frequent use of strategic alliances, as described in Chapter 10).

Perhaps the major reason outsourcing is being used prominently is that few, if any, firms possess the resources and capabilities required to achieve competitive superiority in all primary and support activities. With respect to technologies, for example, research suggests that few companies can afford to develop internally all the technologies that might lead to competitive advantage in the future. By nurturing a few core competencies, a firm increases its probability of developing a competitive advantage. Additionally, by outsourcing activities in which it lacks capabilities, the firm can concentrate fully on those areas in which it can create value.[93]

Smithkline Beecham sells over 400 products all over the world, including well-known Aquafresh, and Gaviscon. Smithkline used to manufacture some of its pharmaceutical products at a Weston, Ontario plant. Now it outsources this manufacturing to companies such as Patheon of Mississauga, Ontario, which offers core manufacturing and integrated supply chain activities. By hiring Patheon, Smithkline can focus on its core capabilities of marketing and research and development and access Patheon's core product development and manufacturing capabilities.[94]

When outsourcing, a firm seeks the greatest value. In other words, a company wants to outsource only to firms possessing a core competence in terms of performing the primary or support activity that is being outsourced. For companies to whom others outsource, being able to create value is the pathway through which they achieve strategic competitiveness and earn above-average returns.

When evaluating resources and capabilities, firms must be careful not to decide to outsource activities in which they can create and capture value. Additionally, companies should not outsource primary and support activities that are used to neutralize environmental threats or complete necessary ongoing organizational tasks. Called "sources of comparative parity" and a "nonstrategic team of resources" in Figure 4.5, firms must verify that they do not outsource capabilities that are critical to their success, even though the capabilities are not actual sources of competitive advantage.

Another risk of outsourcing concerns the firm's knowledge base. As discussed earlier in the chapter, knowledge continues to increase in importance as a source of competence and competitive advantage for firms in the new competitive landscape. In part, organizations learn through a continuous and integrated sharing of experiences employees have as they perform primary and support activities. One reason for the success of a learning organization is that with continuous and integrated sharing of experiences, it is able to evaluate thoroughly the ongoing validity of the key assumptions it holds about the nature and future of its business operations. Outsourcing activities in which the firm cannot create value can have an unintended consequence of damaging the firm's potential to continuously evaluate its key assumptions, learn, and create new capabilities and core competencies. Therefore, managers should verify that the firm does not outsource activities that stimulate the development of new capabilities and competencies.[95]

Occasionally, a firm discovers that areas in which it could perhaps develop a competence can and should be outsourced. This may happen when managers believe their firms lack the skills required to develop a core competence in a particular area. As a result, managers may decide to outsource these activities so the firm can focus on its true core competencies. Bank of Montreal decided to retain ownership of a strategic competency but to outsource it through a wholly owned subsidiary. In 1996, the bank established Cebra. Cebra provides e-commerce solutions through its business advisory services and develops e-commerce alliances. In November 1999, Cebra and Canada Post launched EPOST, a web service that allows consumers and businesses to electronically send and receive mail, pay bills, and find information. Cebra has also helped develop MERX, Canada's Electronic Tendering Service, which gives bidders access to public procurement opportunities.[96] In the next section, important cautions about core competencies are discussed.

## CORE COMPETENCIES—CAUTIONS AND REMINDERS

An attractive attribute of a firm's core competencies is that, unlike physical assets, they tend to become more valuable through additional use. A key reason for this is that they are largely knowledge based.[97] Sharing knowledge across people, jobs, and organizational functions often results in an expansion of that knowledge in competitively relevant ways.[98] On the other hand, evidence and company experiences show that the value of core competencies as sources of competitive advantage should never be taken for granted. Moreover, the ability of any particular core competence to provide competitive advantage on a permanent basis should not be assumed. The reason for these cautions is due to the central dilemma that is associated with the use of core competencies as sources of competitive advantage; all core capabilities simultaneously have the potential to be core rigidities. All capabilities, then, are both strengths and weaknesses. They are strengths because they are a source of competitive advantage and, hence, strategic competitiveness; they are weaknesses because if emphasized when they are no longer competitively relevant, they can be the seeds of organizational inertia.[99] Additionally, as explained in the Strategic Focus on Toyota, some capabilities may be difficult to transfer even within the firm.[100] Toyota has had difficulties in transferring its productions systems to a North American environment.

Events occurring in the firm's external environment create conditions through which core competencies can become core rigidities and create inertia. "Often the flip side, the dark side, of core capabilities is revealed due to external events when new competitors figure out a better way to serve the firm's customers, when new technologies emerge, or when political or social events shift the ground underneath."[101] It really isn't changes in the external environment that cause core capabilities to become core rigidities; rather, it is strategic myopia and inflexibility on the part of a firm's managers. Strategic myopia results in core competencies being emphasized to the point that strategic inertia strangles the firm's ability to grow and to adapt to environmental changes.[102]

The tenure top managers have with a firm may affect their propensity to initiate change. Studies have found that as top management team tenure increases, past actions are increasingly used to guide future decisions, group norms and pressures for conformity are created, individuals with similar experiences and perspectives are hired, and a greater attachment to established policies and practices is exhibited. All of these behaviours increase the likelihood that rather than being a catalyst for organizational change, experienced managers may become a disproportionate source of organizational inertia.[103]

Managers operating in the new competitive landscape must remember that core competencies that are allowed to become core rigidities prevent the firm from changing when necessary. Firms that have achieved strategic competitiveness and earned above-average returns for extended periods of time are sometimes hesitant to change what they are doing. Capabilities are competencies only when they are strategically relevant; that is, when their use permits exploitation of opportunities in the external environment. Rapid and significant changes in the global economy prevent firms from permanently exploiting the same competencies. Firms failing to recognize this reality may quickly find themselves at a competitive disadvantage. Thus, executives must seek to strike a balance between nurturing and supporting existing core competencies while simultaneously encouraging the type of forthright appraisals that will cause the development of new competencies.

Figure 4.8 summarizes how competitive advantage declines. A firm may not adapt well to changes in the external environment, its core competencies may be substituted for by other firms, and/or it may be imitated by competitors.

■ ■ **FIGURE 4.8**

*Declining Competitive Advantage*

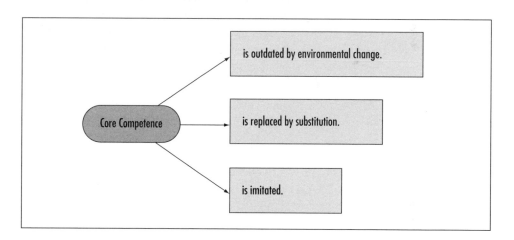

## STRATEGIC INPUTS AND STRATEGIC ACTIONS

As shown in Figure 1.1 in Chapter 1, the results gained through analyses of the external and internal environments provide the strategic inputs a firm needs to develop its strategic intent and strategic mission. The value of intent and mission is that they describe what a firm seeks to achieve in light of its internal competencies and external opportunities.

To close our discussion of strategic inputs, we offer a few final comments about intent and mission. Defined in Chapter 1, strategic intent is the leveraging of a firm's resources, capabilities, and core competencies (hereafter called capabilities for the purposes of this discussion) to accomplish the firm's goals in the competitive environment.[104] Recent evidence suggests that successful firms competing in the global economy have learned how to leverage their capabilities to reach challenging goals.[105]

Strategic managers are challenged to stimulate the formation of stretch goals for each employee, even when some may not understand the importance of doing so.

Individual stretch goals must be consistent with the objective embedded within the firm's strategic intent. When employees are motivated by a well-articulated strategic intent, properly established stretch goals leverage all of a firm's capabilities and may create future success for both individual employees and their firm.[106] Moreover, when handled correctly, pursuing accomplishment of a firm's strategic intent "... causes employees to perform in ways they never imagined possible."[107]

The thoughts of an assistant brand manager at Procter & Gamble's location in Rotterdam, Netherlands, describe positive outcomes from the application of strategic intent. When first exposed to the firm's strategic intent, this employee thought, "You've got to be kidding!" Yet after working toward his personal stretch goals, which were consistent with the firm's strategic intent, he concluded that the concept works. Describing his view about intent, the employee stated that "Even though I might not reach a specific goal, I do get near it, and that is a greater achievement than I would ever have expected."[108]

Accenture (formerly Andersen Consulting) is a firm stretching its capabilities to reach its strategic intent. Viewing itself as the "world's premier business and technology consultancy," the firm intends to become the world's first and foremost full-service consulting emporium, capable of serving clients by rewiring computer systems, recrafting strategies, reeducating employees, and reengineering work processes. Accenture's work in 46 countries reflects its commitment to remain what some believe is the leading global consulting firm.[109] The capabilities Accenture uses to achieve its strategic intent include knowledge, skills, and experiences in terms of logistics and operations strategies, total supply chain management processes, and information and technology strategies.[110] Challenging as it should be, this strategic intent may be reached through effective use of Accenture's capabilities and core competencies.

Strategic intent defines the framework for a firm's strategic mission. The strategic mission is a statement of a firm's unique purpose and the scope of its operations in product and market terms.[111] Because it specifies the products a firm will offer in particular markets, and presents a framework within which the firm will work, the strategic mission is an application of strategic intent.[112] In one small private school, for example, the strategic intent is the vigorous pursuit of excellence. The strategic mission flowing from this intent is to serve intellectually gifted and/or highly motivated students from a six-county region seeking a college preparatory educational experience.

In the case of all firms and organizations, once formulated, the strategic intent and strategic mission are the basis for the development of business-level, corporate-level, acquisition, restructuring, international, and cooperative strategies (see Chapter 5 and Chapters 7 through 10). The first of these strategy types—business-level strategy—is discussed in the next chapter.

# SUMMARY

- In the new competitive landscape, traditional conditions and factors, including labour costs and effective access to financial resources and raw materials, can still provide a competitive advantage but to a lesser degree. In this new landscape, a firm's internal environment (that is, its resources, capabilities, and core competencies) may have a stronger influence on the development of competitive advantage and the formulation and implementation of strategies than do the characteristics and conditions of the external environment. But no competitive advantage lasts forever. Over time, benefits provided by all competitive advantages can be substituted for or duplicated. Because of this, firms are challenged to exploit their current competitive advantages while simultaneously using their resources, capabilities, and core competencies to develop advantages that will be relevant in the future.

- Effective management of core competencies requires careful analysis of a firm's resources (inputs to the production process) and capabilities (capacities for teams of resources to perform a task or activity integratively). To complete these analyses successfully, strategic managers must be self-confident, courageous, and willing to hold people accountable for their work.

- Individually, resources are typically not sources of competitive advantage. Capabilities, which result from groupings of both tangible and intangible resources, are more likely to yield an advantage. A key reason for this is that how the firm forms, nurtures, and organizes to exploit core competencies that are grounded in capabilities is less visible to competitors and, hence, more difficult to understand and costly to imitate.

- The skills and knowledge of the firm's human capital may be the primary basis for all of its capabilities. Capabilities of this type emerge by developing human capital and sharing information regarding how tangible and intangible resources can be combined in strategically relevant ways.

- Not all of the firm's capabilities are core competencies. Only capabilities that are valuable, rare, costly to imitate, and organized to be exploited are sources of sustained competitive advantage and, as such, can be selected as core competencies. Over time, core competencies must be sup-

ported and nurtured, but they cannot be allowed to become core rigidities. Competencies result in competitive advantage over the firm's rivals only when they allow the firm to create value by exploiting external environmental opportunities. When this is no longer the case, the firm's attention must be shifted to other capabilities that do satisfy the four criteria of sustained competitive advantage.

- Value chain analysis is used to identify and evaluate a firm's resources and capabilities. By studying their primary and support activities, firms better understand their cost structure and the activities in which they can create and capture value. Once resources and capabilities are identified by using the value chain, each should be analyzed using the VRIO framework to assess whether they are sources of competitive disadvantage, competitive parity, temporary competitive advantage, or sustained competitive advantage.

- In the cases of primary and support activities that must be performed, but for which the firm lacks the resources and capabilities required to create value, outsourcing is considered. Used frequently in the new competitive landscape, outsourcing is the purchase of a value-creating activity from an external supplier. The firm should outsource only to companies that possess a competitive advantage in terms of the primary or support activity being outsourced. Strategic managers must verify that their firm does not outsource activities in which it can create and capture value. As well, firms must avoid outsourcing nonstrategic capabilities that are not a source of competitive advantage yet are important to the firm's ongoing efforts to develop continuously value-adding knowledge.

- Strategic intent and strategic mission are grounded in the results obtained through analyses of the firm's external and internal environments. Taken together, the results of environmental analyses and the formation of the firm's strategic intent and mission provide the information needed to formulate and implement an array of strategies, including business-level, corporate-level, acquisition, restructuring, international, and cooperative.

# REVIEW QUESTIONS

1. Why is it important for firms to study and gain an understanding of their internal environment?
2. What is value? How do firms earn value, and why is it important that they be able to do so?
3. What are the differences between tangible and intangible resources? Which of these two categories of resources typically contributes more to the development of competitive advantage, and why?
4. What are capabilities? How are capabilities developed?
5. What are the four criteria used to determine which of a firm's resources and capabilities are its core competencies? Why is it important for strategic managers to use these criteria?
6. How is value chain analysis used in organizations? What knowledge can strategic managers gain by using value chain analysis?
7. What is outsourcing? Why is it so valuable to companies competing in the new competitive landscape?
8. Why is it important for firms to prevent their core competencies from becoming core rigidities?
9. What is the relationship between strategic inputs and strategic actions?

# DISCUSSION QUESTIONS

1. Several companies are discussed in the opening case. Which of these companies are likely to have a sustained competitive advantage based on their human resource management capability?
2. Select a store in your local community from which you purchase items. Ask one of the store's strategic managers to describe the value the firm provides to its customers. Do you agree with the strategic manager's assessment? Did the manager describe the value for which you pay when purchasing goods or services from this store? If not, what might account for the difference in opinions?
3. For an organization or club in which you are a member, prepare a list of what you think are its tangible and intangible resources. Using the categories shown in Tables 4.1 and 4.2, group the resources you identified. Show your list to other members of your organization and ask for their assessment. Did they agree with your groupings? If not, why not?

4. Refer to the third question. Was it easier for you to list the tangible or intangible resources? Why?
5. What competitive advantage does your college or university or your place of employment possess? On what core competencies is this advantage based? What evidence can you provide to support your opinions?

# ETHICS QUESTIONS

1. Can an emphasis on developing a competitive advantage result in unethical practices such as the use of questionable techniques to gather information about competitors? If so, do you believe these unethical practices occur frequently? Provide evidence to support your opinion.
2. Can ethical practices facilitate development of a brand name and a corporate reputation? If so, explain how. If not, explain why not.
3. Ethically, are strategic managers challenged to use their firm's resources to help train members of their society to reduce the shortage of skilled workers in their country? Why or why not?
4. What, if any, ethical dilemmas are associated with the use of outsourcing? How should strategic managers deal with them?
5. What ethical issues do strategic managers face when they conclude that their firm cannot earn above-average returns if thousands of employees are not laid off?

# INTERNET EXERCISE

Go to the *Coca-Cola home page* at:
**http://www.coca-cola.com**

Search the Internet for information on Coca-Cola. After you have completed your search, make a list of the company's tangible and intangible resources (see Tables 4.1 and 4.2). How do both sets of resources contribute to Coca-Cola's sustained competitive advantage?

## STRATEGIC SURFING

An increasing number of companies are establishing "internal" or "corporate" universities to facilitate their training needs and help build core competencies. Corporations are using this innovative concept to strengthen their internal environments. Following are several examples of corporate universities:

Motorola University: **http://www.mot.com/MU**
Sears University:
**http://www.sears.com/company/hr/suniv.html**
Dell University:
**http://www.dell.com/dell/careers/benefits/ dellu.htm**
Intel University: **http://wiche.edu/telecom/ membership/Sharing/forms/techintel.html**

## NOTES

1   M. A. Huselid, S. E. Jackson, and R. S. Schuler, 1997, Technical and strategic human resource management effectiveness as determinants of firm performance, *Academy of Management Journal,* 40: 171–88; R. O. Parker and T. E. Brown, 2000, People practices & shareholder value, *Ivey Business Journal,* January/February, 20–26.

2   D. J. Teece, G. Pisano, and A. Shuen, 1997, Dynamic capabilities and strategic management, *Strategic Management Journal,* 18: 509–534; R. G. McGrath, I. C. MacMillan, and S. Venkataraman, 1995, Defining and developing competence: A strategic process paradigm, *Strategic Management Journal,* 16: 251–75.

3   B. Morris, 1996, The brand's the thing, *Fortune,* March 4, 72–80.

4   P. Sellers, 1996, Can Home Depot fix its sagging stock? *Fortune,* March 4, 139–46; The Eagle has crashed, 1994, The Eagle has crashed: Flag-waving Revy blows a US competitor out of the big box hardware market, *Western Report,* November 28, 18–19.

5   P. C. Godfrey and C. W. L. Hill, 1995, The problem of unobservables in strategic management research, *Strategic Management Journal,* 16: 519–33.

6   D. Leonard-Barton, 1995, *Wellsprings of Knowledge: Building and Sustaining the Sources of Innovation* (Boston: Harvard Business School Press); McGrath, MacMillan, and Venkataraman, 1995, Defining and developing competence, 253.

7   A. Reinhardt, I. Sager, and P. Burrows, 1997, Can Andy Grow keep profits up in an era of cheap PCs?, *BusinessWeek,* December 22, 70–77; R. E. Stross, 1997, Mr. Gates builds his brain trust, *Fortune,* December 8, 84–98.

8   Godfrey and Hill, 1995, The problem of unobservables, 522.

9   J. B. Barney, 1996, The resource-based theory of the firm, *Organization* Science, 7: 469–80; J. B. Barney, 1997, *Gaining and Sustaining Competitive Advantage,* (Don Mills, Ontario: Addison-Wesley Publishing); M. E. Porter, 1996, What is strategy? *Harvard Business Review,* 74 (6): 61–78.

10   A. Mehra, 1996, Resource and market based determinants of performance in the U.S. banking industry, *Strategic Management Journal,* 17: 307–22; J. Pfeffer, 1994, *Competitive Advantage through People: Unleashing the Power of the Work Force* (Boston: Harvard Business School Press), 6–14.

11   R. Henderson and W. Mitchell, 1997, The interaction of organizational and competitive influences on strategy and performance, *Strategic Management Journal,* 18 (Summer Special Issue), 5–14; A. A. Lado, N. G. Boyd, and S. C. Hanlon, 1997, Competition, cooperation and the search for economic rents: A syncretic model, *Academy of Management Review,* 22: 110–41; Porter, 1996, What is strategy?; J. B. Barney, 1995, Looking inside for competitive advantage, *Academy of Management Journal Executive,* IX (4): 59–60.

12   S. Ghoshal and C. A. Bartlett, 1995, Changing the role of top management: Beyond structure to processes, *Harvard Business Review,* 73 (1): 96.

13   Barney, 1996, Resource-based theory; Porter, 1996, What is strategy?; M. A. Peteraf, 1993, The cornerstones of competitive strategy: A resource-based view, *Strategic Management Journal,* 14: 179–91.

14   Porter, 1996, What is strategy?, 61.

15   K. E. Marino, 1996, Developing consensus on firm competencies and capabilities, *Academy of Management Executive,* X (3): 40–51.

16   T. A. Stewart, 1997, Does anyone around here know . . . ?, *Fortune,* September 29, 279.

17   C. E. Helfat, 1997, Know-how and asset complementarity and dynamic capability accumulation: The case of R&D, *Strategic Management Journal,* 18: 339–60; C. M. Christensen, 1997, Making strategy: Learning by doing, *Harvard Business Review,* 75 (6): 141–56; R. M. Grant, 1996, Prospering in dynamically competitive environments: Organizational capability as knowledge integration, *Organization Science,* 7: 375–87; D. Lei, M. A. Hitt, and R. Bettis, 1996, Dynamic core competencies through metalearning and strategic context, *Journal of Management,* 22: 247–67; H. Rheem, 1995, The learning organization, *Harvard Business Review* 73 (2): 10; G. Hamel and C. K. Prahalad, 1994, *Competing for the Future* (Boston: Harvard Business School Press).

18   A. Campbell and M. Alexander, 1997, What's wrong with strategy? *Harvard Business Review* 75 (6): 42–51.

19 C. Oliver, 1997, Sustainable competitive advantage: Combining institutional and resource-based views, *Strategic Management Journal,* 18: 697–713; D. J. Collis and C. A. Montgomery, 1995, Competing on resources: Strategy in the 1990s, *Harvard Business*

*Review,* 73 (4): 118–28; B. Wernerfelt, 1995, The resource-based view of the firm: Ten years after, *Strategic Management Journal,* 16: 171–74; J. B. Barney, 1994, Commentary; A hierarchy of corporate resources, *Advances in Strategic Management,* 10A, 113–25.

20  J. H. Dyer, 1996, Specialized supplier networks as a source of competitive advantage: Evidence from the auto industry, *Strategic Management Journal,* 17: 271–91; R. L. Priem and D. A. Harrison, 1994, Exploring strategic judgment: Methods for testing the assumptions of prescriptive contingency theories, *Strategic Management Journal,* 15: 311–24; R. Amit and P. J. H. Schoemaker, 1993, Strategic assets and organizational rent, *Strategic Management Journal,* 14: 33–46.

21  W. Boeker, 1997, Executive migration and strategic change: The effect of top manager movement on product-market entry, *Administrative Science Quarterly,* 42: 213–36; C. R. Schwenk, 1995, Strategic decision making, *Journal of Management,* 21: 471–93.

22  H. W. Jenkins, 1996, 40,000 job cuts! Where does he get off? *Wall Street Journal,* March 5, A15; McGrath, MacMillan, and Venkataraman, 1995, Defining and developing competence, 253.

23  D. Kunde, 1996, Self-control guru, *Dallas Morning News,* February 5, D1, D4; T. A. Stewart, 1996, Looking out for number 1, *Fortune,* January 15, 33–48.

24  M. Farjoun and L. Lai, 1997, Similarity judgments in strategy formulation: Role, process and implications, *Strategic Management Journal* 18: 255–73.

25  H. W. Vroman, 1996, The loyalty effect: The hidden force behind growth, profits, and lasting value (book review), *Academy of Management Executive* X (1): 88–90.

26  W. Kiechel, 1993, Facing up to denial, *Fortune,* October 18, 163–65.

27  H. Ha, 1997, GM seen needing to cut production or raise incentives, *Wall Street Journal Interactive Edition,* http://www.interactive.wsj.com, December 8.

28  P. Sellers, 1996, What exactly is charisma? *Fortune,* January 15, 68–75.

29  Teece, Pisano, and Shuen, 1997, Dynamic capabilities, 513–14; Barney, 1995, Looking inside for competitive advantage, 50.

30  McGrath, MacMillan, and Venkataraman, 1995, Defining and developing competence, 252.

31  T. Chi, 1994, Trading in strategic resources: Necessary conditions, transaction cost problems, and choice of exchange structure, *Strategic Management Journal,* 15: 271–90; R. Reed and R. DeFillippi, 1990, Causal ambiguity, barriers to imitation, and

sustainable competitive advantage, *Academy of Management Review,* 15: 88–102.

32  T. Chi, 1994, Trading in strategic resources: Necessary conditions, transaction cost problems, and choice of exchange structure, *Strategic Management Journal,* 15: 271–90; R. Reed and R. DeFillippi, 1990, Causal ambiguity, barriers to imitation, and sustainable competitive advantage, *Academy of Management Review,* 15: 88–102.

33  N. E. Grund, 1996, Reputation: Realizing value from the corporate image, *Academy of Management Executive* (book review section) X (1): 100.

34  C. J. Fombrun, 1996, *Reputation: Realizing Value from the Corporate Image* (Boston: Harvard Business School Press).

35  R. Furchgott, 1997, Rebel without an engine, *BusinessWeek,* September 15, 8.

36  T. A. Stewart, 1996, Coins in a knowledge bank, *Fortune,* February 19, 230–33.

37  S. Sherman, 1996, Secrets of HP's "muddled team," *Fortune,* March 18, 116–20.

38  McGrath, MacMillan, and Venkataraman, 1995, Defining and developing competence, 252; Porter, 1996, What is strategy?

39  J. B. Quinn, P. Anderson, and S. Finkelstein, 1996, Making the most of the best, *Harvard Business Review,* 74 (2): 71–80.

40  G. Jones, 2000, Accounting for people, *Benefits Canada,* 24(1), January, 9; T. A. Stewart, 1995, Trying to grasp the intangible, *Fortune,* October 2, 157–61.

41  Godfrey and Hill, 1995, The problem of inobservables, 522–23.

42  D. A. Aaker, 1996, *Building Strong Brands* (New York: Free Press).

43  B. Orwell, 1997, Disney is to enter restaurant business, *Wall Street Journal,* October 15, B6.

44  P. Sellers, 1997, Sears, the turnaround is ending, *Fortune,* April 28, 106.

45  Grant, 1996, Prospering in dynamically competitive environments; Lei, Hitt, and Bettis, 1996, Dynamic core competencies; J. B. Quinn, 1994, *The Intelligent Enterprise* (New York: Free Press).

46  Stross, 1997, Mr. Gates builds his brain trust; E. M. Davies, 1996, Wired for hiring: Microsoft's slick recruiting machine, *Fortune,* February 5, 123–24.

47  XWave Solutions, 2000, *Computer World Canada,* 16, (2), January 28, 48.

48  D. Kunde, 1996, Corporations thinking ahead with chief knowledge officers, *Dallas Morning News,* January 14, D1.

49  T. A. Stewart, 1991, Brainpower, *Fortune,* June 3, 44.

50  Helfat, 1997, Know-how and asset complementarity; Lei, Hitt, and Bettis, 1996, Dynamic core competencies.

51  Eid Eid joins NetPCS Networks, 1999, *Computer Dealer News,* 15 (12): March 26, 32.

52  S. Kaufman, 1996, Firm offers essential high-tech component: People, *Dallas Morning News,* January 22, D2.

53  W. Hanley, 1999, Growing up in Silicon Delta: BC's high-tech industry produces stars and struggles, *National Post,* November 24, D1, D2.

54  D. C. Smith, 2000, "Will there be enough excellent profs?" *Report on Prospective Demand and Supply Conditions for University Faculty in Ontario, Council of Ontario Universities,* March, http://www.cou.on.ca.

55  J. Landers, 1995, New jewel in the crown!, *Dallas Morning News,* December 17, H1, H2.

56  Pearce, E., 1999, In Conversation with John Roth: Networking the world, *Ivey Business Journal,* November/December, 24.

57  1999, ICT's worker woes: Canada's information and telecommunication industry struggles to fill vacant job openings, *Computer Dealer News,* 15, (30), October 15, 20.

58  F. F. Reichheld, 1996, Solving the productivity puzzle, *Wall Street Journal,* March 2, A1, A4.

59  1997, Key to success: People, people, people, *Fortune,* October 27, 232.

60  2000, Brain drain and brain gain: The immigration of knowledge workers into and out of Canada, *The Daily, StatsCan,* http://www.statscan.ca:80/Daily/English (Retrieved May 25).

61  M. A. Hitt and R. D. Ireland, 1986, Relationships among corporate level distinctive competencies, diversification strategy, corporate structure, and performance, *Journal of Management Studies,* 23: 401–16; M. A. Hitt and R. D. Ireland, 1985, Corporate distinctive competence, strategy, industry, and performance, *Strategic Management Journal,* 6: 273–93; M. A. Hitt, R. D. Ireland, and K. A. Palia, 1982, Industrial firms' grand strategy and functional importance, *Academy of Management Journal,* 25: 265–98; M. A. Hitt, R. D. Ireland, and G. Stadter, 1982, Functional importance and company performance: Moderating effects of grand strategy and industry type, *Strategic Management Journal,* 3: 315–30; C. C. Snow and E. G. Hrebiniak, 1980, Strategy, distinctive competence, and organizational performance, *Administrative Science Quarterly,* 25: 317–36.

62  M. A. Cusumano, 1997, How Microsoft makes large teams work like small teams, *Sloan Management Review,* 39, (1): 9–20.

63  D. Leonard-Barton, H. K. Bowen, K. B. Clark, C. A. Holloway, and S. C. Wheelwright, 1994, How to integrate work and deepen expertise, *Harvard Business Review, 72,* (5): 123.

64  J. Collins, 1997, The most creative product ever, *Inc.,* May, 82–84.

65  Chi, 1994, Trading in strategic resources, 272, Porter, 1996, What is strategy?

66  C. Ames, 1995, Sales soft? Profits flat? It's time to rethink your business, *Fortune,* June 26, 142–46.

67  A. Taylor, III, 1993, Shaking up Jaguar, *Fortune,* September 6, 66.

68  R. C. Morais, 1997, A methodical man, *Forbes,* August 11, 70–72.

69  This section is drawn primarily from three sources: Barney, 1997, *Gaining and Sustaining Competitive Advantage;* Barney, 1995, Looking inside for competitive advantage, J. B. Barney, 1991, Firm resources and sustained competitive advantage, *Journal of Management,* 17: 99–120.

70  Barney, 1997, *Gaining and Sustaining Competitive Advantage.*

71  Barney, 1995, Looking inside for competitive advantage.

72  This section is drawn primarily from three sources: Barney, 1997, *Gaining and Sustaining Competitive Advantage;* Barney, 1995, Looking inside for competitive advantage, J. B. Barney, 1991, Firm resources and sustained competitive advantage, *Journal of Management,* 17: 99–120.

73  Barney, 1997, *Gaining and Sustaining Competitive Advantage;* Barney, 1995, Looking inside for competitive advantage.

74  Barney, 1991, Firm resources, 108.

75  R. Reed and R. J. DeFillippi, 1990, Causal ambiguity, barriers to imitation, and sustainable competitive advantage, 88–102.

76  Leonard-Barton, 1995, *Wellsprings of Knowledge, 7.*

77  Sherman, 1996, Secrets of HP's "muddled team."

78  S. Ganbauer, 1998, Nestle freshens up supply chain preferences, *Modern Purchasing,* 40, (5), May, 26.

79  Barney, 1991, Firm resources, 111.

80  Amit and Schoemaker, 1993, Strategic assets, 39.

81  Barney, 1997, *Gaining and Sustaining Competitive Advantage.*

82  Ibid.

83  S. Caminiti, 1996, Will Old Navy fill the Gap?, *Fortune,* March 18, 59–62.

84  Ibid., 60.

85  M. E. Porter, 1985, *Competitive Advantage* (New York: Free Press), 33–61.

86  G. G. Dess, A. Gupta, J.-F. Hennart, and C. W. L. Hill, 1995, Conducting and integrating strategy research at the international, corporate, and business levels: Issues and directions, *Journal of Management,* 21: 376; Porter, 1996, What is strategy?

87  T. A. Stewart, 1995, The information wars: What you don't know will you hurt you, *Fortune,* June 12, 119–21.

88  D. Darlin, 1997, Channel change, *Forbes,* August 25, 80; D. Kirkpatrick, 1997, Now everyone in PC's wants to be like Mike, *Fortune,* September 8, 91–92.

89  Outsourcing: How industry leaders are reshaping the American corporation, 1996, *Fortune,* Special Advertising Section.

90  T. Box, 1996, Outsourcing to cut jobs in Arlington, *Dallas Morning News,* March 23, F1, F11.

91  J. Middlemiss, 1998, When third-party service makes sense: some companies outsource customer care to trusted partners and don't lose any sleep over it, *Financial Post,* 91(17), April 25, 27.

92  M. R. Ozanne, 1997, Outsourcing: Managing strategic partnerships for the virtual enterprise, *Fortune,* Special Advertising Section, September 29, S1–S48.

93  H. W. Chesbrough and D. J. Teece, 1996, When is virtual virtuous? Organizing for innovation, *Harvard Business Review* 74, (1): 70.

94  C. MacLean, 1999, Leaving the manufacturing to Patheon: Outsourcer allows drug makers to focus on R&D and marketing, *Plant,* 58 (18), December 20, 16.

95  N. A. Wishart, J. J. Elam, and D. Robey, 1996, Redrawing the portrait of a learning organization: Inside Knight-Ridder, Inc., *Academy of Management Executive* X, (1): 7–20; D. Lei and M. A. Hitt, 1995, Strategic restructuring and outsourcing: The effect of mergers and acquisitions and LBOs on building firm skills and capabilities, *Journal of Management* 21: 835–59.

96  Merx, 2000, *Merx home page,* http:// www.merx. cebra.com (Retrieved May 20); Cebra, 2000, *Cebra home page,* www.cebra.com (Retrieved May 20); Epsot, 2000, *Epsot home page,* www.epsot.ca (Retrieved May 20).

97  J. C. Spender and R. M. Grant, 1996, Knowledge and the firm: Overview, *Strategic Management Journal,* 17 (Winter Special Issue): 5–10.

98  Lei, Hitt, and Bettis, 1996, Dynamic core competencies; Leonard-Barton, 1995, *Wellsprings of Knowledge,* 59–89.

99  M. Hannan and J. Freeman, 1977, The population ecology of organizations, *American Journal of Sociology,* 82: 929–64.

100  G. Szulanski, 1996, Exploring internal stickiness: Impediments to the transfer of best practices within the firm, *Strategic Management Journal,* 17 (Winter Special Issue): 27–44.

101  Leonard-Barton, 1995, Wellsprings of Knowledge, 30–31.

102  R. Sanchez and J. T. Mahoney, 1996, Modularity, flexibility, and knowledge management in procut and organization design, *Strategic Management Journal,* 17 (Winter Special Issue): 63–76; C. A. Bartlett and S. Ghoshal, 1994. Changing the role of top management. Beyond strategy to purpose. *Harvard Business Review,* 72, (6): 79–88.

103  W. Boeker, 1997, Executive migration and strategic change, *Administrative Science Quarterly,* June, 213–36).

104  G. Hamel and C. K. Prahalad, 1989, Strategic intent, *Harvard Business Review,* 67, (3): 63–76.

105  P. Almeida, 1996, Knowledge sourcing by foreign multinationals: Patent citation analysis in the U.S. semiconductor industry, *Strategic Management Journal,* 17 (Winter Special Issue): 155–65.

106  M. S. S. El-Namaki, 1992, Creating a corporate vision, *Long Range Planning,* 25, (2): 119–21.

107  S. Sherman, 1995, Stretch goals: The dark side of asking for miracles, *Fortune,* November 13, 231–32.

108  H. W. Mentink, 1996, An employee's goals, *Fortune,* February 5, 26.

109  J A. Byrne, 1995, Hired guns packing high powered knowhow, *BusinessWeek,* September 18, 92–96.

110  1996, Andersen Consulting advertisement appearing in *Wall Street Journal,* February 6; R. Henkoff, 1993, Inside Andersen's army of advice, *Fortune,* October 4, 78–86.

111  R. D. Ireland and M. A. Hitt, 1992, Mission statements: Importance, challenge and recommendations for development, *Business Horizons,* 35, (3): 34–42.

112  C. Marshall, 1996, A sense of mission, *The Strategist,* 7, (4): 14–16.

# Strategic Actions:
# Strategy Formulation

**PART TWO**

# Chapter Five

## Business-Level Strategy

### LEARNING OBJECTIVES

*After reading this chapter, you should be able to:*

1. Define strategy and explain business-level strategies.
2. Describe the relationship between customers and business-level strategies.
3. Discuss the issues firms consider when evaluating customers in terms of who, what, and how.
4. Define the integrated low-cost/differentiation strategy and discuss its increasing importance in the new competitive landscape.
5. Describe the capabilities necessary to develop competitive advantage through the cost leadership, differentiation, focused low-cost, focused differentiation, and the integrated low-cost/differentiation business-level strategies.
6. Explain the risks associated with each of the five business-level strategies.

## Focus Strategies: Achieving Strategic Competitiveness by Serving Narrow Market Segments

Bang & Olufsen, a Danish company, manufactures upscale electronics products. Using its core competencies in product design and manufacturing, the firm produces an array of "fantastic-looking" luxury items. Among its offerings are $1800 to $5000 stereo speakers, and $15 000 television sets. Striving deliberately for high style and quality, the firm's top-of-the-line products are targeted to audiophiles and video buffs who are willing to pay premium prices. In describing the company's product design, Ole Bek, president of Bang & Olufsen America, noted that he learned much more by window shopping at Louis Vuitton in Paris than by looking at consumer electronics outlets.[*]

To highlight more clearly and consistently the uniqueness of its products and to better serve the specialized interests and needs of its target customers, the firm decided recently to launch a string of impeccably designed stores to sell only its own products. Simultaneously, Bang & Olufsen discontinued the practice of distributing its products through what it considered to be "downscale" shops. The practice of concentrating on its own dedicated shops as the primary means of product distribution is consistent with actions taken by other companies that serve upscale customer needs. Louis Vuitton, for example, sells its bags only in its own boutiques.

Moreover, selling products through its own retailing outlets allows Bang & Olufsen to move even further upscale. Doing this, the firm's executives believe, will allow the company to avoid having to compete against other electronics manufacturers on the basis of price. Bang & Olufsen recognized the disasters that have befallen other European companies (including Ferguson, Brion Vega, and Telefunken) that tried and failed to compete successfully against mainly Asian manufacturers on price. This recognition solidified Bang & Olufsen's strategic decision to focus on the upscale, highly differentiated part of the electronics market.

http://www.bang-olufsen.com
http://www.zeton.com

Purdy's Chocolates also focuses only one particular customer segment. While candy and chocolate bars may provide basic relief to chocoholics, Purdy's has made its product a quality special occasion and seasonal gift. White chocolate snowmen, chocolate bells, and Santas rule the Christmas buying season. While Purdy's stocks elegantly wrapped boxes of cream-filled chocolates and nuts, candied fruit, and ice cream (chocolate coated while you wait), the consistent favourite for Valentine's Day, Easter, Mother's Day, Father's Day, and birthdays is Purdy's hedgehogs—a moulded chocolate with hazelnut cream chocolate filling. As with all their products, Purdy's filling for its hedgehogs is made in its single plant, near Vancouver, with chocolate imported from Belgium. Purdy's ensures the quality of its products through this centralized production, as well as its use of high-quality ingredients, maintaining freshness through strict control of shelf life, and owning its own stores. To allow for further control and a better understanding of its customers, Purdy's has remained a regional business—with no desire to expand its 44 stores any further eastward. Purdy's success was well summarized by one analyst: "They're doing an awful lot of things right. They make it look easy because they're so organised. They've shown throughout their history they understand their market and they're able to respond to changing customer trends while still maintaining a wonderful tradition."

The need for quality doesn't occur only at the consumer level. For any production company, the need for new and innovative production methods is critical. To determine if new processes will work as well in practice as they should in theory, quality scale models of a planned production plant are typically required. However, the personnel needed to engineer and construct such a plant may be needed for only one year in ten. Most major players in the chemical and oil industry now realize that it is less expensive to outsource this function. In steps Zeton, a small private company from Burlington, Ontario. Zeton's specialty is making mockups for industrial giants who need to try out new processes before paying big dollars for a full-scale plant. Technical ability, quality engineering, cost effectiveness, secrecy, and solid quality construction that can be reassembled on the customer's site are important criteria for Zeton's buyers. Since Zeton's products range in price from $150 000 to $15 million, its $45 million in sales may come from just 20 customers. Because of this, their demanding customers are treated very well. When customers outside Canada asked for a local provider, Zeton became an international company. In 1994 it bought out a U.S rival and, in 1996, two European competitors. While integrating such diverse operations can be difficult, Zeton managed to do so and at the same time become recognized as one of Canada's 50 best-managed private companies.

*Since making this statement, Ole Bek has become president of Bang & Olufsen America Inc., taking charge of the distribution of Bang & Olufsen products in the United States, Canada, and Mexico.

Sources: W. Echikson, 1997, Bang & Olufsen's class act gets classier, *BusinessWeek*, October 20, 142F; B. Aarsteinsen, 1998, Shrewd marketing fuels candy company: Purdy's still tasting sweet success *Vancouver Sun*, December 9, Final Edition, D1; D. North, The Meccano millionaires: Life at Zeton Inc. is a dream come true for every kid who ever fooled around with a Meccano set, *Canadian Business*, March 26, 1999, 60 64; The Zeton Company home page (accessed July 5, 1999), http://www.zeton.com.

The three firms mentioned in the opening case implement strategies that are intended to serve customers' unique needs. For this service and the high quality of the products being purchased, these companies' customers are willing to pay premium prices. Please Mum also strives to serve the unique needs of a particular group of customers. Offering products with exceptional style and quality, the essence of the firm's strategic intent and strategy is suggested by the following statements:

*Unlike most others in the clothing field Please Mum has chosen to manufacture almost exclusively in Canada. Please Mum clothes are comfortable, mixable, and matchable. Designed for maximum wear by growing children, they feature "grow cuffs," "double trouble knees" and the quality of 100% preshrunk cotton. Please Mum has established a proud and distinctive niche in the children's clothing market, supported by a world-wide family of passion and quality-conscious moms, dads, and kids ...*

Please Mum designs, manufactures, and markets high-quality, Canadian-made clothing for young people. The Company's basic objective is to design and manufacture its clothes in such a way that they are obviously superior to, and pleasingly different from, competitors' products. The Company's clothes are sold at premium prices to parents who want both the durable, colourful quality of the clothes and exceptional sales service. Along with clean, well-lit, and well-stocked resale outlets, Please Mum outlets help parents shop by providing play areas for young children. If you cannot make it to the store, Please Mum has as expansive group of individual at-home distributors who will bring the selections to a busy parent's home.[1]

To achieve strategic competitiveness and earn above-average returns, companies such as Please Mum analyze their external environment, identify opportunities in that environment, determine which of their internal resources and capabilities are core competencies, and select an appropriate strategy to implement.[2] A **strategy** is an integrated and coordinated set of commitments and actions designed to exploit core competencies and gain a competitive advantage. In this sense, strategies are purposeful and precede the taking of actions to which they apply.[3] An effectively formulated strategy marshals, integrates, and allocates a firm's resources, capabilities, and competencies so it can cope successfully with its external environment.[4] Such a strategy also rationalizes a firm's strategic intent and strategic mission and what will be done to achieve them.[5] Information about a host of variables, including markets, customers, technology, world-wide finance, and the changing world economy[6] must be collected and analyzed to formulate and implement strategies properly. In the final analysis, the test of a strategy's effectiveness is its ability to allow the firm to offer a good or service to customers that provides greater value relative to the value provided by competitors' products.[7]

Recall from Chapters 1 and 4 that core competencies are resources and capabilities that serve as a source of competitive advantage for a firm over its rivals. Strategic competitiveness and the earning of above-average returns hinge on a firm's ability to develop and exploit new core competencies faster than competitors can mimic the competitive advantages yielded by the current ones.[8] When focused on the continuous need to develop new core competencies, firms are able to drive competition in the future as well as the present.[9] Thus, especially in the new competitive landscape, with its continuing globalization and rapid technological changes, only firms with the capacity to improve,

A **strategy** is an integrated and coordinated set of commitments and actions designed to exploit core competencies and gain a competitive advantage.

innovate, and upgrade their competitive advantages over time can expect to achieve long-term success.[10]

As explained in this chapter, successful firms use their core competencies to satisfy customers' needs. The relationship between appropriate strategic actions and achievement of strategic competitiveness is increasingly important in today's turbulent and competitive environment.[11] These relationships are shown in Figure 1.1 in Chapter 1. As displayed in that figure, a firm's strategic inputs (gained through study of the external and internal environments) are used to select the strategic actions (the formulation and implementation of value-creating strategies) that will yield desired strategic outcomes.

Actions taken at Zeton exemplify these relationships. Through an examination of the general, industry, and competitor external environments, Zeton's president Archie Bennett envisioned an opportunity to serve a particular segment of the industrial engineering market—customized-engineered scale models. Today, Zeton is recognized as one of the leaders in a small but highly demanding market.[12] As is the case with Bang & Olufsen and Purdy's Chocolates, focused differentiation is the business-level strategy (defined and discussed later in the chapter) Zeton chose to implement to achieve strategic competitiveness and above-average returns.

The environmental opportunity pursued by Zeton was identified through careful study. Opportunities to continue implementing a chosen business-level strategy can also surface somewhat unexpectedly for established firms. For example, when George Weston, owner of Loblaw Cos., Canada's largest grocery chain—wanted to sell its E.B. Eddy forest products unit so it could refocus on its grocery business, Domtar, which purchased E. B. Eddy, saw an opportunity to expand its operations in the forestry industry.[13] Similarly, in light of a competitor's inability to finance development of a gold mine in South Africa (identified through study of the firm's industry environment), Canadian mining firm Placer Dome was able to buy a 50 percent stake in South Africa's largest known undeveloped gold property. Because of its superior financial position (a source of temporary competitive advantage), Placer Dome's CEO concluded that his company's entry into South Africa was "… ahead of popular market opinion. We have constantly said in any move into South Africa, we would enter gently and our exposure would be limited. The potential rewards of this initial investment far outweigh the risk."[14]

At a broader level, companies committed to the importance of competing successfully in the global economy constantly study developments in the world's markets to identify emerging opportunities to exploit their competitive advantages. The segments most closely linked with strategic competitiveness vary by the type of business-level strategy the firm is using.[15] Consider, for example, Taiwanese PC manufacturers. Collectively, PC manufacturers in Taiwan maintain the third-largest market share position behind the United States and Japan. The low-priced segment of the PC market is targeted by many of Taiwan's PC manufacturers. Competition among firms seeking to serve this segment through the use of the cost leadership business-level strategy is severe. To drive their costs lower and to exploit the competitive advantage their low-cost structures provide, Taiwanese companies are relying more and more on suppliers from mainland China to supply low-priced components. Chinese component suppliers can offer less expensive parts to the Taiwanese PC manufacturers because of their own lower costs, made possible by relatively inexpensive land and labour expenses. Because the Taiwanese firms rely on export to fulfill global demand, completing business transactions with firms in China is not seen as risky: Taiwan does not rely on sales to Chinese customers and hence does not have to worry about the associated credit risks.[16]

Hungary's version of privatization of state-owned firms has helped to put it ahead of other Eastern European countries. Although many Eastern European countries pursued a privatization process in which a voucher scheme was used to make each citizen an owner, Hungary chose to use initial public offerings (IPOs) and direct sales to strategically selected foreign investors. Most of the privatization sales became a combination of domestic and foreign interests. This was a much more difficult approach politically because of the fear of foreign investors and the potential for large-scale layoffs. The main difference was the opportunity to have cash for investment through stronger equity and debt markets relative to the voucher approach.

As a result of the success of its privatization approach, Hungary will likely be the first Eastern European country to join the European Union. In addition, it has management expertise from foreign owners that will allow it to have more cutting-edge technology. Ameritech, for example, in partnership with Deutsche Telekom, has put the Hungarian telecommunications company Matav on a par technologically with its Western European counterparts. Furthermore, through its significant investments, Electrolux has transformed Hungary's appliance industry such that the country is a leader in Eastern Europe. These firms have followed the strategic management process in that they have observed opportunities in the environment and have marshalled their resources in manners that allow them to implement particular business-level strategies in the pursuit of strategic competitiveness. In turn, the firms' strategic actions are creating a vibrant Hungarian economy, even though risks remain—for the country and for firms competing within its borders.[17]

A **business-level strategy** is an integrated and coordinated set of commitments and actions designed to provide value to customers and gain a competitive advantage by exploiting core competencies in specific, individual product markets.

**Business-level strategy**, the focus of this chapter, is an integrated and coordinated set of commitments and actions designed to provide value to customers and gain a competitive advantage by exploiting core competencies in specific, individual product markets.[18] Thus, a business-level strategy reflects a firm's belief about where and how it has an advantage over its rivals.[19]

Customers are the foundation of successful business-level strategies. In the words of one CEO, "When you get people focused on customers, it has a very remarkable effect" on the firm's performance outcomes.[20] Because of their strategic importance, we begin this chapter with a discussion of customers. Three issues are considered in this analysis. Each firm determines (1) *who* it will serve, (2) *what* needs target customers have that it will satisfy, and (3) *how* those needs will be satisfied through implementation of a chosen strategy. For Bang & Olufsen, *who* the firm serves is audiophiles and video buffs; the *what* (or customer need) the company satisfies is for premium top-of-the-line electronics components; and *how* these customer needs are satisfied is through use of Bang & Olufsen's competitive advantages in product design and manufacturing.

Following the discussion on customers, we describe four generic business-level strategies. These strategies are generic because they can be implemented in both manufacturing and service industries.[21] Our analysis of the generic strategies includes descriptions of how each one allows a firm to address the five competitive forces discussed in Chapter 3. In addition, we use the value chain (see Chapter 4) to show examples of primary and support activities necessary to implement each generic strategy successfully. Risks associated with each generic strategy are also presented in this chapter.

Organizational structures and controls required for the successful implementation of business-level strategies are explained in Chapter 12.

A fifth business-level strategy that both manufacturing and service firms are implementing more frequently is considered in the chapter's final section. Some believe that this integrated strategy (a combination of attributes of the cost leadership and differentiation strategies) is essential to establishing and exploiting competitive advantages in the global economy.[22]

# CUSTOMERS: WHO, WHAT, AND HOW

Organizations must satisfy some group of customers' needs to be successful.[23] "Needs" refer to the benefits and features of a good or service that customers want to purchase.[24] A basic need of all customers is to buy products that provide value.

A key reason that firms must be able to satisfy customers' needs is that in the final analysis, returns earned from relationships with customers are the lifeblood of all organizations.[25] Relationships with customers are strengthened when the firm is committed to providing superior value to those it serves. Superior value is often created when a firm's product helps a customer enhance the business's own competitive advantage.[26]

The challenge of identifying and determining how to satisfy the needs of what some business analysts believe are increasingly sophisticated, knowledgeable, and fickle customers is difficult.[27] Moreover, it is only through total satisfaction of their needs that customers develop the type of firm-specific loyalty companies seek. The president of the Ritz-Carlton® Hotel Company describes the relationship between total need satisfaction and customer loyalty: "Unless you have 100% customer satisfaction—and I don't mean that they are just satisfied, I mean that they are excited about what you are doing—you have to improve."[28] Although difficult to earn, the estimate that "raising customer retention rates by five percentage points increases the value of an average customer by 25% to 100%"[29] is another indicator of the value of loyal customers. Increasingly, databases are linked with customer retention rates. Among other useful outcomes, information gleaned from these databases allows a firm to tailor its offerings more precisely to satisfy individualized customer needs.[30]

Strategically competitive organizations in the 21st century will (1) think continuously about who their customers are, (2) maintain close and frequent contacts with their customers, (3) determine how to use their core competencies in ways that competitors cannot imitate, and (4) design their strategies to allow them to satisfy customers' current, anticipated, and even unanticipated needs.[31] Companies study their corporate memory (research stored documents) to enhance their understanding of product attributes that may appeal to current customers. Through these efforts, it might be discovered, for example, that a product being evaluated for possible introduction to the marketplace is quite similar to one the firm produced and sold previously. By analyzing customer reactions to the earlier product, the firm may be able to enhance the value that the new, yet similar, product can offer to customers.[32]

## Who: Determining the Customers to Serve

Customers can be divided into groups based on differences in their needs. Doing this is more effective than deciding that the firm will serve the needs of the "average customer." Averages often do not give in-depth insights about an issue relevant to decisionmakers.

**■ ■ TABLE 5.1**                    **Characteristics of the Average Canadian**

**The Average Canadian:**

Watches television three and one half hours daily (half the amount of the average American).

Takes one half hour per day to read books, magazines and newspapers.

Spends an hour and a half per day eating meals outside of the home,

Has about 40 hours of leisure a week (about the same as the average American).

Spends about $40 per week on food—most of it will go toward meat, dairy and bakery goods.

Owns a refrigerator, and more likely than not, a freezer.

Spends over $400 per year on repairs and renovations to their home.

Participates in civic and voluntary activities 15 to 20 minutes per week.

Spends over $2000 per year on transportation.

In an average week, the average Canadian spends six hours shopping (as does the average American).

Source: Statistics Canada, 1999, *Statistics Canada home page,* http://www.statcan.ca/english/ Pgdb/ People/Families/famil36a.htm (Retrieved October 14).

Table 5.1 shows characteristics of the average Canadian. Though interesting, these descriptors are of less value to a company seeking to target customers than attributes and needs associated with specific and identifiable customer segments.

Almost any identifiable human or organizational characteristic can be used to subdivide a large potential market into segments that differ from one another in terms of that characteristic.[33] Common characteristics on which customers' needs vary are illustrated in Table 5.2.

The experience of Eaton's demonstrates the importance of continuously focusing on the needs of a firm's target customer group. The company's core customers were older than the average Canadian and growing more price-sensitive. As noted in Chapter 1, consumers embraced Wal-Mart's arrival to Canada in 1994, but Eaton's remained unresponsive to consumers' desire for lower prices. Loss of business followed, and Eaton's had to reorganize in 1997.[34] As part of its initial reorganization, Eaton's cut product lines and moved into upscale clothing. This alienated older loyal customers and failed to attract the middle-aged, middle-income customers Eaton's sought. One problem was that Eaton's advertised store changes before they had begun. Potential new customers curious enough to look at the new Eaton's found the same old store. Also, the store's selection of products was not sufficiently fashionable.

Competitors—both speciality retailers and other department stores—occupied the niche Eaton's sought. Others were selling the same clothing lines in stores with similar décor and ambience. While department stores such as The Bay or Sears tried to avoid the extremes in fashion and cater to a wide range of consumers, speciality shops could offer unique selections. Eaton's was perceived as staid and trying to be trendy, and in the end was accepted as neither. Thus, Eaton's was alienating both traditional and prospective

| ■ ■ **TABLE 5.2** | **Basis for Customer Segmentation** |
|---|---|

**Consumer Markets**

Demographic factors (age, gender, income, etc.)

Socioeconomic factors (social class, stage in family life cycle)

Geographic factors (cultural, regional, and national differences)

Psychological factors (lifestyle, personality traits)

Consumption patterns (heavy moderate or light users)

Perceptual factors (benefit segmentation, perceptual mapping)

**Industrial Markets**

End-use segments (industry as identified in the NAICS: North American Industry Classification System).

Product segments (based on technological differences or production economies).

Geographic segments (defined by boundaries between countries or by regional differences within them).

Common buying factor segments (cut across product market and geographic segments).

Customer size segments.

Source: Adapted from S. C. Jain, 2000, *Marketing Planning and Strategy* (Cincinnati: South-Western College Publishing), 120.

consumers.[35] Others who had been paying attention to what their clientele were asking for could count on loyal customers. Wal-Mart, for example, could count on 46 percent of its customers being loyal (recall that there are positive financial effects for customer loyalty).[36]

## Increasing Segmentation of Markets

In the new competitive landscape, many firms have become adept at identifying precise differences among customers' needs. Armed with these understandings, companies segment customers into competitively relevant groups—groups of customers with unique needs. As shown by the following statement, General Motors believes that four of its automobile product groups serve the unique needs of four competitively relevant groups: "The Chevy is squarely aimed at people shopping for a low price. The Pontiac targets performance enthusiasts. The Olds is for upscale buyers who might normally shop for import sport sedans, and the Buick will appeal to older buyers who want premium cars with conservative styling and room for six riders."[37]

Statistics Canada tracks over 30 different sources of ethnic origin, more than 11 visible minority groups, over 10 classes of income, and at least 17 major religious groups.[38] Each group has its own beliefs, aspirations, tastes, and needs (and there may be numerous differences within groups). There are estimates that in the United States, 62 distinct classes of citizens exist.[39] Some believe the trend toward fragmentation into smaller classes and subgroups is accelerating in North America and throughout the world's markets.[40]

Nevertheless, companies' efforts to create a huge set of goods and services intended to satisfy unique needs may be confusing for some customers. This confusion can result from the sheer number of products available to consumers. In fact, North Americans today face by far the widest array of options they have ever confronted. The average number of items in a grocery store grew from about 25 000 to over 30 000 between 1987 and 1997. During this time period, new products emerged on grocers' shelves at incredible rates, peaking at over 22 000 introductions in 1995. Of these introductions, nearly 70 percent fail. Given these realities, companies are challenged to provide sufficient detail to their target customers regarding the superiority of their product relative to competitors' offerings.[41]

Teens and preteens represent a large, competitively relevant group whose purchasing power continues to expand (some of the spending patterns of this group are shown in Table 5.3). This relevance comes from the fact that Canadians age nine to nineteen control $10 billion per year in disposable income. Fifteen-to-nineteen year olds spend the most—about $5 000 each annually. Yet, "tweens" (the 2.4 million Canadians between the ages of nine and fourteen) are increasingly important in spite of the fact that they spend only $600 each per year. This is because younger consumers offer more promising territory for long-term brand loyalty since older teens may have already established such preferences.[42]

When retailer Le Chateau noticed younger customers trying on the smaller sizes of their adult line, the company tested and received an extraordinary response to a junior line of clothes. Le Chateau has now targeted preteens as a separate market with its own brand, distinct icon, and logo. Le Chateau has dedicated space to "tweens" in every store and had opened specialty stores to cater to this group. "They're more aware of the hot brands and they can't wait to spend … They're not bargain hunters. They're open and ready to try on—or discard—trends."[43]

Tailoring products to this market can be difficult, however, since the product demanded can change quickly. There is some evidence to suggest teens and "tweens" can be fickle customers. "Kids will switch. It's just got to be right for their taste, which is difficult because what's right for their taste this week might not be quite right next week."[44] For example, in the mid-1990s the Guess clothing line was judged third in "coolness" by teenagers. By the late 1990s, the brand fell to 23rd.[45]

## What: Determining the Customer Needs to Satisfy

As a firm decides who it will serve, it must simultaneously identify the needs of the chosen customer group that its goods or services can satisfy. Top-level managers play a critical role in efforts to recognize and understand customers' needs. Their capacity to gain valuable insights from listening to and studying customers influences product, technology, and distribution decisions.

Harry Rosen, with $135 million in sales, is Canada's largest upscale men's wear chain (28 percent market share). At Harry Rosen, top-level managers spend significant amounts of time analyzing their customers and solving customer problems. The company's point of sale system allows the firm to identify customers who have not shopped recently, and CEO Rosen will personally call them all to find out why. "We like our customers to shop once or twice a year, but if a customer has skipped four full seasons, then we have concerns that the customer is just not happy."[46] Even though problems are few,

| ■ ■ **TABLE 5.3** | **Spending by Canadian Teens and Preteens** |
|---|---|

There are an estimated 4.1 million Canadians between the ages of 10 and 19. Their numbers are expected to swell to 4.4 million around 2004—about one in seven Canadians.

Nine-to-19 year olds spent $13.5 billion per year. Teenagers spend over $6 billion a year on consumer goods.

Canadian kids influence parent's spending: 80 percent of parents consult with their children before choosing a family vacation, 25 percent consult before deciding what vehicle to buy.

One-third of teens in high school have part-time jobs. As well, many get paid for doing household or community chores.

Teens eat a lot, spending $39 to $55 per week on food. As a group, their food spending could add up to over $7 billion a year.

An estimated 12 percent of those aged 13 to 14 have access to a credit card; the figure rises to 27 percent for those between 15 and 17 years old.

Of the 2.4 million Canadians between the ages of nine and fourteen, 90 percent have influence over the purchase of their clothes and 80 percent have a say in what games and toys, snack foods, and restaurants the family chooses.

Sources: A. Clark, 1999, How teens got the power: Gen Y has the cash, the cool, and a burgeoning consumer culture, *Maclean's* (Toronto Edition), March 22, 42; S. Steinberg, 1998, Have allowance, will transform economy [The tween market], *Canadian Business*, March 13, 58–71; P. Withers, 1998, Move over, boomers: a species called the teenager is making a comeback. *B.C. Business Magazine,* January, 28–33; Canadian Press, 1994, Teens a huge force in consumer market, *Canadian Press Newswire*, November 21.

CEO Rosen spends one to two hours per day calling customers. He personally handles complaints from all of his stores. He has even been known to take a customer call while he is in top-level meetings. Rosen says, "Sometimes I get this silence on the other end of the line, and the person says, 'I didn't really expect to get to speak to you,' but I don't live in some ivory tower, I work in our stores ..."[47] Spending executive time in this manner sends a strong signal to all employees that "our customers are our greatest concern."[48] These efforts by top-level managers may contribute meaningfully to the firm's performance. Designer Hugo Boss was so impressed that Harry Rosen was selected to open and run BOSS stores across the United States. Thus, in firms that achieve strategic competitiveness, such as Harry Rosen, customer contact is a key responsibility for top-level managers as well as marketing and sales personnel.

An additional competitive advantage accrues to firms capable of anticipating and then satisfying needs that were unknown to target customers. Firms able to do this provide customers with unexpected value—that is, a product performance capability or characteristic they did not request, yet do value.[49] Moreover, anticipating customers' needs yields opportunities for firms to shape their industry's future and gain an early competitive advantage (an early competitive advantage is called a "first-mover advantage" and is discussed in Chapter 6). For example, Sprint, a diversified telecommunications company, believes that it "set the standard in long distance with its fibre optic network." In terms of the future, the firm also believes that "by joining with our cable partners in a revolutionary venture, we will be setting the standard once again. We're creating the blueprint that other communications companies will have to follow: a new kind of company that delivers the entire interconnected world of globe-spanning voice, video and data—all from a single source."[50]

## How: Determining Core Competencies Necessary to Satisfy Customers' Needs

Firms use their core competencies to implement value-creating strategies and satisfy customers' needs. One of the strategic imperatives at IBM is to more quickly convert the firm's technological competence into commercial products that customers value. IBM's intensive knowledge of its customers' businesses helps the firm accomplish this objective.[51] Honda's motorcycle, car, lawn mower, and generator businesses are all based on the company's core competence in engines and power trains. Honda continues to bolster its commitment to research and development to strengthen this core competence.[52] At Canon, core competencies in optics, imaging, and microprocessor controls provide the foundation to satisfy customer needs in a range of product markets including copiers, laser printers, cameras, and image scanners. One of the most solid and trusted suppliers in electronics and computers, Hewlett-Packard uses its engineering core competence to produce products that are renowned for their quality.[53]

Next, we discuss the business-level strategies firms implement in the pursuit of strategic competitiveness and above-average returns.

## TYPES OF BUSINESS-LEVEL STRATEGY

Business-level strategies are concerned with a firm's industry position relative to competitors.[54] Companies that have established favourable industry positions are better able to cope with the five forces of competition (see Chapter 3). To position itself, a firm must decide if its intended actions will allow it to perform activities differently or to perform different activities than its rivals.[55] Thus, favourably positioned firms may have a competitive advantage over their industry rivals. This is important in that the universal objective of all companies is to develop and sustain competitive advantages.[56]

Originally, it was determined that firms choose from among four generic business-level strategies to establish and exploit a competitive advantage within a particular competitive scope: cost leadership, differentiation, focused low cost, and focused differentiation (see Figure 5.1). A fifth generic business-level strategy, the integrated low-cost/differentiation strategy, has evolved through firms' efforts to find the most effective ways to exploit their competitive advantages.

When selecting a business-level strategy, firms evaluate two types of competitive advantage: "lower cost than rivals, or the ability to differentiate and command a premium price that exceeds the extra cost of doing so."[57] Having lower costs than rivals denotes the firm's ability to perform activities differently than rivals; being able to differentiate indicates a capacity to perform different activities.[58] Competitive advantage is achieved within some scope. Scope has several dimensions, including the group of product and customer segments served and the array of geographic markets in which a firm competes. Competitive advantage is sought by competing in many customer segments when implementing either the cost leadership or the differentiation strategy. In contrast, through implementation of focus strategies, firms seek either a cost advantage

■ ■ **FIGURE 5.1**

*Four Generic Strategies*

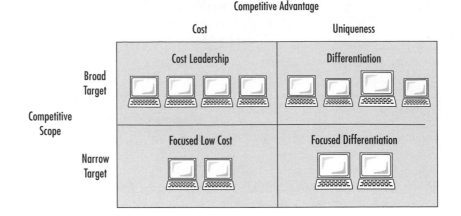

Source: Adapted with the permission of The Free Press, a division of Simon & Schuster from *Competitive Advantage: Creating and Sustaining Superior Performance* by Michael E. Porter, Fig. 1-3, 12. Copyright © 1985 by Michael E. Porter.

or a differentiation advantage in a narrow competitive scope or segment. With focus strategies, the firm "selects a segment or group of segments in the industry and tailors its strategy to serving them to the exclusion of others."[59]

None of the five business-level strategies is inherently or universally superior to the others.[60] The effectiveness of each strategy is contingent on opportunities and threats in a firm's external environment and possibilities permitted by the firm's unique resources, capabilities, and core competencies. It is critical, therefore, for the firm to select a strategy that is appropriate in light of its competencies and environmental opportunities; once selected, the strategy should be implemented carefully and consistently. Some criticized Volkswagen for a perceived failure in terms of these strategic requirements. Indecision regarding the exact segments of the auto industry the firm wanted to compete in and how it intended to compete in chosen segments caused a temporary setback in the firm's stock value.[61]

## The Impact of Corporate-Level Strategy on Business-Level Strategy

Prior to describing business-level strategies, we discuss the impact of corporate-level strategies. Firms that are pursuing limited diversification and operating in only one industry will pursue the business-level strategy appropriate to creating and maintaining value for customers given the firm's resources and capabilities. If the firm is very good at controlling costs, a cost leadership strategy will be appropriate. However, if the firm has an intensely creative group of employees and a customer base willing to pay a premium, differentiation may be more appropriate. If the firm's customer base is willing to pay a premium, the firm has a creative, innovative work force, and the customer base is large enough for sources of cost advantage to be used, an integrated low-cost/differentiation strategy is appropriate.

For firms pursuing related diversification, the same flexibility applies as for firms pursuing limited diversification. However, if the corporate strategy is one of unrelated diversification, it is possible that divisions will be forced, over the long-term, to pursue cost leadership. This is because the tight financial controls that may be imposed in unrelated diversified firms can force divisions to have little discretion in pursuing innovation or creativity over hard financial targets.

## Cost Leadership Strategy

A **cost leadership strategy** is an integrated set of actions designed to produce products at the lowest cost, relative to competitors, with features that are acceptable to customers. A **differentiation strategy** is an integrated set of actions designed to produce products that customers perceive as being different in ways that are important to them.[62] The differentiation strategy calls for firms to sell nonstandardized products to customers with unique needs. The cost leadership strategy should achieve low cost relative to competitors while not ignoring means of differentiation that customers value. Alternatively, the differentiation strategy should consistently upgrade a product's differentiated features that customers value without ignoring costs to customers. Thus, although their nature differs, firms can create value (recall that value is defined in Chapter 3 as the product's set of characteristics and attributes for which customers are willing to pay) through either cost leadership or the differentiation strategy.[63]

> A **cost leadership strategy** is an integrated set of actions designed to produce products at the lowest cost, relative to competitors, with features that are acceptable to customers.
>
> A **differentiation strategy** is an integrated set of actions designed to produce products that customers perceive as being different in ways that are important to them.

Firms seeking competitive advantage by implementing the cost leadership strategy often sell no-frills, standardized products to the most typical customers in the industry. In the new competitive landscape, it is increasingly difficult for firms implementing this type of strategy to differentiate between product features that are standard and those providing benefits that exceed the price the company's target customers are willing to pay.[64]

Successful implementation of the cost leadership strategy requires a consistent focus on driving costs lower, relative to competitors' costs. Firms often drive their costs lower through investments in efficient-scale facilities, tight cost and overhead control, and cost minimizations in such areas as service, sales force, and R&D. For example, Unifi, one of the world's largest texturizers of filament polyester and nylon fibre, makes significant investments in its manufacturing technologies to drive its costs lower in an environment of upward pressure on prices of raw materials and packaging supplies. Already one of the most efficient producers in its industry, the company recently completed a modernization program for texturing polyester. Unifi also intends to modernize and expand its nylon, covered yarn, and dyed yarn operations. Combined, these actions are expected to increase the firm's technological lead over its rivals and further reduce its production costs.[65] Calgary-based Nova Corp.'s chemical business has made similar investments to become the low-cost leader in the manufacture of ethylene and polyethylene. To foster profitable growth as the 21st century begins, the firm intends to use its superior cost position to add pipeline miles in Canada and other locations in North America.[66]

Emerson Electric Co., a U.S. manufacturer that has earned above-average returns during both favourable and unfavourable economic climates, bases its operations on several principles—continuous cost reduction, use of state-of-the-art equipment, and open communications. The firm's adherence to these principles has resulted in impressive outcomes; "Adjusted for inflation, Emerson Electric's revenues have barely increased in the past half-dozen years. Yet in that period its earnings, cash flow and dividends per share have all increased by about 50%."[67]

As described in the Strategic Focus, the cost leadership strategy is being used in one of Magna International's business groups. While reading this Strategic Focus, notice the actions taken in the business group to drive costs lower.

## STRATEGIC FOCUS

### Cost Leadership at Magna International: Cosma Body and Chassis Systems

Aurora, Ontario–based Magna International is a global leader in the engineering, manufacture, and distribution of technologically advanced automotive systems. With facilities in 17 countries and over one-third of sales revenues earned outside North America, Magna attracts business from all the world's major auto manufacturers. In a business where the customers are keenly interested in saving costs, Magna has managed to serve its buyers well by staying on the cutting edge of process innovation.

One example that embodies Magna's cost leadership efforts can be found in its Cosma Body and Chassis Systems Division. Cosma developed and used hydroforming technologies to build the frames for the Chevrolet Silverado and Jeep Sierra with more strength, less weight, and at a lower cost. This shows how the company's commitment to research and development allowed it to become a cost leader in this area.

The frames Cosma makes for these vehicles consist of a front end, middle portion, and rear section. For all these areas, Cosma has saved cost and weight while adding strength. Given the strength and weight requirements, hydroforming and draw-bending were less expensive than traditional welding methods. Compared to the previous method of making the front end of the vehicle frame (welding two stamped pieces of metal together), hydroforming makes the most sense. Precut tubing is inserted into a die that is then filled with water and pressurized to force the tubes together. This procedure eliminated 20 kilograms of metal and welding waste from the front end of the frame.

Cosma considered traditional processes to make the middle portion of the frame, but specifications required bends that could not be done in a conventional way. The solution came when one of the engineers took his children on a tour of a toy-train factory where a movie included a clip about production of rails for real trains. This got him thinking about the problem the company had with the midsection, and the investigation led to new methods of roll-forming and draw-bending of that section. Good ideas come from anywhere and Magna makes a special effort through its "Fair Enterprise System" of profitsharing to encourage employees to come forward with such ideas. Production of the rear section of the truck's frame is done with conventional stamping. The originality here is that the frame's rear section is removable. Since this section is most often damaged in accidents, Cosma engineers decided to make it easier to repair.

By finding unique manufacturing methods to produce what customers want, Cosma and parent Magna have developed what others called the best-engineered frame in its class. The procedures used save customers time and money and help make a vehicle with better handling and a less vibrating ride than earlier products.

All Magna's divisions share this drive for cost leadership though process innovation. New methods and creative ideas from employees feed the effort. With almost $10 billion in sales, Magna's efforts have been dramatically successful.

Source: Magna International, 1999, *Magna International home page*, http://www. magnaint.com (Retrieved October 10); K. DesMarteau, 1999, Magna: Master of automotive innovation, *Bobbin*, April, 99, 58–60; C.A. DeJong; 1999, Silverado strikes gold with water, *Automotive Manufacturing & Production*, Cincinnati, February, 49–51.

As described in Chapter 4, a firm's value chain determines which parts of its operations create value and which do not. Primary and support activities that allow a firm to create value through a cost leadership strategy are shown in Figure 5.2. Companies that cannot link the activities included in this figure lack the resources and capabilities (and hence the core competencies) required to implement the cost leadership strategy successfully.

When implementing the cost leadership strategy, firms must be careful not to ignore completely sources of differentiation (e.g., innovative designs, service after the sale, product quality, etc.) that customers value. Emerson Electric Co. implements what it calls a best-cost producer strategy —"achieving the lowest cost consistent with quality."[68] Thus, while still stressing its capabilities in production, the firm is not ignoring quality control. Therefore, the firm's products provide customers with a level of quality that at least meets, and often exceeds, their expectations relative to the purchase price.

Recently, some worldwide travellers expressed dissatisfaction with the value they received from budget-priced hotels. In the words of one customer in response to her stay in a budget-priced Paris hotel, "Budget to me means clean, comfortable service for a good rate. But what I ended up getting was mediocre for a high price."[69] This feedback shows that customers evaluate a cost leader's product in terms of its cost, relative to the benefits its features provide.

As explained next, effective implementation of a cost leadership strategy allows a firm to earn above-average returns in spite of the presence of strong competitive forces.

## Rivalry with Existing Competitors

Having the low-cost position serves as a valuable defence against rivals. Because of the cost leader's advantageous position, rivals hesitate to compete on the basis of price. Instead, rivals try to compete against cost leaders through some means of differentiation. In South America, for example, top-level executives at Disco SA concluded that they could not compete against giant retailers Wal-Mart and Carrefour of France on the basis of price alone. Offering products at prices nearly as low as its largest competitors, Disco believes that it provides more convenience and service to customers. Carrying a wide range of brands and perishables, Disco stores offer home delivery, telephone ordering, and child-care. Strategically, the firm's executives believe customers will accept a slight increase in product cost in return for the store's conveniences and services.[70] However, if rivals do challenge the firm to compete on the basis of price, the low-cost firm can still earn at least average returns after its competitors have lost theirs through competitive rivalry.[71]

## Bargaining Power of Buyers (Customers)

Powerful customers can force the low-cost leader to reduce its prices, but price will not be driven below the level at which the next-most-efficient industry competitor can earn average returns. Although powerful customers could force the low-cost leader to reduce prices even below this level, they probably would not choose to do so. Still lower prices would prevent the next-most-efficient competitor from earning average returns, resulting in its exit from the market and leaving the low-cost leader in a stronger position. Customers lose their power, and pay higher prices, when forced to buy from a firm operating in an industry without rivals.

*Examples of Value-Creating Activities Associated with the Cost Leadership Strategy.*

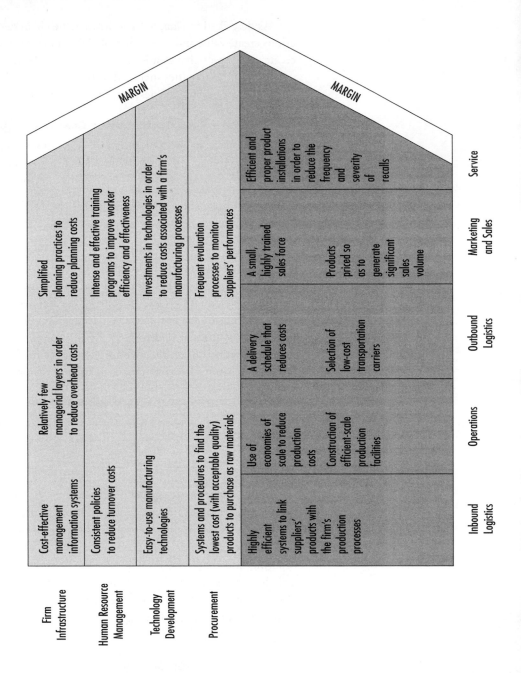

Occasionally, a firm's bargaining power allows it to transfer increased costs to customers. Recently, for example, Unifi incurred substantially higher costs for raw materials and packaging products, but because it is a dominant supplier in many of its markets (up to a 70 percent share in some), Unifi was able to pass through higher costs to customers.[72]

## Bargaining Power of Suppliers

A firm in the low-cost position operates with margins greater than those of its competitors. For example, Emerson Electric Co. earned a net profit margin of nine cents per sales dollar, a figure "… that's far higher than the industry average."[73] Also, analysts' expectations are that the firm's margins should continue to expand, especially in light of its efforts aimed at productivity gains and lower payroll costs (gained partly by directing production to low-wage regions).[74]

Among other benefits, higher margins relative to competitors make it possible for the low-cost firm to absorb price increases from suppliers. When an industry is faced with substantial increases in the cost of its supplies, the low-cost leader may be the only one able to pay the higher prices and continue to earn either average or above-average returns. Alternatively, powerful low-cost leaders may be able to force suppliers to hold down their prices, reducing their margins in the process.

## Potential Entrants

Through continuous efforts to reduce costs to levels below those of competitors, low-cost leaders become very efficient. Because they enhance profit margins, ever-improving levels of efficiency serve as a significant entry barrier to an industry for potential entrants. New entrants must be willing to accept no better than average returns until they gain the experience required to approach the efficiency of the low-cost leader. To earn even average returns, new entrants must have the competencies required to match the cost levels of other competitors.

The low-cost leader's low profit margins (relative to the margins earned by firms implementing a differentiation strategy) make it necessary for the firm to sell large volumes of its product to earn above-average returns. At Acer, the firm's CEO notes that margins on his company's products, including its personal computers, are "shell-thin." "But sell enough of them," he believes, "and a formula emerges: Low margins and high turnover can be a recipe for success."[75] The cost leadership strategy, and the resulting emphasis on high volume and low margins, are the foundation of the firm's 20-plus-year effort to become Taiwan's first global brand-name powerhouse, similar to IBM or Sony.[76] Yet, firms striving to be the low-cost leader must avoid pricing their products at a level that precludes them from earning above-average returns and encourages new industry entrants. Another computer manufacturer, Packard Bell, is sometimes thought to price its products too low in efforts to gain volume. "A favourite with first-time PC buyers seeking the latest multimedia features at rock-bottom prices," [77] Packard Bell is challenged to sell its products at prices that permit the earning of at least average returns.[78]

## Product Substitutes

As compared to its industry rivals, the low-cost leader holds an attractive position in terms of product substitutes. When faced with the possibility of a substitute, the low-cost leader has more flexibility than its competitors. To retain customers, the low-cost leader can reduce its product's price. With still lower prices and features of acceptable quality, the low-cost leader increases the probability that customers will prefer its product, rather than a substitute.

## Competitive Risks of the Cost Leadership Strategy

The cost leadership strategy is not without risks. One risk is that the low-cost leader's manufacturing equipment could become obsolete because of competitors' technological innovations. These innovations may allow rivals to produce at costs lower than those of the original cost leader.

A second risk is too much focus. Because of their focus on continuously driving costs lower, firms implementing a cost leadership strategy sometimes fail to detect significant changes in customers' needs or in competitors' efforts to differentiate what has traditionally been an undifferentiated, commodity-like product. For example, before the launch of Orville Redenbacher's Gourmet Popping Corn, popcorn was considered a humble, commodity-like product. Convinced people would pay more for high-quality popcorn, Orville Redenbacher developed a popcorn hybrid that produced fuller popping corn. He also perfected harvesting and packaging techniques that minimized kernel damage.[79]

A final risk of the cost leadership strategy concerns imitation. Competitors sometimes learn how to imitate the low-cost leader's strategy successfully. When this occurs, the low-cost leader is challenged to find ways to increase the value provided by its good or service. Usually, value is increased by selling the current product at an even lower price or by adding features customers value while maintaining price. Even low-cost leaders must be careful when reducing prices to a still lower level. If the firm prices its good or service at an unrealistically low level (a level at which it will be difficult to retain satisfactory margins), customers' expectations about what they envision to be a reasonable price become difficult to reverse.[80]

## Differentiation Strategy

With the differentiation strategy, the unique attributes and characteristics of a firm's product (other than cost) provide value to customers. Because a differentiated product satisfies customers' unique needs, firms implementing the differentiation strategy charge premium prices. To do this successfully, a "firm must truly be unique at something or be perceived as unique."[81] It is the ability to sell its differentiated product at a price that exceeds what was spent to create it that allows the firm to outperform its rivals and earn above-average returns.

Rather than costs, the focus of the differentiation strategy is on continuously investing in and developing features that differentiate products in ways that customers value. Overall, a firm using the differentiation strategy seeks to be different from its competitors along as many dimensions as possible. The less similarity between a firm's goods or services and those of competitors, the more buffered the firm is from rivals' actions. Commonly recognized differentiated products include Tommy Hilfiger's clothing lines (image), Caterpillar's heavy equipment (committed to rapid delivery of spare parts to any location in the world), Maytag appliances (product reliability), McKinsey & Co. consulting (the highest priced and most prestigious consulting firm in the world), and Rolex watches (prestige and image).

A product can be differentiated in an almost endless number of ways. Unusual features, responsive customer service, rapid product innovations and technological leadership, perceived prestige and status, different tastes, and engineering design and performance are examples of approaches to differentiation. In fact, virtually anything a firm can do to create real or perceived value for customers is a basis for differentiation.

The challenge is to determine which features create value for the customer and then to stress developing the capabilities that will allow the organization to provide that value.

For example, Mountain Equipment Co-operative (MEC) sells high-tech outdoor clothing and equipment to its million-plus members via mail order or from its stores in Vancouver, Edmonton, Calgary, Toronto, and Ottawa. MEC differentiates itself by supplying information and buying guides to its members to aid purchase decisions, and through its design and exclusive retailing of its own tent and clothing line. Thus, the company has developed a competence in knowing the product and being able to educate the consumer. The co-op also supports a number of environmental causes. Since the "urban adventurer" image is a popular one, MEC is doing well—having given more than $2.5 million to various environmental projects over the last dozen years. [82]

http://www.mec.ca

Key to a differentiation strategy is knowing what the customers desire. Waterloo, Ontario–based Open Text is the market leader in knowledge-management software for companies. CEO Tom Jenkins is adamant that companies must be close to their customers. When speaking of the U.S. market, he insists that, "If Canadians make any mistake in the U.S., it would be the same mistake they might make in Vancouver or Calgary, which is not locating salespeople close to your customers." Open Text has acquired 10 U.S. software developers since 1995. To stay close to its customers, the company has 14 offices for sales, distribution, and support in the United States, and 37 worldwide. Since more than 50 percent of the firm's business is in the United States, company president John Shackleton is based in Chicago, and the company maintains five development centres in the U.S. Midwest. [83]

Jean Coutu Group of Longueuil, Quebec was recently voted the "Most Admired Company in Quebec." Almost 500 pharmacy locations and 16 000 employees are associated with the group. Having grown to $2.6 billion in sales, CEO Jean Coutu credits the firm's success to "superior customer service and advice from experienced, qualified pharmacists." [84] When the company moved to locations outside Quebec, management took great care to study the market to get to know its customers. One of the principal owners lived 18 months in Massachusetts to develop a better sense of the New England market before the company bought its first store there. [85]

A leading manufacturer and retailer of distinctive clothing, Roots creates value through implementation of the differentiation strategy. Though style and image are paramount to Roots, control of the quality that supports that image is also vital to the brand. Both the firm's marketing insight and manufacturing expertise are core competencies Roots uses to differentiate its products from competitors' offerings. Additional information about Roots and its differentiation strategy are presented in the Strategic Focus.

## STRATEGIC FOCUS

### Roots: Achieving Strategic Competitiveness through Differentiation

Started in 1973, Roots is Canada's leading independent manufacturer and retailer of high-quality casual clothing for men, women, and children. Roots now leads the "athletic-inspired casual clothing explosion, having achieved international recognition with the Roots beaver logo." The company currently has more than 120 stores (100-plus in Canada, 6 in the United States, and 13 in Asia). Roots products include quality, easily identifiable shoes, jackets, bags, fragrances, watches, glasses, sportswear, and fashion lines for both genders of all ages.

To maintain and enhance the company's differentiation strategy, the company spends significant time and effort to promote the differentiated quality and style of both its clothing and distinctive beaver logo. Because Roots produces custom products for companies such as Arista Records, Castle Rock Entertainment, Columbia Tri-Star, EMI Records, New Line Cinema, Paramount, and Virgin Records, its quality had become widely known among celebrities. This is how Roots first promoted its brand—as casual fashion worn by celebrities.

The most well-known example of the Roots promotional acumen was the firm's outfitting of the 1998 Canadian Winter Olympic Team. Not only did Roots get worldwide attention but also received so many orders for the team's poorboy caps that Roots could not keep up with demand for months. This coup meant hundreds of millions of dollars in free advertising and made the Roots' style recognizable to a huge number of the world's consumers. Knowing a good deal when they see one, Roots has secured the rights to outfitting the next three Canadian Olympic teams.

Differentiating the product as a quality one is not simply a matter of image and style. The company adheres to a motto of quality and integrity. The four acres of Roots's two Toronto production plants and distribution centre maintain the latest equipment for the manufacture of clothing and accessories. Teamwork with task rotation is also used to improve quality by reducing the tedium of an assembly line. Employees learn to produce a product from start to finish and can thus take pride in their work. Eighty percent of Roots goods are made in Canada (most of these in the Toronto factories). In addition, by owning the stores in which its product is sold, Roots ensures that its products are presented to the customer in the best possible way.

Finally, Roots is maximizing its image by taking its brand into new product lines. The company now sells furniture and housewares (e.g., linens and towels) from a specially dedicated store in Toronto. To further promote the Roots style and image, the company opened a 20-room lodge in Reef Point, B.C. (complete with a retail outlet). By using both its image and reputation for quality, Roots has obtained a three-year licensing and retail agreement for the rights to current NHL clubs and "heritage marks." Now when its competitors in the athletic-inspired casual clothing market sell NHL products, Roots will be making money too.

Source: J. McCann, 1998, Tip of the hat to the Roots boys, *Marketing Magazine*, December 21/28, 19; Roots, 1999, *Roots home page*, http://www.roots.com (Retrieved October 16).

A firm's value chain can also be used to determine if it can link the activities required to create value through implementation of the differentiation strategy. Examples of primary and support activities that are used commonly to differentiate a good or service are shown in Figure 5.3. Companies without the core competencies needed to link these activities cannot expect to implement the differentiation strategy successfully.

As explained next, successful implementation of the differentiation strategy allows a firm to earn above-average returns in spite of the presence of strong competitive forces.

## Rivalry with Existing Competitors

Customers tend to be loyal purchasers of products that are differentiated in ways meaningful to them. As their loyalty to a brand increases, their sensitivity to price increases lessens. This relationship between brand loyalty and price sensitivity insulates a firm from competitive rivalry. Thus, McKinsey & Co. is insulated from its competitors, even on the basis of price, as long as it continues to satisfy the differentiated needs of what appears to be a loyal customer group. The same outcome is true for MEC, as long as its "urban adventurer" products continue to satisfy the needs of its customers.

## Bargaining Power of Buyers (Customers)

The uniqueness of differentiated goods or services insulates the firm from competitive rivalry and reduces customers' sensitivity to price increases. Based on a combination of unique materials and brand image, Ralph Lauren's clothes satisfy certain customers' unique needs better than competitors' offerings do. A key reason that some buyers are willing to pay a premium price for this firm's clothing items is that, for them, other products do not offer a comparable combination of features and cost. The lack of perceived acceptable alternatives increases the firm's power relative to its customers.

## Bargaining Power of Suppliers

Because a firm implementing the differentiation strategy charges a premium price for its products, suppliers must provide it with high-quality parts. However, the high margins the firm earns when selling effectively differentiated products partially insulate it from the influence of suppliers; higher supplier costs can be paid through these margins. Alternatively, because of buyers' relative insensitivity to price increases, the differentiated firm might choose to pass the additional cost of supplies onto the customer by raising the price of its unique product.

## Potential Entrants

Customer loyalty and the need to overcome the uniqueness of a differentiated product are substantial entry barriers faced by potential entrants. Entering an industry under these conditions typically demands significant investments of resources and a willingness to be patient while seeking the loyalty of customers.

## Product Substitutes

Firms selling brand-name goods and services to loyal customers are positioned effectively against product substitutes. In contrast, companies without brand loyalty are more subject to their customers switching either to products that offer differentiated features that serve the same function as the current product, particularly if the substitute has a lower price, or to products that offer more features that perform more attractive functions.

■ ■ **FIGURE 5.3**

*Examples of Value-Creating Activities Associated with the Differentiation Strategy*

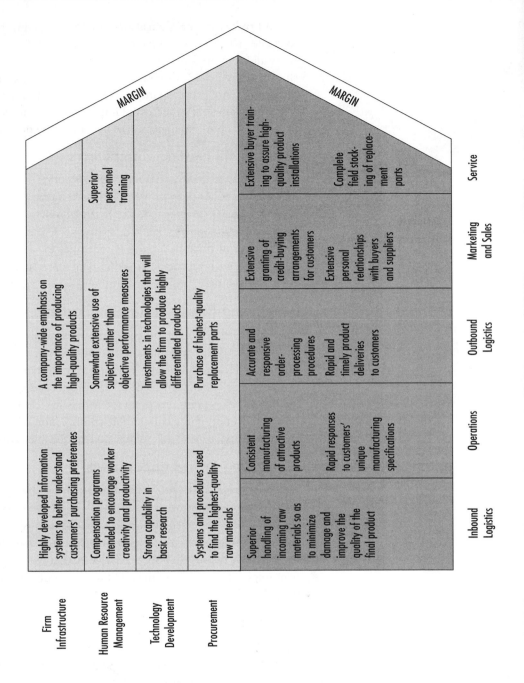

Source: Adapted with the permission of The Free Press, a division of Simon & Schuster from *Competitive Advantage: Creating and Sustaining Superior Performance* by Michael E. Porter, Fig 4-1, 122. Copyright © 1985 by Michael E. Porter.

As our discussion shows, firms can gain competitive advantage through successful implementation of the differentiation strategy. Nonetheless, several risks are associated with this strategy.

## Competitive Risks of the Differentiation Strategy

One risk of the differentiation strategy is that customers might decide that the price differential between the differentiator's and the low-cost leader's product is too significant. In this instance, a firm may be providing differentiated features that exceed customers' needs. When this happens, the firm is vulnerable to competitors that are able to offer customers a combination of features and price that is more consistent with their needs.

Another risk of the differentiation strategy is that a firm's means of differentiation may no longer provide value for which customers are willing to pay. Although we typically think of magazine customers as the readers, an equally, if not more important group are the advertisers that wish to reach a certain target audience. The problem at *Chatelaine* became one where the readership was moving away from the advertisers' target audience. Basically, *Chatelaine*'s demographics, centred on women 25 to 54, had shifted. According to Donna Clark, publisher of *Chatelaine*, "The baby boomer pulled us along with them, and so the demographics had been aging ... How do you stay healthy if you don't add new ... readers?"[86] Thus, Chatelaine needed more new readers among women in the 20- to 30-year-old range to keep readership up and to maintain advertising revenues. To revamp the magazine cost about $2 million, which resulted in a more sophisticated, glossier product. Other changes included a larger up-front health section, clearer feature stories, and elimination of the craft section to regain the differentiated value that readers and advertisers could place on *Chatelaine*.[87]

A third risk of the differentiation strategy is that learning can narrow customers' perceptions of the value of a firm's differentiated features. The value of the IBM name on personal computers was a differentiated feature for which some customers were willing to pay a premium price as the product emerged. However, as customers familiarized themselves with the standard features, and as a host of PC clones entered the market, IBM brand loyalty began to fail. Clones offered customers features similar to those of the IBM product at a substantially lower price, reducing the attractiveness of IBM's product. Even currently, IBM's new lines are failing to meet company expectations. In assessing the situation, one dealer observed that while the Aptiva line possessed some "cool" machines, it simply cost too much for the features provided relative to the combination of features and price of products from competitors such as Compaq and Hewlett-Packard.[88]

## Focus Strategies

In contrast to the cost leadership and differentiation strategies, a company implementing a focus strategy seeks to use its core competencies to serve the needs of a certain industry segment (e.g., a particular buyer group, segment of the product line, or geographic market).[89] A **focus strategy** is an integrated set of actions designed to produce products that serve the needs of a particular competitive segment. Although the breadth of a target is clearly a matter of degree, the essence of the focus strategy "is the exploitation of a narrow target's differences from the balance of the industry."[90] For example, Debaji's Fresh Market has become a landmark for Edmonton food lovers. The Debajis have been able to compete for 15 years with giants such as Loblaws and Canada Safeway by developing a niche market. Debaji's specializes in products that appeal to health-conscious and taste-courageous consumers who are willing to pay well for unusual foods. Nehad Debaji says. "We concentrate on very high quality, value for what

A **focus strategy** is an integrated set of actions designed to produce products that serve the needs of a particular competitive segment.

you pay for."[91] Through successful implementation of a focus strategy, a company can gain a competitive advantage in its chosen target segments even though it does not possess an industry-wide competitive advantage.[92]

The foundation of focus strategies is that a firm can serve a particular segment of an industry more effectively or efficiently than can industry-wide competitors. Success with a focus strategy rests on a firm's ability either to find segments where unique needs are so specialized that broad-based competitors choose not to serve them or locate a segment being served poorly by the broad-based competitors.[93] For example, Street Characters of Calgary created a market niche in what was a nonexistent industry at the time the firm was created: producing lightweight, comfortable mascot costumes for sports teams. Though sports mascots—such as S.J. Sharkie, designed by Street Characters for the NHL's San Jose Sharks—are the foundation of the business, and even though Street Characters' market is worldwide, the 150 or so mascots they create in a year generate only $1.5 million in sales. To sell the product (which can run as high as $30 000), Street Characters provides a range of associated services such as character design, teaching appropriate use of the mascot, providing instructional videos, and performer audition and instruction. Customers are willing to pay the price for Street Characters service because a well-designed mascot can create publicity and aid in merchandising concepts (toys, clothing, etc.) that are far more valuable than the price the firm demands. Street Characters may not develop the full range of marketing that its clients require, but the part it does create commands a premium.[94]

Value can be provided to customers through two types of focus strategies: focused low cost and focused differentiation.

## Focused Low-Cost Strategy

Using one of the watch industry's little-known secrets, Simon Pennell of Vancouver's St. Moritz Watch is producing prestige watches at one-tenth the price of other high-end watchmakers. Pennell's industry secret: with few exceptions, most high-end producers simply assemble parts made by others. Because of his background in the industry, Pennell knew where to buy the components and what they should cost. In an industry where volume discounts and payment schemes that can extend up to two years are normal, St. Moritz has kept costs down by having one set price for each model and giving retailers only 30 days to pay. Being a small producer, St. Moritz avoids direct competition with larger firms by targeting clients who want quality but whose watch sales are too small for larger producers to serve. For example, St. Moritz sells to dive shops and outdoor sports stores, whose customers appreciate their ruggedness and style. The company also serves private-label contracts, including a model for Land Rover, the high-end British sport-utility vehicle maker.[95]

## Focused Differentiation Strategy

Other firms (such as Bang & Olufsen, Purdy's Chocolates, and Zeton, the firms described in the opening case) implement the focused differentiation strategy. The number of ways products can be differentiated to serve the unique needs of particular competitive segments is virtually endless. Consider the following examples.

Toronto's GAP Adventures designs tours to out of the way places such as Borneo and Tibet. In the process of developing its tours, GAP has set the standard for sustainable eco-tourism. GAP tour groups are small, stay in local guesthouses, use local transportation, and interfere as little as possible with the local environment. In the process, tourists get a close-up of the country's real culture and people. GAP owner Bruce Poon Tip says, "If you want the comforts of home, then stay home ..." Currently, GAP operates in more than 20 countries, with over 700 travel packages.[96]

Other firms implementing a focused differentiation strategy include Security Passions, located in Ciudad Juarez, Mexico. For less than $2000, the firm will line a customer's favourite mink coat or leather jacket with bulletproof material. Security Passions developed this product because its town is home to one of Mexico's most notorious drug cartels.[97] Another example is a fourth-generation bread baker who is delighting customers throughout Europe with a variety of unique (and pricey) breads. Among the items he bakes are 10 different Bavarian and French loaves, two types of plaited Jewish challah, and a loaf with very expensive Italian sun-dried onions.[98]

Finally, using its competitive advantages of unimpeachable quality and service, Montreal-based Les Ailes de la Mode's (The Wings of Fashion) three department stores outsell Sears Canada two to one and the Bay three to one on a per square foot basis. Leather couches around a baby grand piano, coat checks, a concierge, a private room for nursing mothers, and, not infrequently, complimentary coffee and dessert are all standards at Les Ailes. If the store does not have an item in stock, employees will get it, even if they have to go to a competitor to buy it.[99]

Firms must be able to complete various primary and support activities in a competitively superior manner to achieve strategic competitiveness and earn above-average returns when implementing a focus strategy. The activities that must be completed to implement the focused low-cost and the focused differentiation strategies are virtually identical to those shown in Figures 5.2 and 5.3, respectively. Similarly, the manners in which the two focus strategies allow a firm to deal successfully with the five competitive forces parallel those described with respect to the cost leadership and the differentiation strategies. The only difference is that the competitive scope changes from industry wide to a narrow competitive segment of the industry. Thus, a review of Figures 5.2 and 5.3 and the text regarding the five competitive forces yields a description of the relationship between each of the two focus strategies and competitive advantage.

## Competitive Risks of Focus Strategies

When implementing either type of focus strategy, a firm faces the same general risks as the company pursuing the cost leadership or the differentiation strategy on an industry-wide basis. However, focus strategies have three additional risks beyond these general ones.

First, a competitor may be able to focus on a more narrowly defined competitive segment and "outfocus" the focuser. For example, a firm might decide that it can better serve the specialized needs of GAP travel's customers—adventurous eco-tourists—by focusing on specific regions or even more out-of-the-way places than GAP does.

Second, a firm competing on an industry-wide basis may decide that the market segment being served by the focus strategy firm is attractive. Molson Breweries moved to address the popularity of microbreweries by producing a micro-brew called "Toronto's Own" to be distributed exclusively within the Greater Toronto Area.[100] The third risk of a focus strategy is that the needs of customers within a narrow competitive segment may become more similar to those of customers as a whole. When this occurs, the advantages of a focus-strategy are either reduced or eliminated.

A risk associated with attracting big competitors is that another focuser may use the strategy to create a national firm. This is what Sleeman's Brewing has done. Sleeman's began as an Ontario microbrewery then became a regional brewer. The firm then had the resources to buy other microbreweries in British Columbia and Quebec to create a national presence and become Canada's third-largest brewer.[101]

Next, we describe a business-level strategy that is being used more prominently in the new competitive landscape. A key reason for this is the requirements of global competition.

## Integrated Low-Cost/Differentiation Strategy

Particularly in global markets, a firm's ability to blend the low-cost and the differentiation approaches may be critical to sustaining competitive advantages. Compared to firms relying on one dominant generic strategy for their success, a company capable of successfully implementing an integrated low-cost/differentiation strategy should be in a better position to adapt quickly to environmental changes, learn new skills and technologies more quickly, and effectively leverage its core competencies across business units and product lines.

A growing body of evidence supports the relationship between implementation of an integrated strategy and the earning of above-average returns.[102] Some time ago, for example, a researcher found that the most successful firms competing in low-profit potential industries were able to effectively combine the low-cost and differentiation strategies.[103] In a more recent comprehensive study, it was discovered that "businesses which combined multiple forms of competitive advantage outperformed businesses that only were identified with a single form."[104]

A key reason firms capable of successfully implementing the integrated strategy can earn above-average returns is that the benefits of this strategy are additive: "differentiation leads to premium prices at the same time that cost leadership implies lower costs."[105] Thus, the integrated strategy allows firms to gain competitive advantage by offering two types of value to customers—some differentiated features (but often fewer than those provided by the product-differentiated firm) and relatively low cost (but not as low as the products of the low-cost leader).

Japan's Mabuchi Motor implements the integrated low-cost/differentiation strategy. This firm produces small electric motors for compact disc players, toy airplanes, and car windows. Mabuchi's focus is singular and consistent. The firm's objective is to produce "high-quality products at low prices, but in limited variety." Costs are kept low by the firm's decision to design and manufacture a limited range of products. The company produces 4.9 million motors daily but fills 55 percent of its orders with just ten different models. These products are differentiated through the firm's "obsession" with its miniature devices. At a modern technical centre, Mabuchi scientists constantly research ways to differentiate their firm's products from competitors' offerings, seeking ways to make their motors "lighter, quieter, hardier, and cheaper."[106] Indicators of Mabuchi's strategic competitiveness include control of more than one-half of the world's market for small motors and routine double-digit operating margins.[107]

Firms must be strategically flexible to implement successfully the integrated low-cost/differentiation strategy. Discussed next are three approaches to organizational work that can increase the strategic flexibility that is associated with implementation of this strategy.

## Flexible Manufacturing Systems

Made possible largely as a result of the increasing capabilities of modern information technologies, flexible manufacturing systems increase the "flexibilities of human, physical and information resources"[108] that are integrated to create differentiated products at low costs. A flexible manufacturing system (FMS) is a computer-controlled process used to produce a variety of products in moderate, flexible quantities with a minimum of manual intervention.[109]

The goal of FMS is to eliminate the low-cost versus product-variety tradeoff inherent in traditional manufacturing technologies. The flexibility provided by an FMS allows a plant to "change nimbly from making one product to making another."[110] When used properly, an FMS can help a firm be more flexible in response to changes in its customers' needs, while retaining low-cost advantages and consistent product quality. Because an FMS reduces the lot size needed to manufacture a product efficiently, a firm's capacity to serve the unique needs of a narrow competitive scope is increased. Thus, an FMS is a significant technological advance that allows firms to produce a large variety of products at a low cost. An example is Montreal's Spectra Premium Industries. The firm designed and built its flexible manufacturing system to produce its new replacement coated-steel gas tanks at industry standard quality but sell them at 50 percent less than original equipment producers.[111]

Effective use of an FMS is linked with a firm's ability to understand constraints these systems may create (in terms of materials handling and the flow of supporting resources in scheduling, for example) and to design an effective mix of machines, computer systems, and people.[112] As a result, this type of manufacturing technology facilitates the implementation of complex competitive strategies, such as the integrated low-cost/differentiation strategy, that lead to strategic competitiveness in global markets.[113]

Incorporated into firms' processes somewhat slowly at first, the number of companies anticipating the use of FMSs in the near future is substantial. It is estimated that the vast majority of the large firms in Japan, Western Europe, and North America (those with more than 10 000 employees) use FMS.[114] Evidence to date suggests, however, that Japanese manufacturing firms have derived greater benefits from investments in FMSs as compared to their North American counterparts. The cause of this outcome may be that FMSs are managed more effectively in Japanese firms.[115]

## Information Networks across Firms

New information networks linking manufacturers with their suppliers, distributors, and customers are another technological development that increases a firm's strategic flexibility and responsiveness.[116] Recent changes in a range of information technologies facilitated the development of competitively valuable information networks. Examples of these technologies include CADD (computer-assisted design and development) systems, CIM (computer-integrated manufacturing) systems, and EDI (electronic data integration). Allen Bradley, Boeing, Ford Motor Co., Hitachi, and Motorola are but a few of the many companies using information networks to coordinate the development, production, distribution, and marketing of their products. Among many benefits, computer-based information links substantially reduce the time needed to design and test new products and allow a firm to compete on the basis of fast delivery (a differentiated feature) and low cost.[117]

## Total Quality Management Systems

Although difficult to implement,[118] many firms have established total quality management (TQM) systems (also see Chapter 6). Important objectives sought through use of TQM systems include increases in the quality of a firm's product and the productivity levels of the entire organization.[119] Enhanced quality focuses customers' attention on improvements in product performance, feature utility, and reliability. This allows a firm to achieve differentiation and ultimately higher prices and market share. An emphasis on quality in production techniques lowers manufacturing and service costs through savings in rework, scrap, and warranty expenses. These savings can result in a competitive advantage for a firm over its rivals. Thus, TQM programs integrate aspects of the differentiation and cost leadership strategies.

Four key assumptions are the foundation of TQM systems. The first assumption is that "the costs of poor quality (such as inspection, rework, lost customers, and so on) are far greater than the costs of developing processes that produce high-quality products and services."[120] The second assumption is that employees naturally care about their work and will take initiatives to improve it. These initiatives are taken only when the firm provides employees with the tools and training they need to improve quality and when managers pay attention to their ideas. The third assumption is that "organizations are systems of highly interdependent parts."[121] Problems encountered in such systems often cross traditional functional (e.g., marketing, manufacturing, finance, etc.) lines. Solving interdependent problems requires integrated decision processes with participation from all affected functional areas. The fourth assumption is that the responsibility for an effective TQM system rests squarely on the shoulders of upper-level managers. These people must openly and totally support use of a TQM system and accept the responsibility for an organizational design that allows employees to work effectively.

As with the other business-level strategies, there are risks associated with use of the integrated low-cost/differentiation strategy.

# Competitive Risks of the Integrated Low-Cost/Differentiation Strategy

The potential of the integrated strategy for above-average returns is significant, but this potential comes with substantial risk. Selecting a business-level strategy calls for firms to make choices about how they intend to compete. Achieving the low-cost position in an industry, or a segment of an industry (e.g., a focus strategy), demands that the firm be able to reduce its costs consistently relative to competitors. Use of the differentiation strategy, with either an industry-wide or a focused competitive scope (see Figure 5.1), results in above-average returns only when the firm provides customers with differentiated products they value and for which they are willing to pay a premium price. One strategy researcher believes that firms pursuing an integrated low-cost/differentiation strategy may do so only under two conditions. One, the way the product/service is differentiated must attract enough customers that it allows for sources of low-cost advantage to be viable. Two, firms who pursue differentiation and move to integrate it with low cost will probably be more successful than firms who pursue low cost and try to integrate it with differentiation. The reason is that differentiation requires creativity and innovation. Firms pursuing differentiation can apply their creativity and innovation to provide unique solutions to achieve lower costs. On the other hand, firms pursuing a low-cost strategy may have stifled creativity and innovation in striving for lower costs. Thus, firms pursuing a low-cost strategy may have destroyed a great deal of the creativity and innovation prerequisite for differentiation.[122]

The firm failing to establish a leadership position in its chosen competitive scope, as the low-cost producer or as a differentiator, risks becoming "stuck in the middle."[123] Being stuck in the middle prevents firms from both dealing successfully with the five competitive forces and earning above-average returns. Some research shows that the lowest-performing businesses are those lacking a distinguishable competitive advantage. Not having a clear and identifiable competitive advantage results from a firm's being stuck in the middle.[124] Such firms can earn average returns only when an industry's structure is highly favourable or when the firm is competing against others in the same position.[125]

Midsize accounting firms (those with as many as 50 partners and 300 employees) appear to be stuck in the middle. These firms lack the size and resources to offer the wide array of services available from the Big Five giants; at the same time, their overhead rates prevent them from matching the low prices charged by small accounting firms and solo practitioners. Thus, these firms' services seem to be too expensive to compete with the low-cost small firms and too undifferentiated to provide the value offered by the large, differentiated accounting firms. In an accounting firm consultant's opinion, these conditions suggest that in the near future midsize accounting firms may be "as extinct as the dodo."[126]

As explained in the Strategic Focus, some firms competing in the specialty coffee business also face the possibility of becoming stuck in the middle. If it materializes, this outcome would be a product primarily of the dynamics of competition within this industry.

Once a firm has selected its business-level strategy, it must both anticipate and be prepared to respond to competitors' actions and responses. For example, Diedrich Coffee's initiation of competitive actions has the potential to affect Starbucks. Diedrich's purchase of Coffee People makes it one of the top three operators of specialty coffee outlets in North America. Diedrich's purchase of Coffee People is part of its strategy to become a 2000-outlet chain itself within the next five years and thus have the size required to compete against Starbucks. Increasing success by competitors will elicit competitive responses from Starbucks and other industry participants. Competitive dynamics such as these are examined in the next chapter. These dynamics take place with respect to all types of strategies (see Chapters 6 through 10), but the majority of competitive actions and competitive responses are initiated in efforts to implement a firm's business-level strategy.[127]

## STRATEGIC FOCUS

### Avoiding Becoming Stuck in the Middle in the Speciality Coffee Business

Evidence suggests that some firms competing in the coffee-bar business may be stuck in the middle. Starbucks, with over 2000 outlets worldwide, is touted as the leader in the industry. Having opened about 400 outlets per year for the last two years, Starbucks is certainly able to drive deep into most markets. Yet, the coffee

*continued*

war in Canada has not yet been won by Starbucks. While Seattle's Starbucks has about 200 outlets in Canada, Toronto's Second Cup is leading the coffee race with about 400 locations. With 42 percent of the specialty coffee market in Canada, Second Cup is the clear leader against Starbucks's 19 percent. In fact, Second Cup's CEO, Randy Powell believes "Our Canadian business is running strong and is actually ramping up and getting stronger."

While both chains possess degrees of vertical integration (controlling operations for coffee sourcing, roasting, packaging, and distribution), their paths are diverging. Starbucks is continuing its international growth and is looking forward to having 5000 outlets. Second Cup has had to refocus its efforts in Canadian coffee operations.

Second Cup did have a U.S. presence with a 70 percent ownership stake in Coffee People and Coffee People's 300-store Gloria Jean's Coffee Beans chain. However, Second Cup had to divest its interest because U.S. operations were not living up to expected performance levels. Coffee People was sold in early 1999 to California's Diedrich Coffee. Along with some cash, Second Cup receives about a 10 percent interest in Diedrich. The latter company's size will likely allow it to be a bigger player in the expected consolidation of the North American retail coffee business. With the cash Second Cup now has, coupled with its knowledge of the Canadian market, analysts expect that the firm will have the resources to make major moves to solidify its position.

Based in part on the prediction that sales in the specialty coffee industry will reach more than $3 billion in the early 2000s (up from only $44 million in 1969), an explosive growth is anticipated in the total number of coffee bars in North America. This growth, which saw the number of total units double between 1996 and 2000, will lead to an industry shakeout. One analyst noted that the intensity of competition in this industry makes it highly improbable that all players in the business will survive. Even more directly, Michael Bergman, chairman of Second Cup, believes that as a result of events occurring in the industry, "You will have the strong, big players and the small, well-run chains that really understand their particular customer. The victims are going to be marginal players in the middle."

Aware of these industry realities, some firms are taking actions in an effort to avoid becoming stuck in the middle. Second Cup's Canadian refocus and Diedrich's growth strategy are two such examples. Established industry participants such as Chock Full O'Nuts—a company that roasts, packs, and markets regular, instant, decaffeinated, and specialty coffees and teas—is another example. In an effort to avoid being stuck in the middle in the coffee specialty business, Chock Full O'Nuts has been expanding its Quikava coffee chain as the foundation of a focused differentiation strategy. Each Quikava unit is a tiny, double-drive-through that sells coffee, sandwiches, and baked goods. Because these units are operating in the red, analysts believe that the company will likely have to more than double its number of stores to reach break-even. In the short run, Chock Full O'Nuts may not have developed a successful specialty coffee business concept—one that will allow it to remain a viable participant in an industry that may experience a shakeout in the near future. However, Starbucks, Second Cup, and Diedrich should not count Chock Full O'Nuts's Quikava out of the game. In 1999, food giant Sara Lee bought Chock Full O'Nuts to better position itself against others in the coffee business. With Sara Lee's backing, Quikava could become another major player in a potentially overcrowded field.

*continued*

Sources: R. Coleman, 1997, Java Juniors, *Dallas Morning News,* June 9, D1, D4; G. Crone, 1999, US expansion a damper on Second Cup's profits, *Financial Post,* Feb. 4, C4; C Edwards, 1999, Sara Lee readies to roast rival: Bids for coffee company, *Financial Post,* May 5, C10; R. M. Greene, 1997, Chock Full O'Nuts, *Value Line,* Aug. 15, 1467; G. Marr, 1999, Starbucks brews up strong growth story, *Financial Post,* Feb. 11, D3; Z. Olijnyk, 1999, Second Cup to sell interest in Coffee People, *Financial Post,* Feb. 10, C4; Chock Full O'Nuts, 2000, *Chock Full O' Nuts home page,* http://www.chockfullonuts.com (Retrieved March 6); Second Cup Coffee, 1999, *Second Cup home page,* http://www.secondcup.com (Retrieved October 12); Bloomberg News, 1997, Upscale coffee chains show signs of overheating, *Dallas Morning News,* August 3, H3.

# SUMMARY

- Business-level strategy is an integrated and coordinated set of commitments and actions designed to provide value to customers and gain a competitive advantage by exploiting core competencies in specific, individual product markets. Five business-level strategies are examined in this chapter. Strategic competitiveness is enhanced when a firm is able to develop and exploit new core competencies faster than competitors can mimic competitive advantages yielded by current competencies.

- Customers are the foundation of successful business-level strategies. When considering customers, firms simultaneously examine three issues: who, what, and how. Respectively, these issues cause the firm to determine the customer groups it will serve, the needs those customers have that it seeks to satisfy, and the core competencies it possesses that can be used to satisfy customers' needs. The increasing segmentation of markets occurring throughout the world creates multiple opportunities for firms to identify unique customer needs.

- Firms seeking competitive advantage through the cost leadership strategy often produce no-frills, standardized products for an industry's typical customer. Above-average returns are earned when firms continuously drive their costs lower than those of their competitors while providing customers with products that have low prices and acceptable levels of differentiated features.

- Competitive risks associated with the cost leadership strategy include (1) a loss of competitive advantage to newer technologies, (2) a failure to detect changes in customers' needs, and (3) the ability of competitors to imitate the low-cost leader's competitive advantage through their own unique strategic actions.

- Through implementation of the differentiation strategy, firms provide customers with products that have different (and valued) features. Because of their uniqueness, differentiated products are sold at a premium price. Products can be differentiated along any dimension that is valued by some group of customers. Firms using this strategy seek to differentiate their products from competitors' goods or services along as many dimensions as possible. The less similarity with competitors' products, the more buffered a firm is from competition with its rivals.

- Risks associated with the differentiation strategy include (1) a customer group's decision that the differences between the differentiated product and the low-cost leader's product are no longer worth a premium price, (2) the inability of a differentiated product to create the type of value for which customers are willing to pay a premium price, and (3) the ability of competitors to provide customers with products that have features similar to those associated with the differentiated product, but at a lower cost.

- Through the low-cost and the differentiated focus strategies, firms serve the needs of a narrow competitive segment (e.g., buyer group, product segment, or geographic area). This strategy is successful when firms have the core competencies required to provide value to a narrow competitive segment that exceeds the value available from firms serving customers on an industry-wide basis.

- The competitive risks of focus strategies include (1) a competitor's ability to use its core competencies to "outfocus" the focuser by serving an even more narrowly defined competitive segment, (2) decisions by industry-wide competitors to serve a customer group's specialized needs that the focuser has been serving, and (3) a reduction in differences of the needs between customers in a narrow competitive segment and the industry-wide market.

- Firms using an integrated low-cost/differentiation strategy strive to provide customers with relatively low-cost products that have some valued differentiated features. The primary risk of this strategy is that a firm might produce products that do not offer sufficient value in terms of low cost or differentiation. When this occurs, the company is "stuck in the middle" and competes at a disadvantage.

## REVIEW QUESTIONS

1. What is a strategy, and what are business-level strategies?
2. What is the relationship between a firm's customers and its business-level strategy? Why is this relationship important?
3. When studying customers in terms of "who," "what," and "how," what questions are firms trying to answer?
4. What are possible impacts of corporate-level strategy on business-level strategies?
5. What is the integrated low-cost/differentiation strategy? Why is this strategy becoming more important to firms?
6. How is competitive advantage achieved through successful implementation of the cost leadership strategy? The differentiation strategy? The focused low-cost strategy? The focused differentiation strategy? The integrated low-cost/differentiation strategy?
7. What are the risks associated with selecting and implementing each of the five strategies mentioned in question 6?

## DISCUSSION QUESTIONS

1. You are a customer of your university or college. What actions does your school take to understand what your needs are? Be prepared to discuss your views.
2. Choose a firm in your local community that is of interest to you. Based on interactions with this company, which business-level strategy do you believe the firm is implementing? What evidence can you provide to support your belief?
3. Assume that you have decided to establish and operate a restaurant in your local community. *Who* are the customers you would serve? *What*

needs do these customers have that you could satisfy with your restaurant? *How* would you satisfy those needs? Be prepared to discuss your responses.
4. What business-level strategy is your business school implementing? What core competencies are being used to implement this strategy?
5. Assume you heard the following comment: "It is impossible for a firm to produce a low-cost, highly differentiated product." Accept or reject this statement and be prepared to defend your position.

## ETHICS QUESTIONS

1. Can a commitment to ethical conduct on issues such as the environment, product quality, and fulfilling contractual agreements affect competitive advantage? If so, how?
2. Is there more incentive for differentiators or low-cost leaders to pursue stronger ethical conduct? Think of an example to support your answer.
3. Can an overemphasis on low-cost leadership or differentiation lead to ethical problems (such as poor product design and manufacturing) that create costly problems (e.g., product liability lawsuits)?
4. Reexamine the assumptions about effective TQM systems presented in this chapter. Do these assumptions urge top-level managers to maintain higher ethical standards? If so, how?
5. A brand image is one a firm can use to differentiate its good or service. Yet, many questions have been raised about the effect brand images have on consumer behaviour. For example, significant concern has arisen about brand images that are managed by tobacco firms and their effect on teen smoking habits. Should firms be concerned about how they form and use brand images? Why or why not?

## INTERNET EXERCISE

Go to the *Hudson's Bay Company home page* at: **www.hbc.com**

The Hudson's Bay Company (HBC) owns both Zellers and The Bay. This combination is unusual in that one of HBC's stores pursues a low-cost strategy and the other a differentiation strategy. Visit HBC's, Zellers', and The Bay's Web sites. Provide examples of how each of the stores supports its respective strategy.

## STRATEGIC SURFING

Canada News Wire provides free access to information and current news stories about Canadian companies. This resource is valuable to managers and students who are interested in learning more about the background, performance, and strategies of Canadian companies. For U.S. companies and internationally, an excellent resource is Hoovers online:

**http://www.newswire.ca**

**http://www.hoovers.com**

## NOTES

1  Please Mum of Prince Rupert BC, 1999, *Please Mum of Prince Rupert BC home page,* http://www.bc-biz.com/pleasemum (Retrieved October 10).

2  This particular view of strategy is mentioned in D. P. Slevin & J. G. Covin, 1997, Strategy formation patterns, performance, and the significance of context, *Journal of Management,* 23: 189–209.

3  A. Campbell & M. Alexander, 1997, What's wrong with strategy? *Harvard Business Review* 75 (6): 42–51; D. J. Collis & C. A. Montgomery, 1995, Competing on resources: Strategy in the 1990s, *Harvard Business Review,* 73 (4): 118–28.

4  C. E. Helfat, 1997, Know-how and asset complementarity and dynamic capability accumulation: The case of R&D, *Strategic Management Journal,* 18: 339–60; A. Seth & H. Thomas, 1994, Theories of the firm: Implications for strategy research, *Journal of Management Studies,* 31: 167.

5  N. Rajagopalan & G. M. Spreitzer, 1997, Toward a theory of strategic change: A multi-lens perspective and integrative framework, *Academy of Management Journal,* 22: 48–79; R. R. Nelson, 1994, Why do firms differ, and how does it matter? in R. P. Rumelt, D. E. Schendel, & D. J. Teece (eds.), *Fundamental Issues in Strategy* (Boston: Harvard Business School Press), 247–69.

6  H. Courtney, J. Kirkland, & P. Viguerie, 1997, Strategy under uncertainty, *Harvard Business Review,* 75 (6): 67–79; P. F. Drucker, 1997, The future that has already happened, *Harvard Business Review,* 75 (5): 20–24.

7  G. S. Day & D. J. Reibstein, 1997, *Wharton on Dynamic Competitive Strategy* (New York: John Wiley & Sons), 3.

8  G. S. Day, 1997, Maintaining the competitive edge: Creating and sustaining advantages in dynamic competitive environments, in G. S. Day & D. J. Reibstein (eds.), 1997, *Wharton on Dynamic Competitive Strategy* (New York: John Wiley & Sons), 48–75; D. Leonard-Barton, 1995, *Wellsprings of Knowledge* (Boston: Harvard Business School Press).

9  C. Oliver, 1997, Sustainable competitive advantage: Combining institutional and resource-based views, *Strategic Management Journal,* 18: 697–713.

10  T. T. Baldwin, C. Danielson, & W. Wiggenhorn, 1997, The evolution of learning strategies in organizations: From employee development to business redefinition, *Academy of Management Executive,* XI (4): 47–58; D. Lei, M. A. Hitt, & R. Bettis, 1996, Dynamic core competences through meta-learning and strategic context, *Journal of Management,* 22: 549–69.

11  C. M. Christensen, 1997, Making strategy: Learning by doing, *Harvard Business Review,* 75 (6): 141–56.

12  D. North, 1999, The Meccano millionaires: Life at Zeton Inc. is a dream come true for every kid who ever fooled around with a Meccano set, *Canadian Business,* March 26: 60–64.

13  Robert Gibbens, 1998, Domtar profit jumps to $20M, *Financial Post,* October 23, Daily Ed., 14; *National Post,* 1998, Weston doubles quarterly profit: Swelled by E.B. Eddy sale, *National Post,* November 20, Final Ed., D4.

14  J. Schreiner, 1998, Placer Dome doubles reserves with $235M South African deal: Gold price drops, as does company's share price, *National Post,* December 1, Final Edition, C3.

15  B. A. Walters & R. L. Priem, 1999, Business strategy and CEO intelligence acquisition, *Competitive Intelligence Review,* 10 (2): 15–22.

16  R. Flannery, 1999, Taiwan PC makers rely more on China, *Wall Street Journal,* October 21, A16.

17  A. Bernasek, 1999, Hungarian rhapsody, *Fortune,* November 8, 46–48; Y. H. Youbir, 1999, Doing business in Hungary, *Thunderbird International Business Review,* 41 (6): 639–54.

18  G. G. Dess, A. Gupta, J.-F. Hennart, & C. W. L. Hill, 1995, Conducting and integrating strategy research at the international, corporate, and business levels: Issues and directions, *Journal of Management* 21: 357–93.

19  Day & Reibstein (eds.), *Wharton on Dynamic Competitive Strategy,* 20.

20  B. Saporito, 1993, How to revive a fading firm, *Fortune,* March 22, 80.

21  M. E. Porter, 1980, *Competitive Strategy* (New York: The Free Press).

22  Lei, Hitt, & Bettis, Dynamic core competencies.

23  Ibid., 149–61; D. F. Abell, 1980, *Defining the Business: The Starting Point of Strategic Planning* (Englewood Cliffs, NJ: Prentice-Hall).

24  A. J. Slywotzky, 1996, *Value Migration* (Boston: Harvard Business School Press), 13.

25  A. W. H. Grant & L. A. Schlesinger, 1995, Realize your customers' full profit potential, *Harvard Business Review,* 73 (5): 59–72.

26  Freightliner: Growing through innovation and agility, 1997, *Fortune,* December 8, S10.

27  T. A. Stewart, 1997, A satisfied customer isn't enough, *Fortune,* July 21, 112–13.

28  T. O. Jones & W. E. Sasser, Jr., 1995, Why satisfied customers defect, *Harvard Business Review, 73* (6): 88–99.

29  T. A. Stewart, 1995, After all you've done for your customers, why are they still not happy? *Fortune,* December 11, 182.

30  J. Hagel, III & J. F. Rayport, 1997, The coming battle for customer information, *Harvard Business Review, 75* (1): 53–65.

31  Slywotzky, *Value Migration,* 13; R. McKenna, 1995, Real-time marketing, *Harvard Business Review, 73* (4): 87–95; S. F. Wiggins, 1995, New ways to create lifetime bonds with your customers, *Fortune,* October 30, 115.

32  V. Griffith, 1997, Treasures in the corporate memory, *Financial Times,* November 10, 14.

33  T. C. Kinnear, K. L. Bernhardt, & K. A. Krentler, 1995, *Principles of Marketing,* 4th ed. (New York: HarperCollins): 149–50.

34  M. Janigan, 1998, Hard times at Eaton's, *Maclean's* (Toronto Edition), November 30, 62; Canadian Press, 1998, New worries beset Eaton's struggle for survival, Canadian Press Newswire, October 30 (via CBCA: Canadian Business and Current Affairs, available at http://delos.lib.sfu.ca:8366/cgi-bin/slri/z3950.CGI/1024975949/?cbca.db).

35  *National Post,* 1999, Fashion director hasn't forgotten the core customer in revitalizing The Bay, *National Post,* April 17, D8; J. Schofield, 1999, The retail revolution: Shoppers are shaking up the market, and Wal-Mart is winning, *Maclean's* (Toronto Edition), March 1, 34.

36  R. Berner, 1997, Kmart makes early-retirement offer to 28,500, *Wall Street Journal,* November 14, B4; M. H. Gerstein, 1997, Kmart Corp., *Value Line,* August 22: 1654; K. Naughton, 1995, Bright lights, big city won't cut it for Kmart, *BusinessWeek,* May 26, 57.

37  Associated Press, 1996, Automakers rolling out new models, *Dallas Morning News,* January 4: D2.

38  Statistics Canada, 1999, Statistics Canada Pages ethnic origin: http://www.StatCan.ca/English/Pgdb/People/Population/demo28a.htm; minorities:http://www.StatCan.ca/english/Pgdb/People/Population/demo40a.htm; earnings: http://www.statcan.ca/english/Pgdb/People/Labour/labor02a.htm; religion: http://www.statcan.ca:80/english/Pgdb/People/Population/demo30a.htm (Retrieved October 8).

39  K. Labich, 1994, Class in America, *Fortune,* February 7, 114–26.

40  K. Labich, Class in America, 114–26.

41  E. Osnos, 1997, Cornucopia of choices proves confusing for today's consumer, *Dallas Morning News,* September 29: D1, D5.

42  P. Withers, 1998, Move over, boomers: A species called the teenager is making a comeback. *B.C. Business Magazine,* January, 28–33; Teens a huge force in consumer market, 1994, Canadian Press Newswire, November 21 (via CBCA: Canadian Business and Current Affairs, available at http://delos.lib.sfu.ca:8366/cgi-bin/slri/z3950.CGI/834403670/?cbca.db).

43  S. Steinberg, 1998, Have allowance will transform economy [The tween market], *Canadian Business,* March 13, 58–71.

44  Ibid., 63.

45  F. Rose & J. R. Emshwiller, 1997, Guess, "coolness" fading, plans sultry ads, *Wall Street Journal,* November 19, B4.

46  C. Cornell, 1999, There's something about Harry: After 40 years, Harry Rosen is working harder than ever, *Profit: The Magazine for Canadian Entrepreneurs,* April, 44–50: 44.

47  Ibid., 46.

48  Ibid., 44.

49  The future for strategy: An interview with Gary Hamel, 1993, *European Management Journal* 14: 179–91.

50  Sprint, 1994, *1994 Annual Report to Shareholders,* 1.

51  G. A. Niemond, 1997, International Business Machines, *Value Line,* October 24, 1099.

52  Honda Motor Company, 1997, *Honda Motor Company home page,* http://www.honda.com (Retrieved December 10).

53  Trendy yet traditional, 1997, *The Financial Times,* November 14, 19.

54  M. E. Porter, 1985, *Competitive Advantage* (New York: The Free Press), 26.

55  M. E. Porter, 1996, What is strategy? *Harvard Business Review, 74,* (6): 61–78.

56  Campbell & Alexander, What's wrong with strategy?, 43; G. Colvin, 1997, The changing art of becoming unbeatable, *Fortune,* November 24, 299–300.

57  M. E. Porter, 1994, Toward a dynamic theory of strategy, in R. P. Rumelt, D. E. Schendel, & D. J. Teece (eds.), *Fundamental Issues in Strategy* (Boston: Harvard Business School Press), 423–61.

58  Porter, What is strategy?, 62.

59  Porter, *Competitive Advantage,* 15.

60  P. M. Wright, D. L. Smart, & G. C. McMahan, 1995, Matches between human resources and strategy among NCAA basketball teams, *Academy of Management Journal,* 38: 1052–74; Porter, Toward a dynamic theory, 434.

61  G. Bowley & H. Simonian, 1997, Volkswagen makes series of U-turns, *The Financial Times,* November 21, 19.

62   Porter, *Competitive* Strategy, 35–40.

63   Campbell & Alexander, What's wrong with strategy?, 42.

64   J. C. Anderson & J. A. Narus, 1995, Capturing the value of supplementary services, *Harvard Business Review,* 73 (1): 75–83.

65   C. Sirois, 1997, Unifi, Inc., *Value Line,* August 22, 1640.

66   J. Arbitman, 1997, Nova Corp., *Value Line,* September 26, 439.

67   S. Lubove, 1994, It ain't broke, but fix it anyway, *Forbes,* August 1, 56–60.

68   Ibid., 56.

69   J. Simmons, 1995, Budget hotels aren't bargains abroad, *Wall Street Journal,* November 17, B1, B4.

70   J. Friedland, 1997, Latin American retailer fights giants, *Wall Street Journal,* September 19, A10.

71   Porter, *Competitive Strategy,* 36.

72   Sirois, Unifi, Inc., 1640.

73   Lubove, It ain't broke, 57.

74   P. M. Seligman, 1997, Emerson Electric, *Value Line,* October 24, 1007.

75   L. Kraar, 1995, Acer's edge: PCs to go, *Fortune,* October 30, 192.

76   J. Moore & P. Burrows, 1997, A new attack plan for Acer America, *BusinessWeek,* December 8, 82–83.

77   Intel filing suggests trouble at PC maker Packard Bell, 1995, *Dallas Morning News,* November 28, D6.

78   Ibid.

79   T. Zorn, 1995, Orville Redenbacher leaves premium legacy, *Dallas Morning News,* September 24, H5.

80   Day & Reibstein (eds.), *Wharton on Dynamic Competitive Strategy,* 10.

81   Porter, *Competitive Advantage,* 14.

82   H. Quan, 1999, Going up against the co-op: Mountain Equipment's dominance makes outdoor clothing a market like no other, *Marketing Magazine,* May 24, 15.

83   *National Post,* 1999, How to succeed in the U.S. market by really really trying, *National Post,* June 3, 76.

84   Jean Coutu, 1999, *Jean Coutu home page,* http://www.jeancoutu.com (Retrieved October 11), CEO's message http://www.jeancoutu.com/finance/english/about_corporation/index.cfm.

85   *National Post,* How to succeed, 76.

86   A. Van den Broek, 1999, Brand makeovers: back-to-back revamps have made Canada's big two women's magazines more distinct than ever, *Marketing Magazine,* April 26, 21–22.

87   Ibid., 22.

88   I. Sager & P. Burrows, 1997, I'm not gonna pay a lot for this Aptiva, *BusinessWeek,* October 13, 59.

89   Porter, *Competitive Strategy,* 38.

90   Porter, *Competitive Advantage,* 15.

91   J. McKinnon, 1998, Edmonton food store competes with niche marketing strategy: Smart independents needn't fear majors, consultant says, *National Post,* November 10, C9.

92   Porter, *Competitive Advantage,* 15.

93   Ibid., 15–16.

94   S. Monte, 1999, Character builders: How a Calgary company is transforming the lowly mascot from cheerleader into mainstream marketing tool, *Profit: The Magazine for Canadian Entrepreneurs,* May, 51.

95   S. Mertl, 1998, Maverick Canadian watchmaker battles big boys, *Canadian Press Newswire,* December 27 (via CBCA: Canadian Business and Current Affairs, available at http://delos.lib. sfu.ca:8366/cgi-bin/slri/z3950.CGI/852851277/?cbca.db).

96   H. Davidson, 1999, 5 entrepreneurs you need to know, *Profit: The Magazine for Canadian Entrepreneurs,* 18 (4) June, 82–92.

97   L. Crawford, 1997, The bullet-proof fashions to die for on wild frontier of Mexico's drug war, *The Financial Times,* November 15, 132.

98   *The Financial Times,* 1997, A cosmopolitan crust, November 23, II.

99   S. Silcoff, 1998, Move over, Timothy Eaton: Quebec retailer Paul Roberge is reinventing how Canadian department stores do business, *Canadian Business,* June 26/July 10, 58, 64.

100  Molson to brew megacity suds, 1999, *Marketing Magazine,* November 23, 1.

101  Z. Olijnyk, 1998, Sleeman Breweries gets toehold in Quebec, *Financial Post,* June 30, 3; A. Bryan, 1998, Sleeman Breweries sheds "micro" tag and eases its way into Quebec with purchase of Boucherville's Seigneuriale, *Montreal Gazette,* June 30, D1; E. Lazarus, 1999, New recipes: Tough times are transforming BC's microbreweries, *Marketing Magazine,* March 1, 17–18.

102  Insights presented in this section are drawn primarily from Dess, Gupta, Hennart, & Hill, Conducting and integrating strategy research, 376–79.

103  W. K. Hall, 1980, Survival strategies in a hostile environment, *Harvard Business Review,* 58 (5): 75–87.

104  Dess, Gupta, Hennart, & Hill, Conducting and integrating strategy research, 377.

105  Porter, *Competitive Advantage,* 18.

106  R. Henkoff, 1995, New management secrets from Japan—really, *Fortune,* November 27, 135–46.

107  Ibid.

108  R. Sanchez, 1995, Strategic flexibility in product competition, *Strategic Management Journal,* 16 (Special Summer Issue): 140.

109  Ibid., 105.

110  D. M. Upton, 1995, What really makes factories flexible? *Harvard Business Review,* 73 (4): 74–84.

111  R. Gibbens, 1998, Spectra takes high road to profit in auto parts, *Financial Post,* July 3, 17.

112  R. S. Russell & B. W. Taylor, III, 1998, Operations Management, 2nd Edition (Upper Saddle River, NJ: Prentice-Hall), 255–57; S. W. Flanders & W. J. Davis, 1995, Scheduling a flexible manufacturing system with tooling constraints: An actual case study, *Interfaces* 25 (2): 42–54.

113  D. Lei, M. A. Hitt, & J. D. Goldhar, 1996, Advanced manufacturing technology, organization design and strategic flexibility, *Organization Studies,* 17: 501–23.

114  E. Mansfield, 1993, The diffusion of flexible manufacturing systems in Japan, Europe and the United States, *Management Science,* 39: 149–59 as quoted in Sanchez, Strategic flexibility in product competition, 141.

115  R. Garud & S. Kotha, 1994, Using the brain as a metaphor to model flexible production systems, *Academy of Management Review,* 19: 671–98.

116  S.A. Melnyk & D.R. Denzler, 1996, *Operations Management: A Value-Driven Approach* (Chicago: Irwin).

117  A. Baxter, 1997, Designs for survival, *The Financial Times,* November 20, 14.

118  T. Y. Choi & O. C. Behling, 1992, Top managers and TQM success: One more look after all these years, *Academy of Management Executive,* XI (1): 37–47; R. K. Reger, L. T. Gustafson, S. M. DeMarie, & J. V. Mullane, 1994, Reframing the organization: Why implementing total quality is easier said than done, *Academy of Management Review,* 19: 565–84.

119  J. D. Westphal, R. Gulati, & S. M. Shortell, 1997, Customization or conformity? An institutional and network perspective on the content and consequences of TQM adoption, *Administrative Science Quarterly,* 42: 366–94.

120  J. R. Hackman & R. Wagemen, 1995, Total quality management: Empirical, conceptual, and practical issues, *Administrative Science Quarterly,* 40: 310.

121  Ibid., 311.

122  J. Barney, 1997, *Gaining and Sustaining Competitive Advantage,* (Don Mills, ON: Addison-Wesley Publishing Company).

123  Porter, *Competitive Advantage,* 16.

124  A. Miller & G. G. Dess, 1993, Assessing Porter's (1980) model in terms of its generalizability, accuracy and simplicity, *Journal of Management Studies,* 30: 553–85.

125  Porter, *Competitive Advantage,* 17.

126  L. Berton, 1995, Midsize accountants lose clients to firms both large and small, *Wall Street Journal,* November 15, A1, A4.

127  Z. Olijnyk, 1999, Second Cup to sell interest in Coffee People: Diedrich to buy for $35m. US company's performance underwhelming, *National Post,* February 10, C4.

# Chapter Six

## Competitive Dynamics

### LEARNING OBJECTIVES

*After reading this chapter, you should be able to:*

1. Define the conditions for undertaking competitive actions.
2. Identify and explain factors affecting the probability that a competitor will initiate a response to competitive actions.
3. Describe first, second, and late movers and the advantages and disadvantages of each.
4. Understand the factors that contribute to the likelihood of a response to a competitive action.
5. Explain the effects of the size of a firm, the speed with which it makes strategic decisions, and implementation, innovation, and quality on the firm's ability to take competitive action.
6. Understand three basic market situations as outcomes of competitive dynamics.
7. Discuss the types of competitive actions most relevant for each of the three stages of an industry evolution.

# Canada's Battle of the Big Boxes

While Sault Ste. Marie, Ontario is home to the world's largest Canadian Tire, the nearest Wal-Mart is safely across the St. Mary's River in Sault Ste. Marie, Michigan. The Ontario city of 80 000 is five times larger than its U.S. neighbour and could easily support a Wal-Mart outlet. Yet the huge Canadian Tire and the lack of a Wal-Mart store reflect the downtown business owners' active fight to keep the world's largest retailer out of the area. It is small wonder there is concern about big-box stores destroying businesses in the city's core. Since Wal-Mart's arrival in Canada, the venerable Canadian institution Eaton's and U.S. retail giant K-Mart have fallen off the Canadian retailing map. While problems at Eaton's and K-Mart began prior to the Wal-Mart invasion, the introduction of this strong new competitor sent a clear signal that competition would be far more intense than it had been in the past.

Big changes occurred at Canadian Tire (CT) in response to Wal-Mart. CT's billion-dollar expansion program has revamped and expanded store locations. The company has stayed with its roots though by focusing on three traditional areas: automotive, sports and leisure, and home products. At the same time, CT has used a number of devices to focus on its customers and maintain its customer base. To make it easy for customers to come in, CT maintained its complete geographic coverage—85 percent of Canadians live within a 15-minute drive of their local Canadian Tire store. To keep customers coming back, CT maintained its use of Canadian Tire Money (cash bonuses that can be used only at Canadian Tire). These tactics seem to be working. Canadian Tire claims that nine of ten adult Canadians shop at Canadian Tire at least twice a year, and 40 percent of Canadians shop at Canadian Tire every week.

Big-box Wal-Mart historically located large stores in rural areas. Store sites were carefully chosen, and the firm distributed its goods in a very efficient manner. Wal-Mart squeezed suppliers for better prices and gave the savings to the consumer. Before the 20th century ended, Wal-Mart built the largest retailing firm in the world—with annual sales of more than $230 billion.

http://www.canadiantire.com
http://www.carrefour.com
http://www.revy.ca
http://www.renodepot.com
http://www.homedepot.com
http://www.rona.ca

Since entering Europe in 1997, Wal-Mart has acquired over 300 stores by absorbing rivals in Germany and Britain. British retailer Tesco responded by making over a half billion dollars in price reductions. To reinforce customer service, Germany's Real gave shoppers five marks if they had to wait more than five minutes at a cashier. France's Carrefour acquired Promodes in late 1999 to create the number-one retailer in Europe (number two in the world). Carrefour now has about 9000 stores in over 25 countries and annual revenues of about $100 billion. To compete against Wal-Mart, Carrefour has reduced prices, remodeled, and relocated other stores. One executive of a rival described Carrefour as "relentless, the toughest competitor I've ever seen anywhere." In addition to its presence in Latin America, Carrefour is strong in Asia. In a sense, Carrefour is trying to be a Wal-Mart for those parts of the world where Wal-Mart has yet to arrive.

Another big-box retailer is Atlanta's Home Depot. It is not unusual for Home Depot big boxes to exceed 100 000 square feet. Today, Home Depot has about 1000 of these stores and opens one more worldwide every 53 hours. Over 50 of its stores are in Canada, a number expected to more than double by 2003—which means opening one store every three weeks.

An assortment of tough competitors—including Canadian Tire—are arrayed against the Home Depot onslaught. Rona, in Boucherville, Quebec, has traditionally been a cooperative network of individually owned stores—much like the U.S. Home Hardware chain, which recently took over Molson's Beaver Lumber. Rona stores now number about 500. Although Rona is over 60 years old, it got into the big-box market only in the mid-1990s. Rona is developing new big-box locations for Ontario, Quebec, and the Maritimes. In order to get a better foothold in Ontario, Rona bought Cashway Building Centres of Ontario and will operate them under the name Rona Cashway. As well, Rona's 1998 agreement with ITM, one of France's leading distributors, gives Rona a buying partner with tens of billions of dollars of purchasing power—enough power to guarantee consumers "your money back plus 10 percent." Not to be outdone, Quebec competitor Reno-Depot will match Rona's price guarantee. Since Reno-Depot is owned by France's Castorama Group, it has their financial and marketing backing. Reno-Depot has repeatedly outdone Rona in locating their big boxes at the choicest sites.

B.C.'s Revy Homecentres opened its first big-box store in 1994. Revy began in 1903 as a sawmill and opened its first retail outlet three years later. To counter the Home Depot threat, Revy has been buying up big-box competitors for several years. Revy bought B.C. rival Lumberland, and entered Home Depot's stronghold, Ontario, by purchasing Lansing Buildall in 1998. Revy is the largest player in Western Canada and hopes to leverage that base to become a contender in an overcrowded Ontario market.

In all these cases, competitors are moving toward looking more like the industry leader. To gain buying power and give customers a one-stop hardware shopping location like Home Depot, Rona, Reno-Depot, and Revy are all moving toward bigger stores, forging links outside Canada, and swallowing up competitors. However, the copying is not just a one-way street. Rona, Reno-Depot, and Revy have been adding features such as providing expertise in home décor.

Home decorating has been so successful for these three competitors that Home Depot is also developing its skills in this area. Accepted standards for the industry in terms of size and service keep changing. With Rona and Reno-Depot moving in from the East, Revy moving in from the West, and Home Depot from the South, the Ontario home improvement market will never be the same.

---

Sources: *Canadian Tire home page,* 2000, http://www.Canadiantire.com (Retrieved July 28); T. Arial, 2000, Battle ready: Revy and Home Depot are set to invade the Quebec hardware market, *Marketing Magazine,* February 21, 11–12; . G. Crone, 2000, Rona's $400m expansion takes in Cashway chain: Hardware wars, *National Post,* February 7, C1, C9; G. Crone, 2000, Home schooling ... *National Post,* January 31, C1, C10; R. Lewandowski, 2000, Le big box battlefield ..., *National Post Business,* January, 65–67; Z. Olijnyk, 1999, Homegrown improvements: Revy is sure it can deliver the goods in the competitive Ontario market. *National Post,* September 20, C3; E. Beck & E. Nelson, 1999, As Wal-Mart invades Europe, rivals rush to match its formula, *Wall Street Journal Interactive,* October 6, interactive.wsj.com/articles; C. Matlack, I. Resch, & W. Zellner, 1999, Engarde, Wal-Mart, *BusinessWeek Online,* September 13, bwarchive.businessweek.com; P. Sellers, 1999, Category killers: They left their competitors with nowhere to hide, *Fortune,* September 27, 223–26; A. Barrett & J. Carreyrou, 1999, French retailers Carrefour, Promodes agree to join in $16.3 billion accord, *Wall Street Journal Interactive,* August 30, interactive.wsj.com/articles; H. Dawley, 1999, Watch out Europe: Here comes Wal-Mart, *BusinessWeek Online,* June 28, bwarchive.businessweek.com; M. Yeates and D. Montgomery, 1999, The changing commercial structure of non-metropolitan urban centres and vacancy rates, *Canadian Geographer,* Winter, 382–99.

---

Wal-Mart and Home Depot's entry into world markets and competitors' reactions typify examples of changes in the 21st-century competitive landscape. Those competing in this more volatile and unpredictable environment must learn how to cope successfully with challenges presented by discontinuous environmental changes, increasing globalization of their industries, and an array of competitive actions and responses being taken by aggressive rivals.[1] Top-level managers must also be willing to make the type of difficult decisions called for by the nature of competitors' actions and responses. In fact, some believe that one of the most important skills linked to strategic competitiveness in the 21st century will be managers' willingness to make significant and sometimes painful decisions.[2] Many of these decisions will be necessitated by the competitive dynamics affecting the firm's operations.

Wal-Mart's entry into European, Latin American, and Chinese markets exemplifies globalization of markets. Competitor's reactions, such as Carrefour's acquisition of Promodes, are examples of the trend toward consolidation in many industries that will allow the remaining competitors to compete effectively. Even if a domestic competitor does not move internationally, it must still make competitive responses to firms who are doing so. Canadian Tire did this by improving store sizes and appearance.

Even market champions such as Wal-Mart need to adjust to changes in the environment. Given its size and market power, communities fear Wal-Mart may wipe out local competitors. Thus, even in Wal-Mart's home market in the United States, there are municipalities that have passed legislation limiting the size of retail establishments.[3] Wal-Mart's response has been to sell merchandise through e-commerce. Although its sales over the Internet are far smaller than Amazon.com's, it is likely Wal-Mart's e-commerce venture will succeed given its brand name, market power, and considerable resources.[4]

---

## INCREASED RIVALRY IN THE NEW COMPETITIVE LANDSCAPE

Conditions in the new competitive landscape are increasing competitive rivalry and require many companies to compete differently in order to achieve strategic competitiveness and earn above-average returns (recall the European retailers' response to Wal-Mart's entering their markets). Professor C.K. Prahalad at the University of Michigan refers to the environment as a competitive battlefield. He suggests that the strategic discontinuities a firm encounters can be positive. For example, the political changes in Eastern Europe opened markets and provided opportunities for firms from Western countries and Asia. Prahalad suggests that the competitive landscape in the 21st century requires a new strategic approach and managerial mind-set.[5]

For instance, increased competitive rivalry requires that firms bring new goods and services to the market more quickly.[6] Compaq has discovered this necessity. In the mid-1990s, Compaq won the competitive battle to become the number-one manufacturer and marketer of personal computers. However, in 1999, Dell overtook Compaq to become number one in this market (see the Strategic Focus in Chapter 3). In fact, Compaq reported a major loss in 1999. Compaq not only lost its leadership in the PC market but also lost major users of Compaq servers to competitors (e.g., Volkswagen and America Online). In addition, Compaq was criticized for having an undeveloped Internet strategy. As a result, Compaq made a number of managerial changes and increased investment in the development of its product line.[7]

The competitive landscape is undergoing fundamental changes, with new entrants transforming industries, often by using new technology.[8] For example, such a change occurred with Amazon.com's entrance into the retail book market. Before Amazon.com's entry, analysts predicted Barnes & Noble would become the "master" of the retail book market. However, Barnes & Noble was "Amazoned," according to *Fortune* magazine. It was almost a year before Barnes & Noble got its book sales on-line and thus, its growth slowed.[9] To increase growth, Barnes & Noble recently expanded on-line sales to include music.[10] However, Amazon.com has been in the on-line music business for some time. In fact, Amazon.com, using its skills in on-line order processing and home delivery, now sells much more than just books.[11]

Interestingly, Amazon.com may face its largest competition from Wal-Mart. While some have described Amazon.com as the Wal-Mart of the Internet, in fact, it is probably the significant presence of Amazon.com and other growing "e-tailers" that has led Wal-Mart and other brick-and-mortar retailers to respond to their growing presence. Competitors such as Chapters have proven that even Amazon.com's position can be attacked from a brick-and-mortar retailer. As discussed in Chapter 1, Chapters moved into the e-tail book market to become Canada's largest online book retailer by being the Canadian competitor and helping customers avoid high exchange rates.[12]

Competitive advantages may come from nontraditional areas in an evolving competitive landscape. This is how U-Haul dominated the consumer-truck rental business in the 1990s. The competitive battle in this industry was fierce. U-Haul was the first to seize on the profit potential in the accessories market (e.g., boxes, packaging, and tape). The company thus maintained very low rental rates to attract many customers, who would then purchase profitable accessories. In contrast, competitors priced their rentals so as to maximize their return from the truck rental business. As a result, U-Haul increased its market share relative to the number-two competitor, Ryder, which ultimately abandoned the rental truck market.[13]

Another phenomenon in the 21st-century landscape is the consolidation of industries. Among the many reasons for this is the need to be large in order to achieve economies of scale to compete effectively in global markets. With freer access to markets in many countries, foreign firms are entering at increasing rates. The enhanced competition has emphasized the need for efficiency, both to offer low prices and, at the same time, to differentiate a firm's products through innovation. Consolidation has occurred in industries ranging from the petroleum industry (e.g., the merger of Exxon and Mobil) and the communications industry (e.g., the merger of BC Tel and Telus) to the on-line book retail industry (e.g., the merger of Indigo and Chapters).

On-line retailing is growing dramatically; on-line sales in 1999 were 2.5 times the amount in 1998. Whether competitors such as Chapters, which has both brick-and-mortar stores and a strong on-line presence, will win against firms such as Amazon.com remains to be seen.[14] Yet, CompUSA's former CEO James Halpin believes there is still a need and demand for physical stores where customers can see, feel, and operate products, as well as have the opportunity to work directly with a salesperson. However, analysts suggest that the environment is too different and uncertain to make definitive predictions at this time.[15]

Significant advances in communication technologies that allow more effective coordination across operations in multiple markets and faster decisionmaking, as well as competitive responses, facilitate the changes occurring in many industries' competitive environments.[16] In addition, new technology and innovations, particularly in the information technology and computer industries, have helped small and medium-sized businesses to compete effectively. Finally, the increasing number of agreements allowing free trade across country borders—such as the 1993 *North American Free Trade Agreement* (NAFTA)—is facilitating a growing cross-border focus.[17]

The changing competitive landscape has even former competitors cooperating in such areas as the development of new technology and forming strategic alliances to compete against other competitors (see Chapter 10).[18] For example, global alliances also have been formed among many of the world's telephone companies to pursue business in Europe. Increasingly, cooperative R&D arrangements are being developed in the competitive environment as well. These arrangements are vehicles through which firms overcome their resource constraints by acquiring skills and capabilities from partners.[19]

This chapter focuses on competitive dynamics. The essence of this important topic is that a firm's strategies and their implementation (see Figure 1.1 in Chapter 1) are dynamic in nature. Actions taken by one firm often elicit responses from competitors that, in turn, typically result in responses from the original firm. This chain of events is illustrated by the chapter's Opening Case, which lists the competitive actions being taken by Canadian retailers competing with Wal-Mart and Home Depot. The series of actions and responses among firms competing within a particular industry creates **competitive dynamics.** This competitive interaction often shapes the competitive position of firms undertaking the business-level strategies described in the previous chapter and, to some extent, the corporate strategies described in Chapters 7, 8, 9, and 10. Thus, because of competitive dynamics, the effectiveness of any strategy is determined not only by the initial move but also by how well the firm "anticipates and addresses the moves and countermoves of competitors and shifts in customer demands over time."[20]

To more effectively explain competitive dynamics, we introduce a model of the phenomenon (see Figure 6.1).

After the overall model is introduced, we examine the factors that lead to competitive attack and potential responses. We follow this examination with a discussion of the incentives of market leadership (first-mover advantages) and its disadvantages. We also discuss the advantages and disadvantages of second and late movers.

After a competitive action is taken, a number of factors affect the potential response. These factors are discussed, and we then examine firms' capabilities to attack

**Competitive dynamics** results from a series of competitive actions and competitive responses among firms competing within a particular industry.

and respond, including the size of the firms, the speed of decisionmaking, innovation, and product and process quality. Following this analysis is a discussion of three different types of competitive markets (slow cycle, standard cycle, and fast cycle) that result from competitive interaction. In particular, we explore the nature of rivalry and propose strategies for competition in fast-cycle markets where competitive rivalry has escalated to an intense level. We examine the strategy of competitive disruption, in which firms capitalize on temporary, compared to sustainable, competitive advantage by cannibalizing their past new-product entries to introduce the next product or process innovation. Finally, we describe competitive rivalry outcomes as industries move through the emerging, growth, and maturity stages.

■ ■ **FIGURE 6.1**

*Competitive Dynamics: Basic Summary Model of Interfirm Rivalry*

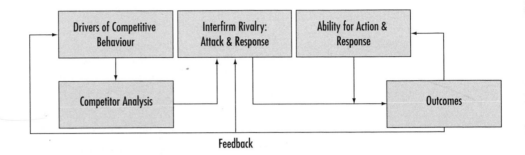

Source: Adapted from M. J. Chen, 1996, Competitor analysis and interfirm rivalry: Toward a theoretical integration, *Academy of Management Review*, 21: 100–34.

## BASIC MODEL OF COMPETITIVE DYNAMICS AND RIVALRY

Over time, firms competing in an industry employ a number of competitive actions and responses.[21] Competitive rivalry exists when two or more firms jockey with one another in the pursuit of an advantageous market position. Competitive rivalry takes place among firms because one or more competitors feel pressure or see opportunities to improve their market position. Rivalry is made possible by competitive asymmetry, which exists when firms differ from one another in terms of their resources, capabilities, and core competencies (see Chapter 4) and in terms of the opportunities and threats in their industry and competitive environments (see Chapter 3). Strategies—especially business-level ones—are formed to exploit the asymmetric relationships among competitors.[22]

In most industries, a firm's competitive actions have observable effects on its competitors and typically cause responses designed to counter the action.[23] In early 1998, for instance, Renault, France's largest car and truck manufacturer, announced plans to increase its output by 500 000 units a year through 2002. In addition, the automaker indicated that it was committed to improving the efficiency of its manufacturing operations to reduce its overall costs. Renault's competitive decisions were made partly in response to Toyota's previously announced intention to build a new small-car manufacturing plant in France. Renault officials believed that the firm's response was required for it to become more competitive in its home market and to prevent Renault from falling behind more efficient rivals such as Toyota.[24] As noted in the Strategic Focus,

Renault must respond to Toyota's strategic action. It is predicted that by 2010, only six major automakers will be operating globally. Although Renault will be a formidable competitor for any firm entering European markets, it is not expected to be one of the surviving global six identified in the Strategic Focus.[25]

## STRATEGIC FOCUS

### Car Wars: The Battle for Survival

The number of automobile manufacturers continues to shrink. The acquisition of Chrysler by Daimler, Ford's purchase of Volvo, and GM's alliance with Honda may foretell the future of the industry. Toyota's CEO, Hiroshi Okuda, suggested that in the 21st century there will be only five or six major automakers. He proposes that a firm's sales volume needs to be at least 5 million vehicles annually in order for the company to compete in global markets.

Consolidation is occurring in the auto industry, as it is in others. Most of the consolidation crosses country borders. Thus, national identity is becoming obsolete. It is predicted that by 2010, each major auto market in the world will have two automakers. Some analysts believe that six firms will remain: Ford and GM in North America, DaimlerChrysler and Volkswagen in Europe, and Toyota and Honda in Asia. Currently, only GM and Ford sell more than 5 million vehicles annually.

The major firms will acquire the healthy, but smaller, firms in Europe (e.g., Renault) and the distressed firms in Asia (e.g., Nissan). Still, this is only speculation, as the dynamism in the competitive environment makes prediction difficult. As the likely survivors, the "big six" automakers noted above must continue to develop and implement effective strategies and respond effectively to competitors' strategic actions to be able to operate successfully and have the resources to acquire and win their battles with competitors. If they do not, they will not survive. For example, DaimlerChrysler is desperately seeking an ally in Asia to help it penetrate Asian markets. Ford owns a significant interest in Mazda, and GM is aligned with Honda. Both also have relationships with other Asian firms (e.g., GM is working on a deal to help improve Daewoo's auto unit). However, DaimlerChrysler does not have alliances with firms from the region—nor are there many available; Nissan has rejected Daimler's overtures. Of course, Renault owns a stake in Nissan. Though Mitsubishi is engaged in talks with Volvo because of a previous relationship between the firms, Daimler did finally acquire a stake in Mitsubishi.

Toyota has announced that it is increasing its manufacturing capacity in North America. Toyota currently sells approximately 1.5 million vehicles in North America despite a capacity to produce only about 1.2 million vehicles. Such expansion may allow Toyota to better serve the lucrative North American market. The company is expected to increase its production of light trucks and sport utility vehicles (SUVs), which account for about 50 percent of the North American market for motor vehicles. This is a highly contested market because of its popularity. In late 1999, for example, Ford and DaimlerChrysler both announced rebates on some of their most profitable light trucks. GM had already offered rebates on some of its vehicles e.g., the Chevrolet Venture minivan. The actions of all three firms have been prompted by competition, particularly from Japanese and European manufacturers.

*continued*

Volkswagen (VW) is another concern in the survival war. While VW has about 19 percent of the Western European auto market, up from 15 percent in 1994, it is experiencing stagnation. Expectations are that it will continue to have problems over the foreseeable future and may be the most vulnerable of the "big six." Concerns grow as the European Union allows freer competition across European country borders and less control over auto dealers. GM's Opel expects to increase its market share in Germany, likely at the expense of VW, which may need a partner in Europe and elsewhere to be among the survivors. On the positive side, VW's sales in the large North American market are quite strong.

Thus, the 21st-century competitive landscape is likely to produce exciting battles and outcomes in the global auto industry. Which firms end up in the shadows of others and which join together to become one of the big six will remain to be seen. Whatever the combinations of firms, their development will make for interesting times.

---

Sources: J. Ball, 1999, Ford, DaimlerChrysler boost rebates on some very profitable light trucks, *Wall Street Journal Interactive,* November 17, interactive.wsj.com/articles; Chrysler in battle of minivan, 1999, *Houston Chronicle,* November 26, 4D; J. Ewing, K. Kerwin, & K. N. Anhalt, 1999, VW: Spinning its wheels? *BusinessWeek Online,* November 22, bwarchive.businessweek.com; J. Ewing, E. Thornton, & M. Ihlwan, 1999, DaimlerChrysler: Desperately seeking an ally, *BusinessWeek Online,* December 13, bwarchive.businessweek.com; Ford: Faith in high prices, 1999, *www.ft.com,* www.ft.com/sea (Retrieved December 24); K. Naughton, K. L. Miller, J. Muller, E. Thornton, & G. Edmondson, 1999, Autos: The global six, *BusinessWeek Online,* January 25, bwarchive.businessweek.com; N. Shirouzu, 1999, Toyota considers boosting capacity in North America, *Wall Street Journal Interactive,* June 29, interactive.wsj.com/articles.

---

Competitive rivalry can have a major effect on a firm's profitability. As rivalry in an industry increases, the average profitability of firms competing in the industry decreases.[26] The intensity of the rivalry is affected not only by the number of competitors but also by the market structure and the firm's strategy. Thus, firms that develop and implement more effective strategies (recall the discussion of business-level strategies in Chapter 5) will fare better than others.[27] Both Eaton's and K-Mart failed in their response to Wal-Mart and are no longer contenders in the Canadian market. In the United States, J.C. Penney's performance suffered from competition. Penney's executives implemented a strategy of differentiation by marketing high-margin private labels as core brands. Yet, the firm failed to fully promote and thus capitalize on its private-label apparel—a lesson apparently not lost on Canadian retailer Zellers when it made certain to promote its Cherokee brand.[28]

As the example of the competitive actions and competitive responses among the retail apparel marketers demonstrates, firms and their competitors are mutually interdependent.[29] **Mutual interdependence** among firms means that strategic competitiveness and above-average returns result only when companies recognize that their strategies are not implemented in isolation from their competitors' actions and responses. Kodak and Fuji Film continue to engage in a series of competitive actions and responses in an effort to establish competitive advantage. Competition in North America with Fuji has affected Kodak's performance. While competitive dynamics between these two rivals has been continuous for the last several years, Fuji was clearly

**Mutual interdependence** among firms means that strategic competitiveness and above-average returns result only when companies recognize that their strategies are not implemented in isolation from their competitors' actions and responses.

successful. Fuji continued to reduce the prices of its film, even during peak selling periods. Most Kodak film stayed 10 to 25 percent higher than Fuji's. As a result, Kodak's market share decreased by about 6 percent, and Fuji's increased by an equal amount.[30] Thus, because they affect strategic competitiveness and returns, the pattern of competitive dynamics and the rivalry it creates are a major concern of firms.[31]

## COMPETITOR BEHAVIOUR AND ANALYSIS

Figure 6.2 illustrates an expanded summary model of interfirm rivalry and response. As seen in the figure, competitor analysis begins with an examination of competitor awareness and motivation to attack and respond to competitive action. Awareness refers to whether or not the attacking or responding firm is cognizant of the competitive market characteristics (such as the market commonality and the resource similarity of a potential attacker or respondent—these terms are defined in a subsequent section).[32] Managers may have "blind spots" in their industry and competitor analyses, due to underestimation or an inability to analyze these factors.[33] Such errors are likely to harm the managers' firms and the industry as well. For example, this lack of awareness may lead decisionmakers to construct additional capacity believing there is sufficient industry demand that they alone will meet. Such actions then lead to industry overcapacity and excessive competition.[34]

■ ■ **FIGURE 6.2**

*Competitor Behaviour and Analysis in the Summary Model of Interfirm Rivalry*

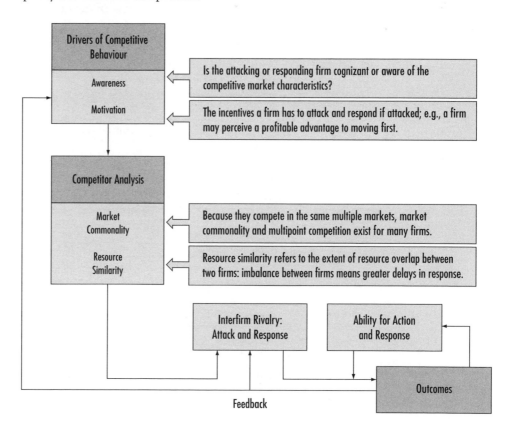

Source: Adapted from M. J. Chen, 1996, Competitor analysis and interfirm rivalry, *Academy of Management Review,* 21: 100–34.

Firms in an industry are likely to exhibit several different types of competitive responses. The reasons for these differences are several but include the number of common markets in which the firm competes with the firm to whose action it is responding, as well as its resources to respond. Also, the response may depend partially on the similarity of the resources among the competitors.[35] Market commonality and resource similarity both affect a firm's motivation to respond to a competitive action. Motivation relates to a firm's incentives to attack and respond if attacked. A firm may perceive advantages to moving first, given the potential for interaction and possible outcomes of the interaction.

As Figure 6.2 suggests, both market commonality and resource similarity mediate the awareness and motivation to undertake actions and responses. In other words, likely action and responses that result in the competitive outcomes will be impacted by a firm's ability to undertake strategic actions and responses. Furthermore, Figure 6.2 illustrates that feedback from the nature of a particular rivalry will also influence a competitor's awareness and motivation to take future actions or responses.

## Competitor Analysis: Market Commonality

Because they compete in the same multiple markets, market commonality exists for many firms; for example, those in the airlines, chemical, pharmaceutical, breakfast cereals, and electronics industries. In the brewery industry, many beer producers compete in the same regional markets.[36] Regional competition is also evident in international markets through "triad" competition—or the necessity for multinational corporations to have businesses in Asia (usually Japan), Europe, and North America.[37] Multimarket overlap presents opportunities for multipoint competition, a situation in which firms compete against each other concurrently in several product or geographic markets.[38] As noted in the opening case, Wal-Mart and Carrefour have numerous opportunities for multipoint competition—particularly in emerging markets such as Latin America and Asia.

Interestingly, research suggests that market commonality and multimarket competition may begin almost by chance. However, the same research also suggests that after it begins, the multimarket competition becomes intentional.[39] Such intentional actions may provide incentives to reduce product lines and avoid entering certain markets.[40] Thus, multimarket competition can become a deterrent to competitive rivalry. However, most multimarket contact is highly complex—as in the airlines industry where routes overlap, and networks of companies create almost innumerable points of competition. As a result, competitive interactions are likely to be complex.

Recent work suggests that firms may take one or more of three different actions in multimarket contact with competitors. First, they may make a thrust, which is a direct attack on a specific competitive market niche, forcing competitors to withdraw resources. Montreal's Suzy Shier stores are locating stores in Mid-Eastern countries such as Oman, Quatar, Bahrain, and Kuwait, using their LaSenza intimate apparel brand. Such actions may serve to cause competitors such as Victoria's Secret to withdraw resources that may be dedicated toward serving these Middle-Eastern markets.[41] The second action that firms may take is a feint, which is an attack on a focal area that is important to a competitor, but not vital to the firm taking the action. The intent is to get the focal firm to commit more resources to the market in question. When British Columbia's Telus bought a 70 percent interest in QuebecTel in April 2000, Quebec was a minor market for Telus. Quebec was a more significant market for Telebec and Bell Canada. Thus, the action by Telus, while it helped Telus build a more national firm, also represented a feint to get its competitors to devote more resources to the Quebec market and away from Western markets where Telus is strong.[42] The final type of action firms may take is a gambit, named from the tactic in chess. In a business gambit, a position is sacrificed to entice a competitor to divert resources to a certain niche.[43] As discussed in Chapter 3, Dell Computer's abandonment of the very large screen monitor market and ensuing public misinformation was used to entice Gateway Computers into this nonviable market.[44]

## Competitor Analysis: Resource Similarity

The intensity of competitive rivalry often is based on a potential response and is of great concern for an attacker. An attacker may not be motivated to target a rival that is likely to retaliate. This is especially true of firms with strategic resources similar to those of a potential attacker.[45] Resource similarity refers to the extent of resource overlap between two firms.[46] Resource dissimilarity also plays a vital role in a competitor's motivation to attack or respond. In fact, the greater "the resource imbalance between the acting firm and competitors or potential responders, the greater will be the delay in response."[47] Although the degree of market commonality is obvious to both firms, strategic resources are difficult to identify because of their causal ambiguity and social complexity (as described in Chapter 4). The difficulty in identifying and understanding the competing firms' resources (including its capabilities and core competencies) also contributes to response delays, especially in instances of resource dissimilarity.

Coca-Cola and Pepsi's decisions to compete in the bottled-water market (as explained in a Strategic Focus later in the chapter) demonstrate an imbalance in resources between the acting firms (Coca-Cola and Pepsi) and their competitors (Perrier Group, Suntory International, McKesson, Great Brands of Europe, and Crystal Geyser). However, the resource dissimilarity between firms such as the Perrier Group on the one hand and Coca-Cola and Pepsi on the other made it difficult for the smaller and less resource-rich companies to implement effective competitive responses.[48]

Because of the intense competition experienced in a number of industries, many firms have inadequate resources to be competitive. For example, Packard Bell NEC, owned jointly by Groupe Bull of France and NEC of Japan, announced in 1999 that it was closing most of its North American operations in the personal computer market. In 1995, Packard Bell was the largest retail PC marketer in North America. However, its fortunes changed quickly with substantial competition from Hewlett-Packard and Compaq, particularly in the low-cost PC market. In 1998 and 1999, Packard-Bell NEC experienced significant net losses. As a result, it no longer had adequate resources to compete in that market.[49] As already discussed, Eaton's demise as an independent Canadian firm was ultimately brought about because it ran out of resources to turn itself around.

Inadequate resources—such as financial, technical, or important capabilities—have forced firms to form alliances to enable them to compete in specific markets. Thus, one of the primary reasons for strategic alliances is the opportunity for partners to share resources. For example, technical, capital, and environmental requirements make conditions in the petroleum industry very competitive. Because of this, joint ventures have become standard in the Canadian oil industry—so much so that the Calgary-based

Petroleum Joint Venture Association (PJVA) has become a world leader in helping industry members create joint ventures and cooperative efforts between each other, outsiders, and regulators. Association president Dennis McGrath says, "Our model agreements have been very helpful to companies for managing their paperwork more efficiently. They spend less time and effort negotiating common boilerplate clauses and more time in production."[50]

Alliances also help firms acquire certain types of resources. For instance, firms may enhance their capabilities by learning from partners, thus improving their resource base.[51] Iogen of Ottawa is supplying its technology in an agreement with Petro-Canada to make ethanol from straw, wood wastes, and grasses. Petro-Can gains knowledge about an alternative energy source, and the ethanol allows the company to reduce carbon dioxide emissions in its fuel. Petro-Can also has agreements with Vancouver's Ballard Power Systems and Methanex to make alternative fuel sources. Partners from around the world can link up in these type of joint efforts. For example, Bermuda's Global Crossing established a joint venture with Hutchison Whampoa of Hong Kong to integrate Hutchison's local fixed phone line network with Global Crossing's international telecommunications capabilities. Global Crossing has also formed a joint venture with Japan's Softbank and Microsoft to build a fibre optic network in Asia.[52] In all of these ventures, each partner has contributed a unique set of resources.

Competitive dynamics have caused firms to move beyond simple alliances to develop more complex networks of relationships. Networks of organizations can provide greater value to consumers, as well as draw on resources from multiple partners. Networks are particularly useful for smaller businesses and in international markets. In fact, the use of networks may allow smaller entrepreneurial businesses to compete with larger and more resource-rich firms. However, managing the networks of relationships is difficult: Firms must formulate and implement network strategies[53] (we discuss these network-based businesses further in Chapters 9 and 11). Next, we examine the likelihood that firms will take strategic actions or respond to them from competitors.

## LIKELIHOOD OF ATTACK

A **competitive action** is a significant competitive move made by a firm that is designed to gain a competitive advantage in a market.

Although awareness and motivation to respond are derived largely from competitors' analyses of market commonality and resource similarity, there are strong incentives to be the first mover in a competitive battle if the attacking firm believes it has the potential to win. A **competitive action** is a significant competitive move made by a firm that is designed to gain a competitive advantage in a market.[54] Some competitive actions are large and significant; others are small and designed to help fine-tune or implement a strategy. The first mover in a competitive interaction may be able to gain above-average returns while competitors consider potential countermoves. Furthermore, the first mover may be able to deter a counterattack, given enough time. As a result, there are significant incentives to be a first mover, and the order of each competitive action and response influences an industry's competitive dynamics. Of greatest importance are first movers, second movers, and late movers.

### First, Second, and Late Movers

A **first mover** is a firm that takes an initial competitive action.

A **first mover** is a firm that takes an initial competitive action. The concept of first movers has been influenced by the work of economist Joseph Schumpeter. In particular, he believed that firms achieve competitive advantage through entrepreneurial and innovative competitive actions.[55] In general, first movers "allocate funds for product innovation and development, aggressive advertising, and advanced research and development."[56] Through competitive actions such as these, first movers hope to gain a competitive advantage. For example, Disco SA was the first supermarket chain to offer on-line shopping in Argentina. Royal Ahold of the Netherlands and Velox Investment of Argentina jointly own Disco. The on-line service alliance represented a natural extension of Disco's shop-by-phone service initiated in 1996. Also in 1996, Disco had a Web site that clients in the company's frequent shopper program could consult about the points they had accumulated and their eligibility for prizes. Importantly, 72 percent of the on-line shoppers previously were customers of other supermarkets. Thus, the on-line service is attracting a significant new clientele to Disco. In addition, the average purchase of a Disco in-store shopper is 14 pesos, while the average purchase of an on-line customer is 100 pesos. As a result, the new service offered by Disco appears to be an unqualified success in all dimensions.[57]

Several competitive advantages can accrue to the firm that is first to initiate a competitive action. Successful actions allow a firm to earn above-average returns until other competitors are able to respond effectively. In addition, first movers have the opportunity to gain customer loyalty, thereby making it difficult for responding firms to capture customers. For instance, Harley-Davidson has been able to maintain a competitive lead in large motorcycles due to intense customer loyalty. Across time, though, the competitive advantage of a first mover begins to erode (recall from Chapter 1 that every competitive advantage can be imitated eventually). The advantages and their duration vary by the type of competitive action and industry.

First-mover advantages also vary on the basis of the ease with which competitors can imitate the action. The more difficult and costly an action is to imitate, the longer a firm may receive the benefits of being a first mover. When core competencies are the foundation of a competitive action, first-mover advantages tend to last longer. Core competence–based competitive actions have a high probability of resulting in a sustained competitive advantage. For example, Labatt Brewing was able to gain new customers after introducing its Ice Beer in 1993. Yet, in spite of Labatt's spending millions to develop the product, Ice Beer was technically simple to produce and was quickly copied by Molson. However, Labatt's trademark on the term "Ice Beer" was a different story; trademarked names cannot be copied. However, Molson was able to get around the trademark by presenting evidence that ice beer was not really an innovation but a 100-year-old German process that Labatt has resurrected. Thus, even hard to imitate features (such as a trademarked name) can sometimes be imitated successfully by second movers.[58]

However, potential disadvantages may result from being the first firm to initiate a competitive action. Chief among these is the degree of risk taken by first movers. The risk of a first move is high, because it is not easy to predict the amount of success a particular competitive action will produce prior to its initiation.[59] Oftentimes, first movers have higher development costs. Both of these occurred in the Ice Beer case noted above. Second movers can avoid costs through reverse engineering (taking apart a new product and then reassembling it to learn how it works). Another potential disadvantage of being a first mover is the dynamic and uncertain nature of many markets in which a firm may compete. In other words, the extent and range of marketplace competition heighten the

A **second mover** is a firm that responds to a first mover's competitive action, often through imitation or a move designed to counter the effects of the action.

potential risk. In fact, in a highly uncertain market, it may be more appropriate to be a second or late mover.

A **second mover** is a firm that responds to a first mover's competitive action, often through imitation or a move designed to counter the effects of the action. When the second mover responds quickly to a first mover's competitive action, it may earn some of the first-mover advantages without experiencing the disadvantages. For example, a fast second mover may gain some of the returns and obtain a portion of the initial customers and thereby customer loyalty, while avoiding some of the risks encountered by the first mover. The firm taking a second action as a competitive response to the first mover can do so after evaluating customers' reactions to the first mover's action.[60] To be a successful first mover or second mover, a company must be able to analyze its markets and identify critical strategic issues.[61] Firms have different capabilities of obtaining information on markets and analyzing that information after it is obtained. These differences explain why some firms are faster to adopt market innovations than are others.[62]

Being second to the market also allows a firm to conduct market research to learn the first mover's actions and improve on them. Thus, being a second mover allows a firm to introduce directed innovation to better meet consumer needs. A second mover has information that is unavailable to a first mover and thus can direct its strategy on the basis of observing what happens to the first mover. Furthermore, being second provides time to perfect the good or service, eliminating potentially irritating "bugs." Hence, the second-mover strategy gains time for R&D to develop a superior product.[63] Sometimes, being first to the market means that the firm will be the first to fail! It is difficult to conduct definitive market research before introducing a new good or service. First, it may be difficult to define precisely the market for a highly innovative product. Second, some market pioneers fail for one of two reasons: They lack sufficient vision for how the product can be used, or they lack the commitment to persist in the long-term. Time may be required to convince consumers to accept a new good or service.[64]

In some instances, it may not be possible to move quickly in response to a first mover's action. For example, if the first mover introduces a sophisticated new product, and competitors have not undertaken similar research and development, considerable time may be required to respond effectively. Therefore, some risks are involved in being a follower in the market. However, there are no blueprints for first-mover success. Followers may be able to respond without significant market development costs by learning from first movers' triumphs and mistakes. Thus, the actions and outcomes of the first firm to initiate a competitive action may provide a more effective blueprint for second and later movers.[65]

New Balance is a second mover in the athletic shoe industry. Accounting for New Balance's success as a second mover is its ability to satisfy baby boomers' needs. The firm's target market is customers with an average age of 42. This compares with 25 for Nike and 33 for Reebok. As a second mover's product, the firm's shoes are not particularly innovative compared to those of the industry leader, Nike. In contrast to many competitors that introduce new models roughly every six weeks, New Balance introduces a new one approximately every 17 weeks. New Balance's competitive success as a second mover appears to be based on its ability to offer high-quality products at moderate prices but in multiple-sized widths. Unlike most companies, which produce shoes in two widths—medium and wide—New Balance offers customers multiple choices, ranging from a narrow AA to an expansive EEEE. The varying widths are a valued competitive feature, in that about 20 to 30 percent of the population has either narrower- or wider-than-average feet.[66]

A **late mover** is a firm that responds to a competitive action, but only after considerable time has elapsed after the first mover's action and the second mover's response.

A **late mover** is a firm that responds to a competitive action, but only after considerable time has elapsed after the first mover's action and the second mover's response. Although some type of competitive response may be more effective than no response, late movers tend to be poorer performers and often are weak competitors. Avon is a late mover in e-commerce. It implemented its Internet-based marketing and sales efforts in 2000, using IBM as a consultant to help in the design and implementation of its system. While analysts think that the change may be a good one for Avon in helping to attract a more upscale customer, Avon is alienating its direct-sales force. The company's Internet sales compete with its sales representatives, who provide direct-sales service. Furthermore, at least six major competitors established Internet sales before Avon. It will be difficult for Avon to gain a reasonable share of this market with the formidable competition.[67]

A successful late mover is Louisiana's Stewart Enterprises, which competes in the funeral home business. Stewart allowed the two larger industry leaders to exhaust their resources competing against each other and then stepped in to claim market share when they could not effectively respond. One leader, Lowen Group of British Columbia, ended up operating under bankruptcy protection and the other, Service International of Texas, was saddled with rising costs and decreasing profits. Both firms had made increasing numbers of acquisitions even as prices rose. Stewart also acquires firms but consolidates them in regions where they can share services that reduce their costs of operation. Thus, Stewart is making increasing investments to prepare for an aging and therefore growing market, while the other two firms are reducing their investments.[68]

## LIKELIHOOD OF RESPONSE

A **competitive response** is a move taken to counter the effects of an action by a competitor.

After firms take a competitive action, the success of the action is often determined by the likelihood and nature of the response by competitors. A **competitive response** is a move taken to counter the effects of an action by a competitor. Firms considering offensive action need to evaluate the potential responses from competition in making their decision to act. An offensive action may escalate rivalry to a point where actions become self-defeating and an alternative strategy may be necessary. A de-escalation strategy is an attempt to reduce overly heated competition that has become self-defeating. As Figure 6.3 shows, the probability of a competitor's response to a competitive action is based on the type of action, the reputation of the competitor taking the action, the competitor's dependence on the market, and the availability of resources to the competitor.

### Type of Competitive Action

A **strategic action** represents a significant commitment of specific and distinctive organizational resources; it is difficult to implement and to reverse.

The two types of competitive actions are strategic and tactical.[69] A **strategic action** represents a significant commitment of specific and distinctive organizational resources; it is difficult to implement and to reverse. Wal-Mart's entry into European markets, Labatt's introduction of Ice Beer, and Avon's implementation of Internet sales are examples of strategic actions.

In contrast to strategic actions, a tactical action is taken to fine-tune a strategy; it involves fewer and more general organizational resources and is relatively easy to implement and reverse. A price increase in a particular market (e.g., in airfares) is an example

■ ■ **FIGURE 6.3**

*Attack and Response in the Summary Model of Interfirm Rivalry*

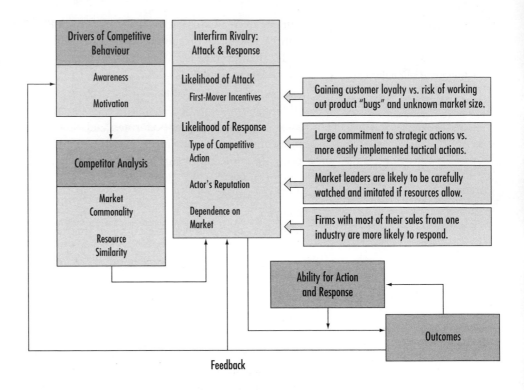

Source: Adapted from M. J. Chen, 1996, Competitor analysis and interfirm rivalry, *Academy of Management Review,* 21: 100–34.

of a tactical action. This action involves few organizational resources (e.g., communicating new prices and changing prices on products), its implementation is relatively easy, and it can be reversed (through price reduction, for example) in a relatively short period of time.

Compared to a tactical action, responses to a strategic action are more difficult, because they require additional organizational resources and time. Compared to strategic actions, tactical actions usually have more immediate effects. For example, the announcement of a price increase in a price-sensitive industry such as white goods (e.g., large home appliances like washers and dryers) could have immediate effects on competitors. Therefore, it is uncommon for competitors not to respond quickly to a competitor's price change, particularly if the announced change represents a price reduction, because without a response, a competing firm may lose market share.

Not all competitive actions elicit or require a response from competitors. On the whole, there are more competitive responses to tactical than to strategic actions.[70] It is usually easier to respond to tactical actions, and sometimes it is necessary, at least in the short term. For example, in the airline industry, responding to changes in a competitor's frequent-flier program is much easier and requires far fewer resources than responding to a major competitor's decision to upgrade its fleet of jets and to form strategic alliances to enter new markets.[71]

## Actor's Reputation

An action (either strategic or tactical) taken by a market leader is likely to serve as a catalyst to a larger number of, and faster responses, from competitors and to a higher probability of imitation of the action. In other words, firms are more likely to imitate the actions of a competitor that is a market leader. For instance, if Coca-Cola enters a new market or introduces a new product, competitors are likely to respond (if they have adequate resources to do so). Pepsi is the most likely competitor to respond, because it has adequate resources and because it is second behind Coca-Cola in most markets. Most market leaders have market power and enjoy special advantages because of their strong positive reputation.[72] Coca-Cola, for instance, enjoys a brand name that is well known globally, and the firm has considerable market power. These advantages create formidable barriers for competitors to overcome in trying to imitate Coca-Cola's actions. For example, Coca-Cola has an extensive bottling and distribution system. Many of the smaller competitors' products (e.g., Dr. Pepper) are bottled and distributed by Coca-Cola's bottlers. Thus, a smaller competitor may have difficulty introducing a new product that is competitive with Coca-Cola's products. Coca-Cola's distributors may refuse to distribute the new product—particularly if it is a cola product.

In addition, firms often react quickly to imitate successful competitor actions. For example, in the personal computer market, IBM quickly dominated the market as a second mover but was imitated by Compaq, Dell, and Gateway. By contrast, firms that take risky, complex, and unpredictable actions are less likely to solicit responses to, and imitations of, their actions.[73] As well, firms that do not initially take large amounts of market share will not illicit responses from major players in the industry. For years, craft brewers such as B.C's Shaftebury Brewing or Albert's Big Rock Brewery could make small inroads into the beer market without a great deal of response from Labatt or Molson.[74] Likewise, Bombardier's jets could meet a demand that industry giants Boeing and Airbus were unlikely to serve. Finally, firms that are known to be price predators (frequently cutting prices to hurt competitors and obtain market share, only to raise prices later) also do not elicit a large number of responses or imitation. In fact, there is less imitation and a much slower response to price predators than to either of the other two types of firms (market leader and strategic player).[75] This is because responses to price predators create price wars and are destructive to many industry participants.

As suggested in the Strategic Focus, there is no single dominant company in the auto industry. GM was once dominant, but its share of the North American auto market decreased from about 35 percent to less than 30 percent in the 1990s. GM, Ford, DaimlerChrysler, and Toyota have the strongest reputations globally. Any firm in the industry is likely to carefully observe a major strategic action by any of those four. If resources allow, other auto companies are likely to respond to the action. However, their response is not only because of the actor's reputation: most auto firms are highly dependent on the industry, so they have no choice but to try to respond to strategic actions of competitors in order to remain viable.

## Dependence on the Market

Firms with a high dependency on a market in which a competitive action is taken are more likely to respond to that action. For example, firms with a large amount of their total sales from one industry are more likely to respond to a particular competitive action taken in that industry than is a firm with businesses in multiple industries (e.g., a conglomerate). Thus, if the type of action taken has a major effect on them, firms are likely to respond, regardless of whether the action is strategic or tactical.

Retail chains in Europe are responding to Wal-Mart's entry into their markets. For example, Tesco and Sainsbury have implemented initiatives to capture the British home-shopping market. Tesco Direct, Tesco's e-commerce effort, is profitable and is predicted to become the world's largest Internet grocery business. The effort may be highly important for Tesco, because Wal-Mart's entry into Britain's grocery market has driven down prices, thereby reducing the margins earned from physical-store sales.[76]

Another example is Toys 'R' Us. It responded with its own Internet toy business to eToys' successful entry into the toy market. While Toys 'R' Us is the major competitor in the toy market and has some other businesses, it does not intend to be "Amazoned," according to analysts.[77] Likewise, Boeing has other businesses, but its core business is the manufacture and marketing of commercial aircraft. Its only global competitor, Airbus Industrie, has decided to develop a super jumbo aircraft that will hold up to 600 passengers. While a few years ago Boeing considered and decided against developing a larger version of its 747, it is now reconsidering this option as a competitive response to Airbus. Unfortunately, there are only six airlines that could use such a large aircraft profitably, thereby limiting the market size. Thus, one or both firms could lose money on a super jumbo aircraft.[78] Of course, Boeing has the resources to develop such an aircraft (said to cost about $3 billion) to respond to Airbus, but not all firms have the resources to respond effectively to competitors' strategic actions.

## Competitors' Availability of Resources

A competitive response to a strategic or tactical action requires organizational resources. Firms with fewer resources are more likely to respond to tactical actions than to strategic ones, because responses to tactical actions require fewer resources and are easier to implement. In addition, a firm's resources may dictate the type of response it makes.

For example, local video stores have limited resources to respond to competitive actions taken by larger competitors such as Rogers or Blockbuster. Usually, a local store cannot imitate the strategic actions of the larger competitors to establish multiple units within a particular geographic area. In contrast, the smaller local firm is far more likely to respond to a larger competitor's tactical action of reduced prices. Yet, because of its lower volume and lack of purchasing power relative to the large chains, initiating a tactical price reduction can also be difficult for the local store. To compete against Rogers or Blockbuster, the local video store often relies on personalized customer service and willingness to stock or search for hard-to-find videos as the sources of its competitive advantage. Focusing instead on mass availability of the most popular titles and holding operating costs low, a large video chain is unlikely to respond to the local store's service-oriented competitive actions, even though it has the resources to do so.[79] As this example suggests, small firms can respond effectively to their larger counterparts' competitive actions, but this may be more difficult to accomplish in a future dominated by electronic markets.

In contrast, AT&T and MCI WorldCom are both resource rich and directly compete against each other in many markets. Thus, they are likely to respond to each others' strategic actions. For example, AT&T is developing its technological capabilities to gain a competitive advantage, particularly in digital communications. MCI WorldCom is trying to acquire the capabilities it needs, exemplified by its latest acquisition of Sprint.

Thus, AT&T is undertaking technological risk, whereas MCI WorldCom is taking greater financial risk.[80]

## FIRMS' ABILITIES TO TAKE ACTION AND RESPOND

As indicated earlier, resource availability and ability to respond affect the probability of a company's response to a competing firm's competitive actions. Firms' abilities therefore moderate the relationship between interfirm rivalry and the competitive outcomes (see Figure 6.4.) In general, four characteristics of firms influence competitive interaction within a market or industry: (1) the relative size of the firm within a market or industry, (2) the speed at which competitive actions and responses are made, (3) the extent of innovation by firms in the market or industry, and (4) the quality of the firm's product.

### Relative Size of Firm

The size of a firm can have two important, but opposite, effects on an industry's competitive dynamics. First, the larger a firm, the greater its market power. Of course, the extent of any firm's market power is measured relative to the power of its competitors. Boeing Company (with roughly a 65 percent share of the world's commercial aircraft market) and Airbus Industrie (with approximately a 33 percent market share) both have substantial market power. However, Boeing's market power exceeds that of Airbus. Thus, Boeing hopes that developing a larger 747 will limit the ability of Airbus to capture the super jumbo aircraft market niche.[81]

■ ■ **FIGURE 6.4**

*Ability for Action and Response in the Summary Model of Interfirm Rivalry*

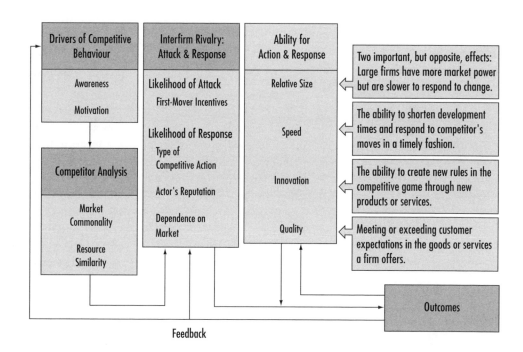

Source: Adapted from M. J. Chen, 1996, Competitor analysis and interfirm rivalry, *Academy of Management Review*, 21: 100–34.

However, size usually reflects more than market power. Often, a firm's market share reflects the general level of its resources, which may even include its R&D capabilities and the perceived quality of its products.[82] The market power and resources of competitors also shape a focal firm's responses.[83] A firm competing against weaker competitors may ignore their actions. However, it may also take actions to which its competitors are unlikely to be able to respond. Indeed, it can even drive them out of the market. For example, in 1999, Intel implemented a tactical price reduction of 41 percent in the price of its Pentium III chips to take sales from its competitors. Actions such as these caused National Semiconductor to exit the PC microprocessor business. The company fell behind in the technology and did not have the resources to increase its technology development.[84]

Problems created by a firm's size are demonstrated by events—both historical and current—in the computer industry. Although the giant in the industry, IBM, was highly successful, it did not invent or even first introduce the microcomputer, which is the primary basis of the industry today. Entrepreneurial ventures, such as Apple Computer, Dell Computer, and Compaq, introduced the innovations in goods and services that revolutionized the industry. Small firms often do this by fostering what Joseph Schumpeter referred to as "creative destruction."[85] As Steven Jobs and Steve Wozniak revolutionized the computer industry, Michael Dell, who was in high school when Apple introduced its computers, revolutionized the way computers were produced and distributed.

The microcomputer market is highly dynamic. Compaq became the number-one manufacturer and seller of personal computers in the 1995–96 period. However, in 1999, Dell overtook Compaq as the top producer of personal computers.[86] Thus, oftentimes the smaller competitor is more innovative and eventually overtakes the top firm. The moral is that it may not be best to grow too large but rather to find a way to continue to operate using a small-firm culture even though the firm is actually large.

Large firms need to use their size to build market power, but they must think and act like a small firm (e.g., move quickly and be innovative) in order to achieve strategic competitiveness and earn above-average returns over the long run. A commitment to the value of each employee and to the use of organizational structures that encourage individuals to demonstrate initiative appears to facilitate large firms' efforts to act entrepreneurially.[87] Xerox, 3M, and Nortel (see the Strategic Focus case in Chapter 14) are large firms that appear to be overcoming the liabilities of size through the creation and support of entrepreneurship.[88]

Pepsi and Coca-Cola's entry into the bottled-water market will make it difficult for the other firms in the industry to compete. Not only can Pepsi and Coca-Cola invest significant resources in promoting their brands of water, they have large and efficient distribution systems. Likely, the survivors of the battle among the small firms will be those that can claim a special niche in the market (e.g., Evian).

The following Strategic Focus explains two situations where Pepsi acted much faster than Coca-Cola. Pepsi moved Diet Pepsi into the Indian drink market within days of the government's announcement allowing the use of artificial sweeteners in soft drinks. Coke was much slower. Also, Coke entered the bottled-water market five years after Pepsi, only after the demand for bottled water began to grow significantly and Pepsi's product became number one in the market. Coke also is experiencing multiple problems that are only exacerbated by the firm's slowness to react to threats and opportunities.

## STRATEGIC FOCUS

### Cola Wars, Water Wars, and Going for the Jugular Vein

Coca-Cola is the dominant firm in the global soft-drink market. It has the largest market share in North America and over 50 percent of the soft-drink market in many of the European countries (e.g., France, Germany, and Spain). Its share of the global soft-drink market is about 50 percent. Because of Coca-Cola's dominant position, along with those of several other competitors (mostly local or regional, except for Pepsi), many of these markets have become saturated. Thus, competitors can no longer enjoy a growing market and must target their competitors' market share. Competitors have largely targeted Coca-Cola.

Coca-Cola withdrew from the Indian market in 1987 because of a nationalist government that wanted it to sell to local firms. Coke returned to India in 1993, but by that time Pepsi was well entrenched without Coca-Cola as a competitor. A local cola firm also gained a major foothold in the market during Coca-Cola's absence. The stakes are high in India, because it is one of the few remaining large markets that is not saturated. Recently, the government approved the use of artificial sweeteners in carbonated drinks. Coca-Cola and Pepsi moved swiftly to introduce their diet colas. In fact, Pepsi introduced Diet Pepsi to the market within two days of the approval. Coca-Cola responded with prominent advertising announcing the arrival of Diet Coke. However, within a week, the Indian Health Ministry announced that it would enforce an old regulation requiring all carbonated drinks to contain at least 5 percent sucrose. Pepsi blamed Coca-Cola for bringing this regulation to the attention of the Indian government. Pepsi believed that Coca-Cola took its action to delay Pepsi so that Coke-Cola could catch up. Pepsi then sought and obtained a court waiver to avoid having to add the sucrose and also won a temporary injunction that allows it to keep selling Diet Pepsi until the court rules on its case. Coca-Cola also sought a waiver and then launched its Diet Coke into the market. Neither company may gain much, even if they win the right to sell their diet drinks: Indians generally do not like the taste of diet drinks and are suspicious of artificial sweeteners.

Pepsi and Coca-Cola are competing in another market as well. In 1994, Pepsi introduced its brand of bottled water, Aquafina. Since that time, Aquafina has become the top-selling brand of bottled water in convenience stores. Five years after Pepsi's introduction of bottled water, Coca-Cola announced that it was entering this market as well. In 1999, Coca-Cola declared that it would begin marketing bottled water under the brand name Dasani. The product will be purified, non-carbonated water fortified with minerals to enhance its taste. Coca-Cola was reluctant to add bottled water to its line of products, preferring instead to encourage consumption of its carbonated soft drinks. However, the popularity of bottled water and Pepsi's success probably lured Coca-Cola into the market, although belatedly. Pepsi and Coca-Cola are expected to battle for sales of their water products. However, both will need to be careful not to substitute sales of water for soft-drink sales (because their margin is much higher on soft drinks).

In the 1990s, consumption of Pepsi's soft drinks increased by only 2 percent, while Coke's consumption increased by 30 percent. Thus, Pepsi managers decided to invest heavily in advertising. In 1999, Pepsi spent almost as much as Coca-Cola did on advertising, even though Pepsi is much smaller. Pepsi used the

*continued*

approximately $4 billion it received from spinning off its bottlers and restaurant operations (now called Tricon) to help finance the new ad campaign.

While Coca-Cola is the clear global leader, all is not well in the company. In 1999, it experienced embarrassing and costly lapses in quality that caused short-term bans of its products in Belgium and France. It also had to withdraw 180 000 bottles of water in Poland after coliform bacteria were discovered in the drink. In addition, Italy's competition authority fined Coca-Cola for anticompetitive practices. Given all of these problems, and the company's slow and ineffective reactions to them, Coca-Cola's CEO, Douglas Ivestor, resigned his position. Coca-Cola also recently announced employee layoffs and a restructuring of its management. Managers at Pepsi are undoubtedly revelling over Coca-Cola's problems.

Sources: M. Benson, 1999, In New York, battle is over city-owned property, *Wall Street Journal Interactive,* September 29, interactive.wsj.com/archive; J. Blitz & B. Liu, 1999, Coca-Cola: $16 million fine from Italian authorities, *www.ft.com,* www.ft.com/sea (Retrieved December 18); N. Deogun & E. Williamson, 1999, Coke, in new breakdown, recalls more water products in Poland, *Wall Street Journal Interactive,* July 6, interactive.wsj.com/articles; D. Foust, 1999, Coke and Pepsi want to make a splash in water, *Businessweek Online,* March 1, bwarchive.businessweek.com; D. Foust, G. Smith, & D. Rocks, 1999, Coke's man on the spot, May 3, bwarchive.businessweek.com; Going for broke, 1999, *The Economist,* August 16, www.economist.com/editorial; It's the real thing: Coca Cola preparing for dive into bottled water market, *Dallas Morning News,* February 20, F12; L. Light, 1999, The Pepsi generation, *Businessweek Online,* March 22, bwarchive.businessweek.com.

## Speed of Competitive Actions and Competitive Responses

Time and speed are important in the 21st century's competitive environment. The speed with which a firm can initiate competitive actions and competitive responses may determine its success. In the 21st century competitive landscape, speed in developing a new product and moving it to the market is becoming critical to both the establishment of a competitive advantage and earning above-average returns.[89]

Tesco and Sainsbury in Great Britain, Carrefour in France, and Canadian Tire in Canada had to respond quickly to Wal-Mart's entry into their markets. Failure to do so could have made them highly vulnerable to Wal-Mart's market power once it became established in their markets. In each country, the firms chose a different way to respond. Carrefour responded by acquiring a major competitor to increase its size, resource base, economies of scale, and breadth and depth of market power. In contrast, Tesco and Sainsbury chose to focus on a market niche in which Wal-Mart has not exhibited strength: e-commerce. Canadian Tire used its geographic coverage and customer loyalty to maintain its customer base in its selected market niches of automotive, sports and leisure, and home products At the same time, Canadian Tire expanded its store size to remain competitive within those selected market niches. For all these companies, their actions were swift and helped the firms continue to be important competitors in their respective markets.

Speed in bringing their products to the marketplace is one of the problems North American automakers have experienced in competing with Japanese firms. Some time ago, Japanese auto companies were able to design a new product and introduce it to the market within three years. In comparison, North American firms required between five and eight years to complete these activities. This time differential made it possible for Japanese firms to design two or three new automobiles and move them to the market in the same time it took a North American automaker to do one. Thereafter, Ford, GM, and DaimlerChrysler all reduced their development time to three to four years. However, Toyota responded by reducing its development time to a minimum of 15 months.

In a global economy, although time is a critical source of competitive advantage, managing for speed requires more than attempting to have employees work faster. Essentially, it requires working smarter, using different types of organizational structures, and shortening the time it takes to bring a car to completion as primary work-related goals.[90] Research has shown that the pace of strategic decisionmaking may be affected by an executive's cognitive ability, use of intuition, tolerance for risk, and propensity to act.[91] Executives who use intuition and have a greater tolerance for risk are predisposed to make faster strategic decisions than those without such characteristics. Also, decisions are likely to occur faster in centralized organizations because they will not have to go through as many levels or receive approval from as many people. More formalized and bureaucratic organizations, however, may find it difficult to make fast strategic decisions[92] because they require more layers of approval.

Jack Welch, former chair and CEO of General Electric, states that speed is the ability sought by all of today's organizations.[93] He suggests that companies are striving to develop products faster, speed up production cycles in moving them to the market, and improve response time to customers. In Welch's opinion, having faster communications and moving with agility are critical to competitive success.

## Innovation

In some industries, such as pharmaceuticals and computers, a third general factor, innovation, has long been known to have a strong influence on a firm's performance.[94] Innovation is increasing in importance in many industries in the 21st-century landscape. The strategic importance of innovation is explored further in Chapter 14. Research suggests that, in today's global economy, innovation, in both products and processes, is becoming linked with above-average returns in a growing number of industries.[95] One study, for example, found that companies with the highest performance also invested the most in research and development. In 1970, U.S. firms held more than two-thirds of the world market in nine of the top fifteen major industries. By 1980, U.S. domination was limited to only three of the industries. The study found that this was due largely to changes in innovation: Non-U.S. firms were more innovative than their U.S. counterparts in many of the industries.[96] In fact, a contributing factor to the productivity and technology problems experienced by U.S. firms has been U.S. managers' unwillingness to bear the costs and risks of long-term development of product and process innovations.[97]

In general, the dynamics of competition among firms in high-tech industries encourage significant allocations to each company's research and development operations.[98] In fact, as the number of competitors increases in an industry, so does the amount of innovation usually produced.[99] In particular, innovation is often a strength of small firms and acts to equalize the competitiveness between large and small firms (see Chapter 14). Innovation is especially important in the computer software industry. While there are different niches, and while separate companies have achieved significant market shares in these niches, Microsoft is probably the best-known and most dominant firm in the software industry. However, Sun Microsystems has targeted Microsoft. Sun acquired the Star Division Corporation, which makes a series of office software known as StarOffice. Sun's primary purpose in acquiring Star is to attack Microsoft with Web-based word-processing and spreadsheet applications. Sun plans to build StarOffice into a free Internet-based service that can be run directly with a Web browser, without the need to load large programs onto the PC. Sun's stated intention is to change the rules of the game. Given that Microsoft earns approximately 40 percent of its revenue from sales of Office, this new challenge could present significant problems for the firm.[100] It also shows the need to continuously bring innovation to the market in the software industry.

In the mobile phone industry, where innovation is important, Ericsson fell behind Nokia. The firm's problems stem primarily from being slow to bring innovations to the market. As a result, Nokia has moved ahead of the Swedish company. In 1999, Ericsson's CEO of only 15 months was forced to resign. His supporters argue that he was treated unfairly since he was given a firm with a poor product life cycle that could not be corrected in a short period of time. While Ericsson's problems can be solved, some analysts have predicted that the firm will need to embark on a process of managed decline.[101]

Firms competing in industries in which the pattern of competitive dynamics calls for innovation-related abilities should recognize that implementing innovations effectively is difficult. Some researchers believe that a failure of implementation, not innovation, increasingly is the cause of many firms' inability to derive adequate competitive benefits from product and process innovations.[102] Among other capabilities, a firm requires executives who are able to integrate its innovation strategy with other strategies (such as the business-level strategies discussed in Chapter 5) and to recruit and select high-tech workers to successfully implement innovations.[103]

Earlier, we suggested that large firms with significant market power that act like small firms—making strategic decisions and implementing them speedily—and that are innovative, are strong competitors and are likely to earn above-average returns. Yet, no matter how large, fast, or innovative an organization is, the quality of its products and services also affects its industry's competitive dynamics and influences the firm's ability to achieve strategic competitiveness in domestic and global markets.

## Quality

Product quality has become a universal theme in the global economy and continues to shape competitive dynamics in many industries.[104] Today, product quality is important in all industry settings and is a necessary, but not sufficient, condition for implementing a firm's strategy successfully. Without quality goods or services, strategic competitiveness cannot be achieved. Yet quality alone does not guarantee that a firm will achieve strategic competitiveness or earn above-average returns. In the words of the president of the National Center for Manufacturing Sciences, a U.S. nonprofit research consortium, "Quality used to be a competitive issue out there, but now it's just the basic denominator to being in the market."[105]

This is the case in the café/bakery business. Accepting product quality as a given, executives of competitors La Madeleine and Corner Bakery believe that their products are more than simply food. They suggest that their establishments and products contribute to a way of life for those interested in purchasing items from neighbourhood bakeries with a family atmosphere.[106]

**Quality** involves meeting or exceeding customer expectations in the goods or services a firm offers.[107] The quality dimensions of goods and services are shown in Table 6.1. As a competitive dimension, quality is as important in the service sector as it is in the manufacturing sector.[108]

Quality begins at the top of the organization. Top management must create values for quality that permeate the entire organization.[109] These values should be built into strategies that reflect long-term commitments to customers, stockholders, and other important stakeholders.[110]

Quality and total quality management are closely associated with the philosophies and teachings of W. Edwards Deming (and, to a lesser extent, Armand Feigenbaum and Joseph Juran).[111] These individuals' contributions to the practice of management are based on a simple, yet powerful, insight: the understanding that it costs less to make quality products than defect-ridden ones.

*(margin note)* **Quality** involves meeting or exceeding customer expectations in the goods or services a firm offers.

---

**■ ■ TABLE 6.1**                    **Quality Dimensions of Goods and Services**

**Product Quality Dimensions**

| | | |
|---|---|---|
| 1. *Performance:* | Operating characteristics |
| 2. *Features:* | Important special characteristics |
| 3. *Flexibility:* | Meeting operating specifications over some period of time |
| 4. *Durability:* | Amount of use before performance deteriorates |
| 5. *Conformance:* | Match with pre-established standards |
| 6. *Serviceability:* | Ease and speed of repair or normal service |
| 7. *Aesthetics:* | How a product looks and feels |
| 8. *Perceived quality:* | Subjective assessment of characteristics (product image) |

**Service Quality Dimensions**

| | |
|---|---|
| 1. *Timeliness:* | Performed in promised period of time |
| 2. *Courtesy:* | Performed cheerfully |
| 3. *Consistency:* | Giving all customers similar experiences each time |
| 4. *Convenience:* | Accessibility to customers |
| 5. *Completeness:* | Fully serviced, as required |
| 6. *Accuracy:* | Performed correctly each time |

Sources: Adapted from J.W. Dean, Jr., & J.R. Evans, 1994, *Total Quality: Management, Organization and Society* (St. Paul, MN: West Publishing Company); H. V. Roberts & B. F. Sergesketter, 1993, *Quality Is Personal* (New York: The Free Press); D. Garvin, 1988, *Managed Quality: The Strategic and Competitive Edge* (New York: The Free Press).

**Total quality management** (TQM) is a "managerial innovation that emphasizes an organization's total commitment to the customer and to continuous improvement of every process through the use of data-driven, problem-solving approaches based on empowerment of employee groups and teams."[112] Actually a philosophy about how to manage, TQM "combines the teachings of Deming and Juran on statistical process control and group problem-solving processes with Japanese values concerned with quality and continuous improvement."[113] Statistical process control (SPC) is a technique used to continually upgrade the quality of the goods or services a firm produces. SPC benefits the firm through the detection and elimination of variations in processes used to manufacture a good or service.[114]

Although there are cynics, when applied properly, principles of total quality management can help firms achieve strategic competitiveness and earn above-average returns.[115] Three principal goals sought when practising total quality management are boosting customer satisfaction, reducing the amount of time required to introduce products into the marketplace, and cutting costs. These are accomplished in several ways; most importantly, by empowering workers to achieve continuous improvements in all aspects of their tasks.[116]

British Telecommunications (BT) uses a TQM system in order to be competitive with firms worldwide. BT managers believe that the firm's TQM system, implemented in 1986, has helped it to compete effectively in global markets.[117] Ironically, Deming's and Juran's ideas on quality and continuous improvement were adapted and implemented by Japanese firms long before many North American firms acknowledged their importance. For this reason, a host of Japanese firms developed a competitive advantage in product quality that was difficult for other firms to overcome.[118] By effectively implementing TQM systems, many North American and Western European firms have overcome the original competitive advantage enjoyed by Japanese firms related to the quality of their products. Deming's 14 points for managing and achieving quality (see Table 6.2) are critical in businesses around the world.

Embedded within Deming's 14 points for management is the importance of striving continuously to improve both the operation of a firm and the quality of its goods or services. In fact, Deming did not support use of the term "TQM," arguing that he did not know what total quality was and that it is impossible for firms to reach a goal of total quality. The pursuit of improvements in quality, Deming believed, should be a neverending process.

Newer methods of TQM use benchmarking and emphasize organizational learning.[119] Benchmarking facilitates TQM by developing information on the best practices of other organizations and industries. This information is often used to establish goals for the firm's own TQM efforts. Benchmarking is a process through which a company can learn from the outcomes of other firms.[120] Because of the importance of quality (of both goods and services) in achieving competitive parity or a competitive advantage, many firms around the world emphasize TQM and integrate it with their strategies.

In sum, relationships between each of the four general abilities (size, speed, innovation, and quality) influence a firm's competitive actions and outcomes. Those responsible for selecting a firm's strategy should understand these relationships and anticipate that competitors will take competitive actions and competitive responses designed to exploit the positive relationships depicted in Figure 6.5. In the next section, we describe the different outcomes of competitive dynamics.

| ■ ■ **TABLE 6.2** | **Deming's 14 Points for Management** |
|---|---|

1. Create and publish to all employees a statement of the aims and purposes of the company or other organization. The management must demonstrate constantly their commitment to this statement.

2. Learn the new philosophy, top management and everybody.

3. Understand the purpose of inspection, for improvement of processes and reduction of costs.

4. End the practice of awarding business on the basis of price tag alone.

5. Improve constantly and forever the system of production and service.

6. Institute training.

7. Teach and institute leadership.

8. Drive out fear. Create trust. Create a climate for innovation.

9. Optimize toward the aims and purposes of the company—the efforts of teams, groups, staff areas.

10. Eliminate exhortations for the workforce.

11. (a) Eliminate numerical quotas for production. Instead, learn and institute methods for improvement. (b) Eliminate management by objective. Instead, learn the capabilities of processes and how to improve them.

12. Remove barriers that rob people of pride of workmanship.

13. Encourage education and self-improvement for everyone.

14. Take action to accomplish the transformation.

Source: Reprinted from *Out of the Crisis,* by W. Edwards Deming. Published by MIT, Center for Advanced Engineering Study, Cambridge, MA 02139. Copyright, 1986 by W. Edwards Deming.

■ ■ **FIGURE 6.5**

*Effects of Firm Size, Speed of Decisionmaking and Actions, Innovations, and Quality on Sustainability of Competitor Actions and Outcomes*

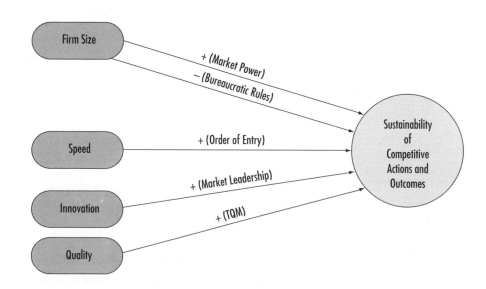

Plus and minus signs indicate effects on performance.

## OUTCOMES OF INTERFIRM RIVALRY

Figure 6.6 illustrates various potential outcomes of interfirm rivalry. In some competitive environments, building a sustainable competitive advantage may be more likely than in others. As discussed in Chapter 4, one of the key determinants of sustainability is whether a firm's products are costly to imitate. Sustainability, therefore, might focus on different markets in which product imitability is largely or partially shielded.[121] In countries whose markets are largely open to international competitors, foreign rivals have made inroads into most major markets. However, even with strong rivalry and an increasing potential for imitability, some markets have been shielded from such competition. These markets are referred to as slow-cycle or sheltered markets. In other markets, product imitability is moderate, so they are labelled standard-cycle markets and are sometimes described as oligopolistic. In still other markets, firms operate in rapid, dynamic, and often entrepreneurial environments. These markets are identified as fast-cycle markets.[122]

■ ■ **FIGURE 6.6**

*Outcomes in the Summary Model of Interfirm Rivalry*

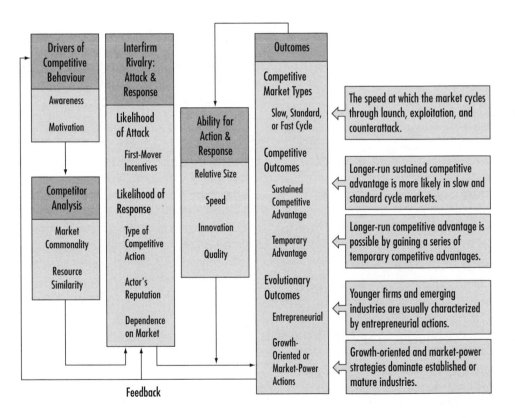

Source: Adapted from M. J. Chen, 1996, Competitor analysis and interfirm rivalry, *Academy of Management Review*, 21: 100–34.

Products in **slow-cycle markets** reflect strongly shielded resource positions wherein competitive pressures do not readily penetrate the firm's sources of strategic competitiveness.

## Competitive Market Outcomes

Products in **slow-cycle markets** reflect strongly shielded resource positions wherein competitive pressures do not readily penetrate the firm's sources of strategic competitiveness. In economics, this situation is often characterized as a monopoly position. A firm that has a unique set of product attributes or an effective product design may dominate its markets for decades, as IBM did with large mainframe computers. This type of competitive position can be established even in markets where there is significant technological change; an example is Microsoft's position with respect to difficult-to-imitate, complex software systems. Of course, conditions have changed for IBM and also for Microsoft, as competitors such as Sun Microsystems close in on Microsoft, and the U.S. government prosecutes the firm for anticompetitive practices.

While concerns about anticompetitive behaviour are not uncommon in North America (e.g., Ottawa's disapproval of the proposed mergers between major Canadian banks in the late 1990s), such prosecution is puzzling to some European observers. For example, the Netherlands is a small country that is home to such corporate giants as Shell Oil and Philips Electronics. Given the large size of these firms and the small size of the country, the nation's fortunes are, in many ways, tied to the successes of these companies and therefore government tends to support their efforts. Thus, as one academic teaching in Holland noted, "If Bill Gates were Dutch, he would be applauded, not attacked."[123] Thus, while some governments may be inclined to interfere in negative ways, others may be positively inclined toward certain competitors or industries. In fact, some firms are protected by regulations or laws prohibiting competition. For example, for a long time, the utilities industries were largely protected as legal monopolies. However, that stance has changed, and competition is now allowed. In contrast, drug manufacturers still maintain a legally protected position under patent laws. Note that shielded advantages may be geographic; thus, the opening of huge emerging markets in Eastern Europe, Russia, China, and India offers strong motivation for firms to pursue such opportunities.

Effective product designs may enable the firms that produced them to dominate their markets for many years, as the examples of Microsoft and IBM show. These firms' advantages are drawn largely from their special core competencies, because their resources and capabilities are difficult to imitate. The sustainability of competitive action associated with a slow-cycle market is depicted in Figure 6.7. Because these markets (and hence the firms that operate in them) are largely protected, they usually enjoy the highest average price increase over time. Alternatively, price increases in standard-cycle markets often vary closely around zero.[124]

Products in **standard-cycle markets** reflect moderately shielded resource positions wherein competitive interaction penetrates a firm's sources of strategic competitiveness; but with improvement of its capabilities, the firm may be able to sustain a competitive advantage.

Standard-cycle markets are more closely associated with the industrial organization economics approach exemplified in Porter's five forces model of competitive strategy (see Chapter 3). In these firms, strategy and organization are designed to serve high-volume or mass markets. The focus is on coordination and market control, as in the automobile and appliance industries.[125] Even though these firms may be able to sustain world-class products for decades (e.g., Coca-Cola), they may experience severe competitive pressures. Extended dominance and, in fact, world leadership are possible through continuing capital investment and superior learning, as was the case with Coca-Cola. However, as described in the last Strategic Focus, Coke is now experiencing substantial competitive pressures in several of its markets. In particular, Pepsi is taking strategic actions much more quickly than Coke. In contrast, less investment is made in

> Products in **standard-cycle markets** reflect moderately shielded resource positions wherein competitive interaction penetrates a firm's sources of strategic competitiveness; but with improvement of its capabilities, the firm may be able to sustain a competitive advantage.

innovation in protected markets. Although it may be difficult to enter standard-cycle markets because of the competitive intensity, if a firm is successful and its strategy duplicated by competitors, more intense competitive pressures can be brought to bear. In that case, the competition may be similar to that found in fast-cycle markets.[126]

■ ■ **FIGURE 6.7**

*Gradual Erosion of a Sustained Competitive Advantage*

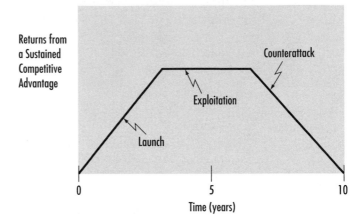

Source: Adapted from I.C. MacMillan, 1988, Controlling competitive dynamics by taking strategic initiative, *Academy of Management Executive,* II, (2) 111–18.

Standard-cycle markets that are intensely competitive may also require innovation (as discussed earlier). For example, a firm can capture market share in the standard-cycle market of brewing by offering innovative products. Unibroue of Chambly, Quebec has gained recognition in Canada for its interpretation of traditional Belgian and French farmhouse styles. In this case, the innovation is the introduction of traditional beer styles rarely found in North America—even as imports. Its U.S. partner, Unibrew USA, has firmly established the brand along the U.S. East Coast as well. The company also expects to match its success in new markets on the U.S. West Coast, and in New Mexico and Texas.[127]

## Competing in Fast-Cycle Markets

Achieving a sustained competitive advantage is possible in slow- and, possibly, standard-cycle markets. However, it is largely impossible to gain a sustained competitive advantage in a fast-cycle market. Figure 6.7 focuses on sustainable competitive advantage. In **fast-cycle markets**, a competitive advantage cannot be sustained; firms attempt to gain temporary competitive advantages by strategically disrupting the market. Usually, there is an entrepreneurial launch stage of the strategy, then a period of exploitation, and, ultimately, a period of counterattack wherein the competitive advantage erodes. In fast-cycle markets, a competitive advantage can even create inertia and expose a firm to aggressive global competitors. Even though GM has economies of scale, a huge advertising budget, an efficient distribution system, cutting-edge R&D, and slack resources, many of its advantages have been eroded by global competitors in Europe and Japan. Fast-cycle markets are the most difficult to manage and are the most volatile. Such markets often experience average price reductions over time. For example, over a recent

In **fast-cycle markets**, a competitive advantage cannot be sustained; firms attempt to gain temporary competitive advantages by strategically disrupting the market.

period, 10 fast-cycle markets experienced price reductions ranging from a minimum of 3.5 percent to a maximum of 29 percent.[128]

A new competitive advantage paradigm is emerging in which a firm seizes the initiative through a series of small steps, as illustrated in Figure 6.8. As the figure indicates, the idea is to create a counterattack before the advantage is eroded. The counterattack actually leads to cannibalizing a firm's own products through the next stage of product evolution and entry. Thus, the focus of this new paradigm is competitive disruption.[129] However, a firm can escalate competition in areas such as price and quality only so far before the dominant competitor seeks to achieve another level of competition focused on factors such as speed and know-how or innovation.

The telecommunications industry reflects a fast-cycle market. It is global in nature and highly dynamic. Firms in the industry have acquired cable companies and are now focusing on wireless communications companies. Most firms in the industry believe that the next generation of telecommunications will be based on wireless transmission. In 1999, Vodafone, a telecommunications firm based in Great Britain, acquired AirTouch Communications, a United States–based firm. Vodafone also has acquired Mannesman, a fast-growing wireless operator based in Germany.[130]

■ ■ **FIGURE 6.8**

*Obtaining Temporary Advantages to Create Sustained Advantage*

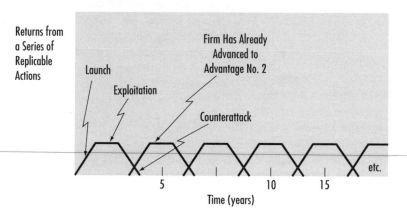

Source: Adapted from I.C. MacMillan, 1988, Controlling competitive dynamics by taking strategic initiative, *Academy of Management Executive,* II, (2): 111–18.

In an allied industry, telecommunications equipment, Nortel recently attacked one of its especially effective competitors: Cisco Systems. Cisco, a fast-growing data communications equipment manufacturer, had developed the router that controls traffic on the Internet. While Nortel was initially slow to respond to Cisco's moves, it had made up for lost ground. Nortel's attack consisted of introducing new software, dramatically reducing hardware prices, and established licensing agreements with Intel and Microsoft. However, Cisco managers referred to Nortel's actions as a fire sale. They suggested that it indicated that the firm was desperate.[131] Yet, as noted in the next strategic focus, given Nortel's major acquisitions to build a world-class contender, one can hardly call the company out of the game.

## STRATEGIC FOCUS

### Fibre Wars: Light-Speed Changes in the Fibre Optics Industry

In the 1880s, Alexander Graham Bell invented the Photophone—a device for sending voices through the air via reflected sunbeams. This was the first device that used light to transmit voice, and it came long before the invention of radio. The idea of using optical fibre to communicate signals was invented in the 1920s and patented in the early 1930s. However, it was not until the late 1950s that a device was available that could adequately transmit a signal about a metre; and, it was not until the late 1970s that optical fibre could be made pure enough to transmit signals over kilometres. It was at this point that the telecommunications industry, having used up most of the available radio frequencies, was becoming desperate for additional ways to transmit information, and optical fibre answered the need. By the 1990s, the Internet brought additional demands for data transmission. The need for fibre optic cable and the devices that help it transmit and receive signals mushroomed.

Market leader Lucent Technologies was spun off from giant AT&T several years ago. The company's 140 000 employees make telecom equipment, software, telecommunications power systems, and integrated circuits. Lucent had sales of almost $60 billion in 1999. While some of Lucent's technology was developed by Bell Labs and gave the company an early technological lead, the firm has developed its broadband (voice, data, and video) networking market through acquisitions. To stay technologically current, some Lucent acquisitions are start-ups that have never generated revenue. For example, Lucent spent almost $6 billion for optical networker Chromatis. Likewise, second-place Nortel made a $9 billion acquisition of no-income Xros.

Brampton, Ontario's, Nortel is perhaps one of the industry's most prolific acquirers. Nortel's CEO John Roth made over $20 billion in acquisitions in 2000. Based on Nortel's market capitalization of around $100 billion, its sales of over $30 billion, and its over 60 000 employees, and in spite of setbacks in the price of Nortel's stock, Roth may still have room to spend on a few more acquisitions. Nortel products include switching, wireless, and broadband network systems. Also, the company is a leader in fibre optic systems for high-capacity data and voice networks. Nortel's acquisitions have allowed it to stay technologically ahead of Lucent and Cisco (particularly in some software segments). It is not only Nortel's acquisitions that keep it going but also John Roth's attitude. While Nortel can call itself a leader, Roth exercises some Canadian reserve by positioning Nortel as a David against Goliaths: "Cisco has a bigger market cap, Lucent has more in sales, Ericsson is ahead of us in wireless." Yet Roth is not all that reserved, "If we rise above them, we will invent a [market] leader to fight against."

Although Cisco Systems has about 85 percent of Nortel's sales, it generates those sales with about 20 000 employees—about one-third of Nortel's workforce. Cisco sells the majority of products that link networks and the Internet, e.g., routers, switches, dial-up access servers, and network management software. Cisco is no stranger to acquisitions either. It has bought more than 40 companies since 1993 and has earmarked billions more for purchases. Cisco also relies on alliances with firms such as IBM, Motorola, and Sun Microsystems to keep its market share.

*continued*

While all three of these companies, and a host of minor players, drove a huge acquisition binge, the stock market for a long time signalled its approval. With market capitalizations that started at $250 billion, it seems that purchasing a company with the next new cutting-edge technology was an acceptable form of hedging a technological bet. Witness Nepean, Ontario's, JDS Uniphase and its $57 billion acquisition of SDL in 2000. That acquisition comes on the heels of its $22 billion acquisition of E-Tek months earlier. JDS Uniphase's fibre optic laser subsystems and equipment are sold to such industry giants as Lucent and Nortel. Yet the firm had only about $2 billion in sales and the size of its acquisitions exceed those of both Lucent and Nortel. Still, this market was so hot—industry sales growth was expected to quadruple between 2000 and 2003—that market analysts felt that a company with $2 billion in sales making about $80 billion in acquisitions was "a better investment than ever." Yet as the U.S. economy slowed and growth predictions fell, stocks such as Nortel sent markets into a tailspin. While hedging one's technological bet may still make some sense, the price of the hedge has been knocked down considerably.

Sources: M Lewis and J. Gatehouse, 2001, Nortel plunges, class actions fly, National Post, A1, A2; Hoovers Online, 2000, Cisco Systems Inc., http://www.hoovers.com/co/capsule/4/0,2163, 13494,00.html (Retrieved August 18); Hoovers Online, 2000, Lucent Technologies, http://www.hoovers.com/co/capsule/6/0, 2163,46656,00.html (Retrieved August 18); Hoovers Online, 2000, Nortel, http://www.hoovers.com/co/capsule/4/0,2163,41824,00.html (Retrieved August 18); C.Y. Chen, 2000, Gorilla in the midst..., Fortune Investor Analysis Online, August 14, http://www.ecompany.com/articles/mag/0,1640,8183,00.html (Retrieved April 27, 2001); J. Hecht, 1999, The lost generation of fiber optics..., Analog Science Fiction and Fact, March: 42–51.

The array of competitive actions and competitive responses occurring over time in the fibre optics telecommunications industry demonstrates the four strategic steps shown in Table 6.3. At different times and with different products, several telecommunications firms have been able to (1) identify a competitive opportunity that disrupted the status quo, (2) create a temporary advantage that was eroded through aggressive responses by their competitors, (3) seize the initiative from their competitors through effective competitive actions, and (4) sustain their momentum by continually offering new products and entering new markets. Thus, firms must exhibit strategic flexibility if they are to be successful competing in fast-cycle markets. When operating under these market conditions, firms must learn how to respond quickly to technological change and market opportunities by offering more new products, broader product lines, and product upgrades more rapidly.[132]

## Competitive Dynamics and Industry Evolution Outcomes

Because industries and markets evolve over time, so do the competitive dynamics among firms in an industry. We have examined how firms interact in a short span of time using an action-response framework, but we have not yet considered how competitive interaction evolves over longer periods of time. Three general stages of industry evolution are relevant to our study of competitive dynamics: the emerging, growth, and mature stages. These are shown in Figure 6.9.

■ ■ **FIGURE 6.9**

*An Action-Based Model of the Industry Life Cycle*

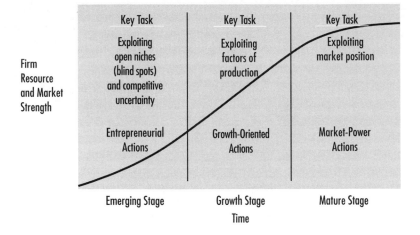

Source: Adapted from C.M. Grimm & K.G. Smith, 1997, *Strategy as Action: Industry Rivalry and Coordination* (St. Paul, MN: West Publishing Co.).

Firms entering emerging industries attempt to establish a niche or an initial form of dominance within an industry. Competitive rivalry for the loyalty of customers is serious. In these industries, depending on the types of products, firms often attempt to establish product quality, technological superiority, or advantageous relationships with suppliers in order to develop a competitive advantage in the pursuit of strategic competitiveness. These firms are striving to build their reputation. As a result, a variety of different competitive strategies may be employed in such an industry. This diversity can be beneficial to many of the firms in the industry, helping them avoid direct competition and gain dominance in market niches.[133] Though speed is important in emerging industries, access to capital is often the critical issue. Thus, it is not uncommon to have strategic alliances develop between a new firm entering the market and a more established firm that wishes to gain a foothold in the new industry.[134]

Firms in emerging industries often rely on top management to develop market opportunities. Steve Jobs and Bill Gates were able to foresee the future possibilities of the microcomputer and the standardized microcomputer operating system. Their vision of an uncertain environment gave rise to Apple Computer and Microsoft, respectively. Thus, firms in an emerging stage take entrepreneurial actions that focus on entrepreneurial discovery in uncertain environments.

Firms in growth-oriented industries are survivors from the emerging-industry stage. In the growth stage, growth-oriented actions are emphasized, which tend to create product standardization as consumer demand creates a mass market with growth potential. Thus, many of these firms are more established, but none the less competitive. In fact, as the industry begins to mature, the variety of strategies that are implemented tends to decrease. Entrepreneurial actions are indeed still taking place, but there is more emphasis on growth-oriented actions. Oftentimes, groups of firms will follow a similar strategy and thus become directly competitive. However, the rivalry between groups may be more indirect.[135] In industries in which there is considerable rivalry both within strategic groups and among firms in separate strategic groups, firms frequently earn below-average returns.[136]

## ■ ■ TABLE 6.3 — Strategic Steps for Seizing the Initiative in Fast-Cycle Markets

1. *Disrupting the status quo*
   Competitors disrupt the status quo by identifying new opportunities to serve the customer and by shifting the rules of competition. These moves end the old pattern of competitive interaction between rivals. Disrupting the status quo requires speed and variety in approach.

2. *Creating a temporary advantage*
   Disruption creates temporary advantages that are based on better knowledge of customers, technology, and the future. Derived from customer orientation and employee empowerment throughout the entire organization, these advantages are short lived and eroded by fierce competition.

3. *Seizing the initiative*
   By moving aggressively into new areas of competition, acting to create a new advantage, or undermining a competitor's old advantage, the firm seizes the initiative. The opponent, thrown off balance, is at a temporary disadvantage and is forced to play catch-up, reacting rather than shaping the future via its own initiatives. The initiator is proactive and forces competitors to be reactive.

4. *Sustaining the momentum*
   Several actions in a row are taken to seize the initiative and create momentum. The firm continues to develop new advantages and does not wait for competitors to undermine them before launching the next initiative. This succession of actions sustains the momentum. Continually offering new initiatives is the only source of sustainable competitive advantage in fast-cycle environments.

Source: Adapted from R.A. D'Aveni, 1995, Coping with hypercompetition: Utilizing the new 7's framework, *Academy of Management Executive,* IX (3): 45–60.

Some of these industries may also be fragmented. Fragmented markets, such as the fast food restaurant market, tend to offer standardized facilities and products but leave decentralized decisionmaking to the local units. The standardization allows for low-cost competition. The primary value added comes from the services that are provided. These markets offer a prime opportunity for franchising because of the ability to standardize facilities, operations, and products.[137]

The Internet access market has become relatively fragmented but also remains an emerging growth industry. While AOL is by far the market leader, there is considerable rivalry in this market, particularly from Microsoft, through Microsoft Net (MSN) and Prodigy. Bill Gates once threatened to buy or bury AOL and, though he has not been able to do it, Microsoft is a formidable foe. As stated by one author, "Microsoft's past is littered with the corpses of old enemies."[138] AOL is strengthened by its acquisition of Netscape and its alliance with Sun Microsystems, another former nemesis of Microsoft.

In response, Microsoft has devised a three-pronged attack on AOL. First, it has developed and brought to market an instant messaging system to compete directly with AOL's. Second, Microsoft is preparing the way for low-cost or free Internet access. This move could be particularly damaging to AOL, as the firm receives 77 percent of its revenues from Internet subscriptions. Third, Microsoft is trying to emphasize broadband communication to revolutionize the Internet as a platform for "infotainment" and commerce. If Gate's half-billion-dollar agreement with Rogers Communications is any indication, Microsoft will certainly be a significant contender in this market.[139] Although AOL is in a good position in the markets it serves, it must be careful because Microsoft has the capability to win competitive battles.[140] AOL's merger with Time Warner has increased its strength and reduced the likelihood that Microsoft will be able to "bury it." In nonfragmented industries, the speed with which new products are developed and introduced to the marketplace becomes an important competitive weapon. Consumers tend to be more sophisticated and expect not only quality products but also product designs that meet their needs. Moving new products that better meet consumers' needs to the market more quickly than competitors results in a competitive advantage.

In mature industries, there are usually fewer surviving competitors. Those that do survive tend to be larger and hold dominant market share positions. Thus, firms in the mature stage emphasize market-power actions, which focus the firm's attention on offering product lines that are profitable and producing those products in an efficient manner. Product innovations and entrepreneurial actions continue but are greatly de-emphasized. Process innovations are emphasized more, because they maintain dominance through cost efficiencies and the quality of products manufactured and provided to customers.[144] Finally, firms in industries in the mature stage frequently seek to expand into international markets or increase their emphasis on international operations and sales to extend a product's life. Thus, growth-oriented actions also continue, even though the primary emphasis is on market-power actions.

In sum, once mature firms have a dominant market share, they seek to exploit their market power and extensive resources and capabilities to maintain dominance. The PC/server operating system market exemplifies a mature industry. Microsoft rather quickly became the dominant force in this industry and has held a virtual monopoly for the last decade. Because of its position, Microsoft provides incremental system's innovation (e.g., Windows 2000). Linux is trying to break the Windows' monopoly through its operating system, which is distributed free by Red Hat and a few other entrepreneurial firms. These firms obtain their revenue by providing support operations for those who adopt Linux. Microsoft is concerned enough to develop an "attack team" designed to monitor and analyze Linux and its distributors. The purpose of this team, as depicted by Microsoft's director of marketing for Windows 2000, is "Getting inside the head of our competitor."[141] This could be a daunting task since Linux was developed by thousands of independent programmers—quite a number of heads for the attack team to get into. Linux has targeted the server market, of which it has captured about 17 percent; Windows holds about 36 percent. The Linux advantage, besides the fact that it is free, is that it is about 50 percent faster than Windows.[142] It will be interesting to observe the competitive battle between the rivals as it plays out.

This chapter is summarized in Figure 6.10, which concludes our emphasis on business-level strategy—although some business-level issues are discussed in subsequent chapters (e.g., Chapters 9, 10, and 12). The next chapter begins our discussion of corporate-level strategy.

■ ■ **FIGURE 6.10**

*Summary Model of Interfirm Rivalry*

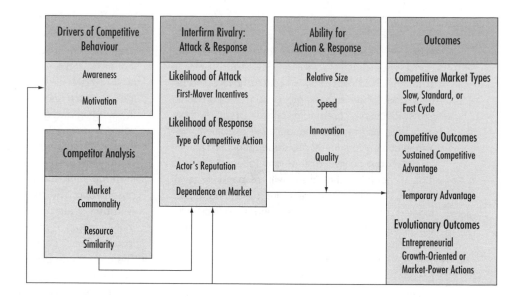

Source: Adapted from M. J. Chen, 1996, Competitor analysis and interfirm rivalry, *Academy of Management Review*, 21: 100–34.

## SUMMARY

- Competitive rivalry entails actions and responses to competitive actions taken by other firms. Competitive attack and response are more likely when awareness, motivation, and abilities to attack or respond are present.

- Market commonality, as determined by multimarket contact in such industries as airlines, is likely to lead to the dampening of a potential attack. However, if an offensive action is taken, a response is more likely in the presence of market commonality.

- Awareness of competitors' ability to attack or respond is facilitated by resource similarity among competitors. Those with similar resources are more likely to attack and respond than are those with less overlap in resources.

- First movers can gain a competitive advantage and customer loyalty in the market. First movers also take more risks; however, they often are higher performers. Second movers—particularly those that are larger and faster—can also gain a competitive advantage and earn at least average returns because they imitate first movers but do not take

some of the risk that first movers take. In fact, some second movers may gain significant market share and outperform the first movers. They do this when they carefully observe the market's reaction and are able to improve the product introduced by the first mover and correct or avoid its mistakes. However, the longer the time required for the second mover to respond, the higher the probability that the first mover will enjoy strong performance gains. Late movers (those that respond a long time after the original action was taken) tend to be lower performers and much less competitive.

- The probability of a response by a competitor to a competitive action is based partially on the extent to which the competitor is dependent on the particular market in which the action was taken. In addition, the probability of response is based on the type of action, the reputation of the firm taking the strategic action (which affects the expectation of the firm's success), and the resources available to the competitor contemplating the response.

- The two types of competitive actions are strategic and tactical. Strategic actions are more long term in nature, require many specific resources, and are difficult to reverse. By contrast, tactical actions tend to be more short term in orientation, require fewer and more general resources, and can be reversed more easily. It is easier to respond to a tactical action, partly since doing so requires fewer resources. In addition, a tactical action is likely to have a shorter-term effect than a strategic action. Responses to strategic actions are more difficult, require more resources, and require a longer-term investment.

- When competitors are highly dependent on a market in which competitive actions are taken, there is a high probability that they will respond to such actions. Yet firms that are more diversified across markets are less likely to respond to a particular action that affects only one of the markets in which they compete.

- The highest probability of a response comes when an action is taken by a market leader. Furthermore, when a market leader takes an action, a competitor is more likely to imitate it. Alternatively, if the firm has a reputation for taking more complex and risky actions, there is a lower probability of response. A price predator is also less likely to elicit a response from competitors.

- Those with a larger resource base are more likely to respond to strategic actions than those with fewer resources. Furthermore, the probability of response is determined not only by the amount of resources but also by the ability to use those resources in taking competitive actions.

- Characteristics important to engaging in competitive actions and responses include the relative size of the acting and responding firms, the function of speed in the market or industry, the importance of innovation in competitive moves, and the quality of the competing firms' products.

- Large firms often have strong market power. However, as firms grow larger, they frequently institute bureaucratic rules, procedures, and structures that have the effect of reducing the probability that a firm will take actions and respond to others' actions. In addition, these rules reduce the speed with which a firm may be able to implement an action or respond to competitors' actions.

- Speed is becoming increasingly important in many industries in order to gain and hold a competitive advantage. In fact, many large firms must act like small firms (i.e., be flexible and agile) to be competitive. This may require that they decentralize many responsibilities and decisions and that they create cross-functional teams in order to speed a number of processes (e.g., the innovation process).

- Both product and process innovation are becoming increasingly important in the competitive posture of many industries. Some research has shown that firms that invest more in R&D and create more innovation tend to have higher performance in multiple industries. Product innovation tends to be more important in emerging and growth industries, and process innovation is more relevant in mature industries.

- Product quality has become critical to maintaining competitive parity in most industries. Total quality management must be infused throughout the organization by top management and integrated with firm strategies. Benchmarking is used to help make comparative judgments about quality relative to other firms' best practices.

- There are three basic market outcomes of competitive rivalry among firms. Slow-cycle markets allow a firm to establish competitive advantage in a near-monopoly situation. Until recently, many utility firms were in this position. Standard-cycle markets allow market situations in which sustainability is possible. Firms that have multimarket contact may dampen competition somewhat. Fast-cycle markets create a situation in which only temporary competitive advantage is possible, such as that in the electronics and pharmaceutical industries.

- In fast-cycle markets, competitive disruption, a new paradigm of competitive action, may be necessary. This usually involves cannibalization of a previous product by reducing prices, while establishing a new product at the high end of the market, with increased performance at a premium price.

- Industry evolution is important in determining the type of competition and competitive actions that are emphasized by a firm. For example, firms in an emerging industry try to establish a reputation and develop a market niche in technology or the quality of products they provide. Their main task is to establish an entrepreneurial action, usually in an uncertain environment. In growth industries, the firm may place special emphasis on innovation to increase economies of scale. The speed of competitive actions taken is also important. The key task is to pursue growth-oriented actions by exploiting factors of production to increase the firm's dominance. In mature industries, with fewer competitors, special emphasis is placed on market-power actions designed to defend the most profitable product lines and processes in order to produce and distribute those products with the greatest efficiency (lowest cost). Entrepreneurial, growth-oriented, and market-power actions are taken at all stages, but the emphasis is different at each stage.

## REVIEW QUESTIONS

1. What two factors contribute to awareness, motivation, and ability in competitor analysis?
2. What are the advantages and disadvantages of being a first mover? A second mover? A late mover?
3. On what four factors is the likelihood of a response to a competitive action based?
4. What is the likelihood of response to a tactical action? A strategic action? Actions taken by market leaders? Explain why in each of these cases.
5. How does size affect strategic actions and responses?
6. Why is speed important in many industries? What can firms do to increase their speed in making and implementing strategic decisions?
7. In what types of industries is innovation important in gaining competitive advantage? Explain the importance of product and process innovations for success in different industries.
8. What are the three types of markets and the nature of rivalry in each?
9. How does industry evolution affect interfirm rivalry? Identify three stages of industry evolution, and briefly explain the types of competitive actions emphasized in those stages.

## DISCUSSION QUESTIONS

1. Read the popular business press (e.g., *National Post Business*, *Fast Company*, *BusinessWeek*, or *Fortune*) and identify a strategic action and a tactical action taken by firms approximately two years ago. Next, use the Internet to search the popular business press to see if, and how, competitors responded to those actions. Explain the actions and the responses, linking your findings to the discussion in this chapter.
2. Why would a firm regularly choose to be a second mover? Likewise, why would a firm purposefully be a late mover?
3. Make a study of Canadian Tire, or choose any large firm, and examine the popular business press to identify how its size, speed of actions,

level of innovation, and quality of goods or services have affected its competitive position in its industry. Explain your findings.
4. Identify a firm in a fast-cycle market. What strategic actions account for its success or failure over the last several years? How has the Internet affected the firm?

## ETHICS QUESTIONS

1. Are there some industries in which ethical practices are more important than in other industries? If so, name the industries that are ethical, and explain how the competitive actions and competitive responses might differ for these industries compared with a typical industry.
2. When engaging in competitive rivalry, firms jockey for a market position that is advantageous, relative to competitors. In this jockeying, what types of competitor intelligence-gathering approaches are ethical? How has the Internet affected competitive intelligence activities?
3. A second mover is a firm that responds to first movers' competitive actions, often through imitation. Is there anything unethical about how a second mover engages in competition? Why or why not?
4. Standards for competitive rivalry differ in countries throughout the world. What should firms do to cope with these differences? How do the differences relate to ethical practices?
5. Could total quality management practices result in firms operating more ethically than before such practices were implemented? If so, what might account for an increase in the ethical behaviour of a firm using TQM principles?
6. What ethical issues are involved in fast-cycle markets?

## INTERNET EXERCISE

With an offer of around 270 billion deutsche marks—about Cdn$200 billion—Chris Gent, the head of Britain's telecommunications giant Vodafone, planned to acquire the traditional German firm, Mannesmann AG, by February 2000. In a last-minute effort in January 2000 to stave off the hostile takeover, Mannesmann attempted to acquire NetCologne to strengthen its position against Vodafone. Look up Vodafone (www.vodafone.co.uk)

and Mannesmann (www.mannesmann.de) on the Web to see how the merger progressed and how each company's stocks reacted to the news.

**http://www.vodafone.co.uk**

**http://www.mannesmann.de**

## STRATEGIC SURFING

The competitive moves of each major Canadian Brewer are carefully watched by the other. However, if you go to the Molson site at

**http://www.molson.com**

or the Labatt site at

**http://www.labatt.com**

you are likely to find little on the topic of competitive moves in the industry. You will however, find a great many activities that would include a day or evening with your favourite beer. Find out what is really brewing in the industry and try

**http://www.realbeer.com**

or look at the corporate news at Labatt's parent

**http://www.interbrew.com**

## NOTES

1  J. Kurtzman, 1998, An interview with C. K. Prahalad, in J. Kurtzman (ed.), *Thought Leaders* (San Francisco: Jossey-Bass), 40–51; C. M. Grimm & K. G. Smith, 1997, *Strategy as Action: Industry Rivalry and Coordination* (Cincinnati: South-Western College Publishing); A. Y. Illinitch & R. A. D'Aveni, 1996, New organizational forms and strategies for managing in hypercompetitive environments, *Organization Science,* 7: 211–20.

2  G. Colvin, 1997, The most valuable quality in a manager, *Fortune,* December 29, 279–80.

3  Target: Wal-Mart, 1999, *Wall Street Journal Interactive Edition,* October 21, www.interactive.wsj.com/articles.

4  N. Byrnes & L. Armstrong, 1999, When Wal-Mart flexes its cybermuscles, *BusinessWeek,* July 26, 82–83.

5  C. K. Prahalad, 1999, Changes in the competitive battlefield, Mastering Strategy (Part Two), *Financial Times,* October 4, 2–4.

6  J. Fox, R. Gann, A. Shur, L. Von Glahn, & B. Zaas, 1999, Process uncertainty: A new dimension for new product development, *Engineering Management Journal,* 10 (3): 19–27.

7  G. McWilliams, 1999, Compaq's losses of big clients may foster plummeting profits, *Wall Street Journal Interactive Edition,* July 22, www.interactive.wsj.com /articles.

8  D. L. Deeds, D. DeCarolis, & J. Coobes, 2000, Dynamic capabilities and new product development in high technology adventures: An empirical analysis of new biotechnology firms, *Journal of Business Venturing,* 15: 211–29; C. V. Callhan & B. A. Pasterneck, 1999, Corporate strategy in the digital age, *Strategy and Business,* 15: 10–14; B. H. Clark, 1998, Managing competitive interactions, *Marketing Management,* 7(4): 8–20.

9  N. Munk, 1999, Title fight, *Fortune,* June 21, 84–94.

10  P. M. Reilly, 1999, Barnesandnoble.com's redesign yields new online music store, *Wall Street Journal Interactive Edition,* July 7, www.interactive.wsj.com/ articles.

11  G. Anders, 1999, Amazon.com buys 35% stake of Seattle online grocery firm, *Wall Street Journal,* May 18, B8.

12  Chapters Online, 2000, *Chapters Online home page,* http:// www.chapters.ca (Retrieved June 24).

13  O. Gadiesh & J. L. Gilbert, 1998, Profit pools: A fresh look at strategy, *Harvard Business Review,* 76 (3): 139–42.

14  V. Himmelsbach, 1999, An online battle of the books, *Computer Dealer News;* September 10, 18–19.

15  L. B. Ward, 2000, Mexican firm buys CompUSA, *Dallas Morning News,* January 25, D1, D11; A. Goldstein, 1999, Rewiring plan: CompUSA to expand offerings amid rising competition, *Dallas Morning News,* March 11, D1, D11; R. Quick, 1999, Online-retailing revenue is seen totaling 2 1/2 times 1998's figures, *Wall Street Journal Interactive Edition,* July 19, www.interactive.wsj.com/articles.

16  E. K. Clemons, 1997, Technology-driven environmental shifts and the sustainable competitive disadvantage of previously dominant companies, in G. S. Day & D. J. Reibstein (eds.), *Wharton on Dynamic Competitive Strategy* (New York: John Wiley & Sons), 99–126.

17  B. S. Silverman, J. A. Nickerson, & J. Freeman, 1997, Profitability, transactional alignment, and organizational mortality in the U.S. trucking industry, *Strategic Management Journal,* 18 (Special Summer Issue): 31–52.

18  R. Gulati, 1999, Network location and learning: The influence of network resources and firm capabilities, *Strategic Management Journal,* 20: 397–420; A. C. Inkpen & P. W. Beamish, 1997, Knowledge, bargaining power, and the instability of international joint ventures, *Academy of Management Review,* 22: 177–202; J. Stiles, 1995, Collaboration for competitive advantage: The changing world of alliances and partnerships, *Long Range Planning,* 28: 109–12.

19  D. B. Holm, K. Eriksson, & J. Johanson, 1999, Creating value through mutual commitment to business network relationships, *Strategic Management Journal*, 20: 467–86; M. Sakakibara, 1997, Heterogeneity of firm capabilities and cooperative research and development: An empirical examination of motives, *Strategic Management Journal*, 18, (Special Summer Issue): 143–64.

20  G. S. Day & D. J. Reibstein, 1997, The dynamic challenges for theory and practice, in G. S. Day & D. J. Reibstein (eds.), *Wharton on Competitive Strategy* (New York: John Wiley and Sons), 2.

21  S. J. Marsh, 1998, Creating barriers for foreign competitors: A study of the impact of anti-dumping actions on the performance of U.S. firms, *Strategic Management Journal*, 19: 25–37; K. G. Smith, C. M. Grimm, & S. Wally, 1997, Strategic groups and rivalrous firm behavior: Towards a reconciliation, *Strategic Management Journal*, 18: 149–57.

22  R. A. Klavans, C. A. Di Benedetto, & J. J. Prudom, 1997, Understanding competitive interactions: The U.S. commercial aircraft market, *Journal of Managerial Issues*, IX (1) 13–36.

23  Day & Reibstein, *Wharton on Competitive Strategy*; M. E. Porter, 1980, *Competitive Strategy* (New York: The Free Press), 17.

24  H. Simonian, 1998, Renault expands horizons, *Financial Times*, January 2, 10.

25  Autos: The Global Six, 1999, *BusinessWeek Online*, January 25, www.businessweek.com/bwarchive.

26  K. Cool, L. H. Roller, & B. Leleux, 1999, The relative impact of actual and potential rivalry on firm profitability in the pharmaceutical industry, *Strategic Management Journal*, 20: 1–14.

27  W. P. Putsis, Jr., 1999, Empirical Analysis of Competitive Interaction in Food Product Categories, *Agribusiness*, 15 (3): 295–311.

28  S. A. Forest, 1999, A penney saved?, *BusinessWeek*, March 20, 64–66.

29  Porter, *Competitive Strategy*.

30  A. Klein, 1999, Shutter snaps on Fisher's leadership at Kodak, *Wall Street Journal*, June 10, B1, B4.

31  J. A. C. Baum & H. J. Korn, 1999, Dynamics of dyadic competitive interaction, *Strategic Management Journal*, 20: 251–78; C. R. Henderson & W. Mitchell, 1997, The interactions of organizational and competitive influences on strategy and performance, *Strategic Management Journal*, 18 (Special Summer Issue): 5–14.

32  W. Ocasio, 1997, Towards an attention-based view of the firm, *Strategic Management Journal*, 18 (Special Summer Issue): 187–206.

33  Grimm & Smith, Strategy as Action, 75–102; K. Krabuanrat & R. Phelps, 1998, Heuristics and rationality in strategic decision making: An exploratory study, *Journal of Business Research*, 41: 83–93.

34  G. P. Hodgkinson & G. Johnson, 1994, Exploring the mental models of competitive strategists: The case for a processual approach, *Journal of Management Studies*, 31: 525–51; J. F. Porac & H. Thomas, 1994, Cognitive categorization and subjective rivalry among retailers in a small city, *Journal of Applied Psychology*, 79: 54–66.

35  N. J. Vilcassim, V. Kadiyali, & P. K. Chintagunta, 1999, Investigating dynamic multifirm market interactions in price and advertising, *Management Science*, 45 (4): 499–518.

36  N. Houthoofd & A. Heene, 1997, Strategic groups as subsets of strategic scope groups in the Belgian brewing industry, *Strategic Management Journal*, 18: 653–66; G. P. Carroll & A. Swaminathan, 1992, The organizational ecology of strategic groups in the American brewing industry from 1975–1988, *Industrial and Corporate Change*, 1: 65–97.

37  L. C. Thurow, 1999, *Building Wealth: The New Rules for Individuals, Companies and Nationals in a Knowledge-Based Economy* (New York: Harper Collins); K. Ohmae, 1985, *Triad Power* (New York: The Free Press).

38  J. Gimeno & C. Y. Woo, 1999, Multimarket contact, economies of scope, and firm performance, *Academy of Management Journal*, 42 (3): 239–59.

39  H. J. Korn & J. A. C. Baum, 1999, Chance, imitative, and strategic antecedents to multimarket contact, *Academy of Management Journal*, 42: 171–93.

40  S. Javachandran, J. Gimeno, & P. R. Varadarajan, 1999, Theory of multimarket competition: A synthesis and implications for marketing strategy, *Journal of Marketing*, 63: 49–66.

41  Z. Olijnyk, 2000, LaSenza lingerie heads east, *National Post*, April 25, C1, C8.

42  R. Gibbens, 2000, Tellus takes aim at Bell with QuebecTel deal, *National Post*, April 1, D1, D8.

43  R. G. McGrath, M. J. Chen, & I. C. MacMillan, 1998, Multimarket maneuvering in uncertain spheres of influence: Resource diversion strategies, *Academy of Management Review*, 23: 724–40.

44  A. Zipser, 1997, In search of greener pastures, Gateway moves on Dell's turf, *Barron's Online*, http://www.interactive.wsj.com, September 15.

45  J. A. Chevalier, 1999, When it can be good to burn your boats, Mastering Strategy (Part Four), *Financial Times*, October 25, 2–3; M. A. Peteraf, 1993, Intraindustry structure and response toward rivals, *Journal of Managerial Decision Economics*, 14: 519–28.

46  Grimm & Smith, *Strategy as Action*, 84; Chen, Competitor analysis.

47  Grimm & Smith, *Strategy as Action*, 125.

48  B. Horovitz, 1997, Coca-Cola, Pepsi tap bottled water market, *USA Today*, August 27, B10.

49  P. Abrahams & L. Kehoe, 1999, NEC and Bull pull out of US market, *www.ft.com,* www.ft.com/hippocampus (Retrieved November 4).

50  O. Edur, 1999, Firm seeks partner with similar interests: sharing resources, *National Post,* Nov. 30, F4.

51  W. Mitchell, 1999, Alliances: Achieving long-term value and short-term goals, Mastering Strategy (Part Four), *Financial Times,* October 18, 6–11.

52  Global crossing and Hutchison form telecom, web joint venture, 1999, *Wall Street Journal Interactive Edition,* November 15, www.interactive.wsj.com/articles.

53  K. P. Coyne & R. Dye, 1998, The competitive dynamics of network-based businesses, *Harvard Business Review,* 76 (1): 99–109.

54  Smith & Grimm, *Strategy as Action,* 53–74.

55  A. A. Lado, N. G. Boyd, & S. C. Hanlon, 1997, Competition, cooperation, and the search for economic rents: A syncretic model, *Academy of Management Review,* 22: 110–41.

56  J. L. C. Cheng & I. F. Kesner, 1997, Organizational slack and response to environmental shifts: The impact of resource allocation patterns, *Journal of Management,* 23: 1–18.

57  M. Wallin, 1999, Supermarket chain to bring online shopping to Argentina, *Wall Street Journal Interactive Edition,* July 30, www.interactive.wsj.com/articles.

58  L. Mills, 1999, As the beer world turns, *Marketing Magazine,* December 20/27: 16; B. Shecter, 1997, Molson and Labatt settle ice beer battle, *Financial Post,* December 16, 4.

59  M. B. Lieberman & D. B. Montgomery, 1988, First-mover advantages, *Strategic Management Journal,* 9: 41–58.

60  K. G. Smith, C. M. Grimm, & M. J. Gannon, 1992, *Dynamics of Competitive Strategy* (Newberry Park, CA: Sage).

61  A. Ginsberg & N. Venkatraman, 1992, Investing in new information technology: The role of competitive posture and issue diagnosis, *Strategic Management Journal,* 13 (Special Summer Issue): 37–53.

62  H. R. Greve, 1998, Managerial cognition and the mimetic adoption of market positions: What you see is what you do, *Strategic Management Journal,* 19: 967–88.

63  M. Zetlin, 1999, When it's smarter to be second to market, *Management Review,* March, 30–34.

64  G. J. Tellis & P. N. Golder, 1996, First to market, first to fail? Real causes of enduring market leadership, *Sloan Management Review,* Winter, 57–66.

65  Smith, Grimm, & Gannon, *Dynamics of Competitive Strategy.*

66  *New Balance home page,* 2000, www.newbalance.com (Retrieved February 1); I. Pereira, 1998, Sneaker company tags out-of-breath baby boomers, *Wall Street Journal,* January 16, B1, B2.

67  E. White, 1999, Avon tries to exploit internet without alienating its 'ladies,' *Wall Street Journal Interactive Edition,* December 28, www.interactive.wsj.com/articles.

68  D. Morse, 2000, Breakthrough product visits funeral homes: Partial casket display, *Wall Street Journal,* January 7, A1, A10; D. Fisher, 1999, Grave dancer, *Forbes,* June 14, 77–78.

69  G. S. Day, 1997, Assessing competitive arenas: Who are your competitors? In G. S. Day & D. J. Reibstein (eds.), *Wharton on Competitive Strategy* (New York: John Wiley & Sons), 25–26.

70  Grimm & Smith, *Strategy as Action,* 134.

71  K. Labich, 1994, Air wars over Asia, *Fortune,* April 4, 93–98.

72  W. J. Ferrier, K. G. Smith, & C. M. Grimm, 1999, The role of competitive actions in market share erosion and industry dethronement: A study of industry leaders and challengers, *Academy of Management Journal,* 42: 372–88.

73  Smith, Grimm, & Gannon, *Dynamics of Competitive Strategy.*

74  Z. Olijnyk, 1998, Sleeman Breweries gets toehold in Quebec, *Financial Post,* June 30, 3; E. Lazarus, 1999, New recipes: tough times are transforming BC's microbreweries, *Marketing Magazine,* March 1, 17–18.

75  Ibid.

76  N. Cope, 1999, Tesco and Sainsbury battle for home-shopping market, *Independent News,* www.independentàinessother/tescoonline (Retrieved December 1).

77  W. Conard, 1999, Toys 'R' Us plans online challenge, *Dallas Morning News,* June 9, D11.

78  Boeing could make bigger 747 models, 1999, *Houston Chronicle,* September 21, 4C.

79  B. Pinsker, 1997, Rental block, *Dallas Morning News,* June 14, C5, C8.

80  S. N. Mehta, 1999, SBC Communications to launch service 'bundles' in two markets, *Wall Street Journal Interactive Edition,* August 24, www.interactive.wsj.com/articles.

81  J. Cole, 1999, Airbus prepares to 'bet the company' as it builds a huge new jet, *Wall Street Journal,* November 3, A1, A10; M. Skapinker, 1998, Airbus boasts year of record orders, *Financial Times,* January 8, 6.

82  L. Krishnamurthi & V. Shankar, 1998, What are the options for later entrants? Mastering Marketing (Part Six), *Financial Times,* October 19, 4.

83  Baum & Korn, Dynamics of dyadic competitive interaction.

84   Intel reduces prices on Pentium III chips, 1999, *New York Times Online,* August 24, www.nytimes.com/library.

85   J. A. Schumpeter, 1961, *Theory of Economic Development* (New York: Oxford University Press).

86   M. A. Hitt, 2000, The new frontier: Transformation of management for the twenty-first century, *Organizational Dynamics,* 28 (Winter): 7–17.

87   J. Kurtzman, 1998, An interview with Charles Handy, in J. Kurtman (ed.), *Thought Leaders* (San Francisco: Jossey-Bass), 134–149; J. Birkinshaw, 1997, Entrepreneurship in multinational corporations: The characteristics of subsidiary initiatives, *Strategic Management Journal,* 18: 207–29.

88   Harvard Business Review Perspectives, 1995, How can big companies keep the entrepreneurial spirit alive? *Harvard Business Review,* 73 (6): 183–92.

89   R. E. Krider & C. B. Weinberg, 1998, Competitive dynamics and the introduction of new products: The motion picture timing game, *Journal of Marketing Research,* 35: 1–15.

90   C. E. Lucier & J. D. Torbilier, 1999, Beyond stupid, slow and expensive: Reintegrating work to improve productivity, *Strategy & Business,* 17, 9–13; R. R. Nayyar & K. A. Bantel, 1994, Competitive agility: A source of competitive advantage based on speed and variety, *Advances in Strategic Management,* 10A, 193–222.

91   S. Wally & J. R. Baum, 1994, Personal and structural determinants of the pace of strategic decision-making, *Academy of Management Journal,* 37: 932–56.

92   Ibid.

93   G. Colvin, 1999, The ultimate manager, *Fortune,* November 22, 185–87; T. Smart & J. H. Dobrzynski, 1993, Jack Welch on the art of thinking small, *BusinessWeek,* Special Enterprise Issue, 212–16.

94   Kurtzman, An interview with Gary Hamel; J. Wind, 1997, Preemptive strategies, in G. S. Day & D. J. Reibstein (eds.), *Wharton on Dynamic Competitive Strategy* (New York: John Wiley & Sons), 256–76; S. C. Wheelwright & K. B. Clark, 1995, *Leading Product Development* (New York: The Free Press).

95   S. A. Zahra, A. P. Nielsen, & W. C. Bogner, 1999, Corporate entrepreneurship, knowledge, and competence development, *Entrepreneurship: Theory and Practice,* 23 (3): 169–89; B. N. Dickie, 1998, Foreword, in J. Kurtzman (ed.), *Thought Leaders* (New York: Jossey-Bass), x–xvii; J. Kurtzman, 1998, An interview with Paul M. Romer, in J. Kurtzman (ed.), *Thought Leaders* (New York: Jossey-Bass), 66–83.

96   L. G. Franko, 1989, Global corporate competition: Who's winning, who's losing, and the R&D factor as one reason why, *Strategic Management Journal,* 10: 449–74.

97   R. E. Hoskisson & M. A. Hitt, 1994, *Downscoping: How to Tame the Diversified Firm* (New York: Oxford University Press).

98   D. L. Deeds, D. DeCarolis, & J. Coombes, 1999, Dynamic capabilities and new product development in high technology ventures: An empirical analysis of new biotechnology firms, *Journal of Business Venturing,* 18: 211–29; K. J. Klein & J. S. Sorra, 1996, The challenge of innovation implementation, *Academy of Management Review,* 21: 1055–80.

99   N. Kim, E. Bridges, & R. K. Srivastava, 1999, A simultaneous model for innovative product category sales diffusion and competitive dynamics, *International Journal of Research in Marketing,* 16: 95–111.

100  D. P. Hamilton, 1999, Sun to challenge Microsoft's Office with purchase of software maker, *Wall Street Journal Interactive Edition,* August 31, www.interactive.wsj.com/articles.

101  N. George, 1999, Ericsson drifts in Nokia's wake, *Financial Times,* July 22, 13.

102  Klein & Sorra, The challenge of innovation implementation.

103  N. Dunne, 1998, American goldmine for high-tech workers, *Financial Times,* January 15, 4; V. Griffith, 1998, Learning to wear two hats, *Financial Times,* January 5, 20; N. Timmins, 1998, Manufacturers face skills shortfall, *Financial Times,* January 9, 4.

104  J. W. Dean, Jr., & D. E. Bowen, 1994, Management theory and total quality: Improving research and practice through theory development, *Academy of Management Review,* 19: 392–419.

105  J. Aley, 1994, Manufacturers grade themselves, *Fortune,* March 21, 26.

106  M. Halkias, 1997, Rising competition, *Dallas Morning News,* November 13, D1, D12.

107  J. Heizer & B. Render, 1996, *Production and Operations Management,* 4th ed. (Upper Saddle River, NJ: Prentice Hall), 75–106.

108  M. van Biema & B. Greenwald, 1997, Managing our way to higher service-sector productivity, *Harvard Business Review,* 75 (4): 87–95.

109  S. Chatterjee & M. Yilmaz, 1993, Quality confusion: Too many gurus, not enough disciples, *Business Horizons,* 36 (3): 15–18.

110  J. Heizer & B. Render, 1999, *Operations Management,* 5th ed. (Upper Saddle River, NJ: Prentice Hall).

111  W. S. Sherman & M. A. Hitt, 1996, Creating corporate value: Integrating quality and innovation programs, in D. Fedor & S. Ghoshal (eds.), *Advances in the Management of Organizational Quality* (Greenwich, CT: JAI Press), 221–44.

112  J. D. Westphal, R. Gulati, & S. M. Shortell, 1997, Customization or conformity: An institutional and net-

work perspective on the content and consequences of TQM adoption, *Administrative Science Quarterly,* 42: 366–94.

113 E. E. Lawler, III, 1994, Total quality management and employee involvement: Are they compatible? *Academy of Management Executive,* VIII (1): 68.

114 R. S. Russell & B. W. Taylor, III, 2000, *Operations Management,* 3rd ed. (Upper Saddle River, NJ: Prentice Hall), 130–65.

115 A. M. Schneiderman, 1998, Are there limits to total quality management? *Strategy & Business,* 11: 35–45; R. Krishnan, A. B. Shani, & G. R. Baer, 1993, In search of quality improvement: Problems of design and implementation, *Academy of Management Executive,* VII (3): 7–20.

116 S. Sanghera, 1999, Making continuous improvement better, *Financial Times,* April 21, 28.

117 Ibid.

118 H. V. Roberts & B. F. Sergesketter, 1993, *Quality Is Personal* (New York: The Free Press).

119 S. B. Sitkin, K. M. Sutcliffe, & R. G. Schroeder, 1994, Distinguishing control from learning in total quality management: A contingency perspective, *Academy of Management Review,* 19: 537–64.

120 J. R. Hackman & R. Wageman, 1995, Total quality management: Empirical, conceptualization and practical issues, *Administrative Science Quarterly,* 40: 309–42.

121 J. R. Williams, 1999, *Renewable Advantage: Crafting Strategy through Economic Time* (New York: The Free Press); J. R. Williams, 1992, How sustainable is your competitive advantage? *California Management Review,* 34, Spring: 29–51.

122 G. S. Day, 1997, Maintaining the competitive edge: Creating and sustaining advantages in dynamic competitive environments, in G. S. Day & D. J. Reibstein (eds.), *Wharton on Dynamic Competitive Strategy* (New York: John Wiley & Sons), 48–75.

123 E. Gedadajlovic, 2000, in conversation with J. Sheppard, July 9, Montreal. Though paraphrased here, the sentiment was succinctly expressed as something along the lines of "If Bill Gates were Dutch, people in Holland would say 'He may be a scoundrel, but he's *our* scoundrel!'"

124 J. R. Williams, 1999, Economic time, *Across the Board,* September, 11.

125 A. D. Chandler, 1990, The enduring logic of industrial success, *Harvard Business Review,* 68 (2): 130–40.

126 J. L. Bower & T. M. Hout, 1988, Fast-cycle capability for competitive power, *Harvard Business Review,* 66 (6): 110–18.

127 W. Loob, 1998, Unibrew moves west, *Celebrator Beer News Online,* www.celebrator.com/9804/LOOB.html (Retrieved August 20, 2000).

128 Williams, Economic time.

129 K. R. Conner, 1995, Obtaining strategic advantage from being imitated: When can encouraging "clones" pay? *Management Science,* 41: 209–25; R. A. D'Aveni, 1995, Coping with hypercompetition: Utilizing the new 7's framework, *Academy of Management Executive,* IX (3): 45–60; K. R. Conner, 1988, Strategies for product cannibalism, *Strategic Management Journal,* 9 (Special Summer Issue): 135–59.

130 S. N. Mehta, 1999, Phone companies expect wireless to usher in the telecom future, *Wall Street Journal Interactive Edition,* November 15, www.interactive.wsj.com/articles.

131 A. Cane, G. Bowley, & R. Taylor, 1999, Nortel counter attack launched against Cisco, *www.ft.com,* www.ft.com/hippocampus (Retrieved November 9).

132 R. Sanchez, 1995, Strategic flexibility in product competition, *Strategic Management* Journal, 16 (Special Summer Issue): 9–26.

133 M. A. Hitt, B. B. Tyler, C. Hardee, & D. Park, 1995, Understanding strategic intent in the global marketplace, *Academy of Management Executive,* IX (2): 12–19.

134 M. A. Hitt, M. T. Dacin, E. Levitas, J. L. Arregle, & A. Borza, 2000, Partner selection in emerging and developed market contexts: Resource-based and organizational learning perspectives, *Academy of Management Journal,* in press.

135 R. E. Miles, C. C. Snow, & M. Sharfman, 1993, Industry variety and performance, *Strategic Management Journal,* 14: 163–77.

136 K. Cool & I. Dierickx, 1993, Rivalry, strategic groups and firm profitability, *Strategic Management Journal,* 14: 47–59.

137 S. A. Shane, 1996, Hybrid organizational arrangements and their implications for firm growth and survival: A study of new franchisers, *Academy of Management Journal,* 39: 216–34.

138 Pricks and kicks, 1999, *The Economist Online,* August 16, www.economist.com/editorial.

139 D. Judge, C. Cormell, M. T. Bitti, and A. Lopez-Pacheco, 1999, Canada's corporate elite 1999: Our 10th annual review of business leadership, *National Post,* November: 73–114.

140 Ibid.

141 D. M. Schroeder, 1990, A dynamic perspective on the impact of process innovation upon competitive strategies, *Strategic Management Journal,* 11: 25–41.

142 Ibid.

# Chapter Seven

## Corporate-Level Strategy

### LEARNING OBJECTIVES

*After reading this chapter, you should be able to:*

1. Define corporate-level strategy and discuss its importance to the diversified firm.
2. Describe the advantages and disadvantages of single-business and dominant-business strategies.
3. Explain three primary reasons why firms move from single-business and dominant-business strategies to more diversified strategies.
4. Describe how related-diversified firms use sharing activities and the transfer of core competencies to create value.
5. Discuss the two ways an unrelated-diversification strategy can create value.
6. Discuss the incentives and resources that encourage diversification.
7. Describe motives that can encourage managers to further diversify a firm.

## CGMI: A Diversified Internet Conglomerate

CMGI was named one of the top five best stocks of the 1990s, with a 57 191 percent increase in the value of a share. Only Cisco Systems, AOL, Dell, and EMC shares superseded this increase in value. In fact, CMGI's performance was better than that of such well-known companies as Charles Schwab, Microsoft, Sun Microsystems, Qualcomm, and Yahoo! The interesting aspect of CMGI's strategy, relative to most firms among the best performers, is that CMGI has used a classic diversification strategy to realize its increase in value. A NASDAQ 100 company, CMGI is in the business of creating and managing a diverse network of Internet companies focused in four areas: Internet advertising and marketing, content and Internet communities, e-commerce, and e-commerce enabling technologies.

CMGI's marketing and advertising companies offer state-of-the-art technologies to help firms establish interactive advertising and marketing. Engage Technologies, which is 80 percent owned by CMGI, is buying Flycast Communications, Inc., and AdSmart (already owned by the CMGI parent). These purchases will allow for more centralization of CMGI's advertising units and make the firm a strong competitor for DoubleClick, the leader in Internet advertising. AdSmart places Internet advertisements for media buyers across a network of 300 Internet sites, 90 percent of which come from CMGI properties. Adforce, another firm partly owned by CMGI, creates on-line ads for clients and measures their effectiveness. Flycast runs direct marketing campaigns on the Internet; it can run a test campaign and adjust it day by day to find what types of buyers should be targeted for specific products, such as golf clubs or winter vacations. Flycast gathers information from 1700 sites, which will be combined with information from the 2000 sites that Engage Technologies has signed up for collecting profile information.

CMGI's e-commerce companies sell directly to consumers or to businesses over the Web. Shopping.com sells everything from digital cameras to in-line skates. Mothernature.com is a purveyor of vitamins and health care supplements.

http://www.aol.com

http://www.carparts.com

http://www.cisco.com

http://www.cmgi.com

http://www.dell.com

Furniture.com, obviously, sells sofas, beds, and other furniture and furnishings. Carparts.com is a site used to find almost any car part imaginable. CMGI often owns a minority, but fairly large, percentage of these e-commerce companies.

Enabling technologies allow a firm to track Web traffic and create anonymous user profiles of those who surf the Web. With the information gathered by these technologies, firms can target their marketing to on-line users by tracking their proclivities for specific Internet sites. The new technologies and services help other e-commerce companies, as well as traditional corporations, exploit the Internet's full potential. Engage Technologies, for instance, a CMGI property, has allowed Lycos (a major portal associated with CMGI) to track and build a record of user behaviour. Each time an Internet surfer arrives at a site, the site can automatically flash ads tailored to the surfer's interest. For example, a consumer who has repeatedly visited the National Park Service Web site automatically sees ads for tents and hiking boots when he or she visits an airline reservation site. Numberoneclickcharge is payment software that allows on-line stores to charge customers a small transaction fee per click for reviews, music, or articles on-line. To help round out its Internet solutions offerings, CMGI also acquired an 80 percent interest in Tallan, Inc., which provides Internet consulting and software services.

Content and Internet community companies, however, are probably the main core engines of CMGI. These companies facilitate increases in traffic, the mainstay of any Internet company's success. CMGI's main portals are Alta Vista and Lycos. The company wants to turn Alta Vista into a "megaportal" site that would be a showcase and jumping-off point for CMGI's other properties, including Raging Bull, which is one of the content companies that has increased traffic at CMGI. Compared to the e-commerce companies, CMGI owns larger percentages of the content and portal companies, with 83 percent and 50 percent respectively, of Alta Vista and Raging Bull.

Raging Bull is an example of what CMGI's CEO, David S. Wetherell, is trying to accomplish through his firm's diversification strategy. In August 1998, Wetherell was searching the Web and found a site called Raging Bull. Three college students who focused on investor chat rooms founded and ran the site from an apartment basement. Wetherell bought 50 percent ownership for $2 million. Raging Bull's core technology operations were taken over and managed by the Web site management company NaviSite, a CMGI Internet insight and infrastructure management company. NaviSite easily began generating ad revenues after receiving services from AdSmart, another CMGI company that provides on-line links for advertisers. All of these partnerships proved significant, as Raging Bull's audience exploded from 200 000 pages a day in January 1999 to over 5 million per day in September 1999. It now is the second–most popular on-line investor forum behind Yahoo! Inc. Raging Bull is an example of CMGI's plan to harness the collective resources of its Internet partners by having them share customers and technology and create strategic partnerships to form a diversified firm composed of Internet companies.

Internet Capital Group (ICG) is another firm that uses a diversification strategy, one that is similar to CMGI's. ICG is a holding company that focuses exclusively on business-to-business (B2B) Internet operations. This is a somewhat different focus from CMGI's. ICG currently owns a percentage of over 50 on-line marketplaces where businesses can trade everything from chemicals, paper, and plastics to cattle and office supplies with other businesses. By the beginning of 2000, ICG's market capitalization had reached $30 billion. In September 1999, the company's shares were trading at $40; by the beginning of 2000, they were at $112. ICG's market capitalization rivals that of Merrill Lynch, and its stock price represented 40 percent of the market capitalization of the entire business-to-business Internet segment. Although it had taken only three of its companies (Breakaway Solutions, Rest Interactive, and Vertical Net) through the IPO process, a number of additional IPOs were planned.

Firms such as CMGI and ICG are not risk-free ventures. These companies continue to show operating losses, and their market capitalization is based on highly valued stock prices that can disappear quite quickly, as was exemplified in the downturn of Internet stocks in early 1999. Only time will tell whether these business models will be successful in the long term.

---

Sources: W. M. Buckeley, 2000, GMGI's Engage will buy 2 other units of conglomerate for $2.5 billion in stock, *Wall Street Journal*, January 20, B10; M. Maremont, 2000, CMGI agrees to buy 80 percent of Tallan for about $715 million in cash, stock, *Wall Street Journal*, February 15, B6; E. Schonfeld, 2000, Investors still can't get enough of Internet capital group, *Fortune*, January 10, 212; C. Taylor, 2000, CMGI—the Internet catalyst, www.cmgi.com/about/main.html; J.G. Auerbach & G. McWilliams, 1999, How CMGI plans to make Alta Vista hot again, *Wall Street Journal*, June 30, B1, B4; T.C. Judge, 1999, Internet evangelists, *BusinessWeek*, October 25, 141–50; T.C. Judge, 1999, One happy family—but for how long? *BusinessWeek*, October 25, 148.

As indicated in the Opening Case, top-level managers at CMGI and Internet Capital Group decided that their firms should be more diversified than other Internet-related companies. CMGI is following a related-linked diversification strategy wherein the businesses function in a way that creates added value for each other. For example, the expertise of NaviSite greatly facilitated the success of Raging Bull's Web page views, and AdSmart facilitated links to Internet advertisers. Thus, the parent corporation, CMGI, and its affiliates significantly fostered the success of the newly added property, Raging Bull, which started as an investor's "chat room" site run by college students. Accordingly, by means of a corporate strategy, CMGI has been able to create increased market power and competitive advantage over other companies.

Canadian company George Weston has operated since 1882 in two business lines: food processing and food distribution (the latter operated by Loblaw's, Canada's largest food distributor). Food processing operations include seafood processing, bakeries, and a dairy. Distribution is through corporate, franchised, associate, and independent outlets including Loblaw's, The Real Canadian Superstore, Provigo, and Dominion Stores (in Newfoundland). In April 2000, George Weston announced that it had agreed to purchase the North American operations of Norse Dairy Systems, a U.S. manufacturer and supplier of ice cream and other ice cream novelties. George Weston is following a related-constrained diversification strategy.

http://www.weston.ca/en/ main01.html

Disney, a large diversified entertainment company, has also sought to leverage its resources and capabilities to forge a set of on-line businesses. Its main portal, go.com, was seeking to compete with Yahoo! Excite, and other major service portals. In 1999, Disney acquired the rest of Infoseek Corporation to incorporate the Infoseek search engine more fully with Disney's other on-line businesses. However, the firm was too late getting into the portal business to compete with Yahoo! and AOL. Disney has now shifted the focus of go.com to that of an entertainment and leisure site. ABC.com is the news and entertainment Web site associated with the Disney TV network, Disney.com is the main e-commerce site that sells Disney-associated products on-line, and ESPN.com is the sports information and entertainment site associated with the Disney-owned cable sports network. Disney also has a stake in e-companies that serve as an incubator for Internet start-ups similar to NaviSite, a CMGI affiliate. Therefore, Disney is using its Internet diversification to build on the strengths that it already has in entertainment and associated products (e.g., toys created from its movie characters).[1]

In Chapters 5 and 6, our discussions focused on the selection and use of business-level strategies. Our discussions of different business-level strategies (Chapter 5) and the competitive dynamics associated with their use (Chapter 6) were focused primarily on firms competing in a single industry or product market.[2] When a firm chooses to diversify its operations beyond a single industry and to operate businesses in several industries, it is pursuing a corporate-level strategy of diversification. As is the case with business-level strategies, a corporate-level strategy of diversification allows a firm to adapt to conditions in its external environment.[3] An influential strategic choice in firms, diversification strategies play a major role in the behaviour of large firms.[4] Strategic choices regarding diversification are, however, fraught with uncertainty.[5]

A diversified company has two levels of strategy: a business-level (or competitive) strategy and a corporate-level (or company-wide) strategy.[6] In diversified firms, each business unit chooses a business-level strategy (appropriate for its industry) to implement to achieve strategic competitiveness and earn above-average returns. But diversified firms must also choose a strategy that is concerned with the selection and management of its businesses. Defined formally, a **corporate-level strategy** is action taken to gain a competitive advantage through the selection and management of a mix of businesses competing in several industries or product markets. In essence, a corporate-level strategy is what makes "the corporate whole add up to more than the sum of its business unit parts."[7] Corporate-level strategy is concerned with two key questions: what businesses the firm should be in and how the corporate office should manage its group of businesses.[8] Roberto Goizueta, the former CEO of Coca-Cola, captured the essence of these two questions by suggesting that top-level executives were responsible for verifying that the firm could develop effective strategies across time and knew how to allocate capital effectively and efficiently.[9] In the current complex global environment, top-level managers should view their firm's businesses as a portfolio of core competencies when seeking answers to these critical questions.[10]

Relating back to Figure 1.1 in Chapter 1, our focus herein is on the formulation of corporate-level strategy. The corporate-level strategy should evolve from the firm's strategic intent and mission. Also, as with business-level strategies, corporate-level strategies are expected to help the firm earn above-average returns (create value).[11] Some have suggested that few corporate-level strategies actually create value.[12] In the final analysis, the value of a corporate-level strategy "must be that the businesses in the portfolio are worth more under the management of the company in question than they would be under any other ownership."[13] Thus, the corporate-level strategy should be expected to contribute a given amount to the returns of all business units that exceeds what those returns would be without the implementation of such a strategy.[14] When managed effectively, corporate-level strategies enhance a firm's strategic competitiveness and contribute to its ability to earn above-average returns.[15] In the 21st century, corpo-

A **corporate-level strategy** is action taken to gain a competitive advantage through the selection and management of a mix of businesses competing in several industries or product markets.

rate-level strategies will be managed in a global business environment characterized by high degrees of risk, complexity, uncertainty, and ambiguity.[16]

A primary approach to corporate-level strategy is diversification, which requires corporate-level executives to craft a multibusiness strategy. One reason for the use of a diversification strategy is that managers of diversified firms possess unique, general management skills that can be used to develop multibusiness strategies and enhance a firm's strategic competitiveness.[17] To derive the greatest benefit from their skills, managers must focus their energies on the tasks associated with managing a diversification strategy.[18] The prevailing theory of diversification suggests that firms should diversify when they have excess resources, capabilities, and core competencies that have multiple uses.[19] Multibusiness strategies often encompass many different industry environments, and, as discussed in Chapter 12, these strategies require unique organizational structures.

This chapter begins by addressing the history of diversification. Included in this discussion are descriptions of the advantages and disadvantages of single-business and dominant-business strategies. We next describe different levels of diversification (from low to high) and reasons firms pursue a corporate-level strategy of diversification. Two types of diversification strategies that denote moderate to very high levels of diversification—related and unrelated—are then examined.

Large diversified firms often compete against each other in several markets. This is called multipoint competition. For instance, Svenska Aeroplan Aktiebolaget (Saab) and DaimlerChrysler AG compete against one another in both automobiles and aircraft engines. Vertical integration strategies designed to exploit market share and gain power over competitors are also explored. Closing the chapter is a brief discussion of questions firms should consider when examining the possibility of becoming a diversified company. For the already-diversified firm, these questions can be used to determine if additional levels of diversification should be pursued.

Of course, there are alternatives to diversification. These options entail long-term contracts, such as strategic alliances and franchising, discussed in Chapter 10, and expanding into new geographic markets, such as international diversification, discussed in Chapter 9.

## HISTORY OF DIVERSIFICATION

In 1950, only 38.1 percent of the *Fortune* 500 U.S. industrial companies generated more than 25 percent of their revenues from diversified activities. By 1974, this figure had risen to 63 percent. In 1950, then, more than 60 percent of the largest *Fortune* 500 industrial companies were either single-business or dominant-business firms; by 1974, this had dropped to 37 percent.[20]

Beginning in the late 1970s, and especially through the middle part of the 1980s, a significant trend toward refocusing and divestiture of business units unrelated to core business activities took place in many firms. In fact, approximately 50 percent of the *Fortune* 500 companies refocused on their core businesses from 1981 to 1987.[21] As a result, by 1988, the percentage of single- or dominant-business firms on the *Fortune* 500 list of industrial companies had increased to 53 percent.[22] Although many diversified firms have become more focused, this is somewhat masked because extensive market and international diversification (compared to product diversification) has occurred that is not included in these statistics. As Chapter 9's discussion reveals, international strategy has been increasing in importance and has led to greater financial performance relative to product diversification.[23]

The trend toward product diversification of business organizations has been most significant among U.S. firms. Nonetheless, large business organizations in Europe, Asia, and other parts of the industrialized world have also implemented diversification strategies. In the United Kingdom, the number of single- or dominant-business firms fell from 60 percent in 1960 to 37 percent in 1980. A similar, yet less dramatic trend toward more diversification occurred in Japan. Among the largest Japanese firms, 60 percent were dominant- or single-business firms in 1958, although this percentage fell only to 53 percent in 1973.

In Canada, a recent study provides support for the notion that publicly traded firms are not as diversified as their counterparts in other countries. Two researchers are completing a study that suggests single business firms are the largest proportion of firms. These two researchers randomly selected 141 firms from the Stern Stewart Canada 300 list and assessed their type of diversification using the criteria from the next section, Levels of Diversification.[24] Figure 7.1 contains the results.

■ ■ **FIGURE 7.1**

*Type of Diversification in Canada among Large Publicly Traded Firms*

| Type of Diversification | Percentage |
|---|---|
| Single | 59% |
| Dominant | 13% |
| Related Constrained | 20% |
| Related Linked | 6% |
| Unrelated | 2% |

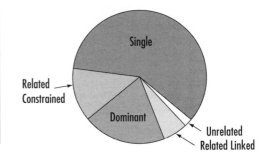

Source: P. Kavanagh & W. G. Rowe, 2000, The Mediating Effect of Risk on the Diversification-firm Value Relationship: A Canadian Perspective, Working Paper, Memorial University of Newfoundland.

The trends toward more diversification, which have been partially reversed due to restructuring (see Chapter 8), indicate that learning has taken place regarding corporate diversification strategies. The main lesson learned is that firms performing well in their dominant business may not want to diversify. Moreover, firms that diversify should do so cautiously, choosing to focus on a relatively few, rather than many, businesses.[25]

Deciding to become more diversified in terms of both product offerings and geographic locations appears to have contributed to Cott's recent difficulties. Originally, Cott produced and sold (at discount prices) an array of private-label beverages including soft drinks, New Age beverages, iced teas, juice drinks, sport drinks, and bottled water. Cott's customers were large retail chains such as Wal-Mart and Safeway. Through effective implementation of its strategy, this Toronto firm grew, in less than 10 years, from a small family business to a multinational corporation with annual sales of over $1 billion. This growth resulted in the firm's becoming the leading worldwide supplier of premium retailer branded beverages and the world's fourth-largest soft drink company. The company believes that product innovation, employee creativity, high-quality products, and world-class packaging are its core competencies.

As one analyst observed recently, the firm followed its initial success with expansions "into things it had no business expanding into, such as the Canadian beer market and faraway countries." In addition to these product and geographic forays, Cott also planned, but did not execute, a strategy that called for it to pattern a major line of private-label foods after the approach it used to sell its private-label soft drinks. Given the problems created by ill-advised diversification efforts, Cott sold its beer business and reorganized its international operations to cut costs.[26] Thus, for Cott, diversification outside its core business area did not result in additional financial returns.

Sometimes, however, the failure to pursue appropriate types of diversification may have a negative effect on the firm's strategic competitiveness. Some analysts believe that this may have been the case recently for AT&T. During the time AT&T was searching for a new CEO, its competitors, such as WorldCom, GTE, and MCI Communications, completed transactions to achieve dominant market positions in different segments of the telecommunications industry. Inactive during the search for its new CEO, AT&T may have lost some opportunities to buy assets required to do battle. As a result, AT&T may find itself competing against a raft of fortified new rivals. The breadth of its rivals' strengths suggests that AT&T is facing the "fight of its life" in everything from local phone services to the Internet. Calling for the firm to pursue a strategy of related diversification, some proposed that AT&T should have been adding to its communications assets at the same time competitors were adding to theirs. AT&T pursued related diversification earlier (in the mid-1990s) when it filled a hole in its wireless services capabilities through the purchase of McCaw Cellular Communications for more than $12 billion.[27]

As the Cott and AT&T examples suggest, strategic competitiveness can be increased when the firm pursues a level of diversification that is appropriate for its resources (especially financial resources) and core competencies and the opportunities and threats that exist in its external environment. For some companies, however, the match between competencies and external environmental conditions indicates that they can flourish by focusing on single or highly related businesses. Two prominent examples include Wal-Mart and Coca-Cola. In fact, when he became Coca-Cola's CEO, Roberto Goizueta went against then-current wisdom when he decided to change the firm from a highly diversified company to one that was focused tightly on its core products. Goizueta explained, "There's a perception in this country that you're better off if you're in two lousy businesses than if you're in a good one—that you're spreading the risk. It's crazy."[28]

Another example of a firm that achieves success through highly focused operations is Mabuchi Motor, a midsize but highly successful Japanese firm. Ninety-nine percent of its annual revenue comes from the sale of motors. The focus on motors allows company scientists to continuously examine ways to improve the motors, such as making them lighter, quieter, more enduring, and cheaper.[29] The Strategic Focus describes two Canadian firms that are becoming more focused.

# LEVELS OF DIVERSIFICATION

Diversified firms vary according to the level of diversification and connection between and among their businesses. Figure 7.2 lists and defines five categories of businesses according to increasing levels of diversification. Besides single- and dominant-business categories, more fully diversified firms are classified into related and unrelated categories. A firm is related through its diversification when there are several links among

## STRATEGIC FOCUS

### Attempting to Refocus to Increase Shareholder Value

Laidlaw, Inc. is the largest operator in school and intercity (Greyhound) bus services, municipal transit, ambulance transportation, and hospital emergency department management. It is headquartered in Burlington, Ontario and has 95 000 employees in Canada and the United States. It diversified in 1993 by getting into ambulance services and again in 1997 by buying EmCare Holdings, a Dallas-based firm in hospital emergency department management. By 1998, Laidlaw had made 38 acquisitions, with almost 75 percent of them in the health care field.

One takeover included a hostile takeover of Safety-Kleen Corp, a North Carolina oil-recycling company. These acquisitions led to losses and dropping share prices. Consequently, in September 1999, Laidlaw announced that it would sell assets related to its health care businesses. Laidlaw intended to divest American Medical Response, the largest ambulance business in the United States, EmCare, and a large share in Safety-Kleen Corp. The company hoped that this would allow it to refocus on its core business and boost its sagging share price. Yet Safety-Kleen continued to drag down company performance. Safety-Kleen sought protection from creditors in Bankruptcy court in June 2000. Still, Laidlaw's diversification efforts exacted a higher price. While most operating subsidiaries were sound, the finances of Laidlaw were a disaster. In June 2001, the corporate parent also sought the protection of the Bankruptcy court.

In another less dramatic example, Bell Canada recently announced it was divesting Nexacor Realty Management, Inc., its wholly owned property management unit. This move to outsource property management functions fits with Bell's divesture plans over the past few years of nontelecommunication real estate assets that are outside its core business. Bell Canada's results will, it expects, lead to a better outcome than Laidlaws.

Sources: *Laidlaw home page*, www.laidlaw.com (retrieved July 23.) M. MacDonald, 1999, Laidlaw prepares for huge asset sale, *The Telegram*, September 14, 34; G. Livingston, 2000, Laidlaw annual meeting, *Canadian Press Newswire*, January 12; 1999, Bell sells property unit to Profac: Property management, *Financial Post*, 2 (43), December 15, C4; J. Aguayo, 1997, The consolidator, *Forbes*, October, 56–57.

business units; for example, units share products or services, technologies, and/or distribution channels. The more links among businesses, the more "constrained" the relatedness of diversification. Unrelatedness refers to a lack of direct links among businesses.

## Low Levels of Diversification

A firm pursuing a low level of diversification focuses its efforts on a single or a dominant business. The Wm. Wrigley Jr. Company is an example of a firm with little diversification. Its primary focus is the chewing gum market.[30] A firm is classified a single business when revenue generated by the dominant business is greater than 95 percent of total sales.[31] Dominant businesses are firms that generate between 70 percent and 95 percent of their total sales within a single category. Because of the sales it generates from breakfast cereals, Kellogg is an example of a dominant business firm.

■ ■ **FIGURE 7.2**

*Levels and Types of Diversification*

**Low Levels of Diversification**

| | | |
|---|---|---|
| Single Business: | More than 95 percent of revenue comes from a single line of business. | ① |
| Dominant Business: | Between 70 and 95 percent of revenue comes from a single line of business. | ①—② |

**Moderate to High Levels of Diversification**

| | | |
|---|---|---|
| Related Constrained | Less than 70 percent of revenue comes from the dominant business, and all businesses share product, technological, and distribution linkages. | |
| Related Linked (Mixed related and unrelated and unrelated) | Less than 70 percent of revenue comes from the dominant business, and there are only limited links between businesses. | |

**Very High Levels of Diversification**

| | | |
|---|---|---|
| Unrelated | Less than 70 percent of revenue comes from the dominant business, and there are no common links between businesses. | |

Hershey Foods Corp. (the largest U.S. producer of chocolate and nonchocolate confectionery items) is another dominant business firm. The bulk of Hershey's revenue is earned through the selling of its confectionery items.[32] To generate interest in its candies across time, the company introduces new products carefully and deliberately. Commenting on this approach, an analyst suggested the following: "Announcing that a new candy is on the way, then keeping it under wraps until it is ready increases sales and sparks a general feeling of enthusiasm for Hershey stock."[33]

Wal-Mart has focused narrowly on discount retailing. However, it recently bought Federal BankCentre, a small savings bank in Oklahoma, to add a customer service feature to its portfolio, noting that 20 percent of Wal-Mart's customers and many of its 780 000 employees lack "an established banking relationship." Wal-Mart currently leases space to banks in about 450 of its stores. The company indicated that it would learn about the business and then test-market its own branches in five stores.[34] Although Wal-Mart is moving into foreign markets and creating a more competitive environment in Europe, it still has a very narrow scope in regard to product diversification. The move into financial services could signal that the firm is increasing its level of diversification. Fishery Products International, of St. John's, Newfoundland, is a very focused firm and is considered to be a single industry business with 100 percent of its revenues coming from its products in the fishing industry. Canadian Tire Corporation is considered to be pursuing a dominant corporate-level strategy.

## Moderate and High Levels of Diversification

When a firm earns more than 30 percent of its sales volume outside a dominant business, and when its businesses are related to each other in some manner, the company is classified as a related-diversified firm. With more direct links between the businesses, the firm is defined as related-constrained. Related-constrained firms share a number of resources and activities among businesses. Examples of related constrained firms include SNC-Lavalin Group and Nortel Networks in Canada, and Campbell Soup, Procter & Gamble, Xerox, and Merck & Company in the United States. If there are only a few links between businesses, the firm is defined as a mixed related and unrelated business, or a related-linked firm (see Figure 7.1). Canadian firms Bombardier and Rogers Communications and U.S. firms Johnson & Johnson, Westinghouse, General Electric, and Schlumberger are examples of related-linked firms. Related-linked firms have less sharing of actual resources and assets and relatively more transfers of knowledge and competencies between businesses. Highly diversified firms, which have no relationships among businesses, are called unrelated-diversified firms. An example of a Canadian firm pursuing an unrelated-diversification strategy is Toromont Industries. Other examples are U.S. firms Dart Group, Tenneco, and Textron, and Thailand's Charoen Pokphand (with department stores and business units operating in the petrochemicals and telecommunications industries, this firm's annual sales revenue approximates $8 billion).[35]

In general, there are more unrelated-diversified firms in the United States than in other countries. In Latin America and other emerging economies such as Korea and India, conglomerates (firms following the unrelated-diversification strategy) continue to dominate the private sector.[36] For example, typically family controlled, these corporations account for more than two-thirds of the 33 largest private business groups in Brazil. Similarly, the largest business groups in Mexico, Argentina, and Colombia are family-owned, diversified enterprises.[37]

Consistent with a global trend of refocusing, some companies decide to become less diversified. Cited historically as perhaps the world's most successful follower of the unrelated-diversification strategy, Hanson nonetheless decided in the mid-1990s to become less diversified and to streamline its operations. Thus, Hanson either sold or spun off a number of its operating businesses; those remaining were structured into four independent business units.[38]

As an industrial manufacturer established more than 100 years ago, Westinghouse Electric implemented the related-linked diversification strategy for many years. The significant reduction in the amount of this firm's diversification began with the August 1995 acquisition of CBS for $5.4 billion in cash. Convinced that the firm's future was in broadcasting, CEO Michael H. Jordan initiated a process that culminated in the official changing of the firm's name to CBS Corporation. To create its broadcasting focus, two business units were sold in 1997 (Thermo King and Westinghouse Power Generation). Jordan intended to complete the sales of the remaining major business units—energy systems, process control, and government operations—by mid-1998.

During these divestitures, CBS Corp. acquired American Radio Systems' radio broadcasting operations. Calling this transaction "strategically attractive," a top-level CBS executive stated, "This investment will significantly strengthen CBS's position in the fast-growing radio industry. It will enable CBS Radio to expand into new top 50 markets and increase its position in its existing markets." Thus, to expand its single product line of broadcasting, a line that includes CBS Network, CBS radio, the TV station group, cable, and "other" broadcasting, CBS Corp. was committed to making selective acquisitions.

Ultimately, Mel Karmazin became CEO of CBS. In talking with Sumner M. Redstone, Viacom's 76-year-old CEO, about taking advantage of a Federal Communications Commission ruling that allowed one company to own two television stations in one market, these CEOs decided to merge their two firms. Viacom bought the assets of CBS and agreed to pay $37 billion in stock to combine the two companies into a new mega-media empire with capabilities comparable to Disney, News Corporation, and AOL Time Warner.[39] Thus, over time, Westinghouse first increased its diversification, then decreased its diversification and became CBS Corporation, and finally increased its diversification when it merged with Viacom. The Strategic Focus describes three Canadian firms that have moderate to high levels of diversification.

## STRATEGIC FOCUS

### *The Range of Diversification: Small Steps to Big Explosions*

Fortis shares are now widely held across Canada. Fortis has become a diversified holding company that owns electrical utilities, property management and hospitality companies, and a finance company. Newfoundland Power is a 100 percent–owned subsidiary and serves approximately 214 000 customers throughout the island portion of Newfoundland. Other power companies are listed as follows

| Company | Ownership | Market | Customers |
|---------|-----------|--------|-----------|
| Maritime Electric | 100% | Prince Edward Island | 64 000 |
| Belize Electricity Ltd. | 67% | Belize, Central America | 51 000 |
| Canadian Niagara Power | 50% | Fort Erie, Ontario | 14 000 |
| Fortis US Energy | 100% | New York State | Power Companies |
| Caribbean Utilities | 20% | Cayman Islands | 18 000 |

Other interests include Fortis Properties and Fortis Trust. Fortis Properties is a wholly owned subsidiary and owns and manages commercial, retail, and hotel properties in the provinces of Newfoundland and Labrador, Nova Scotia, and New Brunswick. Fortis Trust is 100 percent owned and is a licensed trust company operating as a deposit-taking and mortgage-lending institution in Newfoundland, Labrador, and Prince Edward Island.

In total Fortis's many subsidiaries make it a related-linked firm, with Newfoundland Power contributing 68 percent of revenue and Maritime Electric contributing 17 percent. The other 15 percent comes from the firm's other six subsidiaries. The parent firm is considered related-linked because it has not obtained the synergies from the two non-related firms (Fortis Properties and Fortis Trust) that it hoped for when they were being developed. These firms have not been able to share activities in an operational sense. On the other hand, Fortis engaged in corporate relatedness when it transferred Philip Hughes from Maritime Electric to Newfoundland Power so he could become its CEO in 1997.

BCE is Canada's largest telecommunications firm. Its range of activity is certainly greater than that of Fortis. In early 2000, it announced that it was spinning off Nortel Networks. Nortel's market capitalization had tripled in the year prior to the announcement, and BCE's minority share in Nortel had risen to 78 percent of BCE's market value. The divestment brings substantial cash and is expected to allow BCE flexibility in making other investments either in the telephone industry, the Internet industry, or the media industry. This restructuring move by BCE resulted in a more strategically focused firm.

*continued*

The new BCE is now better able to concentrate on becoming a communications powerhouse. BCE's bold transformation strategy allows BCE to focused on the following businesses: Bell Canada, a firm that boasts 21 million points of contact with its customers across Canada; Sympatico, Canada's leading Internet service, reaches one million subscribers across the country; Teleglobe has one of the world's largest international Internet systems and is expanding its reach with its GlobeSystem initiative, which will increase the capacity of its network 200-fold; Bell ExpressVu, Canada's leading satellite TV service reaches 722 000 subscribers through Nimiq, Canada's first high-power direct-broadcast satellite; CTV, Canada's leading private TV network, reaches 99 percent of English Canadians; *The Globe and Mail,* Canada's leading national newspaper, reaches 2 087 800 readers each week; and, BCE Emergis, one of the top e-commerce providers in North America.

Seagram's Company was an example of a very diversified firm, with holdings in entertainment, music, and liquor. From its beginnings in 1924 as Distillers, the Montreal-based firm launched Seagram's V.O. Canadian Whiskey in 1934 and for most of its history remained predominantly in the liquor and distilling business. In 1993, Seagram's announced its intention to purchase 15 percent of Time Warner, and in 1995 it acquired 80 percent of Universal Studios, Inc. (formerly MCA Inc.) from Matsushita Electric Industrial Company (a large Japanese firm). Seagram also sold holdings in DuPont and Tropicana. Seagram's ranked the world's largest recorded music company (with artists Diana Krall, Shania Twain, and U2). The firm announced in mid-2000 that it intended to focus on its three core businesses—liquor, music, and making movies.

In June 2000, Seagram issued a press release confirming that it was in discussions with Vivendi and Canal+, two firms headquartered in France, to create a three-way strategic business combination. The combined firm, Vivendi Universal, would bring together content from the world's largest music company; the second-largest film library; a major film production studio; the second-largest destination theme park company; and the global leader in reference, consumer, and PC-based software game publishing with Vizzavi, Vivendi's new multiple access portal; and the combined global distribution capabilities of Vivendi, Seagram, and Canal+. Seagrams had exploded into something totally unlike the old liquor firm. What was not clear was what would happen to the liquor and distilling business that carried the Seagram name for so long. On December 19, 2000, Vivendi Universal Chair and CEO Jean-Marie Messier and Executive Vice-Chair Edgar Bronfman, Jr. announced that Seagram's Spirits and Wine Business had been sold to Diageo and Pernod Ricard for $8.5 billion. The after-tax proceeds were greater than Seagram's net debt and strengthened Vivendi Universal's balance sheet to help create real and immediate value for Vivendi's shareholders.

Sources: http://www.bce.ca/en/corporate/overview/ (Retrieved February 17, 2001); R. Laver, 2000, BCE divides to conquer: In shedding 37% of Nortel, BCE is building up a powerful war chest for itself in the world of e-commerce, *Maclean's,* 113 (6), 38; Eight decades in Seagram's history, *Seagram home page,* www.seagram.com/company_info (Retrieved May 29, 2000 and February 17, 2001); *Vivendi home page,* 2000, www.vivendi.com (Retrieved November 20); *Newfoundland Power home page,* 2000, www.nfpower.nf.ca (Retrieved November 20); *Fortis home page,* 2000, www.fortis.ca (Retrieved November 20); *Fortis Trust home page,* 2000, www.fortisinc.com/fortis_trust (Retrieved November 20).

# REASONS FOR DIVERSIFICATION

Firms use a diversification strategy as their corporate-level strategy for many reasons. A partial list is shown in Table 7.1. These reasons are discussed throughout the remainder of the chapter in relation to related and unrelated-diversification strategies, incentives, and managerial motives to diversify.

Most firms implement a diversification strategy to enhance the strategic competitiveness of the entire company. This reason describes strategic actions at CMGI, as explained in the Opening Case, and at Internet Capital Group as well. When a diversification strategy enhances strategic competitiveness, the firm's total value is increased. Value is created through either related diversification or unrelated diversification when that particular strategy allows a company's business units to increase revenues or reduce costs while implementing their business-level strategies.

| ■ ■ TABLE 7.1 | Motives, Incentives, and Resources for Diversification |
|---|---|

**Motives to Enhance Strategic Competitiveness**

Economies of scope (related diversification)

        Sharing activities

        Transferring core competencies

Market power (related diversification)

        Blocking competitors through multipoint competition

        Vertical integration

Financial economies (unrelated diversification)

        Efficient internal capital allocation

        Business restructuring

**Incentives and Resources with Neutral Effects on Strategic Competitiveness**

| | |
|---|---|
| Anti-trust regulation | Uncertain future cash flows |
| Tax laws | Firm risk reduction |
| Low performance | Tangible and intangible resource |

**Managerial motives**

Diversifying managerial employment risk

Increasing managerial compensation

Another reason for diversification is to gain market power relative to competitors. In a bid to increase its market power, Toronto-based Teknion purchased United States–based Halcon. In business since 1983, Teknion sells its office furniture directly to companies. Its office systems, modular walls, and desks make up 80 percent of its sales, and bookshelves and other office furniture make up the rest. Halcon focuses on hardwood office furniture such as desks and tables. Michael Herman, Teknion's VP of corporate development, considered the strategic fit a good one and one that would allow

Teknion to combine its office system product offerings with Halcon's capability on the wood side. Teknion earns 30 to 35 percent of its revenue in Canada, 50 to 55 percent in the United States and the rest internationally. Teknion expects to increase revenue by 5 percent with this acquisition.[40]

Other reasons for implementing a diversification strategy may not enhance strategic competitiveness; in fact, diversification could have neutral effects or actually increase costs or reduce a firm's revenues. These reasons include diversification (1) to neutralize a competitor's market power (e.g., to neutralize the advantage of another firm by acquiring a distribution outlet similar to that of the competitor) and (2) to expand a firm's portfolio to reduce managerial employment risk (e.g., if one of the businesses fails, the top executive remains employed in a diversified firm). Because diversification can increase a firm's size and thus managerial compensation, managers have motives to diversify a firm. This type of diversification may reduce the firm's value. Diversification rationales that may have a neutral effect or that may reduce a firm's value are discussed in a later section.

■ ■ **FIGURE 7.3**

*Motives, Incentives, and Resources for Diversification*

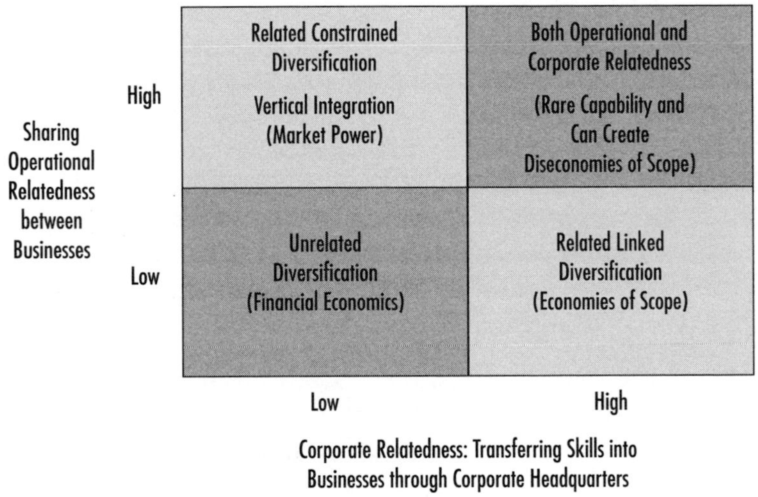

|  | | Corporate Relatedness: Transferring Skills into Businesses through Corporate Headquarters | |
|---|---|---|---|
| Sharing Operational Relatedness between Businesses | **High** | Related Constrained Diversification<br><br>Vertical Integration (Market Power) | Both Operational and Corporate Relatedness<br><br>(Rare Capability and Can Create Diseconomies of Scope) |
| | **Low** | Unrelated Diversification (Financial Economics) | Related Linked Diversification (Economies of Scope) |
| | | **Low** | **High** |

To provide an overview of value-creating diversification strategies, Figure 7.3 illustrates the two dimensions as sources of relatedness. Researchers have studied these independent dimensions of relatedness[41] and have found that resources and key competencies are critical. The vertical dimension of the figure relates to sharing activities (operational relatedness), and the horizontal dimension represents corporate capabilities for transferring knowledge (corporate relatedness). The upper-left quadrant shows a firm with a high degree of capability in managing operational synergy, especially in sharing assets between its businesses. This quadrant also represents vertical sharing of assets through vertical integration. The lower-right quadrant of the figure represents a highly developed corporate capability of transferring a skill to other businesses. This skill is located primarily in the corporate office. Whichever type of relatedness is used, it is based on some kind of knowledge asset that the firm can either share or transfer.[42] Unrelated diversification may also be illustrated here, but its source of value does not come through either operational or corporate relatedness among business units; rather, it comes through financial economies or the restructuring of businesses the firm acquires. The next section examines related diversification.

# RELATED DIVERSIFICATION

**Economies of scope** are cost savings attributed to transferring the capabilities and competencies developed in one business to a new business without significant additional costs.

As suggested earlier in the chapter, related diversification is a strategy through which firms intend to build upon or extend their existing resources, capabilities, and core competencies in the pursuit of strategic competitiveness.[43] Thus, firms that have selected related diversification as their corporate-level strategy seek to exploit economies of scope between business units. Available to firms operating in multiple industries or product markets,[44] **economies of scope** are cost savings attributed to transferring the capabilities and competencies developed in one business to a new business without significant additional costs.

As illustrated in Figure 7.3, firms seek to create value from economies of scope through two basic kinds of operational economies: sharing activities (operating relatedness) and transferring skills or core competencies (corporate relatedness). The difference between sharing activities and transferring competencies is based on how separate resources are used jointly to create economies of scope. Tangible resources, such as plant and equipment or other business-unit physical assets, often must be shared to create economies of scope. Less tangible resources, such as sales forces, also can be shared. However, when know-how is transferred between separate activities, and there is no physical or tangible resource involved, a corporate core competence has been transferred as opposed to an operational sharing of activities.

## Operational Relatedness: Sharing Activities

Sharing activities is quite common, especially among related-constrained firms. At Procter & Gamble, a paper towels business and a baby diapers business both use paper products as a primary input to the manufacturing process. Having a joint paper production plant that produces inputs for both divisions is an example of a shared activity. In addition, these businesses are likely to share distribution sales networks, because they both produce consumer products.

Primary and support value-chain activities were discussed in Chapter 4. In general, primary activities, such as inbound logistics, operations, and outbound logistics, might possess multiple shared activities. Through efficient sharing of these activities, firms may be able to create core competencies. In terms of inbound logistics, the business units may share common inventory delivery systems, warehousing facilities, and quality assurance practices. Operations might share common assembly facilities, quality control systems, or maintenance operations. With respect to outbound logistics, two business units might share a common sales force and sales service desk. Support activities could include the sharing of procurement and technology development efforts. Among pharmaceutical producers, the importance of sharing of activities is driving a number of mergers and acquisitions of firms seeking to reduce their costs.

Jan Leschly, CEO of Smithkline Beecham, and Richard Sykes, CEO of Glaxo Wellcome, both British pharmaceutical firms, have signalled that the two huge firms intend to merge. The merger is valued at $70 billion and will create the world's number-one drugmaker, to be called Glaxo Smithkline. This transaction is one of many that have been signalled among pharmaceutical firms recently. The anticipated acquisition of

Warner-Lambert by several suitor companies and the proposed merger of Monsanto and Pharmacia & Upjohn, are two similar deals. The R&D costs of producing new drugs are forcing these firms to think about sharing laboratories and the capabilities they house. As one business writer said, "Part of what is driving companies to join together is the need to finance the enormous effort required to turn a revolution in human biology into a steady flow of new medicines."[45]

However, in 1996, when Swiss drugmakers Ciba-Geigy and Sandoz joined in a $63 billion merger to form Novartis, CEO Daniel Vasella stated that Novartis was "in a unique position to apply technologies learned from plant genetics to both pharmaceuticals and agricultural businesses." He staked the company's future on genetic engineering. But, especially in Europe, a backlash over genetically modified crops has been undermining the life-sciences concept upon which Novartis is based. In 1999, the whole firm required restructuring because of poor performance in its agribusinesses.[46] Thus, there are risks associated with basing two businesses on a single value proposition to create economies of scope.

Firms expect the sharing of activities across units to result in increased strategic competitiveness and improved financial returns. Other matters, however, affect the degree to which these outcomes will be achieved through sharing activities. For example, firms should recognize that sharing activities requires sharing strategic control over business units. Moreover, one business-unit manager may feel that another is receiving more benefit from the sharing activities. Such a perception could create conflicts between division managers. Sharing activities also is risky because business-unit ties create links between outcomes. For instance, if demand for the product of one business is reduced, there may not be sufficient revenues to cover the fixed costs of running the joint plant. Shared activities create interrelationships that affect the ability of both businesses to achieve strategic competitiveness, as is illustrated in the aforementioned case of Novartis. Sharing activities may be ineffective if these costs are not taken into consideration.

The costs of sharing activities notwithstanding, research shows that the sharing of activities and resources across business units can increase the firm's value. For example, research that examined acquisitions of firms in the same industry (referred to as horizontal acquisitions), such as the banking industry, has found that sharing resources and activities (thereby creating economies of scope) contributed to postacquisition increases in performance and higher returns to shareholders.[47] Research also found that firms that sold off related units in which resource sharing was a possible source of economies of scope produced lower returns than those that sold off businesses unrelated to the firm's core business.[48] Still other research found that firms with more related units had lower risk.[49] These results suggest that gaining economies of scope by sharing activities and resources across businesses within a firm may be important in reducing risk and in earning positive returns from diversification efforts. Further, more attractive results are obtained through the sharing of activities when a strong corporate office facilitates the sharing.[50]

## Corporate Relatedness: Transferring of Core Competencies

Over time, a strategically competitive firm's intangible resources, such as know-how, become the foundation for competitively valuable capabilities and core competencies. Thus, in diversified firms, core competencies are complex sets of resources and capabilities that link different businesses primarily through managerial and technological knowledge, experience, and expertise.[51]

Marketing expertise is an example of a core competence that could be used this way. Because the expense of developing such a competence has already been incurred, and because competencies based on intangible resources are less visible and more difficult for competitors to understand and imitate, transferring these types of competencies from an original business unit to another one may reduce costs and enhance an entire firm's strategic competitiveness.[52] A key reason Philip Morris decided to acquire Miller Brewing was that it believed that a competitive advantage could be achieved by transferring its marketing core competence to Miller.

As a cigarette company, Philip Morris developed a particular expertise in marketing. When Philip Morris purchased Miller Brewing, the beer industry had efficient operations, but no firm in the industry had established marketing competence as a source of competitive advantage. The marketing competence transferred from Philip Morris to Miller resulted in the introduction of improved marketing practices to the brewing industry. These practices, especially in terms of advertising, proved to be the source of competitive advantage that allowed Miller Brewing to earn above-average returns for a period of time. In fact, several years passed before Anheuser-Busch, the largest firm in the brewing industry, developed the capabilities required to duplicate the benefits of Miller's strategy. A strong competitive response from Anheuser-Busch was predictable, however, in that beer is the firm's core business.

Some firms discover that either they are unable to transfer competencies or they transfer competencies that do not help a business unit establish a competitive advantage. One way managers facilitate the transfer of competencies is to move key people into new management positions. Although Philip Morris accomplished competence transfer to Miller Brewing in this way, a business unit manager of an older division may be reluctant to transfer key people who have accumulated knowledge and experience necessary to their own divisions. Thus, managers of a core competence may come at a premium or may not want to transfer, and the top-level managers from the transferring division may not want them to be transferred to a new division to fulfill a diversification objective. Research suggests that transferring expertise in manufacturing-based businesses often does not result in improved performance.[53] However, those businesses in which performance does improve often exhibit a corporate passion for pursuing skill transfer and appropriate coordination mechanisms for realizing economies of scope.

## Market Power

**Market power** exists when a firm is able to sell its products above the existing competitive level or reduce the costs of its primary and support activities below the competitive level, or both.

Related diversification can also be used to gain market power. **Market power** exists when a firm is able to sell its products above the existing competitive level or reduce the costs of its primary and support activities below the competitive level, or both.[54]

One approach to gaining market power through diversification is multipoint competition. Multipoint competition exists when two or more diversified firms compete in the same product areas or geographic markets.[55] For example, when Philip Morris moved into foods by buying General Foods and Kraft, RJR's competitive response was the acquisition of another food company, Nabisco.

If the diversified firms compete head to head in each market, multipoint competition will not create potential gains; instead, it will generate excessive competitive activity.

Over time, if the firms refrain from competition and, in effect, realize mutual forbearance, they are engaged in a form of related diversification that creates value for each firm through less competitive activity (see Chapter 6). Mutual forbearance is a relationship between two or more firms where they realize they are in a situation where their competition is self-destructive and, without formal agreement, cease to engage in it.

Actions taken by Vodafone AirTouch and Mannesmann are an example of multipoint competition. Mannesmann began as a German producer of steel piping, but moved into telecommunications services in 1996 with the purchase of a telecommunications network formerly owned by the German railroad, Deutsche Bahn. By 1997, Mannesmann had more mobile phone customers than Deutsche Telekom. In 1999, Mannesmann purchased a number of mobile assets across Europe. The company paid $1.2 billion for o.tel.o, owned by Veba and RWE, which exited the telecommunications business. Next, Mannesmann purchased the cellular business of Olivetti, OmniTel, for $7.8 billion, because Olivetti was trying to take over Telecom Italia. Then, in a surprise move, Mannesmann acquired British mobile phone company Orange for $34 billion in October 1999.

However, in November 1999, Vodafone AirTouch launched a hostile bid for Mannesmann. Headquartered in Britain, Vodafone AirTouch realized that it had to make this deal because Mannesmann would be the firm's biggest competitor in Europe, especially after it took over Orange, a leading mobile phone service provider in Britain. Mannesmann paid a significant premium of $6000 per subscriber for Orange, which is 70 percent above the industry average cost per subscriber. However, Mannesmann shares had increased 145 percent in 1999, a performance that satisfied shareholders.[56]

In 1998, Christopher Gent, Vodafone's CEO, had paid $60 billion in stock and cash for San Francisco-based AirTouch, beating out a rival offer from Bell Atlantic. However, Gent later structured a transaction with Bell Atlantic, which had acquired GTE's cellular business. The partnership created a network of 20 million cellular customers that would cover 90 percent of the U.S. population. AT&T was now in second place in market share, with 12 million wireless customers. As investors viewed the transaction, they not only approved of the U.S. deal but also could see the cellular global strategy in the combination of Vodafone and AirTouch. Accordingly, the takeover price appreciated 25 percent. Bell Atlantic's stock price did not appreciate significantly, compared to the increases in Vodafone AirTouch stock price. The reason for the difference is the international opportunity seen by shareholders in the Vodafone AirTouch deal. Anticipating an advantage in the future of international cellular calls, Gent decided to pursue the Mannesmann deal.[57]

The preceding example illustrates the potential negative side of multipoint competition. Vodafone AirTouch actions represent a counterattack mode, an exceptional strategic action when multipoint competition exists.[58] Counterattacks are not common in multipoint competition because the threat of a counterattack may prevent strategic actions from being taken, or, more likely, firms may retract their strategic actions with the threat of counterattack.[59]

As noted in Figure 7.3, another approach to creating value by gaining market power is the strategy of vertical integration. **Vertical integration** exists when a company is producing its own inputs (backward vertical integration) or owns its own source of distribution of outputs (forward vertical integration). It is also possible to have partial vertical integration wherein some inputs and outputs are sold through firm units while others are produced or sold through outside firms (see Figure 7.4).

**Vertical integration** exists when a company is producing its own inputs (backward vertical integration) or owns its own source of distribution of outputs (forward vertical integration).

*A Simple Model of Partial
Vertical Integration in the
Pharmaceutical Industry*

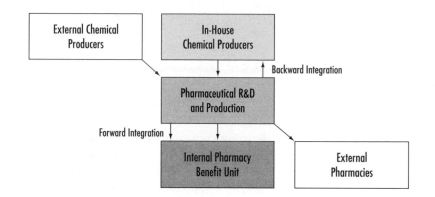

A company pursuing vertical integration is usually motivated to strengthen its position in its core business by gaining market power over competitors. This is done through savings on operations costs, avoidance of market costs, better control to establish quality, and, possibly, the protection of technology. It also happens when firms have strong ties between their assets for which no market prices exist. Establishing a market price would result in high search and transaction costs, so firms seek to vertically integrate rather than remain separate businesses.[60]

In response to prominent threats from their external environment (such as changes in environmental regulations and third-party reimbursement practices) in the early to mid-1990s, some firms competing in the pharmaceutical industry pursued a strategy of vertical integration. More recently, these companies have completed horizontal acquisitions (recall the transaction between Glaxo and Smithkline.) However, in November 1993, Merck & Company, at the time the world's largest prescription drug manufacturer, paid $6.6 billion to acquire Medco Containment Services (one of the largest mail-order pharmacy and managed care companies at the time of its purchase). With Medco, Merck controls a dominant supplier of its products. Contributing further to an increase in Merck's market power as a result of pursuing vertical integration was its opportunity to have detailed and immediate access to information regarding customer's marketing-related needs. In an identical fashion, the former Smithkline Beecham attempted to increase its market power through forward vertical integration by purchasing United Healthcare's pharmacy benefit services unit, Diversified Pharmaceutical Services. Eli Lilly & Company's purchase of McKesson's PCS Health Systems unit was completed for the same strategic reason.[61] Important benefits accruing to Merck & Company, the former Smithkline Beecham, and Eli Lilly as a result of their separate decisions to vertically integrate in a forward direction include reductions in market transaction costs and some additional protection of proprietary technologies.

Of course, there are limits to vertical integration. For example, an outside supplier may produce the product at a lower cost. As a result, internal transactions from vertical integration may be expensive and reduce profitability. Also, bureaucratic costs are incurred in implementing this strategy. And because vertical integration can require substantial sums of capital to be invested in specific technologies, the strategy may be problematic when technology changes quickly. Finally, changes in demand create capacity balance and coordination problems. If one division of a firm is building a part for another internal division, but achieving economies of scale requires the first division to build the part at a scale beyond the capacity of the internal buyer to absorb demand, sales outside the company would be necessary. However, if demand slackens, overcapacity would result because the internal users cannot absorb the total demand. Thus, although vertical integration can create value and contribute to strategic competitiveness, especially in gaining market power over competitors, it is not without risks and costs.

Many manufacturing firms no longer pursue vertical integration. In fact, deintegration is the focus of most manufacturing firms, such as Intel and Dell, and even among large auto firms, such as Ford and General Motors, as they develop independent supplier networks. However, in energy production, vertical integration still may be worthwhile and lead to strategic competitiveness and above-average returns. Duke Power has completed a 510-megawatt power plant near Brownsville, Texas. The plant was built through Duke's construction arm, will be staffed with the firm's operating engineers, and will be provided fuel through Duke's natural gas pipelines. Furthermore, the power will be marketed through the firm's Houston-based power marketing division. Thus, Duke Energy's Texas operations are fully integrated through its energy supply chain.

As deregulation in the electric utility industry in the United States has progressed, other energy companies are also seeking to build their plant capacity to drive costs lower to compete in a more cost-conscious deregulated environment. However, many industry analysts predict that this approach will lead to overcapacity. To deal with that problem, Duke Energy's CEO, Richard Priory, has sought to distinguish himself as an energy asset trader. He acquired PanEnergy, a natural gas supplier and pipeline operator, in 1998. Furthermore, he merged Duke's gas-gathering and -processing business with that of Phillips Petroleum in 1999. Duke has sold other assets in Ohio, Indiana, and Texas at a profit. Priory believes that Duke will have the ability to react and sell quickly if the market becomes overbuilt. With lower costs through its vertical integration strategy, and with the ability to react quickly through the astute buying and selling of assets, Duke Energy hopes to be well positioned for the 21st-century competitive battles in the energy industry.[62]

As Figure 7.3 suggests, some firms may try to seek both operational and corporate forms of economies of scope.[63] Firms that attempt to do this often fail and create diseconomies of scope, because trying to manage two sources of knowledge is extremely difficult. However, if successful, this strategy can create value that is difficult for competitors to imitate. For example, through the leadership of Jack Welch, General Electric's famous former CEO, the firm has been successful both in realizing operational synergy and in transferring knowledge between business units. GE had long possessed the ability to develop operational synergies inside its business groups. Through the use of "sharing best practices" and "boundaryless behaviour," techniques developed through Welch's leadership and support, the firm also possesses the ability to transfer knowledge among its units.[64] In describing the achievements resulting from these abilities, business analysts suggest, "GE is truly firing on all cylinders." For instance, "GE Capital, the world's largest non-bank finance company, boasts investments in 45 e-business companies. And NBC has allied with a host of Net players to capitalize on the convergence of the media, entertainment, and technology industries."[65]

Because knowledge management is so important in consulting firms such as McKinsey and Company and Accenture (formerly known as Andersen Consulting), each company tries to manage both operational and corporate relatedness.[66] Accenture originally focused on consulting in the field of information system implementation, but now the company consults on information systems and technology and provides strategic services and outsourcing (wherein Accenture becomes the computer-processing department for a large firm). Accenture also has diversified industry lines of consulting businesses (financial services, government, oil and gas, etc.). The firm does a lot of sharing across these lines but also has a large knowledge base from which consultants draw and seek to transfer information across lines of industry consulting engagements. Consulting is a business that requires the sharing and transfer of skills in order to remain profitable, especially if business declines and consulting projects become more competitive.[67]

Disney has also been successful in using both operational and corporate relatedness. Disney's strategy is especially successful in comparison to that of Sony, at least as measured by revenues generated from blockbuster movies. Through the use of both operational and corporate relatedness, Disney made $3 billion on the 150 products that came out simultaneously with its movie *The Lion King*. Sony's *Men in Black* was a major hit at the box office and earned $600 million, but box office and video revenues were practically the entire success story. Disney was able to accomplish its great success by sharing knowledge within its movie and distribution divisions, while at the same time transferring knowledge into its retail and product divisions, creating a music CD and producing a video sequel. In addition, there were *Lion King* themes at Disney resorts and Animal Kingdom parks.[68] The next corporate-level strategy considered, unrelated diversification, lacks both operational and corporate relatedness, but, when used appropriately, also creates value.

## UNRELATED DIVERSIFICATION

**Financial economies** are cost savings realized through improved allocations of financial resources based on investments inside or outside the firm.

An unrelated-diversification strategy (see Figure 7.3) can create value through two types of financial economies. **Financial economies** are cost savings realized through improved allocations of financial resources based on investments inside or outside the firm.[69]

The first type of financial economy involves efficient internal capital allocations. This approach seeks to reduce risks among the firm's business units—for example, through the development of a portfolio of businesses with different risk profiles. The approach thereby reduces business risk for the total corporation. The second type of financial economy is concerned with purchasing other corporations and restructuring their assets. This approach allows a firm to buy and sell businesses in the external market with the intent of increasing the total value of the firm.

Toronto-based Onex is an example of a Canadian firm that achieves financial economies through both risk reduction and the buying and selling of other firms to restructure their assets. Onex has been very successful in growing shareholder value when compared to what investors could earn with a very balanced risk-diversified portfolio. A $100 investment in Onex on January 1, 1989 would be worth approximately $1,465 in 2001. A similar investment in the TSE 300 or the S&P 500 would be worth $273 and $533, respectively. Onex operates in the electronics manufacturing services, customer relationship management, airline catering, automotive products, engineered building products, and other industries. Onex made 71 acquisitions since 1990 and achieved a 36 percent growth rate in the last 15 years. This is in comparison to the S&P 500, which grew 15 percent and the TSE 300, which grew 12 percent. Among Onex's operating principles are risk reduction through the deliberate development of a portfolio of businesses that gives appropriate returns for appropriate risks and helping the existing management of acquired businesses increase the value over the long term.

http://www.onex.ca/

# Efficient Internal Capital Market Allocation

Capital allocation is usually distributed efficiently in a market economy by capital markets. Capital is distributed efficiently because investors seek to purchase shares of firm equity (ownership) that have high future cash-flow values. Capital is allocated not only through equity but also through debt, by means of which shareholders and debt-holders seek to improve the value of their investment by investing in businesses with high-growth prospects. In large diversified firms, however, the corporate office distributes capital to divisions to create value for the overall company. Such an approach may provide gains from internal capital market allocation, relative to the external capital market.[70] The corporate office, through managing a particular set of businesses, may have access to more detailed and accurate information regarding those businesses' actual and prospective performance.

Compared with corporate office personnel, investors have relatively limited access to internal information and can only estimate divisional performance and future business prospects. Although businesses that seek capital must provide information to those who will supply the capital (e.g., banks or insurance companies), firms with internal capital markets may have at least two informational advantages. First, information provided to capital markets through annual reports and other sources may not include negative information, but rather emphasize positive prospects and outcomes. External capital sources have limited ability to know specifically what is taking place inside large organizations. Even owners who have access to information have no guarantee of full and complete disclosure.[71]

Second, although a firm must disseminate information, that information becomes available to potential competitors simultaneously. With insights gained by studying such information, competitors might attempt to duplicate a firm's competitive advantage. Without having to reveal internal information, a firm may protect its competitive advantage through an internal capital market.

If intervention from outside the firm is required to make corrections, only significant changes are possible, such as forcing the firm into bankruptcy or changing the dominant leadership coalition (e.g., the top-level management team described in Chapter 13). Alternatively, in an internal capital market, the corporate office may fine-tune corrections by choosing to adjust managerial incentives or suggest strategic changes in a division. Thus, capital can be allocated according to more specific criteria than is possible with external market allocation. The external capital market may fail to allocate resources adequately to high-potential investments, compared with corporate office investments, because it has less accurate information. The corporate office of a diversified company can more effectively perform such tasks as disciplining underperforming management teams and allocating resources.[72]

Some firms still follow the unrelated-diversification strategy.[73] Many of these large diversified business groups are found in southern European countries and throughout the emerging economies of the world. The Strategic Focus on diversified business groups in emerging economies speaks to how many of those business groups are becoming less diversified. As our discussion of these strategic actions suggests, choosing to use the unrelated-diversification strategy may actually decrease a firm's strategic competitiveness.

Implementing the unrelated-diversification business strategy continues to make sense in many economies of the world, as the Strategic Focus points out, especially among emerging economies such as China's. Research also indicates that the conglomerate or unrelated strategy has not disappeared in Europe, where the number of firms using this strategy has actually increased.[74] Although many conglomerates (e.g., ITT and Hansen Trust) have refocused, other unrelated-diversified firms have replaced them. The Achilles heel of the unrelated strategy is that conglomerates in developing economies have a fairly short life cycle because financial economies are more easily duplicated than in the case of operational and corporate relatedness. This is less of a problem in emerging economies, where the absence of a "soft infrastructure" (e.g., effective financial intermediaries, sound regulations, and contract laws) supports and encourages the pursuit of the unrelated-diversification strategy.

## STRATEGIC FOCUS

### Refocusing Large Diversified Business Groups in Emerging Economies

Large firms with portfolios of unrelated businesses throughout the world's emerging economies, as well as in some developed economies, are seeking to refocus their portfolios on a "core." The intention of this type of strategic action is to improve performance. These large diversified business groups, known as the chaebols in South Korea, are actually quite typical of those in capitalist countries that have industrialized since World War II. Many such firms from Asia and Latin America are using a model of Western corporate-level strategies and are refocusing their diversified operations: "Companies are mimicking Corporate America by refocusing, downsizing, merging, and spinning off faltering businesses to become globally competitive." But, at times, this refocusing may not be wholly appropriate in an emerging economy. Nonetheless, many of the firms have followed the pattern in the United States and the United Kingdom, where high levels of diversified operations have been refocused. A number of refocused firms specialize in managing businesses with core technology families to realize related diversification.

However, in emerging economies and in many highly developed economies such as France, Germany, and Italy, these diversified business groups have dominated the competitive landscape for several reasons. Some have argued that the underlying reason for having these conglomerates in the first place has not changed that much, especially in regard to emerging economies. Tarun Khanna and Krishna Palepu, accordingly, argue that the total restructuring of these diversified business groups is flawed. However, the recent financial crises in Asia and Latin America have reinforced the idea among politicians that these large business groups in emerging economies should refocus. In fact, in Korea, for instance, Kim Dae Jung, the president, pressed the chaebols to downscope and invited foreign investors to help in the process by buying some of the assets that the chaebols were forced to spin off.

Nevertheless, in a broad range of emerging economies, such as in Chile, India, and South Korea, it has taken longer than a decade to build institutions that support well-functioning infrastructure markets for capital, management, labour, and technology. The reason these diversified business groups evolved is that the markets for capital, management, labour, and international

*continued*

technology have been internalized in firms in those groups. The main problem is unequal (i.e., asymmetric) information and potential conflicts of interest between buyers and sellers in these markets. Where advanced markets exist, effective intermediaries, sound regulations, and contract laws can minimize the unequal information and any conflicts between buyers and sellers. For instance, in the U.S. financial market, investment bankers play an intermediary role in the allocation of capital to businesses. Furthermore, the Securities and Exchange Commission ensures that investors can rely on corporate disclosure and, thereby, adequate information. In addition, well-developed contract law helps resolve conflicts between buyers and sellers, and hundreds of business schools provide graduates who possess the knowledge required to manage firms successfully through the use of the strategic management process.

However, in emerging economies, these institutional mechanisms are often missing, creating additional transaction costs between businesses. The existence of a "soft infrastructure" (laws, regulatory bodies, and financial intermediaries that facilitate the transactional environment) is as important as that of a hard physical infrastructure such as roads, ports, and telecommunications systems, because the former reduces transaction costs. China, for example, has invested heavily in its physical infrastructure but has made little progress in creating a strong institutional infrastructure. Instead, China has been fostering large diversified business groups, such as the Bashing Iron and Steel Group Corporation in steelmaking, the Haier Group in appliances, the Sichuan Chang Hong Group in televisions, the North China Pharmaceutical Group Corporation in drugs, the Jiangnan Shipyard Group Co. in shipbuilding, and the Peking University Founder Group in computer software. Although Western journalists have been disappointed with the formation of these large diversified corporations because unrelated diversification is often viewed as inefficient in more developed economies, the corporations may be necessary because of the lack of a "soft infrastructure" in China. As in other emerging economies, these large diversified business groups serve as internal capital markets for the allocation of capital by a strong corporate headquarters. Furthermore, they function as a way to manage transactions, often through their own subsidiaries, when the country does not have a well-developed legal infrastructure. The transactions are effective because the corporations have a way of managing them equitably within the firm and through family members or closely affiliated partners. In addition, these diversified companies serve as training grounds for managers in the labour market system, because educational institutions often are unable to train managers via distinctive business programs such as those found in Western educational institutions.

Although large diversified firms such as the chaebols in Korea have been identified as the main cause of that country's economic problems, they in fact were necessary, given the absence of structure in the economy when those firms were first developing. Chile was one of the first emerging economies to seriously pursue market liberalization, and it has succeeded in developing one of the most efficient capital markets. However, the process of reform took more than 25 years and is still not complete. Although financial deregulation began in 1974 with the banking crisis, which was similar to the events in Asia in 1997, it was not until 1990 that the benefits of Chile's reforms started to take effect, when the first American Depository Receipt, La Compaq de Teléfonos de Chile, was listed on a U.S. exchange. In comparison, the Korean and Indian govern-

*continued*

ments have both used banks as instruments of economic development, in a manner similar to bank-lending policies in Malaysia and Indonesia. However, without a sharp-edged capital market such as that found in Chile, when a financial crisis develops, government interference has curtailed the development of basic financial intermediation expertise such as credit analysis.

As an example, Thai Petrochemical Industry, headquartered in Bangkok, Thailand, was recently forced to reorganize because of the Asian financial crisis and high levels of debt. This company and a number of others are part of a large conglomerate owned by Prachai Leophairatana. Leophairatana was having a hard time understanding that when a company goes bankrupt, its lenders, not its owners, have first claims over the remains of the firm. In Thailand, this sort of reasoning seemed unfair to the debtor and his employees. In fact, the government agreed, and the IMF relaxed the requirement to pass foreclosure legislation as part of a bailout package for Thailand. Without appropriate legislation and without suitable bankruptcy laws, it is unlikely that Thailand's financial difficulties can be resolved quickly. Traditionally, conglomerates in emerging economies have been controlled by families, and their main form of financing typically has been through debt, because debt allows family owners to control large business groups with a relatively small amount of equity capital. This approach has been used in Korean companies, and thus they are heavily indebted, even for very risky ventures. In theory, such risky ventures, such as diversifying into semiconductors, should be based on more long-term equity capital because debt requires short-term cash flow.

To restructure these firms in emerging economies, it may be necessary first to change their internal orientation rather than pursue drastic action, as was chosen by the Korean government. Most of these firms have adopted a growth orientation toward financial goals, forgoing some profits. Taking a stronger orientation toward profitability would help make individual firms or divisions more accountable for their operating performance. In addition, the corporate office should take a role in management development by delegating operational authority to large affiliated corporations. Groupwide recruiting, training, and job rotation programs would be helpful as well. These programs would allow executives to receive the training they need, but also enable them to be responsible for a greater profit orientation at the business or division level. Such an orientation would create better financial information internally and ultimately would lead to more transparent transactions in the economy. Rather than placing the blame on Korea's chaebols, which have responded to government policy in the past, the Korean government should focus on building more effective institutions, a result of which would be a weeding out of inefficient groups. Simply blaming the chaebols for the crisis is not helpful. The government should invite foreign competitors and, thereby, promote market competition. Effective intermediaries would then develop, and they would not be isolated from foreign competition. They could familiarize themselves with investment banking, venture capitalists, and new business school techniques. Thus, focusing on developing the "soft infrastructure" may be better for a government than blaming firms that helped them achieve the foundation of economic development, even though the weaknesses had been exposed by the Asian financial crisis.

Sources: T. Khanna & K. Palepu, 1999, The right way to restructure conglomerates in emerging markets, *Harvard Business Review*, 77 (4): 125–34; M. Schuman & J. L. Lee, 1999, Dismantling of Daewoo shows how radically Korea is changing, *Wall Street Journal*, August 17, A1, A10; J. Webber, H. Dawley, E, Malkin, M. Tanikawa, & I. Katz, 1999, International: As the world restructures, *BusinessWeek Online*, June 14, www.businessweek.com; L. Chang, 1998, Big is beautiful, *Wall Street Journal*, April 30, R9; D. McDermott, 1998, Asian recovery focus shifts to Thailand, *Wall Street Journal*, December 9, A19.

# Restructuring

Another alternative, similar to the internal capital market approach, focuses exclusively on buying and selling other firms' assets in the external market.[75] As in the real-estate business, profits are earned through buying assets low, restructuring them, and selling them as high as possible. This restructuring approach usually entails buying the firm, selling off its assets, such as corporate headquarters, and terminating corporate staff members.

Selling underperforming divisions and placing the remaining divisions under the discipline of rigorous financial controls is an added restructuring action that is often used. Rigorous controls require divisions to follow strict budgets and account regularly for cash inflows and outflows to corporate headquarters. A firm that pursues this approach may have to use hostile takeovers or tender offers. Hostile takeovers have the potential to increase the resistance of the target firm's top-level managers. In these cases, corporate-level managers often are dismissed, while division managers are retained.

Creating financial economies through the purchase of other companies and the restructuring of their assets requires an understanding of significant tradeoffs. Success usually calls for a focus on mature, low-technology businesses. Otherwise, resource allocation decisions become too complex because the uncertainty of demand for high-technology products requires information-processing capabilities that are beyond those of the smaller corporate staffs of firms employing the unrelated-diversification strategy. Service businesses are also difficult to buy and sell in this way because of their client or sales orientation. Sales staffs of service businesses are more mobile than those of manufacturing-oriented businesses and may seek jobs with a competitor, taking their clients with them. This is especially so in professional service businesses such as accounting, law, advertising, consulting, and investment banking. These businesses probably would not create value if a firm that was restructuring using an unrelated-diversification strategy acquired them.

Through the strategic leadership of its CEO, L. Dennis Kozlowski, Tyco International completed 109 acquisitions between 1992 and the beginning of 1999. It is not unusual for this firm to conclude a dozen acquisitions per year. Accordingly, Tyco's revenues grew from $3 billion in 1992 to $23 billion in 1999. However, questions raised toward the end of 1999 resulted in a substantial decline in the value of the firm's stock. The main issue of inquiry revolved around concerns about accounting aberrations of the Bermuda-headquartered firm.[76]

Tyco focuses on buying and restructuring businesses in four market segments: disposable medical supplies, valves, fire protection and electronic security, and electrical and electronic components. Although those businesses are not highly profitable, "he [Kozlowski] squeezes the most out of these operations with ultra-lean and decentralized management. His headquarters staff numbers only about 70, centred around four worldwide managers."[77] As they dispose of larger headquarters staffs in acquired companies, streamline operations, and use Tyco financial control systems, Kozlowski and his small headquarters team improve the overall company performance of their diversified operations.

# DIVERSIFICATION: INCENTIVES AND RESOURCES

The economic reasons given in the last section summarize the conditions under which diversification strategies increase a firm's value. Diversification, however, is often undertaken with the expectation that doing so will prevent a firm from losing some of its value. Thus, there are reasons to diversify that are value-neutral. In fact, some research evidence indicates that all diversification moves may lead to tradeoffs and some level of sub-optimization.[78] Nonetheless, several incentives may lead a firm to pursue further diversification.

## Incentives to Diversify

Incentives to diversify come from both the external environment and a firm's internal environment. The term "incentive" implies that managers have some choice regarding whether to pursue the incentive or not. Incentives external to the firm include antitrust regulation and tax laws. Internal firm incentives include low performance, uncertain future cash flows, and an overall reduction of risk for the firm.

### Antitrust Regulation and Tax Laws

Government antitrust policies and tax laws provided incentives for U.S. firms to diversify in the 1960s and 1970s.[79] The application of U.S. antitrust laws to mergers that created increased market power (via either vertical or horizontal integration) was stringent in the 1960s and 1970s.[80] As a result, many of the mergers during that time were unrelated—that is, they involved companies pursuing different lines of business. Thus, the merger wave of the 1960s was "conglomerate" in character. Merger activity leading to conglomerate diversification was actually encouraged by the U.S. government and its federal laws that discouraged horizontal and vertical mergers. Thus, even as late as the mid-1970s (1973–77), 79.1 percent of all U.S. mergers were of a conglomerate type.[81]

Mergers in the 1980s were different, however. Antitrust enforcement ebbed, permitting more and larger horizontal mergers (acquisitions of target firms in the same line of business, such as a merger between two oil companies).[82] In addition, investment bankers became more freewheeling in the kinds of mergers they would try to facilitate; as a consequence, hostile takeovers increased to unprecedented numbers.[83] Conglomerates or highly diversified firms of the 1960s and 1970s became more focused in the 1980s and 1990s as merger constraints were relaxed, and restructuring was implemented.[84]

There are also tax reasons related to diversification. Some companies (especially mature ones) may have activities that generate more cash than they can reinvest profitably. Michael Jensen, a prominent financial economist, believes that such free cash flows (liquid financial assets for which investments in current businesses are no longer economically viable) should be redistributed to shareholders in the form of dividends.[85] Because dividends were taxed more heavily than ordinary personal income, shareholders preferred that companies retained free cash flows for use in buying and building companies in high-performance industries. If the stock value appreciated over the long term, shareholders might receive a better return on those funds than through dividends, because they would be taxed more lightly under capital gains rules. In addition, since acquisitions typically increase a corporation's depreciable asset allowances, the resulting increased depreciation (non-cash-flow expense) produces lower taxable income, thereby providing an additional incentive for acquisitions.

A loosening of regulations (along with a desire to expand product offerings in order to hold onto and build upon existing franchises) has provided incentives for large banks to become more diversified. By acquiring securities firms, investment banks, and other financial services companies, some large banks have diversified their revenue streams considerably. In the United States, John McCoy became Bank One CEO in 1986. "He transformed a family business into a national powerhouse by aggressively acquiring other regional banks." Bank One became the fourth-largest bank in the United States before its diversified growth led to deterioration in its financial performance. As a result, McCoy resigned, and the bank itself may be a takeover candidate because of its low stock price.[86]

In another diversification move, Citigroup was formed from the merger of Travelers and Citibank. Travelers had formerly merged Solomon and Smith Barney, two investment bank and retail brokerage operations, with its insurance and financial products divisions, once financial deregulation occurred. However, the merger creating Citigroup in mid-1999 struggled to deal with the leadership and cultural integration of the banking, credit card, insurance, and investment businesses.[87]

Deregulation moves in the financial services industry have also provided Canadian banks with opportunities. For example, Royal Bank has taken advantage of opportunities to improve its brokerage, trust, and insurance businesses. In addition to Dominion Securities (which Royal acquired control of in 1988), the Royal Financial Group expanded its brokerage business through its acquisition of investment dealer Richardson Greenshields in 1997. Royal Bank purchased Royal Trust in 1993, and trust services were expanded in 1996 and 1997 by the bank's acquisition of the institutional and pension custody businesses of TD Bank, Montreal Trust, and Scotiabank. Purchases of insurance businesses such as Westbury Canadian Life (1996) and the Canadian operations of Mutual of Omaha (1998) and Prudential's Canadian individual life insurance business (2000) allowed for a more solid foundation for RBC Insurance as well.[88]

In addition to the external incentive to diversify based on antitrust regulation and tax laws, a number of incentives internal to the firm increase the likelihood that diversification will be pursued.

## Low Performance

It has been proposed that "high performance eliminates the need for greater diversification,"[89] as in the example of the Wm. Wrigley Jr. Company. Conversely, low performance may provide an incentive for diversification. Firms plagued by poor performance often take higher risks.[90] Interestingly, though, some researchers have found that low returns are related to greater levels of diversification.[91] Poor performance may lead to increased diversification, especially if resources exist to pursue diversification (when the resources do not exist, research has found diversification to be ill-advised).[92] Continued poor returns following additional diversification, however, may slow the pace of diversification and even lead to divestitures. Thus, an overall curvilinear relationship, as illustrated in Figure 7.5, may exist between diversification and performance.[93]

Lockheed Martin may have diversified beyond its capabilities to manage its level of diversification. The company is the largest defence contractor in the world, primarily because it chose to buy post–Cold War defence assets when other firms were selling them. However, the U.S. government has grown uncomfortable with so much power centred in one defence contractor. When Lockheed Martin was forced to drop its $11.6 billion bid for Northrop Grumman, another defence contractor, in the face of government objections, it sought to acquire Comsat Corporation, which launches and delivers satellites. Lockheed Martin has also been interested in General Electric, a British defence company, and other transatlantic deals, to diversify away from the United States. Financial analysts, however, have driven down Lockheed's stock as it ponders these

■ ■ **FIGURE 7.5**

*The Curvilinear Relationship between Diversification and Performance*

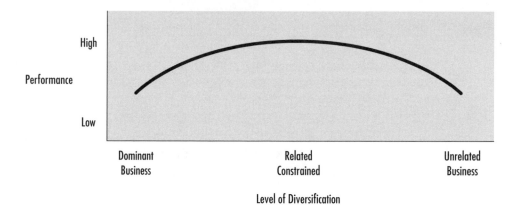

potential deals, because the firm has become so diversified. One analyst questioned, "Has this company just gotten too big and too complex?" In a period when the stock prices of most companies were increasing, Lockheed Martin's price plummeted to a 52-week low at the beginning of the millennium. Although Lockheed's diversification creates strength when the company can integrate its various divisions to bid for contracts, Lockheed's CEO, Peter B. Teets, suggests, "My biggest challenge is to learn how to harness that strength." Evidence suggests that Lockheed Martin's diversification is currently on the downside of the diversification performance curve in Figure 7.5[94]

## Uncertain Future Cash Flows

As a firm's product line matures or is threatened, diversification may be perceived as an important defensive strategy. Small firms and companies in mature or maturing industries sometimes find it necessary to diversify to survive over the long term.[95] Certainly, this was one of the dominant reasons for diversification among railroad firms during the 1960s and 1970s. Railroads diversified primarily because the trucking industry was perceived to have significant negative effects on the demand for rail transportation. Uncertainty, however, can be derived from both supply and demand sources.

Franco Tato is the CEO of ENEL, Italy's state-owned electricity company. Through Tato's leadership, ENEL has diversified its operation to the point where it has moved from a sole focus on electricity to the building of a diversified portfolio that includes telecommunications, water distribution, and Internet services. Accordingly, some have compared ENEL's acquisition spree to becoming a new version of the state-owned IRI, which once owned everything from Italy's telephone lines to Alitalia, the national airline. Furthermore, there are serious questions about whether ENEL is cross-subsidizing its acquisitions with revenues from the electricity side, which would be a questionable practice, because it is a consumer-oriented utility. However, Tato justifies the firm's diversification on the grounds that ENEL's grip on the Italian electricity market is threatened. Deregulation not only in Italy but also across Europe, may mean that ENEL will have to cede 30 percent of its generating capacity to new rivals with cheaper electricity production. One of these rivals may be the state-owned Electricity de France, which is focused on selling its excess electricity across borders. ENEL's plans are to secure overseas contracts to build power stations, because that is a core competence of the company.

However, the main thrust of the firm's diversification strategy is to develop a multiutility that focuses on a portfolio of services in electricity, water, gas, and Internet service, as well as mobile phone customers. One analyst suggested that there might be five to seven large groups of electric producers in Europe. Thus, ENEL's future sources of revenue are threatened. ENEL has responded by using a corporate-level diversification strategy to compete in multiple segments of the utility market.[96]

## Firm Risk Reduction

Research has shown that diversification, particularly unrelated diversification, can aid a firm's likelihood of survival (except when undertaken with insufficient resources).[97] Yet, because diversified firms pursuing economies of scope often have investments that are too inflexible to realize synergy between business units, a number of problems may arise. **Synergy** exists when the value created by business units working together exceeds the value those same units create working independently. But, as a firm increases its relatedness among business units, it also increases its risk of corporate failure,[98] because synergy produces joint interdependence between business units, and the firm's flexibility to respond is constrained. This threat may force two basic decisions.

First, the firm may reduce its level of technological change by operating in more certain environments. This behaviour may make the firm risk averse to, and thus uninterested in, pursuing new product lines that have potential, but are not proven. Alternatively, the firm may constrain its level of sharing activities and forego the benefits of synergy. Either or both decisions may lead to further diversification. The former would lead to related diversification into industries in which more certainty exists. The latter may produce additional, but unrelated, diversification.[99] Research suggests that a firm that pursues a related-diversification strategy is more careful in its bidding for new businesses, whereas a firm that pursues an unrelated-diversification move may more easily overprice its bid. An unrelated bidder may not be aware of all the informational dilemmas that the acquired firm faces.[100]

Boeing, for example, has been diversifying to reduce its dependence on commercial airlines and the frequent cycles in this business line. In 1998, Boeing acquired Rockwell's space division and McDonnell Douglas. Both acquisitions were designed to help Boeing improve its position in commercial space activities. In 2000, Boeing agreed to purchase Hughes Electronics space operations. Hughes divested this unit so that it could better focus on DirectTV and future Internet operations.[101] Boeing also invested in a long-range project with McCaw Cellular and Microsoft to create an Internet-in-the-sky satellite system called Teledesic. The Teledesic system would be the first satellite system with the capability of handling any kind of communication, from voice calls to Internet browsing to video and interactive multimedia. The system would be analogous to throwing a fibre optic net around the world, but in space. Teledesic is different from Motorola's Iridium network, which has been in financial difficulty. The Iridium network was designed to handle only voice communication via mobile phones. These ventures are positioning Boeing as an aerospace firm for the next economic frontier: space. Once it has the Teledesic system in place, Boeing will be a world-class satellite producer and launcher.[102] However, the results of the firm's diversification strategy are as yet uncertain.

**Synergy** exists when the value created by business units working together exceeds the value those same units create when working independently.

## Resources and Diversification

Although a firm may have incentives to diversify, it must possess the resources required to make diversification economically feasible.[103] As mentioned earlier, tangible, intangible, and financial resources may facilitate diversification. Resources vary in their utility for value creation, however, because of differences in rarity and mobility. That is, some resources are easier for competitors to duplicate because they are not rare, valuable, and costly to imitate. For instance, free cash flows may be used to diversify the firm. Because these resources are more flexible and common, they are less likely to create value compared with other types of resources.[104] The earlier-mentioned diversification on the part of steel firms was significantly facilitated by the presence of free cash flows.

Similarly, Anheuser-Busch was a very profitable company, and significant cash flows were created from the success of the brewery business. These resources were used to purchase the St. Louis Cardinals, to invest almost $400 million in the development and operation of the Eagle snack food business, and to acquire the Campbell Taggart bakery business. The use of the resources, however, did not produce significant positive returns for Anheuser-Busch, and as a result, the firm decided to spin off Campbell Taggart, sell the St. Louis Cardinals, and close the Eagle snacks business.[105] Still the world's largest brewing organization, Anheuser-Busch continues to use free cash flows to support its business interests in theme park operations, manufacturing and recycling aluminium beverage containers, rice milling, real-estate development, turf farming, railcar repair and transportation, and paper-label printing, among others.[106] It is the diversification created by this particular mix of businesses that the corporation's executives are able to manage in a way that creates value.

Tangible resources usually include the plant and equipment necessary to produce a product. Such assets may be less flexible: Any excess capacity often can be used only for very closely related products, especially those requiring highly similar manufacturing technologies. Excess capacity of other tangible resources, such as a sales force, can be used to diversify more easily. Again, excess capacity in a sales force would be more effective with related diversification, because it may be utilized to sell similar products. The sales force would be more knowledgeable about related-product characteristics, customers, and distribution channels. Tangible resources may create resource interrelationships in production, marketing, procurement, and technology, defined earlier as sharing activities. Intangible resources are more flexible than tangible physical assets in facilitating diversification. Although the sharing of tangible resources may induce diversification, intangible resources could encourage even more diversification. Clearly, some potential intangible resource synergies could be achieved by Anheuser-Busch. For example, the firm's knowledge of yeast products may have been useful in the operation of Campbell Taggart. It did not, however, produce significant positive synergies between the brewery and bakery businesses, as was hoped by Anheuser-Busch executives.[107]

## Extent of Diversification

If a firm has both the incentives and the resources to diversify, the extent of its diversification will be greater than if it has incentives or resources alone.[108] The more flexibility, the more likely it is that the resources will be used for unrelated diversification; the less flexibility, the more likely it is that the resources will be used for related diversification. Thus, flexible resources (e.g., free cash flows) are likely to lead to relatively greater levels of diversification.[109] Also, because related diversification requires more information processing to manage links between businesses, a small corporate office could manage more unrelated business units.[110]

# MANAGERIAL MOTIVES TO DIVERSIFY

Managerial motives for diversification may exist independently of incentives and resources and include managerial risk reduction and a desire for increased compensation.[111] For instance, diversification may reduce top-level managers' employment risk (the risk of job loss or income reduction). That is, corporate executives may diversify a firm in order to diversify their employment risk, as long as profitability does not suffer excessively.[112] Diversification also provides an additional benefit to managers that shareholders do not enjoy. Diversification and firm size are highly correlated, and as size increases, so does executive compensation.[113] Large firms are more complex and more difficult to manage; thus, managers of larger firms are better compensated.[114] This increased compensation may serve as a motive for managers to engage in greater diversification. Governance mechanisms, such as the board of directors, monitoring by owners, executive compensation, and the market for corporate control, may limit managerial tendencies to overdiversify. These mechanisms are discussed in more detail in Chapter 11.

On the other hand, governance mechanisms may not be strong, and in some instances managers may diversify the firm to the point that it fails to earn even average returns.[115] Resources employed to pursue each line of diversification are most likely to include financial assets (e.g., free cash flows) but may also involve intangible assets. Thus, this type of diversification is not likely to lead to improved performance. The loss of adequate internal governance may result in poor relative performance, thereby triggering a threat of takeover. Although this threat may create improved efficiency by replacing ineffective managerial teams, managers may avoid takeovers through defensive tactics (e.g., golden parachutes and poison pills). Therefore, an external governance threat, although having a restraining influence on managers, does not provide flawless control of managerial motives for diversification.[116]

Most large publicly held firms are profitable because managers are positive agents, and many of their strategic actions (e.g., diversification moves) contribute to the firm's success. As mentioned, governance devices are designed to deal with exceptions to the norms of achieving strategic competitiveness and increasing shareholder wealth in the process. Thus, it is overly pessimistic to assume that managers usually act in their own self-interest as opposed to their firm's interest.[117]

Managers may also be held in check by concerns for their reputation in the labour market. If positive reputation facilitates power, a poor reputation may reduce power. Likewise, a market for managerial talent may deter managers from pursuing inappropriate diversification.[118] In addition, some diversified firms police other diversified firms, acquiring those poorly managed companies in order to restructure their asset base. Knowing that their firms could be acquired if they are not managed successfully, managers are encouraged to find ways to achieve strategic competitiveness.

In summary, although managers may be motivated to increase diversification, governance mechanisms are in place to discourage such action merely for managerial gain. However, this governance is imperfect and may not always produce the intended consequences. Even when governance mechanisms cause managers to correct a problem of overdiversification, these moves are not without tradeoffs. For instance, firms that are spun off may not realize productivity gains, although spinning them off is in the best interest of the divesting firm.[119] Accordingly, the assumption that managers need disciplining may not be entirely correct, and sometimes governance may create consequences that are worse than those resulting from overdiversification.[120]

To receive positive outcomes from a diversification strategy, a company must use a proper amount and type of diversification.[121] The chapter's final Strategic Focus is a recent example of diversification, with final outcomes that are yet to be determined. The transaction is between an Internet provider (AOL) and a media content provider (Time Warner).

As the Strategic Focus suggests, a number of issues are involved in creating an effective diversification strategy. The firm must prepare forthright answers to questions of leadership, the synergistic use of combined resources, and competitive reactions in order for the strategy to improve the company's performance. If the answers to these questions indicate an inability to create value through diversification, then a decision not to become more diversified is required. At the corporate level, value is created through the selection and management of a particular group of businesses that is worth more under the ownership of the acquiring company than it would be under any other ownership.[122]

## STRATEGIC FOCUS

### AOL's Diversification Merger with Time Warner

On January 11, 2000, a merger agreement was announced between AOL, an Internet service provider (ISP), and the media content company Time Warner, whose businesses that include movies, magazines, music, and significant cable TV operations. Both companies have resources and incentives to become more diversified, as Figure 7.5 suggests. In fact, additional levels of diversification solve a number of problems for each firm, but especially for AOL. First, there is much opportunity for resource synergy between the two firms. AOL will be able to advertise *Time* magazine and other Time Warner publications on AOL's Internet sites. Furthermore, Time Warner owns the Book-of-the-Month Club, which gives AOL an opportunity to connect with many new subscribers to its service. In addition, Time Warner music and movies could be made available over the Internet. However, the primary reason for the acquisition is the cable TV assets that provide AOL with broadband speed; Time Warner currently owns the Roadrunner cable modem ISP service. When AT&T bought MediaOne and developed TCI cable modem service, AOL's stock price decreased significantly, because, at the time, AOL did not appear to have a high-speed Internet service option. When the merger with Time Warner is complete, this problem will be solved. Accordingly, many resources will allow for synergistic improvement with both firms.

Some have questioned whether AOL and Time Warner are taking the best course of action. Because AT&T owns 25 percent of Time Warner, AOL must finalize an arrangement with AT&T to get more access to the broadband approach through AT&T's cable operations. The problem is that many service providers have been offering regular modem Internet service for free so that they

*continued*

can get households to spend money on bundled cable TV and local and long-distance telephone services. This development may be especially problematic for AOL because it generates most of its money from its ISP service.

At the time of the announcement of the AOL–Time Warner merger, Yahoo! did not feel that it would need to purchase a company such as Disney; instead, Yahoo! decided that it would rather buy services from a range of media providers, such as Disney and News Corp., as well as from television stations and movie producers. Yahoo! believes that its media needs may be much cheaper to satisfy through purchase on the open market rather than through vertical integration. In addition, Yahoo! can achieve more flexibility that way. Yahoo! feels that the AOL–Time Warner merger is an unproved strategy for an ISP: "It may be more viable for AOL rivals to strike different contract and distribution deals with a number of companies rather than to tie themselves inextricably to one partner."

A number of implementation details also will influence the degree of success that is gained from the diversification created by the AOL–Time Warner merger. Gerald Levin, current CEO of Time Warner, will be the CEO of the new company, while Steve Case, current CEO of AOL, will be the chairman. Case apparently felt that the transaction would not be consummated unless Levin, a very powerful and politically astute individual, was in charge of operations. Fortunately, this plan fit in with Case's leadership style, in that he is more of a strategic thinker than an operations manager. It remains to be seen how successful the efforts to assimilate the two diverse cultures will be: AOL is quite entrepreneurial; in contrast, the culture at Time Warner is stodgier and not focused on running on "Internet time."

AOL's stock price depreciated considerably shortly after the merger was announced, while Time Warner's increased significantly. This combination of events, in which the acquiring firm's stock price declines while that of the target increases, is not unusual. However, how the diverse set of investors will mesh is also an important issue, in that AOL and Time Warner investors have different investment criteria and risk preferences. Nonetheless, several analysts suggested that institutional investors supported the merger. The board of directors will also have an influence on what happens, but only time will tell how the situation will evolve. Eight directors from each firm will be on the board. AOL shareholders will own 55 percent of the newly formed company, Time Warner shareholders 45 percent.

In the long run, the product market and rival's strategic positioning will influence the effectiveness of the merger. AT&T has said that it will not seek to get into media content through such an acquisition. However, the prices of its main products, telecommunications services, are rapidly decreasing, and one wonders whether the company may need to pursue content deals to earn higher profit margins. As mentioned, Yahoo! signalled that it would not get into content in the near future, preferring instead the flexibility to contract for opportunities in that regard with a broad range of providers.

In sum, a number of resources and incentives support the diversification merger between AOL and Time Warner. There also may be managerial motives, especially on the part of Ted Turner (Turner Broadcasting was purchased by Time Warner) and Gerald Levin, who own significant amounts of stock in the new

*continued*

company. Indeed, their net worth has increased with the acquisition. However, the success of the acquisition will depend on a number of leadership, cost, and restructuring issues. Furthermore, how well synergy is realized through the combination of resources will have a significant impact on the well-being of the firm. The reaction by capital and product market players will also play into the success or failure of the diversification move. Finally, conditions placed on the transaction by regulators will influence the success or failure of the merger. Usually, media combinations take longer to pass through the regulatory process, creating at least short-term uncertainty for all parties.

Sources: G. Farrell, 2000, Deal forms multimedia marketer, *USA Today*, January 17, www.usatoday.com; M. Murray, N. Deogun, & N. Wingfield, 2000, Can Time Warner click with AOL? Here are eight things to watch, *Wall Street Journal*, January 14, A1, A16; M. Rose, 2000, Database of merged AOL brings cheers and chills, *Wall Street Journal*, January 14, B6; D. Solomon, 2000, AOL's path to broadband now clear, *USA Today*, January 11, www.usatoday.com; K. Swisher, 2000, Yahoo! posts a loud message: We're not next, *Wall Street Journal*, January 12, B1, B4.

## SUMMARY

- Pursuing a single- or dominant-business corporate-level strategy may be preferable to a more diversified-business strategy, unless a corporation can develop economies of scope or financial economies between business units, or obtain market power through additional levels of diversification. Economies of scope and scale and market power are the main sources of value creation for firm diversification.

- The primary reasons a firm pursues increased diversification are value creation through economies of scope, financial economies, or market power; actions because of government policy, performance problems, or uncertainties about future cash flow; and managerial motivations (e.g., to increase managers' compensation).

- Managerial motives to diversify can lead to over-diversification. On the other hand, managers can also be good stewards of the firm's assets.

- The level of firm diversification is a function of the incentives, firm resources, and the managerial motives to diversify.

- Related diversification can create value by sharing activities or transferring core competencies.

- Sharing activities usually involves sharing tangible resources between businesses. Core competence transfer involves transferring the core competencies developed in one business to another business. It also may involve transferring competencies between the corporate office and a business unit.

- Sharing activities is usually associated with related constrained diversification. Sharing activities is costly to implement and coordinate, may create unequal benefits for the divisions involved in sharing, and may lead to fewer risk-taking behaviours.

- Successful unrelated diversification is accomplished through efficiently allocating resources or restructuring a target firm's assets and placing them under rigorous financial controls.

## REVIEW QUESTIONS

1. What is corporate-level strategy? Why is it important to a diversified firm?

2. Identify the advantages and disadvantages of single- and dominant-business strategies as compared to firms with higher levels of diversification.

3. What are three reasons why firms choose to move from either a single- or a dominant-business position to a more diversified position?

4. How do firms share activities and transfer core competencies to obtain economics of scope, while pursuing a related-diversification strategy?

5. What are the two ways to obtain financial economies when pursuing an unrelated-diversification strategy?

6. What incentives and resources encourage diversification in firms?

7. What motives might encourage managers to engage a firm in more diversification?

## DISCUSSION QUESTIONS

1. This chapter suggests that there is a curvilinear relationship between diversification and performance. How can this relationship be modified so that the negative relationship between performance and diversification is reduced, and the downward curve has less slope or begins at a higher level of diversification?

2. The firms highlighted in *The Globe and Mail*'s Report on Business 1000 are very large, and many of them have some product diversification. Are these firms overdiversified currently and experiencing lower performance than they should? Explain.

3. Is the primary reason for overdiversification industrial policies (such as taxes and antitrust regulation) or because managers pursue self-interest, increased compensation, and reduced risk of job loss? Why? Are the industrial policies in Canada different than those in the United States? Will this have a differential effect on overdiversification in Canada relative to the United States?

4. One rationale for pursuing related-diversification is to obtain market power. In Canada, too much market power, however, may result in a challenge by the federal government (because it may be perceived as anticompetitive). Under what situations might related diversification be considered unfair competition?

5. Assume you have received two job offers—one from a dominant-business firm and one from an unrelated-diversified firm (the beginning net salaries are virtually identical). Which offer would you accept and why?

6. By 2010, do you believe large firms will be more or less diversified than they are today? Why? Will the trends regarding diversification be identical in Canada, Europe, the United States, and Japan? Explain.

7. Go to your university library and obtain the *Canadian Business* Tech 100. This ranking is based on sales and gives the largest 100 technology firms in Canada. Select several from the top ten, go to their Web sites, and assess their level of diversification. Have they stayed focused or become unrelated-diversified firms? The third annual ranking of the Tech 100 was published in the June 12, 2000 issue of *Canadian Business*.

## ETHICS QUESTIONS

1. Assume you overheard the following statement: "Those managing an unrelated-diversified firm face far more difficult ethical challenges than do those managing a dominant-business firm." Based on your reading of this chapter, do you accept or reject this statement? Why?

2. Is it ethical for managers to diversify a firm rather than return excess earnings to shareholders? Provide reasoning in support of your answer.

3. What unethical practices might occur when a firm restructures its operations? Explain.

4. Do you believe ethical managers are unaffected by the managerial motives to diversify discussed in this chapter? If so, why? In addition, do you believe ethical managers should help their peers learn how to avoid making diversification decisions on the basis of the managerial motives to diversify? Why or why not?

## INTERNET EXERCISE

Go to the Report on Business 1000 List at:

**http://www.robmagazine.com/top1000**

Select three firms from the *ROB* 1000 and visit their Web sites. From their Web sites and other Internet resources, determine each firm's level of diversification (see Figure 7.2). For each firm, comment on the appropriateness of its level of corporate diversification given the overall nature of the firm.

## STRATEGIC SURFING

The following Web sites are very helpful for accessing current news stories about Canadian firms. The reports provide current insight into the corporate and business-level company strategies.

**http://www.canada.com/news/cp**

**http://www.robmagazine.com**

**http://www.canadianbusiness.com/index.shtml**

**http://www.nationalpost.com/financialpost/cadbusiness/index.html**

# NOTES

1 B. Orwell, 2000, Disney to recast Go network Web property as entertainment destination, Dow Jones.com archives, www.dowjones.com (Retrieved January 7).

2 M. E. Porter, 1980, *Competitive Strategy* (New York: The Free Press), xvi.

3 T. B. Palmer & R. M. Wiseman, 1999, Decoupling risk taking from income stream uncertainty: A holistic model of risk, *Strategic Management Journal*, 20: 1037–62; K. Ramaswamy, 1997, The performance impact of strategic similarity in horizontal mergers: Evidence from the U.S. banking industry, *Academy of Management Journal*, 40: 697–715.

4 M. A. Hitt, R. E. Hoskisson, & H. Kim, 1997, International diversification: Effects on innovation and firm performance in product-diversified firms, *Academy of Management Journal*, 40: 767–98; W. G. Rowe & P. M. Wright, 1997, Related and unrelated diversification and their effect on human resource management controls, *Strategic Management Journal*, 18: 329–38.

5 D. D. Bergh & M. W. Lawless, 1998, Portfolio restructuring and limits to hierarchical governance: The effects of environmental uncertainty and diversification strategy, *Organization Science*, 9: 87–102; W. Boeker, 1997, Executive migration and strategic change: The effect of top manager movement on product-market entry, *Administrative Science Quarterly*, 42: 213–36; H. A. Haverman, 1993, Organizational size and change: Diversification in the savings and loan industry after deregulation, *Administrative Science Quarterly*, 38: 20–50.

6 M. E. Porter, 1987, From competitive advantage to corporate strategy, *Harvard Business Review*, 65 (3): 43–59.

7 Ibid., 43.

8 Boeker, Executive migration and strategic change; C. A. Montgomery, 1994, Corporate diversification, *Journal of Economic Perspectives*, 8: 163–78.

9 J. Huey, 1997, In search of Roberto's secret formula, *Fortune*, December 9, 230–34.

10 B. Wysocki, Jr., 1999, Corporate America confronts the meaning of a "core" business, *Wall Street Journal*, November 9, A1, A4; J. Kurtzman, 1998, An interview with C.K. Prahalad, in J. Kurtzman (ed.), *Thought Leaders* (San Francisco: Jossey-Bass), 40–51; D. Lei, M. A. Hitt, & R. Bettis, 1996, Dynamic core competences through meta-learning and strategic context, *Journal of Management*, 22: 547–67.

11 C. C. Markides, 1997, To diversify or not to diversify, *Harvard Business Review*, 75 (6): 93–99.

12 C. C. Markides & P. J. Williamson, 1996, Corporate diversification and organizational structure: A resource-based view, *Academy of Management Journal*, 39: 340–67; M. Goold & K. Luchs, 1993, Why diversify? Four decades of management thinking, *Academy of Management Executive*, VII (3): 7–25.

13 A. Roseno & C. Nokkentved, 1997, *Management Processes and Corporate-Level Strategy* (Copenhagen, Denmark: Management Process Institute); A. Campbell, M. Goold, & M. Alexander, 1995, Corporate strategy: The question for parenting advantage, *Harvard Business Review*, 73 (2): 120–32.

14 T. H. Brush, P. Bromiley, & M. Hendrickx, 1999, The relative influence of industry and corporate on business segment performance: An alternative estimate, *Strategic Management Journal*, 20: 519–47; T.H. Brush & P. Bromiley, 1997, What does a small corporate effect mean? A variance components simulation of corporate and business effects, *Strategic Management Journal*, 18: 825–35.

15 J. B. Barney, 1997, *Gaining and Sustaining Competitive Advantage* (Reading, MA: Addison-Wesley).

16 M. A. Hitt, B. W. Keats, & S. DeMarie, 1998, Navigating in the new competitive landscape: Building strategic flexibility and competitive advantage in the 21st century, *Academy of Management Executive*, XII (4): 22–42; T. Mroczkowski & M. Hanaoka, 1997, Effective rightsizing strategies in Japan and America: Is there a convergence of employment practices? *Academy of Management Executive*, XI (2): 57–67.

17 D. J. Collis & C. A. Montgomery, 1998, Creating corporate advantage, *Harvard Business Review*, 76 (3): 70–83.

18 R. Simons & A. Davila, 1998, How high is your return on management? *Harvard Business Review*, 76 (1): 71–80.

19 B. S. Silverman, 1999, Technological resources and the direction of corporate diversification: Toward an integration of the resource-based view and transaction cost economics, *Administrative Science Quarterly*, 45: 1109–24.; D. Collis & C. A. Montgomery, 1995, Competing on resources: Strategy in the 1990s, *Harvard Business Review*, 73 (4): 118–28; M. A. Peteraf, 1993, The cornerstones of competitive advantage: A resource-based view, *Strategic Management Journal*, 14: 179–91.

20 R. P. Rumelt, 1974, *Strategy, Structure and Economic Performance* (Cambridge, MA: Harvard University Press).

21 C. C. Markides, 1995, Diversification, restructuring and economic performance, *Strategic Management Journal*, 16: 101–18.

22 R. E. Hoskisson, M. A. Hitt, R. A. Johnson, & D. S. Moesel, 1993, Construct validity of an objective (entropy) categorical measure of diversification strategy, *Strategic Management Journal*, 14: 215–35.

23 Hitt, Hoskisson, & Kim, International diversification; M. A. Hitt, R. E. Hoskisson, & R. D. Ireland, 1994, A mid-range theory of the interactive effects of international and product diversification on innovation and performance, *Journal of Management,* 20: 297–26.

24 P. Kavanagh, & W. G. Rowe, 2000, *The Mediating Effect of Risk on the Diversification-firm Value Relationship: A Canadian Perspective,* Working Paper, Memorial University of Newfoundland.

25 W. M. Bulkeley, 1994, Conglomerates make a surprising come back with a '90s twist, *Wall Street Journal,* March 1, A1, A6.

26 D. Westell, 1999, Taking the Cott challenge, *Canadian Business,* November 26, 27–28; M. Heinzl & N. Deogun, 1998, Cott loses sparkle due to price war, chairman's health, *Wall Street Journal,* January 6, B8; G. G. Marcial, Why Cott may bubble up, *BusinessWeek,* March 2, 108; Cott Corporation home page, 1998, http://www.cott.com (Retrieved January 13).

27 J. J. Keller, 1997, As AT&T seeks CEO, megadeals pass by, *Wall Street Journal,* October 17, A8.

28 J. Talton, 1997, Late Coke CEO built empire with quiet grace, *Dallas Morning News,* October 26, H3.

29 R. Henkoff, 1995, New management secrets from Japan—really, *Fortune,* November 27, 135–46.

30 A. Bary, 1999, Who wants gum? *Barron's,* September 27, 21–22.

31 Rumelt, Strategy, Structure, and Economic Performance; L. Wrigley, 1970, *Divisional autonomy and diversification* (Ph.D. dissertation, Harvard Business School).

32 J. G. Brenner, 1999, *The Chocolate Wars: Inside the Secret Worlds of Mars and Hershey* (New York: HarperCollins Business).

33 Associated Press, 1997, Psst! Hershey's up to something, *Dallas Morning News,* October 14, D1.

34 E. Nelson, 1999, Wal-Mart, widening its focus, to buy tiny bank, *Wall Street Journal,* June 30, A3.

35 M. Ihlwan, P. Engardio, I. Kunii, & R, Crockett, 1999, Samsung: Howáa Korean electronics giant came out of the crisis stronger than ever, *BusinessWeek Online,* December 20, www.businessweek.com.

36 T. Khanna & K. Palepu, 1997, Why focused strategies may be wrong for emerging markets, *Harvard Business Review,* 75 (4): 41–50.

37 *The Economist,* 1997, Inside story, December 6, 7–9.

38 L. L. Brownlee & J. R. Dorfman, 1995, Birth of U.S. industries isn't without complications, *Wall Street Journal,* May 18, B4.

39 R. Siklos, 1999, Viacom-CBS: They Have It All Now, *BusinessWeek Online,* September 20, www.businessweek.com.

40 G. Crone, 1998, Teknion's US acquisition opens market: Halcon specialist in wood. *National Post,* 1 (51), December 24, D4.

41 M. Farjoun, 1998, The independent and joint effects of the skill and physical bases of relatedness in diversification, *Strategic Management Journal,* 19: 611–30.

42 R. Morck & B. Yeung, 1999, When synergy creates real value, Mastering strategy (Part 7), *Financial Times,* November 8, 6–7.

43 L. Capron, 1999, The long-term performance of horizontal acquisitions, *Strategic Management Journal,* 20: 987–1018; D. J. Teece, G. Pisano, & A. Shuen, 1997, Dynamic capabilities and strategic management, *Strategic Management Journal,* 18: 509–33.

44 M. E. Porter, 1985, *Competitive Advantage* (New York: The Free Press), 328.

45 S. D. Moore, M. Waldholz, & A. Raghavan, 2000, Glaxo Wellcome to buy SmithKline, *Wall Street Journal Interactive Edition,* January 17, www.wsj.com.

46 K. Capell & H. Dawley, 1999, Healing Novartis: As agribiz sours, it shifts to health care, *BusinessWeek Online,* November 1, www.businessweek.com.

47 T. H. Brush, 1996, Predicted change in operational synergy and post-acquisition performance of acquired businesses, *Strategic Management Journal,* 17: 1–24; H. Zhang, 1995, Wealth effects of U.S. bank takeovers, *Applied Financial Economics,* 5: 329–36.

48 D. D. Bergh, 1995, Size and relatedness of units sold: An agency theory and resource-based perspective, *Strategic Management Journal,* 16: 221–39.

49 M. Lubatkin & S. Chatterjee, 1994, Extending modern portfolio theory into the domain of corporate diversification: Does it apply? *Academy of Management Journal,* 37: 109–36.

50 T. Kono, 1999, A strong head office makes a strong company, *Long Range Planning,* 32 (2): 225.

51 Barney, Gaining and Sustaining Competitive Advantage, 367; A. Mehra, 1996, Resource and market based determinants of performance in the U.S. banking industry, *Strategic Management Journal,* 17: 307–22; S. Chatterjee & B. Wernerfelt, 1991, The link between resources and type of diversification: Theory and evidence, *Strategic Management Journal,* 12: 33–48.

52 N. Argyres, 1996, Capabilities, technological diversification and divisionalization, *Strategic Management Journal,* 17: 395–410.

53 C. St. John & J. S. Harrison, 1999, Manufacturing-based relatedness, synergy, and coordination, *Strategic Management Journal,* 20: 129–45.

54 W. G. Shepherd, 1986, On the core concepts of industrial economics, in H. W. deJong & W. G. Shepherd (eds.), *Mainstreams in Industrial Organization* (Boston: Kluwer Publications).

55  J. Gimeno & C. Y. Woo, 1999, Multimarket contact, economies of scope, and firm performance, *Academy of Management Journal*, 42: 239–59; K. Hughes & C. Oughton, 1993, Diversification, multi-market contact and profitability, *Economica*, 60: 203–24.

56  R. Heller, 2000, The man with the big footprint, *Forbes*, January 24, 116–20.

57  J. Ewing & S. Reed, 2000, Can Mannesmann wriggle away?, *BusinessWeek*, January 17, 52–54.

58  A. Karnani & B. Wernerfelt, 1985, Multipoint competition, *Strategic Management Journal*, 6: 87–96.

59  F. I. Smith & R. L. Wilson, 1995, The predictive validity of the Karnani and Wernerfelt model of multipoint competition, *Strategic Management Journal*, 16: 143–60.

60  O. E. Williamson, 1996, Economics and organization: A primer, *California Management Review*, 38 (2): 131–46.

61  E. Karrer-Rueedi, 1997, Adaptation to change: Vertical and horizontal integration in the drug industry, *European Management Journal*, 15: 461–69.

62  C. Palmery, 1999, The integrated BTU, *Forbes*, January 24, 90.

63  K. M Eisenhardt & D. C. Galunic, 2000, Coevolving: At last, a way to make synergies work, *Harvard Business Review*, 78 (1): 91–111.

64  J. A. Byrne, 1998, How Jack Welch runs GE, *BusinessWeek Online*, June 8, www.businessweek.com.

65  *BusinessWeek*, 2000, Live wire Welch, *BusinessWeek*, January 10, 71.

66  M. Sarvary, 1999, Knowledge management and competition in the consulting industry, *California Management Review*, 41 (2), 95–107.

67  T. D. Schellhardt, E. McDonald, & P. Hennessey, 1998, Consulting firms get an unexpected taste of their own medicine, *Wall Street Journal*, October 20, A1, A10.

68  Eisenhardt & Galunic, 2000, Coevolving, 94.

69  D.D. Bergh, Predicting divestiture of unrelated acquisitions; C. W. L. Hill, 1994, Diversification and economic performance: Bringing structure and corporate management back into the picture, in R. P. Rumelt, D. E. Schendel, & D. J. Teece (eds.), *Fundamental Issues in Strategy* (Boston: Harvard Business School Press), 297–321.

70  O. E. Williamson, 1975, *Markets and Hierarchies: Analysis and Antitrust Implications* (New York: Macmillan Free Press).

71  R. Kochhar & M. A. Hitt, 1998, Linking corporate strategy to capital structure: Diversification strategy, type, and source of financing, *Strategic Management Journal*, 19: 601–10.

72  Ibid., P. Taylor & J. Lowe, 1995, A note on corporate strategy and capital structure, *Strategic Management Journal*, 16: 411–14.

73  D. J. Denis, D. K. Denis, & A. Sarin, 1999, Agency theory and the reference of equity ownership structure on corporate diversification strategies, *Strategic Management Journal*, 20: 1071–76; R. Amit & J. Livnat, 1988, A concept of conglomerate diversification, *Journal of Management*, 14: 593–604.

74  Whittington, 1999, In praise of the evergreen conglomerate, 4.

75  S.J. Chang & H. Singh, 1999, The impact of entry and resource fit on modes of exit by multibusiness firms, *Strategic Management Journal*, 20: 1019–35.

76  *BusinessWeek*, 2000, Managers to watch in 2000, *BusinessWeek*, January 10, 69.

77  *BusinessWeek*, 1999, L. Dennis Kozlowski: Compulsive shopper, *BusinessWeek*, January 11, 67.

78  S. Chatterjee & J. Singh, 1999, Are tradeoffs inherent in diversification moves? A simultaneous model for type of diversification and mode of expansion decisions, *Management Science*, 45: 25–41.

79  M. Lubatkin, H. Merchant, & M. Srinivasan, 1997, Merger strategies and shareholder value during times of relaxed antitrust enforcement: The case of large mergers during the 1980s, *Journal of Management*, 23: 61–81.

80  D. L. Smart & M. A. Hitt, 1998, *A Test of the Agency Theory Perspective of Corporate Restructuring*, Working Paper, Texas A&M University.

81  R. M. Scherer & D. Ross, 1990, *Industrial Market Structure and Economic Performance* (Boston: Houghton Mifflin).

82  A. Shleifer & R. W. Vishny, 1994, Takeovers in the 1960s and 1980s: Evidence and implications, in R. P. Rumelt, D. E. Schendel, & D. J. Teece (eds.), *Fundamental Issues in Strategy* (Boston: Harvard Business School Press), 403–22.

83  Lubatkin, Merchant, & Srinivasan, Merger strategies and shareholder value; D. J. Ravenscraft & R. M. Scherer, 1987, *Mergers, Sell-Offs and Economic Efficiency* (Washington, DC: Brookings Institution), 22.

84  P. L. Zweig, J. P. Kline, S. A. Forest, & K. Gudridge, 1995, The case against mergers, *BusinessWeek*, October 30, 122–30; J.R. Williams, B. L. Paez, & L. Sanders, 1988, Conglomerates revisited, *Strategic Management Journal*, 9: 403–14.

85  M. C. Jensen, 1986, Agency costs of free cash flow, corporate finance, and takeovers, *American Economic Review*, 76: 323–29.

86  P. L. Moore 1999, Will a sale be Bank One's salvation? *BusinessWeek Online*, December 23, www.businessweek.com; M. Murray, 1997, Banks look a field to satisfy appetite for expansion, *Wall Street Journal*, July 9, B4.

87  G. Silverman, L. Nathans, J. Rossant, & O. Ullmann, 1999, Citigroup: Is this marriage working? *BusinessWeek Online,* June 7, www.businessweek.com.

88  Royal Bank, 2000, *Royal Bank home page,* http://www.royalbank.com/history/quicktofuture/index.html (Retrieved November 28).

89  Rumelt, *Strategy, Structure and Economic Performance,* 125.

90  R. M. Wiseman & L. R. Gomez-Mejia, 1998, A behavioral agency model of managerial risk taking, *Academy of Management Review,* 23: 133–53; E. H. Bowman, 1982, Risk seeking by troubled firms, *Sloan Management Review,* 23: 33–42.

91  Y. Chang & H. Thomas, 1989, The impact of diversification strategy on risk-return performance, *Strategic Management Journal,* 10: 271–84; R. M. Grant, A. P. Jammine, & H. Thomas, 1988, Diversity, diversification, and profitability among British manufacturing companies, 1972–1984, *Academy of Management Journal,* 31: 771–801.

92  J. P. Sheppard, 1993, Corporate Diversification and Survival, *Journal of Financial and Strategic Decisions,* 6 (1): 113–32.

93  L. E. Palich, L. B. Cardinal, & C. C. Miller, 2000, Curvilinearity in the diversification-performance linkage: An examination of over three decades of research. *Strategic Management Journal,* 21: 155–74.

94  S. Crock, 1999, A lean, mean fighting machine it ain't, *BusinessWeek,* January 11, 41.

95  J. C. Sandvig & L. Coakley, 1998, Best practices in small firm diversification, *Business Horizons,* 41 (3): 33–40; C. G. Smith & A. C. Cooper, 1988, Established companies diversifying into young industries: A comparison of firms with different levels of performance, *Strategic Management Journal,* 9: 111–21.

96  *Financial Times,* 1999, Enel: "Kaiser Franz" nears ambitious goal, *Financial Times,* September 29, www.ft.com; *Financial Times,* 1999, Germany: The monoliths stir, *Financial Times,* September 28, www.ft.com.

97  J. P. Sheppard, 1993, *Corporate Diversification and Survival.*

98  Ibid.

99  N. M. Kay & A. Diamantopoulos, 1987, Uncertainty and synergy: Towards a formal model of corporate strategy, *Managerial and Decision Economics,* 8: 121–30.

100 R. W. Coff, 1999, How buyers cope with uncertainty when acquiring firms in knowledge-intensive industries: Caveat emptor, *Organization Science,* 10: 144–61.

101 J. Cole & A. Pasztor, 2000, Boeing moves closer to satellite-based telecom niche, *Wall Street Journal,* January 14, B4.

102 D. Field, 1999, Boeing diversifies to avoid turbulence; www.usatoday.com (Retrieved February 28); K. Maney & D. Field, 1999, Boeing joins Internet-in-the-sky venture, February 28, www.usatoday.com.

103 Chatterjee & Singh, Are tradeoffs inherent in diversification moves? S. J. Chatterjee & B. Wernerfelt, 1991, The link between resources and type of diversification: Theory and evidence, *Strategic Management Journal,* 12: 33–48.

104 R. Kochhar & M.A. Hitt, 1998, Linking corporate strategy to capital structure, *Strategic Management Journal,* 19: 601–10.

105 R. A. Melchor & G. Burns, 1996, How Eagle became extinct, *BusinessWeek,* March 4, 68–69.

106 Anheuser-Busch Companies, Inc., *Anheuser-Busch home page,* 2000, www.anheuser-busch.com (Retrieved January 18).

107 R. Gibson, 1995, Anheuser-Busch will sell snacks unit, Cardinals, and the club's home stadium, *Wall Street Journal,* October 26, A3, A5; M. Quint, 1995, Cardinals and snack unit are put on block by Busch, *New York Times,* October 26, D2.

108 R. E. Hoskisson & M. A. Hitt, 1990, Antecedents and performance outcomes of diversification: Review and critique of theoretical perspectives, *Journal of Management,* 16: 461–509.

109 Chatterjee & Singh, Are tradeoffs inherent in diversification moves?

110 C. W. L. Hill & R. E. Hoskisson, 1987, Strategy and structure in the multiproduct firm, *Academy of Management Review,* 12: 331–41.

111 W. Grossman & R. E. Hoskisson, 1998, CEO pay at the crossroads of Wall Street and Main: Toward the strategic design of executive compensation, *Academy of Management Executive,* 12 (1): 43–57; A. A. Cannella, Jr. & M. J. Monroe, 1997, Contrasting perspectives on strategic leaders: Toward a more realistic view of top managers, *Journal of Management,* 23: 213–37; S. Finkelstein & D. C. Hambrick, 1996, *Strategic Leadership: Top Executives and Their Effects on Organizations* (St. Paul, MN: West Publishing Company).

112 P. J. Lane, A. A. Cannella, Jr., & M. H. Lubatkin, 1998, Agency problems as antecedents to unrelated mergers and diversification: Amihud & Lev reconsidered, *Strategic Management Journal,* 19, 555–78; D. L. May, 1995, Do managerial motives influence firm risk reduction strategies? *Journal of Finance,* 50: 1291–1308; Y. Amihud & B. Lev, 1981, Risk reduction as a managerial motive for conglomerate mergers, *Bell Journal of Economics,* 12: 605–17.

113 S. R. Gray & A. A. Cannella, Jr., 1997, The role of risk in executive compensation, *Journal of Management,* 23: 517–40; H. Tosi & L. Gomez-Mejia, 1989, The decoupling of CEO pay and performance: An agency theory perspective, *Administrative Science Quarterly,* 34: 169–89.

114  S. Finkelstein & R. A. D'Aveni, 1994, CEO duality as a double-edged sword: How boards of directors balance entrenchment avoidance and unity of command, *Academy of Management Journal, 37*: 1070–1108.

115  R. E. Hoskisson & T. Turk, 1990, Corporate restructuring: Governance and control limits of the internal market, *Academy of Management Review, 15*: 459–77.

116  J. K. Seward & J. P. Walsh, 1996, The governance and control of voluntary corporate spin offs, *Strategic Management Journal, 17*: 25–39; J. P. Walsh & J. K. Seward, 1990, On the efficiency of internal and external corporate control mechanisms, *Academy of Management Review, 15*: 421–58.

117  Finkelstein & D'Aveni, CEO duality as a double-edged sword.

118  E. F. Fama, 1980, Agency problems and the theory of the firm, *Journal of Political Economy, 88*: 288–307.

119  R. A. Johnson, 1996, Antecedents and outcomes of corporate refocusing, *Journal of Management, 22*: 439–83; C. Y. Woo, G. E. Willard, & U. S. Dallenbach, 1992, Spin-off performance: A case of overstated expectations, *Strategic Management Journal, 13*: 433–48.

120  H. Kim & R. E. Hoskisson, 1996, Japanese governance systems: A critical review, in S.B. Prasad (ed.), *Advances in International Comparative Management* (Greenwich, CT: JAI Press), 165–89.

121  Markides, To diversify or not to diversify.

122  Collis & Montgomery, Creating corporate advantage.

# Chapter Eight

## Acquisition and Restructuring Strategies

### LEARNING OBJECTIVES

*After reading this chapter, you should be able to:*

1. Describe why acquisitions have been a popular strategy.
2. List and explain the reasons why firms make acquisitions.
3. Describe seven problems that work against developing a competitive advantage when making acquisitions.
4. Name and describe the attributes of acquisitions that help make them successful.
5. Define restructuring and distinguish among its common forms.
6. Describe how a firm can achieve successful outcomes from a restructuring strategy.

## The Drive for Global Mergers and Acquisitions

Now freed from many regulatory constraints in multiple global markets, telecom firms are using merger and acquisition strategies to develop the economies of scale that are important to competitive success in rapidly changing and cost-sensitive markets and to enter new markets. In early 2000, at a cost of almost $300 billion, Vodafone AirTouch of Britain was set to acquire Mannesmann of Germany. If approved as conceived, the takeover would result in a firm that would dominate the European market with a global base of more than 50 million customers. Reviewing this proposed combination, an analyst stated that "the power that this company will have to call the shots in wireless Internet is enormous." Others believe that "Internet fever" is also a primary driver of what has been seen as a frenzy of merger and acquisition activity among telecommunications companies. For example, MCI WorldCom's proposed $160 billion acquisition of Sprint was necessary, according to MCI's CEO, for the combined company to be a viable competitor in a global arena in which size has an important relationship to profitability. In addition, the acquisition will allow the new firm to become an important participant in Internet-related business transactions. Interestingly, MCI WorldCom is a product of WorldCom's 1998 acquisition of MCI. Yet all the market power that the Sprint acquisition would yield for MCI WorldCom is of critical concern to both North American and European regulators. Because of this concern, regulators studied the deal for a long period of time.

The Internet's commercial potential is also one factor associated with America Online's intended acquisition of Time Warner. According to some analysts, the ability to bundle services together for customers may be the core reason for the acquisition. Describing this possibility, business writers suggested that "Time Warner's extensive cable network can help AOL compete with giants and fast-moving start-ups for the grand prize: the estimated $100 to $150 [U.S.] a month a middle-class household is willing to spend on cable TV, local and long-distance telephone service, and Internet access. Bundling all of that on a single network has become a central strategy of the ... biggest telecom and Internet

http://www.aol.com
http://www.rogers.com
http://www.vodafone.com
http://www.wcom.com

companies." Moreover, it is likely that the commercial potential of bundling "will drive mergers and acquisitions across several industries." Again, all this market power is of grave concern to regulators, and some degree of company restructuring will have to occur before the deal will be completed.

Such service bundling was also the idea behind the Rogers $4 billion bid for Videotron. Rogers' expertise in interactive TV and high-speed Internet was thought to be a good match for Videotron's experience in IP voice over fibre/coaxial cable. The combination would have allowed Rogers to create a company that looks very much like Bell Canada because of its ability to handle telephone and data traffic (but over cable TV lines). Thus, Rogers could have bundled cable, telephone, and Internet connections in a single package. Yet the attraction of becoming a large Internet service provider also drew print media giant Quebecor into the fight. Though Quebecor won the battle, the logic of a Rogers/Videotron association is still likely to create some links between Videotron Rogers and the Quebecor Media division.

Another way the Internet is influencing merger and acquisition activity is through the large number of transactions taking place among Internet firms themselves. An interest in having first-mover advantages influences some of these transactions. By purchasing Internet ventures with strong brand names, the Internet-based firm that acquires them gains access to a critical mass of customers to whom products may be cross-sold. As well, a firm with a strong brand name is harder to dislodge from its market share than competitors without established brands. Examples of acquisitions involving Internet firms acquiring other Internet ventures include Yahoo!'s purchase of Broadcast.com (an Internet broadcaster), Excite@Home's acquisition of iMall (an Internet retailer), and eBay's purchase of Butterfield & Butterfield (an auction house). Amazon.com acquired a host of Internet ventures, including Pets.com and Drugstore.com, in order to expand and diversify its operations.

High levels of acquisition activity among Internet ventures, service providers, and equipment makers had been facilitated by the high valuations of many of these Internet-related companies. These valuations allowed the use of company stock as acquisition currency. However, Internet-related stock valuations dropped through 2000, and into 2001. Equipment provider Nortel dropped two-thirds of its value between July 2000 and February 2001—10 percent of that drop occurring in one day. While the currency companies had used to fund acquisitions—their stocks—have obviously been devalued, some have argued that the value of the companies being acquired are now worth far less because of the decline. Thus, some contend that the price paid for the devalued stocks may accurately reflect the actual value of these acquisitions In addition, these lower values may further dampen the rate of acquisitions as managers at likely targets wait for their firms' valuations to return to more desirable levels.

Finally, venture capital funding had been available at record rates to support growth via acquisitions. This funding is likely to go toward other efforts as future payoffs are now less certain and will probably take longer than was previously the case. Given these factors, the past flood of merger and acquisition activity among Internet-related companies, as well as the number of transactions, is unlikely to continue at the previous torrent.

Sources: T. Corcoran, 2001, Editorial: A whale is beached, The vultures are out, *National Post,* February 20, C15; B. Marotte & K. Damsell, 2000, Pedladeau newest media king, Quebecor boss offers olive branch to rival Rogers by touting future partnerships, *The Globe and Mail,* September 14, B1, B9; B. Quinton, 2000, Hearing IP voices everywhere, *Telephony;* February 14, 19–26; R. Blumenstein, 2000, MCI WorldCom seeks to demonstrate Sprint deal will boost competition, *Wall Street Journal,* January 13, B10; J. Files, 2000, Competition rings in, *Dallas Morning News,* February 6, H1, H2; C. Hill & L. Landro, 2000, Does everybody have to own everything? *Wall Street Journal*, January 12, B1, B4; R. MacLean, 2000, What business is Amazon.com really in? *Inc.,* February, 86–88; *Wire Reports,* 2000, Mannesmann to accept Vodafone's takeover bid, *Dallas Morning News,* February 4, D1, D2; J. Harrison, 1999, Dynamics driving Internet deals, Mergers & Acquisitions, September/October, 49–51; R. Rivlin, 1999, Europeans lift M&A activity in US, *Financial Times,* July 28, 20.

In Chapter 7, we studied corporate-level strategies, focusing on types and levels of product diversification strategies that can build core competencies and create competitive advantage. As noted in that chapter, diversification allows a firm to create value by productively using excess resources.[1] For each strategy we discuss in this book, including diversification strategies and merger and acquisition strategies, the firm creates value only when its resources, capabilities, and core competencies are used productively.[2]

In this chapter, which is related closely to Chapter 7, we explore acquisitions as the dominant means firms use to develop a diversification strategy. In one sense, diversification is a risk management tool, in that its successful use reduces a firm's vulnerability to the consequences of competing in a single market or industry.[3] As suggested in Chapter 1, risk plays a role in the strategies a firm selects to earn above-average returns. In addition, continuous evaluations of risk are linked with a firm's ability to achieve strategic competitiveness.[4]

The purpose of this chapter is to explore acquisition and restructuring strategies. Firms from different industries decide to use an acquisition strategy for several reasons: "Pharmaceutical companies are looking for new products, telecommunications companies are seeking faster ways to get into more households, finance companies want to burst into new services quickly, and high-tech money is constantly chasing creativity."[5] However, acquisition strategies are not without problems. Before describing attributes that evidence suggests are associated with effective acquisitions, we discuss the most prominent problems companies experience when using an acquisition strategy. When acquisitions contribute to poor performance, a firm may deem it necessary to restructure its operations. Closing the chapter are descriptions of three restructuring strategies, as well as the short- and long-term outcomes resulting from their use. Setting the stage for our consideration of all of these topics are brief descriptions of the differences among mergers, acquisitions, and takeovers.

## THE INCREASING USE OF MERGER AND ACQUISITION STRATEGIES

Acquisitions have been a popular strategy among North American firms for many years.[6] Increasingly, acquisition strategies are becoming more popular with firms in other economic regions, including Europe.[7] In fact, in the third quarter of 1999, for the first time the dollar volume of merger and acquisition transactions announced in Europe exceeded the value announced in the United States.[8] As is the case with all strategies, acquisitions indicate a choice a firm has made regarding how it intends to compete.[9] Because each strategic choice affects a firm's performance, the possibility of diversification merits careful analysis.[10] The successful use of an acquisition strategy is another way a firm can differentiate itself from competitors.[11] Being differentiated effectively may benefit the firm in that less direct competition with competitors is experienced when this is the case.[12]

An indicator of the popularity of the acquisition strategy is the labelling of the 1980s as the "merger mania" decade. During that time, depending on whether only acquisitions of entire firms or partial (ownership) acquisitions are counted, the number of acquisitions completed in North America varied from the 30 000 range to over 55 000. The total value of these acquisitions approached $2 trillion.[13] However, the merger and acquisition activity of the 1980s pales in comparison to what occurred in the 1990s.[14] In 1999 alone, about $5 trillion was spent worldwide on mergers and acquisitions, up from about $4 trillion in 1998 and less than $700 billion in 1990. As mentioned in the Opening Case, "the Internet is one key force driving this activity, merger experts say. With the Internet wrecking the traditional sales and distribution formulas for everything from cars to computers, even established companies believe they are at risk."[15] Recently, for example, Staples decided to form alliances with some small Internet companies and acquire others, "to offer an array of small-business services on the Web including payroll management, insurance, and high-speed Internet connections and other phone services." In part, this strategic action was taken as a competitive response to competitor Office Depot's earlier entry into Internet sales, as well as because of the conviction within Staples' top management team that being able to sell on the Internet is "a matter of survival."[16]

Another trend in acquisition strategies is the rapid increase in the number of acquisitions completed between firms based in different countries.[17] These transactions are called cross-border acquisitions.[18] In Chapter 9, we discuss cross-border alliances. Sharing similar characteristics, cross-border acquisitions and cross-border alliances are strategic alternatives firms consider in the pursuit of strategic competitiveness and above-average returns, as are domestic alliances and acquisitions.

The strategic management process (see Figure 1.1) calls for an acquisition strategy to increase a firm's strategic competitiveness as well as its returns to shareholders. Thus, an acquisition strategy should be used only when the acquiring firm will be able to increase its economic value through ownership and the use of an acquired firm's assets.[19]

However, evidence suggests that, at least for acquiring firms, acquisition strategies may not result in these desirable outcomes. Recently, for example, a survey by accounting and consulting firm KPMG estimated that 83 percent of mergers failed to increase shareholder value in acquiring firms; indeed, in 53 percent of the transactions, shareholder value in acquiring firms was actually reduced![20] These results are consistent with those obtained through studies by academic researchers, who have found that shareholders of acquired firms often earn above-average returns from an acquisition, while shareholders of acquiring firms are less likely to do so, typically earning returns from the transaction that are close to zero.[21] Apparently, investors anticipate this state of affairs, as is indicated by the fact that, in approximately two-thirds of all acquisitions, the acquiring firm's stock price falls immediately after the intended transaction is announced. This negative response is viewed by some as an indication of "investors' skepticism about the likelihood that the acquirer will be able both to maintain the original values of the businesses in question and to achieve the synergies required to justify the premium."[22]

# Mergers, Acquisitions, and Takeovers: What Are the Differences?

A **merger** is a strategy through which two firms agree to integrate their operations on a relatively co-equal basis because they have resources and capabilities that together may create a stronger competitive advantage.

An **acquisition** is a strategy through which one firm buys a controlling, or 100 percent, interest in another firm with the intent of using a core competence more effectively by making the acquired firm a subsidiary business within its portfolio.

A **takeover** is a type of an acquisition strategy wherein the target firm did not solicit the acquiring firm's bid.

A **merger** is a strategy through which two firms agree to integrate their operations on a relatively co-equal basis because they have resources and capabilities that together may create a stronger competitive advantage. The transaction between Reckitt & Coleman of the United Kingdom and Benckiser of the Netherlands is an example of a merger. The deal joined firms with complementary products and geographical penetration. Because the merger created the world's leading household cleaning products group, the new firm had substantial market power that was expected to lead to significant cost reductions and improved profitability.[23] An **acquisition** is a strategy through which one firm buys a controlling, or 100 percent, interest in another firm with the intent of using a core competence more effectively by making the acquired firm a subsidiary business within its portfolio.[24] Usually, the management of the acquired firm reports to its counterparts in the acquiring firm. Most mergers are friendly transactions, whereas acquisitions include unfriendly takeovers.

A **takeover** is a type of an acquisition strategy wherein the target firm did not solicit the acquiring firm's bid. For example, Quebecor's $4.9 billion offer for Groupe Videotron was a takeover bid. The bid came on the heels of a bid of $4.2 billion from Rogers Communications. The Chagnon family—who control the majority of Videotron stock—preferred the Rogers bid since it would have had Videotron shareholders become part of a telecommunications company able to take on Bell Canada. However, Quebecor not only made a larger offer but also had the backing of the Caisse de depôt et placement du Quebec. Caisse, the Quebec pension fund administrator, had shareholder agreements with Videotron that effectively vetoed the Rogers deal.[25]

In early 2000, a generally favourable worldwide economic climate and a strong stock market—along with occasional peculiar shareholder arrangements (as shown above)—have created an environment in which few firms were safe from the possibility of a hostile takeover. According to some analysts, in the global economy, "the ability to use stock as a currency and finance enormous transactions means a company can run, but it can't hide" from an unsolicited takeover bid.[26] Even a company as large as General Motors is not immune from takeover speculation. The reason for this is primarily the value of its majority stake in Hughes Electronics. Because of its ownership position in Hughes, GM's assets are worth substantially more than its market capitalization.[27] On a comparative basis, acquisitions occur more commonly than mergers and takeovers. Accordingly, this chapter focuses on acquisitions.

# REASONS FOR ACQUISITIONS

In this section, we discuss reasons that support the active use of an acquisition strategy, as well as a decision to occasionally acquire another company.[28] In contrast to these appropriate reasons, managerial ego does not justify a decision to merge with or acquire another firm. For example, an out-of-control ego might cause a manager to acquire other companies to increase the firm's size, even when doing so may be at the expense of profitability. Hard to detect as a decision criterion in individual transactions, egos nonetheless have been known to influence a number of merger and acquisition decisions.[29]

## Increased Market Power

A primary reason for acquisitions is to achieve greater market power.[30] Defined in Chapter 6, market power exists when a firm is able to sell its goods or services above competitive levels or when the costs of its primary or support activities are below competitors'. Many companies may have core competencies but lack the size to exercise their resources and capabilities. Market power usually is derived from the size of the firm and its resources and capabilities to compete in the marketplace. Therefore, most acquisitions designed to achieve greater market power entail buying a competitor, a supplier, a distributor, or a business in a highly related industry to allow exercise of a core competence and gain competitive advantage in the acquiring firm's primary market. As noted in Chapter 6, Nortel was making $20 billion of acquisitions per year to maintain its market power in switching, wireless, and broadband network systems, as well as its leadership in high-capacity data and voice network fibre optic systems. These acquisitions, as noted earlier, allow Nortel to stay technologically ahead of Lucent and Cisco (particularly in some software segments).[31] Firms use horizontal, vertical, and related acquisitions to increase their market power. These are discussed below.

### Horizontal Acquisitions

The acquisition of a firm competing in the same industry and at the same place in the value chain is referred to as a horizontal acquisition.[32] Horizontal acquisitions increase a firm's market power by exploiting cost-based and revenue-based synergies.[33] For example, Taiwan Semiconductor Manufacturing's acquisition of competitor Worldwide Semiconductor Manufacturing is expected to increase the firm's manufacturing capacity by at least 14 percent (through revenue-based synergies) and preserve its "lead in a contract-manufacturing market that by 2003 will account for 12 percent of the semiconductor industry's total business."[34]

Research suggests that horizontal acquisitions of firms with similar characteristics result in higher performance than when firms with dissimilar characteristics combine operations. Examples of important similar characteristics include strategy, managerial styles, and resource allocation patterns. Similarities in these characteristics make the integration of the two firms proceed more smoothly.[35] When Nepean, Ontario's JDS Fitel merged with San Jose, California's Uniphase, analysts praised the $6 billion deal. Both companies were optoelectronics firms that designed and sold fibre optic telecommunications components and modules. Although their customers are typically the same companies, the components bought from each are different. The combined JDS Uniphase allows buyers more one-stop shopping. Top management of the firm was initially complimentary. JDS founder, Jozef Straus was "a quirky PhD who founded JDS with some co-workers from Northern Telecom ..." and generally avoids the public.[36] Uniphase CEO Kevin Kalkhoven worked well in the spotlight.[37] Though Kalkhoven has since retired, Straus proved equally adept at running the firm and has completed some of the biggest mergers in the firm's history. Though hit by the downturn in tech stocks, the company is seen as very sound operationally.

### Vertical Acquisitions

A vertical acquisition refers to a firm's acquiring a supplier or distributor of one or more of its goods or services. A firm becomes vertically integrated through this type of acquisition, in that it controls additional parts of the value chain (see Chapter 4). Although promising in terms of increasing the firm's performance, vertical acquisitions have the potential to alienate some of a firm's customers. PepsiCo discovered this effect after acquiring Pizza Hut, Taco Bell, and KFC. One objective of these acquisitions was to use the three restaurant chains as distribution channels to sell the company's drinks. Aware of this, Coca-Cola convinced Wendy's and other fast food chains that selling Pepsi in their stores indirectly benefited those of their competitors that PepsiCo owned.[38] As noted in the Strategic Focus near the end of this chapter, Pepsi later spun off its three food units to form Tricon, a separate entity. Thus, firms must balance anticipated benefits of a vertical acquisition with potential risks.[39]

## Related Acquisitions

The acquisition of a firm in a highly related industry is referred to as a related acquisition. Carnival, the large cruise line firm, intended to acquire Fairfield Communities, a rapidly growing company competing in the time-share vacation business. The transaction was to be completed through a $1 billion stock swap. Carnival executives envisioned synergies by attaching the company's well-known brand name to Fairfield's properties in an effort to cross-sell products; cruise customers were to be offered time-share opportunities, while time-share customers were to be given chances to take a Carnival cruise. Also supporting Carnival's interest in this related acquisition was the belief that the firm faced a "dearth of opportunities in cruise-line acquisitions."[40]

However, about a month after the initial announcement, Carnival abandoned its attempt to acquire Fairfield. Influencing this decision was the stock market's reaction to Carnival's strategic intentions. Following the announcement that it sought to acquire Fairfield, the value of each firm's stock dropped dramatically (41 percent for Carnival, 27 percent for Fairfield). Thus, especially when stock swaps are involved, companies must anticipate a careful scrutiny of their merger and acquisition strategies by investors and financial analysts.[41] In this instance, investors apparently were not persuaded that an acquisition based on the firms' apparent relatedness would be in shareholders' best interests.

Acquisitions intended to increase market power are subject to regulatory review, as well as to analysis by financial markets (as in Carnival's intended acquisition of Fairfield). Thus, firms seeking growth and market power through acquisitions must understand the political/legal segment of the external environment (see Chapter 2) in order to successfully use an acquisition strategy. For example, in early 2000, the U.S. Surface Transportation Board voted to impose a 15-month moratorium on all railroad mergers after Canadian National announced its intention to merge with the Burlington Northern Santa Fe.[42] The combined railroad was to have been headquartered in Montreal and would have been the largest in North America. Though the new firm would certainly have possessed market power, the basis for the Surface Transportation Board moratorium effectively thwarted the merger on different grounds. As discussed in the Strategic Focus, the board's assessment was that the proposed transaction would likely cause interruptions in service that would be intolerable for shippers.

## STRATEGIC FOCUS

http://www.cn.ca

http://www.bnsf.com

*The Canadian National and Burlington Northern Santa Fe:*
*A Case of Intentions and Realities in the World of Acquisitions*

At the end of 1999, two of North America's largest railroads announced a merger that would create the continent's largest rail transportation company. Combined, Montreal-based Canadian National (CN) and Fort Worth, Texas–based Burlington Northern Santa Fe (BNSF) would have controlled a total of about 80 000 km of track—twice the distance around the world.

The railroads cover an impressive geographic territory. The CN operates coast to coast in Canada and, through its ownership of the Illinois Central, from Canada to the Gulf of Mexico. BNSF covers the Western two-thirds of the United States and its rails stretch from the U.S. Pacific Northwest and Southern California to the U.S. Midwest and Southeast. BNSF runs the busiest trailer and container-handling rail facility in the world.

The merger is nothing new for either company. In fact, almost all North American railroads have a long history of mergers. The Canadian National itself was created by a set of mergers. At the beginning of the 20th century, the Canadian Northern and the Grand Trunk Railways offered alternatives to the Canadian Pacific. To support these Western railroads, the government built the National Transcontinental Railway in the East. During World War I, the rail system lost regular British financing to the war effort, and the Canadian government pressed railroads into war service with little financial reward. Almost all the major rail carriers fell heavily into debt. To save these lines, the federal government took over a number of them, including the Canadian Northern, and combined it with its own National Transcontinental. By 1923, the government had integrated the ailing Grand Trunk with these other lines to form the "Canadian National."

The Canadian National would remain as much government agency as business enterprise until the early 1990s, when new management sought to make the railway more of a commercially viable venture. By the end of 1995, the railway was financially healthy enough to be privatized. By 1999, the Canadian National possessed enough resources and was run well enough to swallow up the Illinois Central Railroad. This acquisition allowed CN to have links from the West to the East to the Gulf coasts. The next logical step would be to combine the company with another well-run railroad to gain greater geographic coverage. The BNSF offered that coverage. The two roads met at critical points and had complementary geographic coverage (i.e., except for some parallel lines in the West, their routes did not overlap).

The BNSF was no stranger to the merger game either. The story of the BNSF is one of success sandwiched between failure and chaos. When the Pennsylvania and New York Central Railroads merged in 1968—after a century of bitter rivalry—to become Penn Central —it signalled a new regulatory acceptance in the United States of large railroad mergers. It was within this environment that four U.S. railroads with interlocking ownership were granted regulatory approval to merge. In 1970, those railroads became the Burlington Northern (BN). Oddly, the BN was born in the same year that the Penn Central was to become the largest bankruptcy in the United States to that point in time. Saddled with too much debt, conflicts between railway workers that were brought up in

*continued*

different and rivalrous corporate cultures, and poor management, the Penn Central Railroad was driven out of business.

The BN, however, went on to become a successful transportation company that, in 1995, merged with Santa Fe Railway to form BNSF. The merger spurred the giant Union Pacific to acquire Southern Pacific (SP). This combination, however, proved to be disastrous. SP had failed to make adequate investments in physical facilities, and the combined firm required unexpected increases in numbers of locomotives and staff. To reduce costs, Union Pacific had encouraged Southern Pacific personnel to leave the company. The resulting loss of institutional knowledge meant that in many cases sections of the railway could not run properly. At times, more than 1000 railroad cars were stuck in limbo in the Union Pacific system. Rail customers switched to trucking their goods at an increased cost estimated to be close to $2 billion.

The Union and Southern Pacific combination spurred others to merge. The results of these mergers were also poor. The 1998 purchase of Conrail by CSX and Norfolk Southern was labelled "one of the worst mergers in U.S. rail history." The traffic congestion caused by that merger cost the Eastern U.S. division of CN rival Canadian Pacific millions of dollars in additional fuel, crew, and equipment. Union Pacific's acquisition of the Chicago North Western created similar problems at its Chicago and St. Paul terminal areas. Traffic was delayed or misrouted. Shipments that normally move in about two weeks took five weeks. Shippers as far away as British Columbia were affected. Again, many customers gave up on the railroads and found other ways to transport their freight.

It was with these particular merger disasters in mind that the stage was set for scuttling the CN–BNSF merger. There were also reasonable fears that another round of mergers would force the remaining railways into a rapid consolidation. Such moves would cause further deterioration of service in the short run. Thus, immediately after the CN-BNSF merger announcement, forces on both sides of the border sought to halt the merger, in spite of the fact that the merger promised to save the combined company $1.2 billion, CN had done reasonably well at integrating the Illinois Central, and BN had performed similarly with the Santa Fe. The organizational disasters of other rail carriers haunted the rail merger business. Competitors, customers, and government officials publicly voiced objections to the proposed combination.

In addition to public resistance, the merger faced review by the Surface Transportation Board in the United States and the Competition Bureau in Canada. The American body held its hearings first and scheduled 160 witnesses from both the United States and Canada. Rival railways could legitimately object on the grounds that the merger would reduce competition. Shippers saw the potential for the delays that had plagued other mergers. Finally, politicians—especially in Western Canada—were concerned that competition to ship freight to the Port of Vancouver and along Prairie rail lines would virtually disappear because the CN and BNSF rails ran parallel to each other in these areas. While worries about the ability of the two railroads to smoothly integrate began the move to stop the merger, it was the potential exercise of market power by the CN–BNSF that, for

*continued*

now, sealed the merger's fate. In the first part of 2000, U.S. regulators imposed a 15-month moratorium on such alliances. Only four months after the firms announced the combination, they were forced to issue a joint statement calling off the proposed $28 billion merger.

Sources: Canadian National, 2000, *CN home page*, http://www.cn.ca (Retrieved September 16); Burlington Northern Santa Fe, 2000, *BNSF home page*, http://www.bnsf.com (Retrieved September 16); P. Fitzpatrick, 2000, Ottawa looks at hearings on CN rail merger, *National Post*, March 10, C1, C4; CPR asks US authorities to stop CNR BNSF rail mega merger, 2000, *Canadian Press Newswire*, March 3; M. A. Hitt, R.D. Ireland, and R. E. Hoskisson, Chaos on the railroads after acquisition, *Strategic Management, Competitiveness and Globalization*, 3rd Edition: 251–52; Bill Hough, 1997, Book Review: The wreck of the Penn Central by Joseph R. Daughen and Peter Binzen. Review taken from the misc.transport.rail.americas newsgroup, originally posted October 4, 1997, http://prozac.cwru.edu/jer/pc/docs/wreckpc.html (Retrieved September 16, 2000).

## Overcoming of Entry Barriers

Barriers to entry (introduced in Chapter 3) are factors associated with the market, or firms operating in it, that increase the expense and difficulty new ventures face when trying to enter a particular market. For example, well-established competitors may be producing their goods or services in quantities through which significant economies of scale are gained. In addition, enduring relationships with customers often create product loyalties that are difficult for new entrants to overcome. When facing differentiated products, new entrants typically must spend considerable resources to advertise their goods or services and may find it necessary to sell at a price below competitors' to entice customers. Facing the barriers created by economies of scale and differentiated products, a new entrant may find the acquisition of an established company to be more effective than attempting to enter the market as a competitor offering a good or service that is unfamiliar to current buyers. In fact, the higher the barriers to market entry, the greater the probability that a firm will acquire an existing firm to overcome them. Although an acquisition can be expensive, it does provide the new entrant with immediate market access.

Entry barriers firms face when trying to enter international markets (i.e., markets outside their home country) are often quite steep. In response, acquisitions are commonly used to overcome those barriers. Being able to compete successfully in international markets is becoming increasingly critical, in that, in general, global markets are growing at more than twice the rate of domestic markets.[43] At least for large multinational corporations, another indicator of the importance of entering and then competing successfully in international markets is the fact that five emerging markets (Brazil, China, India, Indonesia, and Mexico) are among the 12 largest economies in the world, with a combined purchasing power that is already one-half that of the Group of Seven industrial nations (Britain, Canada, France, Germany, Italy, Japan, and the United States).[44]

### Cross-Border Acquisitions

Acquisitions made between companies with headquarters in different countries are called cross-border acquisitions. These kinds of acquisitions are often made to overcome entry barriers. In Chapter 10, we examine cross-border alliances and the reason for their use.

Cross-border acquisitions and cross-border alliances are strategic alternatives firms consider while pursuing strategic competitiveness. Compared to a cross-border alliance, a firm has more control over its international operations through a cross-border acquisition.[45]

Historically, U.S. firms have been the most active acquirers of companies outside their domestic market. Canada, in particular, feels the effects of this investment. A majority of the approximately one-quarter trillion dollars (Canadian) of Foreign Direct Investment (FDI) in Canada is from U.S. companies.[46] Canadian FDI into other countries exceeds such investment others have into Canada. As well, the largest part, though not a majority, of Canadian FDI is invested in the United States.[47] Although some analysts have decried the degree of U.S. investment in Canada, others have noted that foreign control of Canadian companies, as a percent of assets, has levelled out over the last decade.[48] In addition, Canadians are also buying more U.S. firms than vice versa. For example, in the second quarter of 2000, U.S. companies bought 30 Canadian firms for a total of $4.4 billion, and Canadian companies bought 66 U.S. firms for $6.3 billion.[49]

In the global economy, companies throughout the world are choosing the strategic acquisition option with increasing frequency. Even the traditional predators in the takeover market, U.S. companies, are finding that they are now the prey. In 1999, non-U.S. companies acquired U.S.$271 billion of U.S. firm assets. U.S. firms spent only U.S.$139 billion to buy foreign entities during the same period.[50]

Because of relaxed regulations, the amount of cross-border activity among nations within the European community also continues to increase. Accounting for this growth in a range of cross-border acquisitions, some analysts believe, is the fact that "many large European corporations seem to have come to the conclusion in recent years that they had reached the limits of growth within their domestic markets, and in order to preserve their strategic position, they had to be more aggressive in doing deals in foreign markets."[51] Firms in all types of industries are completing cross-border acquisitions. For example, in the cosmetics industry, Japan's Shiseido created a new division to pursue mergers and acquisitions. With its growth long fuelled by acquisitions, the firm is now committed to emphasizing the cross-border variety, especially with European companies.[52]

Although used increasingly in multiple settings, financial services and telecommunications are industries in which cross-border mergers and acquisitions are prominent as a means of industry consolidation. For example, the Belgian-Dutch financial giant Fortis paid $2.6 billion to acquire American Bankers Insurance Group. At the time, analysts labelled the transaction the latest in a spate of cross-border mergers and acquisitions in the insurance industry.

European pension funds are also expanding rapidly in the global market. A great deal of this growth is occurring through cross-border transactions, with more than two-thirds of 1999's mergers and acquisitions among these firms involving companies outside a firm's domestic market. Analysts also anticipated that Europe's first major cross-border banking merger would take place in the near future. Unicredito SpA of Italy and Banco Bilbao Vizcaya Argentaria, the recently merged Spanish bank, were top candidates for such a transaction.

The global auto industry is also being consolidated through companies' strategic actions, including cross-border acquisitions. The Strategic Focus discusses the reported merger between DaimlerBenz and Chrysler Corporation as an example of consolidation through cross-border acquisitions.

## STRATEGIC FOCUS

### DaimlerBenz and Chrysler Corporation: Will It Be a Successful Union?

At the time of its announcement, the merger between DaimlerBenz and Chrysler Corporation was the world's largest. A horizontal merger, this cross-border transaction was intended to create market power and generate synergies on which the world's preeminent automotive, transportation, and services company could be built. An immediate outcome of the merger was some additional consolidation of the global auto industry.

Each of the former competitors had needs that the merger was supposed to address. Chrysler lacked the infrastructure and management depth required to be a truly global automobile company. DaimlerBenz executives concluded that increasingly intense competitive rivalry in its core luxury-car segment made it necessary for their firm to diversify its product line and distribution channels. Recognizing these respective needs, some analysts believed that the two firms were a complementary fit for at least two reasons. First, Chrysler's dominant market position was in North America as well as a stake in Asian producer Mitsubishi, while DaimlerBenz's presence was stronger in two regions—Europe and South America—where Chrysler lacked a meaningful presence. Second, the companies' product lines were complementary: The bulk of Chrysler's profitability was earned from sport utility vehicles and multipurpose vans, whereas luxury vehicles were the foundation of DaimlerBenz's automotive-based strategic competitiveness.

As discussed previously, horizontal acquisitions can create cost- and revenue-based synergies. DaimlerBenz and Chrysler expected to generate both types of synergies through their merger. For example, the integration of separate operations was expected to reduce costs by about 1.3 billion euros in 1999 alone (Can$1.8 billion). The decision to build the Mercedes M-Class cars and the Jeep Grand Cherokee on the same production line in Graz, Austria, is one of the integration projects that was started immediately in the combined firm. In fact, DaimlerChrysler wanted the Graz facility to showcase its ability to generate cost-based synergies by integrating previously independent manufacturing operations. On the revenue side, the new firm seeks cross-selling synergies by integrating DaimlerBenz's competencies in technological innovations with Chrysler's ability to rapidly introduce new products into the marketplace.

Initial results were encouraging; it appeared that Daimler's decision-making style enabled Chrysler to get products to market quickly. The new firm's 1999 financial performance was heartening as well: operating profit was approximately 11 billion euros for the year, up from 8.6 billion euros in 1998. In addition, company officials were optimistic about the future, predicting that sales volume would climb from 155 billion euros in 1999 to at least 158 billion euros in 2000 and 172 billion euros by 2002. As well, positions articulated by DaimlerChrysler in early 2000 suggested confidence in the results of the cross-border acquisition that formed the company, as well as a commitment to continued growth by using the same strategic option.

Although framed around anticipated benefits, the DaimlerChrysler cross-border transaction has been questioned and criticized. Some thought that inte-

*continued*

grating the firms' computer systems would be quite difficult as would be determining how product development decisions were to be made. Others have noted the difference in corporate cultures. One executive at another automaker noted that "The Chrysler culture was 'Live on the edge; be a little bit crazy." Yet this same commentator noted that Daimler's German culture was "all about order and rules."

Critics also argued that the companies' estimates of cost- and revenue-based synergies were far too optimistic. In fact, by late 2000, reports out of Detroit were that, far from declining, costs were running too high—most notably on new products such as the 2001 minivan and the 2002 Liberty. As costs spiralled upward, North American profits crashed. Before 2000 ended, conditions at Chrysler were projected to create a decline in DaimlerChrysler earnings to half of the previous year. Predictions were for a loss of $1 to $3 billion for Chrysler in 2001.

Compounding this issue was the perception that an acquisition, rather than a merger, had occurred. Actions witnessed in the combined firm quickly indicated that in actuality, DaimlerBenz had acquired Chrysler. Because of the cost problems already noted, Daimler CEO Jurgen E. Schrempp replaced Chrysler's CEO with DaimlerBenz executive Dieter Zetsche. Zetsch brought in Wolfgang Bernhard from Mercedes to be Chrysler's new Chief Operating Officer. To cut costs, the German team quickly demanded that, by 2003, suppliers must reduce their prices by 5 percent, a move that made suppliers angry, and created customer worries about quality.

Currently, DaimlerChrysler is the world's fifth-largest automaker (behind General Motors, Ford, Toyota, and Volkswagen). Company executives noted that one of their key objectives was to become the largest transportation company in the world by 2003. To reach this objective, DaimlerChrysler intended to acquire other firms and form an array of strategic alliances. Yet, with the application of the type of not so subtle management changes made at Chrysler, the firm may have a hard time convincing others to combine with it. However, if it manages to lure others to work with it (the company has a 34 percent stake in Mitsubishi), combinations such as DaimlerChrysler would almost certainly result in further consolidation of the world's auto industry.

Sources: T Burt, 2001, Chrysler prepares for a shakeup of top managers, *National Post,* February 21, C1, C8. A. Taylor III, 2001, DaimlerChrysler gives workers das boot, *Fortune,* February 19, 40; J. Flint, 2001, Chrysler can be fixed, *Forbes;* January 22, 106; J. Muller, J. Green, & C. Tierney, 2001 Chrysler's rescue team *BusinessWeek,* January 15, 48–50; D.C. Steinberg, 2001, Chrysler's cost-cutting has one driver scared, *BusinessWeek,* January 15; M. A. Hitt, J. S. Harrison, & R. D. Ireland, 2001, *Creating Value through Mergers and Acquisitions: A Complete Guide to Successful M&As* (New York: Oxford University Press); J. Ball & S. Miller, 2000, Daimler profit accelerated 87 percent to $1.1 billion in 4th quarter, *Wall Street Journal,* February 29, A17, A19; J. Ball & S. Miller, 2000, DaimlerChrysler is aiming for top spot, *Wall Street Journal,* January 14, A10; S. Miller, 2000, Daimler results climbed to top of expectations for last year, *Wall Street Journal,* February 28, A21, A23; J. Flint, 1999, A letter to Jurgen Schrempp, *Forbes,* May 31, 168; R. Simison & S. Miller, 1999, Making "digital" decisions, *Wall Street Journal,* September 24, B1, B4.

## Cost of New Product Development

Developing new products internally and successfully introducing them into the market-place often requires significant investments of a firm's resources, including time, making it difficult to earn a profitable return quickly.[53] Also of concern to firms' managers are estimates that almost 88 percent of innovations fail to achieve adequate returns from the capital invested in them.[54] Perhaps contributing to these less-than-desirable rates of return is the fact that approximately 60 percent of innovations are successfully imitated within four years after patents are obtained. Because of outcomes such as these, managers often perceive internal product development as a high-risk activity.[55]

Acquisitions are another means through which a firm can gain access to new products and to current products that are new to the firm. Compared to internal product development processes, acquisitions provide more predictable returns as well as faster market entry. Returns are more predictable because the performance of the acquired firm's products can be assessed prior to completing the acquisition.[56] Pharmaceutical firms frequently use acquisitions to enter markets quickly, to overcome the high costs of developing products internally, and to increase the predictability of returns on their investments. For example, the acquisition of Novopharm, Canada's second-largest generic drug company, allowed Israel's Teva Pharmaceutical Industries to get a quick entry point into the North American market.[57] Similarly, acquiring TheraTech gave Watson Pharmaceuticals access to more than 50 patents in advanced drug-delivery systems. Watson intends to use these patented systems to help it create opportunities for new products.[58]

In a broader context, evidence shows that acquisition activity is extensive throughout the pharmaceutical industry. According to business analysts, "There's good reason" for this, in that "patents on stalwart drugs—generating $16 [U.S.] billion in annual revenue—are expiring" in the near future. Compounding the seriousness of this issue is the fact that "some companies don't have adequate substitutes in their research pipelines." Without internally generated products, acquiring other firms, followed by cost reductions, is an attractive strategic option for many of these companies.[59] Recently, large pharmaceutical companies have chosen to acquire a number of small biotechnology firms. For example, Cangene—a firm controlled by Canada's largest generic drug producer, Apotex—made a bid for Mississauga's Hyal Pharmaceutical. Depending on the possible approval and success of Hyal's drug, Solarase, Apotex could have a very inexpensive entry into a treatment for actinic keratosis, a type of precancerous skin condition. For similar reasons, Pharmacia & Upjohn bought Sugen, a San Francisco–based biotech firm specializing in cancer drugs. In addition to citing attractive prices, analysts suggest that these acquisitions are a way for large pharmaceuticals to "fill their pipeline with projects from undervalued biotechnology companies and to get their hands on new products."[60]

## Increased Speed to Market

As indicated earlier, compared to internal product development, acquisitions result in more rapid market entries.[61] In two researchers' words, "Acquisitions remain the quickest route companies have to new markets and to new capabilities."[62] Using new capabilities to pioneer new products and enter markets quickly can create advantageous market positions.[63] As discussed in Chapter 6, the durability of the advantage created by an attractive market position is determined largely by rivals' competitive responses.[64]

Firms seek rapid market entry in many different industries. British Telecommunications (BT), for example, recently spent £175 billion (Can$365 billion ) to acquire Esat Telecom Group, Ireland's second-largest phone company. The acquisition gives BT immediate access to "Ireland's rapidly growing telecommunications market, including in the area of high-speed broadband delivery."[65] In the consumer foods industry, Kraft Foods acquired meat-alternative producer Boca Burger. This acquisition gave Kraft an immediate presence in the rapidly expanding market for soy-based products as alternatives to traditional meat offerings. The attractiveness of soy-based goods gained steam when the U.S. Food and Drug Administration decided to allow companies to equate soy-protein consumption with a reduced risk of heart disease.[66] At a cost of $370 million, PC manufacturer Compaq Computer acquired the custom-assembly operations of Inacom. Stimulating this purchase was new CEO Michael Capellas's conclusion that Compaq needed to be able to accelerate the speed with which it delivered products to major customers. According to Capellas, the "purchase gives us the right capability quickly and cost-effectively."[67] Increasing the speed of its distribution channel was necessary for Compaq to become more competitive with several rivals, especially Dell Computer.

## Lower Risk Compared to Developing New Products

As mentioned earlier, internal product development processes can be risky. Alternatively, because an acquisition's outcomes can be estimated more easily and accurately compared to the outcomes of an internal product development process, managers may view acquisitions as carrying lower risk.[68]

The assessment of risk between an internal product development process and an acquisition may have taken place among managers at Toronto's Corus Entertainment. Recently, Corus acquired TV animator Nelvana—producer of children's TV shows Franklin, Babar, and Pippi Longstocking. The combination will allow Nelvana the funds to expand its children's programming and Corus the access to Nelvana's content for their channels. Corus is also rumoured to be a likely buyer for Cinar Corporation. Cinar's stock was depressed from the investigation, liabilities, and scandal resulting from its problems with obtaining government support. Thus, Corus may end up picking up Cinar inexpensively. The Corus-Nelvana-Cinar combination will likely produce a powerful producer of children's television programming. Assessing the performance of Nelvana before acquiring the company will ensure Corus managers have a reasonably high degree of confidence in the outcomes associated with their intended strategic actions. As a result, Corus managers may have considered more extensive entry into the production of children's television programming through acquisition to be less risky compared to building this business through an internal product development process.[69]

As with other strategic actions discussed in this book, caution must be exercised when a decision is made to acquire new products rather than to develop them internally. In the context of the issue of lower risk, for example, firms should be aware that research evidence suggests that acquisitions have become a common means of avoiding risky internal ventures (and therefore risky R&D investments). In fact, acquisition may become a substitute for innovation.[70] Thus, acquisitions are not a risk-free alternative to entering new markets through internally developed products.

# Increased Diversification

Based on experience and the insights resulting from it, firms typically find it easier to develop and introduce new products in markets served currently by the firm. In contrast, it is harder for companies to develop products—ones that differ from their current lines—for markets in which they lack experience. Thus, it is uncommon for a firm to develop new products internally as a means of diversifying its product lines.[71] Instead, a firm usually opts to use acquisitions as the means to engage in product diversification. The extreme example is Onex Corporation. Onex founder Gerry Schwartz has labelled the firm as "the ninth-largest company in Canada."[72] Onex has bought its way into the field of in-flight meals, computer components manufacturing, movie theatres, and sugar production, among others. In fact, companies that Onex has acquired serve 800 000 airline meals each day (SkyChef Catering) and process more than half of Canada's sugar (BC Sugar Refinery). Through its Celestica purchase, Onex has become the world's third-largest contract manufacturer of electronics products.[73] As well, Onex has an interest in Loew's Theatres—North American's second-largest chain.[74]

Both related-diversification and unrelated-diversification strategies can be implemented through acquisitions. In addition, as discussed in Chapter 9, acquisitions are the most frequently used means for firms to diversify their operations into international markets.[75] Using acquisitions to diversify a firm seems appropriate, in that evidence suggests that acquisitions are the quickest and, typically, the easiest way to change a firm's portfolio of businesses.[76] Yet, acquisitions that diversify a firm's product lines must be undertaken only after careful study and evaluation, in that the more related the acquired firm is to the acquiring firm, the greater the probability that the acquisition will be successful.

Thus, horizontal acquisitions (through which a firm acquires a competitor) and related acquisitions tend to contribute more to strategic competitiveness than do those through which a firm acquires a company operating in product markets that are quite different from those in which it currently competes.[77] This evidence suggests the likelihood of a successful outcome from Philadelphia-based chemical company Rohm & Haas's acquisition of specialty-chemicals and salt manufacturer Morton International. The transaction involved companies offering similar products to similar, yet slightly different, markets. Business writers observed that this "acquisition offers Rohm & Haas multiple platforms for growth in coatings and electronic materials, provides complementary products lines and attractive financial returns, and is based on cultural compatibility of the companies."[78]

Evidence regarding the value of related acquisitions can even be found with very unrelated diversifiers. Onex Corporation is one of Canada's most diversified companies. In some quarters, Onex has a reputation for buying broken-down companies, fixing them up, and selling them off.[79] Yet, it also keeps some of those companies, thereby using acquisitions to support its presence in that industry. When Onex entered the auto parts field in 1990, it made numerous purchases of small, related companies and eight major acquisitions to its initial investment in Automotive Industries (AI). Onex later sold AI with many of the major add-on companies for a healthy profit. However, Onex also took the remaining auto parts firms it owned and quietly bought up dozens of related firms to help create Dura Automotive Systems. By mid-1999, Dura had become a viable competitor through Onex's efforts in setting up some very large deals: a $750 million deal to buy Indiana-based Excel Industries and a $320 million deal to buy Britain's

Adwest Automotive.[80] Thus, while Onex made frequent corporate acquisitions that added to its diversity, it also made purchases to support its portfolio.

## Reshaping the Firm's Competitive Scope

As discussed in Chapter 3, the intensity of competitive rivalry is an industry characteristic that affects a firm's profitability. To reduce the negative effect of an intense rivalry on its financial performance, the firm may use acquisitions as a way to restrict its dependence on a single or a few products or markets. Reducing a company's dependence on single products or markets alters the competitive scope of the company.

Increasingly, some of the world's automobile manufacturers are diversifying their operations to reduce their dependence on the intensely competitive global auto markets. DaimlerChrysler, for example, "is exploring opportunities to expand its presence in financial and computer services, aftermarket sales, and electronics and satellite systems." Company officials believe that, in addition to affording more desirable operating margins, growth possibilities in these areas are now more attractive than either alliances or acquisitions in car manufacturing.[81] Similarly, Ford CEO Jacques Nasser wants to make his company the world's leading consumer services business that specializes in the automotive sector. Nasser wants Ford to tap all sectors in the after-sales market, including repairs, replacement parts, and product servicing. One of the first actions Ford took to reach this objective was the acquisition of Kwik-Fit, the U.K. automotive aftermarket group. To evaluate the success in its efforts to reshape the firm's competitive scope through diversification, "Ford will measure itself against world-class consumer businesses in whatever business they operate rather than the traditional yardsticks of rival automakers."[82]

Japan's largest electronics manufacturer, Hitachi, has $3 billion that it intends to use either to purchase North American and Japanese high-technology companies outright or to buy stakes in them. Recently, Hitachi studied 60 possible acquisitions, half in Japan and half in other nations. According to the president of the company, the acquisitions' primary purpose is to facilitate his objective of "remaking" a firm that he believed had become a sprawling giant in order to increase its competitiveness in the global economy.[83]

As a final note regarding the legitimate reasons for firms to use acquisition strategies, we must include the notion that such acquisitions may have more subtle strategic purposes. For example, JDS Uniphase offered almost $60 billion to acquire SDL and its laser manufacturing abilities. Although JDS can make the reliable, small, and powerful lasers that send signals over optical fibre, SDL is clearly the world leader. Thus, the stated rationale for making the acquisition is to enhance the JDS product line and increase capacity. The SDL acquisition definitely performed this function.

Yet, one analyst argued that there are other, more subtle reasons behind the JDS Uniphase purchase. Corning desperately needed these technologies to stay current in fibre optics, and the JDS move denied its competitor those resources. If Corning elected to bid up the SDL acquisition price, it would have to pay JDS a $1 billion break-up fee for the purchase. If regulators killed the acquisition, they would not do so for several months. In the meantime, JDS could tie up the company, and the resulting uncertainty would mean that SDL would have trouble hiring and innovating. This would effectively freeze SDL's continued development and allow JDS to maintain its dominance in the industry.[84]

Thus, as we have described, there are obvious and subtle legitimate reasons for firms to use acquisition strategies as part of their efforts to increase strategic competitiveness and to improve the likelihood of being able to earn above-average returns. However, also as we have said, acquisition strategies are not risk free. In fact, on the basis of company experience and research findings, it has been suggested that "less than 20 percent of all mergers and acquisitions are successful."[85] This success rate is consistent with the finding discussed earlier in the chapter that the average returns of acquisitions for acquiring firms hover close to zero.

# PROBLEMS IN ACHIEVING ACQUISITION SUCCESS

Reasons supporting the use of acquisition strategies, as well as potential problems accompanying their use, are shown in Figure 8.1. The potential problems are discussed in the sections that follow. A reasonable conclusion to draw from those discussions is that "successful acquisitions involve a well-thought-out strategy in selecting the target, avoiding overpaying, and creating value in the integration process. [In addition], a good acquisition strategy combines the analytical with the intuitive, and the linear with the iterative."[86]

## Integration Difficulties

Integrating two companies following an acquisition can be quite difficult.[87] Integration issues include those of melding two disparate corporate cultures,[88] linking different financial and strategic control systems, building effective working relationships (particularly when management styles differ), and resolving problems regarding the status of the newly acquired firm's executives.[89]

The importance of a successful integration should not be underestimated. Without it, a firm achieves financial diversification, but little else. Thus, as suggested by a researcher studying the process, "managerial practice and academic writings show that the post-acquisition integration phase is probably the single most important determinant of shareholder value creation (and equally of value destruction) in mergers and acquisitions."[90] Firms should also be aware of the large number of activities associated with integration processes. For instance, Intel acquired Digital Equipment's semiconductor division. On the day Intel began to integrate the acquired division into its operations, 6000 deliverables were to be completed by hundreds of employees working in dozens of different countries.[91]

According to research completed by consulting firm Booz-Allen Hamilton, there is a positive relationship between the rapid integration of the acquiring and acquired firms and overall acquisition success. Intentions at Honeywell (AlliedSignal kept the Honeywell name after acquiring it) are consistent with this relationship. According to analysts, "AlliedSignal and Honeywell have set an aggressive six-month timetable to merge their operations into a $24 billion industrial powerhouse that makes everything from aircraft landing systems to home thermostats."[92] To help integrate the two formerly independent firms within six months, Honeywell organized a team that was charged with developing and implementing an integration plan. Rapid integration is one of the guidelines that DaimlerChrysler CEO Jurgen Schrempp recommends companies follow to successfully integrate firms involved in a global merger or acquisition. Schrempp's other guidelines include dealing with unpopular issues immediately and being honest with people regarding the effects the integration will likely have on them.[93]

According to some business writers, Cisco Systems "wears the mantle of M&A king."[94] One reason for this is the firm's ability to quickly integrate its acquisitions into its existing operations. Focusing on small companies with products and services related closely to its own, some analysts believe that the day after the company acquires a firm, employees in that firm feel as though they have been working for Cisco for decades.[95]

■ ■ **FIGURE 8.1**

*Reasons for Acquisitions and Problems in Achieving Success*

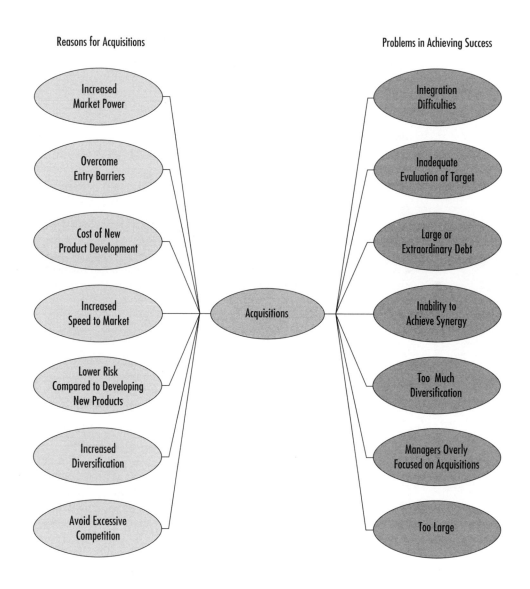

Reasons for Acquisitions

Increased Market Power

Overcome Entry Barriers

Cost of New Product Development

Increased Speed to Market

Lower Risk Compared to Developing New Products

Increased Diversification

Avoid Excessive Competition

Acquisitions

Problems in Achieving Success

Integration Difficulties

Inadequate Evaluation of Target

Large or Extraordinary Debt

Inability to Achieve Synergy

Too Much Diversification

Managers Overly Focused on Acquisitions

Too Large

## Inadequate Evaluation of Target

Due diligence is a process through which a firm evaluates a target firm for acquisition. An effective due-diligence process examines hundreds of items in areas as diverse as those of financing the intended transaction, differences in cultures between the acquiring and target firm, tax consequences of the transaction, and actions that would be necessary to successfully meld the two workforces. Due diligence is commonly performed by investment bankers, accountants, lawyers, and management consultants specializing in that activity, although firms actively pursuing acquisitions may form their own internal due-diligence team.

The failure to complete an effective due-diligence process often results in the acquiring firm paying a premium—sometimes an excessive one—for the target company. In fact, research shows that without due diligence, "the purchase price is driven by the pricing of other 'comparable' acquisitions rather than by a rigorous assessment of where, when, and how management can drive real performance gains. [In these cases], the price paid may have little to do with achievable value."[96] Premiums paid without effective due diligence may also account for research results indicating that the amount of the purchase premium does not predict acquisition success.[97]

The results of some acquisitions in a number of industries suggest a failure to perform adequate due diligence. In 1988, for example, British retailer Marks and Spencer spent $750 million to acquire Brooks Brothers. Even after more than 10 years, the acquisition remains unsuccessful. Initially, Marks and Spencer executives thought that renovating and "upscaling" Brooks Brothers would attract customers and improve the chain's deteriorating performance. These efforts proved unsuccessful, and indeed, some believe that the premium Marks and Spencer paid to acquire Brooks Brothers precluded success, almost irrespective of any actions taken to reverse the chain's fortunes. At twice the sales volume and 75 times the earnings, the acquisition price was the highest one retail analyst had seen paid for a U.S. retailer in his 35-year career. Another analyst called the purchase price "insane."[98] Effective due diligence might have resulted in a decision by Marks and Spencer not to buy Brooks Brothers.

An example of effective due diligence appears to be DaimlerChrysler's 1999 decision not to acquire Nissan Motor Company. DaimlerChrysler was interested in Nissan as a means of expanding Daimler's access to global auto markets, especially those in Southeast Asia. The primary concern for analysts and, apparently, for DaimlerChrysler executives, was Nissan's $22 billion debt. Speaking to this possible acquisition, Robert Lutz, retired vice-chairman of the former Chrysler Corporation, said that DaimlerChrysler "might as well take $5 billion in gold bullion, put it in a huge container, spray paint the word Nissan on the side and drop it into the middle of the Pacific Ocean."[99] An adequate evaluation of the target firm through DaimlerChrysler's due-diligence process appears to be the cause of the company's decision not to acquire Nissan.

## Large or Extraordinary Debt

To finance a number of acquisitions completed during the 1980s and 1990s, some companies significantly increased their levels of debt. Partly making this possible was a financial innovation called junk bonds,[100] a financing option through which risky acquisitions are financed with money (debt) that provides a large potential return to lenders (typically called bondholders). Because junk bonds are unsecured obligations (that is, they are not tied to specific assets such as collateral), interest rates for these high-risk debt instruments sometimes reached between 18 and 20 percent during the 1980s.

Also supporting a decision to increase debt significantly during this period in order to acquire other companies was the belief that debt disciplined managers, causing them to act in shareholders' best interests. This view was grounded in work by finance scholars who argued that the constraints on spending possibilities created by the requirement to service debt obligations caused managers to be more prudent in allocating remaining funds and to behave less opportunistically. This logic resulted in managers sometimes being encouraged by company directors and finance officials to utilize significant leverage to finance large acquisitions.[101]

As the 21st century begins, junk bonds are being used less frequently to finance acquisitions. In addition, the conviction that debt disciplines managers is less strong than it was in the previous two decades. Nonetheless, some firms still take on too much debt to acquire companies. For example, AgriBioTech recently acquired dozens of small seed firms. These acquisitions were used to gain access to the skills necessary to develop genetically enhanced alfalfa and turf grasses and to gain the economies of scope required to distribute products nationwide. But the firm's "acquisition strategy got out of hand. AgriBioTech wound up issuing massive amounts of new shares. Debt, meanwhile, ballooned to $135 million compared to annual revenues of about $409 million." Analysts concluded that the first order of business to turn the firm around was to "clear up the debt mess."[102]

In spite of the issues associated with too much of it, debt can discipline managerial actions because when debt is high, principal and interest payments reach levels that preclude other investments, some of which might be in managers' best interests (e.g., greater amounts of diversification to reduce managerial employment risk). On the other hand, high debt levels increase the likelihood of bankruptcy, which can lead to a downgrade in the firm's credit rating from agencies.[103] In addition, high debt precludes investments in activities that contribute to the firm's long-term success, including R&D, human resource training, and marketing.[104]

Therefore, we conclude that the use of debt has positive and negative effects. On the one hand, leverage can be a positive force in a firm's development, allowing it to take advantage of attractive expansion opportunities. However, too much leverage (e.g., extraordinary debt) can lead to negative outcomes, such as postponing or eliminating investments (e.g., R&D expenditures), which are necessary to maintain strategic competitiveness over the long term. Partly because of debt's potential disadvantages and partly because of a generally favourable global economy, cash and equity offerings were frequently used instead of significant amounts of debt to complete acquisitions during the latter part of the 1990s and into the 21st century. For example, in a transaction between two Quebec firms, Abitibi-Consolidated acquired Donohue for $7 billion in cash and stock. The transaction created market power for the new firm in that it became the world's largest newsprint maker, with 16.3 percent of global newsprint capacity (the next-largest market share holder had 8.2 percent).[105]

## Inability to Achieve Synergy

Derived from the Greek word "synergos," which means "working together," synergy exists when the value created by units working together exceeds the value those units could create working independently (see Chapter 7). Therefore, synergy exists when assets "are worth more when used in conjunction with each other than separately. Synergies can involve physical and non-physical assets,"[106] such as human capital. For shareholders, synergy generates gains in their wealth that they could not duplicate or exceed through their own portfolio diversification decisions.[107] Being able to create synergy when using an acquisition strategy is important, in that doing so is a key justification for using such a strategy, which often results in a firm becoming more diversified.[108]

A firm develops a competitive advantage through an acquisition strategy only when a transaction generates private synergy, which is created when the combination and integration of the acquiring and acquired firms' assets yield capabilities and core competencies that could not be developed by combining and integrating either firm's assets with another company. Private synergy is possible when firms' assets are complementary in unique ways; that is, the unique type of asset complementarity is not possible by combining either company's assets with another firm's assets.[109]

Because of its uniqueness, private synergy is difficult for competitors to understand and imitate. However, private synergy is also difficult to create. For example, Quaker Oats' executives believed that the firm's ownership of Snapple, which came about through an acquisition, would create private synergy. The expectation was that integrating Quaker's own Gatorade products with Snapple's would create complementarities that could not be created through any other combination of each firm's assets with the assets of any other firm. However, that expectation was not realized, and after struggling with the acquisition, Quaker Oats finally divested Snapple. Analysts suggested that there was a lack of complementarity between the sales and marketing activities required by Gatorade's and Snapple's drinks.

Firms experience several expenses when trying to create private synergy through acquisitions. Called transaction costs,[110] these expenses are incurred when firms use acquisition strategies to create synergy. Direct costs include legal fees and charges from investment bankers who complete due diligence for the acquiring firm. Managerial time to evaluate target firms and then to complete negotiations is an example of an indirect cost, as is the loss of key managers and employees following an acquisition.[111] Affecting an acquisition's success, in terms of whether synergy is created, is a firm's ability to account for costs that are necessary to create anticipated revenue- and cost-based synergies. Of the two types of costs, firms tend to underestimate the sum of indirect costs when the value of the synergy that may be created by combining and integrating the acquired firm's assets with the acquiring firm's assets is calculated.

## Too Much Diversification

As explained in Chapter 7, when used properly, diversification strategies lead to strategic competitiveness and above-average returns. In general, firms using related diversification strategies outperform those employing unrelated diversification strategies. However, conglomerates, formed by using an unrelated diversification strategy, also can be successful. For example, Toronto's Onex Corporation, discussed earlier, is highly diversified yet successful, as is the Virgin Group, the U.K.–based firm with interests ranging from cosmetics to trains.[112]

At some point, firms can become overdiversified. The level at which this happens varies across companies. The reason for the variation is that each firm has different capabilities that are required to successfully manage diversification. Recall from Chapter 7 that related diversification requires more information processing than does unrelated diversification. The need for related-diversified firms to be able to process more and more diverse information creates a situation in which they become overdiversified with a smaller number of business units, compared to firms using an unrelated diversification strategy.[113] Regardless of the type of diversification strategy implemented, however, declines in performance usually result from overdiversification,[114] after which different business units are divested.

The pattern of excessive diversification followed by divestments of underperforming business units was observed frequently, but not exclusively, among U.S. firms during the 1960s through the 1980s. While U.S. firms such as ITT became bloated with acquisitions in the 1960s—only to sell off many of these acquisitions in later years, Canadian firms were not immune to overdiversification.[115] Canadian Pacific (CP), at one time or another, went into land and resource development, ships, airlines, film production, steel and paper production, trucking, insurance, and even china making. For most of its history, CP was a diversified company. However, the most peripheral of CP's businesses, most of which were acquired in the 1970s, were dropped in the 1980s.[116] Yet the market still thought of CP as overly diversified. So much so that on the day in 2001 that CP announced that the company would be broken into five pieces (petroleum, hotels, ships, coal, and rail) its stock gained about 10 percent—having risen 25 percent the previous month on rumours of the reorganization.[117]

Even when a firm is not overdiversified, a high level of diversification can have a negative effect on the firm's long-term performance. For example, the scope created by additional amounts of diversification often causes managers to rely on financial rather than strategic controls to evaluate business units' performances[118] (financial and strategic controls are defined and explained in detail in chapters 11 and 12). Essentially, when top-level executives have the breadth and depth of information needed to understand each business unit's objectives and strategy, they are able to use strategic controls to monitor performance. Without such a rich understanding of business units' objectives and strategies, those same executives rely on financial controls to assess the performances of managers and their business units. Financial controls are based on objective evaluation criteria, such as the firm's return on investment (ROI). Executives' reliance on financial controls to judge managerial performance can cause individual business-unit managers to focus on short-term outcomes at the expense of long-term investments. When long-term investments are reduced to levels that jeopardize future success in order to boost short-term profits, a firm may have diversified to the point beyond which its diversification strategy can enhance overall strategic competitiveness.[119]

## Managers Overly Focused on Acquisitions

Typically, a fairly substantial amount of managerial time and energy is required for acquisition strategies to contribute to a firm's strategic competitiveness. Activities with which managers become involved include (1) searching for viable acquisition candidates, (2) completing effective due-diligence processes, and (3) preparing for negotiations.

Top-level managers do not personally gather all data and information required to complete the activities that are part of an acquisition. However, upper-level executives do make final decisions regarding the firms to be pursued as targets, the nature of the negotiations to acquire a firm, and so forth. In a broader sense, the most important responsibility the top management team has in terms of acquisition strategies is to make certain that the firm is using them effectively. Company experiences show that being responsible for, and participating in, many of the activities that are part of an acquisition strategy can divert managerial attention from other matters (e.g., thinking seriously about the firm's purpose and interacting effectively with board members and external stakeholders) that are linked with long-term competitive success.[120]

Another issue that concerns some analysts centres on the possibility that managers who are overly focused on acquisitions may fail to objectively assess the value of outcomes achieved through the use of the firm's acquisition strategy (compared with outcomes that might be achieved by concentrating on using the firm's other strategies more effectively). For example, it has been suggested that Ford Motor Company's acquisition strategy may not be enhancing the firm's strategic competitiveness. Consider the words of an individual who studies the automobile industry: "Ford owns one-third of the stock of Mazda of Japan and essentially runs the company. There have been three Mazda presidents in three years (all from Ford). I wouldn't call that a sign of success. Ford pumped $6 billion into Jaguar over the past decade, and there are signs that this may work out one day, but it will take a decade to earn back the investment. And I don't think Ford will ever earn back its Volvo investment."[121] An option available to Ford is to rely on its technological skills to develop innovative engines, transmissions, suspension systems, and so forth. In other words, some believe that the firm might contribute more positively to its strategic competitiveness by focusing its time and attention on determining actions to take to increase the value of its own automobiles and trucks, instead of using managerial time and energy to expand the firm's product lines by acquiring competitors. Thus, upper-level executives should avoid focusing on the use of an acquisition strategy at the expense of a firm's long-term strategic competitiveness.

Acquisitions can consume significant amounts of managerial time and energy in target firms as well as in the companies that acquire them. Because of the uncertainty that an acquisition creates, some suggest that target firms find themselves in a state of virtual suspended animation during an acquisition.[122] For example, while the target firm's day-to-day operations continue, albeit sometimes at a slower pace, most of the company's executives are hesitant to make decisions with long-term consequences, choosing to postpone such decisions until negotiations have been completed. Thus, evidence suggests that the acquisition process can create a short-term perspective and a greater aversion to risk among top-level executives in a target firm.[123]

## Too Large

Most acquisitions create a larger firm. In theory, the increased size should help a firm gain economies of scale in various organizational functions. These economies can then lead to more efficient operations. For instance, combining the R&D functions of two firms involved in an acquisition should create economies of scale that can be the stimulus to greater innovative output.

Evidence suggests, however, that a larger size creates efficiencies in various organizational functions only when the new firm is not too large. In other words, at some level, the added costs required to manage the larger firm exceed the benefits of efficiency created by economies of scale. As well, when faced with the complexities generated by the larger size, managers—especially those from the acquiring firm—typically decide that more bureaucratic controls should be used to manage the combined firms' operations. **Bureaucratic controls** are formalized supervisory and behavioural rules and policies that are designed to ensure consistency of decisions and actions across different units of a firm. Consistency in terms of decisions and actions can benefit the firm, primarily in

**Bureaucratic controls** are formalized supervisory and behavioural rules and policies that are designed to ensure consistency of decisions and actions across different units of a firm.

the form of predictability and cost reductions. However, across time, relatively rigid and standardized managerial behaviour tends to be the product of strict adherence to formalized rules and policies.

For example, when it announced that it was splitting into five companies, Canadian Pacific credited the need for each former division to, among other things, "capitalize each unit with debt and equity as it deems appropriate … and design equity-based compensation programs targeted to their performance." These possibilities were generally unavailable to the larger organization while one entity.[124] Certainly, in the long run, the diminished degree of flexibility created by use of bureaucratic controls, which accompanies rigid and standardized managerial behaviour, may produce less innovation. Because of innovation's importance to competitive success in the 21st-century landscape (see Chapter 1), the bureaucratic controls that are sometimes used when firms become too large through the use of an acquisition strategy can have a detrimental effect on performance.[125]

# EFFECTIVE ACQUISITIONS

Earlier in the chapter, we noted that acquisition strategies do not consistently produce above-average returns for the acquiring firm's shareholders. Nonetheless, some companies are able to create value via the use of an acquisition strategy.[126] Results from a research study shed light on the differences between unsuccessful and successful acquisition strategies and suggest that there is a pattern of decisions and actions firms can follow that may improve the probability of acquisition strategy success.[127]

The study appears to show that when a target firm's assets are complementary to the acquired firm's assets, an acquisition is more successful. This is because, with complementary assets, integrating two firms' operations creates synergy. In fact, in the firms that were a part of the study, the researchers found that integrating two firms with complementary assets frequently produced unique capabilities and core competencies; a requirement for building strategic competitiveness, as previously described.[128] Thus, the acquisitions were generally highly related to the acquiring firm's businesses. In fact, the acquiring firm maintained its focus on core businesses and leveraged them with the complementary assets and capabilities from the acquired firm. Oftentimes, targets were selected and "groomed" by establishing a working relationship sometime prior to the acquisition. Using a cooperative strategy between the two firms is one way to determine whether firms can work together effectively over an extended period. As discussed in Chapter 10, strategic alliances are sometimes used to test the feasibility of firms trying to work together to pursue mutual interests.[129]

The study's results also show that friendly acquisitions facilitate integration of the firms involved in an acquisition. Through friendly acquisitions, firms work together to find ways to integrate their operations so that positive synergy can be created. In hostile takeovers, animosity often results between the two top-management teams, a condition that in turn often affects relationships and methods of working in the newly created firm. As a result, more key personnel in the acquired firm may be lost, and those who remain may resist the changes necessary to integrate the two firms and create synergy.[130] With effort, cultural clashes can be overcome, and fewer key managers and employees will become discouraged and leave.[131] Thus, successful acquisitions tend to be friendly, although there are exceptions.

Another finding from the study is that a successful acquiring firm generally has conducted effective due-diligence processes that, at a minimum, involve the deliberate and careful selection of target firms and an evaluation of how negotiations should be conducted. Having financial slack (in the form of debt, equity, or cash) in both the acquiring and acquired firms also frequently contributed to success in acquisitions. In a related way, continuing to maintain a low to moderate amount of debt (as opposed to higher levels of debt) in the newly created firm is an important attribute of acquisition success. Indeed, maintaining low or moderate debt was shown to be critical to success even in instances when a substantial amount of leverage was used to finance the acquisition. When substantial debt is used to finance the acquisition, companies with successful acquisitions reduced the debt quickly, partly by selling off assets from the acquired firm. Often, the assets that are sold are not complementary to the acquiring firm's businesses or are performing poorly. Also, the acquiring firm may sell its own lower-performing businesses after making an acquisition. In this way, high debt and debt costs are avoided. Therefore, the debt costs do not prevent long-term investments such as R&D, and managerial discretion in the use of cash flow is relatively flexible. Another attribute of successful acquisition strategies is an emphasis on innovation, as demonstrated by continuing investments in R&D activities. Significant R&D investments show a strong managerial commitment to innovation, a characteristic that is increasingly important to overall competitiveness, as well as acquisition success, in the 21st-century landscape.

Flexibility and adaptability are successful acquisitions' final two attributes. When both the acquiring and the target firms' executives have experience in managing change, they will be more skilled at adapting their capabilities to new environments. As a result, the executives will be more adept at integrating the two organizations, which is particularly important when firms have different organizational cultures. Adaptation skills allow the two firms to integrate their assets more quickly, efficiently, and effectively. In turn, rapid, efficient, and effective integration may quickly produce the desired synergy in the newly created firm.

The attributes and results of successful acquisitions are summarized in Table 8.1. Managers seeking acquisition success should emphasize the seven attributes that are listed. Cisco Systems uses an acquisition strategy quite successfully and employs many of these standards to better ensure the likelihood of acquisition success.

As we have learned, some acquisitions—particularly those characterized by the attributes shown in Table 8.1—enhance strategic competitiveness. Certainly, this is the case with Cisco Systems, which earned U.S.$2.1 billion in net income in fiscal-year 1999 on a sales volume of U.S.$12.1 billion.[132] However, the majority of acquisitions that took place from roughly the 1970s through the 1990s did not enhance firms' strategic competitiveness. In fact, some researchers observe that "history shows that anywhere between one-third [and] more than half of all acquisitions are ultimately divested or spun off."[133] Thus, firms often use restructuring strategies to correct for the failure of a merger or an acquisition. According to Peter Drucker, restructuring strategies are being used more frequently. To support his view, he observes that, on a single, yet typical, day in the business world, the *Wall Street Journal* reported that "Hewlett-Packard was spinning off its $8 billion business in test and measuring instruments, Procter & Gamble was selling its adult-incontinence business to a midsize company, and the Harris Co. was selling its entire semi-conductor business to a small company."[134]

| ■ ■ **TABLE 8.1** | **Attributes of Successful Acquisitions** |
|---|---|
| **Attributes** | **Results** |
| 1. Acquired firm has assets or resources that are complementary to the acquiring firm's core business | High probability of synergy and competitive advantage by maintaining strengths |
| 2. Acquisition is friendly | Faster/more effective integration; possibly lower premiums |
| 3. Acquiring firm selects target firms and conducts negotiations carefully and deliberately | Firms with strongest complementarities are acquired, and overpayment is avoided |
| 4. Acquiring firm has financial slack (cash, equity, or a favourable debt position) | Financing (debt or equity) is easier and less costly to obtain |
| 5. Merged firm maintains low to moderate debt position instead of a higher debt position | Lower financing cost, lower risk (e.g., of bankruptcy), and avoidance of tradeoffs associated with high debt) |
| 6. Has experience with change and is flexible and adaptable | Faster and more effective integration facilitates achievement of synergy |
| 7. Sustained and consistent emphasis on R&D and innovation | Maintain long-term competitive advantage in markets |

# RESTRUCTURING

*Restructuring is a strategy through which a firm changes its set of businesses or financial structure.*

The failure of an acquisition strategy is oftentimes the driver of a restructuring strategy.[135] In other instances, however, firms use a restructuring strategy because of changes in their external and internal environments. For example, different opportunities sometimes surface in the external environment that are particularly attractive to the diversified firm in light of the core competencies that have been developed in its internal environment. In such cases, restructuring may be appropriate to position the firm so that it can create more value for stakeholders, given the environmental changes. Restructuring strategies may also be used to gain the support of financial analysts—individuals who value firms' efforts to operate efficiently and effectively in the challenging global economy.[136] Regardless of the reason for its use, a restructuring strategy changes the composition of a firm's business portfolio.[137]

Defined formally, **restructuring** is a strategy through which a firm changes its set of businesses or financial structure.[138] From the 1970s through the 1990s, divesting businesses from company portfolios and downsizing accounted for a large percentage of firms' restructuring strategies.[139] Firms can adopt three types of restructuring strategies: downsizing, downscoping, and leveraged buyouts.

## Downsizing

*Downsizing is a reduction in the number of a firm's employees and, sometimes, in the number of its operating units, but it may or may not change the composition of business in the company's portfolio.*

Once thought to be an indicator of organizational decline, downsizing is now recognized as a legitimate restructuring strategy.[140] **Downsizing** is a reduction in the number of a firm's employees and, sometimes, in the number of its operating units, but it may or may not change the composition of businesses in the company's portfolio. Thus, downsizing is an intentional proactive management strategy, whereas "decline is an environmental or organizational phenomenon that occurs involuntarily and results in erosion of an organization's resource base."[141]

The late 1980s and the 1990s saw the loss of thousands of jobs in private and public organizations. For example, one study estimates that 85 percent of *Fortune* 1000 firms have used downsizing as a restructuring strategy.[142] Moreover, evidence suggests that, in spite of generally robust economic growth in many nations as the 21st century begins, "the organizational downsizing juggernaut continues unabated."[143]

Firms use downsizing as a restructuring strategy for different reasons. The most frequently cited reason is that the firm expects improved profitability from cost reductions and more efficient operations. For example, Bausch & Lomb recently reduced its global workforce by 7 percent in order to consolidate or restructure its contact-lens operations. The company expected these actions to produce at least $30 million in payroll savings annually, beginning in 2001. Bausch & Lomb anticipated further savings through the phase-out of older equipment in favour of more efficient machinery. To restore sales growth and to "revive a flagging culture of innovation," Procter & Gamble decided to cut 15 000 jobs from its operations. The cuts, called for by the firm's Organization 2005 restructuring plan, accounted for 13 percent of P&G's worldwide workforce. P&G expected annual savings of at least $900 million by 2004 as a result of its downsizing decision. In Japan, Malox, a logistics company and a unit of Mazda Motor Corp., tried for five years to restructure without layoffs. However, cost reductions and improvements in operational efficiency from these actions fell short of Mazda and Ford's expectations. Although downsizing was difficult because of the historical tradition in Japanese companies avoiding layoffs, Malox's executives finally decided to eliminate 100 of its 440 company-wide jobs as a key part of the firm's overall restructuring strategy.[144]

## Downscoping

**Downscoping** refers to divestiture, spin-off, or some other means of eliminating businesses that are unrelated to a firm's core businesses.

Compared to downsizing, downscoping has a more positive effect on firm performance.[145] **Downscoping** refers to divestiture, spinoff, or some other means of eliminating businesses that are unrelated to a firm's core businesses. Commonly, downscoping is described as a set of actions that causes a firm to strategically refocus on its core businesses. A firm that downscopes often also downsizes simultaneously.[146] However, it does not eliminate key employees from its primary businesses in the process, because such action could lead to a loss of one or more core competencies. Instead, a firm that is simultaneously downscoping and downsizing becomes smaller by reducing the diversity of businesses in its portfolio.

Following restructuring through downscoping, a firm can be managed more effectively by its top management team. Managerial effectiveness increases because the firm has become less diversified, allowing the top management team to better understand and manage the remaining businesses, primarily the core and other related businesses.[147]

In general, North American organizations use downscoping as a restructuring strategy more frequently than European companies. Highlighting this reality are research findings indicating that "there is a powerful post-war trend towards the building of more conglomerates among the top 100 domestically-owned French, German and British industrial companies."[148] However, there has been an increase in downscoping by European firms. For example, RWE, the large German energy and industrial group, is restructuring through downscoping. Aiming to become a multi-energy, multiutility company with a 15 percent share of the European energy market by 2010, RWE intends to hold stakes in "companies such as Hechtief, the construction group, E-Plus, the mobile telephone group, or Heidelberger printing machines, as pure financial investments, perhaps as a prelude to spin-offs." Thus, by downscoping, RWE is abandoning the unrelated diversification strategy that drove the firm's growth during the 1980s and 1990s.[149]

Walt Disney is among the firms using downscoping as a restructuring strategy. Disney sold its Fairchild Publications unit to Advance Publications for $650 million. According to analysts at the time, sales of Disney's baseball and hockey teams and other operations (e.g., a magazine called *Los Angeles*) "would fit in with Disney's continuing drive to pare down or dispose of non-core operations. That drive [began in 1999], as Disney faced a deepening earnings slump."[150] ConAgra, a large U.S. food and agricultural products company, performed well in the 1980s through the use of an unrelated diversification strategy. Implemented through an acquisition strategy, the diversification strategy resulted in ConAgra's becoming a conglomerate with roughly 90 independent companies that make products from fertilizers to Slim Jim meat snacks. Analysts argue that the firm's recent profitability problems indicate that it is due for a serious downscoping effort. In response to its difficulties, the firm's top-level managers are restructuring their company's operations into 10 product groups under three main divisions—food service (restaurants), retail (grocery stores), and agricultural products.[151]

Restructuring strategies may require a considerable amount of time before a firm is able to divest a sufficient number of operations so that it can refocus on its core business or businesses. This may or may not prove to be the case with Walt Disney and ConAgra, though it has been for Ralston Purina, which intends to spin off its Eveready battery division, "leaving the once highly-diversified group focused entirely on pet food." However, Ralston has been restructuring almost since it purchased Eveready in 1986, and, analysts say, the firm's "long-running restructuring has seen it dispose of bakeries, baby food [manufacture], animal feed [production], and ski resorts."[152]

Rather than sell off operations to another company in order to downscope, firms may elect to spin them off. In a spinoff, the parent may issue new shares in the company or distribute shares in the spun-off company to its own shareholders. As discussed in the Strategic Focus, spinoffs have a long and mixed history.

## STRATEGIC FOCUS

### Cast Out, Orphaned, or Spun Off?

Decades ago, before LTV—now North America's third-largest steel company—ever got into the metals business, it was one of the conglomerate kings of Wall Street. Yet James Ling, LTV's founder, did as much spinning off of businesses as acquiring them. After buying Wilson & Company—a meat packer, sporting goods producer, and pharmaceutical maker—he broke up the company and sold it as three separate parts. Although the three stocks eventually did take off, the immediate response to the stock issue was less than stellar: initially the stocks were nicknamed "Meatball," "Golfball," and "Goofball," respectively.

*continued*

The market's response to spinoffs has not improved much since those days. Tricon, the spinoff of Pepsi's three underperforming fast-food icons—KFC, Pizza Hut, and Taco Bell—has received mixed reviews. Since 1997, the year Tricon was spun off, annual franchise sales growth has been an anaemic 4 percent. Company revenues have declined from almost $10 billion (U.S.) in 1997 to under $8 billion in 1999. This is due to the fact that Tricon itself is, in a sense, spinning off company-owned stores to franchisees. The firm dropped about 30 percent of its 10 000 company-owned stores between 1997 and 1999—a number about equal to the increase in franchise outlets. Tricon's stock ended 1997 at nearly U.S.$28 per share. The stock rose to almost $48 per share at the end of 1998 before slumping back to about $38 per share at the end of 1999. In strategic downscoping, both the parent and the spinoff should achieve increased shareholder value and accounting performance, yet in this regard the Tricon results have been disappointing.

In case one is tempted to think that spinning off companies is an American phenomenon only, remember that Nortel is a spinoff from BCE. As well, Shaw Communications spun off its media assets to form Corus Entertainment. Corus operates radio and TV stations and is expanding into program production via its purchase of Nelvana. Corus's previous parent, Shaw, has refocused its business and has invested $100 million in 360networks to expand its cable presence. Oddly enough, 360networks is a spinoff from Vancouver's Ledcor Industries.

We should also not restrict our notion of spinoffs to billion-dollar companies either. Guelph, Ontario's Hammond Manufacturing—with 1999 sales of about $170 million—was split up into three pieces. Hammond makes metal cases, transformers, and electronic components. The dry transformer group became a separate company with Bill Hammond as its chair and CEO. His brother Robert stayed on as chair and CEO of Hammond Manufacturing—the metal case producer. Finally, senior managers bought out Hammond's Moloney Electric division, a maker of oil transformers. The restructuring was intended to allow managers to concentrate on their core businesses, increase strategic planning flexibility, and bring the company's stock price out of the basement. The combined company shares were trading at less than half their book value.

It should be noted that spinoffs are not a cure-all for performance problems. AT&T's spinoff of Lucent Technologies and NCR did not significantly improve the performance of either company. Because of the highly disappointing performance of NCR within AT&T, many referred to the change as a castoff. Even Lucent has spinoffs. Its Enterprise Networks office systems division and other slower-growing units were shed so that the company can acquire other firms that will help it compete with rivals Cisco Systems and Nortel. Thus, spinoffs seem to have some benefits but cannot cure all the ills of companies with multiple businesses.

Sources: 360networks, 2000, *360networks home page*, http://www.worldwidefiber.com (Retrieved September 23); Tricon, 2000, *Tricon 1999 Annual Report*, www.tricon.con (Retrieved September 23); C. Howes, 2000, Shaw launches new fibre network ..., *National Post*, July 28, C6; R. Day, 2000, Lucent up on speculation of US$40b spinoff microelectronic unit, *National Post*, June 16, C8; K. Damsell, 2000, Corus swallows Nelvana ..., *The Globe and Mail*, September 19, B1, B11; Canadian Press Newswire, 2000, Brothers to split Hammond Manufacturing, *Canadian Press Newswire*, June 9; B. Critchley, 2000, Pension funds pick sides over Nortel ..., *National Post*, May 2, D3; P. Galuska, 1997, Still waiting for the new NCR, *BusinessWeek*, December 15, 142–46; R. Gibson, 1997, Fast-food spin-off enters Pepsi-free era, *Wall Street Journal*, B1, B10; P. Sellers, 1997, Pepsi's eateries go it alone, *Fortune*, August 4, 27–30; R. Sobel, 1984, *The Rise and Fall of the Conglomerate Kings*, Briarcliff Manor, N.Y.: Stein and Day.

## Leveraged Buyouts

Commonly, leveraged buyouts (LBOs) are used as a restructuring strategy to correct for managerial mistakes or because managers are making decisions that primarily serve their own interests rather than those of shareholders.[153] A leveraged buyout (LBO) is a restructuring strategy whereby a party buys all of a firm's assets in order to take the firm private. Once the transaction is completed, the company's stock is no longer traded publicly. Usually, significant amounts of debt are incurred to finance an LBO. To support debt payments and to downscope the company so that managers can concentrate on the firm's core businesses, the owners of a firm created through an LBO may immediately sell, or attempt to sell, a number of assets.[154] It is not uncommon for those buying a firm through an LBO to restructure the firm to the point that it can be sold at a profit within a five- to eight-year period.

Management buyouts (MBOs), employee buyouts (EBOs), and whole-firm buyouts are the three types of LBOs. EBOs are often called ESOPs—Employee Stock Ownership Plans. In whole-firm buyouts, an entire company, instead of a part of it, is purchased.

In part because of managerial incentives, MBOs, more so than EBOs and whole-firm buyouts, have been found to lead to downscoping, an increased strategic focus, and improved performance.[155] As a case in point, in the mid-1980s, Winnipeg's Dimatec was a money-losing diamond drill bit manufacturer of about 100 employees. Management bought out the company, and through downsizing and downscoping, the managers created an environment conducive to motivating their workforce. They reorganized the work process, introduced a bonus system, and brought in new production equipment and information systems to the company. Ten years later, Dimatec was a multimillion-dollar ISO 9001–certified company with an international clientele and a focused staff of just 52. The firm was recognized by Arthur Andersen Consulting as one of the 50 Best-managed Private Companies in Canada.[156]

Improvements at UAL (United Airlines) and Avis are attributed to EBOs at those firms. At UAL, there has been more of a cooperative spirit with gains in market share and above-average returns.[157] At Avis and a number of U.S. firms that have opted for EBOs, difficulties have surfaced between management and employees. As well, few employee owners have been requested to sit on boards in these firms.[158] These problems are similar to problems experienced with EBOs in Russia: Needed restructuring is hard to accomplish because of employee job security fears,[159] and when change is needed, problems can occur between managers and employees.

Canadian EBOs seem to be somewhat less confrontational. This may be because the more well-known EBOs are a result of a unique combination of a relatively isolated community with a major departing employer and some employee understanding of market and business necessities. For example, Tembec is a leading Canadian integrated forest products company. In 1972, it appeared that Tembec's hometown, Témiscaming, Québec, was about to become a ghost town. The town's main employer shut down the pulp mill, thus shaking the economic foundation of the community. Unwilling to give up, the mill's employees and town's residents purchased the mill. Through their efforts and company-created guidelines to encourage employee ownership, profit sharing, and employee participation, the company has been very successful. Tembec has grown from a few hundred employees in the mid-1970s to an international company with about $2.5 billion of assets in 1999.[160]

Whole-firm LBOs, on the other hand, often produce improvements through downsizing and retrenchment. This approach is illustrated by a buyout of Dr Pepper by Forsmann Little, an LBO specialist. Dr Pepper was successful enough to receive a new infusion of capital through an initial public offering. Subsequently, the firm was purchased by Cadbury Schweppes.[161]

## Restructuring Outcomes

The short- and long-term outcomes resulting from the three restructuring strategies are shown in Figure 8.2. As indicated, downsizing does not usually lead to higher firm performance. Researchers have noted that the majority of downsizing companies do not report productivity increases or any long-term gains in shareholder value.[162] Another researcher's findings about downsizing are also informative. This particular study showed that downsizing contributed to lower returns in U.S. and Japanese firms in the group of companies studied. In effect, these findings indicate that the stock markets in the firms' respective nations evaluated the downsizings negatively (i.e., investors concluded that downsizing would have a negative effect on companies' ability to achieve strategic competitiveness in the long term). An interpretation of the findings is that downsizing occurs as a consequence of other problems in a company.[163] For example, in 2000, Coca-Cola announced a reduction of 21 percent of its 29 000-plus-strong global workforce, including what analysts saw as an "astonishing 40 percent at [the firm's] headquarters." The largest downsizing in the firm's history, this decision was viewed by some as an admission "that the company had gone down the wrong road."[164]

■ ■ **FIGURE 8.2**

*Restructuring and Outcomes*

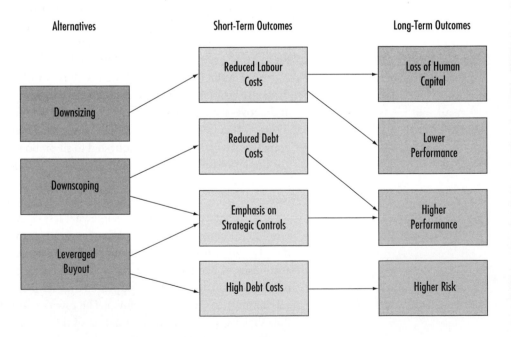

Coca-Cola's decision to reduce its workforce may also demonstrate another concern that often surfaces when firms use downsizing as a restructuring strategy. As shown in Figure 8.2, downsizing tends to result in a loss of human capital in the long term. Losing employees with many years—perhaps even decades—of experience with a firm creates a vacuum in terms of knowledge. As regards Coca-Cola, it has been noted that "analysts and company observers question whether [the firm] is cutting too many people in too many different places."[165] Thus, in general, research evidence and corporate experience suggest that downsizing may be of more tactical (i.e., short-term) than strategic (i.e., long-term) value (see Chapter 6).

As Figure 8.2 indicates, downscoping leads to more positive outcomes in both the short and the long term than does downsizing or engaging in an LBO. Downscoping's desirable long-term outcome of contributing to higher performance is a product of the positive short-term benefits of reduced debt costs and the emphasis on strategic controls that becomes possible once a firm restructures itself to concentrate on its core businesses—businesses that are less diverse in nature and that are more familiar to the top-management team. However, downscoping's positive short- and long-term outcomes are achieved only when the firm uses that restructuring strategy properly—that is, in ways that allow the company to refocus on its core business or businesses.[166]

Although whole-firm LBOs have been hailed as a significant innovation in the financial restructuring of firms, there can be negative tradeoffs. First, the large debt increases the financial risk of the firm, as is evidenced by the number of companies that filed for bankruptcy in the 1990s after having executed a whole-firm LBO. Sometimes, the intent of the owners to increase the efficiency of the bought-out firm and sell it within five to eight years creates a short-term and risk-averse managerial focus. As a result, many of these firms fail to invest in R&D or take other major actions designed to maintain or improve the company's core competence.[167] However, research suggests that in firms with an entrepreneurial mind-set, buyouts can lead to greater innovation.[168]

The strategic competitiveness spawned and above-average returns earned by GE during Jack Welch's tenure as CEO demonstrate the value that can be created by using restructuring strategies effectively. Downscoping was the primary restructuring strategy implemented by GE under Welch's leadership.[169] Toward the end of Welch's time as CEO, GE had become the ninth-largest and second-most-profitable company in the world. Between 1981, when Welch became CEO, and 1999, GE's sales rose 3.7 times (from $27.2 billion to $100.5 billion), while profits grew 5.7 times (from $1.6 billion to $9.2 billion). These outcomes indicate the significant increase in shareholders' wealth that was a product of strategic decisions made at GE while Welch was CEO.[170]

The GE of 1999 was substantially different from the GE of 1981, when Welch assumed the company's top executive position. Under Welch, GE was restructured almost continuously to create greater efficiencies, globalize operations, and develop world-class managers and top-level executives. During his final year as CEO, Welch was passionate about electronic commerce. Believing that electronic commerce was the biggest revolution in business in his lifetime, Welch thought that the Web would change how business was conducted on a global scale and how firms should be organized to compete successfully in light of those changes. Welch intended to include employees, suppliers, and customers in various activities to gather information required to determine how GE should restructure itself to exploit Web-based opportunities.[171]

As we discuss in Chapter 10 and as was mentioned earlier in this chapter, cooperative strategies, such as strategic alliances, are an alternative to merger and acquisition strategies. Citing statistics, Peter Drucker suggests that alliances of all kinds, "such as partnerships, a big business buying a minority stake in a small one, cooperative agreements in research or in marketing, joint ventures, and, often, handshake agreements with few formal and legally binding contracts behind them,"[172] are being completed with greater frequency. Both cooperative strategies and merger and acquisition strategies can lead to competitive success when they are used because there is a match between opportunities in the firm's external environment and competitive advantages formed by internal resources and capabilities.

Before examining cooperative strategies in detail in Chapter 10, however, we turn our attention to an analysis of international strategies. Because of the rapidly expanding global economy, international strategies are becoming more important drivers of strategic competitiveness for firms competing in all industries and countries.

# SUMMARY

- Acquisition strategies are increasingly popular among the world's firms. Because of globalization, deregulation of multiple industries in many different economies, and favourable legislation, among other factors, the number and size of domestic and cross-border acquisitions continues to increase.

- Firms use acquisition strategies to (1) increase market power, (2) overcome entry barriers to new markets or regions, (3) avoid costs of developing new products internally and bringing them to market, (4) increase the speed of new market entries, (5) reduce the risk of entering a new business, (6) become more diversified, and (7) reshape their competitive scope through developing a different portfolio of businesses.

- Among the problems associated with the use of an acquisition strategy are (1) the difficulty of effectively integrating the firms involved, (2) incorrectly evaluating the target firm's value, (3) creating debt loads that preclude adequate investments (e.g., R&D allocations) required for long-term success, (4) overestimating the potential for synergy between the companies involved, (5) creating a firm that is too diversified, given its core competencies and environmental opportunities, (6) creating an internal environment in which managers devote increasing amounts of their time and energy to analyzing and completing additional acquisitions, and (7) developing a combined firm that is too large, necessitating an extensive use of bureaucratic, rather than strategic, controls.

- Although potentially problematic, acquisitions can contribute to a firm's strategic competitiveness.

They do so when (1) the target firm is selected and purchased through careful, detailed analyses and negotiations, (2) the acquiring and target firms have considerable slack in the form of cash or debt capacity, (3) the acquiring firm has a low or moderate level of debt, (4) the newly created firm reduces its debt obligations quickly (especially the debts that were incurred to complete the acquisition) by selling off portions of the acquired firm or some of the acquiring firm's poorly performing companies, (5) the acquiring and target firms have complementary resources that can be the basis of core competencies in the newly created firm, (6) the acquiring and acquired firms have experience in terms of adapting to change (such experience increases the likelihood that the companies' operations will be integrated successfully), and (7) R&D and innovation are emphasized in the new firm.

- In the late 1980s and continuing into the present, restructuring is a strategy firms use to improve their performance by correcting for problems that were created by inappropriate or excessive diversification. Downsizing, a set of actions through which a firm's number of employees and hierarchical levels are reduced, is a restructuring strategy. Although it can lead to short-term cost reductions, they may be realized at the expense of long-term success. The reason for this is that once downsizing begins, the firm is unable to prevent an exodus of employees with skills required for strategic success. These employees might leave the focal firm to obtain positions with less uncertainty in other companies.

- With the goal of reducing the firm's level of diversification, downscoping is the second restructuring strategy. Often, it is accomplished by divesting unrelated businesses. As a result, the firm and its top-level managers are able to refocus on the core businesses. Firms sometimes downsize and downscope simultaneously, a comprehensive process that often yields better results than downsizing alone.

- Leveraged buyouts (LBOs) are the third restructuring strategy. Through an LBO, a firm is purchased so that it can become a private entity. LBOs usually are financed largely through debt. There are three types of LBOs: management buyouts (MBOs), employee buyouts (EBOs), and whole-firm LBOs. Because they provide clear managerial incentives, MBOs have generally been the most successful of the three. Although EBOs have the potential to improve cooperation throughout the firm, power struggles are also a possibility. These struggles are more likely when significant change is required for a firm to improve its performance. In general, whole-firm LBOs have met with mixed success. Oftentimes, the intent is to improve efficiency and performance to a point where the firm can be sold successfully within five to eight years. However, the cost of debt incurred to finance the whole-firm LBO makes it difficult for companies to perform in ways that make them attractive candidates for purchase.

- Commonly, restructuring's primary goal is gaining or re-establishing effective strategic control of the firm. Of the three restructuring strategies, downscoping is aligned the most closely with establishing and using strategic controls. Once refocused on core businesses, as downscoping allows, managers can more easily control the firm because it is less diverse (in terms of products or markets), and the businesses that remain are those about which managers tend to be the most knowledgeable.

## REVIEW QUESTIONS

1. Why are acquisition strategies popular in many firms competing in the global economy?

2. What specific reasons account for firms' decisions to use acquisition strategies as one means of achieving strategic competitiveness?

3. What are the seven primary problems that affect a firm's efforts to use an acquisition strategy successfully?

4. What are the attributes that have been found to be associated with the successful use of an acquisition strategy?

5. What does the phrase "restructuring strategy" mean, and what are the most common forms of restructuring?

6. What are the short- and long-term outcomes associated with the different restructuring strategies?

## DISCUSSION QUESTIONS

1. Evidence indicates that the shareholders of many acquiring firms gain little or nothing in value from the acquisitions. Why, then, do so many firms continue to use an acquisition strategy?

2. Of the problems that affect the success of an acquisition, which one do you believe is the most critical in the global economy? Why? What should firms do to make certain that they do not experience such a problem when they use an acquisition strategy?

3. Use the Internet to read about acquisitions that are currently under way. Choose one of these acquisitions. Based on the firms' characteristics and experiences and the reasons cited to support the acquisition, do you think it will result in increased strategic competitiveness for the acquiring firm? Why or why not?

4. Using the Internet, study recent merger and acquisition activity that is taking place throughout the global economy. Are most of the transactions you found between domestic companies, or are they cross-border acquisitions? What accounts for what you found?

5. What is synergy, and how do firms create it through mergers and acquisitions? In your opinion, how often do acquisitions create private synergy? What evidence can you cite to support your position?

6. What can a top-management team do to ensure that its firm does not become diversified to the point of earning negative returns from its diversification strategy?

7. Some companies enter new markets through internally developed products, while others do so by acquiring other firms. What are the advantages and disadvantages of each approach?

8. How do the Internet's capabilities influence a firm's ability to study acquisition candidates?

## ETHICS QUESTIONS

1. Some evidence suggests that there is a direct and positive relationship between a firm's size and its top-level managers' compensation. If this is so, what inducement does that relationship provide to upper-level executives? What can be

done to influence the relationship so that it serves shareholders' interests?

2. When a firm is in the process of restructuring itself by divesting some assets and acquiring others, managers may have incentives to restructure in ways that increase their power base and compensation package. Does this possibility explain at least part of the reason for the less-than-encouraging outcomes of acquisitions for shareholders of the acquiring firm?

3. When shareholders increase their wealth through downsizing, does this come, to some degree, at the expense of loyal employees—those who have worked diligently to serve the firm in terms of accomplishing its strategic mission and strategic intent? If so, what actions would you take to be fair to both shareholders and employees if you were charged with downsizing or "smartsizing" a firm's employment ranks? What ethical base would you employ to make decisions regarding downsizing?

4. Are takeovers ethical? Why?

5. Internet fever is mentioned in the Opening Case. Is it ethical for managers to acquire other companies just because industry competitors are doing so?

## INTERNET EXERCISE

Trace the history of some recent large mergers and acquisitions using the following Internet information sources: JDS Fitel and Uniphase, Daimler and Chrysler; and Vodafone and Mannesmann. Use any other sources you find to obtain information on the official regulatory agencies that were involved in granting or denying permission for these mergers.

## STRATEGIC SURFING

Many interesting Internet sites offer information on mergers and acquisitions. One good site is the U.S. Federal Trade Commission's (FTC) official site at:

**www.ftc.gov**

With the increasing number of cross-border mergers and acquisitions, the U.S. FTC has been required to work closely with other governments' antitrust enforcers to regulate the new era of the global transaction.

## NOTES

1 R. Whittington, 1999, In praise of the evergreen conglomerate, Mastering Strategy (Part Six), *Financial Times,* November 1, 4–6; M. A. Hitt, R. E. Hoskisson, R. D. Ireland, & J. S. Harrison, 1991, Effects of acquisitions on R&D inputs and outputs, *Academy of Management Journal,* 34: 693–706.

2 P. Moran & S. Ghoshal, 1999, Markets, firms, and the process of economic development, *Academy of Management Review,* 24: 390–412.

3 T. A. Stewart, 2000, Managing risk in the 21st century, *Fortune,* February 7, 202–06.

4 R. Simons, 1999, How risky is your company? *Harvard Business Review, 77* (3): 85–94.

5 S. Sugawara, 1999, Merger mania spawns powerhouses as world enters new century, *Dallas Morning News,* December 31, D11.

6 How M&A will navigate the turn into a new century, 2000, *Mergers & Acquisitions,* January, 29–35.

7 E. Portanger, 2000, Europe sets the stage for more megamergers, *Wall Street Journal,* January 4, A17.

8 How M&A will navigate, 30.

9 C. C. Markides, 1999, A dynamic view of strategy, *Sloan Management Review,* 40 (3): 55–63.

10 H. R. Greve, 1998, Managerial cognition and the mimetic adoption of market positions: What you see is what you do, *Strategic Management Journal,* 19: 967–988.

11 B. Lowendahl & O. Revang, 1998, Challenges to existing strategy theory in a postindustrial society, *Strategic Management Journal,* 19: 755–73.

12 D. L. Deephouse, 1999, To be different, or to be the same? It's a question (and theory) of strategic balance, *Strategic Management Journal,* 20: 147–66.

13 M. A. Hitt, J. S. Harrison, & R. D. Ireland, 2001, *Creating Value through Mergers and Acquisitions: A Complete Guide to Successful M&As* (New York: Oxford University Press); Hitt, Hoskisson, Ireland, & Harrison, Effects of acquisitions, 693–706.

14 A. Rappaport & M. L. Sirower, 1999, Stock or cash? *Harvard Business Review, 77* (6): 147–58.

15 Sugawara, Merger mania, D11.

16 J. Pereira, 2000, Late to the Web, Staples forges dot-com links, *Wall Street Journal,* January 14, B1, B4.

17 M&A scorecard, 2000, *Mergers & Acquisitions,* January, 40–42.

18 Hitt, Harrison, & Ireland, *Creating Value;* K. C. O'Shaughnessy & D. J. Flanagan, 1998, Determinants of layoff announcements following M&As: An empirical investigation, *Strategic Management Journal,* 19: 989–99.

19 J. Anand, 1999, How many matches are made in heaven, Mastering Strategy (Part Five), *Financial Times,* October 25, 6–7.

20 B. Deener, 1999, Mega-deals stifle shares, survey implies, *Dallas Morning News,* November 30, D1, D6.

21 M. C. Jensen, 1988, Takeovers: Their causes and consequences, *Journal of Economic Perspectives,* 1 (2): 21–48.

22 Rappaport & Sirower, Stock or cash? 147–58.

23 E. Robinson, 1999, UK and Dutch cleaning products groups to merge, *Financial Times,* July 28, 13.

24 W. Mitchell, 1999, Recreating the company: Four contexts for change, Mastering Strategy (Part Ten), *Financial Times,* November 29, 4–7.

25 K. Leger, 2000, Videotron shareholders threaten action against Caisse: Rogers takeover dispute, *National Post,* July 5, C3; M. Lewis, 2000, Rogers offers olive branch to Quebecor: Videotron compromise, *National Post,* May 31, C1, C10. Court a real possibility, 2000, Court a real possibility: Rogers, Videotron, Quebecor, Caisse may go before judge next month, *Cablecaster,* 12 (5) May: 16.

26 S. Lipin, 1999, More big firms are ripe for hostile takeover bids, *Wall Street Journal,* November 22, B10.

27 S. Tully, 2000, The new takeover target (Hint: It's in Detroit), *Fortune,* January 10, 28–30.

28 Mitchell, Recreating the company, 7; D. K. Datta, G. E. Pinches, & V. K. Naravyanan, 1992, Factors influencing wealth creation from mergers and acquisitions: A metaanalysis, *Strategic Management Journal,* 13: 67–84; P. C. Haspeslagh & D. B. Jemison, 1991, *Managing Acquisitions: Creating Value through Corporate Renewal* (New York: The Free Press).

29 M. L. Marks, 2000, Egos can make and unmake mergers, *Wall Street Journal,* January 24, A26.

30 P. Haspeslagh, 1999, Managing the mating dance in equal mergers, Mastering Strategy (Part Five), *Financial Times,* October 25, 14–15.

31 C. Y. Chen, 2000, Gorilla in the Midst, *Fortune Investor Analysis Online,* August 14.

32 L. Capron, 1999, Horizontal acquisitions: The benefits and risk to long-term performance, Mastering Strategy (Part Seven), *Financial Times,* November 8, 7–8.

33 L. Capron, 1999, The long-term performance of horizontal acquisitions, *Strategic Management Journal,* 20: 987–1018.

34 R. Flannery, 2000, Big Taiwan chip maker to acquire rival, *Wall Street Journal,* January 10, A7.

35 K. Ramaswamy, 1997, The performance impact of strategic similarity in horizontal mergers: Evidence from the U.S. banking industry, *Academy of Management Journal,* 40: 697–715.

36 J. Vardy, 1999, JDS, Uniphase seen as good corporate fit: Firms have 100% customer overlap, no product overlap, *National Post,* February 2, C6.

37 Ibid.

38 Anand, How many matches, 6–7.

39 R. Gertner & M. J. Knez, 1999, Vertical integration: Make or buy decisions, Mastering Strategy (Part Ten), *Financial Times,* November 29, 12–13.

40 M. Brannigan, 2000, Carnival agrees to buy Fairfield for stock, debt, *Wall Street Journal,* January 25, A8.

41 M. Brannigan, 2000, Carnival, hit by stock dive, calls off talks to acquire Fairfield Communities, *Wall Street Journal,* February 28, A15.

42 CPR asks US authorities to stop CNR BNSF rail mega merger, 2000, *Canadian Press Newswire,* March 3.

43 T. Petzinger, Jr., 2000, So long, supply and demand, *Wall Street Journal,* January 1, R31.

44 J. A. Gingrich, 1999, Five rules for winning emerging market consumers, *Strategy & Business,* 15: 19–33.

45 Hitt, Harrison, & Ireland, *Creating Value,* Chapter 10; D. Angwin & B. Savill, 1997, Strategic perspectives on European cross-border acquisitions: A view from the top European executives, *European Management Review,* 15: 423–35.

46 Based on U.S. FDI of U.S.$111.7 billion from Table 4.2. *Foreign Direct Investment Position in the United States on a Historical-Cost Basis,* 1999, from the U.S. Bureau of Economic Analysis, 2000, http://www.bea.doc.gov/bea/ai/0700dip/table4-2.htm (Retrieved September 18, 2000) and total FDI in Canada of Can$240 billion from *Canada's International Investment Position,* 1999, from Statistics Canada, http://www.statcan.ca/ english/Pgdb/ Economy/Economic/econ08.htm (Retrieved September 18, 2000), as adjusted for currency exchange rates.

47 Based on total Canadian FDI of $257.4 billion (CDN) from *Canada's International Investment Position,* 1999, from Statistics Canada, http://www.statcan.ca/english/Pgdb/Economy/ Economic/econ08.htm (Retrieved September 18, 2000), and Canadian FDI in the U.S. of U.S.$79.7 billion from Table 3.2. *Foreign Direct Investment Position in the United States on a Historical-Cost Basis,* 1999, from the U.S. Bureau of Economic Analysis, http://www. bea.doc.gov/bea/ai/0700dip/table3-2.htm (Retrieved September 18, 2000).

48 P. C. Newman, 1999, The year of living dangerously: in 1999, US takeovers of Canadian companies have taken on a disturbing new reality. The result: "We have become squatters on our own land," *Maclean's* (Toronto Edition), December 20, 50; N. Nankivell, 1999, What's good for the goose: Canadians are mounting more mergers and acquisitions abroad than foreigners are here, *National Post,* March 20, D6.

49 B. Ng, 2000, Mergers and acquisitions activity hits $149b in second quarter: On record pace, *National Post,* July 8, D8.

50 International Investment Data, 2000, *International Investment Data: Foreign Direct Investment in the United States: Capital Inflows,* U.S. Bureau of Economic Analysis, http://www.bea.doc.gov/bea/di/fdi21web.htm (Retrieved September 18).

51 J. N. Deogun, 1999, Made in U.S.A.: Deals from Europe hit record, *Wall Street Journal,* October 25, C1, C18.

52 E. Robinson, 1999, Shiseido pursues M&A, *Financial Times,* July 27, 14.

53 J. K. Shank & V. Govindarajan, 1992, Strategic cost analysis of technological investments, *Sloan Management Review,* 34 (3): 39–51.

54 E. Mansfield, 1969, *Industrial Research and Technological Innovation* (New York: Norton).

55 Hitt, Harrison, & Ireland, *Creating Value;* L. H. Clark, Jr. & A. L. Malabre, Jr., 1988, Slow rise in outlays for research imperils U.S. competitive edge, *Wall Street Journal,* November 16, A1, A5; E. Mansfield, M. Schwartz, & S. Wagner, 1981, Imitation costs and patents: An empirical study, *Economic Journal,* 91: 907–18.

56 M. A. Hitt, R. E. Hoskisson, R. A. Johnson, & D. D. Moesel, 1996, The market for corporate control and firm innovation, *Academy of Management Journal,* 39: 1084–19.

57 J. Greenwood, 1999, Novopharm edges toward deal with Teva: In due diligence. Only business not on the block is biotech unit, *National Post,* October 20, C3.

58 M. Elvekrog, 2000, Watson Pharmaceuticals, *Better Investing,* February, 32–34.

59 R. Wherry, 1999, Pfizer's surpriser, *Forbes,* November 29, 56.

60 J. Greenwood, 1999, Cangene declares interest in Hyal: Skyepharma has offer in, *National Post,* July 20, C5; D. Pilling, 1999, Big boys eye bite-sized bios, *Financial Times,* July 15, 14.

61 F. McCardle & S. Viswanathan, 1994, The direct entry versus takeover decision and stock price performance around takeovers, *Journal of Business,* 67: 1–43.

62 Rappaport & Sirower, Stock or cash? 147.

63 M. Song, A. A. Di Benedetto, & Y. L. Zhao, 1999, Pioneering advantages in manufacturing and service industries: Empirical evidence from nine countries, *Strategic Management Journal,* 20: 811–36.

64 H. Lee, K. G. Smith, C. M. Grimm, & A. Schomburg, 2000, Timing, order and durability of new product advantages with imitation, *Strategic Management Journal,* 21: 23–30.

65 S. Stecklow, 2000, BT rides in to buy Ireland's Esat, topping bid by Norway's Telenor, *Wall Street Journal,* January 12, A18.

66 Kraft Foods agrees to buy Boca Burger, a soy-products firm, 2000, *Wall Street Journal,* January 19, B7.

67 G. McWilliams, 2000, Compaq buying custom-PC lines of Inacom, with Dell in mind, *Wall Street Journal,* January 15, B2.

68 M. A. Hitt, R. E. Hoskisson, & R. D. Ireland, 1990, Mergers and acquisitions and managerial commitment to innovation in M-form firms, *Strategic Management Journal,* 11 (Special Summer Issue): 29–47.

69 K. Damsell, 2000, Corus swallows Nelvana, Broadcaster's $540 million acquisition of animation house part of global ambition, *The Globe and Mail,* September 19, B1, B11.

70 Hitt, Hoskisson, & Ireland, Mergers and acquisitions; J. Constable, 1986, Diversification as a factor in U.K. industrial strategy, *Long Range Planning,* 19: 52–60.

71 Hitt, Hoskisson, Ireland, & Harrison, Effects of acquisitions; Hitt, Hoskisson, & Ireland, Mergers and acquisitions.

72 D. Olive, 1999, Fine-tuning an engine of wealth: you'd never predict that Gerry Schwartz, chairman of Onex Corp, was a car guy. But as Mr Schwartz has shown, he's anything but predictable, *National Post,* February 1, C12.

73 Ibid.

74 Z. Olijnyk, 2001, Schwartz new cinema czar, Buys Loews Cineplex, *National Post,* February 16, C1, C4.

75 J. F. Hennart & S. B. Reddy, 2000, Digestibility and asymmetric information in the choice between acquisitions and joint ventures: Where's the beef? *Strategic Management Journal,* 21: 191–93.

76 D. D. Bergh, 1997, Predicting divestiture of unrelated acquisitions: An integrative model of ex ante conditions, *Strategic Management Journal,* 18: 715–31.

77 J. Anand & H. Singh, 1997, Asset redeployment, acquisitions and corporate strategy in declining industries, *Strategic Management Journal,* 18 (Special Summer Issue): 99–118.

78 J. Harrison, 1999, Following the lead of a changing industry, *Mergers & Acquisitions,* May/June, 60–61.

79 D. Olive, 1999, Fine-tuning an engine of wealth.

80 Ibid.

81 T. Burt, 1999, DaimlerChrysler looks to diversify, *Financial Times,* August 3, 16.

82 J. Griffiths, 1999, Spotlight falls on Japanese, *Financial Times,* May 22, 1: 1999, Fitter future for Ford as Nascar takes the driving seat, *Financial Times,* April 13, 24.

83 P. Landers & R. A. Guth, 2000, Japan's Hitachi plans high-tech shopping spree, *Wall Street Journal,* January 5, A19.

84 D. Stewart, 2000, Can we make the damn parts fast enough: Deal appears to have nothing but upsides, *National Post,* July 11, C8.

85  Marks, Egos can make, A26.

86  Anand, How many matches, 7.

87  Hitt, Harrison, & Ireland, *Creating Value;* D. K. Datta, 1991, Organizational fit and acquisition performance: Effects of post-acquisition integration, *Strategic Management Journal,* 12: 281–97.

88  A. J. Viscio, J. R. Harbison, A. Asin, & R. P. Vitaro, 1999, Post-merger integration: What makes mergers work? *Strategy & Business,* 17: 26–33; H. Aaron, 1994, A poisoning of the atmosphere, *Wall Street Journal,* August 29, A10; P. M. Elsass & J. F. Veiga, 1994, Acculturation in acquired organizations: A force field perspective, *Human Relations,* 47: 453–71.

89  S. DeVoge & S. Spreier, 1999, The soft realities of mergers, *Across the Board,* December, 27–32; A. F. Buono & J. L. Bowditch, 1989, *The Human Side of Mergers and Acquisitions* (San Francisco: Jossey-Bass).

90  M. Zollo, 1999, M&A, The challenge of learning to integrate, Mastering Strategy (Part 11), *Financial Times,* December 6, 14–15.

91  Ibid., 14.

92  N. Knox, 1999, AlliedSignal, Honeywell plan rapid integration of companies, *Dallas Morning News,* June 8, D4.

93  R. L. Simison & S. Miller, 1999, Making 'digital' decisions, *Wall Street Journal,* September 24, B1, B4.

94  H. Goldblatt, 1999, Cisco's secrets, *Fortune,* November 8, 177–82.

95  Anand, How many matches, 7; K. Ohmae, 1999, The Godzilla companies of the new economy, *Strategy & Business,* 18: 130–39.

96  Rappaport & Sirower, Stock or cash?, 149.

97  Viscio, Harbison, Asin, & Vitaro, Post-merger integration, 27.

98  R. C. Morais, 2000, Takeover bait, *Forbes,* January 24, 74–75.

99  Hitt, Harrison, & Ireland, *Creating Value.*

100  G. Yago, 1991, *Junk Bonds: How High Yield Securities Restructured Corporate America* (New York: Oxford University Press), 146–48.

101  M. C. Jensen, 1987, A helping hand for entrenched managers, *Wall Street Journal,* November 4, A6; M. C. Jensen, 1986, Agency costs of free cash flow, corporate finance, and takeovers, *American Economic Review,* 76: 323–29.

102  A. Osterland, 1999, False spring for a seed company, *BusinessWeek,* June 12, 130.

103  M. A. Hitt & D. L. Smart, 1994, Debt: A disciplining force for managers or a debilitating force for organizations? *Journal of Management Inquiry,* 3: 144–52.

104  Hitt, Harrison, & Ireland, *Creating Value.*

105  A. Swift, 2000, Donohue marks the end of its 100-year history and the end of an era in pulp and paper, *National Post,* May 9, C5; C. J. Chipello, 2000, Abitibi agrees to purchase Donohue in $4 billion cash-and-stock accord, *Wall Street Journal,* February 14, A32.

106  T. N. Hubbard, 1999, Integration strategies and the scope of the company, Mastering Strategy (Part 11), *Financial Times,* December 6, 8–10.

107  Hitt, Harrison, & Ireland, *Creating Value.*

108  C. H. St. John & J. S. Harrison, 1999, Manufacturing-based relatedness, synergy, and coordination, *Strategic Management Journal,* 20: 129–45.

109  Hitt, Hoskisson, Ireland, & Harrison, Effects of acquisitions; J. B. Barney, 1988, Returns to bidding firms in mergers and acquisitions: Reconsidering the relatedness hypothesis, *Strategic Management Journal,* 9 (Special Summer Issue): 71–78.

110  O. E. Williamson, 1999, Strategy research: Governance and competence perspectives, *Strategic Management Journal,* 20: 1087–1108.

111  Hitt, Hoskisson, Johnson, & Moesel, The market for corporate control.

112  Whittington, In praise of, 4.

113  C. W. L. Hill & R. E. Hoskisson, 1987, Strategy and structure in the multiproduct firm, *Academy of Management Review,* 12: 331–41.

114  R. A. Johnson, R. E. Hoskisson, & M. A. Hitt, 1993, Board of director involvement in restructuring: The effects of board versus managerial controls and characteristics, *Strategic Management Journal,* 14 (Special Issue): 33–50; C. C. Markides, 1992, Consequences of corporate refocusing: Ex ante evidence, *Academy of Management Journal,* 35: 398–412.

115  R. Sobel, 1984, *The Rise and Fall of the Conglomerate Kings,* Briarcliff Manor, N.Y.: Stein and Day.

116  D. Olive, 2001, Good riddance to bad policy, *National Post,* February 14, C1, C4.

117  P. Fitzpatrick, 2001, CP Splits to unlock value: Five new divisions, *National Post,* February 14, C1, C4.

118  R. E. Hoskisson & M. A. Hitt, 1988, Strategic control systems and relative R&D investment in large multiproduct firms, *Strategic Management Journal,* 9: 605–21.

119  Hitt, Hoskisson, & Ireland, Mergers and acquisitions.

120  Ibid.

121  J. Flint, No guts, no glory, *Forbes,* February 7, 88.

122  Hitt, Hoskisson, Ireland, & Harrison, Effects of acquisitions.

123  R. E. Hoskisson, M. A. Hitt, & R. D. Ireland, 1994, The effects of acquisitions and restructuring (strategic refocusing) strategies on innovation, in G. von Krogh, A. Sinatra, and H. Singh (eds.), *Managing Corporate Acquisitions* (London: Macmillan Press), 144–69.

124  P. Fitzpatrick, 2001, CP splits to unlock value: Five new divisions, *National Post,* February 14, C1, C4.

125 Hitt, Hoskisson, & Ireland, Mergers and acquisitions.

126 K. Ohmae, 2000, The Godzilla companies of the new economy, *Strategy & Business*, 18: 130–39.

127 Hitt, Harrison, & Ireland, *Creating Value.*

128 S. Harrison, M. A. Hitt, R. E. Hoskisson, & R. D. Ireland, 1991, Synergies and post acquisition performance: Differences versus similarities in resource allocations, *Journal of Management,* 17: 173–90; Barney, Returns to bidding firms.

129 M. A. Lubatkin & P. J. Lane, 1996, Psst ... The merger mavens still have it wrong! *Academy of Management Executive,* X (1): 21–39.

130 J. P. Walsh, 1989, Doing a deal: Merger and acquisition negotiations and their impact upon target company top management turnover, *Strategic Management Journal,* 10: 307–22.

131 S. Lublin, 1995, Strategies for preventing post-takeover defections, *Wall Street Journal,* April 28, B1, B8.

132 J. Daly, 1999, John Chambers: The art of the deal, *Business 2.0,* October, 106—16.

133 Anand, How many matches, 6.

134 P. F. Drucker, 2000, The unrecognized boom, *Across the Board,* January, 15–16.

135 R. G. Hoskisson, R. A. Johnson & D. D. Moesel, 1994, Divestment intensity of restructuring firms: Effects of governance, strategy, and performance, *Academy of Management Journal,* 37: 1207–51.

136 S. R. Fisher & M. A. White, 2000, Downsizing in a learning organization: Are there hidden costs? *Academy of Management Review,* 25: 244–51.

137 R. A. Johnson, 1996, Antecedents and outcomes of corporate refocusing, *Journal of Management,* 22: 437–81.

138 J. E. Bethel & J. Liebeskind, 1993, The effects of ownership structure on corporate restructuring, *Strategic Management Journal,* 14 (Special Summer Issue): 15–31.

139 A. Campbell & D. Sadtler, 1998, Corporate breakups, *Strategy & Business,* 12: 64–73; E. Bowman & H. Singh, 1990, Overview of corporate restructuring: Trends and consequences, in L. Rock & R. H. Rock (eds.), *Corporate Restructuring* (New York: McGraw-Hill).

140 Fisher & White, Downsizing in a learning organization, 244.

141 W. McKinley, J. Zhao, & K. G. Rust, 2000, A sociocognitive interpretation of organizational downsizing, *Academy of Management Review,* 25: 227–43.

142 W. McKinley, C. M. Sanchez, & A. G. Schick, 1995, Organizational downsizing: Constraining, cloning, learning, *Academy of Management Executive,* IX (3): 32–44.

143 McKinley, Zhao, & Rust, A sociocognitive interpretation, 227.

144 N. Shirouzu, 2000, Driven by necessity—and by Ford—Mazda downsizes, U.S.-style, *Wall Street Journal,* January 5, A1, A8; A. Edgecliffe-Johnson, 1999, Procter & Gamble to cut 15,000 jobs in restructuring, *Financial Times,* June 10, 1; J. Hechinger, 1999, Bausch & Lomb to cut its work force, restructure contact-lens operation, *Wall Street Journal,* December 3, B14.

145 Hoskisson and Hitt, Downscoping.

146 J. S. Lublin, 1995, Spin-offs may establish new companies, but they often spell the end of jobs, *Wall Street Journal,* November 21, B1, B8; J. Kose, H. P. Lang, & J. Netter, 1992, The voluntary restructuring of large firms in response to performance decline, *Journal of Finance,* 47: 891–917.

147 Johnson, Hoskisson, & Hitt, Board of directors involvement; R. E. Hoskisson & M. A. Hitt, 1990, Antecedents and performance outcomes of diversification: A review and critique of theoretical perspectives, *Journal of Management,* 16: 461–509.

148 Whittington, In praise, 4.

149 R. Atkins, 1999, German business giants evolve to meet new challenges, *Financial Times,* June 24, 23.

150 B. Orwall & M. Rose, 2000, Disney may sell Los Angeles magazine as it pares down noncore operations, *Wall Street Journal,* January 19, B7.

151 B. Copple, 2000, Synergy in ketchup? *Forbes,* February 7, 68–69.

152 A. Edgecliffe-Johnson & M. Marsh, 1999, Ralston plans to spin off Eveready arm, *Financial Times,* June 11, 18.

153 D. D. Bergh & G. F. Holbein, 1997, Assessment and redirection of longitudinal analysis: Demonstration with a study of the diversification and divestiture relationship, *Strategic Management Journal,* 18: 557–71; C.C. Markides & H. Singh, 1997, Corporate restructuring: A symptom of poor governance or a solution to past managerial mistakes? *European Management Journal,* 15: 213–19.

154 M. F. Wiersema & J. P. Liebeskind, 1995, The effects of leveraged buyouts on corporate growth and diversification in large firms, *Strategic Management Journal,* 16: 447–60.

155 A. Seth & J. Easterwood, 1995, Strategic redirection in large management buyouts: The evidence from post-buyout restructuring activity, *Strategic Management Journal,* 14: 251–74; P. H. Phan & C. W. L. Hill, 1995, Organizational restructuring and economic performance in leveraged buyouts: An ex-post study, *Academy of Management Journal,* 38: 704–39.

156 L. Katynski, 1997, Turning it around: How to remake a company into a winner, *Manitoba Business,* May: 25–26.

157  S. Chandler, 1996, United we own, *BusinessWeek*, March 18, 96–100.

158  A. Bernstein, 1996, Why ESOP deals have slowed to a crawl, *BusinessWeek*, March 18, 101–2.

159  I. Filatochev, R. E. Hoskisson, T. Buck, & M. Wright, 1996, Corporate restructuring in Russian privatizations: Implications for US investors, *California Management Review*, 38 (2): 87–105.

160  Tembec, 2000, *Tembec home page*, http://www.tembec.ca (Retrieved September 24).

161  B. Ortega, 1995, Cadbury seeking a new King of pop to oversee no. 3 soft-drink business, *Wall Street Journal*, January 30, B2.

162  Fisher & White, Downsizing in a learning organization, 244.

163  P. M. Lee, 1997, A comparative analysis of layoff announcements and stock price reactions in the United States and Japan, *Strategic Management Journal*, 18: 879–94.

164  H. Unger, 2000, Coke cutbacks show company went down wrong path, *Wall Street Journal*, January 30, H6.

165  Ibid.

166  Johnson, Antecedents and outcomes.

167  W. F. Long & D. J. Ravenscraft, 1993, LBOs, debt, and R&D intensity, *Strategic Management Journal*, 14 (Special Issue, Summer): 119–35.

168  M. Wright, R. E. Hoskisson, L. W. Busenitz, & J. Dial, 2000, Entrepreneurial growth through privatizing: The upside of management tryouts. *Academy of Management Review*, 25 (3): 591–601.

169  Whittington, In praise, 6.

170  T. A. Stewart, 1999, See Jack. See Jack run, *Fortune*, September 27, 124–36.

171  Ibid.

172  Drucker, The unrecognized boom, 15.

# Chapter Nine

## International Strategy

## LEARNING OBJECTIVES

*After reading this chapter, you should be able to:*

1. Explain traditional and emerging motives for firms to pursue international diversification.
2. Explore the four factors that lead to a basis for international business-level strategies.
3. Name and define generic international business-level strategies.
4. Define the three international corporate-level strategies: multidomestic, global, and transnational.
5. Discuss the environmental trends affecting international strategy.
6. Name and describe the five alternative modes for entering international markets.
7. Explain the effects of international diversification on firm returns and innovation.
8. Name and describe two major risks of international diversification.
9. Explain why the positive outcomes from international expansion are limited.

# Technology and Globalization: A Changing Landscape in the 21st Century

Technology and the globalization of business have created a new competitive landscape for the 21st century. In short, technology and globalization have interacted to create an ongoing revolution. In particular, the development and use of new technology facilitate increasing globalization. Two types of technology—the Internet and wireless communications—are having profound effects on the way business is conducted worldwide.

The Internet now allows rapid and effective communication and coordination of units and operations on a global basis. It also facilitates business-to-business (B2B) relationships and increases the speed with which innovations are diffused throughout the world. Although the Internet revolution largely emanated from the United States, the rest of the world now participates. For example, although U.S. firms accounted for about 75 percent of e-commerce in 1998, it is expected that they will account for only about 50 percent of the $8.3 trillion global e-commerce market by 2003. Consumer retailing purchases via the Internet are estimated to triple by 2003. European e-commerce alone is expected to exceed $2.1 trillion by 2004 (a 140 percent annual growth rate).

Likewise, mobile phones are becoming ubiquitous and used for multiple purposes. For example, it is becoming increasingly common for children in middle school (as young as 10 years old) to carry mobile phones in Sweden, and approximately 58 percent of all people in Finland own mobile phones. DoMoCo, a Japanese company, has developed and marketed a mobile phone that allows people to connect to the Internet and perform many of the tasks normally confined to a computer. In fact, mobile phone technology will bring the Internet to locations throughout the world that have been slow to adopt computer-based connections. The number of mobile phones in use is growing at more than twice the rate of new fixed (wired) telephone connections annually. This third generation of mobile telephony will dramatically increase the speed of data transmission and greatly enlarge the number of users of such phones globally. Mobile phones are

http://www.7-eleven.com
http://www.alcan.com

a cheaper and easier (i.e., more user-friendly) means of accessing the Internet than computers and thus will be available to a larger number of people.

The global potential for increased e-commerce worldwide is substantial. For example, although there were 4 million Internet users in China in 1999, it is predicted that by 2001 that country will have 27 million users. The potential for this rapid increase in the number of Internet users in China rests with the introduction of mobile phone connections to the Internet. Firms in other emerging-market countries such as Russia and Bulgaria in Eastern Europe are also increasing their use of e-commerce.

For all of the preceding reasons, many firms are rushing to join the global e-commerce revolution. For instance, Seven-Eleven Japan is leading the development of an e-commerce joint venture with seven other firms to offer goods and services through the Internet and multimedia portals in 8000 Japanese Seven-Eleven outlets. The goal is to expand this service to Seven-Eleven stores globally. Seven-Eleven Japan will hold the largest stake in the venture, followed by Sony, NEC, and Nomura Research Institute, each with a 13 percent share. Interestingly, prior to this joint venture formed in 2000, Seven-Eleven was the hub of e-commerce in Japan.

Another example is Alcan's move to form a global Internet-based procurement market of 14 mining and metals firms—with others expected to join later. Firms in the group include Canada's Barrick Gold and Inco, U.S. aluminium competitor Alcoa, Australian's Broken Hill Proprietary Company, Chile's CODELCO, and South Africa's De Beers. The arrangement will provide access to sources from producers and suppliers in more than 100 countries. There will also be benefits to buyers and suppliers through standardization, simplified transaction processes, and better inventory management.

The increasing importance of e-commerce is shown by Intel's decision to develop "server farms." These farms are intended to provide firms with the capability of conducting e-commerce. Intel located its first farm in Reading, England. The location houses 10 000 Internet servers and a staff of 170. The farms target small firms that do not have the internal resources to support e-commerce activities. Intel projects demand for servers will increase by 2500 percent by 2005. Accordingly, Intel expects to locate server farms throughout Europe to meet fast-growing demand. Indeed, e-commerce activities will extend the reach of even small businesses across the globe.

Sources: Alcan, 2000, *Alcan Aluminium News Page,* http://www.alcan.com/www.Alcan.nsf/Level2-E/LevelNews-E?OpenDocument (Retrieved May 26); J. Borzo, 2000, Court ruling in Russia…, *Wall Street Journal Interactive,* January 6, www.inter active.wsj.com.articles; C. Grande, 1999, E-commerce: U.S to retain global lead, *www.ft.com,* www.ft.com.nbearchive; C. Grande, 2000, Shopping: E-spending will triple by 2003, *www.ft.com,* January 17, www.ft.com.nbearchive; B. Groom, 2000, Intel: Berkshire hosts 90m server farm, *www.ft.com,* January 20, www.ft.com.nbearchive; R. Grover, 2000, Univision peers into Cyberspace, *BusinessWeek Online,* January 9, www.businessweek.com; A. Kaiser, 2000, Bulgaria, LVMH strike deal to team up for online sales, *Wall Street Journal Interactive,* January 6, www.interactive.wsj.com.articles; P. Landers, 1999, In Japan, the hub of E-Commerce is a 7-Eleven, *Wall Street Journal,* November 1, B1, B4; M. J. Mandel, 1999, The Internet economy…, *BusinessWeek Online,* September 27; C. Matlack, J. Ewing, G. Edmondson, & W. Echikson, 1999, Cashing in on an Internet bonanza, *BusinessWeek,* December 13, 62; N. Nakamae, 2000, Seven-Eleven: Online arm to launch, *www.ft.com,* January 7, www.ft.com.nbearchive; Seven-Eleven Japan, NEC, Others JV called 7dream.com, 2000, *Wall Street Journal Interactive,* January 6, www.interactive. wsj.com.articles; Seven-Eleven Japan reveals e-commerce joint venture, 2000, *Wall Street Journal Interactive,* January 6, www.interactive.wsj.com.articles; The world in your pocket, 2000, *Economist.Com,* January 6, www. economist.com/editorial.

In the 1980s, the dramatic success of Japanese firms and products, such as Toyota and Sony, in international markets provided a powerful jolt to managers and awakened them to the importance of international competition and global markets. In the 21st century, Russia and China represent potential major international market opportunities for firms from many countries, including Canada, the United States, Japan, Korea, and the European Community.[1] Russia and China are also formidable competitors, particularly China's low-technology manufacturing industries. However, companies competing in the global marketplace have expressed concerns about the relative attractiveness of the Russian and Chinese markets. The economic crises in Russia in the late 1990s lent credibility to these concerns. Some believe that, for at least a period of time, foreign investors will continue to favour China, because China is more orderly, and Russia remains full of risks. Russia's movement to more of a free-market economy now seems more likely to depend on homegrown developments instead of foreign direct investments (FDI) and other modes firms use to internationalize their operations.[2]

The 21st century may find less focus on a particular region of the world and more emphasis on truly global markets. An emphasis on global markets is facilitated by the developments in technology described in the Opening Case. Parallel developments in the Internet and mobile telephony facilitate communications all over the globe. Furthermore, these developments have led to the e-commerce revolution that is now prevalent in the business world. The information presented in the Opening Case suggests rapid growth of e-commerce globally, which is exemplified by the venture led by Seven-Eleven in Japan. E-commerce is not restricted to large firms. Because Intel's server farms provide the technology necessary for small firms to participate in e-commerce, even small firms can sell their goods and services globally without having (brick-and-mortar) facilities beyond their home location. The increasingly rapid globalization of markets and business is evident all over the world. For example, Brazil's Internet market is expanding quickly. Recently, Terra Brasil, an Internet provider controlled by Telefonica of Spain, acquired ZAZ, the second-largest Internet provider in Brazil. This action followed an announcement by two of Brazil's largest private banks to offer free Internet services. Other free Internet services are expected to enter the Brazilian market, some by way of the current largest service providers.[3]

Thus, the international arena features both opportunities and threats for firms seeking strategic competitiveness in global markets. This chapter examines opportunities facing firms as they seek to develop and exploit core competencies by diversifying into global markets. We also discuss different problems and complexities that can be associated with implementation of the firm's chosen international strategies.[4] National boundaries, cultural differences, and geographical distances no longer pose barriers to business and entry into many markets. Business has become truly global, in markets ranging from drugs and tires to publishing and engineering.[5] Selecting and implementing appropriate international strategies allows the firm to become a global corporation. However, to mould their firms into truly global companies, managers must develop global mind-sets. Traditional means of operating with little cultural diversity and without global competition are no longer effective.[5] Developing a global mind-set among managers without international experience and with little experience of cultural diversity is challenging. Of course, firms experiencing these challenges are slower to change. Providing international experiences may be required to more quickly build global mind-sets among a firm's managers.[6]

For example, Cemex rapidly changed from a domestic cement manufacturer in the Mexican market to a global producer of cement, largely through acquisitions of cement firms in Latin America, Asia, North America, and Europe. In fact, Cemex has played an important role in developing a global cement industry. For example, 60 percent of Asia's cement market is now served by multinationals, up from only 20 percent a few years ago. As Cemex's managers had little experience with global markets, the company established an extensive management development program designed to help its managers build a global mind-set.[7]

In this chapter, as illustrated in Figure 1.1 in Chapter 1, we discuss the importance of international strategy as a source of strategic competitiveness and above-average returns. The chapter focuses on the incentives to internationalize. Once a firm decides to compete internationally, it must select its strategy and choose a mode of entry into international markets. It may enter international markets by exporting from domestic-based operations, licensing some of its products or services, forming joint ventures with international partners, acquiring a foreign-based firm, or establishing a new subsidiary. Such international diversification can extend product life cycles, provide incentives for more innovation, and produce above-average returns. These benefits are tempered by political and economic risks and the problems of managing a complex international firm with operations in multiple countries. Figure 9.1 provides an overview of these choices and outcomes. The relationships among international opportunities, exploration of resources and capabilities that result in strategies, and modes of entry that are based on core competencies are explored in this chapter.

■ ■ **FIGURE 9.1**

*Opportunities and Outcomes of International Strategy*

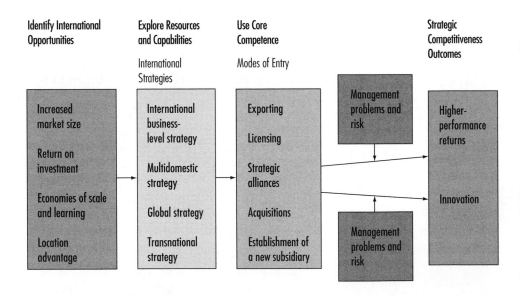

# IDENTIFYING INTERNATIONAL OPPORTUNITIES: THE INTERNATIONAL STRATEGY INCENTIVE

An **international strategy** refers to the selling of products in markets outside the firm's domestic market.

An **international strategy** refers to the selling of products in markets outside the firm's domestic market.[8] One of the primary reasons for implementing an international strategy (as opposed to a strategy focused on the domestic market) is that international markets yield potential new opportunities. Raymond Vernon captured the classic rationale for international diversification.[9] He suggested that typically a firm discovers an innovation in its home country market. Some demand for the product may develop in other countries and, thus, exports are provided by domestic operations. Increased demand in foreign countries justifies direct foreign investment in production capacity abroad, especially as foreign competitors also organize to meet increasing demand. As the product becomes standardized, the firm may rationalize its operations by moving production to a region where manufacturing costs are low. Vernon, thereby, suggests that firms pursue international diversification to extend a product's life cycle.

Another traditional motive for firms to become multinational is to secure needed resources. Key supplies of raw material, especially minerals and energy, are important in some industries. For instance, aluminium producers need a supply of bauxite, tire firms need rubber, and oil companies scour the world to find new petroleum reserves.

Others seek to secure access to low-cost factors of production. Clothing, electronics, watchmaking, and many other industries have moved portions of their operations to foreign locations in pursuit of lower costs. To enhance its cost competitiveness in the deflationary environment at the end of the 1990s, GE continued to shift some of its appliance manufacturing operations to various locations throughout the world. All of the firm's gas ranges are now made in San Luis Potosi, Mexico, through the firm's joint venture with Mabe, a Mexican company. In total, GE employs over 24 000 people in Mexico, primarily to manufacture appliances.[10]

Turkey's wage rates are among the lowest in Europe. In fact, the nation's hourly rates average one-half of those in Portugal, the poorest country in the European Union. Moreover, wages are lower than in some Eastern European countries and many developing nations. Because of these wage rates, coupled with the fact that workers' productivity is increasing by 3.6 percent annually, compared to the OECD average of 2.8 percent, many multinational companies are establishing operations in Turkey. In fact, these investments caused Turkey's economy to grow at a rate that has caused labour shortages.[11]

Though these traditional motives continue to exist, as the above examples show, other emerging motivations have been driving international expansion (see Chapter 1). For instance, pressure has increased for global integration of operations, mostly driven by more universal product demand. As nations industrialize, demand for commodity products appears to become more similar.[12] This nationless or borderless demand for products may be due to lifestyle similarities in developed nations. Also, increases in global communication media facilitate the ability of people in different countries to visualize and model lifestyles in disparate cultures.[13]

The need to go international is particularly important for Canadian companies. Not only is the domestic market a limited one—particularly relative to the United States and Mexico—but potential U.S. competitors entering the Canadian market pose a real threat. Yet, although the first logical market for Canadian firms to enter is the United States, and although Americans may certainly hear less about Canada than Canadians hear about the United States, such knowledge may not assure success. The Strategic Focus discusses some of the promise and some of the pitfalls of taking that first international step to the United States.

## STRATEGIC FOCUS

### The Promise and Pitfalls of Taking That First International Step to the United States

Not only do Canada and the United States share one of the world's longest borders, the same name for their currency (in spite of the difference in value), the same language, and the same economic system, we are each other's main trading partner. Therefore, the United States should be a good place for Canadians to do business. Yet developing profitable operations in the United States can be challenging. Canadian businesses—such as the Second Cup, Canadian Tire, E.D. Smith, and the Future Shop have all discovered that when they tried to replicate their Canadian success in the United States they ended up in shameful retreat. Professor Shawna O'Grady of Queen's University has studied this phenomenon and concludes, "Often, there's not been a lot of strategic thought put behind the decision to enter the U.S. market ... They thought it was just like the Canadian market, only bigger." Yet, as we will see, there are significant differences between markets in the two countries. Even with the retreats noted above, some noteworthy success stories exist.

Longueuil, Quebec's Jean Coutu Group went to the United States and started small and close to home—taking over a five-store chain in New England. The company was conscious of the need to change fundamental attributes of its business. "Jean Coutu" was not easy for Americans to pronounce, so the firm entered the market with the MaxiDrug store name. Its U.S. chain has grown to over 250 stores. As well, Jean Coutu did what many large Canadian retailers consistently fail to do in the United States: get very involved quickly in the day-to-day details of operations and discovering, hands-on, what works, what does not, what local competitors are doing, and what customers expect.

Similarly, Keg Restaurants concentrated on locations in Washington and Oregon—near its Vancouver home. The company thus avoided repeating its earlier failure of entering more distant markets in Texas and Illinois. Again, subtle cultural differences needed attention. For example, food portions had to be larger in the United States, not because the Americans necessarily ate more, but rather because they wanted to be sure they were getting value. Another difference was that Washington and Oregon customers preferred local wines; Canadian wine tastes were more diverse. As well, the Keg's U.S. restaurants do a bigger Thanksgiving business and their bars do a bigger Halloween business than the Canadian locations.

Toronto's TLC (The Laser Center) established leadership in its industry by using its technological lead in laser-vision correction. Since Canadian medical authorities allowed use of the laser equipment before U.S. authorities, TLC was able to train its medical personnel and develop its organizational and marketing capabilities before others could get into the market. TLC began using the laser-vision correction process in Canada in 1993. When American authorities approved the procedure in 1996, TLC entered the U.S. market. Over 40 of TLC's 50 clinics are

*continued*

now in the United States, and 90 percent of TLC's revenues are from the United States.

For many firms, successfully penetrating the U.S. market begins with sales offices. President of Winnipeg's Winpak, Bob Lavery stated, "We set up as a North American company … We didn't think about borders." Within its first year, this manufacturer of food and dairy plastic-packaging products hired sales staff in Atlanta, Chicago, Denver, and Los Angeles, and across Canada—this in spite of not setting up a manufacturing facility in the U.S. for a number of years. Lavery said, "You've got to establish a sales organization in the U.S. first … If you think it necessary to have a sales rep in Montreal, you should find it just as necessary to have one in Chicago."

Acquiring U.S. operations is also essential. Waterloo, Ontario's Open Text has become one of the market leaders in commercial knowledge-management software. Since its founding in 1991, the firm has had sales offices in the United States. As well, Open Text has acquired 10 other software developers in the United States. Having a large corporate research centre near Chicago and being listed on the NASDAQ also gives the firm a U.S. appearance. Open Text views these U.S. attributes as an important tool in gaining U.S. customers. Open Text CEO Tom Jenkins insists that companies have to be prepared to pay the price to be close to their customers. "If Canadians make any mistake in the U.S., it would be the same mistake they might make in Vancouver or Calgary, which is not locating salespeople close to your customers … [and] you have to provide a good product at a fair price and keep your customers happy."

Part of keeping the American customer happy is sometimes very different from keeping the Canadian customer happy. As Canadian Tire (CT) discovered, buying and turning around underperforming U.S. operations is not always easy. CT's purchase of Texas-based White Stores in 1982 failed to provide the company with a viable U.S. base. If a competitor that knew the market could not do well, it will likely be difficult for a newcomer to turn things around. As well, U.S. retailers tend to be more cognizant of the importance of great front-line sales staff. Canadians complain less about the poor service they get, and thus Canadian retailers do not "have to strive for excellence as they do in the U.S." As the Future Shop found, entering a market where there are a great number of already firmly established competitors is also problematic. Even though Future Shop at one time had almost 30 stores (over one-quarter of its outlets) in the northwest U.S., it decided to end its operations there. Profits in the consumer electronics retail industry have been described as "wafer-thin at the best of times," and intense competition in the United States made it impossible for the company to compete in the market.

E.D. Smith and Sons found that not only U.S. consumers but also U.S. workers differed from Canadians. For four years in the early 1990s, the family-run maker of jams, pie fillings, and sauces tried to make its Mississippi plant run correctly. For E.D. Smith, running the plant correctly meant defect-free product with zero shortages. Such goals require a culture with significant employee dedication. Yet Smith found that Canadian culture produces a different corporate culture. The culture and company dedication to the 110 year-old company in Winona, Ontario is very different from the devotion to the newcomer in Byhalia, Mississippi. Thus, the firm could not meet product standards in the United States and had to close its U.S. plant.

*continued*

Yet, companies such as Open Text seem to be doing very well. About 60 percent of Open Text's sales come from North America; but only four percent of these are from Canada. Canadian companies need to recognize that, although the United States is Canada's closest neighbour, it is a different culture to which Canadian businesses need to be sensitive.

Sources: How to succeed in the U.S. market by really really trying, *National Post,* June 3, 1999, 76; S Theobald, 1999, Future Shop pulls plug in US, shares rise, *Canadian Press Newswire,* March 9, http://delos.lib.sfu.ca:8366/cgi-bin/slri/z3950.CGI/216.129.15.13. 700998495/?cbca.db (Retrieved July 24, 2000); T. Belford and K. Vermond, 1999, Mr Smith goes to Mississippi and turns back…, *National Post,* December 15, E14; R. Steiner, 1999, Year after year…, *National Post Business,* October, 70–77.

In some industries, technology is driving globalization because economies of scale necessary to reduce costs to the lowest level often require efficient scale investment greater than that needed to meet domestic market demand.[14] There is also pressure for cost reductions by purchasing from the lowest-cost global suppliers. As well, R&D expertise for a new emerging business start-up may not be found in the domestic market, and firms may need to go far afield in attracting the needed expertise.[15]

New large markets, such as Russia, China, and India also provide a strong incentive because of potential demand. Because of currency fluctuations, firms may desire to have their operations distributed across many countries to reduce the risk of currency devaluation in one country.[16] The unique nature of emerging markets presents major growth opportunities, with both opportunities and challenges.[17] China, for example, differs from Western countries in many respects, including culture, politics, and the precepts of its economic system.[18] It does, however, offer a huge potential market. While its differences from Western countries are numerous, many international firms perceive Chinese markets as almost virgin markets, without exposure to many modern and sophisticated products. With such exposure, these firms believe that demand will develop. However, the differences pose serious challenges for Western competitive paradigms that emphasize the need for possession of the skills to manage financial, economic, and political risks.

Thus, companies seeking to internationalize their operations should also be aware of increased pressure for local country or regional responsiveness, especially where goods or services require customization because of cultural differences.[19] For example, Burger King, with operations in almost 60 nations, tailors its food products from country to country. Burger King offers local traditional dishes such as Broiled Salmon Fish Sandwiches in Chile, Beef Burritos in Mexico, and, of course, Poutine in Canada.[20] Danone, an international French provider of food products, either acquires local companies to meet local needs or uses marketing in an attempt to help local customers acquire new tastes. In recent years, Danone has acquired local water companies in Indonesia, China, and North America. It has also acquired a number of local food providers in Latin America. The firm also has attempted to overcome local resistance toward its products with marketing. Danone is the global leader in providing dairy products, and because of its skill in adapting to international markets, Danone is among the top 10 food and beverage firms (in sales revenue) in the world.[21]

The frequent need for local repair and service is another factor influencing an increased desire for local country responsiveness. This localization may even affect industries that are seen as needing more global economies of scale, such as white goods (e.g., refrigerators and other appliances).[22] Alternatively, it is becoming increasingly common for suppliers to follow their customers, particularly large ones, into international markets. When they do so, the need to find local suppliers is eliminated.[23] However, for large products, such as heavy earthmoving equipment, transportation costs are significant. Employment contracts and labour forces differ significantly as well; it is more difficult to negotiate employee layoffs in Europe than in North America, because of employment contract differences. Often, host governments demand joint ownership, which allows the foreign firm to avoid tariffs. Also, host governments frequently require a high percentage of local procurements, manufacturing, and R&D. These issues increase the need for local investment and responsiveness compared to seeking global economies of scale.

Given the traditional and emerging motivations for expanding into international markets, firms may achieve four basic benefits from international diversification: (1) increased market size; (2) greater returns on major capital investments or on investments in new products and processes; (3) greater economies of scale, scope, or learning; and (4) a competitive advantage through location (e.g., access to low-cost labour, critical resources, or customers). These opportunities to enhance the firm's strategic competitiveness are examined relative to the costs incurred to pursue them and the managerial challenges that accompany both product and geographic international diversification decisions. Higher coordination expenses, a lack of familiarity with local cultures, and a lack of full access to knowledge about political influences in the host country are examples of costs firms incur when pursuing international diversification.[24]

## Increased Market Size

Firms can expand the size of their potential market, sometimes dramatically, by moving into international markets. To expand the size of its markets, Ontario's Royal Group Technologies entered into various joint ventures and ownership arrangements in China, Argentina, Colombia, and Poland. With almost $1 billion in sales, Royal is one of North America's largest extruders of polyvinyl chloride building products. To be closer to its U.S customers, Royal also bought a number of U.S. companies.[25]

Changing consumer tastes and practices linked to cultural values or traditions is not simple. For example, when the cereal market in North America stagnated, cereal makers Kellogg and General Mills looked to international markets to revive their growth prospects. Initial efforts appeared to be successful. However, the dry cereal produced by these firms is not a staple in most European breakfasts. Thus, sales reached a peak, but then began to decline in the late 1990s. Kellogg had to close several manufacturing plants in Europe as its revenues and profits declined.[26]

Following an international strategy is a very attractive option to firms competing in local markets that have limited growth opportunities. For example, Small Fry Snack Foods—one of Canada's largest manufacturers, marketers, and distributors of salty snacks—found a limited domestic market. Small Fry was able to extend its reach into the U.S. market by purchasing the trademarks, distribution system, and other key U.S. assets of the U.S. Humpty Dumpty brand. CEO Gerald Schmalz felt that "this transaction allows us to reunify the Canadian and U.S. Humpty Dumpty brand name and to expand our branded sales into the U.S. [as well as] … providing a tremendous opportunity for further growth."[27]

The size of a particular international market also affects a firm's willingness to invest in R&D to build advantages in that market. Larger markets usually offer higher potential returns and thus generally pose less risk for a firm's investments. The strength of the science base in the country in question also can affect a firm's foreign R&D investments. Most firms prefer to invest more heavily in those countries with the scientific knowledge and talent to produce more effective new products and processes from their R&D.[28]

Given the current transformation of the global auto industry, it is projected that only about six major auto manufacturers will survive over time.[29] However, the surviving firms will be large and wield considerable market power, thereby driving out smaller competitors. In fact, Renault's much-criticized acquisition of the troubled automaker Nissan was completed because of the need to build adequate market power in order to maintain a measure of competitive parity with the other large global automakers (e.g., DaimlerChrysler, GM, Ford, and Toyota). Analysts predict that 8 to 10 years will be required before Renault realizes a return on its investment in Nissan. Furthermore, if Nissan fails to perform, this investment may eliminate Renault's chances to survive as an independent company. Because of the importance of Nissan to Renault's future, the firm has assigned the task of reviving it to tough, but successful, Brazilian-born executive Carlos Ghosn. In turn, he developed and implemented a drastic restructuring of the Japanese automaker that was designed to greatly reduce costs and increase efficiency in its manufacturing operations. Interestingly, Renault is also seeking to acquire other companies, particularly in Asia (especially Korea).[30]

Market size and a firm's market power do not guarantee success, however. For example, analysts argue that the merger between France's Seita and Spain's Tabacalera is unlikely to be successful. They suggest that the combination of two small, inefficient, and poorly managed firms is likely to produce one large, inefficient, and poorly managed firm.[31]

## Return on Investment

Large markets may be crucial for earning a return on significant investments, such as plant and capital equipment and/or R&D. Therefore, most R&D-intensive industries are international. For example, the aerospace industry requires heavy investments to develop new aircraft. To recoup investments, aerospace firms may need to sell new aircraft in both domestic and international markets. This is the case for Boeing and Airbus Industrie. International sales are critical to the ability of each firm to earn satisfactory returns on its invested capital. Airbus is continuing to build its competitive ability. In fact, a merger in 1999 between two of its consortium owners, DASA (a DaimlerChrysler company) and Aerospatiale Matrais, was predicted to enhance the ability of Airbus to compete with Boeing in international markets. Boeing may need to take actions of its own, because Airbus captured more orders for civilian aircraft in 1999 than did Boeing.[32]

In addition to the need for a large market to recoup heavy investment in R&D, the development pace for new technology is increasing. As a result, new products become obsolete more rapidly. Thus, investments need to be recouped more quickly. Beyond this, firms' abilities to develop new technologies are expanding, and because of different patent laws across country borders, imitation by competitors is more likely. Through reverse engineering, competitors are able to take apart a product, learn the new technology, and develop a similar product that imitates the new technology (see Chapters 6 and 14). Because of competitors' abilities to do this relatively quickly, the need to recoup new product development costs rapidly is increasing. Therefore, the larger markets provided by international expansion are particularly attractive in many industries (e.g., computer hardware) because they expand the opportunity to recoup large capital investment and large-scale R&D expenditures.[33] It must be emphasized, however, that the primary reason for making investments in international markets is to produce excellent returns on investments. Thus, expected returns from the investments represent a primary predictor of firms moving into international markets. Still, firms from different countries have different expectations and use different criteria to decide whether to invest in international markets.[34]

## Economies of Scale and Learning

When firms expand their markets, they may be able to enjoy economies of scale, particularly in their manufacturing operations. Thus, to the extent that firms are able to standardize products across country borders and use the same or similar production facilities, coordinating critical resource functions, they are likely to achieve more optimal economic scale.[35] As noted earlier in this chapter, only six global auto firms are expected to survive because of the need for market power and efficiency to compete effectively. For instance, Honda has been a largely successful firm with substantial competencies in the manufacture of engines. However, it has problems competing against several larger and more resource-rich automakers. Ford has $23 billion in cash, whereas Honda has only about $3.2 billion. GM invests approximately $9 billion annually in R&D, while Honda can invest only about $2.6 billion. As a result, some experts do not expect Honda to be one of the surviving global six automakers. A consultant for the firm suggested that Honda would have a chance if it could become large enough to have adequate resources and gain comparable economies of scale. Honda has achieved economies of scale in the development and sale of its engines. It sells about 2 million autos annually, but sells 10 million engines (including lawn mower engines). Honda has formed an alliance with GM to produce engines for some of its vehicles. Thus, perhaps Honda will survive as an independent engine producer.[36]

Firms may also be able to exploit core competencies across international markets. This allows resource and knowledge sharing between units across country borders.[37] It also generates synergy and helps the firm produce higher-quality goods or services at lower cost. In addition, working across international markets provides firms with an opportunity to learn from the different practices they encounter in separate international markets. Even firms based in developed markets can learn from operations in emerging markets.[38]

## Location Advantages

Firms may locate facilities in other countries to lower the basic costs of the goods and/or services provided.[39] For example, they may have easier access to lower-cost labour, energy, and other natural resources. Other location advantages include access to critical supplies/resources and to customers. Once positioned favourably through an attractive location, firms must manage their facilities effectively to gain the full benefit of a location advantage.[40]

For example, in order to gain better access to customers, Markham, Ontario's Image Processing Systems (IPS) developed service bureaus in Holland, Taiwan, and the United States and partnerships with companies and ministries in South Korea, Japan, and China. The IPS staff of about 200 come from 26 universities around the world and speak 11 different languages. IPS Chair and President Terry Graham states that "you must meet foreign buyers on their own turf." About 15 percent of IPS's revenue was generated in Canada, another 17 percent in the United States, 15 percent in Europe, and a whopping 53 percent in Asia. Sales of IPS's automatic display inspection systems—computers coupled with digital cameras to enforce tight quality controls on high-speed production lines—realized sales growth of over 25 000 percent between 1993 and 1998.[41]

As described in the Strategic Focus, the European Union is changing the competitive landscape in Europe and the world. The European Union provides a large and unified market for European and foreign firms that is attracting considerable investment from international companies. In addition, European markets and firms are undergoing substantial changes to take advantage of economies of scale, economies of learning, and advantages of location in the various European markets. The common currency and the integration of capital markets have reduced financial risks and made available significant amounts of capital that were previously unavailable in the separate country markets. Thus, European firms are growing in power and will challenge many of the world's prominent companies, including those from North America and Asia.

## STRATEGIC FOCUS

### The Decade of Europe: 2000–10

Europe is undergoing a substantial transformation. Only a little more than a decade since the dramatic fall of the Berlin wall and the collapse of the socialist regimes in Eastern Europe, a new economic and political architecture is emerging. The transformation is being shaped by technology and the globalization of business. Economically, Europeans have made considerable gains. For instance, gross domestic product (GDP) in the new European Union (EU) increased by over 46 percent during the decade of the 1990s, and the future is even brighter. During the same decade, inflation in the EU decreased by 77 percent, autos per capita increased by 14.6 percent, and even life expectancy increased, from 73 to 74 years. The EU has created a seamless market of over 290 million people. The introduction of the common currency, the Euro, removed two barriers to economic development in Europe: the exchange-rate risk and limited access to capital. The Euro was introduced in 1999 and will be placed in full circulation in 2002. The use of the Euro helps European firms to compete more effectively in global markets. A strong Euro is welcomed in the rest of the world as well; it has helped to ease the economic crisis in Asia by increasing Asian firms' ability to compete in European markets. Europe has become a primary global growth engine. All but one of the EU members (England) have adopted the Euro. The EU has a $6.5 trillion economy, representing approximately 8.1 percent of world trade.

The large pool and free flow of capital provides the means to finance large deals. Furthermore, to be competitive across the European markets and in

*continued*

global markets, firms need to gain market power, achieve economies of scale, and realize synergies. The implementation of the EU and the Euro created and facilitated considerable incentives for large-scale mergers and acquisitions throughout Europe. In fact, one major business publication described the scene as consisting of American-style mergers and acquisitions, with hostile takeovers, substantial debt, and large fees for the investment bankers. Others described it as "buyout fever." European buyouts in 1999 were $100 billion more than in 1998. Consolidation is the watchword in industries ranging from banking to telecommunications. Most activity occurs across country boundaries (e.g., the acquisition of Racal Electronics in the United Kingdom by the French firm Thomson-CSF). Consolidation also is exemplified by Cable & Wireless's acquisition of eight Internet service providers throughout Europe. The companies that were acquired provide access primarily to business customers in Western Europe. The companies are located in Austria, Belgium, France, Italy, Spain, and Switzerland. Cable & Wireless is a multinational firm controlling about 25 percent of the Internet traffic in North America as well.

While significant change engulfs most of Europe, resistance to change is also present. For example, four Italian top executives have forestalled change in their firms. These executives are well over the normal retirement age, and some refer to them as the "corporate gerontocracy." The four executives are Enrico Cuccia of Mediobanca, Cesare Romiti of Fiat, Giovanni Bazoli of Banco Ambrosiano, and Alfonso Desiata of Assicurazioni Generali. These executives actually tightened their grip on power when analysts predicted changes that would likely reduce or even eliminate their power. However, their victory may be short-lived as the EU comes into full bloom: These executives' firms may experience problems competing in the European markets, particularly against large, powerful, and nimble rivals.

In some cases, the new Europe and its firms are gaining significant strength. These gains are exemplified by Airbus Industrie's besting of Boeing in 1999. Airbus garnered orders for 470 new commercial aircraft, compared to Boeing's 391 orders. Thus, Airbus captured 55 percent of the global market for large commercial aircraft. In other sectors, changes have not been kind to some venerable European competitors, e.g., Marks and Spencer, an old and formerly successful British retailer, is now facing major problems. Marks and Spencer targets the "middle market." However, customers have been flocking to discounters and to the high-end market. Marks and Spencer's market has thus been shrinking, and the company has been unable to change its focus to other market niches. Marks and Spencer has tried to compete with the major discounters, but without success. It is also losing its traditional market to more attractive competitors such as Gap.

In European banking, there has been considerable consolidation as well. However, prominent banks, such as Deutsche Bank, have reached beyond Europe. For example, Deutsche Bank acquired Bankers Trust in the United States. For Deutsche Bank to meet its goal of becoming a universal bank, it must compete with the large and formidable U.S. and Japanese banks. At least some of the rationale behind proposed mergers of Canadian banks (e.g., the Royal Bank and the Bank of Montreal) was to address the big international bank threat. Yet, refusal by the Canadian government to agree to such mergers is likely a signal that international targets are more logical partners—versus domestic groupings—in order to produce world class–size banks.

*continued*

In sum, there will be success and failure in the new Europe. Yet one can count on significant change. The EU will, no doubt, be a prominent force in the world economy of the 21st century.

Sources: D. Ball, 2000, How old guard boardroom barons tightened their grip on new Italy, *Wall Street Journal Interactive,* January 13, www.interactive.wsj.com.articles; E. Beck, 2000, Dixons, Marks & Spencer post weak results in a tough year, *Wall Street Journal Interactive,* January 13, www.interactive.wsj.com.articles; P. Engardio & O. Ullmann, 1999, The Atlantic century, *BusinessWeek,* February 8, 64–73; N. George, 2000, SDP backs Swedish entry to euro zone, *www.ft.com,* January 15, www.ft.com.nbearchive; T. Kamm, 1999, Europe's move into the free market spurs a massive corporate workout, *Wall Street Journal Interactive,* December 30, www.interactivewsj.com.articles; D. Michaels & J. Cole, 2000, *Wall Street Journal Interactive,* January 13, www.interactive.wsj.com.articles; K. L. Miller, J. Ewing, S. Reed, & G. Silverman, 1999, Fixing Deutsche Bank, *BusinessWeek,* July 19, 56–58; G. Naik, 2000, Cable & Wireless announces purchase of eight Internet providers in Europe, *Wall Street Journal Interactive,* January 13, www. interactive.wsj.com.articles; J. Peet, 1998, The year of Europe, *The Economist's The World in 1999,* 11–12; S. Reed, 1999, Buyout fever, *BusinessWeek,* June 14, 60–61; S. Reed, 1999, We have liftoff! *BusinessWeek,* January 18, 34–37; S. Reed, J. Rossant, & G. Edmondson, 1999, Deal, *BusinessWeek,* April 5, 50–54; J. Rossant, 1999, Ten years after the wall, *BusinessWeek,* November 8, 57–61; Thomson-CSF announces E1.32 bn Racal deal, 2000, *www.ft.com,* January 13, www.ft.com.nbearchive; F.G. Mathewson and N. C. Quigley, 1998, Canadian bank mergers: Efficiency and consumer gain vs. market power, *C.D. Howe Institute Commentary,* June, 1.

# INTERNATIONAL STRATEGIES

In the previous section, we explored why international strategies may be important and examined some of their advantages. In this section, we describe the types and content of international strategies that might be formulated and then implemented.

An international strategy may be one of two basic types, business or corporate level. At the business level, firms follow generic strategy types: low cost, differentiation, focused low cost, focused differentiation, or integrated low cost/differentiation. At the corporate level, firms can formulate three types: multidomestic, global, or transnational (a combination of multidomestic and global). However, to create competitive advantage, each of these strategies must realize a core competence based on difficult to duplicate resources and capabilities.[42] As discussed in Chapters 5 and 7, a firm expects to create value through the implementation of a business-level and a corporate-level strategy.[43]

## International Business-Level Strategy

Each business must develop a competitive strategy focused on its own domestic market. We discussed business-level generic strategies in Chapter 5 and competitive dynamics in Chapter 6. However, international business-level strategies have some unique features. In pursuing an international business-level strategy, the home country of operation is often the most important source of competitive advantage.[44] The resources and capabilities established in the home country often allow the firm to pursue the strategy beyond the national boundary.

Michael Porter developed a model that describes the factors contributing to the advantage of firms in a dominant global industry and associated with a specific country or regional environment.[45] His model is illustrated in Figure 9.2.

■ ■ **FIGURE 9.2**

*Determinants of National Advantage*

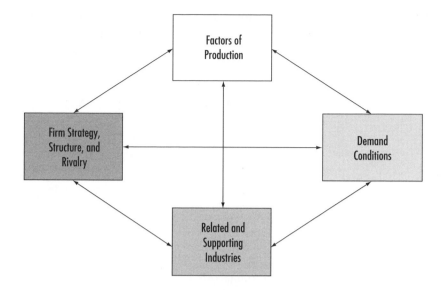

Source: Adapted and reprinted with the permission of The Free Press, a Division of Simon & Schuster from *The Competitive Advantages of Nations* by Michael E. Porter, p. 72. Copyright © by Michael E. Porter.

The first dimension in the model, *factors of production*, refers to the inputs necessary to compete in any industry, such as labour, land, natural resources, capital, and infrastructure (e.g., highway, postal, and communication systems). Of course, there are basic (e.g., natural and labour resources) and advanced (e.g., digital communication systems and highly educated workforces) factors. There are also generalized (highway systems, supply of debt capital) and specialized factors (skilled personnel in a specific industry, such as a port that specializes in handling bulk chemicals). If a country has both advanced and specialized production factors, it is likely that this will serve an industry well in spawning strong home-country competitors that can become successful global competitors. Ironically, countries often develop advanced and specialized factor capabilities because they lack critical basic resources. Some Asian countries, such as Korea, lack abundant natural resources, but the strong work ethic, the large number of engineers, and the systems of large firms have created an expertise in manufacturing. Germany developed a strong chemical industry, partially because Hoechst and BASF spent years developing a synthetic indigo dye to reduce their dependence on imports. This was not the case in Britain because large supplies of natural indigo were available in the colonies.[46]

The second dimension, *demand conditions*, is characterized by the nature and size of the buyers' needs in the home market for the industry's goods or services. The sheer size of a sales segment could produce the demand necessary to create scale-efficient facilities. This efficiency could also lead to domination of the industry in other countries. However, specialized demand may also create opportunities beyond national boundaries. For example, Swiss firms have long led the world in tunnelling equipment because of the need to tunnel through mountains for rail and highway passage. Similarly, Japanese firms have created a niche market for compact, quiet air conditioner units, which are required in Japan because homes are often small and packed together tightly. Under these conditions, large, noisy units would be unacceptable.[47]

*Related and supporting industries* is the third dimension in the model. Italy has become the leader in the shoe industry because of related and supporting industries. The leather supplies necessary to build shoes are furnished by a well-established industry in leather processing. Also, many people travel to Italy to purchase leather goods. Thus, there is support in distribution. In addition, supporting industries in leather-working machinery and design services contribute to the success of the shoe industry. In fact, the design services industry supports many related industries, such as ski boots, fashion apparel, and furniture. In Japan, cameras and copiers have been related industries. In Denmark, the dairy products industry is related to an industry focused on food enzymes.

*Firm strategy, structure, and rivalry*, the final country dimension, also fosters the growth of certain industries. The pattern of firm strategy, structure, and rivalry among firms varies greatly from nation to nation. Earlier, much attention was placed on examining North American enterprise managers; more recently, the Japanese have been scrutinized and emulated. In Germany, because of the excellent technical training system, there is a strong inclination toward methodological product and process improvement. In Japan, unusual cooperative and competitive systems have facilitated cross-functional management of complex assembly operations. In Italy, the national pride of its designers has spawned strong industries in sports cars, fashion apparel, and furniture. In the United States, competition among computer manufacturers and software producers has favoured the development of these industries.

The four basic dimensions of the "diamond" model shown in Figure 9.2 emphasize the environmental or structural attributes of a national economy that may contribute to national advantage. One could therefore conclude that chance or luck has led to the competitive advantage of individual firms in these industries. To a degree this is true, but government policy also contributes to the success and failure of firms and industries. This is certainly the case in Japan, where the Ministry of International Trade and Investment (MITI) has contributed significantly to the corporate strategies followed. Yet each firm must create its own success. Not all firms have survived to become global competitors, given the same country factors that spawned the successful firms. Thus, the actual strategic choices managers make may be the most compelling reason for success or failure. The factors illustrated in Figure 9.2, therefore, are likely to lead to competitive advantages for a firm only when an appropriate strategy is applied, taking advantage of distinct country factors. Hence, the next four subsections explain the cost leadership, differentiation, focused cost leadership, focused differentiation, and integrated cost leadership/differentiation generic strategies (discussed in Chapter 5) in an international context.

## International Cost Leadership Strategy

The international low-cost strategy is likely to develop in a country with a large demand. Usually the operations of such an industry are centralized in a home country, and obtaining economies of scale is the primary goal. Outsourcing of low value-added operations may take place, but high value-added operations are retained in the home country. As such, products are often exported from the home country.

Through a variety of entry modes (entry modes are discussed in detail later in the chapter), Wal-Mart follows this strategy as it continues to globalize operations. The essence of Wal-Mart's international low-cost strategy is demonstrated by founder Sam Walton's words: "We'll lower the cost of living for everyone, not just in America." One of the keys to implementing its low-cost strategy is the firm's advanced retail technology, which enables Wal-Mart to have the correct quantities of goods in the appropriate place at the right time while minimizing inventory costs. The latest variation of this sophisticated system has employees carrying handheld computers that allow them to reorder merchandise. Simultaneously, backroom computers link each store with a sophisticated satellite system.

Wal-Mart started to internationalize its operations in 1991. Since then, the firm has become the largest retailer in Canada and Mexico. Wal-Mart also operates stores in Argentina, Brazil, China, and Indonesia through joint ventures. To continue diversifying internationally, Wal-Mart decided to enter the European market with the purchase of the Wertkauf hypermarket company in Germany. Wal-Mart has also moved steadily into the British market. Wal-Mart usually entered international markets via a joint venture. However, it entered some European markets by acquiring existing large retail operations in each country. Combining its volume with the acquired firms' logistics skills and merchandising savvy will help Wal-Mart to achieve strategic competitiveness in the European markets. Also, Wal-Mart emphasizes customer service along with low prices, thus changing the retailing culture in many European markets (e.g., England).[48] Many analysts believe that Wal-Mart will be successful in European markets. If so, its resources and skills, along with its international cost leadership strategy, will have changed the retailing landscape in Europe and perhaps globally.[49]

There are, of course, risks associated with implementing the international low-cost strategy. A major risk for Wal-Mart is learning quickly how to compete successfully in Europe's unique retailing environment. Does Wal-Mart have the confidence it needs to make small adjustments to satisfy local tastes while maintaining the discipline required to keep prices low? Will European retailers retain their customers by learning how to create value either through differentiation strategies or by driving their costs lower relative to Wal-Mart's? These issues pose strategic challenges to Wal-Mart's executives; but the fact that the company hopes to generate one-third of its profit growth annually through international sales suggests its intentions in Europe and other world markets.[50]

Volkswagen AG (VW) is attempting to implement an international cost leadership strategy in China. VW plans to produce a low-price "people's auto," reaching the huge mass market for autos in China. Few international manufacturers have been able to reach China's mass market, because most Chinese cannot afford expensive products such as autos. Foreign auto manufacturers have been selling their autos chiefly to the government and corporations, a relatively small market. There are about 13 million autos in China, with only 30 percent owned by individuals. However, VW built the original "people's auto" lovingly referred to as the "bug" or "beetle," in Germany. Volkswagen won approval from the Chinese government to produce a compact car over other hopeful firms such as GM. The new auto will be developed and produced by Shanghai VW, a joint venture with Shanghai Automotive Industrial formed in 1984. The company already has 46 percent of the Chinese market with its Santana model, used by many of the taxi fleets in China. The new car will have a small engine (1–1.6 litres) and sell for 100 000 yuan (about $17 500). It is expected on the market by 2002.[51]

## International Differentiation Strategy

A country with advanced and specialized factor endowments is likely to develop an international differentiation strategy. For example, Germany has a number of world-class chemical firms. The differentiation strategy followed by many of these firms to develop specialized chemicals was possible because of the factor conditions surrounding the development of this industry. The Kaiser Wilhelm (later Max Planck) Institutes and university chemistry programs were superior in research and produced the best chemistry education in the world. Also, Germany's emphasis on vocational education fostered strong apprenticeship programs for workers.[52] Today, German companies competing in retailing consumer goods are learning how to improve their service to battle against competitors (e.g., Lands' End) implementing their international differentiation strategies in Germany.[53]

In the Opening Case, we discussed the wireless Internet service offered by Japan's DoMoCo. DoMoCo has captured the Japanese market but is planning to enter global wireless communication and Internet service markets. The company is following a differentiation strategy by offering the world's only i-mode that allows continuous Internet access by cell phone. While some predict that DoMoCo may be the next global wireless communications giant, it must continue to differentiate its product in ways that are attractive to the mass market, because it will face fierce competition in global markets from companies such as Vodafone AirTouch, AT&T, and British Telecom. Yet, DoMoCo should have the resources to compete. In 1999, the firm earned about $7 billion on sales of $50 billion, and it has access to Japanese giant NTT, which owns 67 percent of DoMoCo. To continue its differentiation, DoMoCo is working on a third-generation set of wireless protocols (called 3G) that will permit much higher communication speeds. To maintain its competitive advantage, DoMoCo strongly emphasizes R&D.[54]

As described in Chapter 5, firms may differentiate their products and services through physical characteristics, or they may differentiate their products in the minds of the consumer. As the market for cigarettes in North America has decreased, international markets have become critical to tobacco companies. Generally, greater percentages of the population smoke in countries outside North America, and they certainly tend to be less litigious than consumers in the United States. In those countries, cigarette companies compete largely on brand differences established through advertising.[55]

## International Focus Strategies

Many firms remain focused on small market niches as they pursue international focus strategies.[56] The ceramic tile industry in Italy contains a number of medium and small fragmented firms that produce approximately 50 percent of the world's tile.[57] These tile firms, clustered in the Sassuolo area of Italy, have formed a number of different focus strategies. Firms such as Marazzi, Iris, Cisa-Cerdisa, and Flor Gres invest heavily in technology to improve product quality, aesthetics, and productivity. These firms have close relationships with equipment manufacturers. They tend to emphasize the focused low-cost strategy, while maintaining a quality image. Another group, including Piemme and Atlas Concorde, attempts to compete more on image and design. Firms in this group invest heavily in advertising and showroom expositions. Because they try to appeal to selected customer tastes, they emphasize the focused differentiation strategy.[58]

The efficiency of the highly capitalized domestic institutions, coupled with their large branch networks and use of high-quality, sophisticated technologies, creates a retail banking environment in Spain in which it is difficult for foreign firms to compete successfully. Because of the domestic banks' competitive advantages, foreign rivals now concentrate on niche activities. Because of what they envision as significant growth potential in terms of mutual and pension funds, U.K.–based Barclays is focusing on the private banking sector. Barclays has "scaled back its retail operations in Spain, concentrated on the big cities and focused on asset management of medium to big private accounts according to a carefully elaborated segmentation of potential clients." Barclays operates 180 branches as it competes to serve the unique needs of the private banking market segment in Spain.[59]

## International Integrated Low-Cost/Differentiation Strategy

The integrated strategy has become more popular because of flexible manufacturing systems, improved information networks within and across firms, and total quality management systems (see Chapter 5). Because of the wide diversity of markets and competitors, following an integrated strategy may be the most effective in global markets.[60] Therefore, competing in global markets requires sophisticated and effective management.[61] Japanese heavy equipment manufacturer Komatsu provides a good example of this strategy. Komatsu was able to gain on a strong competitor, Caterpillar, by pursuing the integrated low-cost/differentiation strategy. Caterpillar had a very strong brand image in world markets, but Komatsu was able to overcome this differentiation advantage by improving its image and reducing its costs. As well, in the 1970s, the dollar was strong, which allowed a successful export strategy. Although Komatsu has remained very competitive, it faces critical challenges today due to the competitive actions being taken by Caterpillar.[62]

Compaq also is attempting to employ an integrated cost leadership/differentiation strategy. It needs to maintain low costs so that it can standardize its prices to compete with firms such as Dell. Compaq is doing so by reducing the number of products in its product line and by using the Internet both to purchase supplies from across the globe and to manage the distribution of its products. But Compaq also must continue to differentiate its products to meet international market requirements.[63]

# International Corporate-Level Strategy

The business-level strategies discussed previously are based at least partially on the type of international corporate-level strategy the firm follows. Some corporate strategies give individual country units the authority to develop their own business-level strategies; other corporate strategies largely dictate the business-level strategies used to accomplish standardization of products and sharing of resources across countries. International corporate-level strategy focuses on the scope of a firm's operations through both product and geographic diversification.[64] International corporate-level strategy is required when the firm operates in multiple industries and multiple countries or regions.[65] The strategy is guided by the headquarters unit, rather than by business or country managers. The three international corporate-level strategies are shown in Figure 9.3.

■ ■ **FIGURE 9.3**

*International Corporate-Level Strategies*

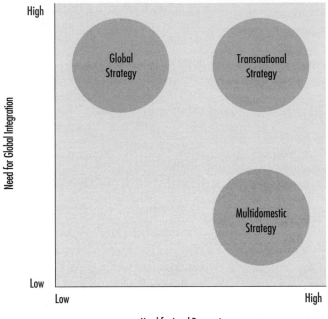

## Multidomestic Strategy

A **multidomestic strategy** is one in which strategic and operating decisions are decentralized to the strategic business unit in each country in order to tailor products to the local market.

**A multidomestic strategy** is one in which strategic and operating decisions are decentralized to the strategic business unit in each country in order to tailor products to the local market.[66] A multidomestic strategy focuses on competition within each country, and it assumes that the markets differ and therefore are segmented by country boundaries. In other words, consumer needs and desires, industry conditions (e.g., number and type of competitors), political and legal structures, and social norms vary by country.

Multidomestic strategies allow for the customization of products to meet the specific needs and preferences of local customers. Therefore, they should be able to maximize competitive response to the idiosyncratic requirements of each market. The use of multidomestic strategies usually expands the firm's local market share because of the attention paid to the needs of the local clientele. However, the use of these strategies also results in more uncertainty for the corporation as a whole, because of the differences across markets and thus the different strategies employed by local country units.[67]

Moreover, multidomestic strategies do not allow for the achievement of economies of scale and thus can be more costly. As a result, firms employing a multidomestic strategy decentralize their strategic and operating decisions to the business units operating in each country. The multidomestic strategy has been more commonly used by European multinational firms because of the varieties of cultures and markets found in Europe.

Bestfoods (makers of Knorr soups, Hellmann's salad dressings, Entenmann's baked goods, and Skippy peanut butter, among others) follows the multidomestic strategy. To implement the multidomestic strategy, Bestfoods's managers are given a great deal of autonomy to adapt products to local tastes. This is necessary, says the firm's CEO, because food brands have geographical limitations. These limitations are exemplified by the following comment from the CEO: "The day I teach Americans to eat Marmite will be the day I teach the French to eat peanut butter."[68] (Marmite is a thick, dark, yeast-based spread that is a staple of the national diet in Britain.)

## Global Strategy

A **global strategy** is one in which standardized products are offered across country markets, and the competitive strategy is dictated by the home office.

Alternatively, a global strategy assumes more standardization of products across country markets.[69] As a result, competitive strategy is centralized and controlled by the home office. The strategic business units operating in each country are assumed to be interdependent, and the home office attempts to achieve integration across these businesses. Thus, a **global strategy** is one in which standardized products are offered across country markets, and the competitive strategy is dictated by the home office. Thus, a global strategy emphasizes economies of scale and offers greater opportunities to utilize innovations developed at the corporate level or in one country in other markets. Accordingly, a global strategy produces lower risk but may forego growth opportunities in local markets, either because those markets are less likely to identify opportunities or because opportunities require that products be adapted to the local market.[70] In effect, the strategy is not responsive to local markets and is difficult to manage because of the need to coordinate strategies and operating decisions across country borders. Thus, achieving efficient operations with a global strategy requires the sharing of resources and an emphasis on coordination and cooperation across countries, and these in turn require centralization and headquarters control. Many Japanese firms have often pursued this strategy with success.[71]

Aggreko, headquartered in England, has become the world's leading provider of power equipment through rentals. Currently, the company operates in 48 countries and employs a global strategy. The firm's fleet of equipment is integrated globally, which allows it to shift equipment to different regions of the world to meet specific needs. One of Aggreko's major competitors, Caterpillar, suffers because its dealers would rather sell than rent equipment. And Caterpillar's dealers are franchises, so the company cannot easily control their actions. Applying the global strategy, Aggreko designs and assembles its equipment in-house to meet the needs of its customers. Aggreko has been highly successful, earning approximately 18 percent on invested capital with a growth in earnings of 14 percent.[72]

## Transnational Strategy

A **transnational strategy** is a corporate-level strategy that seeks to achieve both global efficiency and local responsiveness.

A **transnational strategy** seeks to achieve both global efficiency and local responsiveness. Realizing these goals is obviously difficult, because one goal requires close global coordination while the other requires local flexibility. Thus, "flexible coordination"—building a shared vision and individual commitment through an integrated network—is required to implement the transnational strategy.[73] In reality, it is difficult to achieve a pure transnational strategy because of the conflicting goals. On the positive side, the effective implementation of a transnational strategy often produces higher performance than either of the other two corporate strategies may do alone.[74]

Until the mid-1990s, Ford used a multidomestic strategy with separate, decentralized operations for North America and Europe. However, former CEO Alex Trotman implemented a global strategy in the middle 1990s. Applying this strategy, Ford attempted to build what it called a global auto: the Mondeo. Both the auto and the strategy failed. The new CEO, Jacques Nasser, is now changing Ford's strategy to be transnational. Furthermore, Nasser is restructuring management so that it can respond flexibly to opportunities outside the traditional auto-manufacturing business. Applying the transnational strategy, Ford is trying to standardize some of the components in its various automobiles—Ford, Lincoln, Jaguar, and Volvo—but yet allow design and other differences in the market segments at which each of those brands of automobile is targeted. Through this, Ford is trying to become consumer oriented and be responsive to the various markets across the globe that it serves.[75] The transnational strategy requires that managers think globally but act locally.[76]

The next Strategic Focus describes the changes in Asia's economic landscape. The world's largest continent in both area and population is awakening again. Many Asian firms used a global strategy before the 1998 economic crisis. Most, however, will have to adopt a transnational strategy to be competitive in the 21st-century landscape.

## STRATEGIC FOCUS

### The Reawakening of the Asian Tiger

It looks as if the Asian tiger is reawakening. Asia's economies are bottoming out, and most are starting to grow again. For example, the economies in Malaysia, the Philippines, Korea, Japan, and China experienced growth. Furthermore, the stock markets in most of these countries are on the upswing, portending economic growth. For most countries, 1998 was the year in which they incurred their greatest losses. However, in 1998, Singapore's economy grew, albeit only 1.5 percent, and the country largely avoided the severe problems experienced by most other Asian countries. Still, Singapore is implementing reforms similar to those adopted by many other Asian countries to ensure continued economic prosperity. Asian countries must adapt as globalization continues and powerful forces shape the world economy. The two most prominent of these forces, the Internet and wireless communications, were discussed in the Opening Case.

Japan has the largest economy in Asia and also has suffered significantly. The suffering is greater there than in some other Asian markets because Japan was considered an economic miracle at one time and imitated by many countries around the world. But Japan had what was referred to as a "bubble economy," built on debt and interdependence, and the bubble eventually burst. Because of its economic difficulties, Japan has been subject to more outside influence than ever before.

One of the best examples of Japan's fall is the problem experienced by Mitsubishi. The Mitsubishi group of companies or "kereitsu" is huge and produces over 8 percent of Japan's total output. In the late 1980s, Mitsubishi companies were feared because of their economic power and potential domination of global markets. Today, though, most of Mitsubishi's companies are trying to stem the tide of losses. The organization had to obtain over $2 billion in capital from its member companies to save some of the other member firms from bankruptcy. Although Japanese companies were harmed severely by the economic problems throughout Asia, these firms are beginning to enjoy growth again as the Asian economies expand.

Many foreign firms—particularly financial institutions—are gaining a foothold in Japan. Furthermore, analysts argue that Japan's assets are largely

*continued*

undervalued; thus, they are of substantial value to foreign investors. Some of Japan's best firms, including Honda, Sony, Bridgestone, Canon, and Toyota, survived the crisis and even continued to achieve positive returns when many could not. In fact, these five firms experienced the largest growth in net profits among Japanese firms in 1999. Still, although most of them followed a global strategy, they will have to develop and implement a transnational strategy to compete effectively in global markets, as their competitors from other regions of the world do. Japan will have to become a larger participant in the Internet economy, particularly e-commerce. DoMoCo provides a good start, but more such firms are needed.

China has been the lone shining economic star in Asia, with a growing economy even during the crisis. In fact, China's economy is expected to grow at 7.5 percent annually for at least the foreseeable future. China's GDP grew at 7.1 percent in 1999, and the country is expected to enter the World Trade Organization in 2000.

Interestingly, Chinese firms manufacture products sold globally, but few people know about the companies. For example, Haier, a firm that manufactures and sells household appliances, is one of a small number of companies from China that sell their products outside the local domestic market. There are many more products made in China but marketed under non-Chinese brand names. China leads the world in the export of toys, kitchenware, and textile products.

In many ways, China is undergoing an economic revolution. State enterprises are being transformed to private companies, and dynamic new entrepreneurial companies are growing dramatically. Some suggest that Chinese cities are flush with capital and entrepreneurs. While this is likely an overstatement, the economy does look bright. China has agreed to let many foreign firms enter Chinese markets, although usually requiring that they form a joint venture with a Chinese firm, similar to Volkswagen's venture with Shanghai Automotive Industrial. The critical concern about China is the stability of its reforms. China still has an authoritarian Communist government, and if economic reforms stall, economic growth may come to a halt. In particular, if the government becomes too heavy-handed, it could limit the inflow of foreign capital needed to fuel the country's economic growth. Also, many of the state firms have had problems privatizing and breaking government ties.

The last of the "big three" Asian economies is South Korea. A number of Korean firms suffered significant financial problems during the Asian economic crisis. In particular, Korean groups of companies or "chaebols" were caught with too much debt, were too diversified, and were not flexible enough (primarily due to the massive debt and cross shareholdings). Several of the chaebols have been "downscoping"—ridding themselves of poorly performing diversified businesses. Samsung and Hyundai seem to be improving and likely will again become formidable competitors in global markets, but debate still surrounds the viability of Daewoo. In fact, Hyundai plans to be one of the six survivors in the global auto industry during this decade; however, to do so, the company must reduce its large debt and improve its market capitalization. Also, the South Korean economy remains fragile, and political problems—particularly those associated with dealing with the North Koreans—could spell trouble. South Korea would have difficulty absorbing North Korea in the way West Germany

*continued*

absorbed East Germany, and the German reunification was itself fraught with severe problems during the adjustment.

Sources: B. Bremner, S. Prasso, J. Veale, J. Moore, & J. Barnathan, 1999, Asia: How real is the recovery? *BusinessWeek,* May 3, 56–58; B. Bremner, E. Thorton, & I. M. Kunii, 2000, Mitsubishi: Fall of a kereitsu, *BusinessWeek Online,* January 6, www.businessweek.com; B. Bremner, E. Thornton, I. M. Kunii, & M. Tanikawa, 1999, A new Japan, *BusinessWeek,* October 25, 69–74; China at fifty …; 1999, *The Economist,* October 2, 23–25; China's economy …, 2000, *Wall Street Journal Interactive,* January 13, www.interactice.wsj.com.articles; M. L. Clifford, M. Shari, & B. Einhorn, 2000, Remaking Singapore Inc., *BusinessWeek Online,* January 6, www.businessweek.com; P. Engardio, J. Veale, & M. L. Clifford, 1999, Boom or miracle? *BusinessWeek,* November 8, 50–51; B. Fulford & T. Y. Jones, 1999, Up from Lemons, *Forbes,* June 14, 122–24; J. Grant, 1998, Why Japan is undervalued, *Wall Street Journal,* April 17, A14; J. E. Hilsenrath, 1999, The speed of change, *Wall Street Journal Interactive,* October 25, www.interactive.wsj.com; Japan's growth companies, 1999, *The Economist,* June 26, 69–70; J. L. Lee, 1999, South Korea checks big business groups, *Wall Street Journal,* July 23, A13; Out of the shadows, 1999, *The Economist,* August 28, 50–51; D. Roberts, 1999, China's new revolution, *BusinessWeek,* September 27, 72–78; D. Roberts, 1999, Foreign carmakers get the green light, *BusinessWeek,* July 19, 63; D. Roberts, J. Barnathan, J. Morre, and S. Prasso, 1999, Plans for reform are screeching to a halt …, *BusinessWeek,* February 22, 48–50; J. Sapsford, 1999, U. S. financial firms delve deeper into Japan, *Wall Street Journal,* January 26, A13; The Koreas: Yesterday's war, tomorrow's peace, 1999, *The Economist,* July 10, 3–16; E. Thornton & M. Shari, 1999, Japan's Asian comeback, *BusinessWeek,* November 1, 58–59; P. Wonacott & I. Johnson, 2000, Petrochina prepares to go public …, *Wall Street Journal Interactive,* January 13, www.interactive.wsj.com.

## ENVIRONMENTAL TRENDS

Although the transnational strategy is difficult to implement, emphasis on the need for global efficiency is increasing as more industries begin to experience global competition. To add to the problem, there is also an increased emphasis on local requirements: global goods and services often require some customization to meet government regulations within particular countries or to fit customer preferences and tastes. As well, most multinational firms desire to achieve some coordination and sharing of resources across country markets to hold down costs. Further, some products and industries may be better suited for standardization across country borders than others. As a result, most large multinational firms with diverse products employ a multidomestic strategy for some product lines and a global strategy for others. Perhaps this type of flexibility will be required in many Asian firms if they are to be strategically competitive in the coming years (see Strategic Focus for discussion of the Asian transformation).

### Regionalization

Regionalization is becoming more common in world markets; consequently, a firm's location can affect its strategic competitiveness.[77] Firms must decide whether to compete in all (or many) world markets or to focus on a particular region(s).[78] The advantages of trying to compete in all markets include the economies that can be achieved because of the combined market size. However, if the firm is competing in industries where the international markets differ greatly (in which it must employ a multidomestic strategy), it may wish to narrow its focus to a particular region of the world. In so doing, it can better understand the cultures, legal and social norms, and other factors that are important for effective competition in those markets. For example, a firm may focus on Far East markets only, rather than attempting to compete in the Middle East, Europe, and the Far East simultaneously. Or the firm may choose a region of the world where the markets are more similar, and thus, some coordination and sharing of resources would be possible. In this way, the firm may be able not only to better understand the markets in which it competes but also to achieve some economies, even though it may have to employ a multidomestic strategy.

Regional strategies may be promoted by countries that develop trade agreements to increase the economic power of their regions. The European Union (EU) and the Organization of American States (OAS, in South America) are collections of countries that developed trade agreements to promote the flow of trade across country boundaries within their respective regions.[79] Many European firms have been acquiring and integrating their businesses in Europe to better coordinate pan-European brands as the EU creates more unity in European markets.

The North American Free Trade Agreement (NAFTA), signed by the United States, Canada, and Mexico, is designed to facilitate free trade across country borders in North America and may be expanded to include other countries in South America, such as Argentina, Brazil, and Chile.[80] NAFTA agreements loosen restrictions on international strategies within a region and provide greater opportunity to realize the advantages of international strategies. Contrary to what some might think, NAFTA does not exist for the sole purpose of U.S. businesses going north and south of the border. In fact, Canada's trade surplus with the United States was almost $6 billion per month through the first half of 2000.[81] In fact, Mexico is the number-two trading partner of the United States, and NAFTA greatly increased Mexico's exports to the United States. In December 1999, the U.S. trade deficit with Mexico increased to its highest level, $2.5 billion; the catalyst for Mexico's export boom was NAFTA.[82]

Most firms enter regional markets sequentially, beginning in markets with which they are more familiar. However, they also enter these markets with their largest and strongest lines of business first, followed by their other lines of business after the first ones are successful.[83] After firms decide on their international strategies and whether to employ them in regional or world markets, they must decide how to accomplish such international expansion.[84] Accordingly, the next section discusses how to enter new international markets.

## CHOICE OF INTERNATIONAL ENTRY MODE

International expansion is accomplished through exporting, licensing, strategic alliances, acquisitions, and establishing new wholly owned subsidiaries. These means of entering international markets and their characteristics are shown in Table 9.1. Each has its advantages and disadvantages as described in the following subsections.

### Exporting

Many industrial firms begin their international expansion by exporting goods or services to other countries.[85] Exporting does not require the expense of establishing operations in the host countries, but exporters must establish some means of marketing and distributing their products. Usually, exporting firms develop contractual arrangements with host-country firms. The disadvantages of exporting include the often high costs of

| ■ ■ **TABLE 9.1** | **Global Market Entry: Choice of Entry Mode** |
|---|---|

| Type of Entry | Characteristics |
|---|---|
| Exporting | High cost; low control |
| Licensing | Low cost, low risk, little control, low returns |
| Strategic Alliances | Shared costs, shared resources, shared risks, problems of integration (e.g., two corporate cultures) |
| Acquisition | Quick access to new market, high cost, complex negotiations, problems with merging domestic operations |
| New wholly owned subsidiary | Complex, often costly, time-consuming, high risk, maximum control, potential above-average returns |

transportation and possible tariffs placed on incoming goods. Furthermore, the exporter has less control over the marketing and distribution of its products in the host country and must either pay the distributor or allow the distributor to add to the price to recoup its costs and make a profit. As a result, it may be difficult to market a competitive product through exporting or to provide a product that is customized to each international market. However, evidence suggests that cost leadership strategies enhance the performance of exports in developed countries, whereas differentiation strategies are more successful in emerging economies.[86]

Firms export mostly to countries that are closest to their facilities, because of the lower transportation costs and the usually greater similarity between geographic neighbours. As noted above, Canada and the United States are each other's largest trading partners, with over Can$40 billion of goods crossing the border each month.[87] The largest amounts of exports from Texas businesses go to its neighbour Mexico. The state's exports to Mexico represent more than all other exports from Texas combined.[88]

Small businesses are most likely to use exporting as their mode of international entry. One of the most significant problems with which small businesses must deal is currency exchange rates. Large businesses have specialists to help them manage exchange rates, but small businesses rarely have this expertise. Thus, the change to a common currency in Europe actually is helpful to small businesses operating in European markets. Instead of trying to remain current with 12 different exchange rates (assuming that they are exporting to all EU countries), these firms have to obtain information on only one. Yet, although most Canadians are comfortable with calculating at least the U.S./Canadian exchange rate, small U.S. businesses seem to have a concern about understanding the Euro. Thus, U.S. small businesses continue to rely on the U.S. dollar but often must pay prohibitive surcharges to do so. In general, small businesses operating in international markets must try to understand those markets and manage the business with knowledge of foreign exchange rates to reduce their overall costs and remain competitive.[89]

## Licensing

A licensing arrangement allows a foreign firm to purchase the right to manufacture and sell the firm's products within a host country or set of countries.[90] The licenser is normally paid a royalty on each unit produced and sold. The licensee takes the risks and makes the monetary investments in facilities for manufacturing, marketing, and distributing the goods or services. As a result, licensing is possibly the least costly form of international expansion. As such, licensing is one of the forms of organizational networks that is becoming common, particularly among smaller firms.[91]

Licensing is also a way to expand returns based on previous innovations. For instance, Sony and Philips co-designed the audio CD and now license the rights to companies to make CDs. Sony and Philips collect about 7 cents Canadian for every CD sold.[92] As this example demonstrates, many firms can earn good returns on their past innovations. A continual focus on research and patent licensing allows a firm to gain strong returns from its innovations for many years into the future.[93]

Today, however, the returns to Sony and Philips from CD sales are being threatened. Cheap counterfeit disks imitating the original products are a growth business. Sales of counterfeit disks in China alone are estimated to exceed $1 billion annually. Interestingly, technological advances are contributing to the severity of the problem. In fact, innovation makes it easier for counterfeiters to improvise. Pressing machinery used to manufacture disks is now so advanced and compact that it can be operated in the smallest of quarters. Located commonly in housing tenements, counterfeiters' production lines are difficult for officials to find. Corporations are seeking legal remedies to this situation but have had limited success to date.[94]

Licensing can sometimes represent a great opportunity for the licensing firm. Small Fry Snack Foods, mentioned earlier in this chapter, originally licensed the Humpty Dumpty brand from its U.S. producer. The licence allowed Small Fry to become the sole producer of the brand for Canada. After the U.S. owner of the brand went bankrupt, Small Fry was able to take over the former U.S. licensor and obtain full rights to the brand internationally.[95]

Of course, licensing has its disadvantages. For example, it gives the licenser very little control over the manufacture and marketing of its products in other countries. In addition, licensing provides the least potential returns, because returns must be shared between the licenser and the licensee. Worse, the international firm may learn the technology and produce and sell a similar competitive product after the license expires. Komatsu, for example, first licensed much of its technology from International Harvester, Bucyrus-Erie, and Cummins Engine in order to enter the earthmoving equipment business to compete against Caterpillar. Komatsu then dropped these licenses and developed its own products using the technology it gained from the companies with which it now competes internationally.[96]

## Strategic Alliances

In recent years, strategic alliances have enjoyed popularity as a primary means of international expansion.[97] Strategic alliances allow firms to share the risks and the resources required to enter international markets.[98] Moreover, such alliances can facilitate the development of new core competencies that can contribute to a firm's future strategic competitiveness.[99] In addition, most strategic alliances are with a host-country firm that knows and understands the competitive conditions, legal and social norms, and cultural idiosyncrasies of the country, which should help the firm manufacture and market a competitive product. In return, the host-country firm may find its new access to technology and innovative products attractive. Each partner in an alliance brings knowledge or resources to the partnership.[100] Indeed, partners often enter an alliance with the purpose of learning new capabilities. Common among those desired capabilities are technological skills.[101]

Ford Motor Company has joined an alliance that existed previously between DaimlerChrysler and British Columbia's Ballard Power Systems. This larger alliance, between two manufacturers and an alternative energy company, was organized so the three companies could work together to develop automotive engines and drive trains that produce power more efficiently and cleanly compared to products used currently. By participating in this alliance, Ford and DaimlerChrysler are showing their support for the concept of electric cars that do not need batteries but can create their own electricity with a fuel cell device. Ballard's knowledge as a leader in fuel-cell technology is critical to the work to be completed through the formation of the alliance. In addition to their knowledge regarding electric vehicles, Ford and DaimlerBenz are committing significant amounts of financial resources ($600 million from Ford alone) to this alliance. Thus, the three partners to this alliance are contributing in ways that are intended to result in the alliance's success.[102]

Not all organizations that employ strategic alliances do so for profit. For example, the Terry Fox Foundation's *raison d'etre* is its role as a strategic alliance partner to cancer research organizations. After losing his leg to cancer, Terry Fox embarked on a coast-to-coast "Marathon of Hope" in April 1980 to raise awareness about the need to find a cure for cancer. Starting at St. John's, Newfoundland and running a marathon distance every day for five months, he made it to Thunder Bay, Ontario, before his cancer returned and claimed him the following June. The Foundation, in coordination with other national organizations, sponsors Terry Fox Runs in over 50 countries around the world. Through these fundraising efforts the foundation brings together alliance partners to raise funds internationally.[103] To date, nearly a quarter of a billion dollars has been raised for cancer research in Terry Fox's name.[104] The Union Against Cancer in Geneva then distributes the funding to various agencies for research.

http://www.terryfoxrun.org
http://www.ncic.cancer.ca

Not all alliances are successful; in fact, many fail. The primary reasons for failure include selecting an incompatible partner and conflict between the partners.[105] International strategic alliances are especially difficult to manage.[106] Trust between the partners is critical and did not have time to develop in the much-publicized alliance, called Global One, among Deutsche Telecom, French Telecom, and MCI WorldCom. First, France Telecom became angry when it learned about Deutsche Telecom's attempt to take over Telecom Italia. When MCI WorldCom acquired Sprint without consulting its partners, the alliance was all but dead. Sprint is a member of another European alliance that is a rival of Global One.[107] Fortunately, research has shown that equity-based alliances, over which a firm has more control, tend to produce more positive returns[108] (strategic alliances are discussed in more depth in Chapter 10).

## Acquisitions

With free trade expanding more and more in global markets, cross-border acquisitions have been increasing significantly.[109] In recent years, cross-border acquisitions have comprised over 40 percent of all acquisitions completed worldwide.[110] Acquisitions have been especially popular in Europe, as noted in an earlier Strategic Focus, and are used by European firms to build their market power and extend their reach throughout the European Union. Also, foreign firms use acquisitions to enter the European Union and gain a foothold in its commerce. For example, GE completed 133 acquisitions of European firms during the 1990s. As a result, GE employs about 90 000 people in Europe, and its European operations produce approximately $35 billion in sales annually.[111] Montreal-based information technology services company CGI has expanded its business from about $96 million to about $1.4 billion over the past three years in part through acquisitions. Currently, 75 percent of CGI's revenues come from Canada. However, the company is targeting the United States to make up 50 percent of its North American revenues by 2003. To do this, CGI recently purchased Web-specialist DRT for over $100 million in cash.[112]

As explained in Chapter 8, acquisitions can provide quick access to a new market. In fact, acquisitions may provide the fastest and often the largest initial international expansion of any of the alternatives. As noted earlier, Jean Coutu Group used an acquisition to enter the U.S. market and then used a number of acquisitions to expand its U.S. presence.[113] Although acquisitions have become a popular mode of entering international markets, they are not without their costs. International acquisitions carry some of the same disadvantages as domestic acquisitions (see Chapter 8). In addition, they can be expensive and often require debt financing (which also carries an extra cost). International negotiations for acquisitions can be complex and more complicated than for domestic acquisitions. For example, it is estimated that only 20 percent of the cross-border bids lead to a completed acquisition, compared to 40 percent for domestic acquisitions.[114] Dealing with the legal and regulatory requirements in the host country of the target firm and obtaining appropriate information to negotiate an agreement frequently present significant problems. Finally, the problems of merging the new firm into the acquiring firm often are more complex than in the case of domestic acquisitions. The acquiring firm must deal not only with different corporate cultures but also with potentially different social cultures and practices. Therefore, although international acquisitions have been popular because of the rapid access to new markets, they also carry with them important costs and multiple risks.

Wal-Mart, the world's largest retailer, has used several entry modes to globalize its operations. For example, in China, the firm used a joint-venture mode of entry. To begin the firm's foray into Latin American countries, Wal-Mart also used joint ventures. But in some cases (e.g., Mexico), it acquired its venture partner after entering the host-country's market. As described earlier, Wal-Mart has used acquisitions to enter European markets (e.g., Germany and England). Thus, the most effective mode of entering a particular international market must be carefully considered and selected.

Interestingly, as mergers and acquisitions become more common in Europe, the number of hostile European takeover attempts has increased. For instance, Olivetti made a hostile takeover bid for Telecom Italia, which tried to fend off the takeover with a restructuring plan. Olivetti was not deterred and made a larger offer. Telecom Italia then agreed to be acquired by Deutsche Telecom, but Olivetti entered into a bidding war and eventually won the bid to acquire Telecom Italia. Likewise, Vodafone AirTouch (based in England) actively pursued a hostile takeover of Mannesmann, a German firm. However, Mannesmann actively fought the takeover attempt in almost every way possible. Sometimes, takeover attempts become personal contests between the companies' executives, as opposed to taking the appropriate action for the shareholders.[115]

## New, Wholly Owned Subsidiary

A **greenfield venture** is one in which a new, wholly owned subsidiary is established.

The establishment of a new, wholly owned subsidiary is referred to as a **greenfield** venture. This is often a complex and potentially costly process, but it has the advantage of affording the firm maximum control and, therefore, if successful, has the most potential to provide above-average returns. This is especially true of firms with strong intangible capabilities that might be leveraged through a greenfield venture.[116] The risks are also high, however, because of the costs involved in establishing a new business operation in a new country. The firm may have to acquire the knowledge and expertise of the existing market by hiring either host-country nationals, possibly from competitive firms, or consultants (which can be costly). Still, the firm maintains control over the technology, marketing, and distribution of its products. Alternatively, the company must build new manufacturing facilities, establish distribution networks, and learn and implement appropriate marketing strategies to compete in the new market.

Wingham, Ontario's Westcast Industries—the world's largest supplier of auto exhaust manifolds—is expanding from its North American base through a direct investment in a new plant being built in Hungary. One of Westcast's principle customers, Ford, has been increasing its European presence, e.g., through its purchase of Jaguar and Volvo. Though Westcast sales exceed $350 million, the 100-year-old company sought to maintain responsiveness to Ford as well as quality via its greenfield investment in Hungary.[117]

## Dynamics of Mode of Entry

A firm's choice of mode of entry into international markets is determined by a number of factors.[118] Initially, market entry will often be through export, because this requires no foreign manufacturing expertise and investment only in distribution. Licensing can facilitate the product improvement necessary to enter foreign markets, as in the Komatsu example. Strategic alliances have been popular because they allow a firm to connect with an experienced partner already in the targeted market. Strategic alliances also reduce risk through the sharing of costs. All three modes therefore are best for early market development tactics.

To secure a stronger presence in international markets, acquisitions, or greenfield ventures may be required. Many Japanese automobile manufacturers, such as Honda, Nissan, and Toyota, have gained a presence in Canada and the United States through both greenfield ventures and joint ventures. Toyota has particularly strong intangible production capabilities that it has been able to transfer through greenfield ventures.[119] Both acquisitions and greenfield ventures are likely to come at later stages in the development of an international diversification strategy. In addition, both strategies tend to be more successful when the firm making the investment has considerable resources, particularly in the form of valuable core competencies.[120] Large diversified business groups, often found in emerging economies, not only gain resources through diversification but also have specialized abilities in managing differences in inward and outward flows of foreign direct investment. In particular, Korean chaebols have been adept at making acquisitions in emerging economies.[121]

Thus, to enter a global market, a firm selects the entry mode that is best suited to the situation at hand. In some instances, the various options will be followed sequentially, beginning with exporting and ending with greenfield ventures. In other cases, the firm may use several, but not all, of the different entry modes, each in different markets. The decision regarding the entry mode to use is primarily a result of the industry's competitive conditions, the country's situation and government policies, and the firm's unique set of resources, capabilities, and core competencies.

# STRATEGIC COMPETITIVENESS OUTCOMES

Once the strategy and mode of entry have been selected, firms need to be concerned about overall success. International expansion can be risky and may not result in a competitive advantage. The following strategic competitiveness issues are discussed, as suggested in Figure 9.1.

## International Diversification and Returns

International diversification is the primary international corporate-level strategy. In Chapter 7, we discussed the corporate-level strategy of product diversification. Through this strategy, the firm engages in the manufacture and sale of multiple diverse products. **International diversification** is a strategy through which a firm expands the sales of its goods or services across the borders of global regions and countries into different geographic locations or markets. The number of different markets in which it operates and their importance show the degree to which a firm is internationally diversified. The percentage of total sales is often used to measure a region's or country's importance to the firm.[122]

**International diversification** is a strategy through which a firm expands the sales of its goods or services across the borders of global regions and countries into different geographic locations or markets.

As noted earlier, firms have numerous reasons to diversify internationally. Because of its potential advantages, international diversification should be related positively to firms' returns. Research has shown that, as international diversification increases, firms' returns increase.[123] In fact, the stock market is particularly sensitive to investments in international markets. Firms that are broadly diversified into multiple international markets usually achieve the most positive stock returns.[124] There are also many reasons for the positive effects of international diversification, such as potential economies of scale and experience, location advantages, increased market size, and the opportunity to stabilize returns. The stabilization of returns helps reduce a firm's overall risk.[125] Smaller and newer ventures, as well as larger and established firms can achieve all of these outcomes. Recently, it has been shown that new ventures can enjoy higher returns when they learn new technologies from their international diversification.[126]

Firms in the Japanese automobile industry have found that international diversification may allow them to better exploit their core competencies, because sharing knowledge resources between operations can produce synergy.[127] Also, a firm's returns may affect its decision to diversify internationally. For example, poor returns in a domestic market may encourage a firm to expand internationally in order to enhance its profit potential. In addition, internationally diversified firms may have access to more flexible labour markets, as the Japanese do in the United States, and may thereby benefit from global scanning for competition and market opportunities.[128] As a result, multinational firms with efficient and competitive operations are more likely to produce above-average returns for their investors and better products for their customers than are solely domestic firms.[129] However, as explained later, international diversification can be carried too far.

# International Diversification and Innovation

Michael Porter stated that a nation's competitiveness depends on the capacity of its industry to innovate and suggested that firms achieve competitive advantage in international markets through innovation. Eventually and inevitably, competitors outperform firms that fail to innovate and improve their operations and products. Thus, the only way to sustain a competitive advantage is to upgrade it continually.[130]

International diversification provides the potential for firms to achieve greater returns on their innovations (through larger or more numerous markets) and thus lowers the often substantial risks of R&D investments. Therefore, international diversification provides incentives for firms to innovate. In addition, international diversification may be necessary to generate the resources required to sustain a large-scale R&D operation. An environment of rapid technological obsolescence makes it difficult to invest in new technology and the capital-intensive operations required to take advantage of it. Firms operating only in domestic markets may find such investments problematic due to the length of time required to recoup the original investment. If time is extended, it may not even be possible to recover the investment before the technology becomes obsolete.[131] As a result, international diversification improves a firm's ability to appropriate additional and necessary returns from innovation before competitors can overcome initial competitive advantage created by the innovation. Also, firms moving into international markets are exposed to new products and processes. If they learn about those products and processes and integrate the knowledge into their operations, further innovation can be developed.[132]

The relationship among international diversification, innovation, and returns is complex. Some level of performance is necessary to provide the resources to generate international diversification, which in turn provides incentives and resources to invest in research and development. The latter, if done appropriately, should enhance the returns of the firm, which then provides more resources for continued international diversification and investment in R&D.

Because of the potential positive effects of international diversification on performance and innovation, some have argued that such diversification may even enhance returns in product-diversified firms. International diversification would increase market potential in each of these firms' product lines, but the complexity of managing a firm that is both product diversified and internationally diversified is significant. Therefore, it is likely that international diversification can enhance the returns of a firm that is highly product diversified, but only when it is managed well.

Asea Brown Boveri (ABB) may demonstrate these relationships. This firm's operations involve high levels of both product and international diversification, yet ABB's performance is quite strong. Some believe that the firm's ability to effectively implement the transnational strategy contributes to its strategic competitiveness. To manage itself, ABB assembles culturally diverse corporate and divisional management teams, which are then used to facilitate the simultaneous achievement of global integration and local responsiveness. Evidence suggests that more culturally diverse top-management teams often have a greater knowledge of international markets and their idiosyncrasies[133] (top-management teams are discussed further in Chapter 13). Moreover, an in-depth understanding of diverse markets among top-level managers facilitates intrafirm coordination and the use of long-term, strategically relevant criteria to evaluate the performance of managers and their units. In turn, this approach facilitates improved innovation and performance.[134]

## Complexity of Managing Multinational Firms

Although many benefits can be realized by implementing an international strategy, doing so is complex and can produce greater uncertainty.[135] For example, multiple risks are involved when a firm operates in several different countries. Firms can grow only so large and diverse before becoming unmanageable, or the costs of managing them exceed their benefits. Other complexities include the highly competitive nature of global markets, multiple cultural environments, potentially rapid shifts in the value of different currencies, and the possible instability of some national governments.

# RISKS IN AN INTERNATIONAL ENVIRONMENT

International diversification carries multiple risks.[136] International expansion is difficult to implement, and it is difficult to manage after implementation, because of these risks. The chief risks are political and economic. Taking these risks into account, highly diversified firms are accustomed to market conditions yielding competitive situations that differ from what was predicted. Sometimes, these situations contribute to the firm's strategic competitiveness; on other occasions, they have a negative effect on the firm's efforts.[137] Specific examples of political and economic risks are shown in Figure 9.4.

## Political Risks

**Political risks** are related to instability in national governments and to war, civil or international.

**Political risks** are related to instability in national governments and to war, both civil and international. Instability in a national government creates numerous problems. Among these are economic risks and uncertainty created by government regulation, the existence of many, possibly conflicting, legal authorities, and the potential nationalization of private assets. For example, foreign firms that are investing in Russia may have concerns about the stability of the national government and what might happen to their investments or assets in that country should there be a major change in government. This concern remained when Yeltsin abruptly resigned at the beginning of 2000.

It took five years for Zeneca, a British chemical company, to negotiate with Chinese government officials for the right to build a large herbicide plant in the Eastern province of Jiangsu. An even more direct example of political risk was China's announced policy change in 1999 to reduce sales of cell phones by foreign companies. In addition, in 1999, a top Chinese official declared that ownership by a foreign company in the Chinese Internet was illegal.[138]

## Economic Risks

Economic risks are interdependent with political risks, as noted earlier. Chief among the economic risks of international diversification are the differences and fluctuations in the value of different currencies. With Canadian firms, the value of the dollar relative to other currencies determines the value of their international assets and earnings; for example, a decrease in the value of the Canadian dollar can increase the value of Canadian multinational firms' international assets and earnings in other countries. Furthermore, the value of different currencies can, at times, dramatically affect a firm's competitiveness in global

■ ■ **FIGURE 9.4**

*Risks in the International Environment*

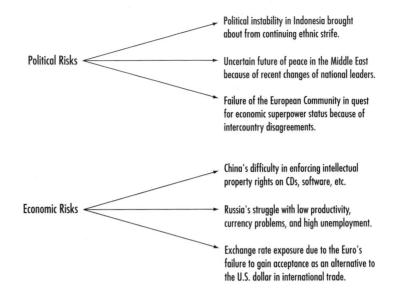

Source: S. Herbst-Bayliss, 2000, Euro sinks to new low as investors return to U.S., *National Post,* April 20: C14; G. Woodard, 2000, Australia's foreign policy after Timor, *International Journal,* 55 (1): 1–14; V. Press, 1999, King Hussein mourned; *Canadian Jewish News,* Fall 11: 22; D. Mandel, 1999, Frustration in Russia, *Canadian Dimension,* May/June: 27–28; R.S. Greenberger, 1996, U.S. sharply attacks China over intellectual property, *Wall Street Journal,* May 1, A3, A4; J. Templeman, 1996, The economy that fell to earth, *BusinessWeek,* January 15, 46.

markets because of its effect on the prices of goods manufactured in different countries. A decrease in the value of the Canadian dollar can aid Canadian firms' exports to international markets because of the price differential of the products.

The Canadian motion picture industry depends greatly on the value of the Canadian dollar relative to the U.S. dollar. Technical talent in the Vancouver film industry is attractive to Hollywood producers due to not only the quality of the work being performed but also the relatively low wages paid. The wage rates are lower because of the low value of the Canadian dollar relative to the U.S. dollar.[139]

## Limits to International Expansion: Management Problems

Research has shown that firms tend to receive positive returns on early international diversification, but they often level off and become negative as the diversification increases past some point.[140] There are several reasons for the limits to the positive effects of international diversification. First, greater geographic dispersion across country borders increases the costs of coordination between units and the distribution of products. Second, trade barriers, logistical costs, cultural diversity, and other differences by country (e.g., access to raw materials and different employee skill levels) greatly complicate the implementation of an international diversification strategy.[141]

Institutional and cultural factors often represent strong barriers to the transfer of a firm's competitive advantages from one country to another. Marketing programs often have to be redesigned and new distribution networks established when firms expand into new countries. In addition, firms may encounter different labour costs and capital charges. In general, it is difficult to effectively implement, manage, and control a firm's international operations.[142]

Wal-Mart made significant mistakes in some Latin American markets. For example, Wal-Mart executives learned that giant parking lots do not draw huge numbers of customers in a country where the shoppers do not have autos. The lots meant that stores were so far away from the bus stops used by many Mexicans for travelling and shopping that potential customers did not come to Wal-Mart stores because they could not easily get their goods home.[143]

The amount of international diversification that can be managed will vary from firm to firm and according to the abilities of each firm's managers. The problems of central coordination and integration are mitigated if the firm diversifies into more friendly countries that have cultures similar to its own country's culture. In that case, there are fewer trade barriers, laws and customs are better understood, and products are easier to adapt to local markets. For example, U.S. firms may find it less difficult to expand their operations into Canada and Western European countries than into Asian countries.[144]

## Other Management Problems

One critical concern firms have is that the global marketplace is highly competitive. Firms that are accustomed to a highly competitive domestic market experience more complexities in international markets, caused not only by the number of competitors encountered but also by the differences among those competitors. For instance, a Canadian firm expanding its operations into a European country may encounter competitors not only from Great Britain, Germany, France, and Spain, but also from countries outside Europe, such as Hong Kong, Japan, Korea, Taiwan, the United States, and possibly even South America. Firms from each of these countries may enjoy different competitive advantages. Some may have low labour costs, others may have easy access to financing and low capital costs, and still others may have access to new high technology. Adapting to all these differences is neither simple nor easy. Finally, attempting to understand the strategic intent of a competitor is more complex because of all these different cultures and mind-sets.[145]

Another problem associated with international diversification focuses on the relationships between the host government and the multinational corporation. For example, while Japanese firms face few trade barriers in North American markets, Canadian firms may encounter many barriers to selling their products and operating in Japanese markets.[146] Regulations have traditionally kept the yen high relative to the U.S. dollar to keep out imports and reduce the value of Japanese exports. As noted earlier, the problem has been reversing itself somewhat, but much more remains to be done to reduce entry barriers. Many firms, such as Toyota and General Motors, are turning to strategic alliances to overcome those barriers. They do so to form interorganizational networks that allow firms to share resources and risks and also help to build flexibility.[147]

# SUMMARY

- International diversification is increasing not only because of traditional motivations but also for emerging reasons. Traditional motives include extending the product life cycle, securing key resources, and having access to low-cost labour. Emerging motivations focus on increased pressure for global integration both as the demand for commodity products becomes borderless and pressure for local country responsiveness is increasing.

- An international strategy usually attempts to capitalize on four important opportunities: potential increased market size; opportunity to earn a return on large investments, such as plant and capital equipment and/or research and development; economies of scale and learning; and potential location advantages.

- International business-level strategies are similar to the generic business-level strategy types: international low cost, international differentiation, international focus, and international integrated low cost/differentiation. However, each of these strategies is usually grounded in some home-country advantage, as Porter's diamond model suggests. The diamond model emphasizes four determinants: factors of production; demand conditions; related and supporting industries; and patterns of firm strategy, structure, and rivalry.

- International corporate-level strategies are classified into three types. A multidomestic strategy focuses on competition within each country in which the firm operates. Firms employing a multidomestic strategy decentralize strategic and operating decisions to the strategic business units operating in each country so each can tailor its goods and services to the local market. A global strategy assumes more standardization of products across country boundaries. Therefore, competitive strategy is centralized and controlled by the home office. A transnational strategy seeks to combine aspects of both multidomestic and global strategies in order to emphasize both local responsiveness and global integration and coordination. The strategy is difficult to implement, requiring an integrated network and a culture of individual commitment.

- Although the transnational strategy is difficult to implement, environmental trends are causing many multinational firms to consider the needs for both global efficiencies and local responsiveness. Most large multinational firms, particularly those with many diverse products, may use a multidomestic strategy for some product lines and a global strategy for others.

- Some firms decide to compete only in certain regions of the world, as opposed to viewing all markets in the world as potential opportunities. Competing in regional markets allows firms and managers to focus their learning on specific markets, cultures, location resources, etc.

- Firms may enter international markets in one of several different ways, including exporting, licensing, forming strategic alliances, making acquisitions, and establishing new, wholly owned subsidiaries, often referred to as greenfield ventures. Most firms begin with exporting and/or licensing because of their lower costs and risks but later may expand to strategic alliances and acquisitions. The most expensive and risky means of entering a new international market is through the establishment of a new, wholly owned subsidiary. Alternatively, it provides the advantages of maximum control for the firm and, if successful, potentially the greatest returns as well.

- International diversification facilitates innovation in the firm by providing a larger market to gain more and faster returns from investments in innovation. In addition, international diversification may generate the resources necessary to sustain a large-scale R&D program.

- In general, international diversification is related to above-average returns, but this assumes effective implementation of international diversification and management of international operations. International diversification can provide greater economies of scope and learning, which, along with the greater innovation, help produce above-average returns.

- Several risks are involved with managing multinational operations. Among these are political risks (e.g., instability of national governments) and economic risks (e.g., currency value fluctuations).

- There are also limits to the ability to manage international expansion effectively. International diversification increases coordination and distribution costs, and management problems are exacerbated by trade barriers, logistical costs, and cultural diversity, among other factors.

- Additionally, international markets are highly competitive, and firms must maintain an effective working relationship with the host government.

## REVIEW QUESTIONS

1. What are the traditional and emerging motives that cause firms to expand internationally?
2. What four factors are a basis for international business-level strategies?
3. What are the generic international business-level strategies? How do they differ from each other?
4. What are the differences among the following corporate-level international strategies: multidomestic, global, and transnational?
5. What environmental trends are affecting international strategy?
6. What five modes of international expansion are available, and what is the normal sequence of their use?
7. What is the relationship between international diversification and innovation? How does international diversification affect innovation? What is the effect of international diversification on firm returns?
8. What are the risks involved in expanding internationally and managing multinational firms?
9. What are the factors that create limits to the positive outcomes of international expansion?

## DISCUSSION QUESTIONS

1. Given the advantages of international diversification, why do some firms choose not to expand internationally?
2. How do firms choose among the alternative modes for expanding internationally and moving into new markets (e.g., forming a strategic alliance versus establishing a wholly owned subsidiary)?
3. Does international diversification affect innovation similarly in all industries? Why or why not?
4. What is an example of political risk in expanding operations into China or Russia?
5. Why do some firms gain competitive advantages in international markets? Explain.
6. Why is it important to understand the strategic intent of strategic alliance partners and competitors in international markets?
7. What are the challenges associated with pursuing the transnational strategy? Explain.

## ETHICS QUESTIONS

1. As firms attempt to internationalize, there may be a temptation to locate where product liability laws are lax to test new products. Are there examples where this motivation is the driving force behind international expansion?
2. Some firms may outsource production to foreign countries. Although the presumed rationale for such outsourcing is to reduce labour costs, examine the liberality of labour laws (for instance, the strictness of child labour laws) and laws on environmental protection in another country to evaluate the ethics of this action.
3. Asia has been experiencing a significant change in both political orientation and economic development. Describe these changes. What strategies should foreign international businesses implement, if any, to influence government policy in these countries? Is there a chance these political changes will reverse? How would business strategy change if Asian politics reverses its current course?

## INTERNET EXERCISE

Go to the Government of Canada's Export Development Corporation at:

**http://www.edc-see.ca**

Or International Business Resources at:

**http://www.ciber.bus.msu.edu/busres.htm**

These sites contain numerous links to other international business sites. Put yourself in the place of the manager of a firm that is thinking about exporting for the first time. Which links on the above site would be valuable to you as a first-time exporter? Explain the merits of each of the links that you feel would be helpful.

Alternately, pick a company making news in today's *Financial Post*. Select one European and one Asian country in which the company might do business. Beginning with the above information sources, determine why the two countries would or would not be a good site for investment.

## STRATEGIC SURFING

To help businesses understand foreign markets, various government agencies produce an array of information on trade and develop "country profiles" that are available to the public free of charge. Information is available at the following Web sites:

The International Development Research Centre at:

**http://www.idrc.ca**

Industry Canada's home page:

**http://www.info.ic.gc.ca**

The CIA World Factbook:

**http://www.odci.gov/cia/publications/nsolo/wfb-all.html**

U.S. State Department Country Reports on Economic Policy and Trade Practices:

**http://www.state.gov/www/issues/economic/trade-reports/index.html**

## NOTES

1. T. Isobe, S. Makino, & D. B. Montgomery, 2000, Resource commitment, entry timing and market performance of foreign direct investments in emerging economies: The case of Japanese international joint ventures in China, *Academy of Management Journal,* June, 43 (3): 468–85.

2. I. Filatotchev, T. Buck T., & V. Zhukov, 2000, Downsizing in privatized firms in Russia, Ukraine and Belarus: Theory and empirical evidence, *Academy of Management Journal,* June, 43 (3): 286–305.; P. Krantz, 2000, How Yeltsin blew Russia's big chance, *BusinessWeek,* January 17, 50.

3. J. Wheatley, 2000, TERRA: Brazil ISP launches free access, *www.ft.com,* January 21, http://news.ft.com/nbearchive.

4. B. L. Kirkman and D. L. Shapiro, 1997, The impact of cultural values on employee resistance to teams: Toward a model of globalized self-managing work team effectiveness, *Academy of Management Review,* 22: 730–57.

5. J. B. White, 1998, There are no German or U.S. companies, only successful ones, *Wall Street Journal,* May 7, A1, A11.

6. B. L. Kedia & A. Mukherji, 1999, Global managers: Developing a mindset for global competitiveness, *Journal of World Business,* 34 (3): 230–51.

7. Bagged cement, 1999, *The Economist,* June 18, www.economist.com/editorial.

8. C. W. L. Hill, 1998, *Global Business Today* (Boston: Irwin/McGraw Hill), 336; B. J. Punnett and D. A. Ricks, 1997, *International Business,* second edition, (Cambridge, MA: Blackwell Publishers), 8.

9. R. Vernon, 1996, International investment and international trade in the product cycle, *Quarterly Journal of Economics,* 80: 190–207.

10. A. Bernstein, S. Jackson, and J. Byrne, 1997, Jack cracks the whip again, *BusinessWeek,* December 15, 34–35.

11. *Financial Times,* 1997, Flexible and cheap, December 12.

12. J. N. Kapferer, 1998, Making brands work around the world, What are global brands and why do they make sense?, *Financial Post,* September 26/28, MGB10, MGB12.

13. Punnett and Ricks, *International Business,* 334–37.

14. S. Batholomew, 1997, National systems of biotechnology innovation: Complex interdependencies in the global system, *Journal of International Business Studies,* 28: 241–66; A. Madhok, 1997, Cost, value and foreign market entry mode: The transaction and the firm, *Strategic Management Journal,* 18: 39–61.

15. W. Kuemmerle, 1997, Building effective R&D capabilities abroad, *Harvard Business Review,* 75, no. 2: 61–70; B. J. Oviatt and P. P. McDougall, 1995, Global start-ups: Entrepreneurs on a worldwide stage, *Academy of Management Executive,* IX, (2): 30–44.

16. J. J. Choi and M. Rajan, 1997, A joint test of market segmentation and exchange risk factor in international capital markets, *Journal of International Business Studies,* 28: 29–49.

17. R. E. Hoskisson, L. Eden, C. M. Lau, & M. Wright, 2000, Strategy in emerging economies. *Academy of Management Journal,* June 43 (3): 249–67; D. J. Arnold & J. A. Quelch, 1998, New strategies in emerging markets, *Sloan Management Review,* 40: 7–20.

18. S. Lovett, L. C. Simmons, & R. Kali, 1999, Guanxi versus the market: Ethics and efficiency, *Journal of International Business Studies,* 30: 231–48; J. L. Xie, 1996, Karasek's model in the People's Republic of China: Effects of job demands, control, and individual differences, *Academy of Management Journal,* 39: 1594–1618.

19. M. A. Hitt, M. T. Dacin, B. B. Tyler, and D. Park, 1997, Understanding the differences in Korean and U.S. executives' strategic orientations, *Strategic Management Journal,* 18: 159–67.

20. Burger King, 2000, *Burger King Company facts pages,* http://www.burgerking.com/company/facts.htm (Retrieved June 29); http://www.burgerking.com/company/latinfacts.htm.

21. G. Edmondson, 1999, Danone hits its stride, *BusinessWeek,* February 1, 52–53.

22. Berstein, Jackson, and Byrne, Jack cracks the whip again.

23  X. Martin, A. Swaminathan, & W. Mitchell, 1999, Organizational evolution in the interorganizational environment: Incentives and constraints on international expansion strategy, *Administrative Science Quarterly,* 43: 566–601.

24  S. Zaheer and E. Mosakowski, 1997, The dynamics of the liability of foreignness: A global study of survival in financial services, *Strategic Management Journal,* 18: 439–64.

25  I. Litvak, 1998, Canadian firms emerge as global players, *National Post,* October 31, MGB3–MGB4.

26  E. Beck & R. Balu, 1998, Europe is deaf to snap! crackle! pop! *Wall Street Journal,* June 22, B1, B8.

27  Small Fry takes big steps into US with Humpty Dumpty assets, 2000, *National Post,* January 26, C8.

28  W. Kuemmerle, 1999, The drivers of foreign direct investment into research and development: An empirical investigation, *Journal of International Business Studies,* 30: 1–24.

29   K. Naughton, K.L. Miller, J. Muller, E. Thornton, and G. Edmondson, 1999, Autos: The global six, *BusinessWeek Online,* January 25, http://www.bwarchive.businessweek.com.

30  K. L. Miller & J. Muller, 1999, Daimler Chrysler: The grace period is over, *BusinessWeek,* March 29, 50; E. Thornton, 1999, Remaking Nissan, *BusinessWeek,* November 15, 70–76; D. Owen, 1999, Renault lifted by news of interest in Korean carmaker, *www.ft.com,* December 30, www.ft.com/nbearchive.

31  Smoke gets in your eyes, 1999, *The Economist,* October 9, 83.

32  G. Edmondson, J. Rae-Dupree, & K. Capell, 1999, How Airbus could rule the skies, *BusinessWeek,* August 2, 54; DASA, Aerospatiale to merge; Deal will also include Airbus, 1999, *Wall Street Journal Interactive,* November 14, www.interactive.wsj.com/articles.

33  W. Shan and J. Song, 1997, Foreign direct investment and the sourcing of technological advantage: Evidence from the biotechnology industry, *Journal of International Business Studies,* 28: 267–84.

34  L. G. Thomas, III & G. Waring, 1999, Competing capitalism: Capital investment in American, German and Japanese firms, *Strategic Management Journal,* 20: 729–48.

35  A. J. Venables, 1995, Economic integration and the location of firms, *The American Economic Review,* 85: 296–00.

36  E. Thornton, K. Kerwin, & K. Naughton, 1999, Can Honda go it alone? *BusinessWeek,* July 5, 42–45.

37  H. Bresman, J. Birkinshaw, & R. Nobel, 1999, Knowledge transfer in international acquisitions, *Journal of International Business Studies,* 30: 439–62; J. Birkinshaw, 1997, Entrepreneurship in multinational corporations: The characteristics of sub-sidiary initiatives, *Strategic Management Journal,* 18: 207–29.

38  Luo & Peng, Learning to compete in a transition economy.

39  S. Makino and A. Delios, 1996, Local knowledge transfer and performance: Implications for alliance formation in Asia, *Journal of International Business Studies,* 27 (Special Issue), 905–27.

40  K. Ferdows, 1997, Making the most of foreign factories, *Harvard Business Review,* 75, (2): 73–88.

41  R. Wright, 1998, Global vision: Image Processing Systems makes awesome machines that see and think, but it took Terry Graham to put IPS on top of the world, *Profit: The Magazine for Canadian Entrepreneurs,* June, 108–12.

42  D. J. Teece, G. Pisano, and A. Shuen, 1997, Dynamic capabilities and strategic management, *Strategic Management Journal,* 18: 509–33.

43  A. Campbell and M. Alexander, 1997, What's wrong with strategy? *Harvard Business Review,* 75, no. 6: 42–51.

44  A. Rugman, 1998, Multinationals as regional flagships, in Part One of As business goes global, *Financial Times,* February 10–11, 6–9.

45  M. E. Porter, 1990, *The Competitive Advantage of Nations* (New York: The Free Press).

46  Ibid., 84.

47  Ibid., 89.

48  Ibid., 89.

49  A. Edgecliffe-Johnson, 1999, A friendly store from Arkansas, *Financial Times,* June 19, 7.

50  N. D. Schwartz, 1998, Why Wall Street's buying Wal-Mart again, *Fortune,* February 16, 92–94.

51  Schwartz, Why Wall Street's buying Wal-Mart again, 94; Sam's travels, 1997, *Financial Times,* December 19, 13.

52  Porter, *Competitive Advantage,* 133.

53  D. Woodruff, 1997, Service with a what? *BusinessWeek,* September 8, 130F–130H.

54  I. M. Kunii & S. Baker, 2000, Amazing DoCoMo, *BusinessWeek Online,* January 9, www.businessweek.com.

55  J. A. Byrne, 1999, Phillip Morris, *BusinessWeek,* November 29, 176–92.

56  T. Burns, 1997, Niche goals bring away results, *Financial Times,* November 17, II; Oviatt and McDougall, Global start-ups.

57  Porter, *Competitive Advantage,* 210–25.

58  M. J. Enright and P. Tenti, 1990, How the diamond works: The Italian ceramic tile industry, *Harvard Business Review,* 68, (2): 90–91.

59  Burns, Niche goals bring away results, 17.

60  D. Lei, M. A. Hitt, and J. D. Goldhar, 1996, Advanced manufacturing technology: The impact on

organization design and strategic flexibility, *Organization Studies,* 17: 501–23.

61 R. D. Ireland and M. A. Hitt, 1999, Achieving and maintaining strategic competitiveness in the 21st century: The role of strategic leadership, *Academy of Management Executive,* 13 (1): 43–57.

62 D. Weimer, 1998, A new Cat on the hot seat, *BusinessWeek,* March 9, 56–61; A. E. Johnson, 1997, Caterpillar pays $1.3 billion for Varity Perkins, *Financial Times,* December 12, 1; P. Marsh and S. Wagstyl, 1997, The hungry Caterpillar, *Financial Times,* December 2, 22.

63 K. J. Delaney, 1999, Compaq boosts role of Internet sales, plans single pricing for firms in Europe, *Wall Street Journal,* December 8, B2.

64 J. M. Geringer, S. Tallman, & D. M. Olsen, 2000, Product and international diversification among Japanese multinational firms, *Strategic Management Journal,* 21: 51–80.

65 M. A. Hitt, R. E. Hoskisson, & R. D. Ireland, 1994, A mid-range theory of the interactive effects of international and product diversification on innovation and performance, *Journal of Management,* 20: 297–326.

66 S. Ghoshal, 1987, Global strategy: An organizing framework, *Strategic Management Journal,* 8: 425–40.

67 T. T. Herbert, 1999, Multinational strategic planning: Matching central expectations to local realities, *Long Range Planning,* 32: 81–87.

68 R. Tomkins, 1998, US market benefits from Knorr know-how, *Financial Times,* January 20, 19.

69 Ghoshal, Global strategy.

70 Y. Luo, 1999, International strategy and subsidiary performance in China, *Thunderbird International Business Review,* 41: 153–78.

71 J. K. Johaansson & G. S. Yip, 1994, Exploiting globalization potential: U.S. and Japanese strategies, *Strategic Management Journal,* 15: 579–601.

72 From desert to tundra, becoming a global power in rental, 1999, *Financial Times,* October 20, 24.

73 C. A. Bartlett & S. Ghoshal, 1989, *Managing across Borders: The Transnational Solution* (Boston: Harvard Business School Press).

74 Luo, International strategy and subsidiary performance in China.

75 J. B. White, 1999, Ford's CEO Nasser ponders giving more authority to regional units, *Wall Street Journal Interactive,* September 17, www.interactive.wsj.com/articles.

76 F. Rose, 1999, Think globally, script locally, *Fortune,* November 8, 157–60.

77 Govindarajan & Gupta, Setting a course; A. Saxenian, 1994, *Regional Advantage: Culture and Competition in Silicon Valley and Route 128* (Cambridge, MA: Harvard University Press).

78 Rugman, Multinationals as regional flagships, 6.

79 L. Allen & C. Pantzalis, 1996, Valuation of the operating flexibility of multinational corporations, *Journal of International Business Studies,* 27: 633–53.

80 J. I. Martinez, J. A. Quelch, & J. Ganitsky, 1992, Don't forget Latin America, *Sloan Management Review,* 33 (Winter): 78–92.

81 U.S. Department of Commerce, 2000, *Trade Statistics with Canada,* http://www.census.gov/foreign-trade/sitc1/2000/c1220.html (Retrieved July 23).

82 H. Przybyla, 2000, Strong U.S. economy pushing trade deficit with Latin America, *Houston Chronicle,* January 21, 1C; 4C.

83 J. Chang & P. M. Rosenzweig, 1998, Industry and regional patterns in sequential foreign market entry, *Journal of Management Studies,* 35: 797–822.

84 V. Govindarajan & A. Gupta, 1998, How to build a global presence, in As business goes global, Part 1, *Financial Times,* February 10–11; Madhok, Cost, value and foreign market entry mode, 41.

85 Punnett & Ricks, *International Business,* 249–50; G. M. Naidu & V. K. Prasad, 1994, Predictors of export strategy and performance of small- and medium-sized firms, *Journal of Business Research,* 31: 107–15.

86 P. S. Aulakh, M. Kotabe, & H. Teegen, 2000, Export strategies and performance of firms from emerging economies: Evidence from Brazil, Chile and Mexico. *Academy of Management Journal,* June, 43 (3): 342–61.

87 U.S. Department of Commerce, 2000, *Trade Statistics with Canada,* http://www.census.gov/foreign-trade/sitc1/2000/c1220.html (Retrieved July 23).

88 A. Dworkin, 1999, Texas exports pinched by global slowdown, *Dallas Morning News,* March 10, D1, D10.

89 J. H. Prager, 1999, Many small businesses continue to have 'euro phobia,' *Wall Street Journal,* April 6, B2.

90 Hill, *International Business,* 436–37.

91 M. A. Hitt & R. D. Ireland, 2000, The intersection of entrepreneurship and strategic management research, in D. L. Sexton & H. Landstrom (eds.) *The Blackwell Handbook of Entrepreneurship* (Oxford, UK: Blackwell Publishers.).

92 B. Schlender, 1995, Sony on the brink, *Fortune,* June 12, 66.

93 J. R. Green & S. Schotchmer, 1995, On the division of profit in sequential innovation, *The Rand Journal of Economics,* 26: 20–33.

94 B. Einhorn, 1997, China's CD pirates find a new hangout, *BusinessWeek,* December 15, 138F.

95 Small Fry takes big steps into US with Humpty Dumpty assets, 2000, *National Post,* January 26, C8.

96 C. A. Bartlett & S. Rangan, 1992, Komatsu limited, in C. A. Bartlett & S. Ghoshal (eds.), *Transnational*

Management: Text, Cases and Readings in Cross-Border Management (Homewood, IL: Irwin), 311–26.

97  A. Jan & M. Zeng, 1999, International joint venture instability: A critique of previous research, a reconceptualization, and directions for future research, Journal of International Business Studies, 30: 397–414; A. C. Inkpen & P. W. Beamish, 1997, Knowledge, bargaining power, and the instability of international joint ventures, Academy of Management Review, 22: 177–202; S. H. Park & G. R. Ungson, 1997, The effect of national culture, organizational complementarity, and economic motivation on joint venture dissolution, Academy of Management Journal, 40: 279–307.

98  Y. Pan & D. K. Tse, 1996, Cooperative strategies between foreign firms in an overseas country, Journal of International Business Studies, 27 (Special Issue): 929–46.

99  M. A. Hitt, B. W. Keats, & S. M. DeMarie, 1998, Navigating in the new competitive landscape: Building strategic flexibility and competitive advantage in the 21st century, Academy of Management Executive, 12 (4): 22–42.

100  B. L. Simonin, 1999, Transfer of marketing know-how in international strategic alliances: An empirical investigation of the role and antecedents of knowledge ambiguity, Journal of International Business Studies, 30: 463–90; M. A. Lyles & J. E. Salk, 1996, Knowledge acquisition from foreign parents in international joint ventures: An empirical examination in the Hungarian context, Journal of International Business Studies, 27 (Special Issue): 877–903.

101  M. A. Hitt, M. T. Dacin, E. Levitas, J.-L. Arregle, & A. Borza, 2000, Partner selection in emerging and developed market contexts: Resource based and organizational learning perspectives, Academy of Management Journal, June, 43 (3): 449–61; J. A. Mathews & D. S. Cho, 1999, Combinative capabilities and organizational learning in latecomer firms: The case of the Korean semiconductor industry, Journal of World Business, 34: 139–56.

102  Ford joins global alliance on electric cars, 1997, Dallas Morning News, December 16, D6.

103  Terry Fox Humanitarian Award Program, 2001, Terry Fox Humanitarian Award Program home page, http://www.terryfox.org (Retrieved February 23) and the links page at http://www.terryfox.org/English/links.html.

104  Terry Fox Foundation, 2001, Terry Fox Foundation home page, http://www.terryfoxrun.org (Retrieved February 23).

105  C. R. Fey & P. W. Beamish, 1999, Strategies for managing Russian international joint venture conflict, European Management Journal, 17: 99–106.

106  M. T. Dacin, M. A. Hitt, & E. Levitas, 1997. Selecting partners for successful international alliances:

Examination of U.S. and Korean Firms, Journal of World Business, 32: 3–16.

107  A. C. Inkpen, 1999, Case study: Global one, Thunderbird International Business Review, 41: 337–53.

108  Y. Pan, S. Li, & D. K. Tse, 1999, The impact of order and mode of market entry on profitability and market share, Journal of International Business Studies, 30: 81–104.

109  M. A. Hitt, R. E. Hoskisson, & H. Kim, 1997, International diversification: Effects on innovation and firm performance in product-diversified firms, Academy of Management Journal, 40: 767–98.

110  M. A. Hitt, J. S. Harrison, & R. D. Ireland, 2001, Creating Value through Mergers and Acquisitions (New York: Oxford University Press).

111  T. A. Stewart, 1999, See Jack. See Jack run, Fortune, September 27, 124–36.

112  K. Restivo, 1999, Canadians eye American SI market: Domestic firms go after projects south of the border. Computer Dealer News, June 18, 1, 47.

113  How to succeed in the U.S. market by really really trying, 1999, National Post, June 3, 76.

114  French Dressing, 1999, The Economist, July 10, 53–54.

115  French Dressing, 1999, The Economist, July 10, 53–54.

116  K. D. Brouthers & L. E. Brouthers, 2000, Acquisition or greenfield start-up? Institutional, cultural and transaction cost influences, Strategic Management Journal, 21: 89–97.

117  J. Terrett, 2000, Westcast earns gold from iron and steel, Plant, April 24: 1.

118  W. C. Kim & P. Hwang, 1992, Global strategy and multinationals' entry mode choice, Journal of International Business Studies, 23: 29–53.

119  D. K Sobek, II, A. C. Ward, & J. K. Liker, 1999, Toyota's principles of set-based concurrent engineering, Sloan Management Review, 40 (2): 53–83.

120  H. Chen, 1999, International performance of multinationals: A hybrid model, Journal of World Business, 34: 157–70.

121  M. Guillen, 2000. Business groups in emerging economies: A resource-based view, Academy of Management Journal, June, 43 (3): 362–80.

122  Hitt, Hoskisson, & Kim, International diversification, 767.

123  A. Delios & P. W. Beamish, 1999, Geographic scope, product diversification, and the corporate performance of Japanese firms, Strategic Management Journal, 20: 711–27.

124  C. Y. Tang & S. Tikoo, 1999, Operational flexibility and market valuation of earnings, Strategic Management Journal, 20: 749–61.

125  M. Geringer, P. W. Beamish, & R. C. daCosta, 1989, Diversification strategy and internationalization: Implications for MNE performance, *Strategic Management Journal,* 10: 109–19; R. E. Caves, 1982, Multinational Enterprise and Economic Analysis (Cambridge, MA: Cambridge University Press).

126  S. A. Zahra, R. D. Ireland, & M. A. Hitt, 2000, International expansion by new venture firms: International diversity, mode of market entry, technological learning and performance, *Academy of Management Journal,* October, 43 (5): 925–50.

127  B. Bremner, L. Armstrong, K. Kerwin, & K. Naughton, 1997, Toyota's crusade, *BusinessWeek,* April 7, 104–14.

128  S. J. Kobrin, 1991, An empirical analysis of the determinants of global integration, *Strategic Management Journal,* 12 (Special Issue): 17–37.

129  M. Kotabe, 1989, Hollowing-out of U.S. multinationals and their global competitiveness, *Journal of Business Research,* 19: 1–15.

130  Porter, *Competitive Advantage.*

131  M. Kotabe, 1990, The relationship between off-shore sourcing and innovativeness of U.S. multinational firms: An empirical investigation, *Journal of International Business Studies,* 21: 623–38.

132  Y. Luo, 1999, Time-based experience and international expansion: The case of an emerging economy, *Journal of Management Studies,* 36: 505–33.

133  S. Finkelstein & D. C. Hambrick, 1996, *Strategic Leadership: Top Executives and Their Effects on Organizations* (St. Paul, MN: West Publishing Company).

134  Hitt, Hoskisson, & Kim, International diversification, 790.

135  W. G. Sanders & M. A. Carpenter, 1998, Internationalization and firm governance: The roles of CEO of compensation, top team composition and board structure, *Academy of Management Journal,* 41: 158–78.

136  D. M. Reeb, C. C. Y. Kwok, & H. Y. Baek, 1998, Systematic risk of the multinational corporation, *Journal of International Business Studies,* 29: 263–79.

137  C. Pompitakpan, 1999, The effects of cultural adaptation on business relationships: Americans selling to Japanese and Thais, *Journal of International Business Studies,* 30: 317–38.

138  J. Harding, 1999, Zeneca's long march, *Financial Times,* March 16, 17; J. Kynge, 1999, Cell phone groups face big cut in China sales, *www.ft.com,* November 10, www.ft.com/nbearchives; M. Forney & L. Chang, 1999, Top Chinese official declares foreign net stakes are illegal, *Wall Street Journal Interactive,* September 15, www.interactive.wsj.com/articles.

139  J. Hunter, 1999, Northern exposure: More TV shows and movies are being filmed in Canada, *Maclean's,* October 11, 68.

140  Hitt, Hoskisson, & Kim, International diversification; S. Tallman & J. Li, 1996, Effects of international diversity and product diversity on the performance of multinational firms, *Academy of Management Journal,* 39: 179–96; Hitt, Hoskisson, & Ireland, A mid-range theory of interactive effects; Geringer, Beamish, & daCosta, Diversification strategy.

141  Porter, *Competitive Advantage.*

142  Hitt, Hoskisson, & Kim, International diversification.

143  A. Sanders, 1999, Yankee imperialist, *Forbes,* December 13, 56.

144  Hitt, Dacin, Tyler, & Park, Understanding the differences.

145  M. A. Hitt, B. B. Tyler, & C. Hardee, 1995, Understanding strategic intent in the global marketplace, *Academy of Management Executive,* 9 (2): 12–19.

146  D. P. Hamilton, M. Williams, & N. Shirouzu, 1995, Japan's big problem: Freeing its economy from over-regulation, *Wall Street Journal,* April 25, A1, A6.

147  N. Athanassiou & D. Nigh, 1999, The impact of U.S. company internationalization on top management team advice networks: A tacit knowledge perspective, *Strategic Management Journal,* 20: 83–92; P. C. Ensign, 1999, The multinational corporation as a coordinated network: Organizing and managing differently, *Thunderbird International Business Review,* 41: 291–322; M. J. H. Oomens & F. A. J. van den Bosch, 1999, Strategic issue management in major European-based companies, *Long Range Planning,* 32: 49–57.

# Chapter Ten

## Cooperative Strategy

## LEARNING OBJECTIVES

*After reading this chapter, you should be able to:*

1. Identify and define different types of cooperative strategy.
2. Explain the rationale for a cooperative strategy in three types of competitive situations: slow-cycle, standard-cycle, and fast-cycle markets.
3. Understand competitive advantages and disadvantages and competitive dynamics of cooperative strategies at the business level.
4. Describe uses of cooperative strategies at the corporate level.
5. Identify appropriate applications of cooperative strategies when pursuing international strategies.
6. Distinguish the competitive risks of cooperative strategies.
7. Understand the nature of trust as a strategic asset in forming cooperative strategies.
8. Describe the two basic management approaches for managing strategic alliances.

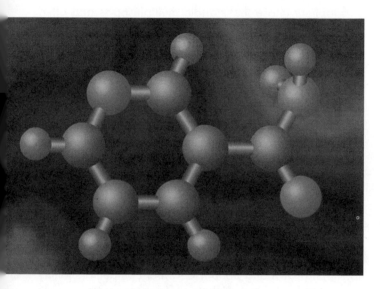

# Firms Collaborating to Compete

Trends in large firms, multinational enterprises, and small entrepreneurial firms have begun to emphasize a cooperative strategy or partnering with other companies. As explained in Chapter 9, large multinational enterprises have formed to exploit firm-specific advantages on a worldwide basis. Yet, many of these large firms have found their potential profits dissipating because internal governance and organizational structure costs outweigh their benefits. To improve this situation, many large multinationals are spinning off businesses they own and forming partnerships with other companies. These firms have moved away from a wholly owned approach and toward managing a business network of partners. The Japanese have created some of the better known of these networks or firms. Often known as vertical keiretsus (a flagship firm with associated suppliers and distributors as partners), these networks have succeeded in forming strong global competitive positions in such diverse fields as consumer electronics (Sony, Matsushita), automobiles (Toyota, Nissan), and computers (NEC, Toshiba).

Microsoft is an example of a firm that has a large system of partnerships with smaller software producers. Nowhere is this more evident than at the Comdex trade show where Microsoft's partner pavilion exhibits the nearly 300 firms that eagerly show their relationship to the giant company. Yet, it would be impossible for even Microsoft to purchase subsidiaries in all the areas of technology where software plays an important role; therefore, it must forge these relationships through partnering. However, not even Microsoft alone can set standards that may be essential for the future of computer-related technologies. One of the most important of these technologies is Bluetooth—a set of short-range radios that allow computers to communicate with other components, such as printers and scanners, without a tangle of wires. Bluetooth will also allow computers to talk with other Bluetooth-enabled devices, e.g., your computer can talk to your coffeemaker, and tell it when to start brewing or, if your laptop says so, that you are not home and do not need coffee. To set up this standard, the Bluetooth Special

http://www.bluetooth.com
http://www.almac.com

Interest Group was formed. Composed of 3Com, Ericsson, IBM, Intel, Lucent, Microsoft, Motorola, Nokia, and Toshiba, the group will develop the standard for these devices

For small firms, forming cooperative relationships with other small companies as well as large ones is becoming a necessity. Though advances in technology, communications, and transportation have created many opportunities for growing small companies, it is difficult for single, entrepreneurial firms to exploit them on their own. Large firms (e.g., auto producers) are winnowing their base and focusing on "tier-one" suppliers (those that handle multiple parts and often supervise other subcontracting suppliers). These actions force smaller firms farther down the supply chain in two opposite directions—specialization and comprehensiveness. Quality is forcing more specialization, while suppliers are expected to provide all-encompassing or "do-it-all" solutions. This forces smaller firms into cooperation with others, even former competitors. Such small-firm networks are being used in Italy and Denmark as well as other places throughout the world.

For Aurora, Ontario's Almac Conveyer, alliances are nothing new. Almac's relationship with General Conveyor goes back a generation. Originally competitors, the two firms found their work complemented each other. On an industrial conveyor system, Almac may design and install the project, General may cut and form metal components, and a third firm, Canaco, may machine parts. Individually the firms are small, but together they claim a "critical mass" of 120 employees.

In the United States, Harry Brown transformed EBC Industries by building alliances with former competitors. Brown and about 50 former competitors jointly market their capabilities to create business that they couldn't generate as individual firms. Moreover, they share information about quality systems, consult with each other before investing in machinery, use each other's sales reps, and refer customers to each other. They can now offer a far more comprehensive product and a single point of contact for a variety of products. However, these alliances are not without their drawbacks; Brown has had to take on the nearly full-time job of coordinating the group's efforts.

Other businesses form hybrid trade associations or work through an umbrella organization such as the Bluetooth Special Interest Group. Usually each network has a leader (and a strategic-centre firm as explained later in the chapter) who champions the network. Though a particular CEO of a company, such as Brown, can be the champion, a third party can also offer an outside perspective to develop the network. Often network brokers, whose very existence is a testimony to the trend, have a flair for getting overburdened CEOs to see usefulness of such business network strategies.

Source: G. Shaw, 2000, The 'Tooth' is Out There, *The Vancouver Sun*, May 18: D13; A. Pletsch, 1999, Almac finds strength in numbers, *Plant*, October 25, 12–13. S. Hamm, A. Cortese, and S.B. Garland, 1998, Microsoft's future, *BusinessWeek*, January 19, 58–69; D. Fenn, 1997, Sleeping with the enemy, *INC Online*, http://www.inc.com, November; A. Rugman and J. D'Cruz, 1997, The theory of the flagship firm, *European Management Journal*, 15: 403–12; D. Bank, 1997, Microsoft emphasizes its role as a partner at Comdex, *Wall Street Journal*, November 19, B4; S.E. Human and K.G. Provan, 1997, An emergent theory of structure and outcomes in small-firm strategic manufacturing networks, *Academy of Management Journal*, 40: 368–404.

Cooperative strategies have become increasingly popular since the mid-1980s.[1] Cooperative strategies can act as a substitute for acquisitions because they possess many of the advantages of acquisitions discussed in Chapter 8 (among them, assistance in new product development, increased speed to market, and lower risk) without the drawbacks (such as assuming a large amount of debt).

While more than 85 percent of Canadian high-technology executives said alliances were essential to their future strategies,[2] such alliances are not important only for high-tech firms. Hamilton, Ontario–based Dofasco and French steelmaker Sollac formed an alliance—DoSol Galva—to take advantage of each firm's unique competencies. Sollac had knowledge in the hot-dipped, zinc-coated steel that is taking the place of electro-galvanized parts in automobiles. Dofasco had the underlying steel capacity, funds to build the zinc-coating line, and the connections to the big three automakers—GM, DaimlerChrysler, and Ford. Because these three auto companies are investing heavily in South America, and Sollac's parent, Usinor, is expanding into the same region, the Dofasco/Unisor connection may allow the companies to greatly expand their South American operations.[3]

Alliances such as DoSol Galva help firms obtain new technology rapidly and reduce the investment necessary to develop and introduce new products, enter new markets, or survive in their current ones. Also, as the opening case shows, cooperative strategies help firms overcome managerial and size limits to growth.[4] An increasing number of small and midsize companies, such as Almac in the opening case, are engaging in cooperative strategies.[5] A Coopers and Lybrand survey of small companies found that such firms participating in alliances increased their revenues faster by generating 23 percent more goods and services than those not involved in them.[6] Alliances have become even more popular in international markets (among firms with headquarters in different countries) in recent years as the Japanese keiretsus mentioned in the opening case demonstrate.[7] DaimlerChrysler and other auto firms have been seeking to develop keiretsu-type networks among their suppliers.[8]

Although strategic alliances, a prominent cooperative strategy, can serve a number of purposes and many are successful, managing them can be difficult.[9] The failure rate for alliances is notably high.[10] A study on the airline industry, for example, found that less than 30 percent of the alliances between international carriers have been successful.[11] As discussed in this chapter, firms must be careful when selecting alliance partners. They need to understand their potential partner's strategic intent and should attempt to develop trust among the partners to facilitate a more effective operation.[12] Because of the high failure rate, top executives who are considering entering into an alliance must develop a good understanding of the appropriate cooperative strategy to use and how to best implement it.

To this point in the book, competition among firms has been our focus. The previous chapters facilitate understanding of competitive advantage and strategic competitiveness through strong positions against external challenges, maximizing of core competencies, and minimizing of weaknesses. This chapter focuses on gaining competitive advantage through cooperation with other firms.[13]

# TYPES OF COOPERATIVE STRATEGIES

**Strategic alliances** are partnerships whereby their resources, capabilities, and core competencies are combined to pursue mutual interests in developing, manufacturing, or distributing goods or services.

**Strategic alliances** are a primary cooperative strategy. Strategic alliances are partnerships between firms whereby their resources, capabilities, and core competencies are combined to pursue mutual interests in developing, manufacturing, or distributing goods or services. Strategic alliances are explicit forms of relationships between firms. They come in three basic types.

A **joint venture** occurs when two or more firms create an independent company, with each of the partners owning equal shares in the new enterprise.

One type of strategic alliance is a **joint venture** in which two or more firms create an independent company. For instance, Fujitsu Siemens Computers, one of the world's largest computer makers, is owned by Japan's Fujitsu and Germany's Siemens. In joint ventures, each partner owns an equal percentage of the equity—50 percent each if two companies are involved. Such 50-50 joint ventures can be large, such as Fujitsu Siemens, or small, such as Royal Ultraframe(a 50-50 joint venture between Canada's Royal Group Technologies and Britain's Ultraframe to manufacture and market sunrooms throughout North America).[14]

An **equity strategic alliance** consists of partners who own different percentages of equity in the new venture.

A second type of strategic alliance is an **equity strategic alliance**, in which the partners own different percentages of equity in the new venture—such as 60 and 40 percent. Many foreign direct investments are completed through equity strategic alliances; the DoSol Galva joint venture discussed in the opening case was 80 percent owned by Dofasco and 20 percent by Sollac. Unisource is an equity strategic alliance among three European telecommunication companies: Netherlands' Koninklijke PTT, Sweden's Telia, and Swiss Telecom PTT. DaimlerChrysler and Mitsubishi, as well as Ford and Mazda, have also formed significant equity strategic alliances. Equity strategic alliances are considered better at transferring know-how between firms because they are closer to hierarchical control than nonequity alliances.[15]

**Nonequity strategic alliances** are formed through contact agreements given to a company to supply, produce, or distribute a firm's goods or services without equity sharing.

Finally, **nonequity strategic alliances** are formed through contract agreements given to a firm to supply, produce, or distribute a firm's goods or services without equity sharing. DaimlerChrysler's network of supplier partners was mentioned earlier; the company's approach to suppliers used to be based on a supplier's ability to build components at the lowest cost without consultation regarding product design or supplier's profit. Suppliers are now involved deeply so that each works closely with DaimlerChrysler engineers. As a result, nonequity alliances have created $1.7 billion in annual savings for the firm; supplier's profits have increased as well.[16] Other types of cooperative contractual arrangements concern marketing and information sharing. Airlines, for example, use flight code–sharing arrangements. Many of these additional relationships demonstrate nonequity strategic alliances.

Although this chapter focuses primarily on the explicit forms of strategic alliances as noted above, there are also implicit cooperative arrangements. One is **tacit collusion**. This is when several firms in an industry cooperate tacitly in reducing industry output below the potential competitive level, thereby increasing prices above the competitive level.[17] Yet most strategic alliances exist not to reduce industry output but to increase learning, facilitate growth, or increase returns and strategic competitiveness.[18]

**Tacit collusion** exists when several firms in an industry cooperate tacitly in reducing industry output below the potential competitive level, thereby increasing prices above the competitive level.

Cooperative agreements may also be explicitly collusive, which is illegal unless regulated by government (as in the telecommunications industries until deregulation). "Mutual forbearance" (another term for tacit collusion) recognizes interdependence and, like explicit collusion, reduces output and increases prices. Mutual forbearance begins with the realization that competition is self-destructive and, without formal agreement, firms cease self-destructive competitive actions and responses.

The following sections explain strategic alliances in depth. We first discuss reasons for engaging in strategic alliances, and then examine strategic alliances at the business-unit, corporate, and international levels. As well, we describe network strategies where the cooperative relations among firms produce multiple alliances, including large consortia and different types of business networks. We then discuss how strategies among multiple alliance partnerships differ from those with two partner alliances. Next, the major risks of pursuing the various types of alliances are considered. Finally, we discuss the importance of trust as a strategic asset to foster cooperative strategies that create competitive advantage and endure over time.

## Reasons for Alliances

A number of different rationales support participation in strategic alliances.[19] The reasons for cooperation differ based on three types of basic market situations: slow-cycle, standard-cycle, and fast-cycle.[20] These three market situations were introduced in Chapter 6. As noted earlier, slow-cycle markets refer to markets that are sheltered or near monopolies such as railroads and, historically, telecommunications companies and utilities. Often, these companies cooperate to develop standards (e.g., to regulate air or train traffic), but because they can also collude to reduce competition, the government usually provides significant regulation to avoid consumer price discrimination. Standard-cycle market cooperation can result from firms trying to avoid overcapacity rather than attempting to increase their opportunities. As such, these cooperative arrangements are often focused on obtaining market power. Fast-cycle markets frequently involve entrepreneurial firms offering new goods or services with short life cycles that are imitated quickly. In these markets, a cooperative strategy is used to increase the speed of product development or market entry as well as to gain strategic competitiveness. The reasons for strategic alliances in each of these markets are listed in Table 10.1.

In slow-cycle markets, firms tend to seek entry into markets that are restricted or try to establish franchises in new markets. For instance, many firms in slow-cycle markets consider cooperative strategic alliances in emerging markets that usually have restricted entry. In emerging markets in Eastern Europe, Russia, Latin America, India, China, and elsewhere, utility firms from developed countries are strongly motivated to form strategic alliances with local partners. Telecommunications firms, for example, have the opportunity to share in establishing a near-monopoly franchise in these emerging markets. Firms operating in emerging markets desire these alliances because they need the expertise and technological know-how that can be provided by firms from developed countries. France's Alcatel has created a strong market position through joint ventures with local partners in Mexico and China.[21] It is also a leading telecommunications equipment supplier in South Africa and other emerging markets.[22] Unisource, itself a joint venture among three national telecommunication monopolies (from Switzerland, Sweden, and Holland), is launching a venture in Hungary to build Hungary's fibre optic cable network.[23]

Cooperation, however, may be difficult to establish in slow-cycle markets. Near-monopolies usually seek to be self-sustaining rather than be maintained jointly by partners. For example, as competition for telecommunications services emerges in Europe, a number of telecommunications firms that were previously state monopolies have

| ■ ■ **TABLE 10.1** | **Reasons for Strategic Alliances by Market Type** |
|---|---|

| Market | Reason |
|---|---|
| Slow Cycle | Gain access to a restricted market |
| | Establish a franchise in a new market |
| | Maintain market stability (e.g., establishing standards) |
| Standard Cycle | Gain market power (reduce industry overcapacity) |
| | Gain access to complementary resources |
| | Overcome trade barriers |
| | Meet competitive challenge from other competitors |
| | Pool resources for very large capital projects |
| | Learn new business techniques |
| Fast Cycle | Speed new goods or service entry |
| | Speed new market entry |
| | Maintain market leadership |
| | Form an industry technology standard |
| | Share risky R&D expenses |
| | Overcome uncertainty |

sought to cooperate and form strategic alliances. The Global One Alliance, formed by France Telecom and Deutsche Telekom, which is also allied with Sprint, has had difficulties. In this joint venture, the two original partners often compete with one another and thereby pull in opposite directions. These partners have significantly different corporate cultures and technical infrastructures and are scrutinized frequently by government agencies. The Unisource alliance mentioned above has had similar difficulties.[24] On the other hand, deregulation and privatization (e.g., in Russia) create opportunities for establishing monopoly franchises in emerging market countries; slow-cycle market firms often seek to take advantage of these opportunities.

In standard-cycle markets, which are often large and oriented toward economies of scale (e.g., automobile and commercial aerospace), alliances are more likely to be between partners with complementary resources, capabilities, and core competencies (see Table 10.1). In these markets where economies of scale are important for competitive advantage or parity, large international alliances are useful because national markets may be too small to support the scale-efficient nature of the businesses. Thus, the increasing globalization of markets presents opportunities to combine resources, capabilities, and competencies. This is a primary reason for alliances among automobile firms such as Ford and Mazda.

Teledesic, based in Seattle, Washington, is a partnership between Craig McCaw and Bill Gates. McCaw and Gates want to circle the globe with 288 satellites supplying high-speed Internet access around the world. Other competing companies also see the potential of this service: companies such as BCE's Telesat and Alcatel's SkyBridge are adding capacity to service wide area networks and the Internet. Since one Alcaltel subsidiary has experience in launching satellites, Teledesic is partnering with Boeing to obtain rights to launch satellites. Boeing is also conveniently headquartered in Seattle, as is Gates's Microsoft. Teledesic's plan to resell the service through local-country telephone companies to overcome regulatory barriers may also give it a competitive edge.[25]

Firms also may cooperate in standard-cycle markets to reduce industry overcapacity and pool resources to meet capital needs. Though mergers can help to overcome overcapacity, they are not forms of cooperative strategy, because the merged firms do not remain independent. The European alliances in aerospace, e.g., Airbus Industrie, have been designed to help the partners become more competitive with North American aerospace firms. Airbus aircraft are produced by a consortium involving France's Aerospatiale and Germany's DaimlerBenz Aerospace, each with 37.9 percent of the business; British Aerospace, with 20 percent, and Spain's Construcciones Aeronauticas, with 4.2 percent.[26] Since most aerospace projects require huge capital outlays, pooling resources is often a rational step. Also, when a firm has a project that requires significant R&D investment, such as aircraft or pharmaceuticals, it may be necessary to seek a partner to share in these outlays.[27] Finally, firms in standard-cycle markets also may form alliances to overcome trade barriers (see Chapter 9) and to learn new business techniques.

Fast-cycle markets, which have short product cycles, such as those among electronics firms, create incentives for cooperation because development, manufacture, and distribution of a new product can happen more quickly. Furthermore, cooperation can lead to the development of standard products in a high-technology market.[28] For instance, Sematech, a cooperative strategic alliance among multiple electronic and semiconductor firms, was important in establishing the adoption of the UNIX standard operating system for workstation computer producers.[29]

Developing an industry technology standard is also a rationale for increased cooperation among fast-cycle market firms. As noted in the opening case, the Bluetooth Special Interest Group will set standards for connecting computers and computer-aided devices. Software and hardware firms, chipmakers, and communications companies are collaborating on coordinating Bluetooth standards. Since the protocols are still uncertain as to how to combine the technologies, and because a different firm holds expertise for each technology, strategic alliances are the preferred approach. As a way to reduce uncertainty—a significant rationale for cooperation—an amalgam of microprocessor companies (e.g., Intel, 3Com, and Motorola), an operating system firm (Microsoft), cell phone providers (e.g., Motorola and Nokia) and Internet switching–device producers (e.g., Ericsson and Lucent) are joining forces to establish this standard.[30] This example suggests the need for cooperation in establishing standards for products that will cross industry boundaries in fast-cycle markets. As such, alliances between firms in fast-cycle markets also may be formed to share risky R&D investments, maintain market leadership, and reduce uncertainty.[31] Each of these rationales is used to pursue strategy at a different level.

## BUSINESS-LEVEL COOPERATIVE STRATEGIES

In this section, we explain four types of business-level cooperative strategies: complementary strategies, competition reduction strategies, competition response strategies, and uncertainty reduction strategies (see Figure 10.1). Following our discussion of these four general types of business-level cooperative strategies is an assessment of the potential competitive advantages associated with each one.

■ ■ **FIGURE 10.1**

*Types of Business- and Corporate-Level Strategic Alliances*

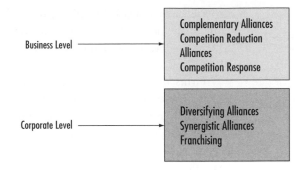

## Complementary Alliances

Complementary strategic alliances are designed to take advantage of market opportunities by combining partner firms' assets in complementary ways to create new value.

**Complementary strategic alliances** are designed to take advantage of market opportunities by combining partner firms' assets in complementary ways to create new value.[32] As the development of the Bluetooth standard suggests, firms often form alliances because they lack certain resources or competencies held by other companies. As Figure 10.2 illustrates, there are two types of complementary strategic alliances, vertical and horizontal. The vertical complementary strategic alliance involves distribution, supplier, and outsourcing functions that are at different stages in the value chain. Benetton and Marks and Spencer are successful clothing firms that use alliances for suppliers and distributors of their products.

Although firms may bring complementary resources and capabilities to a strategic alliance, the role of complementors outside the alliance cannot be neglected. Complementors create products complementary to the industry's product or service. The existence of complementors has been important in the creation and continuation[33] of many industries.[34] For example, electrical appliances and other electronic devices depend upon the availability of a reliable standard electrical supply. The household appliance industry could not have been developed until sufficient numbers of homes had reliable standard electrical current. The Internet, as it is today, is impossible without servers, high-speed optical fibre connections, phone lines, modems, and browsers. Thus, the desirability of use for one product increases as the availability of complementary products increases.[35] The desirability of using a personal computer increased when affordable operating systems and a range of programs became readily available. As operating systems became easier to use, the number of people who desired personal computers increased. Businesses recognize the need to bring the producers of complementary products on board early in the development process in order to make systems work together. Video game producer Nintendo recognized this when it created its next generation Gamecube system to be more easily programmable by game developers.[36]

Within complementary strategic alliances, many large firms have adopted a supply partnership approach that does not entail ownership positions. Traditionally, large firms have preferred vertical integration (ownership of the supply source). This has been especially true of North American automobile producers. In comparison, Japanese automakers use supply partnerships in a system of cooperation and competition between partner suppliers.[37] Performance of supply partnerships suggests that they provide an effective substitute for vertical integration.[38] DaimlerChrysler, as noted earlier, has been developing a keiretsu-type network of partners among its suppliers.[39] Just-in-time inventory systems for suppliers and distributors require significant amounts of cooperation between partnering firms. Such systems can reduce costs for both parties and increase the solidarity of the relationship between manufacturers and their suppliers and distributors.

Outsourcing (discussed in Chapter 4) has been an important means of reducing costs and the basis for an increasing number of strategic alliances. For instance, many large firms outsource their information technology (IT) function;[40] because the technology changes so fast, keeping cutting-edge expertise on staff may be expensive. Thus, a growing number of traditional consulting firms have added managing outsourced functions, such as IT, as part of their services.

As noted in Chapter 5, Magna International has increased its revenues by performing outsourced manufacturing and design work for North American and European automakers.[41] Though Magna faces increased competition, it possesses the capabilities to not only manufacture goods effectively but also design high value–added goods. In fact, Magna can perform initial design, engineering, and development of whole vehicles and thus has become a strong supplier. This sort of significant outsourcing might concern traditional automakers because it could give their suppliers more power, resulting in increased costs.

As Chapter 4 indicates, outsourcing critical resources and capabilities can also harm development and maintenance of core competences. Firms need to ensure that critical functions are not outsourced in order to maintain their core competencies.[42] Partnerships with firms completing work that is outsourced may not be necessary when a purchase is nonstrategic. Since partnerships can be expensive, it may be better to manage the relationship using a free market approach.[43] Thus, a balanced approach is required; a firm does not want to outsource a strategic competence nor enter into a costly partnership, so selectively choosing partners where they are critical to complement capabilities in suppliers is important.

Some firms that have market power use it in detrimental ways. Manufacturing suppliers and retailers, for example, have traditionally seen each other as adversaries. For instance, Wal-Mart's power over Rubbermaid is not the most effective approach to foster a relationship with a supplier. Victims will seek ways to resist as Rubbermaid did in its relationship with Wal-Mart (see Chapter 3). Working together often encourages partners to provide greater value to customers than when they try to exploit their power. Understanding this dynamic has been the key to Marks and Spencer's success.[44] Research also shows that such "soft" relationship aspects are important to the long-term success of foreign exporters.[45]

Horizontal complementary strategic alliances (partners at the same stage in the value chain) are often used to increase the strategic competitiveness of the partners involved. Although horizontal chain alliances usually focus on long-term product and service technology development,[46] many competitors also form joint marketing agreements. Some of these agreements not only reduce costs but also increase revenues and market power. As described in the Strategic Focus, European airlines have formed many joint marketing agreements inside and outside Europe. For example, Lufthansa and Scandinavian Airlines have outlined a strategic alliance in Europe and extended their reach internationally.[47] Their Star Alliance system contains Air Canada, Lufthansa, Scandinavian Airlines, Thai Airways International, and United Airlines.[48] Since these

■ ■ **FIGURE 10.2**

*Vertical and Horizontal Complementary Strategic Alliances*

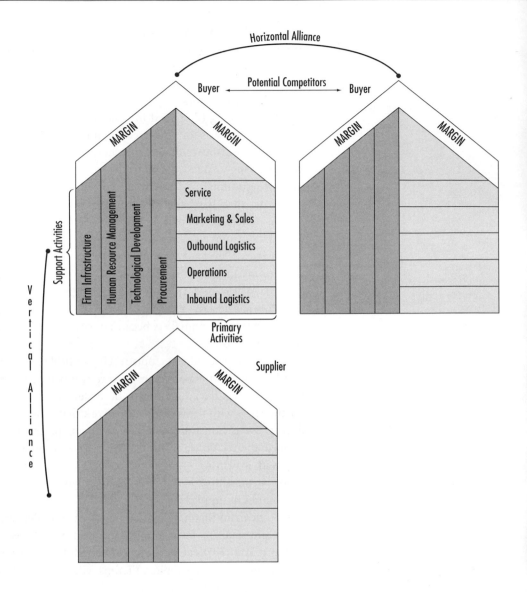

partnerships can increase market power substantially and reduce competition, there have been calls to regulate the international airline links and route allocations.[49]

A few observations may be useful about horizontal versus vertical alliance situations. The perception of partner trustworthiness may be different in horizontal alliances where the potential partners are competitors and in vertical alliances where the partners are buyers and suppliers. For example, the relationship that Chrysler is developing with its supplier network may be built on trustworthiness that has evolved through previous business transactions.

Horizontal alliances, formed among competitors, may have less of a basis for trust. For example, the level of trust among airlines may be quite low because they continue to compete, even with current partners, on many routes. It is not likely that horizontal alliances, therefore, will prove long lasting. This seems to be clear in the airline alliance systems discussed in the Strategic Focus, which appear to be quite tenuous and opportunistic. Such alliances, although they do provide scale advantages, do not appear to be fertile ground for trust and long-standing partnerships.

## STRATEGIC FOCUS

### The Star Alliance System: An Example of a Horizontal Airline Alliance

In May 1997, Lufthansa Airlines announced its Star Alliance with Air Canada, Scandinavian Airlines, Thai Airways International, and United Airlines. Since that time, the Star Alliance has broadened its agreements to include All Nippon Airways, Australian Airlines, Air New Zealand, Cathay Pacific Airlines, Lufthansa, Singapore Airlines, and several others. The alliance had the potential to offer "seamless global service." The Star alliance was, in part, a response to the Global Alliance system composed of Delta, Swissair, Sabena, Austrian Airlines, and Singapore Airlines. Star began by destroying the Global alliance system, by wooing Global member Singapore Air.

Around the same time, KLM Royal Dutch Airlines, Northwest, and Alitalia also created a competing network airline system. This agreement caused Alitalia to alter its alliance with Continental. KLM negotiated an agreement with Continental to create a four-airline group called the Wings alliance. While revenue-sharing arrangements were a sticking point in the partners' negotiations, creation of the four-firm group finally occurred.

The next major grouping—the "Oneworld Alliance" of American Airlines, British Airways, Canadian Airlines, Cathay Pacific, and Qantas—was formed in 1999. Again, this was an alliance formed by creating a defection from another alliance—this time it was Cathay Pacific who defected from the Star alliance. Aer Lingus, Finnair, Iberia, and LanChile have since joined the Oneworld group. Air Canada's takeover of Canadian Airlines meant the loss of Canadian to the Oneworld alliance.

Air France, Europe's third-largest airline (behind British Airways and Lufthansa), has also leapt into the fray. Air France has joined with Delta to create a fourth major airline group. This group, called the "Atlantic Excellence" alliance, also brings together the remnants the Global alliance group—Swissair, Austrian Airlines, and Sabena Belgian World Airlines. In addition, Swissair brings its own regional "Qualiflyer Group" of 10 major and regional European airlines.

The instability among these alliances may cause partners to rethink their alliance plans. For instance, prior to an attempted agreement between American Airlines and British Airways (BA), BA had a relationship with USAir. To form the BA-American alliance, the former alliance with USAir had to be broken. When Singapore Air joined the Star Alliance, it had to break its alliance with Swissair and Delta. As with the USAir-BA alliance, the changeover to the Star Alliance created mistrust of forming future alliances with competitors. Similarly, Cathay Pacific had to opt out of its alliance agreement with Star when Cathay defected to Oneworld. In the meantime, Japan Airlines (JAL) managed to arrive in the new millennia unattached.

*continued*

Although the Air Canada-Canadian combination creates concerns of monopolistic power domestically, the existence of the alliances exacerbates the problem. Between Oneworld partners British Airways and Air Canada, there is a virtual monopoly on direct Canada-London flights. European Community governments were so concerned about the possibility of the Oneworld alliance creating potential monopolistic power that even the BA-American Airlines component of that alliance has yet to be able to win unqualified approval from regulators.

Sources: *Canadian Air home page,* 2000, http://www.cdnair.ca (Retrieved May 25); *Star alliance home page,* 2000, http://www. star-alliance.com (Retrieved May 25); *Oneworld home page,* 2000, http:// www.oneworldalliance.com (Retrieved May 25); M. A. Taverna and G. Thomas, 1999, Star signs up Singapore, *Aviation Week & Space Technology,* October 25, 28–30; Another Airline Alliance, 1999, *World Trade,* 12, (9): 14; J. Ott, 1999, Alliances spawn a web of global networks, *Aviation Week & Space Technology,* August 23, 52–53; T.Y. Jones, 1998, Musical chairs, *Forbes,* January 12, 60–63; C. Goldsmith, 1997, Lufthansa looks to broaden its alliances, *Wall Street Journal,* September 15, A18; H. Banks, 1997, Trans-Atlantic headache, *Forbes,* September 8, 165.

## Competition Reduction Strategies

In the heat of rivalry, many firms may seek to avoid destructive or excessive competition. One means of avoiding such competition is tacit collusion or mutual forbearance. This may be accomplished in some markets through cartels such as OPEC that seek to manage the price and output of companies (e.g., oil companies in member countries) in a specific industry.

In the mid-1990s, Russia had a huge surplus of aluminium. When these aluminium-manufacturing firms were privatized, they began to export the metal in large quantities, undercutting the Western price by as much as 50 percent, which caused the world price to drop precipitously. The Aluminium Association, a trade association of aluminium manufacturers claimed that Russia was "dumping" aluminium below market rates. The Russians argued that they needed foreign hard currency to deal with a difficult transitional economy; to cut them off from foreign markets would create a difficult political problem. As a result, there was a meeting by government and industry officials in Brussels in 1994 that resulted in a government pact calling for "voluntary" cuts in production. Although the politicians claimed this was not a cartel, it had the same result: production cuts to sustain a world price.[50] Aluminium prices in the late 1990s increased, from near $1.50 per kilogram to about $2.25 in 1997.[51] Though aluminium markets suffered a setback in 1998, prices rebounded to about $2.25 per kilogram through 1999 and into the new millennia. Though Alcan's agreement with Alusuisse of Zurich will reduce competition, it cannot be considered an alliance because the companies expect to fully integrate through merger.[52] Given the desire to more fully integrate their activities, merger was preferred over an alliance. However, Alcan's formation of a global Internet-based procurement marketplace with over a dozen other metals producers may reduce some competition in raw materials markets since the group will include their major competitor, Alcoa.[53]

Japan's economy entails a number of entrenched cartels and significant collusion. Even though economic and political forces have been working against cartels and collusion, about 50 percent of the manufacturing industries in Japan engage in some form of price-fixing. Because some cartels date back to the 1600s, such anticompetitive activity in Japan is accepted and tolerated, which makes it difficult to change cartels and collusive practices. Although the situation is complex, it has been argued that cartels and collusion have given Japanese competitors excessive returns against which it is difficult for international firms to compete.[54] Some have argued that problems suffered by Asian economies such as South Korea were the result of large Korean conglomerate-like industrial groups'—chaebols—following collusive practices similar to the Japanese keiretsus. The problem is that cartels restrict output while government restricts imports, and as a result, the countries' currencies have been devalued. Cartels have proven to be problematic for countries' competitiveness in a global economy.[55]

Of course, there is an opposing view. Some claim Japan's firms are less profitable because domestically they are hypercompetitive against each other.[56] For instance, Japan has 10 car firms compared to three competing in North America. These firms engage in intense competitive battles. Yet, if this is harmful, why do the 10 auto firms continue to survive? Part of the answer lies in Japan's industrial policies, such as directions from government regarding industrial sector investment decisions.

More telling is the comparison between South Korea and Taiwan. Industrial policy in South Korea placed economic development in the hands of large family-dominated chaebols. In Taiwan, investment decisions are more decentralized because small and medium-sized firms dominate economic development. Though the large chaebols have developed economies of scale and scope in manufacturing, and moved into more technologically complex industries, their image is not that of leading edge technology firms.[57] Taiwan, on the other hand, has many small firms that often collaborate with one another in industries such as electronic components, computer peripherals, and machine tools. In the economic downturn among Asian nations, Taiwan's economic development approach seems to have fared better than South Korea's. Close chaebol-government ties may have led Korean companies to make less effective investments due to government guarantees. More capital was in the hands of a larger number of investors in Taiwan, resulting in less collusion and better investment decisions. For instance, Korea, like Japan, has too many auto producers; it has five offerings through the chaebols when its economy can really support only two, even with an export-oriented strategy.[58]

Reduction of competition also can be accomplished through industry trade organizations or government policy that is designed to reduce excessive competition, as the aluminium example illustrates above.[59] Some firms follow pricing rules that have developed without direct coordination among competitors. For instance, banks have set rules for lowering or raising mortgage or prime interest rates, which keeps the pricing system for interest rates coordinated among competitors.

Sometimes firms use direct collusion. Toys 'R' Us colluded with toy producers to not sell popular toy lines to its chief competitors, warehouse clubs such as Costco. By getting toy producers to refuse to sell their products to these large, powerful retailers, the price could be higher for toy producers and Toys 'R' Us.[60] Such collusion is illegal, however.

## Competition Response Strategies

As Chapter 6 suggests, some firms enter into strategic alliances to respond to competitors' major strategic actions. For example, as competition for telecommunications services in emerging markets has mushroomed, alliance formation in these areas has increased. Mexico is a country in which these developments are being witnessed; when MCI formed an alliance in Mexico with Grupo Financiero Banamex in January 1994, it was followed by other strategic alliances among competitors to battle for this emerging market. Specifically, AT&T and Grupo Alpha and Sprint and Texmex formed partnerships in November and December 1994, respectively.[61]

The airline alliances mentioned in the Strategic Focus are generally complementary but may also be considered competition response alliances. Susan Snider, director of international alliances for Delta Air Lines, said, "Alliances are not an option anymore. The only way you can fill in the voids is through global partnerships."[62] As businesses go global, travellers are demanding more seamless travel. If one airline can provide it through an alliance system, others are forced to form similar alliances.

## Uncertainty Reduction Strategies

Strategic alliances also can be used to hedge against risk and uncertainty.[63] For instance, a law implementing telecommunications deregulation went into effect on January 1, 1998, in Europe. The law dismantled inefficient state monopolies and opened a $130 billion market for competition. To deal with the uncertainty involved, a number of firms formed alliances throughout the world. Examples of these alliances are explored in the Strategic Focus.

## STRATEGIC FOCUS

### *Alliances Help Firms Overcome Uncertainty*

In Europe, the large telecommunications monopolies have been confronting the uncertainty of the regulatory change with alliances. As of January 1, 1998, a competitor from any country in the Common Market could offer traditional phone services to all customers in any other country. It could do this by either renting part of the country monopoly provider's network or by building its own new network. In anticipation of this, several giant telecommunications monopoly providers formed alliances as mentioned earlier (e.g., the Unisource alliance between the Netherlands' Koninklijke PTT, Sweden's Telia, and Swiss Telecom PTT).

Though Spain won the opportunity to postpone deregulation until 1999, it changed its mind and has offered alternatives to Telefonica de Espana's monopoly. Retevision is the second firm offering international and interprovincial telephone service in Spain. The Global One alliance of Deutsche Telekom, France Telecom, and Sprint has expressed an interest, as has Cable Europa. As well, the Retevision enterprise is supported by a consortium led by the Spanish Utility Empresa Nationalde Electricidad and Telecom Italia.

Although much of the uncertainty leading to the formation of these alliances has been caused by deregulation, technology and anxiety regarding potential demand also leads to multiple alliances. The technical standards for high-definition TV (HDTV), which use digital technology, are beset with difficulties. Since HDTV is digital video, it could potentially be played on specialized TVs as well as computer monitors. The digital medium also means that the signals can be broadcast over normal TV transmitters, cable networks, telephone lines, and satellites. Coordinating all these disparate carriers and receivers, as well as

*continued*

those who must use specialized equipment to produce the content to be transmitted, requires the involvement of numerous parties. There are more than 30 members representing broadcasters, television, cable operators, satellite providers, and equipment suppliers participating in the Canadian Digital Television Technology (CDTV) Working Group. This group, and others like it around the world, have been formed to share the risk and uncertainty associated with the market potential of HDTV. However, realizing that, ultimately, digital television is expected to be worth billions of dollars in sales to broadcasters and consumers, agreeing upon a standard for transmission is critical.

Like the Bluetooth standard mentioned earlier in the chapter, cooperation on HDTV standards is guided by what we might call the "Ghost of Betamax." When home video cassette recorders (VCRs) were introduced, there was no agreed-upon industry standard. Sony produced VCRs using its proprietary standard, "Betamax." Beta offered smaller tapes and better colour. However, Sony was unwilling to license the technology to producers. With a potential market worth billions of dollars, other electronics firms were unwilling to let Sony monopolize the VCR market. Turning to the only alternative they could, these producers adopted Matsushita's "VHS" standard. Though VHS was considered technologically inferior, it could be affordably licensed. The sheer number of manufacturers producing VHS VCRs meant that Beta captured a smaller and smaller percent of the market. The death for Beta came when video rental stores, wanting to mini-mize inventories, resisted stocking both Beta and VHS and selected the more popular VHS format. The triumph of VHS was not only a loss for Sony—whose Beta system lost out—but also a loss for the industry as a whole, because the technologically inferior VHS system became the de facto standard. No manufacturer wants to end up producing another Beta, but no industry wants to end up adopting a technologically inferior standard. Thus, this ghost of Betamax haunts manufacturers who wish to avoid the uncertainties that occurred with the introduction of the home VCR and prompts firms to form standards setting relationships with others.

---

Sources: D. Coxe, 1999, Visions of techno-sugarplums: Owning the best of the best is rarely a losing proposition, *National Post,* December 24: C8; C. Darling, 1999, First Canadian HDTV test facility to transmit this fall, *Broadcaster,* 58 (7): 14–17; A. Manson, 1999, PC workstations make inroads in digital content creation. *Computer Dealer News,* June 18, 33; C. Vitzthum, 1997, Retevision will offer services charging Telefonica's might, *Wall Street Journal Interactive Edition,* http:// www.wsj.com, December 31; G. Naik, 1997, Firms vie to ring in new year in Europe, *Wall Street Journal,* December 18, A18; D. Caruso, In debate on advanced TV, FCC can be assertive, *The New York Times on the Web,* http://www.nytimes.com, June 17.

Not only do deregulation and technical standards push firms to engage in alliances but also political risk is a factor. Vancouver's Placer Dome hedged its approximately $350 million bet on its South African investment by taking a 50 percent interest in the Western Areas of Johannesburg. By sharing the risk, Placer Dome reduces some of the uncertainty that could come from a potentially unstable government.[64] For the same reasons, when Toronto's Manulife entered the insurance market in Vietnam, it did so through a joint venture.[65]

In summary, uncertainty can come from a number of sources: regulatory, technological, demand, and political. Regardless of the source of uncertainty, it leads to firms working together to manage the uncertainty in a collaborative way through strategic alliances. These systems of alliances, however, are often short lived once the uncertainty disappears.

## Assessment of Competitive Advantage

Although all alliances are undertaken for strategic purposes, they will not necessarily realize complementary assets, achieve strategic competitiveness, and earn above-average returns. For instance, alliances to reduce competition are more likely to achieve competitive parity than competitive advantage. In fact, they are usually undertaken to blunt or slow other competitive strategic or tactical moves, which more than likely results in only average returns. An alliance that is formed by a firm lagging behind its competitors for the purpose of improving its capabilities is also likely to achieve no more than competitive parity.

Complementary alliances, however, are more likely to create competitive advantage, achieve strategic competitiveness, and earn above-average returns. When potential complementary capabilities between two firms are realized, there is usually a cost-saving advantage or creation of new capabilities or both, which enhances performance. Furthermore, when a firm is able to enter a market quicker through alliance activities than it could otherwise, it may gain at least a short-term competitive advantage. Many supplier and distributor agreements are of this nature.

Uncertainty reduction strategies, however, are likely to realize only average returns because they attempt to buffer uncertainty and rely, to some degree, on luck. This type of alliance increases the number of options a firm has and thus increases its flexibility and ultimate survival.[66] As such, these alliances are important because, without them, a firm may experience below-average returns. For example, earlier entrants into the market have established relationships with key firms and, thus, may create stronger barriers to the entry of new competitors.

## CORPORATE-LEVEL COOPERATIVE STRATEGIES

Strategic alliances designed to facilitate product and/or market diversification are called **corporate-level cooperative strategies**.

**Diversifying strategic alliances** allow a firm to expand into new product or market areas without an acquisition.

Strategic alliances designed to facilitate product and/or market diversification (see Chapter 7) are called **corporate-level cooperative strategies**. The three types of corporate-level cooperative strategies are diversifying, synergistic, and franchising (see Figure 10.1).

**Diversifying strategic alliances** allow a firm to expand into new product or market areas without an acquisition. Large diversified firms generally seek growth through mergers and acquisitions, as explained in Chapters 7 and 8. However, two firms that do not want to merge can still achieve diversified growth by forming a strategic alliance.[67]

South Korea's Samsung Group is a large conglomerate, or chaebol, that used strategic alliances to expand into new markets first. Samsung invested billions of dollars to develop cars with Nissan; thorough Samsung Aerospace, the company headed a strategic alliance with the Chinese government and aerospace contractors to develop a 100-seat jetliner, and became a part owner of movie producer DreamWorks SKG.[68] The late 1990s' financial crisis throughout much of Asia led to severe financial problems for Samsung because of its far-flung investments.[69]

Samsung's problems exemplify a good point, however. Though strategic alliances can be used to aid in diversification, alliances are also subject to the same limits as logical corporate diversification, as discussed in Chapters 7 and 8. In Samsung's case, its overdiversification led to the firm's being overextended at a critical juncture. This overextension meant that when the Asian financial flu came around, Samsung essentially caught financial pneumonia.

Joint ventures have some similar strategic characteristics to mergers and acquisitions. Legal restrictions can constrain the ability of firms to make major acquisitions. Historically, governments have tried to prevent horizontal acquisitions that created excessive market power. Such acquisitions may be prohibited because they are viewed as fostering explicit collusion. Acquisitions lack the flexibility that is accommodated by strategic alliances. As mentioned earlier, strategic alliances are similar to financial options that create flexibility and reduce risk when moving into uncertain markets.[70] Large diversified firms may adopt diversifying strategic alliances to increase flexibility and reduce risk. Firms also may use a strategic alliance as an experimental step prior to acquisition.[71] If the alliance proves successful, the firm can then acquire its alliance partner. If potential business partners have unique resources or capabilities that cannot be imitated easily by competitors, strategic alliances may be more efficient than acquisitions because these characteristics may be lost in the acquisition process. To buy them on the open market may be very expensive because of their unique qualities and value.[72]

Additionally, some firms are using alliances as a preliminary step to ease the difficulty of other forms of restructuring.[73] For instance, DaimlerBenz Aerospace (DASA) had significant performance problems, given a downturn of the defence industry. DASA and Thomson, a French missile component and armament firm, formed a joint venture known as TDA. This alliance, along with others, allows DASA and Thomson to circumvent local politics in both countries, and provides more flexibility to consolidate operations and alleviate excess capacity in the defence and aerospace industries.[74]

**Synergistic strategic alliances** create joint economies of scope between two or more firms. They are similar to horizontal strategic alliances at the business level, but they create synergy across multiple functions or multiple businesses between partner firms. Two firms might, for example, create joint research and manufacturing facilities that they both use to their advantage and thus attain economies of scope without a merger. Sony Corporation shares its know-how through strategic alliances with multiple small firms. A key reason Sony forms these strategic alliances is to acquire commercially useful economies of scope without incurring the costs of acquisitions.[75]

As mentioned in the Opening Case, the main corporate strategy of Microsoft historically has been its strategic use of partnerships; Microsoft got its start through a strategic alliance with IBM. In launching its entry into personal computers, IBM relied on Intel for logic chips, Microsoft for operating system software, Epson for peripherals, and a number of Asian vendors for other components.[76] With various versions of Windows, Microsoft achieved a strong market reliance on PC manufacturer partnerships. The Windows operating systems was sold with virtually every new PC. Microsoft also used collaboration to establish its Internet browser, Explorer, and to pursue a multimedia strategy with a joint venture with NBC called MSNBC.

The centrepiece of Bill Gates's strategy is to take large chunks of the corporate market by dominating the server and mainframe world. To do this, Microsoft has developed Windows versions for servers that were made possible because Intel produced

Synergistic strategic alliances create joint economies of scope between two or more firms.

chips (e.g., Pentium chips) that run at speeds high enough to be competitive with chips that run servers produced by competitor firms. This has allowed traditional PC partners such as Compaq and Hewlett-Packard to produce machines that run at chip speeds sufficient to allow them to be used as servers when Microsoft server software is installed.

In part, the server versions of Windows have been more profitable than other versions because they are being sold by larger, higher-margin computer firms, in partnership with Microsoft. Often, when a large server network system is sold, the selling firm leaves an agent on site to serve the client. Microsoft, coming from the PC market, has no extensive sales service capability, and needs others to address these problems.[77]

Microsoft's successes at partnerships have brought inordinate market power to the firm and Bill Gates in particular. The concern that Microsoft dominates the industry has lead to a 10-year battle with U.S. antitrust authorities, the threat of a court order to split the firm in two, and unfounded rumours that Microsoft would pack its bags and move its headquarters up the road from Seattle, and out of the United States to Vancouver B.C.[78] Daniel Goodhope, a special assistant in the Texas Attorney General's office, likened Microsoft's form of collaboration as similar to the fictional *Star Trek* race called the Borg. Part flesh and part machine, the Borg beings prowl the universe conquering other races. Goodhope uses the Borg's prime directive as a metaphor for Microsoft: "Resistance is futile. You will be assimilated."[79] Gates claims that being a software company, Microsoft simply wants to move into every business where software matters.

**Franchising** is an alternative to diversification that may be considered a cooperative strategy based on contracting. Franchising provides an alternative to vertical integration and has been a popular strategy.[80] It allows relatively strong centralized control and facilitates knowledge transfer without significant capital investment.[81] Approximately one-third of all retail sales in Canada and the United States are made through franchised outlets.[82] Firms often diversify because focus on a single business is risky (i.e., potential for loss of demand for goods and services without counterbalancing demand from other markets). Service firms may diversify some of their business and financial risk by creating franchises. Many food service firms (e.g., The Great Canadian Bagel Company and Mr. Sub) use this cooperative alternative to diversify into new markets. Firms in a wide array of industries have created nationwide chains through franchising. Franchising reduces financial risk because franchisers invest their own capital to expand the service. This capital investment motivates franchisers to perform well by perpetuating the quality, standards, and reputation of the original business. As such, franchising may provide growth at less risk than diversification. Of course, the franchising firm loses some control, but the franchise contract usually provides for performance and quality audits.

In real estate, many large referral networks that served local brokers are losing market share to firms that are wholly owned or have strong national or international alliance systems. As firms downsize and outsource, there is a demand for property management services and stronger relationships with client companies. As firms expand globally, there is also a need to offer services in more international areas. Thus, large chains with strong national and international affiliations are providing a broader range of service than networks offered. Colliers International Property Consultants developed a system that can offer broker partners a 12-person research department that a purely local firm could not support.[83]

*Franchising is an alternative to diversification that may be considered a cooperative strategy based on contracting.*

Therefore, strong relationships are created as the local independent firm broker systems are breaking down. Networks of affiliate independent brokers can work, but they must assume the appearance of a corporation.

## Motives for Corporate-Level Cooperative Strategies

Because corporate-level cooperative strategies involve not only motives for obtaining competitive advantage but also for reducing risk, assessment of the effects of these motives is essential (for a related discussion, see motives for diversification in Chapter 7). Managers have incentives to increase sales when performance is low as well as to increase their salaries by expanding the size of the business. Alliances, similar to diversification, can help managers achieve both of these objectives. For example, managers can expand the size of the business and thus increase their compensation. Unless a corporation has strong corporate governance to guard against managers using strategic alliances inappropriately (see Chapter 11 regarding governance mechanisms), they may be used for purposes that do not enhance a firm's strategic competitiveness. Managers, for example, may use the intricacy of alliance networks to enrich their own position in the firm. Alliances built on a CEO's contacts and relationships may be lost if that person leaves the company; he or she may be the only one who effectively understands the complex web of relationships existing in the corporate network of alliance partners.[84] These understandings can entrench the manager, making dismissal, if needed, difficult.

Alternatively, the capability to manage a large number of strategic alliances may exist in very few firms and may be difficult for competitors to imitate. In this light, managing a cooperative network may also result in a competitive advantage for the firm. Research shows that firms capable of learning from their collaborations develop know-how that can be distinguished from mere experience with strategic alliances.[85] Though networks of alliances can be used to diversify a firm, create competitive advantage, and possibly to enrich managers' positions, the cost and difficulty of managing them should not be underestimated. Monitoring these relationships and maintaining cordial and trusting relations requires time and effort. Such costs should be considered before entering into numerous strategic alliances.[86]

## INTERNATIONAL COOPERATIVE STRATEGIES

Multinational corporations have typically achieved higher performance than firms operating in a solely domestic market.[87] As domestic economies have grown more global, the importance of international cooperative strategies has also increased.[88] Often, firms that develop distinct resources and capabilities in home markets may be able to leverage them by making direct investments internationally (versus licensing or exporting). For Canadian firms, going international is essential if they are to compete with their U.S. counterparts, if only to retain a local customer base.[89] For example, going international may allow a firm the buying power with vendors necessary to compete with international competitors coming into the Canadian market. Cooperative strategies (e.g., international strategic alliances) are a common mode for making such investments in international markets.

Firms can create more corporate flexibility and extend or leverage their core competencies in new geographic regions by developing international strategic alliances.[90] However, such alliances are more complex and risky than domestic ones. For example, there is a higher failure rate for international joint ventures than for international green-field ventures (establishing a wholly owned subsidiary).[91] Although strategic alliances allow partner firms to share risks, and thus are less risky for each individual partner than a greenfield venture, they are difficult to manage. The need to coordinate and cooperate to share skills and knowledge entails significant processing of information on the part of all partner managers.[92] Where substantial demands are placed on partners' managers to achieve quick returns, there is less alliance success. Thus, although international coop-erative strategies can have significant positive outcomes, care must be taken when choosing the particular partners, managers, and ventures to ensure success.[93]

As indicated in Chapter 9, some countries regard local ownership as an important national policy objective. India strongly prefers to license local companies as opposed to foreign ownership or joint ventures with a local firm or wholly foreign owned sub-sidiaries. Thus, in some countries, managers may not have the full range of entry mode choices. Investment by foreign firms may be allowed only through cooperative agree-ments such as joint ventures. This is often true in newly industrialized and developing countries. For instance, international joint ventures represent 52 percent of the value of new manufacturing ventures in China.[94] Joint ventures can be helpful to foreign part-ners because a local partner can provide information about local markets, capital sources, and management skills.

Generally, Western governments, though nervous about foreign ownership in some industries, are less concerned than many other governments. This is particularly true in the European Community (EC) where cross-border investment is extensive. In the EC, firms have increased direct control over subsidiaries and use pan-European strategies rather than individual country strategies. In other words, firms establish a strategy for all of their operations in Europe as opposed to a different strategy for each European country. However, the trade agreements generally spawned more cooperative ventures between partners from those countries that were a party to the agreement. These trade agreements promote freer trade and therefore increase the opportunity for more foreign direct invest-ment, at least from firms headquartered in countries covered by the agreement.

Though there may be countries in the EC that are more powerful than others (e.g., Germany or Britain), no one single country is dominant across a wide array of industries. This is not the case for participants in the North American Free Trade Agreement (NAFTA); the U.S. dominates the group. This being the case, there is growing concern in Canada regarding U.S. domination of the Canadian economy. This is not only a concern about the relative disparity in economic power but also a concern over foreign direct ownership, location of corporate headquarters, and the citizenship of stockholders.[95]

Canadian Pacific Chair David O'Brien has expressed his concern about what he calls "the great Canadian fire sale."[96] In the last two years of the millennium, hundreds of Canadian companies, over $40 billion in assets, were sold. Firms sold included MacMillan Bloedel and Club Monaco, which were sold to U.S. firms.[97] Critics question where real power is centred in firms that claim Canadian headquarters.[98] It has been claimed that Nortel Networks, though headquartered in Brampton, Ontario, is mostly run from Dallas, Texas.[99] Ownership of Canadian firms has been questioned. The Canadian National Railway has more U.S. shareholders than Canadian ones. Nortel, Four Seasons Hotels, and Imax are listed on both the Toronto Stock Exchange and U.S. exchanges; the U.S. exchanges are far more active in their trading of these stocks. With sentiments such as these, it may well serve companies on both sides of the 49th parallel to enter into joint ventures arrangements rather than deals where moves are perceived to be a takeover by a firm in the other country.

Others argue that Canadian takeovers of foreign firms far exceed the number of foreign firms buying Canadian firms. Over the last decade, foreign control of Canadian companies, as a percent of assets, has levelled out.[100] The argument is that what we are likely seeing is simply increasing globalization, and we are likely to see more of this, particularly if further EC integration proves successful. Such success may create impetus to further NAFTA scope and membership. Expanding NAFTA to include other countries may somewhat lessen the dominance of the United States in the group.

Although U.S. industrial dominance may be perceived as a problem—especially in developing countries around the world—it is also an opportunity for Canadian firms. Canadian companies have the image of technically being at least on par with U.S. companies but with the decided advantage that they are not "American." Even the Americans recognize this advantage. For example, Calgary's Jupiter International Resources, a company with revenue of less than $500 000, struck a $40 million deal to operate electric power plants in developing countries with a subsidiary of Caterpillar. Jupiter International will run the 50-50 joint venture called Jupiter Power.[101] As a Canadian firm, Jupiter managers have the technical expertise, close geographical and cultural proximity to the United States, and the advantage of not being Americans. Since a great many of the world's largest corporations are based in the United States,[102] concerns about American economic dominance are not limited to Canada. Thus, all other things being equal, people may prefer to avoid domination by the Americans and deal with people perceived to be culturally less aggressive than the Americans: the Canadians.[103]

Yet, as trade agreements have proliferated globally, the rules of competition have changed and, therefore, cooperative strategies have likewise changed. More than 100 countries are signatories to the World Trade Organization (WTO) and the International Monetary Fund (IMF). With other treaties, such as NAFTA, only a few countries are involved. In either case, strategies have to be changed to adjust to the agreements. As well, if these agreements come under sufficient fire or are expanded, cooperative strategies will need to change accordingly.

## Strategic Intent of Partner

With the increased number of international cooperative strategies comes a greater variance in the partner's strategic intent. For example, a partner may intend to learn a technology and use it later to become a competitor. Thus, it is important to assess potential partners' strategic intent in forming cooperative relationships.[104]

Emerging economies, such those in the former USSR, have a distinct need for foreign investment and technology transfer. Although most of economy in that region has been privatized, there has been no large influx of capital; the process was intended more to establish private property rights. As the nature of the economy changes, there is a dire need for new investment, but the people are wary of foreign investment in their country.[105] They are quite sensitive about the strategic intent of foreign partners who want to establish cooperative agreements and operations in their country, although this is beginning to change with more market-oriented and entrepreneurial managers.[106]

A recent partnership, for example, between state-owned Georgian Oil and Calgary-based CanArgo Energy, could be an example for other international alliances between

Eastern and Western partners. Georgian Oil gave CanArgo the footing it needed to develop operations after the companies signed a production-sharing contract. The agreement gives CanArgo the right to conduct commercial ventures in the region. CanArgo managed to secure a loan with World Bank agencies to fund the development of the oilfield. In return, CanArgo gives a portion of its oil to Georgian Oil.[107]

Some countries, and the firms within them, have distinct needs for the transfer of technology to facilitate their economic development. Oftentimes, companies in these countries, especially in Asia, have an organizational culture that promotes and facilitates learning. These firms then have the strategic intent in cooperative arrangements of learning from their partner(s).[108]

The degree to which one partner may learn from another is impacted by numerous factors, particularly: (1) learning rates, (2) absorptive capacity, and (3) concentration within the company. *Learning rates* refers to a natural ability to absorb knowledge. For example, placing people into the joint venture who have the ability to learn most skills quickly will improve learning rates. *Absorptive capacity* refers to the ability of individuals to acquire knowledge in a specific field already known to them. For example, a joint venture to produce an optical fibre communications network might involve a laser manufacturer and an optical fibre producer. The laser manufacturer can raise its absorptive capacity in the optical fibre field by contributing to the joint venture people who already have an extensive knowledge of optical fibres. Simply, it's easier to learn a bit more about a topic you already know than to start from the basics. Finally, *concentration within the company* refers to concentrating the knowledge gleaned from the joint venture partner in such a way as to be useful. For example, when these people return from the joint venture, firms that keep the group together to debrief them regarding the knowledge they have acquired will be able to employ that knowledge better than if the group is disbursed throughout the firm.[109]

Firms with different strategic intents may realize a loss of the competitive advantage of their core competence if their alliance partner learns it. Therefore, one way to prevent this is to carefully control technology and knowledge transfer.[110]

On the other hand, Texas Instruments (TI) and Hitachi began conducting joint research in 1988 and incrementally expanded their relationship. During the early part of the relationship, managers from the two firms had to bridge cultural differences. For example, there were differences in decisionmaking processes. TI used an approach in which managers held a meeting to discuss an issue, then spent time brainstorming, then made a decision. Hitachi executives, on the other hand, more commonly held informal discussions and came to a decision prior to the meeting, which was used to ratify the final decision. Over time, the two companies learned to work together effectively and eventually developed a joint venture to produce memory chips. Though it took almost six months of negotiations, it was decided that the new venture would sell its chips to both companies at the same time, and Hitachi and TI would then be free to sell the chips in competition with each other. TI's executives suggest that it intends to provide better services for its customers to differentiate itself from Hitachi.[111]

## NETWORK STRATEGIES

To this point, our focus has been on the cooperative relations between two (or a very few) firms, such as joint ventures or contractual arrangements.[112] However, networks are an important complement to other forms of cooperative strategy. Often, networks of smaller firms work together because they are located in geographic industrial districts. Networks such as these are described in the Strategic Focus.

## STRATEGIC FOCUS

### Cooperative Strategy Often Develops in Economic Districts

Cooperative strategy has been fostered widely in the Silicon Valley of California where many electronic, computer, and biotech firms create innovation and cooperative relationships between large and start-up firms. The Ottawa region—home to Corel and Newbridge Networks, among others—is known as Silicon Valley North. Ottawa's high-tech sector fosters a sense of community; CEOs of some larger companies will not uncommonly sit on the boards of smaller firms to aid them in getting started. In a similar way, B.C.'s Lower Mainland—which has been called the Silicon Delta—has produced the likes of Ballard Power, Creo Products, QLT PhotoTherapeutics, and PMC Sierra.

The "Cambridge phenomenon" was a phrase coined more than a decade ago as Britain tried to create its own Silicon Valley. The Cambridge area of Britain has a network of technologically able and entrepreneurial people. Some 1200 "knowledge-based" companies are located here, employing 30 000 people and generating more than £3 billion of sales. About 85 percent of the start-up companies in the area survive beyond five years, which is well above the British norm of 50 percent. Cambridge University has been a magnet for technological developments. It boasts 50 Nobel prize winners and has many research institutes such as the Laboratory for Molecular Biology where Watson and Crick first discovered the structure of DNA.

Throughout Italy, a number of cooperative districts can be found, focusing on specific industry groups. In northeast Lombardy, the small town of Lumezzane is the world leader in silverware, faucet, and valve production with more than 2000 small companies manufacturing these items. In this town of 24 000, most companies have 20 or fewer employees with each worker specializing in particular crafts, such as shaping forks, sculpting their edges, and polishing specific pieces of silverware.

There is a tight network among family, friends, and colleagues in Lumezzane. For example, when a business is threatened with bankruptcy, a set of phone calls usually yields a group of six to eight unofficial "trustees" who help bring the company safely back into the black. Townspeople are fiercely loyal to Lumezzane; they usually don't sell their businesses to outsiders, and they tend to live in Lumezzane even though better housing prices are available in nearby Brescia.

Once a region acquires a reputation as being conducive to conducting certain types of business, firms in that industry tend to locate there. Given Vancouver's geographic proximity to Hollywood and the known quality technical talent, the city acquired a reputation as Hollywood North. It is home to film and TV producers, Lions Gate Entertainment (its work includes *Mission to Mars* and the *X-files*) and computer animators Mainframe Entertainment (its series include *Reboot* and *Beasties*). Also, movie production has been attracted by the devalued Canadian dollar, which allows films to be produced less expensively.

*continued*

There are numerous districts such as these throughout the world where cooperative strategy is often developed among smaller and larger companies. For instance, clothes design districts are found around Montreal and New York City. Commonly referred to by those in the trade as the rag or "shmatte business," these areas frequently foster, and are fostered by, significant interrelationships between networks of firms or operators that are often competitors and collaborators.

Sources: P. Keitenbrouwer, 2000, Canadian clothing industry's seamy side, *National Post,* April 1, D1; G. Landriault, 1999, Angels, startups and taxes: Ottawa high-tech pioneer Denzil Doyle discusses the industry's money problem, *Computer Dealer News,* November, 26, 25; W. Hanley, 1999, Growing up in Silicon Delta: BC's high-tech industry produces stars and struggles, *National Post,* November 24, D1, D2; J. Hunter, 1999, Northern exposure: More TV shows and movies are being filmed in Canada, *Maclean's,* October 11, 68; K. Damsell, 1998, Movers and shakers, *Financial Post,* June 27, R2; T. Mueller, 1997, A town where cooperation is king, *BusinessWeek,* December 15, 155; T. Buerkle, 1997, Cambridge: Britain's I-technology hotbed, *International Herald-Tribune,* October 8, 13; R. Pouder and C.H. St. John, 1996, Hot spots and blind spots: Geographical clusters of firms and innovation, *Academy of Management Review,* 21: 1192–1225.

A **network strategy** involves a group of interrelated firms that works for the common good of all.

A **network strategy** involves a group of interrelated firms that work for the common good of all.

Although clustered groups of firms often form cooperative networks, it does not mean that the firms in the district are more competitive.[113] The intent of network strategy is to increase performance of a network of firms.[114] The relationships may be formal or informal. Examples of such networks include Japanese keiretsus and North American R&D consortia.

In the 1950s, the emphasis was on larger and stronger firms, as product diversification grew popular and larger firms expanded into new product and geographic markets. Similarly, in the multinational and matrix organizations of the 1970s, a combination of functional and divisional structures was used to create large firms of enormous strength and complexity. More recently, however, a newer type of strategy, known as a network, has emerged. The structural characteristics of a network organization are discussed in Chapter 12. Herein, we outline the strategic approach of these networks. There are three types of networks: stable, dynamic, and internal.[115]

Stable networks often appear in mature industries with largely predictable market cycles and demand. In Japan, these relationships usually include some shared ownership among the network firms as part of a keiretsu.[116] Among North American firms, ties have grown stronger and, thus, stable relationships are more common. For example, in the athletic footwear and apparel business, Nike has long-established relationships with a network of suppliers and distributors throughout the world.

Dynamic networks often emerge in industries where rapid technological innovations are introduced, frequently because of the short life cycles of products. Waterloo, Ontario's Mitra Imaging has made a substantial business of being a contract developer of medical archiving software. To get into this industry quickly, Mitra worked with the medical systems divisions of Agfa, Fuji, Kodak, General Electric, Philips, and Siemens. Using knowledge gained from the experience with this range of partners, Mitra entered a joint venture with Agfa to take the next step in developing software that integrates radiology and other images, along with patient history and current patient information.[117]

Internal networks can also be implemented to facilitate firm operations. For example, the global electric products firm Asea Brown Boveri (ABB) buys and sells a multitude of products across many country boundaries using an internal network for coordination. Benetton, serving as a chief broker among many independent specialist suppliers and distributors, has an external network similar to ABB's internal network.[118]

Each of these network types has a focal **strategic centre** or firm that manages the network. The main bank is the strategic centre in horizontal Japanese keiretsus that entail loosely coupled, diverse businesses. The primary relationship among these diverse businesses is common ownership and arrangements with the same bank or set of banks. In vertical keiretsus, such as Toyota and Nissan, a dominant firm manages a supplier network.[119] Firms such as Apple, Benetton, IKEA, Nike, Nintendo, and Sun Microsystems are strategic centres associated with network structures. These companies are not "virtual firms" where all central competence is outsourced;[120] instead, they have capabilities and core competencies that allow them to shift important activities to other companies, which creates value when these companies are better able to perform such activities.[121]

The virtual company is the ultimate form of network and can be powerful. When U.S. online grocer Peapod began, it spent tens of millions of dollars to develop its own warehouses and distribution centres. In contrast, Canadian online grocer Peachtree created relationships with existing grocers to stock and deliver its products. The total start-up cost was less than $5 million. The only real product provided by Peachtree is the Internet site and coordination of the grocers—local grocers provide the rest. While the investment cost may be low, the arrangement makes Peachtree vulnerable to its network partners. If the partners do not perform well, the virtual company may fail.[122]

## R&D Consortia and Other Network Strategies

R&D consortia represent a form of a network strategy where there is a strong need for cooperation among firms (often direct competitors) in an industry.[123] These network organizations have been in existence for some time in Japan, Korea, and more recently in the European Union.[124] For example, the Japanese government's industrial policy and the Japanese Machine Tool Building Association (a trade group) have fostered the successful development of the machine tool industry in Japan.[125] The Japanese machine tool industry accounted for less than 1 percent of world production in 1955; by the 1990s, it accounted for 28 percent of world output. In contrast, the North American share of world machine tool production declined from about 40 percent in 1955 to less than 10 percent in the early 1990s.

In high-technology industries, where there is significant uncertainty, coalitions among firms are likely to form to develop an industry technological standard, thus reducing uncertainty. The VHS Alliance, coordinated by Matsushita to sponsor VCR standards, Ericsson's support of Bluetooth, and the Technical Workstation Alliance created to develop and sponsor the UNIX operating system standards are three examples of this phenomenon.[126] Such alliances may be developed by a sponsoring firm that offers a technology license at a low cost to induce other firms to adopt its technology. In these cases, there is an incentive to make the consortium as large as possible so there is broad

**Strategic centre** refers to the firm that manages a network.

http:// www.peachtree.ca

acceptance of the standard industry-wide. Yet, these firms still often compete with one another, and participating firms are concerned with potential disproportionate gains by rivals. Disproportionate gains are most likely when alternative standards are being proposed; the firms proposing a standard try to make it functionally equivalent to their pre-alliance technology. Interestingly, alliance partners frequently compete in similar markets.[127] Therefore, R&D consortia tend to develop naturally as competition evolves.

Finally, interlocks between boards of directors—where the same person is the member of two different boards—can provide links between companies. Such links can provide significant guidance and industry knowledge to both firms. In fact, research has shown that, next to financial resources, the existence of long-term board interlocks is the most critical factor in long-term corporate survival.[128]

## COMPETITIVE RISKS WITH COOPERATIVE STRATEGIES

Even as companies attempt to cooperate, they also compete, both with firms in and outside their alliances. As such, there are significant risks with a cooperative strategy, including such actions or outcomes as poor contract development, misrepresentation of partner firms' competencies, failure of partners to make complementary resources available, being held hostage through specific investments associated with the alliance or the partner, and misunderstanding of a partner's strategic intent.

Although there are incentives to cooperate in strategic alliances, there are also incentives to act opportunistically. If a poor contract is developed, the partnership is likely to dissolve in time. The strategic intent of the parties forming an alliance should be identified and incorporated into the contract to guard against potential opportunistic behaviours.

Partnerships may dissolve because firms misrepresent their potential competencies to partners. Such misrepresentation is more likely when a partner offers intangible resources such as "knowledge of local conditions." Some partnerships may fail because partners refuse to allow their complementary resources to be available to the venturing firm. Contractual arrangements can sometimes discourage this form of adverse behaviour, but once a firm makes an investment, in a joint venture for example, the local partner may hold those assets hostage if foreign countries do not have laws protecting them.

An alliance between Publicis of Paris and Foote, Cone & Belding (FCB) of Chicago, two premier advertising agencies, suited the needs of each partner. Publicis needed FCB's experience in North and South America, and FCB could use help to support its international clients. However, the trust between the two chief executives who formed the alliance began to dissolve soon after the deal was struck. The divorce came in 1997 after many aspersions were cast on both sides; but that did not end the fight. Publicis then made a hostile takeover bid for the parent of FCB, True North Communications. Both companies, but especially FCB, are worse off than before the alliance was established.[129]

In addition to the moral hazards (potential cheating by partner firms), there are other risks. One of those risks is having the ability to form and manage a joint venture effectively. Prior experience may not be adequate for collaborative strategies to endure. Another risk is having the ability to collaborate. Alternatively, it may be difficult to identify trustworthy partners with whom to collaborate.

Another risk of cooperative strategies is that the parties in the alliance may lose autonomy and flexibility. For example, cooperating partners frequently commit to some form of joint decision and/or joint planning to increase the participation and commitment of both parties in the alliance. However, attempts to reach consensus between the two independent organizations is likely to slow decisionmaking, possibly resulting in lost market opportunities. This risk is particularly acute in fast-cycle markets where speed and flexibility are key competitive dimensions.

■ ■ **FIGURE 10.3**

*Managing Competitive Risks in Cooperative Strategies*

Substitutes for alliances include mergers and acquisitions or internal development of new products. To the extent that there are reasonable substitutes (e.g., acquisitions) and significant risks, such cooperative strategies may lose their attractiveness. The increasing number of strategic alliances suggests that they may be imitated easily by competitors and that many firms perhaps form alliances with other companies because their competitors have done so. The different risks and means of managing them in strategic alliances are shown in Figure 10.3.

## TRUSTWORTHINESS AS A STRATEGIC ASSET

A component critical to the success of alliances is trust between partners.[130] The fact that there are incentives to pursue cooperative strategies does not mean that partnering firms have the capability to manage such cooperative relationships and maintain them. Corning, over time, has developed a strong reputation for collaborative venturing. Because of Corning's reputation, potential partners know that a strategic alliance is likely to be successful because the company has a reputation for being trustworthy.

If a firm takes advantage of other firms in cooperative relationships, it will develop a reputation that will prevent future cooperative opportunities; potential partners will consider the firm untrustworthy.[131] Several Japanese steel companies were involved in a joint venture to develop the Quintette and Bullmoose coal mines in northeast British Columbia. To fully realize the mines' potential, $220 million was spent to build the neighbouring town of Tumbler Ridge, $550 million was spent to build new rail lines, and $280 million to upgrade rail and port facilities. With over a billion dollars of public infrastructure, government was betting heavily that user fees and taxes paid by the venture would pay off. However, the coal market suffered a general price drop, and with it came demands from partners for tax relief for the mines and lower than contracted prices for its coal. All of this not only meant a loss of tax revenues for the government and a threat to the existence of Tumbler Ridge but also created a great deal of mistrust between the workers and the companies and governments involved.[132]

Thus, trustworthiness is a strategic asset in cooperative relations because it can be rare. Because not all aspects of a cooperative relationship can be specified in a contract, trustworthiness is an important attribute. As previously mentioned, horizontal strategic alliances have been found to be successful in developing and bringing new products to the market. However, because this form of cooperation often occurs between competitors, trust is critical to its success. Over time, collaborators gain knowledge about the reliability of partner firms as well as knowledge about partner capabilities.[133]

## STRATEGIC APPROACHES TO MANAGING ALLIANCES

Two basic approaches to managing assets and liabilities are associated with cooperative strategies (see Figure 10.3).[134] One approach, based on minimizing alliance costs, requires that firms develop capabilities to create effective partner contracts and to monitor such contracts. The other approach, focused on maximizing value-creation opportunities, requires trustworthy partners with complementary assets and emphasizes trusting relationships. The first approach may produce successful joint ventures, but it is costly to write protective contracts and to develop effective monitoring systems. Furthermore, protective contracts and monitoring systems shield parts of the organization from both participating partners. Although monitoring systems can largely prevent opportunism and cheating among partner firms, they also preclude spontaneous opportunities that might develop between cooperating partners. Thus, they may preclude both firms from realizing the venture's full potential.

If trust can be used as a strategic asset in choosing partners, monitoring costs will be lower, and opportunities between collaborating firms can be maximized. This second approach to governance is referred to as opportunity maximizing because partners in such alliances are able to pursue potential rent-generating opportunities that would be unavailable to partners in more contractually restricted alliances.[135] Thus, it is important for firms to consider both the assets and liabilities of monitoring systems that will be used to manage the alliance.[136] For example, AT&T entered an alliance with a smaller credit card technology firm to develop a new credit card service. To ensure secrecy so the alliance could maintain a critical lead in the industry, no contract was used for the first months of this relationship. During this time, the firms worked collaboratively, sharing information and resources, while relying on the character and goodwill of each other to guide the relationship. The partners were more concerned with maximizing alliance opportunities than minimizing potential opportunism from alliance partners.[137]

In summary, trust is not required for cooperation between two parties, but without it, monitoring costs will be higher. Furthermore, trust will increase risk-taking behaviour between partners to take advantage of opportunities.[138] Trust has distinct advantages, but it also has increased liabilities associated with the risks of cooperative strategies.

Our focus in the next major section of the book is the strategic actions taken to implement formulated strategies. The first topic examined is corporate governance: how firms align managers' interests with those of the shareholders and control their operations to affect their strategic competitiveness.

# SUMMARY

- Cooperative strategies can act as a substitute for acquisitions because they possess many of the advantages of acquisitions (assistance in new product development, increased speed to market, and lower risk) without the drawbacks (assuming a large amount of debt).

- Strategic alliances are partnerships between firms whereby resources, capabilities, and core competencies are combined to pursue mutual interests. Usually, firms' complementary assets are combined in strategic alliances. Strategic alliances have three basic varieties: joint ventures, equity strategic alliances, and nonequity strategic alliances.

- Other types of cooperative strategies are usually implicit rather than explicit. These include mutual forbearance or tacit collusion, in which firms in an industry tacitly cooperate to reduce industry output below the potential competitive output level and thereby raise prices above the competitive level. Firms might also explicitly collude, which is an illegal practice unless it is sanctioned through government regulations such as in the case of electric and telecommunications utilities.

- Cooperative strategies are often used at the business-unit level. We identified four types of business-level strategic alliances. Complementary strategic alliances are firm partnerships created to take advantage of market opportunities that combine assets between partner firms in ways that create value. Often, vertical complementary strategic alliances are organized in a way to facilitate supply or distribution. Outsourcing strategies are also of this type when complementarities are possible.

- Horizontal complementary strategic alliances facilitate business-level strategies. These alliances include marketing agreements and joint product development between competitors and other complementary firms (e.g., domestic and international airlines).

- Competition reduction and response alliances are formed to respond to competitive interactions between firms. Competition reduction alliances are proposed to avoid excessive competition and are used to respond to competitors' actions.

- Uncertainty also fosters the use of strategic alliances. Strategic alliances can be used to hedge against risks if there is significant uncertainty about performance or new technologies.

- All business-level strategic alliances may not result in strategic competitiveness and above-average returns. Complementary alliances are most likely to create strategic competitiveness, whereas competition reduction and competitive response alliances are more likely to achieve competitive parity. Uncertainty reduction alliances may prevent a firm from experiencing below-average returns.

- The role of complementors outside an alliance is important in the creation and continuation of many industries. Complementors create products complementary to the industry's product or service (e.g., operating systems and programs are complementary products to personal computers). The desirability of one product increases as the availability of complementary products increases.

- Strategic alliances can be used at the corporate level. Corporate-level diversifying strategic alliances reduce risk but can be very complex. Strategic alliances may also help avoid government sanctions against horizontal mergers. Also, strategic alliances may be used as an experimental step before acquisition.

- Corporate-level synergistic alliances create economies of scope between two firms. Such alliances facilitate achievement of synergy across multiple businesses and functions at the corporate level.

- Franchising is an additional corporate-level cooperative strategy that provides an alternative to diversification. Firms with a franchising strategy can diversify their risk associated with a single business (even with distributors in many markets) without adding new products. McDonald's has used this strategy extensively.

- A number of international cooperative strategies exist. Many firms pursue cooperative international strategies because some countries regard local ownership as an important national policy objective. Trade agreements have facilitated an increased number of cooperative ventures as firms are allowed to participate in more foreign investments. This is particularly true in emerging markets where local partners are often essential. International strategic alliances can be risky; one of the most serious errors managers make in forming foreign ventures is not understanding the strategic intent of the partner.

- The degree to which one partner may learn from another is impacted by learning rates (a natural ability to absorb knowledge), absorptive capacity (the ability of individuals to acquire knowledge in a specific field already known to them) and concentration within the company (concentrating the knowledge gleaned from the joint venture partner in such a way as to be useful).

- Adding to the number of cooperative strategies is the network organization. Network organizations are associations of firms with formal or informal relationships that work for the common good of all. These networks can be one of three types: stable, dynamic, or internal.

- Stable networks appear in mature industries with predictable cycles and market demands. The Japanese horizontal keiretsu is an example of this type of network.

- Dynamic networks produce rapid technological innovations, where product life cycles are short and shifts in consumer tastes alter frequently. Often, these networks are formed to create more stability and facilitate adoption of a new industry technology standard such as the VHS format in video cassette recorders.

- Internal networks occur in firms with established entities across countries to facilitate coordination linking head office and subsidiaries. ABB and Benetton are firms with significant internal networks.

- A number of competitive risks are associated with cooperative strategies. If a contract is not developed appropriately, or if a potential partner firm misrepresents its competencies or fails to make available promised complementary resources, failure is likely. Furthermore, a firm may be held hostage through asset-specific investments made in conjunction with a partner, which may be exploited.

- Trust is an important asset in strategic alliances. Firms recognize other firms that have a reputation for trustworthiness in cooperative strategic relations. This suggests that firms pursuing cooperative relations have two competing objective functions, one fostering strong governance/contract development capabilities and another focusing on selecting trustworthy partners where complementary assets exist.

# REVIEW QUESTIONS

1. What are the three types of cooperative strategies?
2. What are the different rationales for cooperative strategies in slow, standard, and fast-cycle markets?
3. What are the advantages and disadvantages of the four different types of cooperative strategies at the business level?
4. How are cooperative strategies used at the corporate level of strategic analysis? When would these strategy types be used, and what are the potential problems associated with each?
5. How are cooperative strategies applied in international operations?
6. What are the four competitive risks of engaging in cooperative strategies?
7. Why is trust important in cooperative strategies?
8. How is the cost minimization approach different from the opportunity maximization approach to managing strategic alliances?

# DISCUSSION QUESTIONS

1. Select an issue of the *Financial Post* or *Wall Street Journal* and identify all of the articles that focus on cooperative strategies. Classify the particular type of cooperative strategy and identify the strategic objective of each cooperative venture.
2. Find two articles describing a cooperative strategy, one where trust is being used as a strategic asset and another where contracts and monitoring are being emphasized. Examine the differences between the management approaches and describe advantages and disadvantages of each approach.
3. Choose a *Financial Post* 500 or *Fortune* 500 firm that has a significant need to outsource some aspect of its business such as its information technology function. Describe the potential outsourcing opportunities available and explain the approach you would use to achieve the outsourcing objective.
4. Find an example of a research consortia and examine its organization and strategic approaches. Provide an alternative strategy using the network organization that you think would be equivalent in performance.

5. How can corporate-level cooperative strategies help achieve a boundaryless organization? Describe the advantages and disadvantages to such an organization.

## ETHICS QUESTIONS

1. Think about the idea of asset-specific investment and hostage-taking in cooperative relations. Is hostage-taking, as described in the chapter, a central problem in strategic alliances, or is it more of a problem in vertical relationships between firms (e.g., suppliers, distributors)? Please explain.

2. "A contract is necessary because most firms cannot be trusted to act ethically in a cooperative venture such as a strategic alliance." Explain whether you think this statement is true or false.

3. Ventures in foreign countries without strong contract law are more risky because managers are subject to bribery and lack of commitment once assets have been invested in the country. How can managers deal with these problems?

4. Monopoly firms are regulated in Canada. However, a monopoly enterprise is often considered unethical if it seeks to enter an emerging country. Explain why.

5. Firms with reputations for ethical behaviour in strategic alliances are likely to have more legitimate venture opportunities than firms without this reputation. How do firms develop such positive reputations?

## INTERNET EXERCISE

The following companies have information about their business alliances on their Web sites:

Air Canada: **http://www.aircanada.ca**
Ericsson: **http://www.ericsson.se**
General Magic: **http://www.genmagic.com**

Select one of these companies. Go to its Web site and locate the section that discusses the company's business alliances. Then write a critique of how an involvement in business alliances helps the company achieve its business objectives and what potential difficulties may arise from such alliances.

## STRATEGIC SURFING

The *Alliance Analyst* is the only management publication dedicated solely to the topic of strategic alliances. Although it is not available on-line, the *Alliance*

*Analyst* does maintain a Web site that features past articles and other alliance-related information.

**http://www.allianceanalyst.com**

## NOTES

1  A. N. Brandenburger & B. J. Nalebuff, 1996, *Co-opetition* (New York: Doubleday).

2  J. L. Schaan & M. J. Kelly, Michael, 1999, Why most alliances just don't work: Firms must manage their relationship, not just business, *National Post*, December 21, C7.

3  Dofasco's $180m joint-venture ..., 1999, Dofasco's $180m joint-venture plant part of new strategy, Eyeing South America. Galvanizing line first North American deal for Sollac, *National Post*, September 30, C5.

4  D. Fenn, 1997, Sleeping with the enemy, *INC Online*, http://www.inc.com, November; S.A. Shane, 1996, Hybrid organizational arrangements and their implications for firm growth and survival: A study of new franchisers, *Academy of Management Journal*, 39: 216–234.

5  S. E. Human & K. G. Provan, 1997, An emergent theory of structure and outcomes in small-firm strategic manufacturing networks, *Academy of Management Journal*, 40: 368–404.

6  S. Gruner, 1996, Benchmark: Partnering for products, *INC Online*, http://www.inc.com, February.

7  S. H. Park & G. R. Ungson, 1997, The effect of national culture, organizational complementarity, and economic motivation on joint venture dissolution, *Academy of Management Journal*, 40: 279–307; A. Rugman & J. D'Cruz, 1997, The theory of the flagship firm, *European Management Journal*, 15: 403–12.

8  J. H. Dyer, 1996, How Chrysler created an American keiretsu, *Harvard Business Review*, 74, no 4: 42–56.

9  D. Fenn & S. Greco, 1997, Details, details, details, *INC home page*, http://www.inc.com, July.

10  S. H. Park & M. Russo, 1996, When cooperation eclipses competition: An event history analysis of joint venture failures, *Management Science*, 42: 875–90.

11  Airline alliances: Flying in formation, 1995, *The Economist*, July 22, 59.

12  T. Saxton, 1997, The effects of partner and relationship characteristics, *Academy of Management Journal*, 40: 443–62; Park & Ungson, The effect of national culture, organizational complementarity and economic motivation on joint venture dissolution.

13  B. Gomes Casseres, 1996, *The Alliance Revolution: The New Shape of Business Rivalry* (Cambridge, MA: Harvard University Press).

14  Royal acquires, 1999, Royal acquires Quebec extruder, enters joint venture, *Canadian Plastics*, April, 10;

Siemens joins forces, 1999, Siemens joins forces with Fujitsu to create computer giant, *National Post,* June 18, C10.

15 D. C. Mowery, J. E. Oxley, & B. S. Silverman, 1996, Strategic alliances and interfirm knowledge transfer, *Strategic Management Journal,* 17 (Special Winter Issue): 77–92.

16 Dyer, How Chrysler created an American keiretsu.

17 J. B. Barney, 1997, *Gaining and Sustaining Competitive Advantage* (Reading, MA: Addison Wesley), 255.

18 B. Kogut, 1988, Joint ventures: Theoretical and empirical perspectives, *Strategic Management Journal,* 9: 319–32.

19 A. A. Lado, N. G. Boyd, & S. C. Hanlon, 1997, Competition, cooperation, and the search for rents: A syncretic model, *Academy of Management Review,* 22: 110–41; F. J. Contractor & P. Lorange, 1988, Why should firms cooperate? The strategic and economic bases for cooperative strategy, in F. J. Contractor & P. Lorange (eds.), *Cooperative Strategies in International Business,* (Lexington, MA: Lexington Books).

20 E. E. Bailey & W. Shan, 1995, Sustainable competitive advantage through alliances, in E. Bowman & B. Kogut (eds.), *Redesigning the Firm* (New York: Oxford University Press); J. R. Williams, 1992, How sustainable is your competitive advantage? *California Management Review,* 34 (2): 29–51.

21 J. Kahn, 1996, Alcatel's local call paying off in China, *Wall Street Journal,* January 15, A5.

22 J. C. Huertas & J. P. Chapon, 1997, Alcatel awarded major contract in South Africa, *Alcatel home page,* http://www.alcatel.com (Retrieved July 23), press release.

23 M. Feher, 1997, Unisource to invest $250 Mln in Hungary Telecoms Co., *Wall Street Journal Interactive Edition,* http://www.wsj.com (Retrieved December 22).

24 J. L. Schenker & J. Pressley, 1997, Feared French-German telecom venture poses little threat so far, *Wall Street Journal Interactive Edition,* http://www.wsj.com, December 23.

25 K. Chapman, 1999. Wans in the sky, *ComputerWorld Canada,* May 7, 38–39; P. Wayner, 1997, Sky-high dreams for the Internet, *The New York Times on the Web,* http://www.nyt.com, May 22.

26 J. Tagliabue, 1997, Airbus partners agree to form independent corporation. *The New York Times on the Web,* http://www.nyt.com, January 14.

27 N. Templin, 1995, Strange bedfellows: More and more firms enter joint ventures with big competitors, *Wall Street Journal,* November 1, Al, A12.

28 C. W. L. Hill, 1997, Establishing a standard: Competitive strategy and technological standards in

winner-take-all industries, *Academy of Management Executive,* XI (2): 7–25.

29 R. Axelrod, W. Mitchell, R.E. Thomas, D.S. Bennett, & E. Bruderer, 1995, Coalition formation in standard-setting alliances, *Management Science,* 41: 1493–1508; L. D. Browning, J. M. Beyer, & J. C. Shetler, 1995, Building cooperation in a competitive industry: Sematech and the semiconductor industry, *Academy of Management Journal,* 38: 113–51.

30 G. Shaw, 2000, The 'Tooth' is Out There, *The Vancouver Sun,* May 18, D13;

31 Hill, Establishing a standard.

32 Park & Ungson, The effect of national culture, organizational complementarity, and economic motivation on joint venture dissolution; R. Johnston & P. Lawrence, 1988, Beyond vertical integration—The rise of the value adding partnership, *Harvard Business Review,* 66 (4): 94–101.

33 In some cases the lack of complementors will make the industry disappear. For example, as the both the music industry and stereo producers switched from vinyl analog platters to digital compact discs, the makers of turntables left that industry to produce CD players. The turntable manufacturing industry essentially ceased to exist because there were no albums being produced to be played on turntables.

34 The economics literature looks at these relationships under the rubric of cross-elasticity of demand.

35 C. W. L. Hill, 1997, "Establishing a standard: Competitive strategy and technology standards in winner take all industries," *Academy of Management Executive,* 11 (1): 7–25; C. Shapiro and H. R. Varian, 1999, *Information Rules: A Strategic Guide to the Network Economy* (Boston: Harvard Business School Press).

36 Video Senki, 2001, *Video Senki home page,* http://www.video-senki.com/feat/gamecube.html (Retrieved January 30); Console eXtreme, 2001, *Console eXtreme, home page,* http://www.consolextreme.com/nintendo (Retrieved January 30).

37 X. Martin, W. Mitchell, & A. Swaminathan, 1995, Recreating and extending Japanese automobile buyer-supplier links in North America, *Strategic Management Journal,* 16: 589–19; J. Dyer & W. S. Ouchi, 1993, Japanese style partnerships: Giving companies a competitive edge, *Sloan Management Review,* 35 (1): 51–63; B. Asanuma, 1989, Manufacturer-supplier relationships in Japan and the concept of relation-specific skill, *Journal of the Japanese and International Economies,* 3: 1–30.

38 J. H. Dyer, 1996, Specialized supplier networks as a source of competitive advantage: Evidence from the auto industry, *Strategic Management Journal,* 17: 271–91; J. T. Mahoney, 1992, The choice of organizational form: Vertical financial ownership versus other

methods of vertical integration, *Strategic Management Journal,* 13: 559–84.

39  J. H. Dyer, How Chrysler created an American keiretsu.

40  L. Willcocks & C. J. Choi, 1995, Cooperative partnership and "total" IT outsourcing: From contractual obligation to strategic alliance? *European Management Journal,* 13 (1): 67–78.

41  M. Heinzl, 1995, Magna International profits on big three outsourcing, *Wall Street Journal,* August 24, B5.

42  R. A. Bettis, S. R Bradley, & G. Hamel, 1992, Outsourcing and industrial decline, *Academy of Management Executive,* VI (1): 7–22.

43  V. Kapoor & A. Gupta, 1997, Aggressive sourcing: A free-market approach, *Sloan Management Review,* 39 (1): 21–31.

44  K. Nirmalya, 1996, The power of trust in manufacturing-retailer relationships, *Harvard Business Review,* 74 (6): 92–106.

45  N. F. Piercy, C. S. Katsikeas, & D. W. Cravens, 1997, Examining the role of buyer-seller relationships in export performance, *Journal of World Business,* 32 (1): 73–86.

46  M. Kotabe & K. S. Swan, 1995, The role of strategic alliances in high technology new product development, *Strategic Management Journal,* 16: 621–36.

47  B. Coleman, 1995, Lufthansa and Scandinavian Airlines unveil plans for a strategic alliance, *Wall Street Journal,* May 12, A9.

48  E. McDowell, 1995, Delta seeks to expand its tie with three airlines in Europe, *New York Times,* September 9, 34.

49  M. Brannigan, 1995, Airlines' "code sharing" helps them, hinders travelers, *Wall Street Journal,* October 13, B1; T. H. Oum & A. J. Taylor, 1995, Emerging patterns in intercontinental air linkages and implications for international route allocation policy, *Transportation Journal,* 34 (Summer): 5–27.

50  E. Norton & M. DuBois, 1994, Foiled competition: Don't call it a cartel, but world aluminum has forged a new order, *Wall Street Journal,* June 9: A1, A6.

51  C. Adams, 1998, Aluminium companies earnings increased in the fourth quarter, *Wall Street Journal Interactive Edition,* http://www.wsj.com, January 8.

52  Alcan plans purchases, alliances: CEO Bougie says he aims to boost revenues, share price, 2000, *National Post,* April 28, C6; K. Damsell, 2000, Solid results add to Alcan's appeal: Buoyant metal market. Cost controls, merger underline positive trend, *National Post,* January 26: D1, D3.

53  Alcan, 2000, *Alcan Aluminium News Page,* http://www.alcan.com/WWWAlcan.nsf/Level2-E/LevelNews-E?OpenDocument (Retrieved May 26).

54  D. P. Hamilton & N. Shirouzu, 1995, Japan's business cartels are starting to erode, but change is slow, *Wall Street Journal,* December 4: Al, A6.

55  G. Melloan, 1997, This year's economic lesson: Japan's model failed, *Wall Street Journal,* December 30, A11.

56  H. Tezuka, 1997, Success as the source of failure? Competition and cooperation in the Japanese economy, *Sloan Management Review,* 39 (2): 83–93.

57  G. R. Ungson, R. M. Steers, & S. H. Park, 1997, *Korean Enterprise: The Quest for Globalization* (Cambridge, MA: Harvard Business School Press), 163.

58  M. Ihlwan & B. Bremner, 1998, Korea Inc. balks, *BusinessWeek,* January 19, 44–46.

59  R. Brahm, 1995, National targeting policies, high technology industries, and excessive competition, *Strategic Management Journal,* 16 (Special Issue, Summer): 71–92.

60  J. M. Broder, 1997, Toys 'R' Us led price collusion, judge rules in upholding F.T.C., *The New York Times on the Web,* http://www.nytimes.com, October 1.

61  C. Torres, 1996, Mexican phone competition heats up, *Wall Street Journal,* April 23, Al5.

62  As quoted in T.Y. Jones, 1998, Musical chairs, *Forbes,* January 12, 60–63.

63  R. G. McGrath, 1997, A real options logic for initiating technological positioning investments, *Academy of Management Review* 22: 974–96; B. Kogut, 1991, Joint ventures and the option to expand and acquire, *Management Science,* 37: 19–33.

64  John Schreiner, 1998, Placer Dome doubles reserves with $235M South African deal: Gold price drops, as does company's share price, *National Post,* December 1, Final Edition, C3.

65  Z. Olijnyk, 1999, Manulife launches joint venture in Vietnam, *National Post,* June 21, C1, C6.

66  K. Singh, 1997, The impact of technological complexity and interfirm cooperation on business survival, *Academy of Management Journal,* 40: 339–67.

67  J.-F. Hennart & S. Ready, 1997, The choice between mergers/acquisitions and joint ventures in the United States, *Strategic Management Journal,* 18: 1–12.

68  S. Glain, 1995, Korea's Samsung plans very rapid expansion into autos, other lines, *Wall Street Journal,* March 2, A1, A11.

69  M. Ihlwan & B. Bremner, 1998, Korea Inc. balks, *BusinessWeek,* January 19, 44–46.

70  H. Ingham & S. Thompson, 1994, Wholly owned versus collaborative ventures in diversifying financial services, *Strategic Management Journal,* 15: 325–34.

71  J. Bleeke & D. Ernst, 1995, Is your alliance really a sale? *Harvard Business Review,* 73 (1): 97–105.

72  J. B. Barney, 1988, Returns to bidding firms in mergers and acquisitions: Reconsidering the relatedness hypothesis, *Strategic Management Journal*, 9 (Special Summer Issue): 71–78.

73  A. Nanda & P. J, Williamson, 1995, Use joint ventures to ease the pain of restructuring, *Harvard Business Review*, 73 (6): 119–28.

74  C. Covault, 1995, German, French firms merge armaments units, *Aviation Week & Space Technology,* January 30, 25.

75  U. Gupta, 1991, Sony adopts strategy to broaden ties with small firms, *Wall Street Journal,* February 28, B2.

76  M. J. Yoshino & U. S. Rangan, 1995, *Strategic Alliances: An Entrepreneurial Approach to Globalization* (Cambridge, MA: Harvard Business School Press).

77  D. Kirkpatrick, 1997, Gates wants all your business— and he's starting to get it, *Fortune,* May 26, 58–68.

78  P. Kennedy & B. McKenna, 2000, Rumours fly of Microsoft moving north, *The Globe and Mail,* June 3, B1.

79  S. Hamm, A. Cortese, & S. B. Garland, 1998, Microsoft's future, *BusinessWeek,* January 19, 58.

80  S. A. Shane, 1996, Hybrid organizational arrangements and their implications for firm growth and survival: A study of new franchisers, *Academy of Management Journal*, 39: 216–34; R. Martin & R. Justis, 1993, Franchising, liquidity constraints and entry, *Applied Economics*, 25: 1269–77; S. W. Norton, 1988, Franchising, brand name capital, and the entrepreneurial capacity problem, *Strategic Management Journal*, 9 (Special Summer Issue): 105–14.

81  P. Ingram & J. A. C. Baum, 1997, Opportunity and constraint: Organizations' learning from the operating and competitive experience of industries, *Strategic Management Journal*, 18 (Special Summer Issue): 75–98.

82  G. F. Mathewson & R. H. Winter, 1985, The economies of franchise contracts, *Journal of Law and Economics,* 28: 503–26.

83  J. Holusha, 1997, As industry changes, networks feel a ripple, *The New York Times on the Web,* http://www.nyt.com, January 26.

84  R. E. Hoskisson, W. P. Wan, & M. H. Hansen, 1998, Strategic alliance formation and market evaluation: Effects of parent firm's governance structure, in M. A. Hitt, J. Ricart & R.D. Nixon (eds.), *Managing Strategically in an Interconnected World* (London: John Wiley & Sons).

85  B. L. Simonin, 1997, The importance of collaborative know-how: An empirical test of the learning organization, *Academy of Management Journal*, 40: 1150–74.

86  P. J. Buckley & M. Casson, 1996, An economic model of international joint venture strategy, *Journal of International Business Studies*, 27: 849–76; J. E. McGee, M. J. Dowling, & W. L. Megginson, 1995, Cooperative strategy and new venture performance: The role of business strategy and management experience, *Strategic Management Journal*, 16: 565–80.

87  M. A. Hitt, R. E. Hoskisson, & H. Kim, 1997, International diversification: Effects on innovation and firm performance in product diversified firms, *Academy of Management Journal*, 40: 767–98; R. Morck & B. Yeung, 1991, Why investors value multinationality, *Journal of Business*, 64 (2): 165–87.

88  L. K. Mytelka, 1991, *Strategic Partnerships and the World Economy* (London: Pinter Publishers).

89  I. A. Litvak, 1999, Canadian firms emerge as global players …, *National Post,* October 31, MGB3–MGB4.

90  J. Hagedoorn, 1995, A note on international market leaders and networks of strategic technology partnering, *Strategic Management Journal*, 16: 241–50.

91  J. Li, 1995, Foreign entry and survival: Effects of strategic choices on performance in international markets, *Strategic Management Journal*, 16: 333–51.

92  R. Madhavan & J. E. Prescott, 1995, Market value impact of joint ventures: The effect of industry information-processing load, *Academy of Management Journal*, 38: 900–15.

93  J. L. Johnson, J. B. Cullen, & T. Sakano, 1996, Setting the stage for trust and strategic integration in Japanese-U.S. cooperative alliances, *Journal of International Business Studies*, 27: 981–1004; J. M. Geringer, 1991, Measuring performance of international joint ventures, *Journal of International Business Studies*, 22 (2): 249–63.

94  *The Bulletin of the Ministry of Foreign Trade and Economic Cooperation of the People's Republic of China,* 1995, issues no. 1 and no. 2.

95  M. Janigan, 2000, The fear of losing control: a "moderate economic nationalism" rises in, of all places, the business community, *Maclean's* (Toronto Edition), July 1, 60–62.

96  P. C. Newman, 1999, The year of living dangerously: In 1999, US takeovers of Canadian companies have taken on a disturbing new reality. The result: "We have become squatters on our own land" *Maclean's* (Toronto Edition), December 20, 50.

97  Ibid.

98  Ibid.

99  Ibid.

100  N. Nankivell, 1999, What's good for the goose: Canadians are mounting more mergers and acquisitions abroad than foreigners are here, *National Post,* March 20, D6.

101 C. Howes, 1999, Jupiter over the moon with Caterpillar deal [to operate electric power plants], *National Post,* January 20, C3.

102 Fortune, 2000, *The Fortune home page,* http://www.fortune.com/fortune/global500 (Retrieved June 11). About one-third of the world's largest 100 corporations are headquartered in the United States.

103 R. Peterson, 1998, How is entrepreneurship different in Canada? *Financial Post,* March 4, 1998, Daily Edition, 4.

104 M. T. Dacin, M. A. Hitt, & E. Levitas, 1997, Selecting partners for successful international alliances: Examinations of U.S. and Korean firms, *Journal of World Business,* 32 (1): 3–16; M. A. Hitt, M. T. Dacin, B. B. Tyler, & D. Park, 1997, Understanding the differences in Korean and U.S. executives' strategic orientations, *Strategic Management Journal,* 18: 159–68.

105 M. Wright, R. E. Hoskisson, I. Filatotchev, & T. Buck, 1998, Revitalizing privatized Russian enterprises, *Academy of Management Executive,* 12, no 2: 74–85; I. Filatotchev, R.E. Hoskisson, T. Buck, & M. Wright, 1996, Corporate restructuring in Russian privatizations: Implications for U.S. investors, *California Management Review,* 38 (2): 87–105.

106 S. M. Puffer, D. J. McCarthy, & A. I. Naumov, 1997, Russian managers' beliefs about work: Beyond the stereotypes, *Journal of World Business,* 32 (2): 258–75.

107 K. Hanson, 1999, Local links called key in emerging markets: Minimizes risks, *National Post,* October 13, C8.

108 G. Hamel, 1991, Competition for competence and interpartner learning with international strategic alliances, *Strategic Management Journal,* 12: 83–103.

109 K. Onti & R. Kumar, 2000, Differential learning in alliances in *Cooperative Strategy: Economics, Business and Organisational Issues,* D. Faulkner & M. DeRond (eds.): 119–34.

110 G. Hamel, 1991, Competition for competence and interpartner learning with international strategic alliances, *Strategic Management Journal,* 12: 83–103.

111 Dacin, Hitt, & Levitas, Selecting partners for successful international alliances; Templin, 1995, Strange bedfellows: More and more firms enter joint ventures.

112 C. Jones, W. S. Hesterly, & S. P. Borgatti, 1997, A general theory of network governance: Exchange conditions and social mechanisms, *Academy of Management Review,* 22: 911–45; T. J. Rowley, 1997, Moving beyond dyadic ties: A network theory of stakeholder influences, *Academy of Management Review,* 22: 887–910.

113 R. Pouder & C. H. St. John, 1996, Hot spots and blind spots: Geographical clusters of firms and innovation, *Academy of Management Review,* 21: 1192–1225.

114 Rugman & D'Cruz, 1997, The theory of the flagship firm; D.B. Holm, K. Eriksson, & J. Johanson, 1996, Business networks and cooperation in international business relationships, *Journal of International Business,* Studies 27: 1033–53.

115 R. Miles & C. C. Snow, 1994, *Fit, Failure and the Hall of Fame: How Companies Succeed or Fail* (New York: The Free Press).

116 M. L. Gerlach, 1992, *Alliance Capitalism: The Social Organization of Japanese Business* (Berkeley, CA: University of California Press).

117 H. Solomon, 1999, Waterloo-based Mitra forms new firm with Agfa, *Computing Canada,* May 14, 16–17.

118 J. Levine, 1996, Even when you fail, you learn a lot, *Forbes,* March 11, 58–62.

119 T. Nishiguchi & J. Brookfield, 1997, The evolution of Japanese subcontracting, *Sloan Management Review,* 39 (1) 89–101; T. Nishiguchi, 1994, *Strategic Industrial Sourcing* (New York: Oxford University Press).

120 W. Davidow & M. Malone, 1992, *A Virtual Corporation: Structuring and Revitalizing the Corporation of the 21st Century* (New York: Harper Business).

121 G. Lorenzoni & C. Baden-Fuller, 1995, Creating a strategic center to manage a web of partners, *California Management Review,* 37 (3): 146–63.

122 Z. Olijnyk, 2000, Online grocer Peachtree on trading shelf today, *National Post,* March 22, C3; H. W Chesbrough & D. J. Teece, 1996, When is virtual virtuous? Organizing for innovation, *Harvard Business Review,* 74 (1): 65–73.

123 P. Olk & C. Young, 1997, Why members stay in or leave an R&D consortium: Performance and conditions of membership as determinants of continuity, *Strategic Management Journal,* 18: 855–77; M. Sakakibara, 1997, Hetergeneity of firm capabilities and cooperative research and development: An empirical examination of motives, *Strategic Management Journal,* 18 (Special Summer Issue): 143–64.

124 Brahm, National targeting policies.

125 S. Kotha & A. Nair, 1995, Strategy and environment as determinants of performance: Evidence from the Japanese machine tool industry, *Strategic Management Journal,* 16: 497–518.

126 G. Saloner, 1990, Economic issues in computer interface standardization, Economic Innovation and New Technology 1: 135–56.

127 Axelrod, Mitchell, Thomas, Bennett, & Bruderer, Coalition formation in standard-setting alliances.

128  J. P. Sheppard, 1994, Strategy and Bankruptcy: An Exploration into Organizational Death, *Journal of Management:* 20 (4): 795–833.

129  R. A. Melcher & G. Edmundson, 1997, A marriage made in hell, *BusinessWeek,* December 22, 40–42.

130  J. B. Barney & M. H. Hansen, 1994, Trustworthiness: Can it be a source of competitive advantage? *Strategic Management Journal,* 15 (Special Winter Issue): 175–203.

131  M. J. Dollinger, P. A. Golden, & T. Saxton, 1997, The effect of reputation on the decision to joint venture, *Strategic Management Journal,* 18: 127–40; C. W. L. Hill, 1990, Cooperation, opportunism, and the invisible hand: Implications for transaction cost theory, *Academy of Management Review,* 15: 500–13.

132  P. Parker, 1997, Canada-Japan coal trade: An alternative form of the staple production model, *Canadian Geographer,* Fall, 248–67.

133  R. Gulati, 1996, Social structure and alliance formation patterns: A longitudinal analysis, *Administrative Science Quarterly,* 40: 619–652.

134  J. H. Dyer, 1997, Effective interfirm collaboration: How firms minimize transaction costs and maximize transaction value, *Strategic Management Journal,* 18: 535–56; M. Hansen, R. E. Hoskisson, & J. B. Barney, 1997, *Trustworthiness in strategic alliances: Opportunism minimization versus opportunity maximization,* Working Paper, Brigham Young University.

135  P. Moran & S. Ghoshal, 1996, Theories of economic organization: The case for realism and balance, *Academy of Management Review,* 21: 58–72.

136  A. Parke, 1993, Strategic alliance structuring: A game theoretic and transaction cost examination of interfirm cooperation, *Academy of Management Journal,* 36: 794–829.

137  C. S. Sankar, W. R. Boulton, N. W. Davidson, C. A. Snyder, & R. W. Ussery, 1995, Building a world-class alliance: The universal card—TSYS case, *Academy of Management Executive,* IX (2): 20–29.

138  R. C. Mayer, J. H. Davis, & F. D. Schoorman, 1995, An integrative model of organizational trust, *Academy of Management Review,* 20: 709–34.

# Strategic Actions: Strategy Implementation

**PART THREE**

# Chapter Eleven

## Corporate Governance

## LEARNING OBJECTIVES

*After reading this chapter, you should be able to:*

1. Define corporate governance and explain why it is used to monitor and control managers' strategic decisions.
2. Explain how ownership came to be separated from managerial control in the modern corporation.
3. Define an agency relationship and managerial opportunism and describe their strategic and organizational implications.
4. Explain how four internal corporate governance mechanisms—ownership concentration, board of directors, executive compensation, and the multidivisional (M-form) structure—are used to monitor and control managerial decisions.
5. Discuss trends among the three types of compensation executives receive and their effects on strategic decisions.
6. Describe how the external corporate governance mechanism—the market for corporate control—acts as a restraint on top-level managers' strategic decisions.
7. Discuss the use of corporate governance in Germany and Japan.
8. Describe how corporate governance mechanisms can foster ethical strategic decisions and behaviours on the part of top-level executives.

# Abitibi-Consolidated: Corporate Governance and the Board Battle for CEO

The 12-person board of directors at Abitibi-Consolidated has splintered in its approach to handling a potentially divisive situation. Three members of Abitibi's board (all from Quebecor—Abitibi's largest shareholder with 11 percent of the outstanding shares) are unhappy with the performance of the current CEO, John Weaver. Two of these members are Karl Peladeau, the CEO of Quebecor, and Michel Desbiens, Abitibi's former chair, who resigned as chair after an attempt to unseat Mr. Weaver failed. Quebecor has launched an all-out attack with the purpose of replacing Weaver with Michel Desbiens. Mr. Desbiens is also the former CEO of Donohue, which was taken over by Abitibi in April 2000 when Quebecor sold its controlling stake.

The other nine Abitibi board members apparently considered that a three-member committee of the board was the most appropriate and efficient manner for directors to deal with the current situation in the interests of all shareholders. Unfortunately, this committee excluded any of the board members from Quebecor. Quebecor's CEO claims that shareholder value is being lost under Weaver's stewardship. Abitibi spokesperson Denis LeClerc has suggested that Peladeau and Desbiens have acted and spoken in a manner that is detrimental to shareholder value. Apparently, some board members consider that Donohue's cost-conscious and cash flow–oriented culture is being lost under Weaver's leadership, and they want him replaced with Desbiens. The head of the new committee has warned that the increasingly bitter showdown regarding the performance of senior management at Abitibi is potentially in breach of securities laws and corporate governance rules.

A recent *Globe and Mail* article described former Ontario Premier David Peterson as possibly "the unluckiest director in Canada." One reporter explained, "Of the nearly dozen publicly traded companies in which he holds directorships, four are involved in high-profile legal or financial struggles." This

http://www.abicon.com
http://www.quebecor.com

same article elaborates on the issue of performance of directors and their firms in general. While some attribute Mr. Peterson's difficulties to "the turbulent conditions rocking modern businesses ... Critics ... argue that Mr. Peterson's difficulties are the result of a director who is overly stretched by myriad corporate responsibilities." This example illustrates an important corporate governance issue: on how many boards should a director be allowed to serve? A second, and perhaps more important issue, is CEO succession.

One *BusinessWeek* special report classified AT&T's board of directors as one of the worst in the United States. Four of ten money managers and governance experts who responded to a *BusinessWeek* survey classified AT&T's board in this category. They accused it of harmful acquisitions (e.g., the acquisition of NCR), a number of costly write-offs, including the NCR acquisition, and layoffs and spin-offs where AT&T lost a significant amount of its human capital, including personnel working at Bell Labs.

Campbell Soup Company, on the other hand, won the honours in the *BusinessWeek* survey for the best board of directors for the second consecutive year. Chairman David W. Johnson sought to build the reputation of its board as a progressive governance pioneer. Outside directors took control of the search for the new CEO and therefore created a new role for boards in management succession. In addition, Campbell has initiated performance evaluations for board members, making individual members more concerned with self-improvement and more attuned to creating effective processes. Typically, boards are packed with trusted friends and colleagues who rarely challenge the CEO's policies and directives. This has given a country club atmosphere to the perception of many boards. Campbell's board members have been trained to focus on one purpose: acting in the shareholders' best interest.

Furthermore, as the Campbell example illustrates, board members are taking more control of the leadership succession process. Outside directors are becoming less dependent on the CEO and the company. It is being suggested that a minimum of inside managers and no consultants who work with the firm be on the board. Also of concern is the idea of interlocking directorships, where CEOs serve on each other's boards.

Sources: B. Marotte, 2000, Abitibi warns of securities law breach, *The Globe and Mail,* November 4, B1; A. Bryant, 1998, How the mighty have fallen and managed to profit handsomely, *The New York Times on the Web,* http://www.nytimes.com, January 5; S. Lipin, 1998, AT&T to buy Teleport for $11.3 billion, *Wall Street Journal,* January 9, A3, A6; T. Elstrom, 1997, Honeymoon in Jersey, *BusinessWeek,* December 15, 40; J. A. Byrne, R. Grover, and R. A. Melcher, 1997, The best and worst boards: Our special report on corporate governance, *BusinessWeek,* December 8, 91–98; J. J. Keller, 1997, AT&T's board faces many twists and turns in search for new CEO, *Wall Street Journal,* October 13, A1, A6; J. A. Byrne, 1997, AT&T: How to turn a dud into a dynamo, *BusinessWeek,* December 8, 95; K. Day, 1997, Big investors say Walter's exit is latest sign that directors are unequal to their task, *Washington Post,* July 18, G1.

As the opening case illustrates, corporate governance is increasingly important as a part of the strategic management process.[1] If the board makes the wrong decision in selecting the firm's strategic leader—the CEO—the whole firm, as well as its shareholders, suffers. This may be the case at Abitibi and AT&T. David Peterson's case indicates the heightened interest surrounding the performance of directors and their firms in general. On the other hand, solid governance procedures can create credibility for the firm and its strategy as in the instance of Campbell.[2]

**Corporate governance** is a relationship among stakeholders that is used to determine and control the strategic direction and performance of organizations.

**Corporate governance** is a relationship among stakeholders that is used to determine and control the strategic direction and performance of organizations.[3] At its core, corporate governance is concerned with identifying ways to ensure that strategic decisions are made effectively.[4] Additionally, governance can be thought of as a means used in corporations to establish order between parties (the firm's owners and its top-level managers) whose interests may be in conflict.[5] Thus, corporate governance reflects and enforces the company's values.[6] In modern corporations, a primary objective of corporate governance is to ensure that the interests of top-level managers are aligned with shareholders' interests. Corporate governance involves oversight in areas where owners, managers, and members of boards of directors may have conflicts of interest. These areas include the election of directors, general supervision of CEO pay and more focused supervision of director pay, and the corporation's overall structure and strategic direction.[7]

Effective governance of the modern organization is of interest to shareholder activists, businesspeople, business writers, and academic scholars. One reason for this interest is the belief held by some that corporate governance mechanisms have failed to adequately monitor and control top-level managers' strategic decisions.[8] This perspective is causing changes in governance mechanisms in corporations throughout the world, especially with respect to efforts intended to improve the performance of boards of directors.[9] This attention, however, is understandable for a second and more positive reason; namely, evidence suggests that a well-functioning corporate governance and control system can result in a competitive advantage for an individual firm.[10] For example, with respect to one governance mechanism—the board of directors—it has been suggested that the board's role is rapidly evolving into a major strategic force in business firms.[11] Thus, in this first chapter describing strategic actions used to implement strategies, we describe monitoring and controlling mechanisms that, when used properly, ensure that top-level managerial decisions and actions contribute to the firm's strategic competitiveness and its ability to earn above-average returns.

Effective corporate governance is also of interest to nations. One researcher noted that:

"Every country wants the firms that operate within its borders to flourish and grow in such ways as to provide employment, wealth, and satisfaction, not only to improve standards of living materially but also to enhance social cohesion. These aspirations cannot be met unless those firms are competitive internationally in a sustained way, and it is this medium- and long-term perspective that makes good corporate governance so vital."[12]

Corporate governance, then, reflects the standards of the company, which, in turn, collectively reflect the societal standards.[13] Thus, in many individual corporations, shareholders are striving to hold top-level managers more accountable for their decisions and the results they generate. As with individual firms and their boards, nations that govern their corporations effectively may gain a competitive advantage over rival countries.

In a range of countries, but especially in Canada, the United States, and the United Kingdom, the fundamental goal of business organizations is to maximize shareholder value.[14] Traditionally, shareholders are treated as the firm's key stakeholder because they are the company's legal owners. The firm's owners expect top-level managers and others influencing the corporation's actions (e.g., the board of directors) to make decisions that will result in the maximization of the company's value and, hence, their own wealth.[15]

In this chapter's first section, we describe the relationship that is the foundation of the modern corporation. The majority of this chapter is then devoted to an explanation of various mechanisms owners use to govern managers and ensure that they comply with their responsibility to maximize shareholder value.

Four internal governance mechanisms and a single external mechanism are used in the modern corporation (see Table 11.1). The four internal governance mechanisms examined here are (1) ownership concentration, as represented by types of shareholders and their different incentives to monitor managers, (2) the board of directors, (3) executive compensation, and (4) the multidivisional (M-form) organizational structure. (As explained in Chapter 12, in addition to governing managers' decisions, the M-form structure is the one required to implement successfully different types of related and unrelated corporate-level diversification strategies.)

| ■ ■ TABLE 11.1 | Corporate Governance Mechanisms |
|---|---|
| **Internal Governance Mechanisms** | |
| Ownership Concentration | Relative amounts of stock owned by individual shareholders and institutional investors |
| Boards of Directors | Individuals responsible for representing the firm's owners by monitoring top-level managers' strategic decisions |
| Executive Compensation | Use of salary, bonuses, and long-term incentives to align manager's interests with shareholders' interests |
| Multidivisional Organizational Structure | Creation of individual business divisions to closely monitor top-level managers' strategic decisions |
| **External Governance Mechanisms** | |
| Market for Corporate Control | The purchase of a firm that is underperforming relative to industry rivals in order to improve its strategic competitiveness |

We next consider the market for corporate control, an external corporate governance mechanism. Essentially, the market for corporate control is a set of potential owners seeking to "raid" undervalued firms and earn above-average returns on their investments by replacing ineffective top-level management teams.[16] The chapter's focus then shifts to the issue of international corporate governance. We briefly describe governance approaches used in German and Japanese firms whose traditional governance structures are being affected by the realities of competing in the global economy. In part, this discussion suggests the possibility that the structures used to govern global companies in many different countries, including Canada, Germany, Japan, the United Kingdom, and the United States, are becoming more, rather than less, similar. Closing our analysis of corporate governance is a consideration of the need for these control mechanisms to encourage and support ethical behaviour in organizations.

Before we begin, we need to highlight two matters related to corporate governance. First, research results suggest that the mechanisms explained in this chapter have the potential to positively influence the governance of the modern corporation. This evidence is important, because development of the modern corporation has placed significant responsibility and authority in the hands of top-level managers. The most effective of these managers hold themselves accountable for their firm's performance and respond positively to the demands of the corporate governance mechanisms explained in this chapter.[17] Second, it is the appropriate use of a variety of mechanisms that results in the effective governance of a corporation. The firm's owners should not expect any single mechanism to govern the company effectively across time. It is through the proper use of several governance mechanisms and their integrative relationship with an organization's corporate-level strategy that owners are able to govern the corporation in ways that maximize strategic competitiveness and increase the financial value of their firm.[18] With multiple governance mechanisms operating simultaneously, it is also possible for some of the governance mechanisms to conflict.[19] Later, we review how these conflicts can occur.

## SEPARATION OF OWNERSHIP AND MANAGERIAL CONTROL

Historically, founder-owners and their descendants managed firms. In these cases, corporate ownership and control resided in the same person(s). As firms grew larger, "... the managerial revolution led to a separation of ownership and control in most large corporations, where control of the firm shifted from entrepreneurs to professional managers while ownership became dispersed among thousands of unorganized stockholders who were removed from the day-to-day management of the firm."[20] These changes created the modern public corporation, which is based on the efficient separation of ownership and managerial control. A basic legal premise supporting this efficient separation is that the primary objective of a firm's activities should be to increase the corporation's profit and the financial gains of the owners—the shareholders.[21]

The separation of ownership and managerial control allows shareholders to purchase stock, which entitles them to income (residual returns) from firm operations after expenses have been paid. This right, however, requires that they also take a risk that the firm's expenses may exceed its revenues. To manage this investment risk, shareholders seek to maintain a diversified portfolio by investing in several companies to reduce their overall risk.[22]

In small firms, managers often are the owners, so there is no separation between ownership and managerial control, but as firms grow and become more complex, owners/managers may contract with managerial specialists. These managers oversee decisionmaking in the owner's firm and are compensated on the basis of their decision-making skills. Managers, then, operate a corporation through use of their decision-making skills and are viewed as agents of the firm's owners.[23] In terms of the strategic management process (see Figure 1.1 in Chapter 1), managers are expected to form a firm's strategic intent and strategic mission and then formulate and implement the strategies to realize them. Thus, in the modern public corporation, top-level managers, especially the CEO, have primary responsibility for initiating and implementing an array of strategic decisions.

As shareholders diversify their investments over a number of corporations, their risk declines (the poor performance or failure of any one firm in which they invest has less overall effect). Shareholders thus specialize in managing their investment risk; managers specialize in decisionmaking. Without management specialization in decision-making and owner specialization in risk-bearing, a firm probably would be limited by the abilities of its owners to manage and make effective strategic decisions. Therefore, the separation and specialization of ownership (risk-bearing) and managerial control (decisionmaking) is theoretically economically efficient.

## Agency Relationships

An **agency relationship** exists when one or more persons (the principal or principals) hire another person or persons (the agent or agents) as decisionmaking specialists to perform a service.

The separation between owners and managers creates an agency relationship. An **agency relationship** exists when one or more persons (the principal or principals) hire another person or persons (the agent or agents) as decisionmaking specialists to perform a service.[24] Thus, an agency relationship exists when one party delegates decisionmaking responsibility to a second party for compensation (see Figure 11.1).[25] In addition to shareholders and top-level managers, other examples of agency relationships include consultants and clients and insured and insurer. Moreover, within organizations, an agency relationship exists between managers and their employees as well as between the firm's owners and top-level executives.[26] In the modern corporation, managers must understand the links between these relationships and the firm's effectiveness.[27] Although the agency relationship between managers and their employees is important, this chapter focuses on the agency relationship between the firm's owners (the principals) and top-level managers (the principals' agents) because this relationship is related directly to the strategies implemented by managers.

■ ■ **FIGURE 11.1**

*An Agency Relationship*

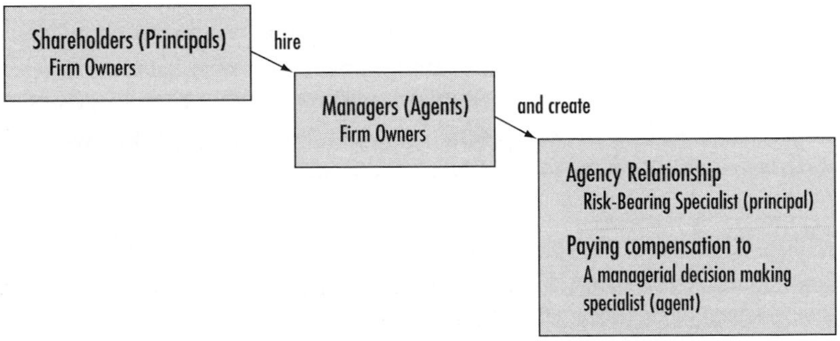

The separation between ownership and managerial control can be problematic. Research evidence documents a variety of agency problems in the modern corporation.[28] Problems can surface because divergent interests exist between the principal and the agent, or because shareholders often lack direct control of large publicly traded corporations. Problems arise when an agent makes decisions that result in the pursuit of goals that conflict with those of the principals. Thus, when ownership and control are separated, a relationship is formed that potentially allows divergent interests (between principals and agents) to surface, which can lead to managerial opportunism.[29]

**Managerial opportunism** is the seeking of self-interest with guile.

**Managerial opportunism** is the seeking of self-interest with guile (i.e., cunning, deceit).[30] Opportunism is both an attitude (e.g., an inclination or proclivity) and a set of behaviours (i.e., specific acts of self-interest that are sought with guile).[31] Although few agents act opportunistically, the inclination and proclivity to engage in opportunistic behaviours varies among individuals and across cultures.[32] The problem for principals, however, is that it is impossible to know beforehand the few agents who will engage in opportunistic behaviour. Because a top-level manager's reputation is an imperfect guide to future behaviour, and because opportunistic behaviour cannot be observed until it has taken place, principals establish governance and control mechanisms on the assumption that some agents might act opportunistically.[33] Thus, the principals' delegation of decisionmaking responsibilities to agents creates the opportunity for conflicts of interest to surface. Top-level managers, for example, may make strategic decisions that maximize their personal welfare and minimize their personal risk.[34] Decisions such as these may prevent the maximization of shareholder wealth. For example, decisions regarding product diversification demonstrate these possibilities.

## Product Diversification as an Example of an Agency Problem

As explained in Chapter 7, corporate-level strategies involving product diversification can enhance a firm's strategic competitiveness and increase its returns, both of which serve the interests of shareholders and top-level managers. However, because product diversification can provide two benefits to managers that shareholders do not enjoy, top-level executives sometimes prefer more product diversification than do shareholders.[35]

The first managerial benefit occurs because of the positive relationships between diversification and firm size and between firm size and executive compensation. Thus, increased product diversification provides an opportunity for higher compensation for top-level managers through growth in firm size.[36]

The second managerial benefit is that product diversification and the resulting diversification of the firm's portfolio of businesses can reduce top-level managers' employment risk.[37] Managerial employment risk is the risk of job loss, loss of compensation, and loss of managerial reputation. These risks are reduced with increased diversification because a firm and its upper-level managers are less vulnerable to the reduction in demand associated with a single or a limited number of product lines or businesses. Furthermore, the firm may have free cash flows over which top-level managers have discretion. Free cash flows are resources generated after investment in all projects that have positive net present values within the firm's current product lines.[38] In anticipation of positive returns, managers may decide to use these funds to invest in products that are not associated with the current lines of business, even if the investments increase the firm's level of diversification. The managerial decision to consume free cash flows to increase the firm's diversification inefficiently is an example of self-serving and opportunistic managerial behaviour. In contrast to managers, shareholders may prefer that free cash flows be returned as dividends so they will have control over their reinvestment decisions.[39]

Curve S in Figure 11.2 depicts shareholders' optimal level of diversification. Owners seek the level of diversification that reduces the risk of the firm's total failure while simultaneously increasing the company's value through the development of economies of scale and scope (see Chapter 7). Of the four corporate-level diversification strategies shown in Figure 11.2, shareholders might prefer the diversified position noted by point A on curve S—a position that is located between the dominant business and related-constrained diversification strategies. Of course, the optimum level of diversification sought by owners varies from firm to firm. Factors that affect shareholders' preferences include the firm's primary industry, the intensity of rivalry among competitors in that industry, and the top management team's experience with implementing diversification strategies.

■ ■ **FIGURE 11.2**

*Manager and Shareholder
Risk and Diversification*

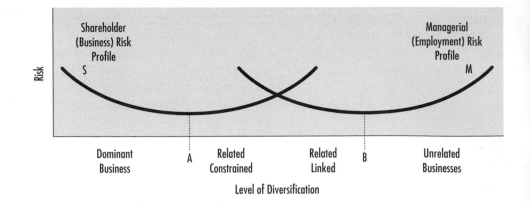

As with principals, upper-level executives—as agents—seek what they perceive to be an optimal level of diversification. Declining performance resulting from too much product diversification increases the probability that a firm will be acquired through the market for corporate control. Once acquired, the employment risk for the firm's top-level managers increases substantially. Furthermore, a manager's employment opportunities in the external managerial labour market are affected negatively by a firm's poor performance. Therefore, top-level managers prefer diversification, but not to a point that it increases their employment risk and reduces their employment opportunities.

Curve M (in Figure 11.2) shows that executives prefer higher levels of product diversification than shareholders. Top-level managers might prefer the level of diversification shown by point B on curve M. In general, shareholders prefer riskier strategies with more focused diversification and reduce their risk through holding a diversified portfolio of equity investments. However, managers cannot work for a diverse portfolio of firms to balance their employment risk. As such, top-level managers may prefer more diversification in order to maximize firm size and executive compensation and reduce employment risk. Product diversification, therefore, is a potential agency problem that could result in principals incurring costs to control their agents' behaviours.

## Agency Costs and Governance Mechanisms

The potential conflict illustrated in Figure 11.2, coupled with the fact that principals do not know which few managers might act opportunistically, demonstrates why principals establish governance mechanisms. But establishing and using the governance mechanisms discussed in this chapter is not without costs. **Agency costs** are the sum of incentive, monitoring, and enforcement costs, and individual financial losses incurred by principals, because it is impossible to use governance mechanisms to guarantee total compliance by the agent.[40]

In general, managerial interests may prevail when governance mechanisms are weak. For example, the firm's level of diversification will move closer to curve M in Figure 11.2 when governance mechanisms allow managers a significant amount of autonomy in making strategic decisions. If, however, the board of directors controls managerial autonomy, or if other strong governance mechanisms are used, the firm's diversification level will approach that desired by shareholders (see curve S).

**Agency costs** are the sum of incentive, monitoring, and enforcement costs, and individual financial losses incurred by principals, because it is impossible to use governance mechanisms to guarantee total compliance by the agent.

In the following sections, we explain the effects of various means of governance on managerial decisions to formulate and implement the firm's different strategies, especially corporate-level diversification strategies. We focus on this strategy type because the relationship between principals and agents, developed through the use of governance mechanisms, is observed easily. Moreover, this relationship is critical in diversified firms. The failure to govern strategic decisions properly in companies implementing diversification results in significant negative effects on the firm's performance as measured by strategic competitiveness and financial returns.[41]

# OWNERSHIP CONCENTRATION

**Ownership concentration** is defined by both the number of large-block shareholders and the total percentage of shares they own.

**Large-block shareholders** typically own at least 10 percent of a corporation's issued shares. In the United States, the cutoff is 5 percent.

**Ownership concentration** is defined by both the number of large-block shareholders and the total percentage of shares they own. In Canada, **large-block shareholders** typically own at least 10 percent of a corporation's issued shares. In the United States, the cutoff is 5 percent. Ownership concentration as a governance mechanism has been researched extensively.[42] One reason for this level of interest and analysis is that large-block shareholders are increasingly active in their demands that corporations adopt effective governance mechanisms to control the decisions of their managerial agents.[43]

In general, diffuse ownership (a large number of shareholders with small holdings and few if any large-block shareholders) produces weak monitoring of managerial decisions. Among other problems, diffuse ownership makes it difficult for owners to coordinate their actions effectively. An outcome of weak monitoring might be diversification of the firm's product lines beyond the shareholders' optimum level. Higher levels of monitoring could encourage managers to avoid levels of diversification that exceed shareholders' preferences. Such monitoring could also disallow excessive compensation paid to managers by holding down diversification and thereby the size of the firm. In fact, research evidence shows that ownership concentration is associated with lower levels of firm diversification.[44] Thus, with high degrees of ownership concentration, the probability is greater that managers' strategic decisions will be intended to maximize shareholder value.

Typically, shareholders monitor managerial decisions and firm actions through the board of directors. Shareholders elect members to their firm's board. Elected members are expected to oversee managerial agents and to ensure that the corporation is operated in ways that will maximize shareholders' wealth.

## The Growing Influence of Institutional Owners as Large-Block Shareholders

A classic work by Berle and Means published in the 1930s argued that the "modern" corporation had become characterized by a separation of ownership and control.[45] This change occurred as firm growth prevented founder-owners from maintaining their dual positions as owners and managers of their corporations. More recently, another shift has occurred. Ownership of many modern corporations is now concentrated in the hands of institutional investors rather than individual shareholders.[46]

**Institutional owners** are financial institutions such as stock mutual funds and pension funds that control large-block shareholder positions.

**Institutional owners** are financial institutions such as stock mutual funds and pension funds that control large-block shareholder positions. Because of their prominent ownership positions, institutional owners, as large-block shareholders, are a powerful governance mechanism.[47] Institutions of these types now own more than 50 percent of the stock in large U.S. corporations. Of the top 1000 corporations, these funds own, on average, 59 percent of the stock.[48] Pension funds alone are expected to control at least one-half of corporate equity by 2000.[49] In Canada, The Fraser Institute estimates that institutions own 65 to 70 percent of publicly traded stocks. Thus, as these ownership percentages suggest, institutional owners have both the size and incentive to discipline ineffective top-level managers and are able to significantly influence a firm's choice of strategies and overall strategic decisions.[50]

Research evidence indicates that institutional and other large-block shareholders are becoming more active in efforts to influence a corporation's strategic decisions. Initially, the focus seemed to be on the accountability of CEOs. After focusing on the performance of many CEOs, which has contributed to the ouster of a number of them, shareholder activists and institutional investors are targeting what they perceive as ineffective boards of directors.

Anthony J.F. O'Reilly, former CEO of H.J. Heinz, was the target of activist shareholders, even though his corporation had earned above-average returns. O'Reilly held lavish parties for company officials and analysts, and activists believe that a stronger board would have reined in such costly events. Both Teachers Insurance and Annuity Association—Retirement Equities Fund (TIAA-CREF) and California Public Employees' Retirement System (CalPERS) believed that Heinz's board of directors was an example of what a board should not be: "a cozy club of loyalists headed by a powerful and charismatic chieftain."[51]

CalPERS provides retirement and health coverage to more than one million current and retired public employees.[52] It is the largest public employee pension fund in the United States, with a portfolio approximating $135 billion invested in more than 1200 companies. As an active institutional owner, the organization's actions have earned it a reputation for bullying some U.S. companies into adopting its recommendations. CalPERS is generally thought to act aggressively to promote decisions and actions that it believes will enhance shareholder value in companies in which it invests. To pressure boards of directors to make what it believes are needed changes, CalPERS annually issues a target list of companies in which it owns stock that it believes are underachieving. This list is based on corporations' relative rates of shareholder return, their degree of responsiveness to CalPERS' inquiries, labour practices, and the percentage of shares owned by CalPERS. Once published, CalPERS usually demands meetings with top-level managers from companies included on the list and is known to flex its muscle to oust directors when its requests are denied.[53] According to CalPERS officials, the intent of these sessions is to persuade corporate boards to force management to initiate appropriate strategic changes inside the targeted company. Based on inputs from this institutional investor, some believe that top-level executives at various companies, including GM, IBM, and Kodak, have lost their jobs.

Public pension funds such as CalPERS also must achieve strategic success through their operations, but research results suggest that the activism of large public pension funds such as CalPERS has not been universally successful. These findings indicate that activists' proposals to top-level managers that are not focused on firm performance issues can have a negative effect on the company's efforts to earn above-average returns. Thus, questions exist regarding the practice of shareholder activists and the long-term performance effects of their actions on targeted firms.[54]

In Canada, the Royal Bank was the subject of opposition by the Ontario Teachers Pension Plan Board (OTPPB) at its annual 2001 meeting. The OTPPB was opposed to the Royal Bank's removing the cap on the amount of common stock ($10 billion) that could be issued and the amount of first preferred shares ($5 billion) that could be issued. The Royal Bank wanted more funding flexibility and to bring its capital structure more in line with some other banks and most Canadian companies. The OTPPB considered that this was similar to giving the bank a blank cheque and that the bank had not given a clear reason for removing the cap. They also considered that the removal of the cap could lead to the dilution of shareholders' existing holdings. The OTPPB is one of the largest pension funds in Canada ($70 billion in assets) and has a history of making its wishes known in the boardrooms of Canadian corporations.[55]

The Strategic Focus discusses the Ontario Municipal Employees Retirement System, recent changes in institutional shareholder activism, and the strategic approach of institutional investors in their pursuit of increased investments in international companies. As these institutional investors begin to invest overseas, they are actively trying to change corporate governance procedures. Also, as pointed out in the Strategic Focus, institutional investors may consider taking board seats on firms in which they are invested heavily.

## STRATEGIC FOCUS

### Institutional Shareholder Activism

When some select Canadian banks (National Bank and Royal Bank) held their annual shareholders' meetings, shareholder activist Yves Michaud was there to challenge management. Michaud—a retired Quebec politician, newspaper publisher, and diplomat—questioned the banks' policies on executive compensation, the CEO/chair split, and length of service of directors. A controversial figure, Michaud has been accused of merely seeking media attention, although he has gained limited legal and regulatory victories. His is not the only voice addressing management actions in Canada. Institutional investors are, in their own way, speaking out.

The Ontario Municipal Employees Retirement System (OMERS) has launched its own less vocal effort that challenges top managers. OMERS has published its Proxy Voting Guidelines to ensure that companies are focused on generating long-term shareholder value for shareholders through appropriate corporate governance mechanisms. OMERS states that it will vote against the following: stock option clauses that violate the guidelines' criteria, golden parachutes, most poison pills, leveraged buyouts if they violate shareholder interests, greenmail transactions, and unlimited or excessive share issues. In other words, OMERS would not support moves by management to obtain overly generous stock options, bonuses for being fired, or self-destructive takeover defences.

In the United States, many of the rules of corporate governance have changed because of activist shareholders such as public pension funds like the California Public Employees' Retirement System (CalPERS). Historically, CalPERS has been proud of its intolerance of poor corporate performance. The policies of institutional activists such as CalPERS have changed the way most boards are

*continued*

http://www.omers.com
http://www.calpers.ca.gov

structured and managed: boards are not overly large now so that they can have more effective group processes; most board members are composed of outside directors who are nonemployees and independent; and outside directors chair key committees such as the audit and compensation committees. Also, the U.S. Security and Exchange Commission has required new proxy rules because activist investors have pushed for more accurate information on those who perform the corporate governance role (e.g., board members and large stockholders).

Shareholder activism is also in evidence in other areas of the world. In Europe, the International Corporate Governance Network drew 35 people to an inaugural meeting in London. Its second meeting in Paris drew 125 people. As well, institutional shareholder activists such as CalPERS have established corporate governance principles for their international investments. CalPERS has established corporate governance principles for Britain, France, Germany, and Japan (where it has large holdings). CalPERS funds invested in the shares of non–U.S. based companies have more than tripled (from $12 billion in 1993 to over $36 billion).

Britain has a set of guidelines aimed at developing more effective board structures and has improved on the disclosure of compensation. France has also been improving. However, Germany and Japan have large bank ownership stakes and in Japan, cross-ownership between companies is common. Therefore, concerns have been raised about companies' ability to appoint independent directors, one of its key principles, in these countries.

The Internet has been extremely helpful in the crusade for better corporate governance. For example, CalPERS now posts its votes on proxy issues on its Web site. Since the company started posting these votes, its Web site received over 30 000 hits per month. By accessing the Web site, investors found that CalPERS intended to withhold votes for the election of directors at Tyson Foods, Emerson Electric, and Micron Technology in January 2000 alone. The reasons for their actions were also posted. These directors had business or personal relationships with the company or top executives, and those relationships, CalPERS believed, could compromise the boards' decisions.

While the Caisse de dépôt et placement du Québec (CDP) does not necessarily want to call itself an "activist" shareholder, the organization's managers are greatly concerned about corporate governance issues. With about $23 billion in Canadian Equity assets—and an almost equal amount in foreign equity assets—the CDP tends to take its responsibility as a shareholder quite seriously. In a recent year, CDP analyzed and took positions on nearly 1000 shareholder proposals—including 325 votes regarding senior management compensation, 50 votes on board characteristics, and 24 votes on poison pills. CDP has created and maintained a governance code regarding how the Caisse should vote its proxies. The CDP code supports shareholder proposals and code of procedures for annual meetings; the CDP code opposes top-management compensation that is not a function of corporate results and any form of corporate contribution to political parties. Philippe Gabelier (CDP's Vice-President of Institutional and Public Affairs) summed up the institutional investors' perspective

*continued*

quite well when he said, "It is important to make an effort to ensure that governance rules ... [are] ... introduced or improved, to ensure that principles associated with sound corporate democracy are embraced wherever capital is at risk, whether at home or abroad."

---

Sources: B. Marotte, 2000, Profile: Yves Michaud: Bank basher with a difference, Southam News, February 21, 1997, http://www.ottawacitizen.com/business/970221/ 791773.html (Retrieved November 14, 2000); OMERS, 2000, *OMERS Proxy Voting Guidelines*, http://www.omers.com/investments/pvg/pvg.pdf (Retrieved November 14); Now a gadfly can bite 24 hours per day, 2000, *BusinessWeek Online*, February 6, www.businessweek.com; P. Gabelier, 1999, *Corporate Governance, A Business Matter* (Notes for a speech by Philippe Gabelier, Vice-President, Institutional and Public Affairs of the Caisse de dépôt et placement du Québec at the Canadian Corporate Shareholder Services Association, Montreal, http://www. lacaisse.com/diffusion/discours/090999-all-e.html (Retrieved September 9); *CalPERS home page,* 1998, http://www.calpers.ca.gov; T. A. Stewart, 1997, A visitor from the dark side, *The Pathfinder Network*, http://www.fortune.com (Retrieved November 10); S. Webb, 1997, CalPERS sets its sight overseas, *Wall Street Journal*, October 20, C1, C18; S. S. Hemmerick, 1997, CalPERS lends muscle to governance effort, *Pensions & Investments*, March 31, 20.

## Shareholder Activism: How Much Is Possible?

In the United States, the Securities and Exchange Commission (SEC) has issued several rulings that support shareholder involvement and control of managerial decisions. One such action is the easing of the rule regarding communications among shareholders. Historically, shareholders could communicate among themselves only through what had proved to be a cumbersome and expensive filing process. With a simple notification to the SEC of the intended meeting, shareholders can now meet to discuss a corporation's strategic direction. If a consensus on an issue exists, shareholders can vote as a block. For example, the 20 largest shareholders of Philip Morris own approximately 25 percent of the firm's stock. Coalescing around a position and voting as a block would send a powerful message to Philip Morris' top-level managers and its board of directors. This voting capability has been referred to as shareholder empowerment.

In Canada, shareholder empowerment was formally recognized in the Toronto Stock Exchange's 1994 Dey report, "Where were the Directors?"

*An effective system of shareholder governance depends on an informed and responsive shareholder community ... Our sense is that the investor community wants to be more responsive to corporate initiatives ... Shareholders increasingly want to behave like owners and influence corporate performance by having a larger say in the governance of the corporation. Institutional shareholders, because of, amongst other things, their substantial resources and influence, are in a particularly good position to contribute to the corporate governance process. A more active shareholder community is essential to an enhanced level of corporate governance.*[56]

The exchange noted the growing acceptance of the need for solid corporate governance when it revisited the topic in 1999. The 1999 report noted that, "it is clear that most corporations take the TSE guidelines seriously. Many of the largest companies that account for the greatest proportion of Canadian equity investment are leaders in corporate governance. A number of the TSE guidelines are now broadly accepted business practices."[57]

Others argue that even greater latitude should be extended to those managing the funds of large institutional investor groups. Allowing these individuals to hold positions on the boards of directors of corporations in which their organization has significant investments might allow fund managers to better represent the interests of those they serve.[58] This capability would foster more direct disciplining of poor-performing or dissident top-level managers when needed.

The type of shareholder and board of director activism we have described sometimes provokes reactions from top-level managers. Unintended, and not always anticipated, these reactions require still further attention by those monitoring the decisions being made by the firm's agents. A reaction articulated by one corporate CEO demonstrates this issue. When asked to evaluate results achieved through shareholder activism, the CEO believed that at least some of the actions requested by shareholder activists exceed the roles specified by the separation of ownership and managerial control. When this occurs, the CEO argued, owners and directors begin to micromanage the corporation, which is not their job. Faced with the micromanaging, executives may reduce their managerial employment risk. Implementing strategies with greater diversification, as explained earlier, is one path top-level managers can pursue to achieve this objective. O'Reilly, for instance, did not increase Heinz's diversification, but he held ownership positions and board responsibilities in a number of other enterprises.[59] Of course, such a course reduced the time he was able to spend on Heinz's strategic issues.

For this reason, a number of CEOs are deciding to decline to be outside directors on other firms' boards. CEOs that are on too many boards have been criticized; the National Association of Corporate Directors (NACD) in the United States has urged that CEOs hold no more than three directorships in publicly held firms. The Toronto Stock Exchange's Dey Report on corporate governance expressed similar feelings but stopped short of specifying the number of directorships. "While we agree there must be a limit to the number of appointments, we have concluded that a specific guideline is unnecessary. The nominating committee, in assessing the suitability of an individual to be elected to a board, will take into account the individual's other commitments, resources, and time available for input to the board."[60] Gordon Bethune of Continental Airlines asks, "How much time do I want to spend doing somebody else's work?" Instead of serving on other firms' boards, top-level managers, such as those at Continental Airlines, increasingly desire to spend time improving their own firm's performance. Improved performance reduces the likelihood that a firm will become a takeover candidate.[61]

Executives may protect themselves against employment risks when institutional investors have major investments in their firm. Besides the offensive protection of doing a better job, they may seek defensive protection from a possible acquisition. Evidence suggests that the number of executives receiving such protection is increasing. In 1987, 35 percent of U.S. public companies offered severance packages to top-level executives in case a firm changed hands. Within 10 years, that number had jumped to 57 percent. A golden parachute, a type of managerial protection that pays a guaranteed salary for a specified period of time in the event of a takeover and the loss of one's job, is sought by many top-level managers, particularly the CEO.

Canadian firms are certainly not immune to golden parachutes. One *Canadian Business* article recently noted several high-profile Canadian cases. For example, Bill Fields—former Hudson's Bay Company (HBC) CEO—received a $5.95 million termination payout. Field's predecessor at HBC was George Kosich. Kosich pocketed $2.17 million when he was terminated from HBC. Within a year of leaving HBC, he was hired and fired from Eaton's (at a price estimated to be over $1 million). Jim Bullock received an estimated $2.5 million for being fired from Laidlaw. Finally, George Watson at Transcanada Pipeline received $4.4 for his early retirement.[62]

Golden parachutes are not the only item that a firm can use to dissuade would-be takeover suitors. There are a number of other anti-takeover provisions that allow a firm to defend itself from a takeover attempt.[63] A more recently developed protection is called "the golden goodbye." A golden goodbye provides automatic payments to top-level executives if their contracts are not renewed, regardless of the reason for nonrenewal. Michael Ovitz, former president of Walt Disney, had a five-year contract that included a U.S.$10 million golden goodbye. However, when he stepped down after only one year on the job, he was still able to collect U.S.$93 million in cash and stock options.[64] Similarly, John R. Walter received a severance package valued at U.S.$26 million after working at AT&T for only eight months. In theory, the golden-goodbye arrangement protects top-level managers working at corporations whose long-term prospects are uncertain.

In general though, the degree to which institutional investors can actively monitor the decisions being made in all of the companies in which they are invested is questionable. CalPERS, for instance, targets just 12 firms at a time. The New York Teachers Retirement Fund, another activist institutional investor, focuses on 25 of the 1300-plus companies in its portfolio. Given limited resources, even large-block shareholders tend to concentrate on corporations in which they have significant investments. Thus, although shareholder activism has increased, institutional investors face barriers to the amount of active governance they can realistically employ.[65]

Institutional activism should create a premium on companies with good corporate governance. However, sometimes trustees for these funds—particularly large private pension funds—have other business relationships with companies in the fund's portfolio, which prevents effective monitoring. In addition, a recent phenomenon is the increase in managerial ownership of the firm's stock. There are many positive reasons for managerial ownership, including the use of stock options to link managerial pay to the performance of a firm. However, an unexpected outcome has been reduced support for shareholder-sponsored proposals to repeal anti-takeover provisions. Institutional owners generally support the repeal of these provisions, and managerial owners generally oppose their repeal. Thus, managerial ownership provides managers with power to protect their own interests.[66] This suggests that other means of governance are needed. Next, we examine one of these governance mechanisms: the board of directors.

## BOARDS OF DIRECTORS

As we have described, the practices of large institutional investors have resulted in an increase in ownership concentration in firms. Nonetheless, diffuse ownership still describes the status of most firms,[67] which means that monitoring and control of managers by individual shareholders is limited in large corporations. Furthermore, large financial institutions, such as banks, are prevented from directly owning firms and from having representatives on boards of directors. These conditions highlight the importance of the board of directors for corporate governance. Our analysis of the board of directors shows that, although they are imperfect, there is a respected body of thought and research supporting the view that boards of directors can positively influence both managers and the companies they serve.

The **board of directors** is a group of elected individuals whose primary responsibility is to act in the owners' interests by formally monitoring and controlling the corporation's top-level executives.[68] This responsibility is a product of the legal systems in Canada and the United States, which "… confer[s] broad powers on corporate boards to direct the affairs of the organization, punish and reward managers, and protect the rights and interests of shareholders."[69] Thus, an appropriately structured and effective board of directors protects owners from managerial opportunism. Board members are seen as stewards of their company's resources, and the way they carry out these responsibilities affects the society in which their firm operates.[70]

Generally, board members (often called directors) are classified in one of three groups (see Table 11.2). *Insiders* are active top-level managers in the corporation who are elected to the board because they are a source of information about the firm's day-to-day operations.[71] *Related outsiders* have some relationship with the firm—contractual or otherwise—that may create questions about their independence, but these individuals are not involved with the corporation's day-to-day activities. *Outsiders* are individuals elected to the board to provide independent counsel to the firm and may hold top-level managerial positions in another company or have been elected to the board prior to the beginning of the current CEO's tenure.[72]

> The **board of directors** is a group of elected individuals whose primary responsibility is to act in the owners' interests by formally monitoring and controlling the corporation's top-level executives.

| ■ ■ TABLE 11.2 | Classification of Board of Directors Members |
|---|---|
| **Insiders** | |
| The company's CEO and other top-level managers | |
| **Related Outsiders** | |
| Individuals not involved with the company's day-to-day operations, but who have a relationship with the firm | |
| **Outsiders** | |
| Individuals who are independent of the firm in terms of day-to-day operations and other relationships | |

Some argue that many boards are not effectively fulfilling their primary fiduciary duty to protect shareholders. Among other possibilities, it may be that boards are a managerial tool—a tool that largely rubber-stamps managers' self-serving initiatives.[73] In general, those critical of boards as a governance device believe that inside managers dominate boards and exploit their personal ties with them. A widely accepted view is that a board with a significant percentage of its membership from the firm's top-level executives tends to result in relatively weak monitoring and control of managerial decisions.[74] Board critics advocate reforms to ensure that independent outside directors represent a significant majority of the total board's membership.[75] Practitioners and academics, however, disagree over the most appropriate role of outside directors in a firm's strategic decisionmaking process.[76]

Because of external pressures, board reforms have been initiated. To date, these reforms have generally called for an increase in the number of outside directors, relative to insiders, serving on a corporation's board. For example, the New York Stock Exchange requires listed firms to have board audit committees composed solely of outside directors. Similarly, in Canada, the Dey Report on Corporate Governance suggested establishing a separate audit committee composed of only outside directors.[77] As a result of these external pressures, boards of large corporations now have more outside members.[78] Research shows that outside board members can influence the strategic direction of companies and thus play an important role on boards of directors.[79] Therefore, there are potential strategic implications associated with the movement toward having corporate boards dominated by outsiders.

Alternatively, a large number of outside board members can also present some problems. Outsiders do not have contact with the firm's day-to-day operations. This lack of contact precludes easy access to the rich information about managers and their skills that is required to evaluate managerial decisions and initiatives effectively. Valuable information may be obtained through frequent interactions with insiders during board meetings. Insiders possess such information by virtue of their organizational positions. Thus, boards with a critical mass of insiders can be informed more effectively about intended strategic initiatives—both in terms of the reasons for them and the outcomes expected through their accomplishments.[80] Without this type of rich strategic information, outsider-dominated boards may emphasize financial, as opposed to strategic, evaluations. Such evaluations shift risk to top-level managers, who, in turn, may make decisions to maximize their interests and reduce their employment risk. Reductions in R&D investments, additional diversification of the firm, and pursuit of greater levels of compensation are examples of decisions managers could make to achieve these objectives.

## Enhancing the Effectiveness of the Board of Directors as a Governance Mechanism

Our discussion has suggested that the board of directors is an important source of control and governance in the modern corporation. Because of this importance, and as a result of increased scrutiny from shareholders, particularly large institutional investors, the performances of individual board members and of entire boards are being evaluated more formally and with greater intensity.[81] Some believe that directors increase the probability of fulfilling their responsibilities effectively when they are honest and act with prudence and integrity for the good of the entire firm and are committed to reaching independent judgments on an informed basis rather than rubber-stamping management proposals.[82]

Given the demand for greater accountability and improved performance, many boards of directors have initiated voluntary changes. Such changes include (1) increasing the diversity of board members' backgrounds (e.g., select a greater number of directors from public service, academic, and scientific settings; increase the percentage of ethnic minorities on boards; and have more members from different countries), (2) strengthening internal management and accounting control systems, and (3) establishing and consistently using formal processes to evaluate the board's performance.

Changes such as these should result in enhancing the effectiveness of the board of directors as a means of control.

The following Strategic Focus also indicates that other innovative board approaches are being pursued. Managers are becoming more interested and aggressive in putting outside directors on their company's boards. One reason for this is that CEOs are finding that including a top-notch outside director can increase a firm's stock price. McKinsey & Co., in a hypothetical survey, found that when companies in which outsiders constituted a majority of the board, owned significant amounts of stock, were subjected to formal evaluation, and were not personally tied to top management, institutional shareholders were willing to pay up to 11 percent more for their shares.[83]

Boards are now becoming more involved in the strategic decisionmaking process, so they must work collaboratively. Research shows that boards working collaboratively make higher-quality strategic decisions, and they make them faster.[84] Boards also are becoming more involved in decisions regarding succession, as opposed to blindly supporting the incumbent's choice. In general, however, boards have relied on precedence (past decisions) for guidance in the selection process. Also, they are more likely to consider inside candidates before looking for outside candidates.[85] Also, top boards, it seems, are becoming smaller, especially in high-technology firms.

Increasingly, outside directors are being required to own significant equity stakes as a prerequisite to holding a board position. A recent study also suggests that inside director performance increases if those directors hold an equity position. The announcement of an inside director with less than 5 percent ownership decreases shareholder wealth, but an insider with ownership between 5 and 25 percent increases shareholder wealth. This way, an inside director's knowledge of the firm can be used appropriately. Lastly, an inside director's relationship to the CEO does not necessarily lead to CEO entrenchment if the inside director has a strong ownership position.[86]

## STRATEGIC FOCUS

### Examples of Boards of Directors Reforms

Shareholder activism has pressured many boards to undertake significant reforms. Many CEOs are also seeking to use the board as a way to improve strategy and corporate performance. In Canada, the Conference Board of Canada, whose own Board of Directors includes about 30 Canadian CEOs, suggests that best governance practices contribute to an organization's long-term performance. In the United States, the Business Roundtable, which includes 200 CEOs of the largest U.S. companies, has openly endorsed ideas on corporate governance once considered radical. Similar to the Conference Board of Canada, the Business Roundtable endorses the belief that the utmost duty of both management and corporate boards is to ensure that shareholder wealth is created.

During the time that Louis E. Platt was CEO at Hewlett-Packard (HP), he indicated that he benefited significantly from his board and their appropriate level of independence. He suggested a need to have an effective balance between collaboration and independence for a board to function appropriately. HP's board emphasizes three fundamental elements that create effective governance. First, there is an emphasis on performance. If the firm is not performing

*continued*

well, the board is not likely to be performing well either. This is the foundational governance principle. The second element is to make sure that each board member is an effective representative of the company's shareholders. Board service then is not just supplemental income for board members. They must realize that if something goes wrong, shareholders expect accountability from not only the company managers but also board members for not performing well as their representatives. Finally, HP's board seeks to have a culture of openness between the CEO and board members. If the company stumbles, and the board struggles to deal effectively with its poor performance, the board may have been kept in the dark about the real issues facing the company.

HP's board, in coordination with the CEO, has developed a set of guidelines and duties for directors and has established the following mission statement: "The mission of the board of directors of Hewlett-Packard Company is to monitor and support management in creating long-term value for its shareholders, customers and employees in an ethically and socially responsible manner while maintaining the standard of excellence that has become associated with Hewlett-Packard."

Although the board's approach has improved governance substantially, and HP's performance is exemplary, Albert Dunlap, former CEO of Sunbeam, pursued a more radical approach to board reform. When he came to Sunbeam, the first thing he did was to pay the board 100 percent in stock. He also had them buy stock in the firm as a condition of being on the board. He did this at Scott Paper, where it was considered revolutionary. He has even undertaken to put governance activists on his boards. For instance, Charles Elson, a law professor and a noted writer and theorist on the role of the board and the value of shareholder activism, was put on Sunbeam's board. As a legal academic, buying 5000 shares at $23 per share was a significant commitment; Elson indicated that the investment was significantly more than he had equity in his home. However, he obviously had to put his money where his mouth was because he had been writing about governance activism for some time. Dunlap has also suggested board term limits of five years.

Interestingly, Dunlap believes that the CEO should also be the chairperson. This view is contrary to many of the governance views held by institutional investors. It is also contrary to practice in Canada where 69 percent of companies are believed to have a non-CEO chair or lead director. In support of this belief, Dunlap states, "The professional chairman comes to that meeting, and although these are capable, well-meaning people, they don't have enough background in the company to raise the important issues. They are not conversant enough with what's going on. The board meeting becomes highly inefficient, and many times misses the most important points." However, he also suggests that he needs a strong board: "If you don't have a strong board, you will fail. I need people who will stand up and say, 'That's nonsense.'"

He also suggests that a board should never have more than 10 people. In fact, the ideal board would probably have eight people, according to Dunlap. One other insider would be useful on the board, the chief financial officer, because he or she has to be so intimately involved in board communications. Dunlap would also seek to have a board with a variety of backgrounds to help a company deal with international, marketing, and financial market issues.

*continued*

Dunlap has criticized the typical board as "a group of CEOs who have failed miserably running companies, and yet they are on a multiplicity of other boards."

Although Al Dunlap has run large companies, his approach is similar to that of smaller more entrepreneurial firms such as those found in Silicon Valley. Because today's firms are intensely competitive, the role of the board of directors has become a lot less ceremonial and more proactive in the oversight and actual running of the corporation. The high-technology sector has an approach that may be useful in creating more successful boards. For most high-technology boards, their role is to be active in the strategic direction of the company. Rather than sheer oversight, each director brings to the board some specialized skill in specific areas (sales and marketing, legal, technical, financial, etc.). The board helps the CEO by asking difficult questions to ensure that the strategic direction is sound and viable. This model appears to be helping high-technology firms, given their success in recent years.

Sources: D. A. H. Brown & D. L. Brown, 1999, *Who Does What?* Ottawa: The Conference Board of Canada Report, 267–99. J. A. Byrne, 1997, Governance: CEOs catch up with shareholder activists, *BusinessWeek*, September 22, 36; J. A. Byrne, 1997, The CEO and the board, *BusinessWeek,* September 15, 106–16; Reforming the Board, 1997, *The Economist*, August 9, 16–17; A. Dunlap, 1997, On "Dunlapping" the Board, *Corporate Board*, January–February, 102–08; D. J. Berger, 1997, The Silicon Valley board, *Corporate Board*, July–August, 105–10; L. E. Platt, 1997, Governance the H-P Way, *Directors & Boards*, 21 (4): 20–25; Charles Elson: The board outsider goes inside, 1997, *Corporate Board*, March–April, 32.

In Canada, there have been mixed results regarding suggested TSE guidelines for corporate boards of directors governance reform. The highest level of compliance has been in board size, involvement in strategic planning, a majority of unrelated/outside board members, internal controls and management information systems, and satisfactory compensation to directors. The guidelines with the lowest level of compliance are a process for assessing individual board member effectiveness, meeting occasionally without senior managers present, position descriptions for directors, and a process for the assessment of board effectiveness.

The results from a November 1998 survey of the CEOs of 1250 TSE-listed companies (Table 11.3) show the rate at which the TSE's guidelines are being followed. The response rate of over 50 percent (635 CEOs replied to the survey) demonstrates that the majority of top managers of major Canadian corporations are concerned with governance issues.[87]

Beside the board reforms mentioned in the Strategic Focus, a number of analysts have suggested that women need more representation on boards. In a 1998 census of women on boards of directors in Canada, Catalyst, a non-profit organization, found that "women hold just 6.2 percent of the board seats on the companies of the 1998 *Financial Post* 500—257 out of 4154 total seats. When the boards of each of the top 20 crown corporations, financial institutions and insurance companies are included, the proportion of women increases to 7.5 percent—372 of 4950 total seats. Of Canada's most influential companies, Catalyst finds that less than half—234 of 560 companies or 41.7 percent—have any women board members. Of these, 94 companies (16.8 percent) have

| ■ ■ **TABLE 11.3** | **Percentage of TSE Corporate Governance Guidelines by Canadian Companies Listed on the Toronto Stock Exchange** |
| --- | --- |

| TSE Guideline | % Adoption |
| --- | --- |
| Board size suitable for individual accountability | 95 |
| Strategic planning involvement | 79 |
| Board constituted with majority of unrelated directors | 77 |
| Internal controls and management information systems | 76 |
| Satisfactory compensation to directors | 76 |
| Independence: Non-CEO chair or lead director | 69 |
| Only non-management members on nominating committee (if committee exists) | 68 |
| Risk management systems in place | 60 |
| Orientation for new directors | 49 |
| Explicit attention to governance | 48 |
| Position descriptions and objectives for CEO | 48 |
| Independence: Known procedure by which directors can retain outside advisors | 39 |
| Separate nominating committee | 33 |
| Succession planning for senior management | 28 |
| Communication policy | 25 |
| Process for assessing director effectiveness, other than ad hoc discussions with chair | 24 |
| Independence: Board meets occasionally without management present | 21 |
| Position descriptions for directors | 18 |
| Process for assessing board effectiveness | 18 |

Source: R. M. Corbin, 1999, *Report on Corporate Governance,* 1999. Five Years to the Dey, Toronto Stock Exchange: 3.

multiple women on their boards." In the United States, women hold approximately 10.6 percent of board seats.[88] Korn/Ferry International, an executive search firm, reports that 71 percent of boards surveyed had at least one woman on the board, up from 46 percent a decade ago. Catalyst notes that among the *Fortune* 500, 84 percent have at least one woman on their board. The Korn/Ferry survey reported that although their influence was increasing, female board members believed their opinions were weighed less heavily in executive succession and compensation decisions. Thus, it appears that more board reform is necessary in regard to diversity and board functioning.[89]

## Board Member Compensation in Canada

Board members in Canada are compensated at a lower level than their counterparts in the United States. A recent study by Spencer Stuart Canada's president, Andrew MacDougall, shows that average board members' total compensation (including stock and options) for 100 Canadian companies was $46 249 in 2000. This was up 6 percent from 1999 and was much lower than the $72 199 paid to board members in the United States in 2000. Nortel Networks paid the highest at approximately $86 250. Air Canada paid each director an average of $79 000 and Atco, an energy and industrial conglomerate, paid an average of $74 000. Seventy percent of Canadian boards polled for the Spencer Stuart survey considered that Canadian directors are not paid enough.[90] The next section examines executive compensation and its impact as a corporate governance mechanism.

# EXECUTIVE COMPENSATION

A reading of the business press shows that the compensation of top-level managers, and especially CEOs, generates a great deal of interest and strongly held opinions. Two researchers noted that, "… to observe CEO pay is to observe in an indirect but very tangible way the fundamental governance processes in large corporations. Who has power? What are the bases of power? How and when do owners and managers exert their relative preferences? How vigilant are boards? Who is taking advantage of whom?"[91]

**Executive compensation** is a governance mechanism that seeks to align managers' and owners' interests through salary, bonuses, and long-term incentive compensation such as stock options.

**Executive compensation** is a governance mechanism that seeks to align managers' and owners' interests through salary, bonuses, and long-term incentive compensation such as stock options.[92] Stock options are a mechanism used to link executives' performance to the performance of their company's stock.[93] Increasingly, long-term incentive plans are becoming a critical part of compensation packages in North American firms. The use of longer-term pay helps firms cope with or avoid potential agency problems.[94] Because of this, the stock market generally reacts positively to the introduction of a long-range incentive plan for top executives.[95] Nevertheless, sometimes the use of a long-term incentive plan prevents major stockholders (e.g., institutional stockholders) from pressing for changes in the composition of the board of directors, because they assume that the long-term incentives will ensure that the top executives will act in the best interests of the shareholders. Alternatively, stockholders largely assume that top-executive pay and the permanence of a firm are more aligned when firms have boards that are dominated by outside members.[96]

Using executive compensation effectively as a governance mechanism is particularly challenging in firms implementing international strategies. For example, evidence suggests that the interests of owners of multinational corporations are served best when there is less uniformity among the firm's foreign subsidiaries' compensation plans rather than more.[97] The reward structure given to CEOs varies by country and by region. Thus, reward structures, which appropriately reflect local market levels for pay and benefits, tend to best serve shareholder's interests.[98] For example, although annual bonuses through incentive compensation represent a significant portion of many executives' total pay, the percentage of the total that such incentives make up may vary greatly between locations. For example, annual bonuses compose an average of about 19 percent of the CEO's total compensation in France, approximately 30 percent in Canada, about 45 percent in the United Kingdom, and about 60 percent in the United States.[99] Such figures underscore the differences in compensation across countries. Table 11.4 contains data for the ten CEOs with the highest levels of compensation in Canada in 1999.

| ■ ■ TABLE 11.4 | CEO Compensation in Canada | | | | |
|---|---|---|---|---|---|
| **CEO** | **Company** | **Salary (000s)** | **Bonus (000s)** | **Other (000s)** | **Total (000s)** |
| Tony Comper | Bank of Montreal | 1304 | 268 | 22 780 | 24 352 |
| Stephen Bachand | Canadian Tire | 944 | 165 | 15 750 | 16 859 |
| Gerald W. Schwartz | Onex | 966 | 10 103 | 0 | 11 069 |
| John A. Roth | Nortel Networks | 1185 | 6124 | 3308 | 10 617 |
| Renato Zambonini | Cognos | 378 | 558 | 8937 | 9873 |
| Frank Hasenfratz | Linamar | 469 | 1589 | 5655 | 7719 |
| Richard J. Currie | George Weston | 1450 | 1000 | 4924 | 7374 |
| John Cleghorn | Royal Bank | 978 | 1000 | 5334 | 7312 |
| Pierre Lessard | Metro | 562 | 526 | 5693 | 6781 |
| John Hunkin | CIBC | 793 | 0 | 5549 | 6342 |

Source: D. Olive, 2000, CEO Scorecard 2000: How much they were paid—and how they performed, *National Post Business*, November, 98–186.

## A Complicated Governance Mechanism

For several reasons, executive compensation, especially long-term incentive compensation, is complicated. First, the strategic decisions made by top-level managers are typically complex and non-routine; as such, direct supervision of executives is inappropriate for judging the quality of their decisions. Because of this, there is a tendency to link the compensation of top-level managers to measurable outcomes such as financial performance. Second, an executive's decision often affects a firm's financial outcome over an extended period of time, making it difficult to assess the effect of current decisions on the corporation's performance. In fact, strategic decisions are more likely to have long-term, rather than short-term, effects on a company's strategic outcomes. Third, a number of variables intervene between top-level managerial decisions and behaviour and firm performance. Unpredictable economic, social, or legal changes (see Chapter 3) make it difficult before implementation to discern the effects of strategic decisions. Thus, although performance-based compensation may provide incentives to managers to make decisions that best serve shareholders' interests, such compensation plans alone are imperfect in their ability to monitor and control managers.

Although incentive compensation plans may increase firm value in line with shareholder expectations, they are subject to managerial manipulation. For instance, annual bonuses may provide incentives to pursue short-term objectives at the expense of the firm's long-term interests. Supporting this conclusion, some research has found that bonuses based on annual performance were negatively related to investments in R&D,

which may affect the firm's long-term strategic competitiveness.[100] Although long-term performance-based incentives may reduce the temptation to underinvest in the short run, they increase executive exposure to risks associated with uncontrollable events, such as market fluctuations and industry decline.[101] The longer the focus of incentive compensation, the greater the long-term risks that are borne by top-level managers. In addition, the nature of this long-term compensation could lead to another problem. As top-level managers' own personal wealth increases because it is tied to their firms' performance, it is possible that they will become risk-averse and want to diversify their own risk. Of course they cannot do this in the same manner as a shareholder, so they may further diversify their firms to diversify the risk to their own personal wealth. This could mean that the very thing stock/stock option compensation is designed to curtail—managerial opportunism—may actually encourage top-level managers to further diversify to the detriment of shareholders.

## The Effectiveness of Executive Compensation

In recent times, many stakeholders, including shareholders, have been angered by the compensation received by some top-level managers, especially CEOs. For example, the top compensation received by an executive in 1998 was the approximately $850 million awarded to Michael Eisner, CEO of Disney. In 1999, the highest reported top-executive compensation was more than $1 billion, for Charles Wang, CEO of Computer Associates. However, the firm lost a lawsuit filed by a shareholder in which the award exceeded the amount provided by the company's long-range incentive compensation plan. The court ruled that Mr. Wang, along with the president and executive vice-president of Computer Associates, had to return about 9.5 million shares of stock that were awarded. The value of the stock returned was about $800 million in total for the three executives.[102]

The primary component of such large compensation packages is stock options and stock. In fact, the average amount of the stock held by top executives and directors of firms reached 21 percent in the 1990s, partly because of the long-term incentive plans that compensate executives in stock options and stock.[103] The primary reasons for compensating executives in stock is that the practice affords incentives to keep the stock price high. Hence, this practice should align the interests of managers and owners. However, there may be some unintended consequences: Research has shown that managers who own more than 1 percent of their firm's stock are less likely to be forced out of their jobs, even when the firm is performing poorly.[104] As well, CEOs have their own unique perspective regarding their compensation. George Fisher, chairman and CEO of Eastman Kodak, stated that "We all should be compensated based on competitive issues. If you want a world-class shortstop, you pay. The good news is that many CEOs are getting well-compensated for really good performances."[105] Indeed, it is the rare CEO who does not sincerely believe that she or he has earned a reward.[106] Thus, some executives argue that they are being rewarded for effectively making critical decisions that affect their firm's performance in the highly competitive global economy.[107]

Among several challenges facing board directors striving to use executive compensation to align managers' interests with shareholders' interests is the determination of what represents "fair" compensation for top-level managers. As guidance for making this decision, board directors should remember that the most important criterion to consider is shareholder wealth creation. This is necessary because the economic principles on which executive compensation is based are concerned not with fairness but with productivity.[108]

Executive compensation is an imperfect means of corporate governance. (Individually, each governance mechanism discussed in this chapter is imperfect.) The dissatisfaction with executive compensation being expressed by shareholders and other stakeholders as well may have surfaced because of the mechanism's imperfection and/or ineffective use. Specifically, there is criticism of excessive stock option packages such as that of Michael Eisner at Disney.[109] It is possible that members of corporate boards of directors have not been effective in their use of this governance mechanism. If executive compensation plans are not aligning top-level managers' interests with the interests of other stakeholders, especially those of shareholders, appropriate changes must be made. For instance, one proposal is that, to be awarded the intended stock option, the executive must outperform peer companies. Alternatively, boards may be rewarding mediocre performance when the stock market is going up in general, and executives are able to take advantage of the increased value without appropriate accountability.

Thus, the proactive positions concerning executive compensation taken by institutional investors and individual shareholders have been effective. Input from these stakeholders should result in modifications to executive compensation that will improve its value as a means of corporate governance.

A company's organizational structure also influences the alignment of principals' and agents' interests. As indicated in the next section, structure can be an especially valuable governance mechanism in diversified firms.

## THE MULTIDIVISIONAL STRUCTURE

An organizational structure, particularly the multidivisional (M-form) structure, serves as an internal governance mechanism by controlling managerial opportunism.[110] The corporate office that is a part of the M-form structure, along with the firm's board of directors, closely monitors the strategic decisions of managers responsible for the performance of the different business units or divisions of the corporation. Active monitoring of an individual unit's performance suggests a keen managerial interest in making decisions that will maximize shareholders' wealth. Still, while the M-form may limit division managers' opportunistic behaviours, it may not limit corporate-level managers' self-serving actions. For example, research suggests that diversified firms using the M-form structure are likely to implement corporate-level strategies that cause them to become even more diversified.[111] In fact, one of the potential problems with divisionalization in the M-form structure is that it is often used too aggressively.[112] Beyond some point, diversification serves managers' interests more than it serves shareholders' interests (see Chapter 6).

In addition, because of the diversification of product lines (breadth of businesses), top executives may not have adequate information to evaluate the strategic decisions and actions of divisional managers (depth). To complete their evaluations, they must focus on the resulting financial outcomes achieved by individual business units. While waiting for these financial outcomes, division managers may be able to act opportunistically.

Where internal controls are limited because of extensive diversification, the external market for corporate control and the external managerial labour market may serve as the primary controls on managers' decisions and actions, such as pursuing acquisitions to increase the size of their firm and their compensation.[113] Because external markets lack access to relevant information from inside the firm, they tend to be less efficient than internal governance mechanisms for monitoring the decisions and performance of top executives. Therefore, in diversified firms, corporate executive decisions can be controlled effectively only when other strong internal governance mechanisms (e.g., the board of directors) are used in combination with the M-form structure. When used as a single governance mechanism, the M-form structure may actually facilitate overdiversification and inappropriately high compensation for corporate executives.[114]

## MARKET FOR CORPORATE CONTROL

The **market for corporate control** is composed of individuals and firms that buy ownership positions in (or take over) potentially undervalued corporations so they can form new divisions in established diversified companies or merge two previously separate firms.

The market for corporate control is an external governance mechanism that becomes active when a firm's internal controls fail.[115] The **market for corporate control** is composed of individuals and firms that buy ownership positions in (or take over) potentially undervalued corporations so they can form new divisions in established diversified companies or merge two previously separate firms. Because they are assumed to be the party responsible for formulating and implementing the strategy that led to poor performance, the top-management team of the purchased corporation is usually replaced. Thus, when operating effectively, the market for corporate control ensures that managerial incompetence is disciplined.[116] This governance mechanism should be activated by a firm's poor performance relative to industry competitors. A firm's poor performance, often demonstrated by the earning of below-average returns, is an indicator that internal governance mechanisms have failed—that is, their use did not result in managerial decisions that maximized shareholder value. This market has been active for some time. The 1980s were known as a time of merger mania in the United States, with approximately 55 000 acquisitions valued at approximately $1.3 trillion. However, there were many more acquisitions in the 1990s, and the value of mergers and acquisitions in that decade was more than $10 trillion.[117]

Throughout 1999, Teleglobe's decreasing profits prompted analysts to speculate that the firm was an attractive takeover target. Teleglobe, operator of Canada's third-largest undersea fibre optic network, was finally bought by BCE in 2000—though not without adjustments to the initial offer because of Teleglobe's continued poor performance.[118]

Both Unilever and Dreyer's Grand Ice Cream made overtures to ice cream–maker Ben & Jerry's. Ben & Jerry's is a socially conscious firm, and socially conscious investors feared that, should the firm be taken over, it would lose this focus. Those investors tried to stop the takeover attempt by buying enough stock to make a takeover infeasible. As a group, the investors would have been a form of a white knight that rescues a takeover target. For Ben & Jerry's, the white knight did not arrive on time, and in 2000 the firm was acquired by Unilever—with some agreements regarding the continuation of the firm's socially conscious policies.[119] British Telecommunications served as a white knight for Esat, Ireland's second-largest telecommunications company.[120] In other cases, the firm may withstand the takeover without external help. This occurred when Philip Green, a retail entrepreneur, unsuccessfully tried to take over Marks and Spencer, the venerable British retailer. Green became concerned because of the likely fight that managers at Marks and Spencer would put up and the potential harm that a prolonged hostile takeover fight could have on the Marks and Spencer business.[121] Firms targeted for hostile takeovers may use multiple defence tactics to fend off the takeover attempt. We discuss managerial defence tactics in the next section.

## Managerial Defence Tactics

Historically, the increased use of the market for corporate control has enhanced the sophistication and variety of managerial defence tactics that are used to reduce the influence of this governance mechanism (such defences are summarized in Table 11.5). The market for corporate control tends to increase risk for managers. As a result, managerial pay is often increased indirectly through golden parachutes (where a CEO can receive up to three years' salary if his or her firm is taken over). Among other outcomes, takeover defences increase the costs of mounting a takeover and can entrench incumbent management while reducing the chances of introducing a new management team.[122]

| ■ ■ TABLE 11.5 | A Basic List of Management Takeover Defences |
| --- | --- |

**Golden Parachute**
Increases the cost of making changes at the takeover target due to the need to pay fired executives high-priced severance packages.

**Greenmail**
Where company money is used to repurchase stock from a corporate raider to avoid the takeover of the firm and the amount paid includes a premium.

**Poison Pill**
A tactic when the takeover target does something to make itself unpalatable to the suitor (e.g., assume a large amount of debt and then issue dividends with the money).

Some defence tactics require the type of asset restructuring that results from divesting one or more divisions in the diversified firm's portfolio. Others necessitate only financial structure changes such as repurchasing shares of the firm's outstanding stock.[123] Some tactics (e.g., a change in the place of incorporation) require shareholder approval, but the greenmail tactic (wherein money is used to repurchase stock from a corporate raider to avoid the takeover of the firm) does not. These defence tactics are controversial, and the research on their effects is inconclusive. Most institutional investors oppose the use of defence tactics. As noted earlier, OMERS, CDP, and CalPERS have taken actions to stop or eliminate poison pills from several firms.[124] However, some defence tactics may be appropriate. For example, shareholders of Canadian Occidental Petroleum approved a poison pill designed to stop a takeover by the parent company, Occidental Petroleum. Canadian Occidental's managers claimed that the parent firm was trying to force Canadian Occidental to give it the Canadian affiliate's lucrative oil operations in Yemen. The parent firm threatened to take over the firm with several partners and then divide and sell its assets. However, with the poison pill, the parent company cannot take over the firm and is likely to sell its 29 percent stake in the Canadian firm.[125]

A potential problem with the market for corporate control is that it may not be totally efficient. A study of several of the most active corporate raiders in the 1980s showed that approximately 50 percent of their takeover attempts targeted firms with above-average performance in their industry—corporations that were neither undervalued nor poorly managed.[126] The targeting of high-performance businesses may lead to acquisitions at premium prices and to decisions by target firm managers to establish what may prove to be costly takeover defence tactics to protect their corporate positions.

Although the market for corporate control lacks the precision possible with internal governance mechanisms, the fear of acquisition and influence by corporate raiders is an effective constraint on the managerial growth motive.[127] The market for corporate control has been responsible for significant changes in many firms' strategies and has, when used appropriately, served the best interests of corporate owners—the shareholders. For instance, the announcement of Compaq's purchase of Digital Equipment shares lifted the Digital share price by 25 percent.[128] Although unthinkable a few years ago, Digital has been performing poorly recently, and the link with Compaq appears to be a positive result for Digital shareholders.

Next, we address the topic of international corporate governance primarily through a description of governance structures used in Germany and Japan.

# INTERNATIONAL CORPORATE GOVERNANCE

Comparisons of corporate governance structures used in other economic systems with the one used in Canada, the United Kingdom, and the United States are interesting given their differences.[129] In this section, we describe the governance structures used in Germany and Japan, among others. Our brief discussion of the governance of German and Japanese corporations shows that the nature of corporate governance in these two nations is being affected by the realities of the global economy and the competitive challenges that are a part of it.[130] Thus, while the stability associated with German and Japanese governance structures has been viewed historically as an asset, some believe that it may now be a burden.

We chose to examine Germany and Japan here because of their prominent positions in the global economy. Furthermore, their governance structures contrast with those of Canada, the United States, and the United Kingdom,[131] providing an opportunity to increase understanding.

## Corporate Governance in Germany

In many private German firms, the same individual is still the owner and manager. In these instances, there is no agency problem. Even in publicly traded corporations, there is often a dominant shareholder.

Historically, banks have been at the centre of the German corporate governance structure, which is the case in many continental European countries such as Italy and France. As lenders, banks become major shareholders when companies they had financed earlier seek funding on the stock market or default on loans. Although stakes are usually under 10 percent, there is no legal limit on how much of a firm's stock banks can hold (except that a single ownership position cannot exceed 15 percent of the bank's capital). Today, various types of specialized institutions—savings banks, mortgage banks, savings and loan associations, leasing firms, and insurance companies—are also important sources of corporate funds.

Through their own shareholdings and by casting proxy votes for individual shareholders who retain their shares with the banks, three banks in particular—Deutsche, Dresdner, and Commerzbank—exercise significant power. Although individual shareholders can tell the banks how to vote their ownership position, they generally elect not to do so. A combination of their own holdings with their proxies results in majority positions for these three banks in many German companies. These banks, as well as others, monitor and control managers both as lenders and as shareholders by electing representatives to supervisory boards.

German firms with more than 2000 employees are required to have a two-tier board structure. Through this structure, the supervision of management is separated from other duties normally assigned to a board of directors, especially the nomination of new board members. Thus, Germany's two-tiered system places the responsibility to monitor and control managerial (or supervisory) decisions and actions in the hands of a separate group.[132] One of the reasons underlying this division is that stronger management is less likely to have interests that coincide with those of the owners of the business. The application of this principle is to place all the functions of direction and management in the hands of the management board—the *Vorstand*—except appointment to the *Vorstand* itself, which is the responsibility of the supervisory tier—the *Aufsichtsrat*. Employees, union members, and shareholders appoint members to the *Aufsichtsrat*.

As implied by our discussion of the importance of banks in Germany's corporate governance structure, private shareholders do not have major ownership positions in their country's firms. Historically, continental Europeans have held the belief that the control of large corporations is too important an asset to be left only to the discretion of public shareholders.[133] Large institutional investors such as pension funds and insurance companies are also relatively insignificant owners of corporate stock. Thus, at least historically, top-level managers in German corporations generally have not been dedicated to the proposition that their decisions and actions should result in maximization of shareholder value. However, this lack of emphasis on shareholder value is changing in some German firms. Many German companies, such as chemical producer BASF, are listing on stock exchanges outside Germany—a move that often requires more transparency and accounting disclosure.[134] As this practice continues, German firms will likely move toward a greater emphasis on creating shareholder value.

## Corporate Governance in Japan

Attitudes toward corporate governance in Japan are affected by the concepts of obligation, family, and consensus. In Japan, obligation does not result from broad general principles; rather, it is a product of specific causes or events. In this context, an obligation "… may be to return a service for one rendered or it may derive from a more general relationship, for example, to one's family or old alumni, or one's company (or Ministry), or the country. This sense of particular obligation is common elsewhere but it feels stronger in Japan."[135] As part of a company family, individuals are members of a unit that envelops their lives to an unusual degree. Company families command the attention and allegiance of parties from the top to the bottom in corporations. Moreover, a keiretsu (defined in Chapter 10) is more than an economic concept—it, too, is a family. Consensus, the most important influence on the Japanese corporate governance structure, calls for the expenditure of significant amounts of energy to win the hearts and minds of people when possible, as opposed to proceeding by edict of top-level managers. Consensus is highly valued, even when a firm's commitment to it results in a slow and cumbersome decisionmaking process.

As in Germany, banks play a more important role in financing and monitoring large public firms in Japan. The bank owning the largest share of stocks and largest amount of debt—the main bank—has the closest relationship with the company's top-level managers. The main bank not only provides financial advice to the firm but also is responsible for closely monitoring managerial agents. Thus, Japan has a bank-based financial and corporate governance structure, and the United States has a market-based financial and governance structure.

Aside from lending money (debt), a Japanese bank can hold up to 5 percent of a firm's total stock; a group of related financial institutions can hold up to 40 percent. In many cases, main-bank relationships are part of a horizontal keiretsu, in which a group of firms are tied together by cross-shareholdings. Thus, firms in such a keiretsu develop interrelationships and are interdependent. A keiretsu firm usually owns less than 2 percent of any other member firm; however, each member firm typically has a stake of that size in every firm in the keiretsu. As a result, somewhere between 30 percent and 90 percent of a firm is owned by other members of the keiretsu. Thus, a keiretsu is a system of relationship investments.

As is the case in Germany, Canada, and the United States, Japan's corporate governance structure is changing. For example, because of their continuing development as economic organizations, the role of banks in the monitoring and control of managerial behaviour and firm outcomes is less significant than in the past.[136] The Asian economic crisis in the latter part of the 1990s made the governance problems in Japanese corporations transparent. The problems were readily evidenced in the large and once-powerful Mitsubishi kereitsu. Many of its core members lost substantial amounts of money in the late 1990s.[137] Toyota's board of directors ousted its president because he demanded changes in its governance system and argued against rescuing other firms in the Toyota kereitsu.[138]

Still another change in Japan's governance system has occurred. In past years, the market for corporate control was nonexistent. However, Cable & Wireless of Great Britain advanced the first hostile bid for another firm in 1999 for International Digital Communications. In 2000, another hostile bid was made by a Japanese investment firm to take over Shoei Co., a large real estate and electric parts firm. A 14 percent premium was offered, but Shoei's board quickly rejected it. The CEO of the investment company criticized the passivity of Japanese shareholders.[139]

## Global Corporate Governance

The 21st-century competitive landscape (see Chapters 1 and 6) and the global economy are fostering the creation of a relatively uniform governance structure that will be used by firms throughout the world.[140] As markets become more global and customer demands more similar, shareholders are becoming the focus of managers' efforts in an increasing number of companies. Investors are becoming more and more active throughout the world. Changes in governance are evident in many countries and are moving the governance models closer to the North American corporation. In turn, however, North American firms are becoming increasingly tied to financial institutions with higher debt levels and increased institutional investor activism. Thus, regardless of their national origin, the structures used to govern corporations will tend to become more similar than is the case today.

This is illustrated in the Strategic Focus about corporate governance reforms taking place in companies around the world. The Japanese model of corporate governance that has been followed by Korean chaebols, large conglomerate firms, is being questioned, and reforms in governance are expected. European countries such as France and Italy, which have bank-centred governance approaches, are moving to more shared ownership. In Italy and other Western European countries, much of this increased focus on equity markets is coming through privatization of large previously state-owned enterprises. The privatization process has also fostered much of the increases in equity in Russia and Eastern Europe as well. It is interesting to note that research has found that privatization has not led to decreases in employment as was previously feared by countries that had initiated the privatization process.[141] China is also undertaking reforms that have affected corporate governance. Although China has not truly privatized, except through the joint venture process, it has decentralized its system to provide much more local control.

## STRATEGIC FOCUS

### Reforms in International Corporate Governance

In both developed and developing economies, corporate governance is being reformed. In Canada, the Conference Board of Canada and the Toronto Stock Exchange's Committee on Corporate Governance in Canada have made several recommendations for reform. Some of these recommendations are board size suitable for accountability; strategic planning involvement; board constituted with majority of unrelated directors; internal controls and management information systems; satisfactory compensation to directors; and, non-CEO chair or lead director. Table 11.3 contains several more recommendations and the adoption rate by Canadian companies as of 1999.

For several decades, intellectuals and policymakers worried that the North American financial system was forcing businesses to pursue short-term profits at the expense of long-term investment. In fact, a national commission headed by Professor Michael Porter of Harvard Business School recommended significant changes to the U.S. approach to capitalism. Many looked to the Japanese and German systems and found that the capital was more "patient" in those economies. Therefore, it was suggested that the U.S. system of corporate governance become more relationship oriented, as was the case with the financial systems in Japan and Germany.

However, the financial systems across Asia, many of which are based on the Japanese-style approach, such as the Korean model, had serious difficulties in 1997 and into 1998. Many of the Asian and continental European economies are bank- and debt-based. A World Bank study found that total bank loans in the United States equal 50 percent of the nation's gross domestic product. This compares with 100 percent in Malaysia, 150 percent in Japan, and 170 percent in Germany. The bond market, on the other hand, totals 100 percent of annual U.S. gross domestic product, compared with 90 percent in Germany, 75 percent in Japan, 50 percent in Korea, and less than 10 percent in Thailand and Indonesia. Therefore, in most of Asia and a significant part of

*continued*

Europe, banks are at the centre of providing capital. Additionally, in many of these economies, banks can hold equity, unlike the U.S. economy, where the *Glass Stegall Act* prevents banks from having equity holdings. For this reason, the Germanic and Japanese approaches have been credited with providing patient and long term—oriented capital to corporations.

France, as well as Italy, has significant bank-oriented financial systems. France, for instance, has been undergoing gradual but significant changes as demands for increasing shareholder value have become more important. As in Italy, France's system has been based on cross-shareholdings and reciprocal board memberships. However, with the large numbers of mergers, privatizations, and restructurings taking place, shareholders are becoming more influential in the governance of large corporations. One active investor in France, G. Guy Wyser-Pratte, suggests, "France is a banana republic when it comes to corporate governance." It is difficult for shareholder power to prosper in a country such as France. The Paris Bourse lists only 681 stocks of French companies, compared with more than 2100 on the London Stock Exchange and more than 7700 on the New York and NASDAQ exchanges combined. Investor anger has been growing in France over the lack of information available on top executives' compensation. As well, a recent French report recommended that the positions of CEO and chairman of the board be held by different individuals. That report also recommended reducing the tenure of board members and disclosing their pay.

Italy's stock market is even smaller, compared to Germany, France, and Spain. Italy's system of corporate governance also includes significant amounts of cross-shareholdings and reciprocal board arrangements between and among companies.

In South Korea, changes went much further: Principles of corporate governance were adopted that "provide proper incentives for the board and management to pursue objectives that are in the interests of the company and the shareholders and facilitate effective monitoring, thereby encouraging firms to use resources more efficiently."

Of course, some systems of corporate governance are built to focus not solely on shareholder concerns. For instance, in the Netherlands and Germany, a two-tiered system of corporate governance is at work. German corporations have a supervisory board with half the members representing shareholders and the other half representing employees. Shareholders have the ultimate control over the supervisory board and thus have the ability to influence decisions. The chairman is one of the shareholder representatives and in cases where voting results in a deadlock, he or she can cast an additional vote to break the logjam. However, there have been some recent challenges to the two-tiered board system. The argument by corporate officials is that the constant search for social consensus among workers and managers has led to a compromise of Germany's competitive edge in world markets. This lack of competitiveness creates large levels of unemployment, not only in Germany but also in other countries such as France where corporate governance has not been incisive.

Board reforms have also been taking place in emerging economies such as Russia and China. In Russia, privatization of numerous banks, combined with broad licensing rules, has allowed the Russian bank industry to become 75 percent private. Furthermore, privatized firms have wrestled control from "red directors" (former communist managers who were previously managers of state-

*continued*

owned enterprises) as investment companies. Such concentrated ownership after the privatization process has allowed many Russian firms to be more rapidly revitalized than would have been the case under less diffused ownership.

Although there are significant differences between the Russian approach and the Chinese approach, China is adopting a corporate governance-restructuring scheme as well. The China approach has decentralized operations by giving local control to previously centralized state enterprises. This is a separation of ownership approach—one that requires accountability in terms of spending and debt payment by these local managers over financial resources. Improvements could be made by providing performance-based incentives for managers, better private financial institutions, and a stronger application of bankruptcy law for poor performance. These issues, as well as stronger private enterprises, would ensure more effective corporate governance.

Sources: C. P. Erlich & D. S. Kang, 1999, South Korea: Corporate governance reform in Korea: The remaining issues—Part I: *East Asian Executive Reports*, 21: 11–14; S. Iskander, 1999, Salary disclosure in France: Transparency or voyeurism? *Financial Times*, July 26, 11–12; R. M. Corbin, 1999, *Report on Corporate Governance*, 1999, *Five Years to the Dey*, Toronto Stock Exchange; "More consensus" in Germany, 1997, *Financial Times*, December 18, 11; Italian governance, 1997, *Financial Times*, December 15, 18; A. Murray, 1997, New economic models fail while America Inc. keeps rolling, *Wall Street Journal*, September 8, A1, A13; Comic opera: Italy's stock exchange, 1997, *The Economist*, August 30, 54–55; S. Douma, 1997, The two-tier system of corporate governance, Long Range Planning, 30 (4): 612–15; S. Li and T. Zhu, 1997, Put onus on managers in China, *Asian Wall Street Journal Weekly*, July 21, 12; A. Osterland, 1997, France is a banana republic: Corporate governance is changing in France … slowly, *Financial World*, July–August, 40–43; Co-termination, 1997, Industry Week, July 21, 54; A. Jack, 1997, New tricks for old dog, *Financial Times*, June 26, 29; J. S. Abarbanell and A. Meyendorff, 1997, Bank privatization in post-Communist Russia: The case of Zhilsotsbank, *Journal of Comparative Economics*, 25: 62–97; S. Liesman, 1997, Outsiders at Russia's Rao Gazpron vie for crucial first seat on firm's board, *Wall Street Journal*, June 25, A18.

## GOVERNANCE MECHANISMS AND ETHICAL BEHAVIOUR

In this chapter's final section, we discuss the need for governance mechanisms to support ethical behaviours. The governance mechanisms described in this chapter are designed to ensure that the agents of the firm's owners—that is, the corporation's top executives—make strategic decisions that best serve the interests of the entire group of stakeholders as described in Chapter 1. In Canada and the United States at least, shareholders are recognized as a company's most significant stakeholder. As such, the focus of governance mechanisms is on the control of managerial decisions to increase the probability that shareholders' interests will be served, but product market stakeholders (e.g., customers, suppliers, and host communities) and organizational stakeholders (e.g., managerial and nonmanagerial employees) are important as well.[142] In this regard, at least the minimal interests or needs of all stakeholders must be satisfied by outcomes achieved through the firm's actions. Without satisfaction of at least minimal interests, stakeholders will decide to withdraw their support or contribution to one firm and provide it to another (e.g., customers will purchase products from a supplier offering an acceptable substitute).

John Smale, an outside member of General Motors' board of directors, believes that all large capitalist enterprises must be concerned with goals in addition to serving shareholders. In Smale's opinion, "A corporation is a human, living enterprise. It's not just a bunch of assets. The obligation of management is to perpetuate the corporation, and that precedes their obligation to shareholders."[143] The argument, then, is that the firm's strategic competitiveness is enhanced when its governance mechanisms are designed and implemented in ways that take into consideration the interests of all stakeholders. Although subject to debate, some believe that ethically responsible companies design and use governance mechanisms that serve all stakeholders' interests. There is, however, a more critical relationship between ethical behaviour and corporate governance mechanisms.

Evidence demonstrates that all companies are vulnerable to a display of unethical behaviours by their employees, including, of course, top executives. For example, HFS acquired CUC International. Shortly after completing the transaction and attempting to merge the two businesses to create the newly named Cendant Corporation, significant accounting irregularities appeared in the figures provided by the former CUC executives. Investigations suggested fraud. When the accounting irregularities were announced, Cendant's stock price fell from over $47 per share to slightly more than $12 per share. The company had to restate its financial results, reducing profits by hundreds of millions of dollars. A class-action lawsuit filed by stockholders claimed negligence by Cendant's executives and board of directors. In late 1999, Cendant settled the suit for a record $4.2 billion.[144]

The decisions and actions of a corporation's board of directors can be an effective deterrent to unethical behaviours. In fact, some believe that the most effective boards participate actively in setting boundaries for business ethics and values. Once formulated, the board's expectations related to ethical decisions and actions by all of the firm's stakeholders must be communicated clearly to top executives and other managers in the firm. Moreover, these executives and managers should be made to understand that the board will hold them fully accountable for the development and support of an organizational culture that results in only ethical decisions and behaviours. As explained in Chapter 13, CEOs can be positive role models for ethical behaviour.

It is only when the proper controls of governance mechanisms are in place that strategies are formulated and implemented in ways that result in strategic competitiveness and above-average returns. As this chapter's discussion suggests, corporate governance mechanisms are a vital, yet imperfect part of firms' efforts to implement strategies successfully. A consultation paper titled *Standards of Sound Business and Financial Practices,* published by the Canada Deposit Insurance Corporation in August 2000 promotes these standards for member organizations in the financial services sector. The standards emphasize the need for "good corporate governance, effective strategic management, proactive risk assessment and an embedded control environment."[145] The next chapter discusses organizational structure and controls and how structures and controls that appropriately follow from the strategy being pursued may be a source of strategic competitiveness.

# SUMMARY

- Corporate governance is a relationship among stakeholders that is used to determine the firm's direction and control its performance. How firms monitor and control top-level managers' decisions and actions, as called for by governance mechanisms, affects the implementation of strategies. Effective governance that aligns managers' interests with shareholders' interests can result in a competitive advantage for the firm.

- In the modern corporation, there are four internal governance mechanisms—ownership concentration, board of directors, executive compensation, and the multidivisional structure—and one external governance mechanism—the market for corporate control.

- Ownership is separated from control in the modern corporation. Owners (principals) hire managers (agents) to make decisions that will maximize the value of their firm. As risk specialists, owners diversify their risk by investing in an array of corporations. As decisionmaking specialists, top-level managers are expected by owners to make decisions that will result in the earning of above-average returns. Thus, modern corporations are characterized by an agency relationship that is created when one party (the firm's owners) hires and pays another party (top-level managers) because of his or her decisionmaking skills.

- Separation of ownership and control creates an agency problem when an agent pursues goals that are in conflict with the principals' goals. Principals establish and use governance mechanisms to control this problem.

- The number of large-block shareholders and the percentage of shares they own define ownership concentration, an internal governance mechanism. With significant ownership percentages such as those held by large mutual funds and pension funds, institutional investors often are able to influence top-level managers' strategic decisions and actions. Thus, unlike diffuse ownership, which tends to bring about relatively weak monitoring and control of managerial decisions, concentrated ownership results in more active and effective monitoring of top-level managers. An increasingly powerful force in Canada and the United States, institutional owners are actively using their positions of concentrated ownership in individual companies to force managers and boards of directors

to make decisions that maximize a firm's value. These owners have caused executives in prominent companies to lose their jobs because of their failure to serve shareholders' interests effectively.

- In Canada, the United States, and the United Kingdom, the board of directors, composed of insiders, related outsiders, and outsiders, is a governance mechanism shareholders expect to represent their collective interests, especially because ownership is diffuse. The percentage of outside directors on most boards now exceeds the percentage of insider directors, which seems appropriate. These individuals are expected to be more independent of a firm's top-level managers than are those selected from inside the firm.

- A highly visible and often criticized governance mechanism is executive compensation. Through the use of salary, bonuses, and long-term incentives, the mechanism is intended to strengthen the alignment of managers' and shareholders' interests. A strong emphasis on executive incentives has widened the gap between the pay of the typical worker and CEOs. A firm's board of directors has the responsibility of determining the degree to which executive compensation is succeeding as a governance mechanism and to initiate all appropriate corrective actions when required.

- As an internal governance mechanism, the multidivisional (M-form) structure is intended to reduce managerial opportunism and align principals' and agents' interests as a result. The M-form makes it possible for the corporate office to monitor and control managerial decisions in the individual divisions in diversified firms. However, at the corporate level, the M-form may actually stimulate managerial opportunism, resulting in top-level executives overdiversifying.

- In general, evidence suggests that shareholders and board directors have become more vigilant in their control of managerial decisions. Nonetheless, these mechanisms are insufficient to govern the diversification of many large companies. As such, the market for corporate control is an important governance mechanism. Although it, too, is imperfect, the market for corporate control has been effective in causing corporations to downscope and reduce their degree of inefficient diversification.

- Corporate governance structures used in Germany and Japan differ from each other and from the one used in Canada and the United States. Historically, the governance structure in Canada and the United States has focused on maximizing shareholder value. In Germany, employees, as a stakeholder group, have a more prominent role in governance than is the case in Canada and the United States. Until recently, Japanese shareholders played virtually no role in the monitoring and control of top-level managers. However, these systems are becoming more similar as are many governance systems in both developed countries such as France and Italy and developing countries such as Russia and China.

- Effective governance mechanisms ensure that the interests of all stakeholders are served. Thus, long-term strategic success results when firms are governed in ways that permit at least minimal satisfaction of capital market stakeholders (e.g., shareholders), product market stakeholders (e.g., customers and suppliers), and organizational stakeholders (managerial and nonmanagerial employees). Moreover, effective governance causes the establishment and consistent use of ethical behaviour as the firm formulates and implements its strategies.

## REVIEW QUESTIONS

1. What is corporate governance? What factors account for the considerable amount of attention corporate governance receives from several parties, including shareholder activists, business press writers, and academic scholars? Why are governance mechanisms used to control managerial decisions?

2. What does it mean to say that ownership is separated from control in the modern corporation? What brought about this separation?

3. What is an agency relationship? What is managerial opportunism? What assumptions do owners of modern corporations make about managerial agents? What are the strategic implications of these assumptions?

4. How are the four internal governance mechanisms—ownership concentration, boards of directors, executive compensation, and the multidivisional (M-form) structure—used to align the interests of managerial agents with those of the firm's owners?

5. What trends exist in terms of executive compensation? What is the effect of increased use of long-term incentives on executives' strategic decisions?

6. What is the market for corporate control? What conditions generally cause this external governance mechanism to become active? How does this mechanism constrain top-level managers' decisions?

7. What is the nature of corporate governance mechanisms used in Germany and Japan?

8. How can corporate governance mechanisms foster ethical strategic decisions and behaviours on the part of managerial agents?

## DISCUSSION QUESTIONS

1. The roles and responsibilities of top-level managers and members of a corporation's board of directors are different. Traditionally, executives have been responsible for determining the firm's strategic direction and implementing strategies to achieve it, whereas the board has been responsible for monitoring and controlling managerial decisions and actions. Some argue that boards should become more involved with the formulation of a firm's strategies. In your opinion, how would the board's increased involvement in the selection of strategies affect a firm's strategic competitiveness? What evidence can you offer to support your position?

2. Do you believe that large Canadian firms have been overgoverned by some corporate governance mechanisms and undergoverned by others? Provide an example of a Canadian business firm to support your belief.

3. How can corporate governance mechanisms create conditions that allow top-level managers to develop a competitive advantage and focus on long-term performance? Search the Canadian business press to find an example of a firm in which this occurred and prepare a brief description.

4. Some believe that the market for corporate control is not an effective governance mechanism. If this is an accurate view, what factors might account for the ineffectiveness of this method of monitoring and controlling managerial decisions?

5. Assume that you overheard the following comments: "As a top-level manager, the only agency relationship I am concerned about is the one between me and the firm's owners. I think that it would be a waste of my time and energy to worry about any other agency relationship."

How would you respond to this person? Do you accept or reject this view? Be prepared to support your position.

## ETHICS QUESTIONS

1. As explained in this chapter, the use of corporate governance mechanisms should establish order between parties whose interests may be in conflict. Do firm owners have any ethical responsibilities to managers when using governance mechanisms to establish order? If so, what are they?

2. Is it ethical for a firm's owner to assume that agents (managers hired to make decisions that are in the owner's best interests) are averse to work and risk? Why or why not?

3. What are the responsibilities of the board of directors to stakeholders other than shareholders?

4. What ethical issues are involved with executive compensation? How can we determine if top-level executives are paid too much?

5. Is it ethical for firms involved in the market for corporate control to target companies performing at levels exceeding the industry average? Why or why not?

6. What ethical issues, if any, do top-level managers face when asking their firm to provide them with either a golden parachute or a golden goodbye?

7. How can governance mechanisms be designed to ensure against managerial opportunism, ineffectiveness, and unethical behaviours?

8. Is it ethical for shareholders to expect managers to be risk-takers when shareholders can diversify their risk by investing in a diversified portfolio of stocks but managers cannot diversify the risk to their personal wealth if their wealth (gained through stock options) is tied up in the related-diversified firm in which they work?

## INTERNET EXERCISE

Go to Ontario Municipal Employees Retirement System at:

**http://www.omers.com/**

To ensure an acceptable return on their investment, the major stockholders of public corporations are becoming increasingly involved in corporate governance issues. The Ontario Municipal Employees

Retirement System is one of the largest pension plans in Canada. It has 271 000 members and total net assets of $34.9 billion. It has a very diverse investment program in many companies worldwide and considers itself a long-term investor. Its primary purpose is to generate long-term shareholder value to comply with the OMERS pension promise. It has published OMERS Proxy Voting Guidelines to let boards of directors of companies in which it has invested know the expectations OMERS has for corporate governance. These guidelines are available at:

**http://www.omers.com/investments/pvg/pvg.pdf.**

## STRATEGIC SURFING

In the United States, Corporate Governance is a Web site dedicated solely to corporate governance issues. The site is extensive and contains information pertaining to a broad spectrum of corporate governance issues. Executive Paywatch is another site of interest to observers of corporate governance issues. This site is sponsored by the AFL-CIO and monitors the compensation packages of the CEOs of major American corporations.

**http://www.corpgov.net**
**http://www.aflcio.paywatch.org/ceopay**

## NOTES

1 R. D. Ward, 1997, *21st Century Corporate Board* (New York: John Wiley & Sons).

2 J. A. Byrne, R. Grover, & R. A. Melcher, 1997, The best and worst boards: Our special report on corporate governance, *BusinessWeek*, December 8, 91–98.

3 R. K. Mitchell, B. R. Agle, & D. J. Wood, 1997, Toward a theory of stakeholder identification and salience: Defining the principle of who and what really counts, *Academy of Management Review*, 22: 853–86.

4 J. H. Davis, F. D. Schoorman, & L. Donaldson, 1997, Toward a stewardship theory of management, *Academy of Management Review*, 22: 20–47.

5 M. M. Blair, 1999, For whom should corporations be run? An economic rationale for stakeholder management, *Long Range Planning*, 31: 195–200; O. E. Williamson, 1996, Economic organization: The case for candor, *Academy of Management Review*, 21: 48–57.

6 J. Magretta, 1998, Governing the family-owned enterprise: An interview with Finland's Krister Ahlstrom, *Harvard Business Review*, 76 (1): 112–23.

7 E. F. Fama & M. C. Jensen, 1983, Separation of ownership and control, *Journal of Law and Economics,* 26: 301–25.

8 Ward, *21st Century Corporate Board.*

9 C. Arnolod & K. Breen, 1997, Investor activism goes worldwide, *Corporate Board,* 18 (2): 7–12.

10 M. Kroll, P. Wright, L. Toombs, & H. Leavell, 1997, Form of control: A critical determinant of acquisition performance and CEO rewards, *Strategic Management Journal,* 18: 85–96; J. K. Seward & J. P. Walsh, 1996, The governance and control of voluntary corporate spinoffs, *Strategic Management Journal,* 17: 25–39.

11 J. D. Westphal & E. J. Zajac, 1997, Defections from the inner circle: Social exchange, reciprocity and diffusion of board independence in U.S. corporations, *Administrative Science Quarterly,* 42: 161–212; Ward, *21st Century Corporate Board.*

12 J. Charkham, 1994, *Keeping Good Company: A Study of Corporate Governance in Five Countries* (New York: Oxford University Press), 1.

13 A. Cadbury, 1999, The future of governance: The rules of the game, *Journal of General Management,* 24: 1–14.

14 Cadbury Committee, 1992, *Report of the Cadbury Committee on the Financial Aspects of Corporate Governance* (London: Gee).

15 C. K. Prahalad & J. P. Oosterveld, 1999, Transforming internal governance: The challenge for multinationals, *Sloan Management Review,* 40 (3): 31–39.

16 M. A. Hitt, R. A. Harrison, & R. D. Ireland, 2001, *Creating Value through Mergers and Acquisitions: A Complete Guides to Successful M&As* (New York: Oxford University Press); M. A. Hitt, R. E. Hoskisson, R. A. Johnson, & D. D. Moesel, 1996, The market for corporate control and firm innovation, *Academy of Management Journal,* 39: 1084–1119; J. P. Walsh & R. Kosnik, 1993, Corporate raiders and their disciplinary role in the market for corporate control, *Academy of Management Journal,* 36: 671–700.

17 Davis, Schoorman, & Donaldson, Toward a stewardship theory of management, 20–47.

18 C. Sundaramurthy, J. M. Mahoney, & J. T. Mahoney, 1997, Board structure, antitakeover provisions, and stockholder wealth, *Strategic Management Journal,* 18: 231–46; K. J. Rediker & A. Seth, 1995, Boards of directors and substitution effects of alternative governance mechanisms, *Strategic Management Journal,* 16: 85–99.

19 R. E. Hoskisson, M. A. Hitt, R. A. Johnson, & W. Grossman, 2000, Conflicting voices: The effects of ownership heterogeneity and internal governance on corporate strategy, Paper presented at the Strategic Management Society, Vancouver, B.C.

20 G. E. Davis & T. A. Thompson, 1994, A social movement perspective on corporate control, *Administrative Science Quarterly,* 39: 141–73.

21 M. A. Eisenberg, 1989, The structure of corporation law, Columbia Law Review 89, (7): 1461, as cited in R. A. G. Monks & N. Minow, 1995, *Corporate Governance* (Cambridge, MA: Blackwell Business), 7.

22 R. M. Wiseman & L. R. Gomez-Mejia, 1999, A behavioral agency model of managerial risk taking, *Academy of Management Review,* 23: 133–53.

23 E. E. Fama, 1980, Agency problems and the theory of the firm, *Journal of Political Economy,* 88: 288–307.

24 M. Jensen & W. Meckling, 1976, Theory of the firm: Managerial behavior, agency costs, and ownership structure, *Journal of Financial Economics,* 11: 305–60.

25 H. C. Tosi, J. Katz, & L. R. Gomez-Mejia, 1997, Disaggregating the agency contract: The effects of monitoring, incentive alignment, and term in office on agent decision making, *Academy of Management Journal,* 40: 584–602; P. C. Godfrey & C. W. L. Hill, 1995, The problem of unobservables in strategic management research, *Strategic Management Journal,* 16: 519–33.

26 P. Wright & S. P. Ferris, 1997, Agency conflict and corporate strategy: The effect of divestment on corporate strategy, *Strategic Management Journal,* 18: 77–83.

27 T. M. Welbourne & L. R. Gomez Meiia, 1995, Gainsharing: A critical review and a future research agenda, *Journal of Management,* 21: 577.

28 P. Wright, S. P. Ferris, A. Sarin, & V. Awasthi, 1996, Impact of corporate insider, blockholder, and institutional equity ownership on firm risk taking, *Academy of Management Journal,* 39: 441–63.

29 P. B. Firstenberg & B. G. Malkiel, 1994, The twenty-first century boardroom: Who will be in charge? *Sloan Management Review,* Fall, 27–35, as cited in C. M. Daily, 1996, Governance patterns in bankruptcy reorganizations, *Strategic Management Journal,* 17: 355–75.

30 O. E. Williamson, 1996, *The Mechanisms of Governance* (New York: Oxford University Press), 6; O. E. Williamson, 1993, Opportunism and its critics, *Managerial and Decision Economics,* 14: 97–107.

31 S. Ghoshal & P. Moran, 1996, Bad for practice: A critique of the transaction cost theory, *Academy of Management Review,* 21: 13–47.

32 Williamson, Economic organization, 50.

33 Godfrey & Hill, The problem of unobservables in strategic management research, 519–33.

34 Y. Amihud & B. Lev, 1981, Risk reduction as a managerial motive for conglomerate mergers, *Bell Journal of Economics,* 12: 605–17.

35 R. E. Hoskisson & T. A. Turk, 1990, Corporate restructuring: Governance and control limits of the internal market, *Academy of Management Review,* 15: 459–77.

36 S. Finkelstein & D. C. Hambrick, 1989, Chief executive compensation: A study of the intersection of markets and political processes, *Strategic Management Journal,* 16: 221–39; H. C. Tosi & L. R. Gomez-Mejia, 1989, The decoupling of CEO pay and performance: An agency theory perspective, *Administrative Science Quarterly,* 34: 169–89.

37 Hoskisson & Turk, 1990, Corporate restructuring, 459–77.

38 M. S. Jensen, 1986, Agency costs of free cash flow, corporate finance, and takeovers, *American Economic Review,* 76: 323–29.

39 C. W. L. Hill & S. A. Snell, 1988, External control, corporate strategy, and firm performance in research intensive industries, *Strategic Management Journal,* 9: 577–90.

40 A. Sharma, 1997, Professional as agent: Knowledge asymmetry in agency exchange, *Academy of Management Review,* 22: 758–98.

41 R. Comment & G. Jarrell, 1995, Corporate focus and stock returns, *Journal of Financial Economics,* 37: 67–87.

42 A. Shleifer & R. W. Vishny, 1986, Large shareholders and corporate control, *Journal of Political Economy,* 94: 461–88.

43 J. A. Byrne, 1997, The CEO and the board, *BusinessWeek,* September 15, 107–16.

44 R. E. Hoskisson, R. A. Johnson, & D. D. Moesel, 1994, Corporate divestiture intensity in restructuring firms: Effects of governance, strategy, and performance, *Academy of Management Journal,* 37: 1207–51.

45 A. Berle & G. Means, 1932, *The Modern Corporation and Private Property* (New York: Macmillan).

46 M. P. Smith, 1996, Shareholder activism by institutional investors: Evidence from CalPERS, *Journal of Finance,* 51: 227–52.

47 J. D. Bogert, 1996, Explaining variance in the performance of long-term corporate blockholders, *Strategic Management Journal,* 17: 243–49.

48 M. Useem, 1998, Corporate leadership in a globalizing equity market, *Academy of Management Executive,* XII.

49 C. M. Daily, 1996, Governance patterns in bankruptcy reorganizations, *Strategic Management Journal,* 17: 355–75.

50 Useem, Corporate leadership in a globalizing equity market; R. E. Hoskisson & M. A. Hitt, 1994, *Downscoping: How to Tame the Diversified Firm* (New York: Oxford University Press).

51 Byrne, The CEO and the board, 109.

52 E. Schine, 1997, CalPERS' grand inquisitor, *BusinessWeek,* February 24, 120.

53 CalPERS highlights retailers in its list of underperformers, 1996, *Wall Street Journal,* February 7, Cl8.

54 B. Rehfeld, 1997, Low-cal CalPERS, *Institutional Investor,* March 31, 4–12; Smith, Shareholder activism.

55 K. Howlett, 2001, Teachers oppose Royal's stock bylaw, *Globe & Mail,* February 20, B3.

56 P. J. Dey, 1994, *Where Were the Directors,* Toronto: Toronto Stock Exchange, 12.

57 R. M. Corbin, 1999, *Report on Corporate Governance, 1999, Five Years to the Dey,* Toronto Stock Exchange, 3.

58 M. J. Roe, 1993, Mutual funds in the boardroom, *Journal of Applied Corporate Finance,* 5, 4: 56–61.

59 Byrne, The CEO and the board, 114.

60 P. J. Dey, 1994, Where Were the Directors, 32–33.

61 J. S. Lublin, 1997, More CEOs decide: No time for seats, *Wall Street Journal,* October 28, A2.

62 J. Gray, 2000, The Golden Parachute Club, *Canadian Business,* June 12, http://www.canadian-business.com/magazine_items/2000/june12_00_parachutes.shtml; *Bloomberg Business News,* 1996, More companies add severance package for execs, survey says, *Dallas Morning News,* July 6, F3.

63 Sundaramurthy, Mahoney, & Mahoney, Board structure, antitakeover provisions, and stockholder wealth, 231–46; C. Sundaramurthy, 1996, Corporate governance within the context of antitakeover provisions, *Strategic Management Journal,* 17: 377–94.

64 R. Grover & E. Schine, 1997, At Disney, Grumpy isn't just a dwarf, *BusinessWeek,* February 24, 38.

65 B. S. Black, 1992, Agents watching agents: The promise of institutional investors voice, *UCLA Law Review,* 39: 871–93.

66 C. Sandaramurthy & D. W. Lyon, 1998, Shareholder governance proposals and conflict of interests between inside and outside shareholders, *Journal of Managerial Issues,* 10: 30–44.

67 Rediker & Seth, Boards of directors, 85.

68 J. K. Seward & J. P Walsh, 1996, The governance and control of voluntary corporate spinoffs, *Strategic Management Journal,* 17: 25–39.

69 P. Mallete & R. L. Hogler, 1995, Board composition, stock ownership, and the exemption of directors from liability, *Journal of Management,* 21: 861–78.

70 D. P. Forbes & F. J. Milliken, 1999, Cognition and corporate governance: Understanding boards of direc-

tors as strategic decision-making groups, *Academy of Management Review*, 24: 489–505.

71  B. D. Baysinger & R. E. Hoskisson, 1990, The composition of boards of directors and strategic control: Effects on corporate strategy, *Academy of Management Review*, 15: 72–87.

72  E. J. Zajac & J. D. Westphal, 1996, Director reputation, CEO-board power, and the dynamics of board interlocks, *Administrative Science Quarterly*, 41: 507–29.

73  J. D. Westphal & E. J. Zajac, 1995, Who shall govern? CEO/board power, demographic similarity, and new director selection, *Administrative Science Quarterly*, 40: 60–83.

74  R. P. Beatty & E. J. Zajac, 1994, Managerial incentives, monitoring, and risk bearing: A study of executive compensation, ownership, and board structure in initial public offerings, *Administrative Science Quarterly*, 39: 313–35.

75  A. Bryant, 1997, CalPERS draws a blueprint for its concept of an ideal board, *New York Times*, June 17, C1.

76  I. M. Millstein, 1997, Red herring over independent boards, *New York Times*, April 6, F10; W. Q. Judge, Jr., & G. H. Dobbins, 1995, Antecedents and effects of outside directors' awareness of CEO decision style, *Journal of Management*, 21: 43–64.

77  R. M. Corbin, 1999, *Report on Corporate Governance, 1999. Five Years to the Dey*, Toronto Stock Exchange: 35; I. E. Kesner, 1988, Director characteristics in committee membership: An investigation of type, occupation, tenure and gender, *Academy of Management Journal*, 31: 66–84.

78  R. M. Corbin, 1999, *Report on Corporate Governance*, 35.

79  T. McNulty & A Pettigrew, 1999, Strategists on the board, *Organization Studies*, 20: 47–74.

80  S. Zahra, 1998, Governance, ownership and corporate entrepreneurship among the *Fortune* 500: The moderating impact of industry technological opportunity, *Academy of Management Journal*, 41.

81  J. A. Conger, D. Finegold, & E. E. Lawler III, 1998, Appraising boardroom performance, *Harvard Business Review*, 76, (1): 136–48; J. A. Byrne & L. Brown, 1997, Directors in the hot seat, *BusinessWeek*, December 8, 100–04.

82  H. Kaback, 1996, A director's guide to board behavior, *Wall Street Journal*, April 1, A14.

83  J. A. Byrne, 1997, Putting more stock in good governance, *BusinessWeek*, September 15, 116; A. Bianco & J. A. Byrne, 1997, The rush to quality on corporate boards, *BusinessWeek*, March 3, 34–35.

84  C. A. Simmers, 2000, Executive/board politics in strategic decision making, *Journal of Business and Economic Studies*, 4: 37–56.

85  W. Ocasio, 1999, Institutionalized action and corporate governance, *Administrative Science Quarterly*, 44: 384–416.

86  S. Rosenstein & J. G. Wyatt, 1997, Inside directors, board effectiveness, and shareholder wealth, *Journal of Financial Economics*, 44: 229–50.

87  R. M. Corbin, 1999, *Report on Corporate Governance, 1999. Five Years to the Dey*, Toronto Stock Exchange, 3.

88  Catalystwomen.org, 2000, 1998 Catalyst Census of Women Board Directors of Canada, *Catalystwomen.org* home page, http://catalystwomen.org/research/research34.html (Retrieved November 12); E. Cetera, 1997, *BusinessWeek*, October 13, 44.

89  A boardroom gender gap, *BusinessWeek*, November 24, 1997, 32.

90  G.Dixon, 2001, Nortel board of directors highest paid in Canada, survey says, *Globe & Mail*, February 19, B1.

91  D. C. Hambrick & S. Finkelstein, 1995, The effects of ownership structure on conditions at the top: The case of CEO pay raises, *Strategic Management Journal*, 16: 175.

92  L. R. Gomez-Mejia & R. Wiseman, 1997, Reframing executive compensation: An assessment and review, *Journal of Management*, 23: 291–374.

93  S. Finkelstein & B. K. Boyd, 1998, How much does the CEO matter?: The role of managerial discretion in the setting of CEO compensation, *Academy of Management Journal*, 41: 179–99; I. Kristol, 1996, What is a CEO worth? *Wall Street Journal*, June 5, A14.

94  S. Finkelstein & B. K. Boyd, 1998, How much does the CEO matter?, 179–99.

95  W. G. Sanders & M. A. Carpenter, 1998, Internationalization and firm governance: The roles of CEO compensation, top team composition and board structure, *Academy of Management Journal*, 41: 158–78.

96  J. D. Westphal & E. J. Zajac, 1999, The symbolic management of stockholders: Corporate governance reform and shareholder reactions, *Administrative Science Quarterly*, 43: 127–53.

97  K. Roth & S. O'Donnell, 1996, Foreign subsidiary compensation: An agency theory perspective, *Academy of Management Journal*, 39: 678–703.

98  S. Fung, 1999, How should we pay them? *Across the Board*, June: 37–41.

99  C. Peck, H. M. Silvert, & K. Worrell, 1999, Top executive compensation: Canada, France, the United Kingdom, and the United States, *Chief Executive Digest*, 3: 27–29.

100  R. E. Hoskisson, M. A. Hitt, & C. W. L. Hill, 1993, Managerial incentives and investment in R&D in large multiproduct firms, *Organization Science*, 4: 325–41.

101  K. A. Merchant, 1989, *Rewarding Results: Motivating Profit Center* Managers (Cambridge, MA: Harvard Business School Press); J. Eaton & H. Rosen, 1983, Agency, delayed compensation, and the structure of executive remuneration, *Journal of Finance,* 38: 1489–1505.

102  W. M. Bulkeley, 1999, Software firm executives ordered to return million in stock options, *Wall Street Journal Interactive,* November 10, www.interactive.wsj.com/articles; J. Reingold & R. Grover, 1999, Executive pay, *BusinessWeek,* April 19, 72–118.

103  C. G. Holderness, R. S. Kroszner, & D. P. Sheehan, 1999, Were the good old days that good? Changes in managerial stock ownership since the Great Depression, *Journal of Finance,* 54: 435–69.

104  J. Dahya, A. A. Lonie, & D. A. Power, 1998, Ownership structure, firm performance and top executive change: An analysis of UK firms, *Journal of Business Finance and Accounting,* 25: 1089–1118.

105  C. Duff, 1996, Top executives ponder high pay, decide they're worth every cent, *Wall Street Journal,* May 15, Bl.

106  Kristol, What is a CEO worth?, A14.

107  L. Uchitelle, 1996, Performance pay made 1995 bonus year for executives, *Houston Chronicle,* March 30, C3.

108  D. Machan, 1996, The last article you will ever have to read on executive pay? No way! *Forbes,* May 20, 176–234.

109  J. Reingold, 1997, The folly of jumbo stock options, *BusinessWeek,* December 22, 36–37.

110  O. E. Williamson, 1985, *The Economic Institutions of Capitalism: Firms, Markets and Relational Contracting* (New York: Macmillan Free Press).

111  B. W. Keats & M. A. Hitt, 1988, A causal model of linkages among environmental dimensions, macro organizational characteristics, and performance, *Academy of Management Journal,* 31: 570–98.

112  O. E. Williamson, 1994, Strategizing, economizing, and economic organization, in R. P. Rumelt, D. E. Schendel, & D. J. Teece (eds.), *Fundamental Issues in Strategy* (Cambridge, MA: Harvard Business School Press), 380.

113  Hoskisson & Turk, Corporate restructuring: Governance and control limits of the internal market.

114  M. A. Hitt, R. E. Hoskisson, & R. D. Ireland, 1990, Mergers and acquisitions and managerial commitment to innovation in M-form firms, *Strategic Management Journal,* 11 (Special Summer Issue): 29–47.

115  Hitt, Hoskisson, Johnson, & Moesel, The market for corporate control and firm innovation; Walsh & Kosnik, Corporate raiders.

116  Mallette & Hogier, Board composition, 864.

117  Hitt, Harrison, & Ireland, *Creating Value through Mergers and Acquisitions.*

118  K. Leger, 2000, BCE trims offer for troubled Teleglobe: Monty defends offer, *National Post,* June 20, C5.

119  Hechinger & J. Pereira, 2000, Socially conscious investors fear Ben and Jerry's could lose its flavor, *Wall Street Journal Interactive,* February 6, www.interactive.wsj.com/articles.

120  C. Daniel, J. M. Brown, & V. Skold, 2000, ESAT: Board supports $2.4bn BT bid, *www.ft.com,* February 3, www.ft.com/nearchive.

121  S. Voyle, 2000, M&S beats of Green threat, *www.ft.com,* February 17, www.ft.com/nbearchive.

122  Sundaramurthy, Mahoney, & Mahoney, Board structure, antitakeover provisions, and stockholder wealth.

123  R. A. Johnson, R. E. Hoskisson, & M. A. Hitt, 2000, *The effects of environmental uncertainty on the mode of corporate restructuring,* Working Paper, University of Missouri.

124  B. Marotte, 2000, Profile: Yves Michaud: Bank basher with a difference, *Southam News,* February 21, 1997, http://www.ottawacitizen.com/business/970221/791773.html (Retrieved November 14, 2000); OMERS, 2000, *OMERS Proxy Voting Guidelines,* http://www.omers.com/investments/pvg/pvg.pdf (Retrieved November 14); J. A. Byrne, 1999, Poison pills: Let shareholders decide, *BusinessWeek,* May 17, 104.

125  T. Carlisle, 2000, Canadian oil firm sets defense against Occidental's takeover bid, *Wall Street Journal Interactive,* February 6, www.interactive.wsj.com/articles.

126  Walsh & Kosnik, Corporate raiders.

127  S. Johnston, 1995, Managerial dominance of Japan's major corporations, *Journal of Management,* 21: 191–209.

128  E. Ramstad & J. G. Auerback, 1998, Compaq buys Digital, an unthinkable event just a few years ago, *Wall Street Journal,* January 28, A1, A14.

129  Useem, Corporate leadership in a globalizing equity market.

130  Our discussion of corporate governance structures in Germany and Japan is drawn from Monks & Minow, *Corporate Governance,* 271–99; Charkham, *Keeping Good Company,* 6–118.

131  Brown & Brown, 1999, *Who Does What?*; H. Kim & R. E. Hoskisson, 1996, Japanese governance systems: A critical review, in B. Prasad (ed.), *Advances in International Comparative Management* (Greenwich, CT: JAI Press), 165–89.

132  S. Douma, 1997, The two-tier system of corporate governance, *Long Range Planning,* 30, (4): 612–15.

133  A. Osterland, 1997, France is a banana republic; Corporate governance is changing in France … slowly, *Financial World,* July–August, 40–43; B.

Riley, 1996, French leave for shareholders, *Financial Times,* June 23.

134 J. Chang, 2000, BASF lists shares on NYSE; record earnings are expected, *Chemical Market Reporter,* June 12: 1, 25; Shake it up, 1997, *Wall Street Journal,* July 15, A18; G. Steinmetz, 1996, Satisfying shareholders is a hot new concept at some German firms, *Wall Street Journal,* March 6, A1, A6.

135 Charkham, *Keeping Good Company,* 70.

136 J. Fiorillo, 2000, While Tokyo's commitment to reform waivers, *Wall Street Journal Interactive,* January 12, www.interactive.wsj.com/articles.

137 B. Bremner, E. Thornton, & I. M. Kunii, 1999, Fall of a Keiretsu, *BusinessWeek,* March 15, 87–92.

138 E. Thornton, 1999, Mystery at the top, *BusinessWeek,* April 26, 52.

139 P. Landers, 2000, Hostile bid for Tokyo's Shoei marks a milestone for Japan, *Wall Street Journal Interactive,* February 6, www.interactive.wsj.com/articles; M. Almieda, 2000, Japanese hostile-takeover bid marks a departure from corporate model, *Wall Street Journal Interactive,* February 6, www.interactive.wsj.com/articles.

140 J. B. White, 2000, The company we'll keep, *Wall Street Journal Interactive,* January 17, www.interactive.wsj.com/articles.

141 W. L. Megginson, R. C. Nash, & M. van Randenborgh, 1994, The financial and operating performance of newly privatized firms: An international empirical analysis, *Journal of Finance,* 49: 403–52.

142 E. Freeman & J. Liedtka, 1997, Stakeholder capitalism and the value chain, *European Management Journal,* 15 (3): 286–95.

143 A. Taylor, III, 1996, GM: Why they might break up America's biggest company, *Fortune,* April 29, 84.

144 Hitt, Harrison, & Ireland, 1999, Creating value through mergers and acquisitions; Cendant reaches preliminary agreement to settle common stock securities class action for $2.83 billion, 1999, *Cendant Press Release,* December 7.

145 W. A. Bradshaw, 2001, eyes wide SHUT: Must directors be the last to know when something is really going wrong in an organization? *CAmagazine,* January/February: 24.

# Chapter Twelve

## Organizational Structure and Controls

## LEARNING OBJECTIVES

*After reading this chapter, you should be able to:*

1. Explain the importance of integrating strategy implementation and strategy formulation.
2. Describe the dominant path of evolution from strategy to structure to strategy again.
3. Identify and describe the organizational structures used to implement different business-level strategies.
4. Discuss organizational structures used to implement different corporate-level strategies.
5. Identify and distinguish among the organizational structures used to implement three international strategies.
6. Describe organizational structures used to implement cooperative strategies.

## The New Structure of Microsoft

Although Microsoft has $257 000 of income per employee, versus the average of $17 000 for the Standard & Poor 500 stock index, the company's top executives are restructuring the firm in a way that will barely resemble the one that got them to that position. Microsoft had its largest market capitalization, $414 billion, in 1999 and has had a revenue growth of 30 percent annually. Why, then, does the firm feel that it must do something different to top this amazing performance for a 24-year-old company? In fact, Bill Gates is taking over as the chief software architect and stepping down as the CEO, and Steve Ballmer is taking over the top position.

In explaining why Microsoft is changing its leadership and structural arrangements, Bill Gates simply said, "The Internet has changed everything. In order to respond to these changes, Microsoft needs to give people the power to do anything they want, anywhere they want and on any device." Accordingly, the new vision, "Microsoft Vision 2.0," is directed at giving Microsoft programmers freedom to develop programs that do not revolve around Windows software, and for Microsoft, that is a significant change. For example, although Microsoft lost to AT&T in the bid for MediaOne Group, a large cable TV operation, it did receive a nonexclusive contract with MediaOne to provide set-top software for the interactive boxes that will facilitate using the Web through the home cable television platform, whereby consumers will also be able to hook up their PCs at lightning-fast speeds.

This Microsoft vision includes a new organizational structure that divides the company's product development into six different divisions. Two groups will target corporate leaders and knowledge workers. Two others emphasize home PC buyers and those who shop for computer and video games at stores. Another group is concerned with software developers. Finally, the last group is aimed at Web surfers and those who shop on the Web.

In the previous structure, products were split by technology, one focusing on Windows application software (such as Microsoft Word and associated software

http://www.microsoft.com
http://www.gm.com

products) and the other on operating systems. The operating systems division focused on a range of systems, from Windows NT down to the stripped-down Win CE for handheld consumer devices. Accordingly, there was no distinction based on customers. Previously, this division had focused on technology for technology's sake and not on the basis of what consumers wanted. Thus, under the new structural arrangement, there will be fewer arcane technological features with the operating systems so that even less sophisticated consumers will obtain what they need and desire, without confusing them unnecessarily about technological aspects.

Previously, the power structure was such that Gates and Microsoft President Steven A. Ballmer made the division heads come to them for almost all decisions. With decisions large and small being funnelled through this top pair, there was a decisionmaking bottleneck. Thus, the structure was functionally oriented (focused on technology) and centralized. With 30 000 employees, 183 different products, and at least 5 layers of management and staffers, there were significant complaints about bureaucratic red tape. Decisionmaking was very slow, and many key employees were leaving because their ideas were not being heard, or there was little opportunity to develop the ideas because of the centralized decisionmaking. The new structure is closer to the multidivisional structure adoption that often follows increased product diversification.

Although the talent drain is one problem that Microsoft's restructuring is intended to slow down through more divisional independence and decentralization, the loss of key employees likely will continue to be a competitive challenge. The hope is that the new structure will give the company an opportunity for fresh ideas to take hold and develop. Along these lines, Microsoft has been considering offering a "tracking stock" (issues of stock focused on specific company assets) that would give its Internet properties a focus for investors. It would allow investors to separate Internet stock valuations and protect Microsoft's cash cow, the Windows software business, from wild price swings, because of the focus on the Internet. Furthermore, a tracking stock would enable business-level managers to cash in on their entrepreneurial ideas. General Motors has had a tracking stock for Hughes that has risen much more rapidly than shares of General Motor's common stock, because of the DirectTV assets targeted by the tracking stock. Thus, the tracking stock allows better market value adjustment, given information on the type of asset, and provides an incentive for up-and-coming creative management talent to stay with Microsoft.

Whether such a structural change will work and whether Gates and Ballmer will be able to give up control are questions that will be tested over time. These two executives are used to delving into every decision, but that approach has slowed decisionmaking. Another potential pitfall is that the different product groups might undertake conflicting strategies now that they are ostensibly independent. However, if the change helps Microsoft to stay focused on its customers, the company is likely to increase its already outstanding performance.

Sources: *Microsoft home page,* 2000, www.microsoft.com (Retrieved March 1); D.J. Greene, 2000, A chat with the new guy in product development, *BusinessWeek,* January 31, 43; D. Bank, 1999, Microsoft will split into five divisions that deal with customers and rivals, *Wall Street Journal Interactive Edition,* www.wsj.com (Retrieved March 30); P. Gillin, 1999, Microsoft's Ballmer details reorg, *Computerworld,* April 5, 12; M. Moeller, S. Hamm, and T.J. Mullaney, 1999, Remaking Microsoft, *BusinessWeek,* May 17, 106–14; M. Moeller and K. Rebello, 1999, Visionary-in-chief: A talk with Chairman Bill Gates on the world beyond Windows, *BusinessWeek,* May 17, 114–16; E. Nee, 1999, Microsoft gets ready for a new game, *Fortune,* April 26, 107–12.

In the previous chapter, we described mechanisms companies use to govern their operations and to align various parties' interests, especially the interests of top-level executives, with those of the firm's owners. Governance mechanisms can influence a company's ability to implement formulated strategies successfully and thereby facilitate competitive advantage.[1]

In this chapter, our focus is on the organizational structures and controls used to implement the strategies discussed previously (e.g., business-level, Chapter 5; corporate-level, Chapter 7; international, Chapter 9; and cooperative, Chapter 10). Moreover, as the discussion about actions taken at Microsoft suggests, the proper use of an organizational structure and its accompanying integrating mechanisms and controls can contribute to the firm's strategic competitiveness.[2] In fact, the most productive global competitors are those with effective product innovation skills and an organizational structure in place that facilitates successful and timely applications of internal capabilities and core competencies.[3] Thus, organizational structure influences managerial work and the decisions made by top-level managers.[4]

Organizational structure alone, however, does not create a competitive advantage;[5] rather, a competitive advantage is created when there is a proper match between strategy and structure. For example, it may be that what makes 3M's competitive advantage somewhat sustainable "… is its unique blend of practices, values, autonomous structures, funding processes, rewards, and selection and development of product champions."[6] Similarly, the Acer Group, manufacturer of Acer personal computers, is known as an innovative competitor. Some analysts believe that Acer's unique organizational structure (which the CEO labels "global brand, local touch") contributes significantly to the firm's strategic competitiveness.[7] On the other hand, ineffective strategy/structure matches may result in strategic rigidity and failure given the complexity and need for rapid changes in the new competitive landscape.[8] Thus, strategic leaders (see Chapter 13) seek to develop an organizational structure and accompanying controls that are superior to those of their competitors.[9] Using competitively superior structures and controls explains in part why some firms survive and succeed while others do not.[10] Bill Gates and Steve Ballmer, the executives at Microsoft who have implemented the new structure outlined in the Opening Case, can expect that the organizational structure will contribute to the firm's future success. As with the other parts of the strategic management process, top-level managers bear the final responsibility to make choices about organizational structures that will enhance firm performance.[11] Following its acquisition of Digital Equipment Corporation (DEC), Compaq Computer Corporation executives, for example, must make structural decisions that will facilitate a successful integration of DEC's businesses into their own. Following its acquisition of Digital Equipment Corporation (DEC), Compaq Computer Corporation executives, for example, did not make good structural decisions, and a successful integration of DEC's businesses into their own continues to cause problems. When Vivendi acquired the Canadian firm Seagram in the summer of 2000, both companies' share prices fell sharply; a trend that analysts attributed in part to organizational structure decisions to shed traditional assets such as beverages.[12]

Selecting the organizational structure and controls that result in effective implementation of chosen strategies is a fundamental challenge for managers, especially top-level managers. A key reason is that in the global economy, firms must be flexible, innovative, and creative to exploit their core competencies in the pursuit of marketplace opportunities.[13] Executives also require a certain degree of stability in their structures so that day-to-day tasks can be completed efficiently. Accessible and reliable information is required for executives to reach decisions regarding the selection of a structure that can provide the desired levels of flexibility and stability. By helping executives improve their decisionmaking, useful information contributes to the formation and use of effective structures and controls.[14]

This chapter first describes the pattern of growth and accompanying changes in an organizational structure experienced by strategically competitive firms. For example, the success of Microsoft mentioned in the Opening Case necessitated the subsequent change in structural arrangement. The chapter's second major section discusses organizational structures and controls that are used to implement different business-level strategies. The dominant structures and control characteristics that contribute to the effective implementation of each of the business-level strategies described in Chapter 5 are explained in this part of the chapter.

The implementation of corporate-level strategy is then described, with the transition from the functional to the multidivisional structure highlighted. This major structural innovation took place in several firms during the 1920s, including DuPont. In fact, noted business historian Alfred Chandler cites DuPont as the innovator in both the strategy of diversification and the multidivisional structure.[15] Specific variations of the multidivisional structure are discussed in terms of their relationship with effective implementation of related and unrelated diversification strategies.

Because of the increasing globalization of many industries, the number of firms implementing international strategies continues to grow; the trend toward globalization is significant and pervasive.[16] For example, Quebec-based Naya, a bottler of mineral water, was recently purchased by French food group Groupe Danone, as part of a global strategy that includes a related acquisition in Turkey and a partnership with an Italian firm to market in Poland.[17]

To cope successfully with the strategic challenges associated with discontinuous changes, the firm must develop and use organizational structures that facilitate meaningful conversations among all stakeholders regarding opportunities and threats facing the company at different points in time.[18] In the chapter's final two sections, we discuss the use of organizational structures to implement cooperative strategies and several issues concerning organizational forms of interest to those responsible for using a firm's strategic management process effectively.

## EVOLUTIONARY PATTERNS OF STRATEGY AND ORGANIZATIONAL STRUCTURE

All firms require some form of organizational structure to implement their strategies. In this section, we describe how organizational structures have evolved in response to managerial and organizational needs. Principally, structures are changed when they no longer provide the coordination, control, and direction managers and organizations require to implement strategies successfully.[19] The ineffectiveness of a structure typically results from increases in a firm's revenues and levels of diversification. In particular, the formulation of strategies involving greater levels of diversification (see Chapter 7) demands structural change to match the strategy. Some structures become elaborate, and others become focused on financial rather than strategic control.

**Organizational structure** is a firm's formal role configuration, procedures, governance and control mechanisms, and authority and decisionmaking processes.

**Organizational structure** is a firm's formal role configuration, governance and control mechanisms, and authority and decisionmaking processes.[20] Influenced by situational factors including company size and age, organizational structure reflects managers' determination of what the firm does and how it completes that work given its chosen strategies.[21] Strategic competitiveness can be attained only when the firm's selected structure is congruent with its formulated strategy.[22] As such, a strategy's potential to create value is reached only when the firm configures itself in ways that allow the strategy to be implemented effectively. Thus, as firms evolve and change their strategies, new structural arrangements are required. Additionally, existing structures influence the future selection of strategies.[23] Accordingly, the two key strategic actions of strategy formulation and strategy implementation continuously interact to influence managerial choices about strategy and structure.

Figure 12.1 shows the growth pattern many firms experience. This pattern results in changes in the relationships between the firm's formulated strategies and the organizational structures used to support and facilitate their implementation.

■ ■ **FIGURE 12.1**

*Strategy and Structure Growth Pattern*

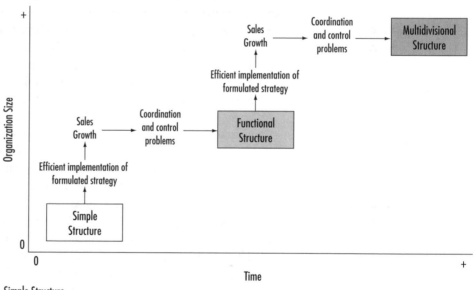

## Simple Structure

A **simple structure** is an organizational form in which the owner-manager makes all major decisions directly and monitors all activities, while the staff serves as an extension of the manager's supervisory authority.

A **simple structure** is an organizational form in which the owner-manager makes all major decisions directly and monitors all activities, while the staff serves as an extension of the manager's supervisory authority. This structure involves little specialization of tasks, few rules, and limited formalization. Although important, information systems are relatively unsophisticated, and owner-managers participate directly in the firm's day-to-day operations. Typically, firms that offer a single product line in a single geographic market use this structure. Because of the small organization size, the simple structure is used frequently in firms implementing either the focused low-cost or focused differentiation strategy. Restaurants, repair businesses, and other specialized enterprises are examples of firms whose limited complexity calls for the use of the simple structure. In this structure, communication is frequent and direct, and new products tend to be introduced to the market quickly, which can result in a competitive advantage. Because of these characteristics, few of the coordination problems that are common in larger organizations exist.

The simple structure, the operations it supports, and the strategies being implemented in these companies play important roles in the success of various economies. Job creation data are one indicator of this importance; companies in the United States with between 100 and 500 employees became the largest job creators in the last decade.[24] The value of small firms to the United Kingdom's economy has also been recognized; some analysts in the United Kingdom believe that the simple organizational structure may result in competitive advantages for some small firms relative to their larger counterparts. In Canada, SMEs (small and medium enterprises) have accounted for a disproportionate share of employment increases in the last decade or so.[25] Although the contribution of SMEs to job creation in the Canadian economy is perhaps not as dramatic as the American case, it is significant nonetheless.

A broad-based openness to innovation, greater structural flexibility, and an ability to respond more rapidly to environmental changes are examples of these potential competitive advantages.[26] Thus, although large corporations are indeed vital to the health of the world's economies, the importance of small firms should not be overlooked. The simple organizational structure properly supports the implementation of the focused strategies that are chosen most often by small firms (see Chapter 5).

However, as the small firm grows larger and more complex, managerial and structural challenges emerge. For example, the amount of competitively relevant information requiring analysis increases substantially. These more complicated information processing needs place significant pressures on the simple structure and the owner-manager. Commonly, owner-managers lack the organizational skills and experiences required to manage effectively the specialized and complex tasks involved with multiple organizational functions. Owner-managers or the top-level managers employed by the small firm's owner bear the responsibility to recognize the inadequacy of the firm's current organizational structure and the need to change to one that is consistent with the firm's strategy.[27]

The experiences of Yo! provide a useful illustration. Established as a sushi restaurant in London, England, this company achieved immediate success. In its first year of operation, Yo! grew by adding products related directly to its restaurant business, such as a London-wide sushi delivery service and an event catering service. After its first year of operation, the company's founder announced ambitious plans to move the Yo! name into new areas including supermarkets and hotels. The objective was to establish Yo! as a mass-market youth brand. Initial product line expansions included clothing for young adults and children and toys. A more contemporary style of hotel—to be called Yotel—was also planned. Beyond this, the founder also believed that there was "… an opportunity for Yo! at the convenience-store level, providing a new retail environment involving home delivery and Internet shopping."[28] These ambitious growth objectives, however, created significant pressures on Yo!'s managers and its simple organizational structure. As the firm's product lines become more diverse (recall that increased product diversity signals a change in strategy), an appropriate response to the pressures the firm and its top-level managers face includes movement to a functional organizational structure or perhaps even one of the forms of the multidivisional structure.

## Functional Structure

To coordinate more complex organizational functions, firms such as Yo! should abandon the simple structure in favour of the functional structure. The functional structure is used by larger firms implementing one of the business-level strategies and by firms with low levels of diversification (for instance, companies implementing either the single- or dominant-business corporate-level strategy).

The **functional structure** consists of a chief executive officer and limited corporate staff, with functional line managers in dominant organizational areas such as production, accounting, marketing, R&D, engineering, and human resources (see Figure 12.2). This structure allows for functional specialization, thereby facilitating knowledge-sharing and idea development.[29] Because the differences in orientation among organizational functions can impede communication and coordination, the central task of the CEO is to integrate the decisions and actions of individual business functions for the benefit of the entire corporation.[30] This organizational form also facilitates career paths and professional development in specialized functional areas.

The **functional structure** consists of a chief executive officer and limited corporate staff, with functional line managers in dominant organizational areas such as production, accounting, marketing, R&D, engineering, and human resources.

■ ■ **FIGURE 12.2**

*Functional Structure*

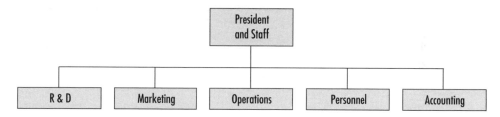

An unintended negative consequence of the functional structure is the tendency for functional-area managers to focus on local versus overall company strategic issues. Such emphases cause specialized managers to lose sight of the firm's overall strategic intent and strategic mission. When this situation emerges, the multidivisional structure often is implemented to overcome this difficulty.

Another condition that encourages a change from the functional to the multidivisional structure is greater diversification (that is, when an organization moves from a form of limited diversification to related-constrained, related-linked, or unrelated diversification). Strategic success often leads to growth and diversification. Deciding to offer the same products in different markets (market diversification) and/or choosing to offer additional products (product diversification) creates control problems. The multidivisional structure provides the controls required to deal effectively with additional levels of diversification. In fact, the firm's returns may suffer when increased diversification is not accompanied by a change to the multidivisional structure.

## Multidivisional Structure

The chief executive's limited ability to process increasing quantities of strategic information, the focus of functional managers on local issues, and increased diversification are primary causes of the decision to change from the functional to the multidivisional (M-form) structure. According to Alfred Chandler, "The M-form came into being when senior managers operating through existing centralized, functionally departmentalized

… structures realized they had neither the time nor the necessary information to coordinate and monitor day-to-day operations, or to devise and implement long-term plans for the various product lines. The administrative overload had become simply too great."[31]

The **multidivisional (M-form) structure** is composed of operating divisions where each division represents a separate business or profit centre, and the top corporate officer delegates responsibilities for day-to-day operations and business-unit strategy to division managers (see Figure 12.3). Because the diversified corporation is the dominant form of business in the industrialized world, the M-form is being used in most of the corporations competing in the global economy.[32] However, only effectively designed M-forms enhance a firm's performance. Thus, for all companies, and perhaps especially for related- and unrelated-diversified firms, performance is a function of the goodness of fit between strategy and structure.[33]

Chandler's examination of the strategies and structures of large American firms documented the M-form's development.[34] Chandler viewed the M-form as an innovative response to coordination and control problems that surfaced during the 1920s in the functional structures being used by large firms such as DuPont and General Motors.[35] Among other benefits, the M-form allowed firms to greatly expand their operations.

> The **multidivisional (M-form) structure** is composed of operating divisions where each division represents a separate business or profit centre and the top corporate officer delegates responsibility for day-to-day operations and business-unit strategy to division managers.

### ■ ■ FIGURE 12.3

*Multidivisional Structure*

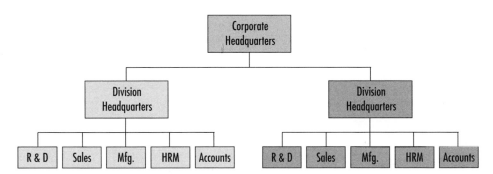

### Use of the Multidivisional Structure at DuPont and General Motors

Chandler's studies showed that firms such as DuPont began to record significant revenue growth through the manufacture and distribution of diversified products while using the functional structure. Functional departments such as sales and production, however, found it difficult to coordinate the conflicting priorities of the firm's new and different products and markets. Moreover, the functional structures being used allocated costs to organizational functions rather than to individual businesses and products. This allocation method made it virtually impossible for top-level managers to determine the contributions of separate product lines to the firm's return on its investments. Even more damaging for large firms trying to implement newly formulated diversification strategies through use of a functional structure that was appropriate for small companies and for those needing proprietary expertise and scale[36] was the increasing allocation of top-level managers' time and energies to short-term administrative problems. Focusing their efforts on these issues caused executives to neglect the long-term strategic issues that were their primary responsibility.

To cope with similar problems, General Motors CEO Alfred Sloan, Jr. proposed a reorganization of the company.[37] Sloan conceptualized separate divisions, each representing a distinct business that would be self-contained and have its own functional hierarchy. Implemented in 1925, Sloan's structure delegated day-to-day operating responsibilities to division managers. The small staff at the corporate level was responsible for determining the firm's long-term strategic direction and for exercising overall financial control of semiautonomous divisions. Each division was to make its own business-level strategic decisions, but because the corporate office's focus was on the outcomes achieved by the entire corporation rather than the performance of separate units, corporate office personnel could supersede decisions made by division heads. Sloan's structural innovation had three important outcomes: "(1) it enabled corporate officers to more accurately monitor the performance of each business, which simplified the problem of control; (2) it facilitated comparisons between divisions, which improved the resource allocation process; and (3) it stimulated managers of poor performing divisions to look for ways of improving performance."[38]

## The Use of Internal Controls in the Multidivisional Structure

The M-form structure holds top-level managers responsible for formulating and implementing overall corporate strategies; that is, they are responsible for the corporate-level acquisition and restructuring, international, and cooperative strategies that we examined in Chapters 7 through 10.

Strategic and financial controls are the two major types of internal controls used to support implementation of strategies in larger firms.[39] Properly designed organizational controls provide clear insights to employees regarding behaviours that enhance the firm's competitiveness and overall performance.[40] Diversification strategies are implemented effectively when firms use both types of controls appropriately. For example, as the Opening Case illustrates, Microsoft is implementing a multidivisional structure. Currently, the company has good strategic control; however, it will need a better balance, with more of an emphasis on financial control, to create the appropriate incentives for managers of their new product-oriented divisions. If Ballmer and Gates do not allow division heads to develop stronger financial control of their divisions and evaluate the performance of those divisions with better financial controls (recall the idea of tracking stock, which could facilitate improved financial control and evaluation by the stock market), a control imbalance will remain, with Gates and Ballmer having too much centralized control.

**Strategic control** entails the use of long-term and strategically relevant criteria by corporate-level managers to evaluate the performance of division managers and their units. Strategic control emphasizes largely subjective judgments and may involve intuitive evaluation criteria. Behavioural in nature, strategic controls typically require high levels of cognitive diversity among top-level managers. Cognitive diversity captures the differences in beliefs about cause-effect relationships and desired outcomes among top-level managers' preferences.[41] Corporate-level managers rely on strategic control to gain an operational understanding of the strategies being implemented in the firm's separate divisions or business units. Because strategic control allows a corporate-level evaluation of the full array of strategic actions—those concerned with both the formulation and implementation of a business-unit strategy—corporate-level managers must have a deep understanding of a division's or business unit's operations and markets.[42] The use of strategic controls also demands rich strategic information exchanges between corpo-

**Strategic control** entails the use of long-term and strategically relevant criteria by corporate-level managers to evaluate the performance of division managers and their units.

rate and divisional managers. These exchanges take place through both formal and informal (i.e., unplanned) face-to-face meetings.[43]

As diversification increases, strategic control can be strained.[44] Sometimes, this strain results in a commitment to reduce the firm's level of diversification. For example, CIBC's departure from most forms of insurance coverage has been characterized as strategic re-focusing. Kenn Lalonde, chief executive of CIBC Insurance stated that the bank's retreat from the business was "… another step in CIBC's strategy to focus our investments and growth in those areas that we believe will deliver the greatest return to our shareholders." The move was seen as one of several moves made by the bank's chairman, John Hunkin, to focus on core operations.[45] Difficulties encountered when attempting to use strategic controls to evaluate the performance of these units and those managing them may have contributed to the divestment decisions.

**Financial control** entails objective criteria (e.g., return on investment) that corporate-level managers use to evaluate the returns being earned by individual business units and the managers responsible for their performance. Because they are oriented to financial outcomes, an emphasis on financial controls requires divisional performance to be largely independent of other divisions.[46] As such, when the firm chooses to implement a strategy calling for interdependence among the firm's different businesses, such as the related-constrained corporate-level strategy, the ability of financial control to add value to strategy implementation efforts is reduced.[47]

Implicit in the earlier discussion on strategic controls is the point that this also includes the use of financial controls. However, as Figure 12.4 illustrates, as the level of diversification increases, the ability to use strategic controls is curtailed until an organization loses strategic control when it moves past an appropriate level of diversification. At this point the organization commences using financial controls only. This is an important point to remember when moving to unrelated diversification from related diversification. The use of financial controls only curtails creativity and innovation in an organization, and maintaining creativity and innovation is critical to maintaining and enhancing above-average future returns.

Now that we have covered the basic organizational structures and controls available, we discuss how those structures and controls can be employed to implement different business-level strategies.

**Financial control** entails objective criteria (e.g., return on investment) that corporate-level managers use to evaluate the returns being earned by individual business units and the managers responsible for their performance.

■ ■ **FIGURE 12.4**

*The Relationship between Corporate-Level Strategy and Controls*

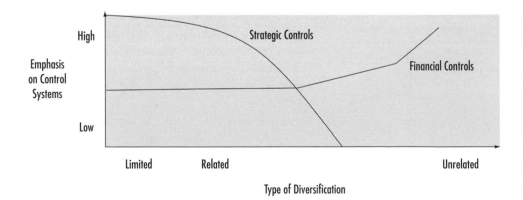

# IMPLEMENTING BUSINESS-LEVEL STRATEGIES: ORGANIZATIONAL STRUCTURE AND CONTROLS

As discussed in Chapter 5, business-level strategies establish a particular type of competitive advantage (typically either low cost or differentiation) in a particular competitive scope (either an entire industry or a narrow segment of it). Effective implementation of the cost leadership, differentiation, and integrated low-cost/differentiation strategies occurs when certain modifications are made to the characteristics of the functional structure based on the unique attributes of the individual business-level strategies.

## Using the Functional Structure to Implement a Cost Leadership Strategy

The structural characteristics of specialization, centralization, and formalization play important roles in the successful implementation of the cost leadership strategy. *Specialization* refers to the type and numbers of job specialties that are required to perform the firm's work.[48] For the cost leadership strategy, managers divide the firm's work into homogeneous subgroups. The basis for these subgroups is usually functional areas, products being produced, or clients served. By dividing and grouping work tasks into specialties, firms reduce their costs through the efficiencies achieved by employees specializing in a particular and often narrow set of activities.

*Centralization* is the degree to which decisionmaking authority is retained at higher managerial levels. Today, the trend in organizations is toward decentralization—the movement of decisionmaking authority down to people in the firm who have the most direct and frequent contact with customers. However, to coordinate activities carefully across organizational functions, the structure used to implement the cost leadership strategy calls for centralization. Thus, when designing this particular type of functional structure, managers strive to push some decisionmaking authority lower in the organization while remaining focused on the more general need for activities to be coordinated and integrated through the efforts of a centralized staff.

The cost leadership strategy is one often chosen by firms that produce relatively standardized products in large quantities; consequently, formalization is necessary. Formalization is the degree to which formal rules and procedures govern organizational activities.[49] To foster more efficient operations, R&D efforts emphasize process innovation, that is, improvements in the manufacturing process.

As summarized in Figure 12.5, successful implementation of the cost leadership strategy requires an organizational structure featuring strong task specialization, centralization of decisionmaking authority, and formalization of work rules and procedures. Typically, there are fewer layers, simpler reporting relationships, focus on a narrower range of business functions, and a smaller corporate staff.[50] This type of functional structure encourages the emergence of a low-cost culture—a culture in which all employees seek to find ways to drive their firm's or unit's costs lower than rivals' costs. Using highly specialized work tasks, low-cost leader Southwest Airlines strives continuously to increase the efficiency of its production and distribution systems. For example, Southwest was one of the first carriers to sell tickets on the Internet. A travel industry consultant concluded that Southwest's simple fares and schedule make it easy to sell travel directly to consumers on the Internet.[51] Similarly, some European carriers that are preparing for privatization, including Air France, TAP Air Portugal, Alitalia, and LOT of Poland, are seeking to develop a low-cost culture that may prove to be critical to their success as deregulated firms competing in the global marketplace.[52] In Canada, Calgary's discount airline WestJet was described in *Canadian Business* as strategically analogous to Southwest. WestJet maintains a low-cost strategy by operating with only one type of plane, fast turnaround times to maximize use of its planes, a nonunion work force motivated by profitsharing, and very little debt. WestJet then passes the cost savings on to customers through very low fares.[53]

■ ■ **FIGURE 12.5**

*Functional Structure for Implementation of a Cost Leadership Strategy*

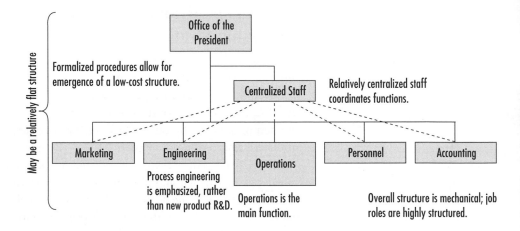

## Using the Functional Structure to Implement a Differentiation Strategy

The differentiation strategy is implemented successfully when a functional structure is used in which decisionmaking authority is decentralized. Unlike the cost leadership strategy, in which the coordination and integration of organizational function activities occurs through centralization of decisionmaking authority, the functional structure used to implement the differentiation strategy demands that people throughout the firm learn how to coordinate and integrate their activities effectively. This means cross-functional linkages, isolated pockets of intense creative efforts, and the willingness to explore structures necessary to take advantage of new opportunities. The implementation of the differentiation strategy is facilitated if there is a consensus style of decisionmaking among the top-management team members. Research suggests that the performance of a strategic business unit (SBU) pursuing a differentiation strategy increases if a consensus style is used. This is particularly true when a differentiation strategy is implemented in a stable environment; it is more difficult to implement a consensus style when the market being pursued by the firm is dynamic and changing.[54]

The marketing and R&D functions are often emphasized in the differentiation strategy's functional structure. For example, because of its commitment to continuous product innovation across all of its operations, R&D is emphasized in several of FAG Kugelfischer's business units to facilitate implementation of the differentiation strategy in those individual units. This emphasis is suggested by the following comment: "All our efforts in the R&D field have only one objective—improving the performance parameters of our products for the benefit of our customers in such a way that new machinery equipped with them constitutes a clear advance in terms of purchasing costs, service, and maintenance."[55] As is the case at FAG, an emphasis on R&D in firms implementing the differentiation strategy typically is focused on those activities required to develop new products. Centralized staffs ensure that the efforts of those working in these two critical functions are integrated successfully. To properly control new product development, a centralized research facility may be established, and to maintain efficiency, the manufacturing facility also may be partially centralized. This allows integration of new products quickly while maintaining the highest possible efficiency.[56] Alternatively, many firms use decentralized cross-functional teams composed of representatives from marketing, R&D, and manufacturing to integrate these functions for new product design, manufacturing, and introduction to the marketplace.

To capitalize on emerging trends in key markets, the firm implementing the differentiation strategy often makes rapid changes based on ambiguous and incomplete information. Such rapid changes demand that the firm use a relatively flat organizational structure to group its work activities (in a relatively flat structure, workers are likely to have a number of tasks included in their job descriptions). The implementation of the differentiation strategy is affected negatively when the firm has extensive centralization and formalization, especially in a rapidly changing environment. Thus, the overall organizational structure needs to be flexible and job roles less structured. Additional characteristics of the form of the functional structure used to implement the differentiation strategy are shown in Figure 12.6.

■ ■ **FIGURE 12.6**

*Functional Structure for Implementation of a Differentiation Strategy*

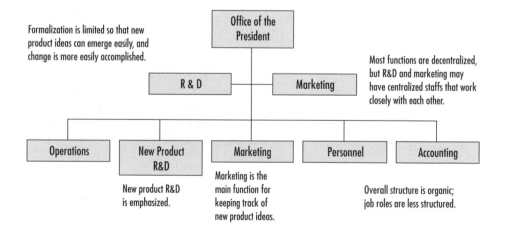

## Using the Functional Structure to Implement an Integrated Low-Cost/Differentiation Strategy

To implement the integrated low-cost/differentiation strategy, companies seek to provide value that differs from that offered by the low cost and the differentiated firm—low cost, relative to the cost of the differentiated firm's product, and valuable differentiated features, relative to the features offered by the low-cost firm's product.

Global firms, especially, are formulating the integrated low-cost/differentiation strategy more frequently, but they are finding it difficult to implement. The primary reason is that the strategic and tactical actions required to implement the low-cost and the differentiation strategies are not the same. For example, to achieve the low-cost position, relative to rivals, emphasis is placed on production and manufacturing process engineering, with infrequent product changes. In contrast, to achieve a differentiated position, marketing and new product R&D are emphasized. But, as explained earlier, the structural characteristics used to emphasize new product development differ from those needed to emphasize process engineering. To implement this strategy successfully, managers are challenged to form an organizational structure that allows the development of differentiated product features while costs, relative to rivals' costs, are reduced. Often, the functional structure has to be supplemented by horizontal coordination, such as cross-functional teams and a strong organizational culture to implement this strategy effectively.

Toyota Motor Corporation has achieved its role of world leader in the auto industry primarily because of its ability to implement cost leadership and differentiation simultaneously.[57] The key to Toyota's success has been the differentiated design and manufacturing process that the company has implemented concurrently through its integrated product design process. Toyota does this first by mapping the design space and defining feasible regions of overlap for product and process design. Second, it looks for intersections of feasible sets for this overlap. Finally, Toyota establishes the feasibility of the overlapping design before committing to it. Overall, comparing the Toyota system to others, one author concluded: "Toyota considers a broader range of possible designs and delays certain decisions longer than other automotive companies, yet has what may be the fastest and most efficient vehicle development cycles in the industry."[58]

## Using the Simple Structure to Implement Focused Strategies

As noted earlier, many focused strategies—strategies through which a firm concentrates on serving the unique needs of a narrow part or scope of the industry—are implemented most effectively through the simple structure. At some point, however, the increased sales revenues resulting from success necessitate changing from a simple to a functional structure. The challenge for managers is to recognize when a structural change is required to coordinate and control effectively the firm's increasingly complex operations.

The intent of companies manufacturing regional soft drinks is to serve the needs of a narrow group of customers better than giants Coca-Cola and PepsiCo. People targeted by the regional manufacturers are those with individualized tastes for soft drinks. To describe these firms and their products, an analyst noted that, "obscure soft drinks … are thriving in local markets … These regional or 'cult' brands … eschew marketing [and are] relying on the appeal of long histories, local pride and wild formulas, including one derived from … a failed pharmaceutical experiment."[59] Revolving around flexible production functions, these manufacturers have low levels of specialization and formalization. For example, Woodbridge Ontario's Lola Beverages began as one man's craving for a product that had not been made in over a decade: the Lola Iceberg ("a double handful of fruit-flavoured liquid contained in a squeezable, waxed cardboard pyramid"). The brand was originally sold only in southern Ontario and Quebec from 1959 to 1982. Its demise in 1982 was due to problems at the producer relating to family reasons (rather than a decline in sales). Founder Tony Romanelli obtained rights to the trademark and with a company of just a couple of others, revived the product. Like other regional or "cult" brands, Lola serves a narrow group of customers with individualized tastes.[60]

Service Performance Corporation (SPC) also uses the simple organizational structure. Serving approximately 100 customers, SPC provides janitorial and facilities services in office buildings, malls, airports, laboratories, and manufacturing facilities. The firm's founder/CEO believes that service is his company's only product. To describe the character of SPC's organizational structure, the CEO noted that his nine-year-old company had retained its "aversion to bureaucracy." The simple structure is used to help all employees focus on what is believed to be the firm's competitive advantage—superior customer service.[61]

## Movement to the Multidivisional Structure

The above-average returns gained through successful implementation of a business-level strategy often result in diversification of the firm's operations. This diversification can take the form of offering different products (product diversification) and/or offering the same or additional products in other markets (market diversification). As explained in Chapter 7, increased product and/or market diversification demands that firms formulate a corporate-level strategy as well as business-level strategies for individual units or divisions (see Figure 7.1 to review the different corporate-level strategies and their respective levels of diversification). With greater diversification, the simple and functional structures must be discarded in favour of the more complex, yet increasingly necessary multidivisional structure.

---

## IMPLEMENTING CORPORATE-LEVEL STRATEGIES: ORGANIZATIONAL STRUCTURE AND CONTROLS

Effective use of the multidivisional structure helps firms implement their corporate-level strategy (diversification). In this section, we describe three M-form variations (see Figure 12.7) that are required to implement the related-constrained, related-linked, and unrelated diversification strategies.

■ ■ **FIGURE 12.7**

*Three Variations of the Multidivisional Structure*

The **cooperative form** (of the multidivisional structure) is an organizational structure that uses many integration devices and horizontal human resource practices to foster cooperation and integration among the firm's divisions.

## Using the Cooperative Form to Implement the Related-Constrained Strategy

To implement the related-constrained strategy, firms use the cooperative form of the multidivisional structure. The **cooperative form** is an organizational structure that uses many integration devices and horizontal human resource practices to foster cooperation and integration among the firm's divisions. The cooperative form (see Figure 12.8) emphasizes horizontal links and relationships more than the two other variations of the multidivisional structure described later in the chapter. Cooperation among divisions that are formed around either products or markets served is necessary to realize economies of scope and to facilitate the transferring of skills.[62] Increasingly, it is important for these links to allow and support the sharing of a range of strategic assets, including employees' "know-how" as well as tangible assets such as facilities and methods of operations.[63]

■ ■ **FIGURE 12.8**

*Cooperative Form of the Multidivisional Structure for Implementation of a Related-Constrained Strategy*

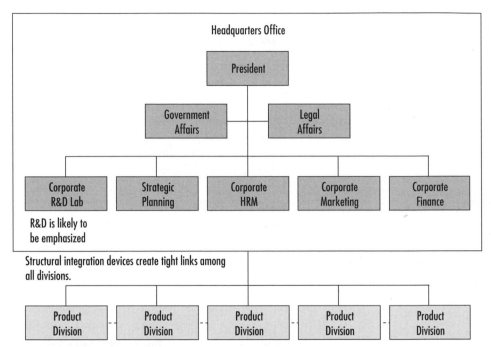

To facilitate cooperation among divisions that are either vertically integrated or related through the sharing of strategic assets, some organizational functions (e.g., human resource management, R&D, and marketing) are centralized at the corporate level. Work completed in these centralized functions is managed by the firm's central administrative, or headquarters, office. When the central office's efforts allow exploitation of commonalties among the firm's divisions in ways that yield a cost or differentiation advantage (or both) in the divisions as compared to undiversified rivals, the cooperative form of the multidivisional structure is a source of competitive advantage for the diversified firm.[64]

Besides centralization, a number of structural integration links are used to foster cooperation among divisions in firms implementing the related-constrained diversification strategy. Frequent direct contact between division managers encourages and supports cooperation and the sharing of strategic assets. Sometimes, liaison roles are established in each division to reduce the amount of time division managers spend facilitating the integration and coordination of their units' work. Temporary teams or task forces may also be formed around projects and may require the efforts of many people from separate divisions to achieve desired levels of divisional coordination. Formal integration departments might be formed in firms requiring the work of temporary teams or task forces on a continuous basis. Ultimately, a matrix organization evolves in firms implementing the related-constrained strategy. A matrix organization (see Figure 12.9) is an organizational structure in which there is a dual structure combining both functional specialization and business product or project specialization.[65] Although complicated, effective matrix structures can lead to improved coordination among a firm's various divisions.[66] A major problem is that employees sometimes find it difficult to be reporting to two bosses, the functional area boss and the product or project boss.

■ ■ **FIGURE 12.9**

*A Typical Product and Functional Matrix Structure*

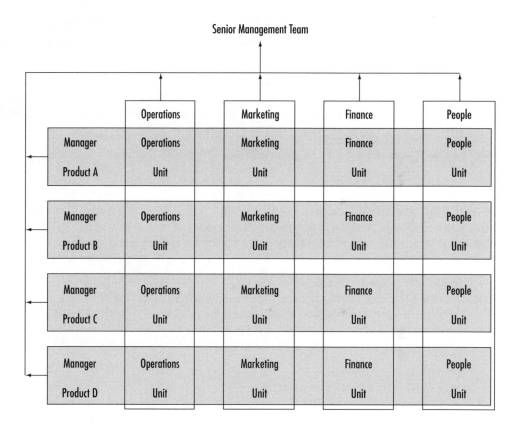

As implied by the horizontal procedures used for coordination that we described earlier, information processing must increase dramatically to implement the related-constrained diversification strategy successfully. But, because cooperation among divisions implies a loss of managerial autonomy, division managers may not readily commit themselves to the type of integrative information processing activities demanded by this organizational structure. Moreover, coordination among divisions sometimes results in an unequal flow of positive outcomes to divisional managers. In other words, when managerial rewards are based at least in part on the performance of individual divisions, the manager of the division able to derive the greatest marketplace benefit from the sharing of the firm's strategic assets might be viewed as receiving relative gains at others' expense. In these instances, performance evaluations are emphasized to facilitate sharing of strategic assets. Furthermore, using reward systems that emphasize overall company performance besides outcomes achieved by individual divisions helps overcome problems associated with the cooperative form.

The use of the cooperative form of the multidivisional structure in three companies is described in the Strategic Focus. Notice that each firm is implementing the related-constrained diversification strategy, which, it seems, results in a match between strategy and structure within these companies.

## STRATEGIC FOCUS

### Using the Cooperative Form of the Multidivisional Structure to Achieve Strategic Competitiveness

Montreal-based Bombardier is a worldwide manufacturer of transportation-related equipment. It has production facilities in eight countries, in addition to Canada. The firm's corporate organizational structure features four product divisions—transportation, recreational products, aerospace, and services. Shared across the four product divisions is the firm's set of technological capabilities and competencies. As a source of competitive advantage, these capabilities and competencies allow Bombardier to introduce innovative products continuously and rapidly. To describe the factors contributing to his firm's strategic competitiveness, Bombardier's CEO, Robert Brown, observed, "We're selling technology, and we're selling new products. That's what makes us a success."

Bombardier has introduced a stream of innovative products. In the aerospace division, for example, the firm is offering the Learjet 45. A midsize plane that is priced like a light jet, the Learjet 45 is capable of nonstop transcontinental flights. Bombardier's factories will be kept busy for the next several years filling booked orders. In the near future, the aerospace division will introduce a plane that analysts believe will yield even greater results for Bombardier. With capacity already in the 40-to 70-seat range, Bombardier plans to introduce the next level of the Canadair Regional Jet Series, which expand the plane series' range up to 90 passengers. The transportation division is building 680 highly automated New York City subway cars for nearly $1 billion. Another project (yielding $419 million in sales revenue) is the manufacture of Amtrak's first high-speed trains, for service on Amtrak's Boston-Washington route. The recreational products division is introducing an entirely new product called the Neighbourhood Vehicle (NV). Essentially a "souped-up golf cart," the NV is targeted to those living in retirement or gated communities. Bombardier Services, the company's fourth division, was created in 1996 so the firm could develop a stronger presence in the growing worldwide market for support, maintenance, and training services related to commercial aircraft and defence products.

E. W. Scripps is a diversified U.S. provider of information and entertainment. The firm is engaged in TV broadcasting, cable network program production, newspaper publishing, and media licensing (Scripps' United Media distributes Dilbert®, Peanuts®, and 150 other comic strips). To increase its strategic competitiveness, E. W. Scripps engaged in a yearlong strategic realignment of its assets. Operations that were divested include book publishing and a cable-TV distribution system. The firm's corporate-level strategy now calls for it

*continued*

"... to be a provider of information and entertainment to particular consumer categories." To implement this strategy, three product divisions have been formed—publishing, broadcast, and entertainment. Personnel in the three divisions cooperate with one another to integrate and coordinate their operations when doing so increases the firm's competitive ability. Facilitating these integration and coordination attempts is Scripps' targeting of particular geographic locations in all three product divisions. Essentially, the firm seeks to cluster its media operations in midsize, high-growth Sun Belt markets such as Florida and Texas.

A similar organizational realignment was undertaken at Quebecor for acquisition. Quebecor's $5.9 million purchase of Videotron and French-language broadcaster TVA made the Montreal-based company a very different firm from the commercial printing giant that it had been. In order to make the purchase fit into a reasonable corporate structure, Quebecor formed Quebecor Media, which would include Quebecor's cable interests, its Netgraphe Internet division, Canoe Internet portal, TVA, and Quebecor's Sun newspaper chain. The commercial printing operations would then be free to concentrate their efforts as a separate division.

Sources: *E. W. Scripps home page,* 2000, http://www.scripps.com (Retrieved November 8); *Plant,* 2000, Bombardier launches 4000 jobs, August: 1; *Cablecaster,* 2000, Court a real possibility: Rogers, Videotron, Quebecor, Caisse may go before judge next month, *Cablecaster,* 12 (5): 16. *Bombardier home page,* 1998, http://www. bombardier.com (Retrieved February 4); *E. W. Scripps home page,* 1998, http://www.scripps.com (Retrieved February 4); J. Weber, W. Zellner, and G. Smith, 1998, Loud noises at Bombardier, *BusinessWeek,* January 26, 94–95; J. P. Miller, 1997, E. W. Scripps turns page, and spots new opportunities, *Wall Street Journal,* September 23, B4.

When there are fewer and/or less constrained links among the firm's divisions, the related-linked diversification strategy should be implemented. As explained next, this strategy can be implemented successfully through use of the SBU form of the multidivisional structure.

## Using the SBU Form to Implement a Related-Linked Strategy

The strategic business unit (SBU) form of the multidivisional structure consists of at least three levels, with the top level being corporate headquarters; the next level, SBU groups; and the final level, divisions grouped by relatedness (either product or geographic market) within each SBU.

The **strategic business unit (SBU) form** of the multidivisional structure consists of at least three levels, with the top level being corporate headquarters; the next level, SBU groups; and the final level, divisions grouped by relatedness (either product or geographic market) within each SBU (see Figure 12.10). The firm's business portfolio is organized into those related to one another within a SBU group and those unrelated in other SBU groups. Thus, divisions within groups are related, but groups are largely unrelated to each other. Within the SBU structure, divisions with similar products or technologies are organized to achieve synergy. Each SBU is a profit centre that is controlled by the firm's headquarters office. An important benefit of this structural form is that individual decisionmakers, within their strategic business unit, look to SBU executives rather than headquarters personnel for strategic guidance. A major problem with the SBU structure is that the SBUs are unrelated to each other, which makes it difficult to create synergies and gain economies of scope. Another problem is the increased bureaucracy if the managers at corporate headquarters do not give the SBU autonomy and protection from the stringent financial controls inherent in this type of structure.

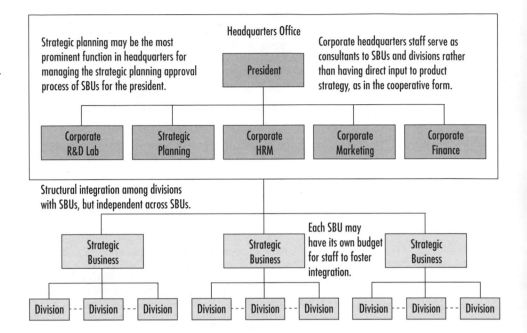

### ■ ■ ■ FIGURE 12.10

*SBU Form of the Multidivisional Structure for Implementation of a Related-Linked Strategy*

Nobuyuki Idei, CEO of Sony, is taking the opportunity to restructure the great Japanese consumer products firm, given the trend toward restructuring in Japan. In fact, job cuts led to a postwar unemployment peak there of 4.4 percent in 1999. Although Sony has had $50 million in revenues due to flat-screen TVs, digital video cameras, and many other differentiated products, its margins have not been significant relative to revenues. For example, Sony's PlayStation video games have contributed only 15 percent of Sony's total sales but make up 42 percent of Sony's operating profits. Accordingly, Idei has been trying to shift the firm to make better use of software (e.g., music, films, and games) in its televisions and audio gear in order to increase Sony's profitability. To accomplish this, Sony's 10 internal companies are being regrouped, "into four autonomous units focused on products and networks." In addition, Idei will cut headquarters staff from about 2500 to several hundred over the next few years. Sony's global workforce of 170 000 will be cut by 10 percent, and factories will go from 70 to 55 by 2003. The restructuring now matches the SBU structure with the company's 10 internal companies organized into four strategic business units. Each unit will receive research funds and will be required to justify its existence on the basis of profitability. The units will also be required to cooperate among themselves within each strategic group. For instance, Sony may build a new PlayStation that doubles as a video player or a high-capacity game feature on its notebook computers. Sony is well positioned to compete in this market because it is the only firm that has a successful computer, television producer, and video game player. Thus, Sony is one of the few companies that has the opportunity to integrate software and content across a broad range of consumer electronics products.[67] The company will implement this strategy through the SBU structure.

The organizational structure of a large diversified firm such as Sony can be complex. This complexity is a reflection of the size and diversity of a diversified firm's operations. Consider the case of General Electric (GE). Implementing the related-linked corporate-level strategy, the firm called for integration among divisions within SBUs, but independence among SBUs. GE managers expect to be able to "walk, think, and talk" like a small firm and to make decisions and introduce innovative products at a pace equivalent to smaller competitors.[68] Recently, GE's structure featured 10 major SBUs as noted in Table 12.1.[69] Note that even though we have simplified the list, the depth and breadth of GE's activities is still somewhat difficult to grasp even when grouped into SBUs.

**■ ■ TABLE 12.1                    GE's SBUs**

| Business Unit | Businesses |
|---|---|
| Aircraft Engines | The world's largest producer of large and small jet engines for commercial and military aircraft |
| Appliances | Produces GE, Hotpoint and other brands, as well as several private-label brands |
| Capital Services | Diversified financial services with comprehensive solutions to increase client productivity/efficiency. |
| Industrial Systems | A leading supplier of products used to distribute, protect, operate, and control electrical power and equipment, as well as a supplier of services for commercial and industrial applications |
| Lighting | A leading supplier of lighting products for global consumer, commercial, and industrial markets |
| Medical Systems | A world leader in medical diagnostic imaging technology, services, and health care productivity |
| Plastics | A world leader in versatile, high-performance engineered plastics used in the computer, electronics, data storage, office equipment, automotive, building and construction, and other industries |
| Power Systems | A world leader in the design, manufacture, and servicing of gas, steam, and hydroelectric turbines and generators for power production, pipeline, and industrial applications |
| Transportation Systems | Manufacturer of more than half of the diesel freight locomotives in North America; its locomotives operate in 75 countries worldwide |
| NBC | Global media company that operates the NBC TV Network, 13 television stations, CNBC, MSNBC (in partnership with Microsoft), and maintains equity interests in the A&E (Arts and Entertainment) Television Network and The History Channel. NBC also has an interest in Internet businesses, with equity stakes in CNET, Talk City, iVillage, Telescan, Hoover's, 24/7 Media, Snap.com, XOOM.com and NBCi (the seventh largest Internet site and the first publicly traded Internet company integrated with a major broadcaster) |

Source: *GE home page*, 2000, www.ge.com (Retrieved March 1).

For firms as large as GE, structural flexibility is as important as strategic flexibility (recall the discussion in Chapter 6 indicating a need for firms to have strategic flexibility). Through a combination of strategic and structural flexibility, GE is able to respond rapidly to opportunities as they emerge throughout the world. Amidst the firm's flexibility, Welch sets precise performance targets and monitors them throughout the year. Thus, GE is run such that the bureaucracy is removed so that the company has a small-firm culture, but managers are held accountable to a leader who seeks to understand the company's many businesses.[70] In sum, one analyst noted that GE is not so much a collection of businesses as it is, "a repository of information and expertise that can be leveraged over a huge installed base."[71] It would appear that GE has been able to create synergies and economies of scope while avoiding the problems inherent in another layer of bureaucracy.

## Using the Competitive Form to Implement the Unrelated Diversification Strategy

Firms implementing the unrelated diversification strategy seek to create value through efficient internal capital allocations or by restructuring, buying, and selling businesses.[72] The competitive form of the multidivisional structure is used to implement the unrelated diversification strategy. The **competitive form** is an organizational structure in which the controls used emphasize competition between separate (usually unrelated) divisions for corporate capital. To realize benefits from efficient resource allocations, divisions must have separate, identifiable profit performance and must be held accountable for such performance. The internal capital market requires organizational arrangements that emphasize competition rather than cooperation between divisions.[73]

To emphasize competitiveness among divisions, the headquarters office maintains an arms-length relationship and does not intervene in divisional affairs except to audit operations and discipline managers whose divisions perform poorly. In this situation, the headquarters office sets rate-of-return targets, monitors the outcomes of divisional performance,[74] and allocates cash flow on a competitive basis, rather than automatically returning cash to the division that produced it. The competitive form of the multidivisional structure is illustrated in Figure 12.11.

The **competitive form** is an organizational structure in which the controls used emphasize competition between separate (usually unrelated) divisions for corporate capital.

■ ■ **FIGURE 12.11**

*Competitive Form of the Multidivisional Structure for Implementation of an Unrelated Strategy*

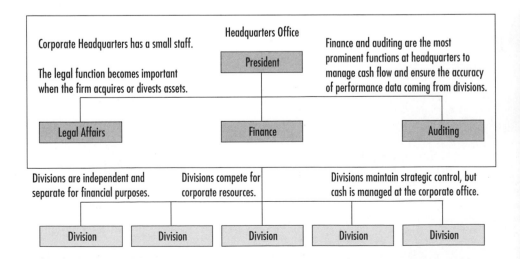

Headquarters Office

Corporate Headquarters has a small staff.

The legal function becomes important when the firm acquires or divests assets.

President

Finance and auditing are the most prominent functions at headquarters to manage cash flow and ensure the accuracy of performance data coming from divisions.

Legal Affairs

Finance

Auditing

Divisions are independent and separate for financial purposes.

Divisions compete for corporate resources.

Divisions maintain strategic control, but cash is managed at the corporate office.

Division   Division   Division   Division   Division

A diversified supplier of hardware items to U.S. discount retailers, Newell Rubbermaid Company uses the competitive form of the multidivisional structure to implement its unrelated diversification strategy. The company's strategy is to market a multiproduct offering of brand-name consumer products to mass retailers, "emphasizing excellent customer service."[75] Committed to growth by acquisition, Newell Rubbermaid added product lines that share no common characteristics to the firm's independent divisions. Supplying primarily large firms such as Wal-Mart, Newell Rubbermaid sells many products, including household products, hardware, and home furnishing and office products. Newell Rubbermaid's competitive advantage is created at the corporate level. Using a small corporate headquarters staff, the firm has developed a sophisticated electronic logistics system, which is used as the basis for each division's logistics with its customers. Although not related to each other, each of Newell Rubbermaid's divisions creates value from the lower cost and improved customer relations provided by the system.[76]

Table 12.2 shows the characteristics of these three major forms of structures. As shown in the table, differences are seen in the degree of centralization, the focus of performance appraisal, the horizontal structures (integrating mechanisms), and the incentive compensation schemes necessary to implement the three corporate-level strategies of related-constrained, related-linked, and unrelated diversification successfully. The most centralized and most costly organizational form is the cooperative structure. The least centralized, with the lowest bureaucratic costs, is the competitive structure. The SBU structure requires partial centralization and involves some of the mechanisms necessary to implement the relatedness between divisions. Also, the divisional incentive compensation awards are allocated according to both SBU and corporate performance. In the competitive structure, the most important criterion is divisional performance.

---

**■ ■ TABLE 12.2    Characteristics of the Structures Necessary to Implement the Related-Constrained, Related-Linked, and Unrelated Diversification Strategies**

| Structural Characteristics | Cooperative M-form (Related-Constrained Strategy)* | SBU M-form (Related-Linked Strategy)* | Competitive M-form (Unrelated Diversification Strategy)* |
|---|---|---|---|
| Centralization of operation | Centralized at corporate office | Partially centralized (in SBU) | Decentralized to divisions |
| Use of integrating mechanisms | Extensive | Moderate | Nonexistent |
| Divisional performance appraisal | Emphasizes subjective criteria | Uses a mixture of subjective and objective criteria | Emphasizes objective (financial or ROI) criteria |
| Divisional incentive compensation | Linked to overall corporate performance | Mixed linkage to corporate, SBU, and divisional performance | Linked to divisional performance |

*Strategy implemented with structural form.

Earlier in the chapter, we indicated that, once formed, an organizational structure could influence a firm's efforts to implement its current strategy and the selection of future strategies. Using the multidivisional structure as the foundation for the discussion, the explanation in the next section exemplifies the relationship between structure and strategy.

# THE EFFECT OF STRUCTURE ON STRATEGY

As explained earlier, the M-form is a structural innovation intended to help managers deal with the coordination and control problems created by increasing product and market variety. Once established, however, the M-form structure has the potential to positively influence the firm's diversification strategy.[77] Strong and appropriate incentives, those that encourage managers to pursue additional marketplace opportunities, coupled with improved accountability and superior internal resource allocations from the corporate office, may stimulate additional diversification. Furthermore, these additional levels of diversification can result in greater returns on the firm's investments.[78] Eventually, however, there is a tendency for the M-form to encourage inefficient levels of diversification. Following a comprehensive review of research evidence, some researchers noted that there is a growing body of evidence that suggests that adoption of the M-form structure facilitates the pursuit of inefficient diversification.[79] Again, this cause/effect relationship—that is, the influence of the M-form on a firm's pursuit of additional diversification—is not inherently negative. The complicating factor is that at some point, the additional amounts of diversification stimulated by the M-form become inefficient, thereby reducing the firm's strategic competitiveness and its returns.

Other theory and research suggests that once the M-form influences the pursuit of more diversification that yields inefficient strategic outcomes, the relationship between structure and strategy may reverse in direction.[80] In other words, firms that become inefficiently diversified implement strategies that result in less efficient levels of diversification. One researcher found, for example, that half of the diversified acquisitions made by unrelated-diversified firms were later divested because the set of businesses lacked focus.[81] Another discovered that a decrease in the diversified scope of M-form firms was associated with an improvement in shareholder wealth. This finding, too, suggests that these firms' diversification had become inefficient.[82] An example of a firm that recently changed its diversification strategy to increase its efficiency and strategic competitiveness is described in the Strategic Focus. Sara Lee reduced its level of diversification, and to achieve all of the potential gains from this corporate-level decision, the firm will also need to change its organizational structure to facilitate implementation of a less diversified strategy. Sara Lee's commitment to lower levels of diversification exemplifies the idea that diversified companies are out of vogue. This preference results in decisions in firms ranging from AT&T to ITT to split up into separately traded companies that focus on their core businesses.[83]

## STRATEGIC FOCUS

### A Cake Maker Gets Lean: Changes at Sara Lee

Founded by a Canadian entrepreneur, Sara Lee Corporation became a global manufacturer and marketer of high-quality, brand-name products for consumers throughout the world. The firm has operations in more than 40 countries and sells its products in over 140 nations. Using the SBU form of the multidivisional structure to implement the related-linked diversification strategy, Sara Lee was, until recently, organized into four separate businesses: packaged meats and bakery (39 percent of sales revenue), coffee and grocery (14 percent), household and body care (9 percent), and personal products (38 percent). Famous brand names included in Sara Lee's portfolio of businesses were Hanes, Polo Ralph Lauren, Spalding, Carter's, L'eggs, Bali, Champion, Hillshire Farm, Jimmy Dean, Sanex, and Kiwi, among others. For many years, the company's growth was fuelled by what its leaders viewed to be strategic acquisitions.

By 1997, the company was generating record profits, but its stock was languishing. Sara Lee's CEO and chairman, John Bryan, described the firm's status with the financial community as follows: "We were pretty boring to Wall Street, and there was a clamour to do something." The "something" Bryan and other Sara Lee top-level managers decided upon was to "deverticalize" their corporation. Deverticalization would largely reduce Sara Lee's level of diversification. In fact, this restructuring program was intended to fundamentally reshape Sara Lee in a manner that executives believed better prepared their firm to compete in the 21st century.

In September 1997, Bryan announced Sara Lee's plan to deverticalize. The conglomerate intended to sell $4.5 billion of its assets, including entire divisions and multiple manufacturing operations. According to Bryan, the firm's "... deverticalization program was designed to enable us to focus our energies and talents on the greatest value-creating activities in our business, which are building and managing leadership brands. Minimizing the degree to which our business is vertically integrated reduces the capital demands on our company while enhancing our competitiveness." As a less diversified corporation, the intention was for Sara Lee to become a firm similar to Nike and Coca-Cola, allocating significant amounts of resources to marketing and outsourcing some manufacturing. Management intended to move away from manufacturing the component parts of the company's brand-name goods. Executives believed that the deverticalization program would generate as much as $4.5 billion within a three-year period.

To reach its objective of building branded leadership positions through deverticalization, Sara Lee divested substantial portions of its U.S. yarn and textile operations. The first of the divestments in this product line was announced on January 5, 1998, when National Textiles agreed to purchase nine of Sara Lee's yarn and textile operations. Although Sara Lee would still make and market the clothes, the company would no longer supply its own yarn. The yield to Sara Lee from this transaction was approximately $900 million over a three-year period. In April 1998, Sara Lee announced the sale of its DEVN Tobacco group. DEVN, headquartered in the Netherlands, sold cut tobacco under various names, including Drum, Amphora, Douwe Egberts, and Van Nelle. The sale to the Imperial Tobacco Group generated about $1.5 billion. In August 1998, Sara Lee

*continued*

http://www.saralee.com

Corporation restructured and deverticalized elements of its household and body care operations for a gain of about $300 million. In late September 1998, Sara Lee generated over $700 million from similar moves in its packaged meats operations. Other sales and changes followed. The company employed the funds to buy back stock and secure a strong presence in the coffee market through purchases of Chock Full O'Nuts, and Nestle's U.S. coffee operations (Hills Brothers, MJB, and Chase & Sanborn).

The results of these divestments and of the less diversified strategy that Sara Lee will follow at the corporate level demand a different organizational structure. Possible structural choices include the cooperative form of the multidivisional structure and even the functional structure (if Sara Lee's final set of divestments results in a highly focused firm—one with low levels of diversification). Wall Street's reaction to Sara Lee's deverticalization program was positive. On the day of the program's announcement, the company's stock rose 14 percent.

Sources: *Sara Lee Corporation home page,* 2000, http://www.saralee.com (Retrieved November 8); Separate and fit, 1997, *The Economist,* September 20, 69; R. Lowenstein, 1997, Remember when companies made things? *Wall Street Journal,* September 18, C1; R. Melcher, 1997, A finger in fewer pies, *BusinessWeek,* September 29, 44; J. P. Miller, 1997, Sara Lee to retreat from manufacturing, *Wall Street Journal,* September 16, A3, A10.

Our discussion now turns to an explanation of organizational structures used to implement the three international strategies explained in Chapter 9.

# IMPLEMENTING INTERNATIONAL STRATEGIES: ORGANIZATIONAL STRUCTURE AND CONTROLS

Although important for many firms, competing successfully in global markets is perhaps especially critical for large companies. For example, "a British survey has ranked Nortel Networks as the best of the world's big multinationals when it comes to actually making money overseas, helping boost Canada to second place among 12 nations ranked in the poll."[84] Nortel Networks is active in over 100 countries and territories around the world.

General Motors, a very large international firm, is altering its structure to reflect changes in strategy by merging its manufacturing of cars and trucks in North America. "For GM, the merger is the latest step in a long series of moves aimed at taking a company that for decades had been run largely as individual fiefdoms into a single global organization."[85] The move is designed to integrate the work of engineers with that of manufacturing and marketing personnel. International strategies such as those chosen by GM's top executives cannot be implemented successfully without using the proper organizational structure.[86]

## Using the Worldwide Geographic Area Structure to Implement the Multidomestic Strategy

The multidomestic strategy is a strategy in which strategic and operating decisions are decentralized to business units in each country to facilitate tailoring of products to local markets. Through this strategy, Campbell Soup customizes its products to local tastes. For example, the firm's cream of pumpkin soup is Australia's best-selling canned soup. In Hong Kong, Campbell sells watercress-and-duck-gizzard soup.[87] However, it is sometimes difficult for firms to know how local their products should or can become. Lands' End, for example, is one of the U.S. mail-order firms being lured by the promise of the European market for its products and services. Interested in adapting to local preferences, the firm's director of international operations observed that the most difficult part of achieving this objective is to know in which areas to be local.[88]

Firms implementing the multidomestic strategy often attempt to isolate themselves from global competitive forces by establishing protected market positions or by competing in industry segments that are most affected by differences among local countries. The **worldwide geographic area structure** (see Figure 12.12) is used to implement the multidomestic strategy. This structure emphasizes national interests and facilitates managers' efforts to satisfy local or cultural differences.

The Body Shop, which pioneered the trend toward nature represented by "green" cosmetics, has been changing its centralized structure to create a stronger focus on regions of the world. This restructuring to the worldwide geographic area structure was proposed after Patrick Cournay took over the CEO position from the company's founder, Anita Roddick. The change includes "shifting centralized management from the company's base in Littlehampton [in the United Kingdom] to regional units in the U.K., Europe, the Americas and Asia."[89] Along with the structural change, the Body Shop is changing its approach to sourcing from local manufacturers linked to the regional centres. However, these manufacturers "would have to uphold the company's ban on animal testing, and other 'green' guidelines."[90]

The **worldwide geographic area structure** emphasizes national interests and facilitates managers' efforts to satisfy local or cultural differences.

■ ■ **FIGURE 12.12**

*Worldwide Geographic Area Structure for Implementation of a Multidomestic Strategy*

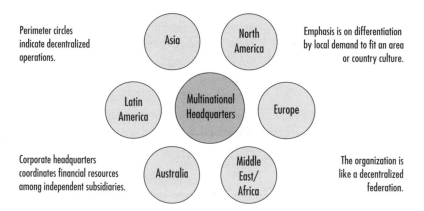

Because implementing the multidomestic strategy requires little coordination between different country markets, there is no need for integrating mechanisms among divisions in the worldwide geographic area structure. As such, formalization is low, and coordination among units in a firm's worldwide geographic area structure is often informal. Because each European country has a distinct culture, the multidomestic strategy and the associated worldwide geographic structure were a natural outgrowth of the multicultural marketplace. Friends and family members of the main business who were sent as expatriates into foreign countries to develop the independent country subsidiary often developed this type of structure originally. The relationship to corporate headquarters by divisions took place through informal communication among "family members."[91]

The primary disadvantage of the multidomestic strategy and worldwide geographic area structure combination is the inability to create global efficiency. As the emphasis on lower-cost products has increased in international markets, the need to pursue worldwide economies of scale and scope has increased. These changes have fostered use of the global strategy.

## Using the Worldwide Product Divisional Structure to Implement the Global Strategy

The global strategy is a strategy in which standardized products are offered across country markets and where competitive strategy is dictated by the firm's home office. International scale and scope economies are sought and emphasized when implementing this international strategy. Because of the important relationship between scale and scope economies and successful implementation of the global strategy, some activities of the firm's organizational functions are sourced to the most effective worldwide providers.

The worldwide product divisional structure (see Figure 12.13) is used to implement the global strategy. The **worldwide product divisional structure** is an organizational form in which decisionmaking authority is centralized in the worldwide division headquarters to coordinate and integrate decisions and actions among disparate divisional business units. This form is the organizational structure of choice for rapidly growing firms seeking to manage their diversified product lines effectively.[92] Integrating mechanisms also create effective coordination through mutual adjustments in personal interactions. Such integrating mechanisms include direct contact between managers, liaison roles between departments, temporary task forces or permanent teams, and integrating roles. As managers participate in cross-country transfers, they are socialized in the philosophy of managing an integrated strategy through a worldwide product divisional structure. A shared vision of the firm's strategy and structure is developed through standardized policies and procedures (formalization) that facilitate implementation of this organizational form.

The **worldwide product divisional structure** is an organizational form in which decisionmaking authority is centralized in the worldwide division headquarters to coordinate and integrate decisions and actions among disparate divisional business units.

■ ■ **FIGURE 12.13**

*Worldwide Product Divisional Structure for Implementation of a Global Strategy*

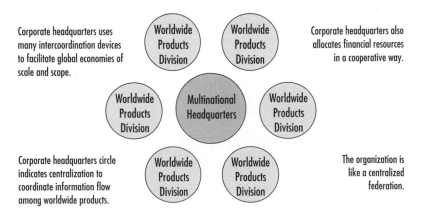

Corporate headquarters uses many intercoordination devices to facilitate global economies of scale and scope.

Corporate headquarters also allocates financial resources in a cooperative way.

Corporate headquarters circle indicates centralization to coordinate information flow among worldwide products.

The organization is like a centralized federation.

Worldwide Products Division

Worldwide Products Division

Worldwide Products Division

Multinational Headquarters

Worldwide Products Division

Worldwide Products Division

Worldwide Products Division

Two primary disadvantages of the global strategy and its accompanying worldwide product divisional structure are the difficulty involved with coordinating decisions and actions across country borders and the inability to respond quickly and effectively to local needs and preferences. As explained in the Strategic Focus, H. J. Heinz uses the worldwide product divisional structure to meet the conflicting demands of coordination and response in implementing its global strategy. Notice that this structure is expected to contribute to the firm's efforts to improve its international operations.

## STRATEGIC FOCUS

### Using the Worldwide Product Divisional Structure as a Means of Increased Internationalization

Headquartered in Pittsburgh, Pennsylvania, H. J. Heinz is a worldwide food producer. Perhaps known best for its ubiquitous ketchup, the firm also sells infant foods, condiments, pet foods, tuna, and is involved with weight-control products and programs as well. Heinz has a strong international presence, deriving 45 percent of sales revenue from operations outside the United States. However, the firm's CEO, William R. Johnson, believes that Heinz has yet to derive full strategic benefit from efforts to internationalize its business. As such, he is convinced that Heinz can improve its overall corporate performance through renewed efforts to compete successfully outside the firm's domestic U.S. markets. Committed to the global strategy rather than the multidomestic strategy, organizational structure plays a key role in the strategic actions Johnson is taking to enhance Heinz's strategic competitiveness.

Under the leadership of Anthony O'Reilly, Johnson's predecessor, Heinz used the worldwide geographic area structure to implement the multidomestic international strategy. Through this structure, decisions were decentralized to business units in various countries or regions to facilitate the tailoring of the company's products to local tastes. Johnson, however, is organizing Heinz in terms of product categories rather than geographic areas. In this manner, "... tuna managers in Europe will work with tuna managers in Asia, Latin America, and other regions, allowing the best brand manager to advise all the countries." Through the operations supported by this structure, Heinz seeks to create additional value by emphasizing its brand names.

One indicator of the new organizational structure was the establishment of a new worldwide products division. Created in 1998, the Specialty Pet Food division was given the responsibility of marketing Heinz's specialty pet foods on a global basis. In particular, marketing efforts were to be focused on introducing Heinz's specialty pet food brands (e.g., Nature's Recipe, Vet's Choice, and Martin Pet Foods) to Europe and other developing pet food markets such as South America, Asia, Australia, and South Africa. In commenting about this new division, then-current CEO O'Reilly suggested that Specialty Pet Foods was an example of Heinz's commitment to reorganize its corporate structure to support the firm's growth initiatives and its desire to continue building international operations.

*continued*

Johnson has other strategic actions that he wants Heinz to initiate. Implementation of these actions, too, will be supported by use of the worldwide product divisional structure. For example, he wants his firm to continue test-marketing products that have been successful in one country in other locations. Frozen tuna filets and flavoured tuna, which have sold well in Europe, were tested recently in the United States. In fact, attempts to cross-sell products among different nations are an important component to Heinz's desire to exploit the value of its brand names internationally.

To evaluate more effectively the performance of individual worldwide products divisions, personnel at Heinz's headquarters have assumed a more prominent role. One result of these evaluations is the decision to consider selling Weight Watchers, the weight-control business that makes frozen foods and offers weight-control classes. Although successful in the United Kingdom, the program has been a disappointment in North America. It remains to be seen whether Heinz's global strategy will improve the company's international operations.

Sources: Heinz makes appointments at three international affiliates; Announces formation of Specialty Pet Food unit, 1998, *Infoseek*, February 4, http://www.infoseek.com; R. Balu, 1997, Heinz's Johnson to divest operations, scrap management of firm by regions, *Wall Street Journal*, December 8, B22; Separate and fit, 1997, *The Economist*, September 20, 69.

## Using the Combination Structure to Implement the Transnational Strategy

The transnational strategy is an international strategy through which a firm seeks to both provide the local responsiveness that is the focus of the multidomestic strategy and achieve the global efficiency that is the focus of the global strategy. The **combination structure** has characteristics and structural mechanisms that result in an emphasis on both geographic and product structures. Unilever Group, for example, uses the combination structure, dividing its operations into 14 business groups. Some of the groups are framed around emerging markets; others are framed around the company's European food and drink businesses.[93] Thus, this structure has the multidomestic strategy's geographic area focus and the global strategy's product focus. The following company statement shows the approach this structure supports:

> The **combination structure** has characteristics and structural mechanisms that result in an emphasis on both geographic and product structures.

*Unilever describes itself as international, not global, because it does not attempt to enter all markets with the same product. Half of Unilever's business is in food, where it is often essential to take a local view. Only a few products—like ice cream, tea, and olive oil—successfully cross national or regional borders. Similarly, in detergents, the formulation Unilever sells in South Africa will differ from the one in France because washing habits, machines, clothes, and water quality are all different. Personal wash products, on the other hand, need to vary less, so there are strong international brands like Lux and Dove. The Unilever portfolio includes a balanced mix of local, regional and international brands, which take account of the differences as well as the similarities in consumer needs.[94]*

The fits between the multidomestic strategy and the worldwide geographic area structure and the global strategy and the worldwide product divisional structure are apparent. However, when a firm seeks to implement both the multidomestic and global strategies simultaneously through a combination structure, the appropriate integrating mechanisms for the two structures are less obvious. The structure used to implement the transnational strategy must be simultaneously centralized and decentralized, integrated and nonintegrated, and formalized and nonformalized. These seemingly opposing structural characteristics must be managed by a structure that is capable of encouraging all employees to understand the effects of cultural diversity on a firm's operations. Moreover, the combination structure should allow the firm to learn how to gain competitive benefits in local economies by adapting capabilities and core competencies that often have been developed and nurtured in less culturally diverse competitive environments.

In the next section, we focus on implementation of the dominant forms of the cooperative strategies that were discussed in Chapter 10.

# IMPLEMENTING COOPERATIVE STRATEGIES: ORGANIZATIONAL STRUCTURE AND CONTROLS

Increasingly, to implement cooperative strategies, companies develop multiple rather than single joint ventures or strategic alliances. Because the global marketplace accommodates many interconnected relationships among firms, networks of firms compete through an array of cooperative arrangements or alliances.[95] When managed effectively, cooperative arrangements can contribute positively to each partner's ability to achieve strategic competitiveness and earn above-average returns.

To facilitate the effectiveness of a strategic network—a grouping of organizations that has been formed to create value through participation in an array of cooperative arrangements such as a strategic alliance—a strategic centre firm may be necessary. A strategic centre firm facilitates management of a strategic network. Through its management, the centre firm creates incentives that reduce the probability of any company taking actions that could harm its network partners, and the centre firm identifies actions that increase the opportunity for each firm to achieve competitive success through its participation in the network.[96] Illustrated in Figure 12.14, the strategic centre firm is vital to the ability of companies to create value and increase their strategic competitiveness. The four critical aspects of the strategic centre firm's function are:

*Strategic outsourcing:* The strategic centre firm outsources and partners with more firms than do the other network members. Nonetheless, the strategic centre firm requires partners to be more than contractors. Partners are expected to solve problems and to initiate competitive courses of action that can be pursued by the network.

*Capability:* The strategic centre firm has core competencies that are not shared with all network partners. To increase the network's effectiveness, the centre firm attempts to develop each partner's core competencies and provides incentives for network firms to share their capabilities and competencies with partners.

*Technology:* The strategic centre firm manages the development and sharing of technology-based ideas among network partners.

*Race to learn:* The strategic centre firm emphasizes to partners that the principal dimension of competition in competitive environments is between value chains and networks of value chains. As a result, a strategic network is as strong as its weakest value-chain link. As a value-chain link, a strategic network seeks to develop a competitive advantage in a primary or support activity (see Chapter 4). The need for each firm to be strong for the benefit of the entire network encourages positive rivalry among partners to learn rapidly and effectively.[97] The most effective strategic centre firms learn how to manage learning processes occurring among network members.

The dominant problem in single venture cooperative arrangements is the lack of ability to control innovation and learning. However, a well-managed strategic network can overcome this problem. Therefore, as explained in the following discussions, the managerial role of the strategic centre firm is critical to the successful implementation of business-level, corporate-level, and international cooperative strategies.

■ ■ **FIGURE 12.14**

*A Strategic Network*

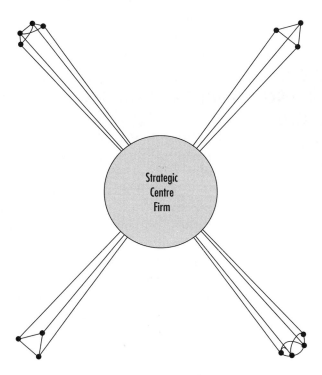

## Implementing Business-Level Cooperative Strategies

As noted in Chapter 10, there are two types of complementary assets at the business level—vertical and horizontal. Vertical complementary strategic alliances are formed more frequently than horizontal alliances. Focused on buyer-supplier relationships, vertical strategic networks usually have a clear strategic centre firm. Japanese vertical keiretsus such as those developed by Toyota are structured this way. Acting as the strategic centre firm, Toyota fashioned its lean production system around a network of supplier firms.

A strategic network of vertical relationships in Japan such as the network between Toyota and its suppliers often includes the following implementation issues. First, the strategic centre firm encourages subcontractors to modernize their facilities and provides them with technical and financial assistance if necessary. Second, it reduces its transaction costs by promoting longer-term contracts with subcontractors so that supplying partners increase their long-term productivity, rather than continually negotiating short-term contracts based on unit pricing. Third, the centre firm provides engineers in upstream companies (suppliers) better communication with contractees. Thus, the contractees and centre firms become more interdependent and less independent.[98]

The lean production system pioneered by Toyota has been diffused throughout the Japanese and U.S. automobile industries. However, no automobile producer is able to duplicate the effectiveness and efficiency Toyota derives from use of this manufacturing system.[99] A key factor accounting for Toyota's ability to derive a competitive advantage from this system is the cost to imitate the structural form used to support its application. In other words, Toyota's largely proprietary actions as the strategic centre firm in the network it created are ones that competitors are unable to duplicate.

In vertical complementary strategic alliances, such as the one between Toyota and its suppliers, the company that should function as the strategic centre firm is obvious. However, this is not always the case with horizontal complementary strategic alliances. For example, the large airline alliances (discussed in a Strategic Focus in Chapter 10) have been quite unstable over the years, and a number of network partners have changed from one network to another or become partners in several networks.[100] Delta Airlines, for instance, recently changed allegiances in Europe from an affiliation with Swiss Air and Sabena to Air France.[101] This instability is usually caused by continuing rivalries among cooperating partners. A problem common to all of these ventures is the difficulty of selecting the strategic centre firm. The distrust that formed among the network airline companies through years of aggressive competition prevented them from agreeing on which firm should function as the strategic centre of a network. Because it is unclear which firm should be the dominant strategic centre firm in a horizontal complementary strategic alliance, these types of alliances tend to be far less stable than vertical complementary strategic alliances.

## Implementing Corporate-Level Cooperative Strategies

In some types of corporate-level cooperative strategies, it is difficult to choose a strategic centre firm. For example, it is difficult for a strategic centre firm to emerge in a centralized franchise network, such as McDonald's.

McDonald's has formed a centralized strategic network in which its corporate office serves as the strategic centre for its franchisees. Recently, McDonald's performance has been mediocre, and a new CEO, Jack M. Greenberg, has been trying to improve the network. Although McDonald's has had success with its Teenie Beanie Babies and Furby dolls promotions, without an improved menu and delivery system, the success is not likely to last. Long a favourite of children, McDonald's does not inspire the same degree of enthusiasm in their parents. Developed through the strategic centre's centralized R&D function, a new product aimed at adults was introduced. Called the Arch Deluxe, this food item was pitched as "the burger with a grown-up taste." However, the Arch Deluxe was not successful, and one analyst suggested that McDonald's was a brand in need of radical surgery.

To cope with its problems, McDonald's, as a strategic centre firm, initiated a series of actions. Framed around the need to improve the quality of its products and speed their delivery, the company developed a "just-in-time kitchen" concept for use by franchisees. This new production system is designed to move made-to-order sandwiches to customers without increasing the preparation time. As part of the system, a computer-monitored machine dumps frozen fries into a basket that in turn is dunked into hot oil for cooking. The machine then shakes the fries and dumps them into bins for serving. Simultaneously, robot machines quickly prepare drinks ordered by the customer. Preventing the full use of the system's capabilities, however, was the delay in supplying all franchisees with the equipment. Thus, as the strategic centre firm in its centralized franchise network, McDonald's still faces significant challenges.[102]

Unlike McDonald's corporate-level cooperative strategy, Corning's strategy has resulted in the implementation of a system of diversified strategic alliances that has required the company to implement a decentralized network. Over time, Corning has focused on intangible resources, such as a reputation for being a trustworthy and committed partner, to develop competitively successful strategic partnerships. In this situation, the strategic network has loose connections between joint ventures or multiple centres, although Corning is typically the principal centre. However, the joint ventures are less dependent on the strategic centre firm and, consequently, require less managerial attention from it.[103]

## Implementing International Cooperative Strategies

Competing in multiple countries dramatically increases the complexity associated with attempts to manage successful strategic networks formed through international cooperative strategies.[104] A key reason for this increased complexity is the differences among countries' regulatory environments. These differences are especially apparent in regulated industries such as telecommunications and air travel.

■ ■ **FIGURE 12.15**

*A Distributed Strategic Network*

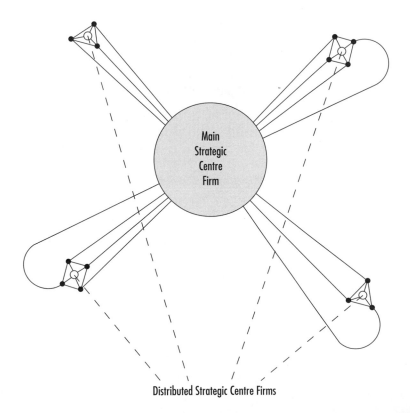

**Distributed Strategic Centre Firms**

As shown in Figure 12.15, many large, multinational firms form distributed strategic networks with multiple regional strategic centres to manage their array of cooperative arrangements with partner firms.[105] Several large multinational firms illustrate these networks. Swedish firms such as Ericsson (telecommunications exchange equipment) and Electrolux (white goods, washing machines) have strategic centres located in countries throughout the world instead of only in Sweden where they are headquartered. Ericsson, for example, is active in more than 100 countries and employs over 85 000. Divided into five business areas (public telecommunications, radio communications, business networks, components, and microwave systems), the firm has cooperative agreements with companies throughout the world.

A world leader in electrical engineering, Asea Brown Boveri Group (ABB) is involved with a significant number of distributed strategic networks. Organized into four key business segments (power generation, power transmission and distribution, industrial and building systems, and financial services), ABB features 1 000 companies and 36 separate business areas. With a new, global 11-member board of directors representing seven nationalities, ABB considers itself a truly global company—one without a single country home. The firm has formed strategic networks in its key world areas of the Americas, Europe (including the former Soviet Union), the Middle East and North Africa, sub-Sahara Africa, and Asia Pacific.[106]

## CONTEMPORARY ORGANIZATIONAL STRUCTURES: A CAUTIONARY NOTE

Contemporary organizational structures such as those used to implement international cooperative strategies emerge typically in response to social and technological advances.[107] However, the redesign of organizations throughout society—indeed globally—necessarily entails losses as well as gains.[108] For example, Nortel's outsourcing of a variety of corporate services—including payroll, employee training, human resource centres, accounts payable, and employee expenses—was a deal reportedly worth nearly $1 billion over five years.[109] Similarly, DuPont, the world's largest chemicals concern, decided recently to scrap most of its central support groups. Primarily, these groups provided information technology, communications, and other services to the company's main operating divisions. The gains expected from this decision included elimination of some corporate bureaucracy and reductions in the amount of time required for production innovations to reach the marketplace. The primary loss associated with these kinds of gains concerned personnel. Although some workers were to be transferred to other positions, many lost their jobs.[110]

With new organizational forms, many workers become deskilled—that is, their abilities are not sufficient to perform successfully in a new structure that often demands constant innovation and adaptation. This may describe the situation for some of the workers that are to be assigned to new positions within DuPont. The learning organization that is a part of new organizational forms requires that each worker become a self-motivated, continuous learner.[111] At least in the short run, a number of employees lack the level of confidence necessary to participate actively in organizationally sponsored learning experiences. Moreover, the flatter organizational structures that accompany contemporary structures can seem intrusive as a result of their demand for more intense and personal interactions with internal and external stakeholders. Combined, these conditions may create stress for many.

These realities do not call for managers to abandon efforts to adopt organizational structures that have the greatest probability of facilitating successful implementation of a firm's strategies. The challenge for those responsible for effective use of the strategic management process depicted in Figure 1.1 of Chapter 1 is to respond to various issues associated with the development and use of new organizational structures in ways that will enhance the productivity of individuals and the firm.[112] As explained in the next chapter, this responsibility belongs to strategic leaders.

# SUMMARY

- Organizational structure is a formal configuration that largely determines what a firm will do and how the firm will complete its work. Different structures are required to implement different strategies. A firm's performance increases when strategy and structure are matched properly.

- Business-level strategies are usually implemented through the functional structure. The cost leadership strategy requires a centralized functional structure—one in which manufacturing efficiency and process engineering are emphasized. The differentiation strategy's functional structure decentralizes implementation-related decisions, especially those concerned with marketing, to those involved with other functional areas. Focus strategies, used in small firms, require a simple structure until such time that a firm begins to compete in multiple markets and/or sells multiple products.

- The evolution from the functional structure to the three types of the multidivisional structure (M-form) occurred from the 1920s to the early 1970s. The cooperative M-form, used to implement the related-constrained corporate-level strategy, has a centralized corporate office and extensive integrating mechanisms. Divisional incentives are linked to overall corporate performance. The related-linked SBU M-form structure establishes separate profit centres within the diversified firm. Each profit centre may have divisions offering similar products, but the centres are unrelated to each other. The competitive M-form structure, used to implement the unrelated diversification strategy, is highly decentralized, integrating mechanisms are nonexistent, and objective financial criteria are used to evaluate each unit's performance.

- Initially, an organizational structure is chosen in light of support required to implement a firm's strategy. Once established, however, structure influences strategy. This is observed most prominently in the M-form structure, stimulating additional diversification in the diversified firm.

- The multidomestic strategy, implemented through the worldwide geographic area structure, emphasizes decentralization and locates all functional activities in the country or geographic area. The worldwide product divisional structure is used to implement the global strategy. This structure is centralized to coordinate and integrate different functions' activities to gain global economies of scope and scale. Decisionmaking authority is centralized in the firm's worldwide division headquarters. The transnational strategy—a strategy through which the firm seeks the local responsiveness of the multidomestic strategy and the global efficiency of the global strategy—is implemented through the combination structure. Because it must be simultaneously centralized and decentralized, integrated and nonintegrated, and formalized and nonformalized, the combination structure is difficult to organize and manage successfully.

- Increasingly important to competitive success, cooperative strategies are implemented through organizational structures framed around strategic networks.

# REVIEW QUESTIONS

1. Why is it important that the strategic actions of strategy implementation and strategy formulation be integrated carefully?

2. What is the meaning of the following statement: "In organizations, there is a consistent path of structure following strategy and then strategy following structure"?

3. What organizational structures are used to implement the cost leadership, differentiation, integrated low-cost/differentiation, and focused business-level strategies?

4. What organizational structures are used to implement the related-constrained, related-linked, and unrelated corporate-level diversification strategies?

5. What organizational structures should be used to implement the multidomestic, global, and transnational international strategies?

6. What is a strategic network? What is a strategic centre firm? What roles do they play in organizational structures used to implement cooperative strategies?

## DISCUSSION QUESTIONS

1. Why do firms experience evolutionary cycles where there is a fit between strategy and structure punctuated with periods in which strategy and structure are reshaped? Provide examples of prominent Canadian firms that have experienced this pattern.

2. Select an organization (for example, an employer, a social club, or a nonprofit agency) in which you currently hold membership. What is this organization's structure? Do you believe this organization is using the structure that is appropriate, given its strategy? If not, what structure should be used?

3. Examine the popular Canadian business press to find a firm using the multidivisional structure. Which form of the multidivisional structure is the firm using? Why is it appropriate for the M-form to be in use in this firm?

4. Through reading the Canadian business press, locate one firm implementing the global strategy and one implementing the multidomestic strategy. What organizational structure is being used in each firm? Are these structures allowing each firm's strategy to be implemented successfully? Why or why not?

5. Identify a businessperson in your local community. Provide definitions of strategic and financial controls to him or her. Ask the businessperson to describe to you the use of each type of control in his or her business. In which type of control does the businessperson have the greatest confidence, and why?

## ETHICS QUESTIONS

1. When a firm changes from the functional structure to the multidivisional structure, what respon-

sibilities do you believe it has to current employees?

2. Are there ethical issues associated with the use of strategic controls? With the use of financial controls? If so, what are they?

3. Are there ethical issues involved in implementing the cooperative and competitive M-form structures? If so, what are they? As a top-level manager, how would you deal with them?

4. Global and multidomestic strategies call for different competitive approaches. What ethical concerns might surface when firms attempt to market standardized products globally or when they develop different products/approaches for each local market?

5. What ethical issues are associated with the view that the "redesign of organizations throughout the society—indeed globally—necessarily entails losses as well as gains"?

## INTERNET EXERCISE

Go to Nortel's home page at:

**http://www.nortelnetworks.com/corporate**

Use the Internet to conduct research on Nortel. How would you describe Nortel's organizational structure? Does Nortel's structure appropriately complement its competitive strategies?

## STRATEGIC SURFING

*The Economist* is a high-quality British magazine available on-line. The magazine publishes thoughtful articles on economics, politics, international business, management, and other issues. Search *The Economist* and find an example of a firm that illustrates the distributed strategic network.

**http://www.economist.com**

## NOTES

1 R. A. Johnson & D. W. Greening, 1999, The effects of corporate governance and institutional ownership on types of corporate social performance, *Academy of Management Journal*, 42: 564–76.

2 R. J. Kramer, 1999, Organizing for global competitiveness: The corporate headquarters design, *Chief Executive Digest*, 3 (2): 23–28; D. J. Teece, G. Pisano, & A. Shuen, 1997, Dynamic capabilities and strategic management, *Strategic Management Journal*, 18: 509–33.

3   A. Sharma, 1999, Central dilemmas of managing innovation in large firms, *California Management Review,* 41 (3): 146–64; C. Hales & Z. Tamangani, 1996, An investigation of the relationship between organizational structure, managerial role expectations and managers' work activities, *Journal of Management Studies,* 33: 731–56.

4   S. E. Human & K. Provan, 1997, An emergent theory of structure and outcomes in small-firm strategic manufacturing networks, *Academy of Management Journal,* 40: 368–403.

5   D. Miller & O. J. Whitney, 1999, Beyond strategy: Configuration as a pillar of competitive advantage, *Business Horizons,* 42 (3): 5–7; M. H. Overholt, 1997, Flexible organizations: Using organizational design as a competitive advantage, *Human Resource Planning,* 20, (1): 22–32.

6   J. R. Galbraith, 1995, *Designing Organizations* (San Francisco: Jossey-Bass), 6.

7   J. Kurtzman, 1998, An interview with Stan Shih, in J. Kurtzman (ed.), *Thought Leaders* (San Francisco: Jossey-Bass), 85–93.

8   A. Y. Ilinitch, R. A. D'Aveni, & A. Y. Lewin, 1996, New organizational forms and strategies for managing in hypercompetitive environments, *Organization Science,* 7: 211–20.

9   D. A. Nadler & M. L. Tushman, 1997, *Competing by Design: The Power of Organizational Architecture* (New York: Oxford University Press).

10  E. F. Suarez & J. M. Utterback, 1995, Dominant designs and the survival of firms, *Strategic Management Journal,* 16: 415–30.

11  R. A. Heifetz & D. L. Laurie, 1997, The work of leadership, *Harvard Business Review,* 75, (1): 124–34; R. H. Hall, 1996, *Organizations: Structures, Processes, and Outcomes* (6th ed.) (Englewood Cliffs, NJ: Prentice-Hall), 106–07.

12  K. Leger, 2000, Seagram name to be dropped: US$30b merger. Talks confirmed, new name would be Vivendi Universal, *National Post,* June 15, C1, C9; M. Fraser, 2000, Stodgy Vivendi puts on the ritz: French utility would become media powerhouse, *National Post,* June 15, C1, C9.

13  H. W. Volberda, 1996, Toward the flexible form: How to remain vital in hypercompetitive environments, *Organization Science,* 7: 359–74.

14  D. Sull, 1999, Why good companies go bad, *Harvard Business Review,* 77 (4): 42–52; Nadler & Tushman, *Competing by Design,* 9.

15  A. D. Chandler, Jr., 1990, *Scale and Scope: The Dynamics of Industrial Capitalism* (Cambridge: The Belknap Press of Harvard University Press), 182–83.

16  J. A. Chesley & M. S. Wenger, 1999, Transforming an organization: Using models to foster a strategic conversation, *California Management Review,* 41 (3): 54–73.

17  T. Ebden, Danone acquires Naya's trademark Quebec plant, *Globe & Mail Metro Edition,* June 17, B4.

18  G. Hamel, 1997, Killer strategies, *Fortune,* June 23, 82.

19  C. H. Noble, 1999, The eclectic roots of strategy implementation research, *Journal of Business Research,* 45: 119–34.

20  Galbraith, *Designing Organizations,* 13; R. R. Nelson, 1994, Why do firms differ, and how does it matter? in R. P. Rumelt, D. E. Schendel, & D. J. Teece (eds.), *Fundamental Issues in Strategy* (Cambridge, MA: Harvard Business School Press), 259.

21  L. Donaldson, 1997, A positivist alternative to the structure-action approach, *Organization Studies,* 18: 77–92; Hales and Tamangani, An investigation of the relationship, 738; Nelson, Why do firms?, 259.

22  B. C. Esty, 1997, A case study of organizational form and risk shifting in the savings and loan industry, *Journal of Financial Economics,* 44: 57–76; C. W. L. Hill, 1994, Diversification and economics performance: Bringing structure and corporate management back into the picture, in R. P. Rumelt, D. E. Schendel, & D. J. Teece (eds.), *Fundamental Issues in Strategy* (Cambridge, MA: Harvard Business School Press), 297–321.

23  W. B. Werther, Jr., 1999, Structure driven strategy and virtual organization design, *Business Horizons,* 42 (2): 13–18.

24  R. Waters, 1997, Return of the downsizers, *Financial Times,* December 19, 13.

25  Statcan, 2000, Have small firms created a disproportionate share of new jobs in Canada? A reassessment of the facts (*Analytical Studies Branch research paper series*),http://www.statcan.ca/english/IPS/Data/11F0019MPE94071.htm (Retrieved November 6).

26  V. Griffith, 1997, Lumbering giants, *Financial Times,* December 15, 10.

27  J. J. Chrisman, A. Bauerschmidt, & C. W. Hofer, 1998, The determinants of new venture performance: An extended model, *Entrepreneurship Theory & Practice,* 23: 5–29; H. M. O'Neill, R. W. Pouder, & A. K. Buchholtz, 1998, Patterns in the diffusion of strategies across organizations: Insights from the innovation diffusion literature, *Academy of Management Review,* 23: 98–114.

28  *YoSushi home page,* 2000, http://www.yosushi.com (Retrieved November 7); M. Carter, 1998, The world according to Yo!, *Financial Times,* January 26, 11.

29  Galbraith, *Designing Organizations,* 25.

30  P. Lawrence & J. W. Lorsch, 1967, *Organization and Environment* (Cambridge, MA: Harvard Business School Press).

31  H. M. O'Neill, R. W. Pouder, & A. K. Buchholtz, 1998, Patterns in the diffusion of strategies across organizations: Insights from the innovation diffusion literature, *Academy of Management Review,* 23: 98–114.

32  W. G. Rowe & P. M. Wright, 1997, Related and unrelated diversification and their effect on human resource management controls, *Strategic Management Journal,* 18: 329–38; D. C. Galunic & K. M. Eisenhardt, 1996, The evolution of intracorporate domains: Divisional charter losses in high-technology, multidivisional corporations, *Organization Science,* 7: 255–82.

33  G. G. Dess, A. Gupta, J. F. Hennart, & C. W. L. Hill, 1995, Conducting and integrating strategy research at the international, corporate, and business levels: Issues and directions, *Journal of Management,* 21: 357–93.

34  A. D. Chandler, 1962, *Strategy and Structure: Chapters in the History of the American Industrial Enterprise* (Cambridge, MA: The MIT Press).

35  O. E. Williamson, 1994, Strategizing, economizing, and economic organization, in R. P. Rumelt, D. E. Schendel, & D. J. Teece (eds.), *Fundamental Issues in Strategy* (Cambridge, MA: Harvard Business School Press), 361–401.

36  Galbraith, *Designing Organizations,* 27.

37  J. Greco, 1999, Alfred P. Sloan, Jr. (1875–1966): The original "organization" man, *Journal of Business Strategy,* 20 (5): 30–31.

38  R. E. Hoskisson, C. W. L. Hill, & H. Kim, 1993, The multidivisional structure: Organizational fossil or source of value? *Journal of Management,* 19: 269–98.

39  Rowe & Wright, Related and unrelated diversification, 329–38.

40  C. M. Farkas & S. Wetlaufer, 1996, The ways chief executive officers lead, *Harvard Business Review,* 74, (3): 110–22.

41  C. C. Miller, L. M. Burke, & W. H. Glick, 1998, Cognitive diversity among upper-echelon executives: Implications for strategic decision processes, *Strategic Management Journal,* 19: 39–58; D. J. Collis, 1996, Corporate strategy in multibusiness firms, *Long Range Planning,* 29: 416–18.

42  M. A. Hitt, R. E. Hoskisson, R. A. Johnson, & D. D. Moesel, 1996, The market for corporate control and firm innovation, *Academy of Management Journal,* 39: 1084–1119.

43  R. E. Hoskisson, M. A. Hitt, & R. D. Ireland, 1994, The effects of acquisitions and restructuring (strategic refocusing) strategies on innovation, in G. von Krogh, A. Sinatra, & H. Singh (eds.), *Managing Corporate Acquisitions* (London: Macmillan Press), 144–69.

44  R. E. Hoskisson & M. A. Hitt, 1988, Strategic control and relative R&D investment in large multiproduct firms, *Strategic Management Journal,* 9: 605–21.

45  *Canadian Press Newswire,* 2000, Some facts on CIBC's sale of its insurance operations, June 22.

46  Collis, Corporate strategy, 417.

47  M. A. Hitt, R. E. Hoskisson, & R. D. Ireland, 1990, Mergers and acquisitions and managerial commitment to innovation in M-form firms, *Strategic Management Journal,* 11 (Special Summer Issue): 29–47.

48  S. Baiman, D. F. Larcker, & M. V. Rajan, 1995, Organizational design for business units, *Journal of Accounting Research,* 33: 205–29; Hall, Organizations, 13.

49  Ibid., Hall, 64–75.

50  J. B. Barney, 1997, *Gaining and Sustaining Competitive Strategy,* (Don Mills, ON: Addison-Wesley Publishing), 215–16.

51  T. Maxon, 1996, Southwest to let surfers use 'Net to arrange flights, *Dallas Morning News,* April 30, D1.

52  V. Boland, 1998, Airlines prepare to hit runway to privatization, *Financial Times,* January 26, 17.

53  P. Verburg, 2000, Reach for the bottom: When WestJet introduced bargain flights to Western Canada, competitors lost their shirts. How the downmarket is moving east, *Canadian Business,* March 6: 42–48.

54  C. Homburg, H. Krohmer, & J.P. Workman, Jr., 1999, Strategic consensus and performance: The role of strategy type and market-related dynamism, *Strategic Management Journal,* 20: 339–57.

55  *FAG home page,* 2000, http://www.fag.com (Retrieved November 8); FAG Kugelfischer, 1996, *Annual Report,* 22.

56  V. Govindarajan, 1988, A contingency approach to strategy implementation at the business-unit level: Integrating administrative mechanisms with strategy, *Academy of Management Journal,* 31: 828–53.

57  P. S. Adler, B. Goldoftas, & D. I. Levin, 1999, Flexibility versus efficiency? A case study of model changeovers in the Toyota production system, *Organization Science,* 10: 43–68.

58  D. K. Sobek, II, A. C. Howard, & J. K. Liker, 1999, Toyota's principles of set-based concurrent engineering, *Sloan Management Review,* 40 (2): 67–83.

59  R. Frank, 1996, Moxie, Big Red, other cult drinks thrive on being hometown heroes, *Wall Street Journal,* May 6, B1, B5.

60  J. Lau, 1997, It's old, it's cold, it's hot again, *Canadian Business,* August: 26–30.

61  Service Performance Corporation, 1998, *Fortune, Special Advertising Section,* February 2, S2.

62  C. C. Markides & P. J. Williamson, 1996, Corporate diversification and organizational structure: A resource-based view, *Academy of Management Journal,* 39: 340–67; C. W. L. Hill, M. A. Hitt, & R. E. Hoskisson, 1992, Cooperative versus competitive structures in related and unrelated diversified firms, *Organization Science,* 3: 501–21.

63  J. Robins & M. E. Wiersema, 1995, A resource-based approach to the multibusiness firm: Empirical analysis of portfolio interrelationships and corporate financial performance, *Strategic Management Journal,* 16: 277–99.

64  C. C. Markides, 1997, To diversify or not to diversify, *Harvard Business Review,* 75, (6): 93–99.

65  Nadler & Tushman, *Competing by Design,* 99.

66  Hall, Organizations, 186; J. G. March, 1994, *A Primer on Decision Making: How Decisions Happen* (New York: The Free Press), 117–18.

67  I. M. Kunii, E. Thornton, & J. Rae-Dupree, 1999, Sony's shake-up, *BusinessWeek,* 52–53.

68  P. J. Frost, 1997, Bridging academia and business: A conversation with Steve Kerr, *Organization Science,* 8: 335.

69  *GE home page,* 2000, www.ge.com (Retrieved March 1).

70  J. A. Byrne, 1998, How Jack Welch runs GE, *BusinessWeek Online,* June 8, www.businessweek.com.

71  T. A. Stewart, 1999, See Jack. See Jack run Europe. *Fortune,* September 27, 127.

72  R. E. Hoskisson & M. A. Hitt, 1990, Antecedents and performance outcomes of diversification: A review and critique of theoretical perspectives, *Journal of Management,* 16: 461–509.

73  C. W. L. Hill, M. A. Hitt, & R. E. Hoskisson, 1992, Cooperative versus competitive structures in related and unrelated diversified firms, *Organization Science,* 3: 501–21.

74  J. B. Barney, 1997, *Gaining and Sustaining Competitive Advantage* (Reading, MA: Addison-Wesley), 420–33.

75  *Newell Rubbermaid home page,* 2000, http://www.newellco.com (Retrieved February 24).

76  Collis, Corporate strategy, 418.

77  Williamson, Strategizing, economizing, 373.

78  B. W. Keats & M. A. Hitt, 1988, A causal model of linkages among environmental dimensions, macro organizational characteristics, and performance, *Academy of Management Journal,* 31: 570–98.

79  Hoskisson, Hill, & Kim, The multidivisional structure, 276.

80  R. E. Hoskisson, R. A. Johnson, & D. D. Moesel, 1994, Corporate divestiture intensity: Effects of governance strategy and performance, *Academy of Management Journal,* 37: 1207–51; R. E. Hoskisson & T. Turk, 1990, Corporate restructuring, governance and control limits of the internal capital market, *Academy of Management Review,* 15: 459–71.

81  S. J. Chang & H. Singh, 1999, The impact of entry and resource fit on modes of exit by multibusiness firms, *Strategic Management Journal,* 20: 1019–35; M. E. Porter, 1987, From competitive advantage to corporate strategy, *Harvard Business Review,* 65, (3): 43–59.

82  C. C. Markides, 1992, Consequences of corporate refocusing: Ex ante evidence, *Academy of Management Journal,* 35: 398–412.

83  S. Lipin, 1998. Cognizant, a D&B spin-off, to split in two, *Wall Street Journal,* January 15, A3.

84  J. Partridge, 2000, Nortel tops UK survey of global firms [Templeton Global Performance Index], *The Globe and Mail* Metro Edition, April 27, B1, B5.

85  G. L. White, 2000, GM to unify manufacturing of cars, trucks, *Wall Street Journal,* January 27, B22.

86  M. A. Hitt, M. T. Dacin, B. B. Tyler, & D. Park, 1997, Understanding the differences in Korean and U.S. executives' strategic orientations, *Strategic Management Journal,* 18: 159–67.

87  L. Grant, 1996, Stirring it up at Campbell, *Fortune,* May 13, 80–86.

88  C. Rahweddeer, 1998, U.S. mail-order firms shake up Europe, *Wall Street Journal,* January 6, A15.

89  E. Beck, 1999, Body Shop gets a makeover to cut costs, *Wall Street Journal,* January 27, A18.

90  Ibid.

91  Bartlett & Ghoshal, *Managing across Borders.*

92  Ibid.

93  C. Rohwedder, 1996, Unilever reorganizes its management as a first step in broad restructuring, *Wall Street Journal,* March 14, A11.

94  *Unilever home page,* 1998, http://www.unilever.com (Retrieved February 5).

95  B. Gomes-Casseres, 1994, Group versus group: How alliance networks compete, *Harvard Business Review,* 72 (4): 62–74.

96  G. R. Jones, 1998, *Organizational Theory* (Reading, MA: Addison-Wesley), 163–65.

97  P. Dussauge, B. Garrette, & W. Mitchell, 2000, Learning from competing partners: Outcomes and duration of scale and link alliances in Europe, North America and Asia, *Strategic Management Journal,* 21: 99–126; G. Lorenzoni & C. Baden-Fuller, 1995, Creating a strategic centre to manage a web of partners, *California Management Review,* 37, (3): 146–63.

98  T. Nishiguchi, 1994, *Strategic Industrial Sourcing: The Japanese Advantage* (New York: Oxford University Press).

99  W. M. Fruin, 1992, *The Japanese Enterprise System* (New York: Oxford University Press).

100  M. Skapinker, 1999, Airlines bent on bigamy ruffle alliances, *Financial Times,* June 23, 8.

101  D. Harbrecht, 1999, A talk with Air France's pilot as he hooks up with Delta, *BusinessWeek Online,* June 22, www.businessweek.com.

102  D. Leonhardt, A. T. Palmer, 1999, Getting off their McButts, *BusinessWeek,* February 22, 84-88; S. S. Branch, 1997, What's eating McDonald's? *Fortune,* October 13, 122–25.

103 *Corning home page,* 2000, www.corning.com (Retrieved February 24); J. R. Houghton, 1990, Corning cultivates joint ventures that endure, *Planning Review,* 18 (5): 15–17.

104 C. Jones, W. S. Hesterly, & S. P. Borgatti, 1997, A general theory of network governance: Exchange conditions and social mechanisms, *Academy of Management Review,* 22: 911–45.

105 R. E. Miles, C. C. Snow, J. A. Mathews, G. Miles, & J. J. Coleman, Jr., 1997, Organizing in the knowledge age: Anticipating the cellular form, *Academy of Management Executive,* XI, (4): 7–20.

106 *ABB Home Page,* 1998, http://www.abb.com (Retrieved February 5); Nadler and Tushman, *Competing by Design,* 89.

107 Chandler, *Scale and Scope.*

108 B. Victor & C. Stephens, 1994, The dark side of the new organizational forms: An editorial essay, *Organization Science,* 5: 479–82.

109 J. Partridge, 2000, Nortel tops UK survey of global firms, *Globe & Mail* Metro Edition, April 27, B1, B5.

110 R. Waters, 1998, New DuPont shake-up to slash bureaucracy, *Financial Times,* January 8, 3; A. Barrett, 1997, At DuPont, time to both sow and reap, *BusinessWeek,* September 29, 107-08.

111 M. A. Hitt, B. W. Keats, & S. M. DeMarie, 1998, Navigating in the new competitive landscape: Building competitive advantage and strategic flexibility in the 21st century, *Academy of Management Executive,* 12 (4): 22–42.

112 R. D. Ireland & M. A. Hitt, 1999, Achieving and maintaining strategic competitiveness in the 21st century: The role of strategic leadership, *Academy of Management Executive,* 13 (1) 34–57.

# Chapter Thirteen
## Strategic Leadership

### LEARNING OBJECTIVES

*After reading this chapter, you should be able to:*

1. Define strategic leadership and describe the importance of top-level managers as an organizational resource.
2. Differentiate among the concepts of strategic, visionary, and managerial leadership.
3. Define top-management teams and explain their effects on a firm's performance and its ability to innovate and make appropriate strategic changes.
4. Discuss the value of strategic leadership for determining the firm's strategic direction and explain the role of strategic leaders in exploiting and maintaining core competencies.
5. Describe the importance of strategic leaders in developing a firm's human capital.
6. Define organizational culture and explain the importance of what must be done to sustain an effective culture.
7. Describe what strategic leaders can do to establish and emphasize ethical practices in their firms.
8. Discuss the importance and use of organizational controls.

## Strategic Leadership in the 21st Century

Given changes toward a new competitive landscape mentioned in this book (in particular, see Chapters 1, 3, and 6), the role of strategic leaders is changing accordingly. As a result, leaders must manage this change process in a way that facilitates competitive success, which means more than just providing a well-designed solution. Change requires an effective implementation process, commitment from people throughout the organization, and the collective intelligence of employees at all levels, particularly those who need to use each other as resources. Working across internal and external organizational boundaries, employees must learn to work together to find solutions. Employees may look to the strategic leader for relief from stress in times of change, but rather than protecting them from outside threats, it is the role of leaders to stimulate their employees to adapt. Instead of maintaining norms, leaders encourage employees to change the way business is done from seemingly immutable practices bound by cultural heritage and history.

One CEO who has focused on strategic success and led his company through incredibly tough times over the last 15 years is Victor L. Young. Young became the CEO of FPI when several bankrupt Atlantic Coast fishing companies were consolidated into one on December 31, 1984. During the consolidation phase (1984 to 1986), Young's strategic focus was the return of these companies from the various levels of government that had supported them to the private sector. His leadership focus was "pulling ourselves up by our own bootstraps." FPI went public in April 1987. From 1987 to 1989, FPI's strategic focus was shareholder value growth, and Young's leadership focus was to be the number-one seafood company in the world. From 1990 to 1993, FPI's strategic focus was survival, and Young's leadership focus was to embrace change. The strategic focus from 1994 to 1995 was transition with a leadership focus to successfully re-invent FPI. These respective foci changed in 1996 to turnaround and creating momentum toward profitability. In 1998, the foci returned to growing shareholder wealth and being the number-one seafood company in the world.

FPI's strategic focus and Young's leadership focus changed so much over the 16-year period from 1984 to 2000 because FPI lost access to its major raw material supply—groundfish—in and around the waters of Newfoundland and Labrador. From 1987 to 1994, FPI lost over 90 percent of its previous core business (from 172 700 tonnes of groundfish in 1987 to 10 800 tonnes in 1994). Extreme ocean conditions, poor scientific data, overfishing, improved technology, and increased seal populations led to a federal government moratorium on the catching of groundfish in 1993. This loss required a major restructuring within FPI that took place from 1993 to 1997.

In 1987, FPI had 66 active vessels, 19 active plants, and 8600 employees. By 1995, the numbers had been reduced to 12 vessels, 9 plants, and 2600 employees. Between 1991 and 1992, FPI wrote down $85 million in assets. In 1993, Young led FPI through a transition that would see it change from a North Atlantic-based harvesting, procurement, processing, and marketing business to a global seafood enterprise that sells a wide range of products in more than 15 countries and sources raw material from more than 30 countries. In his 1993 Report to Shareholders, Young said that FPI would transition from a vertically integrated fishing company to an international seafood enterprise. By 1997, he was able to say that, after seven years, FPI had been reinvented from a Newfoundland fishing company to a successful global enterprise.

There were several keys to FPI's successful transition. First, Young had a very high level of ethical values. These values permeate FPI. Even in the most difficult period, the employees of FPI trusted what he said. He was up-front regarding plant closures, vessel deactivation, and employee layoffs. Second, he constantly praised FPI's employees for their exemplary response to a period of incredible uncertainty. However, he not only praised their resilience, energy, innovation, and dedication but also credited these qualities for FPI's renewed sense of corporate momentum in all his Reports to Shareholders. Third, he emphasized going international. Fourth, he stressed product innovation to enable FPI to meet and exceed the expectations of its seafood customers for quality and value. Fifth, he constantly stressed teamwork. Sixth, he never lost sight of the importance of achieving shareholder value. Seventh, he accentuated the importance of the partnerships being developed between FPI and its suppliers around the world and particularly the inshore fishers in Newfoundland and Labrador. Finally, he commenced a program of capital investment in 1996. By 1998, FPI had two new, world-class, state-of-the-art shrimp-processing facilities and a new crab-processing facility. By 1999, FPI had 15 active vessels, 11 active plants, and 3400 employees.

Young defines strategic leadership as a process of focusing an organization on the task of achieving shareholder value for the long term. He talks about motivating and energizing talented people to embrace the "shareholder value" concept and to "make it happen." He stresses that the process is a dynamic one that is influenced and altered by an ever-changing business environment. This environment varies from firm to firm, industry to industry, time period to time period. It is this environment of constant change and the need to respond to it that defines and redefines the dynamics of strategic leadership.

Although competitive trends are forcing firms to adapt, and outside leaders are often brought in to facilitate change to meet competitive challenges, significant changes require special leadership skills. Leaders who take an interest in employees and develop a firm's human capital are needed. "Slash and burn" CEOs who pursue significant downsizing (e.g., Sunbeam's Al Dunlap or AT&T's Robert Allen) are giving way to a new, less autocratic type of boss. For instance, Matthew Barrett was hired by Bank of Montreal to help rebuild employee morale and reduce customer complaints. The board decided on a CEO who was a great listener and could capture the imagination of Bank of Montreal's employees. Barrett used phrases such as "high-quality human capital," "value-added relationships," and "learning organization." John F. Welch, Jr., the renowned CEO of General Electric, is celebrated as one of the world's most effective CEOs because of his stress on quality and customer service. He also spends 30 percent of his time on leadership development within GE. The Royal Bank of Canada, under the leadership of John Cleghorn, invested $100 million in employee training in 1997. Cleghorn states that unless the Royal Bank continues to invest heavily in the recruitment, training, and development of its best people, it will not achieve its objectives. He is using attrition and slow employment growth rather than layoffs to build commitment and loyalty among the bank's employees.

Another leader, Russ Edwards, the CEO of Winnipeg-based Westman Group, a steel products manufacturer and distributor, has created a very positive culture among his 600 employees. Russ tries to be on a first-name basis with all employees. He knows this is difficult, so he enforces a policy of employees' having their first name on their hard hat so people get known in the plant. He talks to employees and lets them know that his door is always open or that he is only a phone call away. He believes that this results in higher employee satisfaction and allows them to take pride in their work. He links increases in operational efficiency to encouraging feedback from his employees. Because change is an essential and ongoing process, successful strategic managers will be able to make tough decisions such as downscoping and be sensitive to employee relationships.

In summary, strategic leaders are now required to be managers who can help firms operate efficiently and provide visionary leadership, in order to empower managers to develop good product ideas and to motivate people to make the changes necessary for long-term viability.

---

Sources: V. L. Young, Presentation to MBA Strategic Management students, Memorial University of Newfoundland, April 7, 1998. Bank of Montreal, *Annual Reports, 1996–1998;* Fishery Products International, *Annual Reports, 1993–1998;* Royal Bank of Canada, *Annual Reports, 1997–1998;* R. Gage, 1999, Entrepreneur of the year: Steel-Willed, *Manitoba Business,* May, 5–10; J. Helyar and J. S. Lublin, 1998, Do you need an expert on widgets to head a widget company? *Wall Street Journal,* January 21, A1, A10; A. A. Cannella, Jr. and M. J. Monroe, 1997, Contrasting perspectives on strategic leaders: Toward a more realistic view of top managers, *Journal of Management,* 23: 213–37; S. Walsh, 1997, Captains Courteous: Era of the brutal boss may be giving way to a new sensitivity at the top, *Inside Washington Post,* http://www.washingtonpost.com (Retrieved August 31); R. A. Heifetz and D. L. Laurie, 1997, The work of leadership, *Harvard Business Review* 75, (1): 124–34; R. Laver, 1999, Nortel's driving force, *Maclean's,* August 2, 13–14; R. E. Hoskisson and M. A. Hitt, 1994, *Downscoping: Taming the Diversified Firm* (New York: Oxford University Press).

---

The examples of significant strategic changes with which CEOs are confronted in the opening case emphasize the importance and outcomes of effective strategic leadership. As this chapter makes clear, it is through effective strategic leadership that firms are able to use the strategic management process successfully (see Figure 1.1). Thus, as strategic leaders, top-level managers must guide their firms in ways that result in the formation of strategic intent and strategic mission. This may lead to goals that stretch everyone in the organization to improve their performance.[1] Moreover, strategic leaders are then challenged to facilitate the development of appropriate strategic actions and determine how to implement them, culminating in strategic competitiveness and above-average returns[2] (see Figure 13.1).

This chapter begins with a definition of strategic leadership and its importance as a potential source of competitive advantage. Then, we discuss the differences among managerial leadership, visionary leadership, and strategic leadership. Next, we examine top management teams and their effects on firm innovation, strategic change, and performance. Closing the chapter are descriptions of the six key components of effective strategic leadership: determining strategic direction, exploiting and maintaining core competencies, developing human capital, sustaining an effective organizational culture, emphasizing ethical practices, and establishing balanced organizational control systems.

■ ■ **FIGURE 13.1**

*Strategic Leadership and the Strategic Management Process*

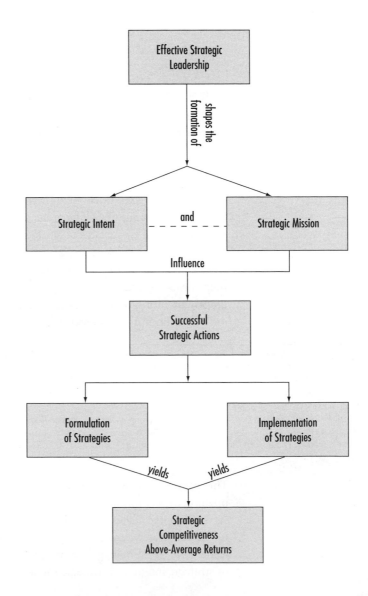

The impermanence of success is well documented by the change in leadership at Compaq Computer. Compaq's former CEO, Eckhard Pfeiffer, had been highly successful in leading Compaq to the number-one position in the personal computer market. In 1998, Compaq seemed to be at the top of its game. However, problems ensued in 1999 and, in a short period of time, Compaq became stagnant and was unseated as the number-one producer of personal computers by Dell. Compaq's board of directors forced Pfeiffer to resign. Pfeiffer's successor, Michael Capellas, is trying to reenergize the firm, to make it more innovative. He believes that this is necessary because, in the high-technology industry, the constant, substantial speed of change may relegate Compaq to a second-class seat. A short time after taking the job, Capellas made significant changes; he restructured the organization and eliminated redundant and overlapping programs. Analysts believe that his actions are on track. One analyst observed that Compaq executives must start thinking outside the box and partner more with solution providers rather than box pushers. Capellas is trying to do just that.[3]

# STRATEGIC LEADERSHIP

The word "strategy" originated with the Greeks. Originally, *strategos* alluded to a role such as a general in command of an army. Subsequently, it referred to the psychological and behavioural skills with which the general occupied the role and came to mean the "art of the general." By 450 B.C., it had come to mean managerial skills such as administration, leadership, oration, and power. And by 330 B.C., it meant the ability to employ forces to defeat opposing forces and to develop a unified system of global governance.[4]

**Strategic leadership** is defined as the ability to influence those with whom you work in your organization to *voluntarily* make decisions on a day-to-day basis that enhance the long-term viability of the organization while at the same time maintaining the short-term financial stability of the organization.[5] This definition of strategic leadership makes several presumptions:

> **Strategic leadership** is the ability to influence those with whom you work in your organization to *voluntarily* make decisions on a day-to-day basis that enhance the long-term viability of the organization while at the same time maintaining the short-term financial stability of the organization.

- It presumes an ability to influence those with whom one works—subordinates, peers, and superiors.
- It presumes that the leader understands the emergent strategic process, which Henry Mintzberg[6] says is more important than the intended strategic process.
- It presumes a shared vision of what the organization is to be, so that the day-to-day decisionmaking, or emergent strategic process, is consistent with this vision.
- It presumes agreement on the opportunities that can be taken advantage of, and the threats that can be neutralized, given the resources and capabilities of the organization.[7]
- It presumes visionary leadership on the part of those with areas of responsibility that entail many characteristics, such as a willingness to take risks.
- It presumes managerial leadership on the part of those with areas of responsibility that entails many characteristics, such as an intended rational way of looking at the world.
- It presumes that visionary leadership and managerial leadership can exist together.
- It presumes that strategic leadership synergistically combines visionary leadership and managerial leadership.
- Finally, it presumes a belief in their strategic leaders' ability to change their organizations in such a way that the environment in which their organizations operate

will also change versus a belief that the actions they take are constrained by the environment and organization in which they work.

In the next two sections, the concepts of managerial and visionary leadership are discussed. A major portion of this discussion is based on the classic *Harvard Business Review* (HBR) article by Abraham Zaleznik.[8]

# A COMPARISON OF MANAGERIAL, VISIONARY, AND STRATEGIC LEADERSHIP

A **managerial frame of reference** is the set of assumptions, premises, and accepted wisdom that bounds—or frames—a manager's understanding of the firm, the industry(ies) in which it competes, and the core competencies it uses in the pursuit of strategic competitiveness.

In the 21st century, many managers who work in nations around the world will be challenged to change their frames of reference to cope with the rapid and complex changes occurring in the global economy. A **managerial frame of reference** is the set of assumptions, premises, and accepted wisdom that bounds—or frames—a manager's understanding of the firm, the industry or industries in which it competes, and the core competencies it uses in the pursuit of strategic competitiveness. A frame of reference is the foundation on which a manager's mind-set is built (see Chapter 4).

A firm's ability to achieve strategic competitiveness and earn above-average returns is compromised when leaders fail to respond appropriately and quickly to mind-set-related changes that an increasingly complex and global competitive environment demands. Research suggests that a firm's "long-term competitiveness depends on managers' willingness to challenge continually their managerial frames" and that global competition is more than product versus product or company versus company—it is also a case of "mind-set versus mind-set, managerial frame versus managerial frame."[9] Competing on the basis of mind-set demands that strategic leaders learn how to deal with diverse and cognitively complex competitive situations. One of the most challenging mind-set changes is overcoming one's own success when change is required. For instance, it was a particular mind-set that led to Wal-Mart's low-pricing strategy victory over Zellers when Wal-Mart bought Woolco and moved into Canada. Being able to successfully complete challenging assignments that are linked to achieving strategic competitiveness early and frequently in one's career appears to improve a manager's ability to make appropriate changes to his or her mind-set.[10]

## Managerial Leadership

Organizations implicitly and explicitly train their people to be managerial leaders for several reasons. For example, in governments some of these reasons are public accountability for every penny spent, unrelated diversification as an organization, the political context, and, for most governments, an enormous debt load. These factors lead to the imposition of a financial control system that enhances the use of managerial leadership and curtails the use of strategic and visionary leadership. Regarding goals, managerial leaders adopt impersonal, passive attitudes toward goals, meaning that goals arise from necessity rather than desires, dreams, etc. These goals are based on the organization's history and are deeply embedded in the history/culture of the organization as it currently stands.[11] Managerial leaders view work as an enabling process that involves some combination of ideas and people interacting to establish strategies and make decisions. In this process, they negotiate and bargain and/or use rewards, punishments, and/or other forms of coercion.[12]

In their relations with others, managerial leaders relate to people according to their role in the decisionmaking process. Although managerial leaders may seek out involvement with others, they will maintain a low level of emotional involvement in these relationships. They may lack empathy; managerial leaders need order, not the potential chaos inherent in human relations.[13] Managerial leaders see themselves as conservators and regulators of the existing order of affairs with which they personally identify. Strengthening and perpetuating the existing institution enhances these managers' self-worth. For example, if they feel that they are members of an institution and contributing to that institution's well-being, they will consider that a mission in life has been fulfilled and will feel rewarded for having measured up to an ideal. This reward transcends material gains and answers the more fundamental desire for personal integrity that is achieved by identifying with existing institutions.[14] However, when the institution they have devoted their career to perpetuating and strengthening gets ripped apart and put back together again during a restructuring, they feel as if they are being torn apart too.

Managerial leaders influence only the actions/decisions of those with whom they work.[15] They are involved in situations/contexts characteristic of day-to-day activities[16] and are concerned with and more comfortable in functional areas of responsibilities.[17] They possess more expertise about their functional areas.[18] Managerial leaders may make decisions that are not subject to value-based constraints,[19] which does not mean that they may not be moral, ethical people on a personal level, but that as managers they may not include values in their decisionmaking because of certain pressures, such as being financially responsible. These leaders engage in, and support, short-term, least-cost behaviour activities, to enhance financial performance figures in the short term.[20] They focus on managing the exchange and combination of explicit knowledge and ensuring compliance to standard operating procedures.[21] They use a linear thought process. Finally, managerial leaders believe in determinism—that is, they believe that their organization's internal and external environments determine what they do.[22]

To summarize, **managerial leaders** want stability and order, and to preserve the existing order. They are more comfortable handling day-to-day activities, and are short-term oriented. They guide without a strategic vision constrained by values and by using explicit knowledge. We need to emphasize that this is not a bad way to be—it is more a recognition of some of the defining characteristics of managerial leadership. Organizations need managerial leadership; however, it is possible that managerial leaders lead too many organizations. In the longer term, managerial leadership causes organizational performance to decline.

**Managerial leaders** want stability and order, and to preserve the existing order. They are more comfortable handling day-to-day activities, and are short-term oriented. They guide without a strategic vision constrained by values and by using explicit knowledge.

## Visionary Leadership

Visionary leadership is touted as the cure for many of the ills that affect organizations in today's fast-changing environment. Unfortunately, these types of leaders are not readily embraced by organizations and may not be appropriate for most organizations if they do not have the support of managerial leaders. Being visionary and having an organizational tendency to use visionary leaders is risky. Ultimately, visionary leadership requires power to influence the thoughts and actions of people. This means putting power in the hands of one person, which entails risk on several dimensions. First, there is the risk of equating power with the ability to achieve immediate results; second, there is the risk of losing self-control in the desire for power; and third, the presence of visionary leaders may undermine the development of managers who become anxious in the relative disorder that visionary leaders tend to generate.

Because they are relatively more proactive, visionary leaders have attitudes toward goals that are opposite to those of managerial leaders. Visionary leaders shape ideas as opposed to reacting to them. They exert influence in a way that determines the direction an organization will take by altering moods, evoking images and expectations, and establishing specific desires and objectives. Their influence changes the way people think about what is desirable, possible, and necessary.[23] Visionary leaders strive to develop choices and fresh approaches to long-standing problems. They create excitement in work. Visionary leaders work from high-risk positions; in fact they seek out risky ventures, especially when the rewards are high.[24]

Visionary leaders are concerned with ideas and relate to people in intuitive and empathetic ways, focusing on what events and decisions mean to people. With visionaries in charge, human relations are more turbulent, intense, and sometimes even disorganized. This may intensify individual motivation and produce unanticipated, positive outcomes.[25] With respect to their sense of self, visionary leaders feel separate from their environment and, sometimes, other people. The key point is that visionary leaders work in but do not belong to organizations. Their sense of identity does not depend on their work, roles, or memberships but on their created sense of identity, which may result from major events in their lives.[26]

Visionary leaders influence the opinions and attitudes of others within their organizations.[27] They are concerned with ensuring the future of an organization through the development and management of people.[28] Visionaries immerse themselves in complexity, ambiguity, and information overload. Their task is multifunctional, and because they have a much more complex integrative task,[29] they come to know less than their functional area experts about each of the functional areas for which they are responsible.[30]

Visionaries are more likely to make decisions that are based on values,[31] and they are more willing to invest in innovation, human capital, and creating/maintaining an effective culture to ensure long-term viability.[32] Visionary leaders focus on tacit knowledge and develop strategies as communal forms of tacit knowledge that promote the enactment of a vision.[33] They utilize nonlinear thinking, and they believe in strategic choice—that is, they believe that their choices make a difference in what their organizations do, and these differences affect their organizations' environments.[34]

In summary, visionary leadership is future oriented and concerned with risk-taking, and visionary leaders are not dependent on their organizations for their sense of identity. Under these leaders, organizational control is maintained through socialization and the sharing of, and compliance to, a commonly held set of norms, values, and shared beliefs. Organizations need visionary leadership to ensure their long-term viability; however, organizations that are led by visionaries without the constraining influence of managers are probably more in danger of failing in the short term than those led by managers. One solution is a combination of managers and visionaries to lead organizations with visionaries having more influence than managers.[35] This was the solution used by IBM from 1956 to 1970 with Thomas Watson, Jr. (the visionary leader) as CEO and his Chief Financial Officer as the managerial leader. A better solution is to have an individual who can exercise both visionary and managerial leadership. Herein is the problem; Zaleznik argues that leaders and managers are different, and that no one person can exercise both types of leadership simultaneously.[36] His perspective suggests that visionary leaders and managerial leaders are at opposite ends of a continuum and that trying to be both causes the individual to end up in the centre, unable to exercise either style of leadership.

This is not an unreasonable perspective when we consider the following: managerial leaders want stability and order, and to preserve the existing order, whereas, **visionary leaders** want creativity, innovation, and chaos, and to change the existing order. An organization in a transition phase being driven by a visionary is very hard on managerial leaders. The organization they have worked so hard to build, and that is part of their identity, is being ripped apart and put together as something else. Under visionary leaders, this will be more the norm than the stability and order experienced under managerial leadership. In fact, the environment being created by today's technological and global forces is one of change and complexity. John Kotter, one of the foremost experts on organizational leadership, suggests that organizations need leaders to cope with change and managers to cope with complexity.[37]

Having said this, it is necessary to reiterate and emphasize that both visionary and managerial leadership are vital for long-term viability and short-term financial stability. As we said earlier, visionary leadership without managerial leadership may be more detrimental to organizational performance in the short term.[38] Having visionary and managerial leadership can be accomplished by having the two different organizational mind-sets that each entail co-exist—but with visionary being more influential than managerial. However, an organization will be more viable in the long term, and better able to maintain its financial stability in the short term, if strategic leadership is prevalent in that organization. To conceptualize strategic leadership, it is necessary to think of visionary leadership and managerial leadership as existing on separate continuums that are perpendicular to each other. This allows the conceptualization of strategic leadership as a synergistic combination of visionary and managerial leadership that was not possible under previous thinking.

## Strategic Leadership

Earlier, strategic leadership was defined as the ability to influence those with whom you work in your organization to voluntarily make decisions on a day-to-day basis that enhance the long-term viability of the organization while at the same time maintaining the short-term financial stability of the organization. Strategic leaders are different from managerial and visionary leaders; they are a synergistic combination of managerial and visionary leadership. This means that a strategic leader creates more wealth[39] than a combination of two individuals—one of whom is a visionary leader and one of whom is a managerial leader.[40] Strategic leaders emphasize ethical behaviour.[41] Strategic leaders are probably very rare in most organizations.[42] They oversee operating (day-to-day) and strategic (long-term) responsibilities.[43] They formulate and implement strategies for immediate impact and the preservation of long-term goals to enhance organizational growth, survival, and long-term viability.[44] Strategic leaders have strong, positive expectations of the performance they expect from their superiors, peers, subordinates, and themselves. They use strategic controls and financial controls—with the emphasis on strategic controls.[45] They utilize and interchange tacit and explicit knowledge both on the individual and organizational levels.[46] And they use both linear and nonlinear thinking patterns. Finally, they believe in strategic choice—that is, they believe

---

**Visionary leaders** want creativity, innovation, and chaos, and to change the existing order.

**Strategic leaders** manage the paradox created by the managerial and visionary leadership models. They use metaphors, analogies, and models to allow the juxtaposition of apparently contradictory concepts by defining boundaries of mutual co-existence. They guide the organizational knowledge-creation process by encouraging contradictory combinative capabilities.

that their choices make a difference in what their organizations do, and this will affect their organizations' environments.[47]

In summary, **strategic leaders** manage the paradox created by the use of managerial and visionary leadership models. They use metaphors, analogies, and models to allow the juxtaposition of apparently contradictory concepts by defining boundaries of mutual co-existence. They guide the organizational knowledge-creation process by encouraging contradictory combinative capabilities—that is, the organization's ability to combine individual, group, and organizational tacit and explicit knowledge to generate organizational and technological innovations.[48] Organizations need to let a critical mass of their managers develop the skills and abilities that are required to exercise strategic leadership.[49] This means that managerial leaders need to bear with those who are strategic leaders as they create chaos, destroy order, take risks, and maybe destroy a part of the organization that is near and dear to them. This does not mean throwing out managerial leadership—it means including visionary and managerial leadership to enhance long-term viability and short-term financial stability. In fact, strategic leaders need to understand what managerial and visionary leaders bring to the organization and utilize the skills, knowledge, and abilities of both.

Multifunctional in nature, strategic leadership involves managing through others, managing an entire enterprise rather than a functional subunit, and coping with change that seems to be increasing exponentially in today's new competitive landscape. Because of the complexity and global nature of this new landscape, strategic leaders must learn how to influence human behaviour effectively in an uncertain environment. By word and/or personal example and through their ability to dream pragmatically, strategic leaders meaningfully influence the behaviours, thoughts, and feelings of those with whom they work.[50] The ability to manage human capital may be the most critical of the strategic leader's skills.[51] In the opinion of one well-known leadership observer, the key to competitive advantage "… will be the capacity of top leadership to create the social architecture capable of generating intellectual capital … By intellectual capital, I mean know-how, expertise, brainpower, innovation (and) ideas."[52] Strategic leaders also establish the context through which stakeholders (e.g., employees, customers, and suppliers) are able to perform at peak efficiency.[53]

Strategic leaders are willing to make candid, courageous, yet pragmatic, decisions—decisions that may be difficult yet necessary in light of internal and external conditions facing the firm.[54] Strategic leaders solicit corrective feedback from their peers, superiors, and employees about the value of their difficult decisions. Often, this feedback is sought through face-to-face communications. The unwillingness to accept feedback may be a key reason other talented executives fail, highlighting the need for strategic leaders to consistently solicit feedback from those affected by their decisions.[55]

The primary responsibility for strategic leadership rests at the top—in particular, with the CEO, but other commonly recognized strategic leaders include members of the board of directors, the top-management team, and division general managers. Regardless of title and organizational function, strategic leaders have substantial decision-making responsibilities that cannot be delegated.[56]

Strategic leadership is an extremely complex but critical form of leadership. Strategies cannot be formulated and implemented to achieve above-average returns without strategic leadership. Because it is a requirement of strategic success, and because organizations may be poorly led and overmanaged, firms competing in the new competitive landscape are challenged to develop strategic leaders.[57] Wayne Calloway, PepsiCo's former CEO, has suggested that "… most of the companies that are in life-or-death battles got into that kind of trouble because they didn't pay enough attention to developing their leaders."[58]

## Constraints on Strategic Leadership

Unfortunately, there are many organizations that constrain the exercise of strategic leadership. Some of these constraints can be examined using government as an example, because some of the principles that affect large businesses also affect governments. Governments are sometimes thought of as a monopoly with the power to impose their will on the people. However, governments compete for human resources with other organizations, with other governments for tax dollars from their constituents, and with other governments for new businesses to set up in their country, state, or province.[59] Unfortunately, they also grow large and unrelated diversified. This high level of diversification *plus* the massive debt loads of many state/provincial and national governments *plus* public accountability for every cent spent *plus* the political context of an election every four years forces governments to use financial controls only and to shove the use of strategic controls aside. This forces leaders with the potential to be strategic leaders to do one of three things: (1) to be managerial leaders, (2) to leave the organization, or (3) to fight within the system, which uses the strategic energy they should be expending on leading and managing their part of the organization.[60]

Is strategic leadership possible in this type of organization? The answer is "probably not" except under two very hard to impose conditions: autonomy and protection.[61] Giving a subunit some autonomy could enhance the exercise of strategic leadership in the sub-unit if the autonomy is coupled with protection from those to whom the strategic leaders report. In this way, the subunit can exercise strategic controls, as well as financial controls. Unfortunately, as the subunit becomes more successful and achieves visibility because it is taking risks and "bruising" the bureaucracy, it is much more difficult to maintain this autonomy and to be protected from the managerial leadership of the organization. Especially when that leadership controls financially and bureaucratically because the organization is unrelated diversified, has a massive debt load, operates in a political context, and must be publicly accountable for every dollar it spends. Doug House, a professor of sociology who was seconded to the provincial government of Newfoundland and Labrador from Memorial University of Newfoundland, considers it difficult to exercise strategic leadership in government:

*The organization of the Newfoundland and Labrador public service is very bureaucratic and hierarchical. There is a place for everyone and everyone should know his or her place. Communications go up the hierarchy from officer to manager to director to assistant deputy minister to deputy minister, and possibly to the minister, and down the hierarchy in a reverse chain. Much gets lost or reinterpreted along the way, and it is often a slow process. Not surprisingly, the public and the business community who deal with government as 'clients,' often complain about 'red tape' and 'bureaucracy.'*

*Such a system is not well suited to dealing with change. To the extent that change has to occur—and able senior officials recognize that it does—they prefer that it takes place at a modest pace under their control and direction. They are naturally skeptical about and resistant to premiers, ministers, and other agencies that want to initiate a lot of change on a number of fronts within a short period of time.*

*This system also tends to select out or mould certain personality types for career success. The premium is on reliability, steadfastness, and loyalty to the service rather than on creativity, innovation, and critical thinking. People who do not fit the mould either stagnate, leave, or are forced out of the service. Creative individuals are usually damned with faint praise in epithets such as 'He's a smart guy but he can't manage people' or 'She's got some good ideas, but she's a bit of a loose cannon.'[62]*

## MANAGERS AS AN ORGANIZATIONAL RESOURCE

As the introductory discussion suggests, top-level managers are an important resource for firms seeking to effectively formulate and implement strategies.[63] A key reason for this is that the strategic decisions made by top managers influence how the firm is designed and whether performance outcomes will be achieved. Thus, a critical element of organizational success is having a top-management team with superior managerial skills.[64]

Managers often use their discretion (or latitude of action) when making strategic decisions, including those concerned with the effective implementation of strategies.[65] Managerial discretion differs significantly across industries. The primary factors that determine the amount of a manager's (especially a top-level manager's) decision discretion include (1) external environmental sources (e.g., industry structure, rate of market growth in the firm's primary industry, and the degree to which products can be differentiated), (2) characteristics of the organization (e.g., size, age, resource availability, and culture), and (3) characteristics of the manager (e.g., commitment to the firm and its strategic outcomes, tolerance for ambiguity, skills to work with different people, and aspiration level) (see Figure 13.2). Because strategic leaders' decisions are intended to help the firm gain a competitive advantage, the way in which managers exercise discretion when determining appropriate strategic actions is critical to the firm's success.[66] In addition to determining new strategic initiatives, top-level managers also develop the appropriate organizational structure and reward systems of a firm. (In Chapter 11, we described how organizational structure and reward systems affect strategic actions taken to implement different types of strategies.) Furthermore, top-level managers have a major effect on a firm's culture,[67] organizational activities, and performance.[68] The significance of this effect should not be underestimated.

Financial markets observe the degree to which top-level managers influence a firm's performance. For example, when Eric Schmidt, chief technology officer at Sun Microsystems, was hired to be Novell's chairman of the board and CEO after a seven-month search, Novell's stock price gained 9 percent. In reaction, Sun's stock price declined 2.5 percent. The market's reaction may have been due in part to Schmidt's broad experience with the Internet; Novell may also be able, with Schmidt's help, to establish important alliances with companies such as Oracle, Netscape Communications, and Sun to foster sales for Novell networking software. Novell should

■ ■ **FIGURE 13.2**

*Factors Affecting
Managerial Discretion*

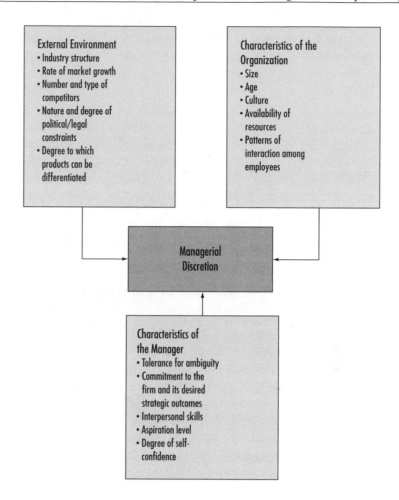

Source: Adapted from S. Finkelstein and D. C. Hambrick, 1996, *Strategic Leadership: Top Executives and Their Effects on Organizations* (St. Paul, Minn: West Publishing Co.).

have been a stronger player in Internet services and has been losing business to Microsoft.[69] Thus, a strategic leader's experience and judgment, and the quality of the decisions based on them, is often of keen interest to various stakeholders, including current and potential shareholders.[70]

As the following discussion shows, the decisions and actions of some strategic leaders result in their becoming a source of competitive advantage for their firm. Consistent with the criteria of sustainability discussed in Chapter 4, strategic leaders can be a source of competitive advantage only when their work is valuable, rare, costly to imitate, and when organizations are organized to exploit and nurture their strategic leaders.

Strategic leaders focus their work on the key issues that ultimately shape the firm's ability to earn above-average returns. For example, Lynton Wilson, CEO of Bell Canada Enterprises (BCE) from 1992 to 1998, focused his energies on determining how his company could be a market leader and then restructured BCE to support this focus.[71] CEOs such as Wilson take actions to gain desired results. They delegate day-to-day operations to others so they can ask "big picture" questions of their managers, suppliers, shareholders, and customers. Strategic leaders also travel to other companies to study successful work processes, and they build time into their schedules to think.

One of the most important issues strategic leaders consider is the source of their firm's competitive advantage. Finding ways to release employees' brainpower influences the degree to which the firm's expertise is applied throughout the company in a competitively relevant fashion.[72] Frank Stronach, former Chair of Magna International, an auto-parts manufacturer, instituted a "Fair Enterprise" policy in 1971. The policy is codified in the company's charter of rights and determines the annual percentage of profits shared among employees, management, and shareholders. It includes a comprehensive dispute-resolution system. Stronach put this policy in place because of his strong belief that the three forces that drive business (management, labour, and capital) must be in harmony or the company will not make a quality product. He strongly believed in the power of his employees and says that traditional businesses do not focus on human capital. Stronach is described as dangling a carrot in front of every one of his plant managers to ensure quality products.[73]

## Top-Management Teams

The top-management team is composed of the key managers who are responsible for formulating and implementing the organization's strategies. Typically, **the top-management team** includes the officers of the corporation as defined by the title of vice-president and above and/or by service as a member of the board of directors.[74] The quality of the strategic decisions made by a top-management team affects the firm's ability to innovate and engage in effective strategic change.[75]

### Top-Management Team, Firm Performance, and Strategic Change

The job of top-level executives is complex and requires a broad knowledge of firm operations, as well as the three key parts of the firm's external environment. Therefore, firms try to form a top-management team that has the appropriate knowledge and expertise to operate the internal organization, yet also deal with external stakeholders. This normally requires a heterogeneous top-management team. A **heterogeneous top-management team** comprises individuals with different functional backgrounds, experiences, and education. The more heterogeneous a top-management team is, with varied expertise and knowledge, the more capacity it has to provide effective strategic leadership in terms of strategy formulation. Members of a heterogeneous top-management team benefit from discussing the different perspectives advanced by separate team members. In many cases, these discussions increase the quality of the top-management team's decisions, especially when a synthesis emerges from the contesting of diverse perspectives that is generally superior to the individual perspectives.[76] For example, heterogeneous top-management teams in the airline industry had the propensity to take stronger competitive actions and reactions.[77] The net benefit of these actions was positive in terms of market share and above-average returns.

It is also important that the top-management team members function cohesively. For example, some believe that an apparent inability to work together as a board affected the selection process for the new CEO at AT&T.[78] In general, the more heterogeneous and larger the top management team is, the harder it is for the team to implement strate-

**The top-management team** includes the officers of the corporation as defined by the title of vice-president and above and/or by service as a member of the board of directors.

A **heterogeneous top-management team** comprises individuals with different functional backgrounds, experiences, and education. The more heterogeneous a top-management team is, with varied expertise and knowledge, the more capacity it has to provide effective strategic leadership in terms of strategy formulation.

gies effectively.[79] The research finding that comprehensive and long-term strategic plans can be inhibited by communication difficulties when top managers of a firm come from different backgrounds and have different cognitive skills may account for these implementation-related difficulties[80]. Having members who have substantive expertise in the firm's core functions and businesses is also important to the effectiveness of a top-management team. In a high-technology industry, it may be critical for a firm to have R&D knowledge and expertise included on the top-management team, particularly when growth strategies are being implemented.[81]

The characteristics of top-management teams are related to innovation and strategic change.[82] For example, more heterogeneous top-management teams are associated positively with innovation and strategic change. Thus, firms that need to change their strategies are more likely to do so if they have top-management teams with diverse backgrounds and expertise. A top-management team with various areas of expertise is more likely to identify environmental changes (opportunities and threats) or changes within the firm that require a different strategic direction.[83]

## CEO and Top Management Team Power

As suggested in Chapter 11, the board of directors is an important mechanism for monitoring a firm's strategic direction and for representing the interests of stakeholders, especially those of shareholders. In fact, higher performance normally is achieved when the board of directors is involved more directly in shaping a firm's strategic direction.[84] Certainly, the shareholders of Westcoast Energy, based in Vancouver, and Enbridge, based in Calgary, will be interested in the performance of Alliance Pipeline. They respectively own 23.6 percent and 21.4 percent stakes in Alliance. The Alliance board recently replaced Chief Executive Officer Dennis Cornelson with board chair Norman Gish. Alliance's board may have made the move for any of several reasons. First, the board may have wanted a change in strategy from one of combativeness to one of cooperation with other firms in the pipeline industry. This may lead to future co-operation with rival TransCanada in northern Canada instead of the current hostile posture. Second, there may have been a personality clash between the CEO and the board. Third, the board may not have thought that Mr. Cornelson was the appropriate person to lead the transition to an operating company. Finally, the board may have wanted someone more experienced.[85]

Boards of directors, however, may find it difficult to direct the strategic actions of powerful CEOs and top-management teams. It is not uncommon for a powerful CEO to appoint a number of sympathetic outside board members or have inside board members who are on the top-management team and report to the CEO. Therefore, the CEO may have significant control over the board's actions. "A central question is whether boards are an effective management control mechanism ... or whether they are a 'management tool' ... a rubber stamp for management initiatives ... and often surrender to management their major domain of decision-making authority, which includes the right to hire, fire, and compensate top management."[86]

CEOs and top-management team members can also achieve power in other ways. Holding the titles of chairperson of the board and chief executive officer usually gives a CEO more power than the one who is not simultaneously serving as chair of the firm's board.[87] Although the practice of CEO duality (i.e., when the CEO and the chairperson of the board are the same) has become more common in Canadian and U.S. businesses, it "… has recently come under heavy criticism—duality has been blamed for poor performance and slow response to change in firms such as General Motors, Digital Equipment Corporation, and Goodyear Tire and Rubber."[88] Although it varies among industries, duality occurs most commonly in the largest firms. Increased shareholder activism has brought CEO duality under increased scrutiny and attack in European firms as well. Historically, an independent board leadership structure—one in which the positions of CEO and chair were not held by the same person—was believed to enhance a board's ability to monitor top-level managers' decisions and actions, particularly in terms of the firm's financial performance.[89] Stewardship theory, on the other hand, suggests that CEO duality facilitates effective decisions and actions. In these instances, the increased effectiveness gained through CEO duality accrues from the individual who wants to perform effectively and desires to be the best possible steward of the firm's assets. Because of this person's positive orientations and actions, extra governance and the coordination costs resulting from an independent board leadership structure would be unnecessary.[90]

To date, the question of the effect of duality on the firm's strategic outcomes is unresolved. In a study of the relationship between duality and firm performance, researchers found that (1) the stock market is indifferent to changes in a company's duality status, (2) changes in a company's duality status have a negligible effect on its financial performance, and (3) "there is only weak evidence that duality status affects long-term performance, after controlling for other factors that might impact that performance."[91] Thus, it may be that, in general, the potential for managerial abuse created through CEO duality is unrealized in many firms.

Top-management team members and CEOs who have long tenures—on the team and in the organization—have an increased ability to influence board decisions.[92] Moreover, long tenure is known to restrict the breadth of an executive's knowledge base. With the limited perspective associated with a restricted knowledge base, long-tenured top-level managers typically develop fewer alternatives to evaluate when making strategic decisions.[93] As well, long tenure and a restricted knowledge base increase an executive's ability to forestall or avoid board involvement in strategic decisions. However, managers of long tenure also may be able to exercise more effective strategic control, thereby obviating the need for board of director involvement because effective strategic control generally produces higher performance.[94]

In the final analysis, boards of directors should develop an effective relationship with the firm's top-management team. The relative degrees of power to be held by the board and top-management team members should be examined in light of an individual firm's situation. For example, the abundance of resources in a firm's external environment and the volatility of that environment may affect the ideal balance of power between boards and top-management teams.[95] Through the development of effective working relationships, boards, CEOs, and other top-management team members are able to serve the best interests of the firm's stakeholders.

As noted earlier, the type of strategic leadership that results in successful implementation of strategies is exemplified by several key actions. The most critical of these are shown in Figure 13.3. The remainder of this chapter is devoted to explaining each action. Note that many of these actions interact with each other. For example, developing human capital through executive training contributes to establishing a strategic direction, fostering an effective culture, exploiting core competencies, using effective organizational control systems, and establishing ethical practices.

■ ■ **FIGURE 13.3**

*Exercise of Effective Strategic Leadership*

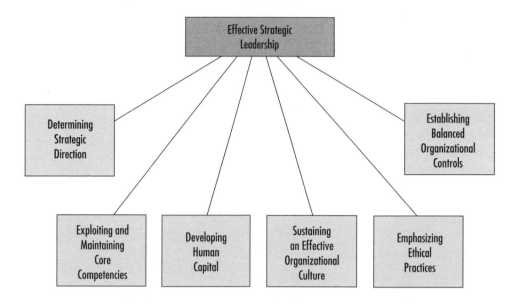

## DETERMINING STRATEGIC DIRECTION

Determining the strategic direction of a firm refers to the development of a long-term vision of a firm's strategic intent. A long-term vision, a philosophy with goals, normally looks at least five to ten years into the future and is the ideal image and character the firm seeks[96] The ideal long-term vision has two parts, core ideology and envisioned future. Although the core ideology motivates employees through the company's heritage (e.g., the "HP way" at Hewlett-Packard), the envisioned future encourages employees to stretch beyond their expectations of accomplishment and requires significant change and progress to attain.[97] The envisioned future serves as a guide to many aspects of a firm's strategy implementation process, including motivation, leadership, employee empowerment, and organizational design. Certainly, Young's vision for FPI (see Opening Case) has not changed—to be the number-one seafood company in the world.[98] For firms competing in many different industries, evidence suggests that the most effective long-term vision is one that has been accepted by those affected by it.[99]

To determine the firm's long-term vision, managers must take a sufficient amount of time to think about how it should be framed. Areas requiring executive thought include an analysis of the firm's external and internal environments and its current performance levels. Most top-level managers ask people with a range of skills to help them analyze various aspects of the firm's operations. Macroeconomists, for example, through their study of trends in the global economy, often provide insights to strategic leaders.[100]

Once the vision is determined, CEOs must motivate employees to achieve them. Some, but not all, top-level managers are thought to be charismatic strategic leaders. Theory suggests that charisma comes through interactions between leaders and followers. These interactions have been studied by examining impression management where framing, scripting, staging, and performing by the strategic leader relate to attribution of charisma by followers.[101] Although charisma is perceived as helpful, it is not a requirement for strategic leadership success. Noncharismatic people often have other skills and traits—intelligence, vision, ambition, and toughness, for example—that provide benefits similar to those gained when one is thought to be charismatic.[102] In certain situations, charismatic CEOs might facilitate better performance; in others, charisma might reduce leadership credibility. Jack Welch, General Electric's CEO, combines outrageous self-confidence, high-strung passion for ideas he unabashedly borrows, unforgiving candour, and charisma.[103]

Other CEOs who are typically not described as charismatic include Wal-Mart's David Glass. Though a fierce competitor, this earnest boss stands no chance in a personality contest with the larger-than-life Sam Walton. To inspire associates, Glass wisely milks the late founder's legacy. General Motors' current chair and former CEO, Jack Smith, is thought by some to be as charismatic as his name; he eschews TV cameras and the press. A pragmatic consensus-builder, he accumulated power by giving it away. He made GM shine even though he doesn't and, despite his lack of charisma, Smith is considered to be a strategic leader.

A charismatic CEO may help gain employees' commitment to a new vision and strategic direction. Nonetheless, for all firms, it is important not to lose sight of the strengths of the organization when making changes required by a new strategic direction. Achieving this objective demands the balancing of a firm's short-term needs while adjusting to a new vision and maintaining its long-term survival by emphasizing its current and valuable core competencies.

## EXPLOITING AND MAINTAINING CORE COMPETENCIES

Examined in Chapters 1 and 4, core competencies are resources and capabilities that serve as a source of sustained competitive advantage for a firm over its rivals. Typically, core competencies relate to an organization's functional skills, such as manufacturing, finance, marketing, and research and development. As shown by the following descriptions, firms develop and exploit core competencies in many different functional areas in order to implement their strategies. Strategic leaders must verify that the firm's competencies are emphasized in strategy implementation efforts. Hewlett-Packard and Intel, for example, have core competencies in terms of competitive agility (an ability to act in a variety of competitively relevant ways) and competitive speed (an ability to act quickly when facing environmental and competitive pressures).[104] Young is pushing FPI to achieve core competencies in sourcing raw material anywhere in the world, in marketing finished goods to worldwide markets, and in new product development.[105]

In firms that are related diversified, core competencies are exploited effectively when they are developed and applied across different organizational units (see Chapter 7). Whirlpool has well-known core competencies that are emphasized to create value across country borders.[106] Some argue that the development, nurturing, and application of core competencies within multinational firms facilitates management of the complex relationships across businesses operating in different international markets.[107] Core competencies, however, cannot be developed or exploited effectively without appropriate human capital.

# DEVELOPING HUMAN CAPITAL

**Human capital** refers to the knowledge and skills of the firm's entire workforce.

**Human capital** refers to the knowledge and skills of the firm's entire workforce. Employees, from this perspective, are viewed as a capital resource that requires investment. One study found that much of the development of industry in the United States could be attributed to the effectiveness of its human capital. One-third of the growth in the U.S. gross national product from 1948 to 1982 was attributed to increases in the education level of the workforce. Fifty percent of this growth resulted from technical innovations and knowledge that also are based strongly on education. Only 15 percent of the growth of the U.S. gross national product during this time was attributed to investment in capital equipment.[108] Outcomes such as these support the position, as discussed in Chapter 4, that "… as the dynamics of competition accelerate, people are perhaps the only truly sustainable source of competitive advantage."[109] This suggests that the role of human resource management should be increasing in importance.[110] In turn, the effective development and management of the firm's human capital—that is, of all of the firm's managerial and nonmanagerial personnel—may be the primary determinant of a firm's ability to formulate and implement strategies successfully.[111]

For individuals, active participation in company-sponsored programs to develop their abilities is highly desirable; in that being able to upgrade one's skills continuously leads to more job and economic security.[112] Increasingly, part of the development required to be selected as a strategic leader is international experience. One business analyst noted, "With nearly every industry targeting fast-growing foreign markets, more companies are requiring foreign experience for top management positions."[113] Thus, companies committed to the importance of competing successfully in the global economy provide opportunities for their future strategic leaders to work in locations other than their home nation. Also, because foreign sources of management capabilities are becoming important, managing inpatriation (the process of transferring host-country or third-country national managers into the home/domestic market of multinational firms) is becoming more important to build global core competencies.[114]

Through participation in effective training and development programs, the probability increases that a manager will be a successful strategic leader. Among other outcomes, these programs build skills, inculcate a common set of core values, and give a systematic view of the organization, thus promoting the firm's strategic vision and organizational cohesion. Furthermore, they help strategic leaders improve skills that are critical to completing other tasks associated with strategic leadership (e.g., determining the firm's strategic direction, exploiting and maintaining core competencies, and developing an organizational culture that supports ethical practices). Analysts recognize GE for the skills of its current top leadership and its commitment to the institutional development of strategic leaders. Its annual expenditure on training and leadership development is currently about $800 million, approximately half of what it spends on research and development. These programs are focused on helping employees develop strategic leadership skills and on promoting Welch's vision for GE. This vision consists of "how to anticipate change, how to cope with change, how to change a very big company that does many things well."[115] Welch spends 30 percent of his time teaching leadership in GE's training and leadership development seminars.

Programs that gain outstanding results in the training of future strategic leaders become a competitive advantage for a firm. GE's system of training and developing future strategic leaders is comprehensive and thought to be among the best.[116] As such, this training system may be a source of competitive advantage for the firm. Similarly, Avon has been particularly effective at hiring, training, and promoting women managers. Four of its eight top officers are women, and 95 percent of its sales come from Avon Ladies. Performance at the cosmetics, toiletries, and fragrance company shows that this not only has been good for diversity but also has also helped improve returns substantially.[117]

As discussed in Chapter 8, millions of managers, strategic leaders, and nonmanagerial personnel have lost jobs in recent years through the restructuring, downscoping, and downsizing in many companies. As noted in the Opening Case, from 1987 to 1995, FPI strategically downscoped by divesting 82 percent of its ships and 53 percent of its plants and dropped from 8600 employees to 2600 employees. During the 1990s, Sears shed 50 000 people; and, in 1996, AT&T announced layoffs of up to 40 000 employees. The view of AT&T's former CEO, Robert Allen, about his firm's job reductions captures the sentiment of many strategic leaders facing this reality:[118] "My company had to make the necessary, even painful changes today or forfeit the future."[119]

Regardless of the cause, layoffs can result in a significant loss of knowledge that is possessed by a firm's human capital. Although it is also not uncommon for restructuring firms to reduce their expenditures/investments in training and development programs, restructuring may be an important time to increase investment in such development. These firms have less slack and cannot absorb as many errors; moreover, many employees may be placed into positions without all of the skills or knowledge necessary to perform required tasks effectively.[120] In the final analysis, a view of employees as a resource to be maximized rather than a cost to be minimized facilitates successful implementation of a firm's strategies. The effectiveness of implementation processes also increases when strategic leaders approach layoffs in a manner that employees believe is fair and equitable.[121] As described next, human capital is an important part of the firm's ability to develop and sustain an effective organizational culture.

## SUSTAINING AN EFFECTIVE ORGANIZATIONAL CULTURE

An **organizational culture** consists of a complex set of ideologies, symbols, and core values that is shared throughout the firm and influences the way it conducts business.

An **organizational culture** consists of a complex set of ideologies, symbols, and core values that is shared throughout the firm and influences the way it conducts business. Evidence suggests that a firm can develop core competencies both in terms of the capabilities it possesses and the way the capabilities are used to produce strategic actions. In other words, because it influences how the firm conducts its business and helps regulate and control employee behaviour, organizational culture can be a source of competitive advantage.[122] Thus, shaping the context within which the firm formulates and implements its strategies—that is, shaping the organizational culture—is a central task of strategic leaders.[123] Konosuke Matsushita outlined core values for Matsushita Electric in 1929 that are still considered to be the reason their workforce is a source of sustained competitive advantage today. Matsushita's remarkably aligned and inspired 265 000 employees believe they are not only building products but are pursuing the noble and just cause of "progress and development of society and the well-being of people through our business activities."[124]

Hewlett-Packard provides another example of the potential power of culture. The core values of this firm's culture are in the basic belief that "men and women want to do a good job, a creative job, and that if they are provided the proper environment, they will do so."[125] Of interest to shareholders of HP will be the impact of an outsider CEO on the HP Culture. Carleton (Carly) Fiorina was asked to leave Lucent Technologies and to become the new CEO of HP in July 1999. It is expected that, among other objectives, she will translate the bureaucratic, consensus-style culture into the era of the Net-Speed and dispose of HP's bad habits and retain the good ones by using a scalpel not a machete.[126] An effective organizational culture encourages and supports an entrepreneurial orientation.

## Entrepreneurial Orientation

Organizational culture often encourages (or discourages) the pursuit of entrepreneurial opportunities, especially in large firms.[127] Successful outcomes derived through employees' pursuit of entrepreneurial opportunities are a major source of growth and innovation for firms competing in today's complex, globalized environment.[128] Innovation, and a CEO that has nurtured a culture that fosters it, may account for Bombardier's recent successful innovations. Laurent Beaudoin, the 59-year-old chief executive of Montreal-based Bombardier, has moved ahead with a number of product innovations over the last several years. Although Bombardier has had performance difficulties, the CEO is counting on a number of new products to increase returns. He has sought to foster innovation in three of the firm's diversified businesses—aerospace, transportation, and recreational products. In 1998, Bombardier offered the Learjet 45, a midsize plane priced like a light jet but capable of nonstop transcontinental flights. A number of regional jet airlines such as American Eagle have placed orders for the plane. Its Global Express, a top of the line executive jet, has also presold a number of planes. Bombardier has also redesigned its subway cars and has a $1 billion contract from New York City featuring automatic announcements and electronic information signs. Its American Flyer high-speed rail trains started carrying Amtrak passengers from Boston to Washington at 150 miles per hour in 1999. The company has moved into jet skis as an offshoot from its snowmobile business, and it has developed a new two-passenger golf cart featuring an electronic motor capable of 25 miles per hour. It expects to establish a strong market share in this $33 million market as noted elsewhere in this book; the product can also be used as a neighbourhood vehicle in gated or retirement communities. Bombardier also expects to introduce a new sporty all-terrain recreational vehicle to compete with models sold by Honda and Yamaha. Even though quite diversified, Bombardier is resolute in selling new technology and products in all of its product lines.[129]

Five dimensions characterize a firm's entrepreneurial orientation (EO).[130] In combination, these dimensions influence the activities a firm uses in efforts to be innovative and to launch new ventures. Discussed in Chapter 14, one of the key ways new ventures are launched in large firms is through internal corporate entrepreneurship. Particularly for firms seeking first-mover advantages (see Chapter 6), an entrepreneurial orientation among employees is critical.

Autonomy is the first of an EO's five dimensions. Autonomy is an active part of a firm's culture when employees are able to take actions that are free of stifling organizational constraints. Generally, autonomy allows individuals and groups to be self-directed. The second dimension, innovativeness, "reflects a firm's tendency to engage in and support new ideas, novelty, experimentation, and creative processes that may result in new products, services, or technological processes."[131] Cultures with a tendency toward innovativeness encourage employees to think beyond existing knowledge, technologies, and parameters in efforts to find creative ways to add value. Third, risk-taking reflects willingness by employees and their firm to accept risks in the pursuit of marketplace opportunities. These risks can include assuming significant levels of debt and allocating large amounts of other resources (e.g., people) to uncertain projects. Often, these risks are accepted to seize marketplace opportunities that can substantially increase the firm's strategic competitiveness and its returns. The fourth EO dimension, proactiveness, describes a firm's ability to be a market leader rather than a follower. Proactive organizational cultures constantly use processes to anticipate future market needs and to satisfy them before competitors learn how to do so. Finally, competitive aggressiveness is a firm's propensity to take actions that allow it to outperform its rivals consistently and substantially. Thus, the key dimensions that characterize an EO include autonomy, a willingness to innovate and take risks, and a tendency to be aggressive toward competitors and proactive relative to marketplace opportunities.[132]

These business attributes are illustrated in the Strategic Focus about Fastenal, a service-oriented business focusing on selling fasteners (such as specialized nuts and bolts) to industrial companies. CEO Bob Kierlin has developed an entrepreneurial culture in the firm that provides a commonplace set of products in a way that creates value for its customers.

## STRATEGIC FOCUS

### Fastenal's Culture for Selling Nuts and Bolts

Bob Kierlin founded Fastenal Company in 1967 in Winona, Minnesota. It has become the largest fastener distributor in the United States through a service-oriented business network. In addition to an in-house manufacturing division and a quality assurance department, Fastenal has a strategic system of distribution centres and a fleet of over 60 trucks and trailers with 660 branches in 48 states, Canada, and Puerto Rico. Fastenal has been on the *Forbes'* 200 Best Small Companies list for the last 10 years. When it first made the list in 1988, the company had annual sales of $22.5 million. In 1997, its sales were $339 million; almost enough to push it off the small company list. Notwithstanding this phenomenal growth, the company's average return on equity has been 26.6 percent over the last five years, and 28.5 percent in 1997.

When Kierlin is asked to describe the reasons for this success, he says, "Just believe in people, give them a chance to make decisions, take risks, and work hard." Furthermore, he suggests, "We could have made this work selling cabbages." In essence, Kierlin and his top officers have facilitated an entrepreneurial culture to stimulate the kind of growth and returns experienced by Fastenal.

This success apparently has nothing to do with Kierlin's salary; He is paid $120,000 annually, an amount that has remained constant for the past 10 years. He receives no options, bonuses, or long-term incentives. He admits, however, that his net worth is tied to the stock price, which has provided better shareholder returns than Coca-Cola or General Electric. Total returns to shareholders over the past five years have been 39.3 percent annually. This performance has

*continued*

come through selling nuts and bolts—49 000 different kinds of fasteners, from grade-eight hex nuts to weld studs to pin-bolt drive anchors—in 620 stores across Canada, the United States. Furthermore, Fastenal's gross margins are 53 percent, approximately 15 percentage points higher than rivals.

Kierlin fosters a culture of decentralized decisionmaking. Fastenal's branches can bypass the company's central purchasing department, which happens in 42 percent of purchases. Often, management-level decisionmaking is pushed down to entry-level positions. One branch decided that it required improved deliveries to increase sales, so to ensure that it was stocked properly, deliveries were received daily. Fastenal's main focus is to furnish customers with exemplary service and charge them premiums for the value that is created by having the product available on time. The premium price works primarily because Fastenal's sales are focused on replacement parts for industrial and other kinds of machines. The company has successfully implemented a focused differentiation strategy (see Chapter 4). When something breaks, Fastenal employees provide the necessary parts in a timely manner. Rich Schmidt of Machinery Services, says, "As far as Fastenal goes, we never get told no." Of course, this kind of service builds loyalty and allows Fastenal to charge its premium price. Usually, a large factory is not likely to quibble over a $3 bolt when its machine is down.

Many construction and equipment manufacturers outsource their inventory function to Fastenal, which means the company can cut, machine, or mould virtually any fastener or other product that it has in inventory or available from suppliers. Although such custom purchases account for only 4 percent of revenues, this is an effective sales tool and builds customer loyalty.

To foster the significant growth of Fastenal, Kierlin has kept the organizational structure very flat. There are only three management levels between branch managers and Fastenal's president, Will Oberton, who is 39 years old. Often, new employees work as few as six months before being given their own store to manage. Compensation for sales people after three years is likely to be split between bonus and base salary. There is no stock option, retirement plan, or other pension plan available; Kierlin believes that employees should be responsible for their own retirement.

Some on Wall Street have been concerned about Fastenal's exceedingly strong growth rate and expect the fastener market to be saturated soon. Kierlin responds that he thought the smallest population that would justify a Fastenal store's presence was 25 000, but with new product lines that have similar margins to nuts and bolts, Kierlin feels that his firm can enter communities as small as 8000 people. Accordingly, Fastenal has begun to sell power tools, saws, drills, and sanders under the FastTool brand. Although people like to comparison shop for tools that cost upward of $150, they are less likely to haggle over accessories such as drill bits, saw blades, sandpaper, and safety accessories. The margins for these replacement products rival those of fastener lines. Kierlin also suggests that the company's oldest stores are its most profitable stores; and, as such, sales continue to grow in already established stores. Therefore, with new lines it appears Fastenal may be able to maintain its high growth level.

*continued*

Although the new locations and product lines give potential for the new growth, Kierlin is quick to remind analysts that it's not the new stores and products lines that allow for success, it's the way people are treated. Fastenal gives employees a chance to make decisions and take risks and provides incentives to work hard. In essence, it's the entrepreneurial culture that Kierlin has created at Fastenal that is the true source of underlying success.

Sources: B. Pappas and R. Boone, Jr., 1997, The best of the best, *Forbes magazine online*, http://www.forbes.com, November 3; *Fastenal Company home page*, http://www.fastenal.com; R. Teitelbaum, 1997, Who is Bob Kierlin—and why is he so successful? *Fortune*, December 8, 254–58.

## Changing Organizational Culture and Business Reengineering

Changing organizational culture is more difficult than maintaining it, but strategic leaders recognize when change is needed. Incremental changes to the firm's culture typically are used to implement current strategies. However, more significant and sometimes even radical changes to organizational culture are needed to support the selection of strategies that differ from those the firm has implemented historically. Regardless of the reasons for change, shaping and reinforcing a new culture requires effective communication and problemsolving, along with the selection of the right people (those who have the values managers wish to infuse throughout the organization), effective performance appraisals (establishing goals and measuring individual performance toward those goals that fit with the new core values), and appropriate reward systems (rewarding the desired behaviours that reflect the new core values).[133]

Evidence suggests that cultural changes succeed only when the firm's CEO, other key top-management team members, and middle-level managers support them actively.[134] In fact, for large-scale changes, approximately one-third of middle-level managers need to be effective change agents. These change agents "… have a nice balance of capabilities: They are technically skilled people who are also very capable in personal relationships. They're an odd combination. On the one hand, they're tough decision-makers who are highly disciplined about performance results. But they also know how to get lots of people energized and aligned in the same direction."[135]

One catalyst for change in organizational culture, particularly for critical changes, is the selection of new top-management team members from outside the corporation. Company founder and CEO Michael Dell of Dell Computer, who pioneered the direct marketing of computers to customers, recruited executives from companies such as Motorola, Hewlett-Packard, and Apple Computer to deal with problems the firm encountered in late 1993 and early 1994.[136] Interestingly, Dell is 10 years younger than the next youngest member of the newly formed top management team.[137]

## EMPHASIZING ETHICAL PRACTICES

The effectiveness of strategy implementation processes increases when they are based on ethical practices. Ethical companies encourage and enable people at all organizational levels to exercise ethical judgment. Alternately, if unethical practices evolve in an organization, they act like a contagious disease.[138] To properly influence employee judgment and behaviour, ethical practices must shape the firm's decisionmaking process and be an integral part of an organization's culture. Once accepted, ethical practices serve as a moral filter through which potential courses of action are evaluated.[139]

As discussed in Chapter 11, managerial opportunism occurs when managers take actions that are in their own best interests but not in the firm's best interests. In other words, managers take advantage of their positions to make decisions that benefit them to the detriment of the owners (shareholders).[140] An implicit assumption of the agency model described in the discussion of corporate governance in Chapter 11 is that top-level managers may act as opportunistic agents who will capitalize on every chance to maximize personal welfare at the expense of shareholders. Individual opportunism is well documented by Wall Street insider trading scandals and other actions taken by those who financed large leveraged buyouts and acquisitions.[141] Other potential problems that have been documented include questionable hiring practices and a willingness to commit fraud by understating write-offs that reduce corporate returns.[142] In addition, it is possible that very high CEO compensation is a sign of opportunism being pursued by those in the upper echelons of management.[143]

Another set of studies sheds light on these issues. Research examining managers' ethical values and beliefs in the mid-1980s and again in the early 1990s showed little change. At both times, managers emphasized utilitarian goals; that is, the achievement of economic gains for the organization's stakeholders. In fact, the earlier survey found that one of the primary reasons some managers emphasized ethical practices was to achieve greater profits. Some argue that the managerial and organizational gains are mutually beneficial. In other words, firms that establish and maintain ethical practices are more likely to achieve strategic competitiveness and earn above-average returns. A key reason for this is that a reputation for ethical practices attracts loyal customers.[144]

On the other hand, recent evidence suggests that at least some individuals from different groups—including top-level executives and business students—may be willing to commit either illegal actions (e.g., fraud) or actions that many think are unethical. In one study, researchers found that 47 percent of upper-level executives, 41 percent of controllers, and 76 percent of graduate-level business students expressed a willingness to commit fraud (as measured by a subject's willingness to misrepresent his or her company's financial statements). Moreover, these researchers discovered that 87 percent of the managers made at least one fraudulent decision out of a total of seven situations requiring a decision. Another finding is that the more an individual valued a comfortable life and/or pleasure, and the less he or she valued self-respect, the greater the probability that a fraudulent decision would be made.[145]

Another study's results appear to have important implications for organizations and those who manage them.[146] The study found that although cheating was observed, there was reluctance to report it. An unwillingness to report wrongdoing calls for the development of comprehensive organizational control systems to assure that individuals' behaviours are consistent with the firm's needs and expectations.

Thus, the findings from these studies seem to support the need for firms to employ ethical strategic leaders—those who include ethical practices as part of their long-term vision for the firm, who desire to do the right thing, and for whom honesty, trust, and integrity are important.[147] Strategic leaders who consistently display these qualities inspire employees as they work with others to develop and support an organizational culture in which ethical practices are the expected behavioural norms. FPI's corporate commitment is to the values of quality, honesty, innovation, and teamwork. One of this text book's authors was taken aback at the emphatic response of one FPI plant manager when he heard Mintzberg's "strategy as a ploy" concept. The plant manager stated quite forcefully that someone who tried a ploy strategy at FPI would be let go so fast that "their heads would still be spinning long after they were let go." There is no doubt that this philosophy permeates FPI, and employees deviate from it at risk of their jobs or worse.

As our discussion suggests, strategic leaders are challenged to take actions that increase the probability that an ethical culture will exist in their organization. When these efforts are successful, the practices associated with an ethical culture become institutionalized in the firm; that is, they become the set of behavioural commitments and actions accepted by most of the firm's employees and other stakeholders with whom employees interact. Actions that strategic leaders can take to develop an ethical organizational culture include (1) establishing and communicating specific goals to describe the firm's ethical standards (e.g., developing and disseminating a code of conduct), (2) continuously revising and updating the code of conduct, based on inputs from people throughout the firm and from other stakeholders (e.g., customers and suppliers), (3) disseminating the code of conduct to all stakeholders to inform them of the firm's ethical standards and practices, (4) developing and implementing methods and procedures to use in achieving the firm's ethical standards (e.g., use of internal auditing practices that are consistent with the standards), (5) creating and using explicit reward systems that recognize acts of courage (e.g., rewarding those who use proper channels and procedures to report observed wrongdoings), and (6) creating a work environment in which all people are treated with dignity.[148] The effectiveness of these actions increases when they are undertaken simultaneously, because the six major actions are mutually supportive. A failure to develop and engage in all six actions reduces the likelihood that the firm can establish an ethical culture. Moreover, when strategic leaders engage successfully in these actions, they serve as moral role models for the firm's employees and other stakeholders. Organizational control systems can help to foster ethical practices and other areas important for the exercise of strategic leadership.

# ESTABLISHING BALANCED ORGANIZATIONAL CONTROLS

Organizational controls have long been viewed as an important part of strategy implementation processes. Controls are necessary to help ensure that firms achieve their desired outcomes of strategic competitiveness and above-average returns.[149] Defined as the "… formal, information-based … procedures used by managers to maintain or alter patterns in organizational activities," controls help strategic leaders build credibility, demonstrate the value of strategies to the firm's stakeholders, and promote and support strategic change.[150] Most critically, controls provide the parameters within which strategies are to be implemented as well as corrective actions to be taken when implementation-related adjustments are required. In this chapter, we focus on two organizational controls—strategic and financial—that were introduced in Chapter 12. Our discussion of organizational controls in this chapter emphasizes strategic and financial controls because strategic leaders are responsible for their development and effective use. Table 13.1 contains several characteristics of a strategically controlled organization and a financially controlled organization.

As explained in Chapter 12, financial controls, which focus on short-term financial outcomes, are often emphasized in large corporations. In contrast, strategic control focuses on the content of strategic actions, rather than their outcomes. Some strategic actions can be correct, but poor financial outcomes may still result because of external conditions such as recessionary economic problems, unexpected domestic or foreign government actions, or natural disasters.[151] Therefore, an emphasis on financial control often produces more short-term and risk-averse managerial decisions because financial outcomes may be due to events beyond managers' direct control. Alternatively, strategic controls encourage lower-level managers to make decisions that incorporate moderate and acceptable levels of risk because outcomes are shared between the business-level executives making strategic proposals and the corporate-level executives evaluating them.

Successful strategic leaders synergistically combine strategic control and financial control (they do not eliminate financial control) with the emphasis on strategic control and with the intent of achieving more positive long-term returns.[152] In fact, most corporate restructuring, especially downscoping, is designed to refocus the firm on its core businesses, thereby allowing top-level executives to re-establish strategic control of their separate business units.[153]

Effective use of strategic control by top-level managers is frequently integrated with appropriate autonomy for the various subunits so they can gain a competitive advantage in their respective markets. Strategic control can be used to promote the sharing of both tangible and intangible resources among interdependent businesses within a firm's portfolio. In addition, the autonomy provided allows the flexibility necessary to take advantage of specific marketplace opportunities. As a result, strategic leadership promotes the simultaneous use of strategic control and autonomy.[154]

The Strategic Focus on diversified business groups suggests the importance of diversified firms maintaining a balanced control orientation. Because large diversified business groups have not maintained this balance, many throughout the world have to restructure their operations. For instance, those in South Korea have had significant problems as the currency crisis in Southeast Asia has revealed problems in their diversification strategies.

As our discussion suggests, organizational controls establish an integrated set of analyses and actions that reinforce one another. Through effective use of strategic controls, strategic leaders increase the probability that their firms will gain the benefits of carefully formulated strategies but not at the expense of the financial control that is a critical part of the strategy implementation process. Effective organizational controls provide an underlying logic for strategic leadership, focus attention on critical strategic issues, support a competitive culture, and provide a forum that builds commitment to strategic intent.

A major problem for strategic leaders is to ensure that their organizations do not become too diversified and therefore able to use only financial controls, which means leaders are able to exercise only managerial leadership even if they have the ability to exercise strategic leadership. Corporate control systems determine how business units are controlled, which determines how divisional general managers control their human resources.[155] Consequently, CEOs who financially control divisions but expect strategic leadership from their general managers may get managerial leadership over the long term.

| ■ ■ **TABLE 13.1** | **Characteristics of Strategic and Financial Control Systems** |
| --- | --- |

**Strategic Controls**

High level of interaction among divisions

High level of interaction between corporate HQ and divisions

Ability to share resources and capabilities among divisions

Ability to transfer core competencies among divisions

Information-sharing among divisions

Corporate managers possess an in-depth knowledge of what is done in divisions

A long-term perspective and a willingness to accept risky ventures

Relatively more is spent on:

> Research and development
>
> Managerial/employee training and development
>
> Capital and equipment
>
> Market research

A good system to monitor product market/operational/financial data

Open communication between corporate and divisional managers

Employees evaluated on the basis of an open, subjective appraisal of what was done to achieve financial results

**Financial Controls**

A least-cost behaviour approach

Capital funds are channelled to divisions that yield higher financial returns (and financial returns are the only criteria used)

A short-term perspective and risk avoidance

Corporate managers have a superficial knowledge of divisional operations

Competition among divisions

Managers and employees are evaluated on the basis of short-term financial criteria

Relatively less is spent on:

> Research and development
>
> Managerial/employee training and development
>
> Capital and equipment
>
> Market research

Focus is on:

> Short-term ROI
>
> Cash flow
>
> Revenue growth
>
> Market share

## STRATEGIC FOCUS

### Synergistically Combining Controls in Large, Diversified Business Groups

Large, diversified business groups are diversified across a wide range of businesses. They often have practical financial interlocks among their holdings, and, in many cases, family ownership and control. These diversified business groups dominate private-sector industrial and service activities in many of the world's economies. In North America, family ownership is quite prevalent, and in the world economy as a whole, the number is certainly over 50 percent. Many diversified business groups (unrelated-diversified firms or conglomerates) have been refocusing because of the market for corporate control and the ability of large investors to buy diffuse equity holdings and keep firms from overdiversifying into too many product markets.

In some developing markets, diversified business groups have provided advantages that allow them to exist more prominently throughout the world. In these emerging markets, equity markets are usually illiquid and banks, some of which are nationalized, provide most financing. Also, large business groups provide a significant training ground for managers in economies with few business schools. Cross-holding among business groups also facilitates contract enforcement where contract laws are often unpredictable. Thus, many economies have diversified business groups such as the chaebols in South Korea and the large diversified business groups in India and throughout Southeast Asia. Furthermore, many developed economies throughout Europe, such as Italy, France, and Sweden, have large diversified business groups.

Strategic leaders are seeing that the control systems they have implemented to manage large diversified business groups are becoming critical as economies become more liberal (regarding trade policies) and experience currency shocks such as those in Southeast Asia. In South Korea, many strategic leaders of the chaebols have been reorganizing to refocus on core businesses and maintain a better balance between strategic and financial controls. For example, the Hyundai Group has indicated during a financial crisis that it would scrap plans to build a $5 billion steel mill and would relinquish management of its money-losing newspaper operation. It also indicated that it would sell or merge unprofitable affiliates that can operate independently. Hyundai has 58 affiliates and sales of over $50 billion. It did not specify which of its 58 affiliates would be affected by the restructuring. Likewise, LG Group said it would cut 90 business lines worth $1.48 billion. Samsung also suggested that it would restructure. As with Hyundai and LG, Samsung promised that it would adopt consolidated financial statements and eliminate cross-guarantees between affiliates for loans, which would provide greater transparency for the group's accounting procedures. Samsung plans to focus on three or four core industries but, like the others, declined to name them. Because the chaebols are largely family-owned, it has been difficult to understand their operation, governance, and control procedures.

Ssangyong's restructuring has been defying the usual convention of diversified business groups in South Korea. Although it is one of the largest chaebols, Kim Suk Joon has taken his company through a long and painful restruc-

*continued*

turing that included selling its prized automobile company to a rival. Many chaebols have been too proud to scale back and often delay unveiling restructuring plans until days before declaring default. Six of the largest chaebols sought court protection from creditors in 1997. Ssangyong sold off its profitable paper company to Procter & Gamble for $46.7 million and sold a California cement company, Riverside Cement, to Texas Industries. Although Ssangyong's restructuring gives it an advantage because it readily undertook the restructuring process relative to other chaebols, the lesson is still the same; they have all over-expanded and overdiversified because their leaders did not have adequate strategic controls in place.

Ahlstrom Corporation, a large Finnish conglomerate, restructured its governance and control systems as it confronted more competitive markets. As with many Asian firms, the Finnish conglomerate was controlled by over 200 family owners. To manage the operation professionally and yet include family involvement, the Ahlstrom owners formed a family assembly that allowed them to have formal communications between family members and the board and the CEO. Furthermore, family assemblies often served as an informal sounding board for the CEO and board of directors. For instance, the family council drafted a document—the Ahlstrom Family Values and Policies—that was discussed extensively and serves as a constitution for the corporation. Ahlstrom ultimately reorganized its diversified holdings into more focused business groups after downscoping by selling off some holdings. Once the holdings were sold off and organized into four groups, the family restructured the operation so that each business group has its own board. There is an industrial holding company above the four business groups, and above that is a main board. This structure has provided much better corporate governance that is closer to the operations and allows each business group with its own subsidiaries and divisions to run more efficiently with better balance between financial controls and strategic controls, as well as better governance of management. Therefore, from a strategic leadership point of view, this structure allows for more family members to be involved and to ensure that the company is running according to the family constitution.

Family-owned companies of expatriate Chinese run many business groups in Southeast Asia. Traditionally, these firms have been in consumer industries that are nontechnical, such as shipping, commodity trading, hotel, real estate and financial services, and other light industries. As these firms seek to move into high-tech industries, such as chemicals and electronics, they have had to move away from the family-managed business concept to more professional managerial techniques. This adjustment is due partly to the change in capital markets where more transparency is required and where contracting law is becoming more prominent. Before these economic shocks, business operations were run mostly on the basis of relationships among family members and friends. Businesses are now being forced to implement better and more professional control systems, as have other diversified business groups throughout the world.

Diversified business operations have also been found in India. Many Indian groups have also been restructuring, as have those in Southeast Asia such as the chaebols in Korea and the Ahlstrom Group in Western Europe. Their leaders are seeking to develop a synergistic combination balance between

*continued*

financial controls and strategic controls us their economies become more liberalized and open to foreign competition. Synergistically combining strategic and financial controls with the emphasis on strategic controls is believed to enhance performance more than using financial or strategic controls alone.

Sources: P. Ghemawat and T. Khanna, 1998, The nature of diversified business groups: A research design and two case studies, *Journal of Industrial Economics,* in press; J. Magretta, 1998, Governing the family-owned enterprise: An interview with Finland's Krister Ahlstrom, *Harvard Business Review,* 76 (1): 112–23; M. Cho, 1998, Samsung to sell units, focus on core industries, *Wall Street Journal,* January 22, A15; M. Schuman, 1998, Samsung weighs retreat on auto output, *Wall Street Journal,* January 21, A7; M. Cho, 1998, Hyundai, LG Groups to trim operations, *Wall Street Journal,* January 20, A14; M. Schuman, 1997, Seoul survivor: A giant resists the crisis, *Wall Street Journal,* December 24, A8; T. Khanna and K. Palepu, 1997, Why focused strategies may be wrong for emerging markets, *Harvard Business Review,* 75 (4): 41–50; M. Weidenbaum, 1996, The Chinese family business enterprise, *California Management Review,* 38 (4): 141–56.

## SUMMARY

- Strategic leadership is required to use the strategic management process successfully, including the strategic actions associated with the implementation of strategies. Strategic leadership entails the ability to influence those with whom you work in your organization to voluntarily make decisions on a day-to-day basis that enhance the long-term viability of the organization while at the same time maintaining its short-term financial stability

- Managerial, visionary, and strategic leadership are different types of leadership. Managerial leaders want stability and order, and to preserve the existing order. They are more comfortable handling day-to-day activities, and are short-term oriented. They guide by using explicit knowledge and without a strategic vision constrained by values.

- Visionary leadership is future oriented and concerned with risk-taking, and visionary leaders are not dependent on their organizations for their sense of identity. Under these leaders, organizational control is maintained through socialization and the sharing of, and compliance to, a commonly held set of norms, values, and shared beliefs.

- Strategic leaders manage the paradox created by the use of managerial and visionary leadership models. They use metaphors, analogies, and models to allow the juxtaposition of apparently contradictory concepts by defining boundaries of mutual co-existence. They guide the organizational knowledge creation process by encouraging contradictory combinative capabilities—that is, the organization's ability to combine individual, group, and organizational tacit and explicit knowledge to generate organizational and technological innovations.

- Top-level managers are an important resource requirement for firms to develop and exploit competitive advantages. In addition, strategic leaders can be a source of competitive advantage. Top executives exercise discretion in making critical strategic decisions.

- The top-management team is composed of key managers who formulate and implement strategies. Generally, they are officers of the corporation and/or members of the board of directors.

- There is a relationship among top-management team characteristics, firm strategy, and performance. For example, a top-management team that has significant marketing and R&D knowledge often enhances the firm's effectiveness as the team steers the firm toward implementation of growth strategies. Overall, most top-management teams are more effective when they have diverse and heterogeneous skills.

- When boards of directors are involved in shaping strategic direction, firms generally improve their strategic competitiveness. Alternatively, boards may be less involved in strategic decisions about strategy formulation and strategy implementation when CEOs have more power. CEOs obtain power when they appoint people to the board and when they simultaneously serve the firm as its CEO and board chair.

- Strategic leadership has six components: determining the firm's strategic direction, exploiting and maintaining core competencies, developing human capital, sustaining an effective organizational culture, emphasizing ethical practices, and establishing balanced organizational controls.

- Often requiring a significant amount of thinking and time to form, determining strategic direction refers to the development of a long-term vision of the firm's strategic intent. A charismatic leader can help achieve strategic intent.

- Strategic leaders must verify that their firm exploits its core competencies, which are used to create and deliver products that create value for customers, to implement strategies. In related-diversified and large firms, in particular, core competencies are exploited effectively when they are shared across units and products.

- A critical element of strategic leadership and effective strategy implementation processes is the ability to develop the firm's human capital. Effective strategic leaders and firms view human capital as a resource to be maximized rather than as a cost to be minimized. Resulting from this perspective is the use of programs intended to train current and future strategic leaders so they will have the skills needed to nurture and develop the rest of the firm's human capital.

- Shaping the firm's culture is a central task of strategic leadership. In the new competitive landscape, an appropriate organizational culture encourages the development of an entrepreneurial orientation among employees and an ability to change the culture as necessary. Reengineering can facilitate this process.

- In ethical organizations, employees are encouraged to exercise ethical judgment and to display only ethical practices. Ethical practices can be promoted through several actions, including those of setting specific goals to describe the firm's ethical standards, using a code of conduct, rewarding ethical behaviours, and creating a work environment in which all people are treated with dignity.

- The final component of strategic leadership is the development and use of effective organizational controls. It is through organizational controls that strategic leaders provide the direction the firm requires to flexibly, yet appropriately, use its core competencies in the pursuit of marketplace opportu-

nities. Best results are obtained when there is a synergistic combination between strategic and financial controls with the emphasis on strategic controls.

## REVIEW QUESTIONS

1. What is strategic leadership? In what ways are top-level managers considered important resources for an organization?

2. Define managerial leadership and visionary leadership. How do they differ from strategic leadership?

3. What is a top-management team, and how does it affect a firm's performance and its abilities to innovate and make appropriate strategic changes?

4. How does strategic leadership affect determination of the firm's strategic direction?

5. Why is it important for strategic leaders to ensure that their firm exploits its core competencies in the pursuit of strategic competitiveness and above-average returns?

6. What is the importance of human capital and its development for strategic competitiveness?

7. What is organizational culture? What must strategic leaders do to sustain an effective organizational culture?

8. As a strategic leader, what actions could you take to establish and emphasize ethical practices in your firm?

9. What are organizational controls? Why are strategic controls and financial controls, two types of organizational controls, an important part of the strategic management process? Which is the more important and why?

## DISCUSSION QUESTIONS

1. Choose a CEO of a prominent firm who you believe exemplifies strategic leadership. What actions does this CEO take that demonstrate strategic leadership? What are the effects of these actions on the firm's performance?

2. Select a CEO of a prominent firm who you believe exemplifies managerial leadership. What actions does this CEO take that exemplify managerial leadership? How have these actions affected the firm's performance?

3. Select a CEO of a prominent firm who you believe exemplifies visionary leadership. What actions does this CEO take that exemplify

visionary leadership? How have these actions affected the firm's performance?

4. What are managerial resources? What is the relationship between managerial resources and a firm's strategic competitiveness? Take two prominent firms in your community and discuss their managerial resources and the impact of these resources on each firm's strategic competitiveness.

5. By examining popular press articles, select an organization that has recently gone through a significant strategic change. While reading these articles, collect as much information as you can about the organization's top-management team. Does your analysis suggest that there is a relationship between the top-management team's characteristics and the type of change the organization experienced? If so, what is the nature and outcome of that relationship?

6. In light of your reading of this chapter and popular press accounts, select a CEO who you feel has exhibited vision. Has the CEO's vision been realized? If so, what were the effects of this realization? If the vision has not been realized, why not?

7. Identify a firm in which you believe strategic leaders have emphasized and developed human capital. What do you believe are the effects of this emphasis and development on the firm's performance?

8. Select an organization that you think has a unique organizational culture. What characteristics of that culture make it unique? Has the culture had a significant effect on the organization's performance? If so, what is that effect?

9. As discussed in this chapter, strategic leadership occasionally requires managers to make difficult decisions. In your opinion, is it ethical for managers to make these types of decisions without being willing to receive feedback from employees about the effects of those decisions? Be prepared to justify your response.

10. Why is the strategic control exercised by a firm's strategic leaders important for long-term competitiveness? How do strategic controls differ from financial controls?

## ETHICS QUESTIONS

1. As an employee with less than one year of experience in a firm, what actions would you pursue if you encountered unethical practices by your CEO?

2. What are the ethical issues involved, if any, with the firm's ability to develop and exploit a core competence in the manufacture of goods that may be harmful to consumers (e.g., cigarettes)? Be prepared to discuss the reasons for your response.

3. As a strategic leader, would you feel ethically responsible for the development of your firm's human capital? Why or why not? Do you believe your position is consistent with the majority or minority of today's strategic leaders?

4. Select an organization, social group, or volunteer agency in which you hold membership that you believe has an ethical culture. What factors caused this culture to be ethical? Are there events that could occur that would cause this culture to become less ethical? If so, what are they?

## INTERNET EXERCISE

Go to *Report on Business* magazine's 50 Best-Paid CEOs in Canada at:

**http://www.robmagazine.com/top1000/index.html**

Each year ROB magazine publishes profiles of the best-paid CEOs in Canada. Select three of these CEOs and research their attributes by a thorough Internet search. In what ways do these CEOs exemplify strategic leadership? Do these CEOs have attributes in common? Explain your answer.

Or, go to Canadian Business Performance 2000 at:

**http://www.ca.nbus.com/cgibin/cbm2000.p15**

This Web site provides the names of the top 25 firms in terms of sales in Canada in 1998. Select three CEOs from this list and research their attributes. In what ways do these CEOs exemplify strategic leadership? Do these CEOs have attributes in common? Explain your answer.

## STRATEGIC SURFING

*CEO Express* is a Web site designed specifically for busy executives. The site contains a menu of links to sites that appeal to CEOs and other business leaders. A similar site is referred to as *The CEO Homepage*. This site contains links to on-line versions of business publications valuable to CEOs and other top managers.

**http://www.ceoexpress.com**
**http://ceohomepage.com/bizpubs.html**

# NOTES

1 K. R. Thompson, W. A. Hochwarter, and N. J. Mathys, 1997, Stretch targets: What makes them effective? *Academy of Management Executive*, XI, (3): 48–59.

2 R. D. Ireland and M. A. Hitt, 1999, Achieving and maintaining strategic competitiveness in the 21st century: The role of strategic leadership, *Academy of Management Executive*, XII, 13 (1), 43–57; D. Lei, M. A. Hitt, and R. Bettis, 1996, Dynamic core competencies through meta-learning and strategic context, *Journal of Management*, 22: 547–67.

3 D. Silverman, 2000, CEO brings new life to stagnant Compaq/Capellas moves firm back to profitability, *Houston Chronicle*, January 25, 1B; Merger Brief, 2000, The digital dilemma, *The Economist*, July 22, 19, 67–68.

4 R. Evered, 1980, So What is Strategy? Working Paper, Naval Postgraduate School, Monterey; J. B. Quinn, 1980, *Strategies for Change: Logical Incrementalism*, (Homewood, Ill.: Richard D. Irwin; H. Mintzberg and J. B. Quinn, 1996, *The Strategy Process: Concepts, Contexts, Cases*, 3rd Edition (Upper Saddle River, New Jersey: Prentice Hall).

5 W. G. Rowe, 2001, Creating wealth in organizations: The role of strategic leadership, *The Academy of Management Executive*, 15 (1), 81–94.

6 H. Mintzberg, 1987, Five Ps for strategy, *California Management Review*, Fall in H. Mintzberg and J. B. Quinn, 1996, *The Strategy Process: Concepts, Contexts, Cases*, 3rd Edition (Upper Saddle River, New Jersey: Prentice Hall), 10–17; H. Mintzberg, 1987, Crafting strategy, *Harvard Business Review*, July–August in H. Mintzberg and J. B. Quinn, 1996, *The Strategy Process: Concepts, Contexts, Cases*, 3rd Edition (Upper Saddle River, New Jersey: Prentice Hall), 101–09.

7 J. B. Barney, 1997, *Gaining and Sustaining Competitive Advantage* (New York: Addison-Wesley Publishing Company), 65–133.

8 A. Zaleznik, 1977, Managers and leaders: Are they different? *Harvard Business Review*, May–June, 67–78.

9 G. Hamel and C. K. Prahalad, 1993, Strategy as stretch and leverage, *Harvard Business Review*, 71, (2): 75–84.

10 S. Sherman, 1995, How tomorrow's best leader's are learning their stuff, *Fortune*, November, 27, 99; R. Calori, G. Johnson, and P. Sarnin, 1994, CEOs' cognitive maps and the scope of the organization, *Strategic Management Journal*, 15: 437–57.

11 Zaleznik, 1977 Managers and leaders: Are they different?, 70–71.

12 Ibid, 71–72.

13 Ibid, 72–74.

14 Ibid, 74–75.

15 L. T. Hosmer, 1982, The importance of strategic leadership, *Journal of Business Strategy*, 3 (2), Fall, 47–57.

16 D. Schendel, 1989, Introduction to the Special Issue on "Strategic Leadership," *Strategic Management Journal*, Special Issue, 10, 1–3.

17 D. Hambrick, 1989, Guest's editor's introduction: Putting top managers back in the strategy picture, *Strategic Management Journal*, Special Issue, 10, 5–15.

18 Ibid, 5–15.

19 Hosmer, 1982, The importance of strategic leadership; R. Evans, 1997, Hollow the leader, *Report on Business*, November, 56–63; L. Sooklal, 1991, The leader as a broker of dreams, *Human Relations*, 44 (8), 833–56; A. Zaleznik, 1990, The leadership gap, *The Academy of Management Executive*, 4, (1), 7–22.

20 C. W. L. Hill and R. E. Hoskisson, 1987, Strategy and structure in the multiproduct firm, *Academy of Management Review*, 12 (2), 331–41; R. E. Hoskisson and M. A. Hitt, 1994, *Downscoping: Taming the Diversified Firm* (New York: Oxford University Press) ; A. Zaleznik, 1990, The leadership gap, 7–22.

21 G. Hedlund, 1994, A model of knowledge management and the N-Form corporation, *Strategic Management Journal*, 15 (Special Issue), Summer, 73–90; B. Kogut and U. Zander, 1992, Knowledge of the firm, combinative abilities, and the replication of technology, *Organization Science*, 3, 383–97.

22 R. Trigg, 1996, *Ideas of Human Nature: An Historical Introduction* (Cambridge, MA: Blackwell Publishers); J. Child, 1972, Organizational structure, environment and performance: The role of strategic choice, *Sociology*, 6, 1–22.

23 Zaleznik, 1977, Managers and leaders: Are they different?, 70–71.

24 Ibid., 71–72.

25 Ibid., 72–74.

26 Zaleznik, 1977, Managers and leaders: Are they different?, 74–75; A. Zaleznik, 1990, The leadership gap, *The Academy of Management Executive*, 4 (1), 7–22.

27 Hosmer, 1982, The importance of strategic leadership, 47–57.

28 Schendel, 1989, Introduction to the Special Issue on "Strategic Leadership," 1–3.

29 Hambrick, 1989, Guest's editor's introduction: Putting top managers back in the strategy picture, 5–15; H. Mintzberg, 1973, *The Nature of Managerial Work*, Chapters 15–17, (New York: Harper and Row).

30 Hambrick, 1989, Guest's editor's introduction: Putting top managers back in the strategy picture, 5–15.

31 Evans, 1997, Hollow the leader, 56–63; Hosmer, 1982, The importance of strategic leadership, 47–57;

Sooklal, 1991, The leader as a broker of dreams, 833–56; Zaleznik, 1990, The leadership gap, 7–22.

32  Hoskisson and Hitt, 1994, Downscoping: Taming the diversified firm.

33  M. Polanyi, 1966, *The Tacit Dimension* (Garden City, NY: Anchor); R. Reed and R. J. deFillippi, 1990, Causal ambiguity, barriers to imitation, and sustainable competitive advantage, *Academy of Management Review*, 15, 88–102; R. Nelson and S. Winter, 1982, *An Evolutionary Theory of Economic Change* (Cambridge, Mass: Belknap Press,); H. Itami, 1987, *Mobilizing Invisible Assets* (Cambridge, MA: Harvard University Press); J. Kotter and J. Heskett, 1992, *Corporate Culture and Performance* (New York: The Free Press); W. G. Ouchi and M. Maguire, 1975, Organizational control: Two functions, *Administrative Sciences* 20, 559–69; E. H. Schein, 1993, On dialogue, culture, and organizational learning, *Organizational Dynamics*, 22 (2), 40–51.

34  R. Trigg, 1996, *Ideas of Human Nature: An Historical Introduction;* J. Child, 1972, Organizational structure, environment and performance: The role of strategic choice, 1–22; H. Mintzberg, B. Ahlstrand, and J. Lampel, 1998, *Strategy Safari,* Chapter 5 (New York: The Free Press).

35  J. P. Kotter, 1990, What leaders really do, *Harvard Business Review,* May–June.

36  Zaleznik, 1977, Managers and leaders: Are they different?, 74–75; Zaleznik, 1990, The leadership gap, 7–22.

37  Kotter, 1990. What leaders really do.

38  Kotter, 1990, What leaders really do.

39  W. G. Rowe, 2001, Creating wealth in organisations: The role of strategic leadership, 81–94.

40  Ibid.

41  Ireland and Hitt, 1999, Achieving and maintaining strategic competitiveness in the 21st century, 43–57.

42  J. Conger, 1991, Inspiring others: The language of leadership, *The Academy of Management Executive,* 5 (1), 31–45; M. Nathan, 1996, What is organizational vision? Ask chief executives, *The Academy of Management Executive,* 10, (1), 82–83.

43  Hambrick, 1989, Guest's editor's introduction: Putting top managers back in the strategy picture, 5–15; Schendel, 1989, Introduction to the Special Issue on "Strategic Leadership," 1–3.

44  Hoskisson and Hitt, 1994, Downscoping: Taming the diversified firm.

45  Ibid.

46  I. Nonaka, 1994, A Dynamic Theory of Organizational Knowledge Creation, *Organization Science*, 5 (1), 14–37; I. Nonaka and H. Takeuchi, 1995, *The Knowledge Creating Company,* (New York: Oxford University Press).

47  Trigg, 1996, *Ideas of Human Nature: An Historical Introduction;* Child, 1972, Organizational structure, environment and performance: The role of strategic choice, 1–22.

48  I. Nonaka and H. Takeuchi, 1995, *The Knowledge Creating Company;* Kogut and Zander, 1992 Knowledge of the firm, combinative abilities, and the replication of technology, 383–97; S. Sherman and W. Glenn Rowe, 1996, Leadership and strategic value: A resource-based typology, *Proceedings of the Texas Conference on Organizations,* March 1.

49  H. Mintzberg, 1975, The manager's job: Folklore and fact, *Harvard Business Review,* July–August. Reprinted in *Harvard Business Review on Leadership,* 1998 (Boston: Harvard Business School Press).

50  H. Gardner, 1995, *Leading Minds: An Anatomy of Leadership* (New York: Basic Books); S. Sherman, 1995, How tomorrow's best leaders are learning their stuff, *Fortune,* November 27, 90–102.

51  J. B. Quinn, P. Anderson, and S. Finklestein, 1996, Managing professional intellect: Making the most of the best, *Harvard Business Review,* 74 (2), 71–80.

52  M. Loeb, 1994, Where leaders come from, *Fortune,* September 19, 241–42.

53  M. F. R. Kets de Vries, 1995, Life and Death in the Executive Fast Lane (San Francisco: Jossey-Bass).

54  Loeb, Where leaders come from, 241; N. Nohria and J. D. Berkley, 1994, Whatever happened to the take-charge manager? *Harvard Business Review,* 72, (1): 128–37.

55  M. Hammer and S. A. Stanton, 1997, The power of reflection, *Fortune,* November 24, 291–96.

56  S. Finkelstein and D. C. Hambrick, 1996, *Strategic Leadership: Top Executives and Their Effects on Organizations* (St. Paul, Minn.: West Publishing Company), 2.

57  J. A. Byrne and J. Reingold, 1997, Wanted: A few good CEOs, *BusinessWeek,* August 11, 64–70; Kotter, 1990 What leaders really do.

58  Sherman, How tomorrow's best, 102.

59  W. G. Rowe, 2001, Creating wealth in organizations: The role of strategic leadership, 81–94.

60  Ibid.

61  Ibid.

62  J. D. House, 1999. *Against the Tide: Battling for Economic Renewal in Newfoundland and Labrador,* Toronto: University of Toronto Press.

63  H. P. Gunz and R. M. Jalland, 1996, Managerial careers and business strategy, *Academy of Management Review,* 21: 718–56.

64  C. M. Christensen, 1997, Making strategy: Learning by doing, *Harvard Business Review,* 75 (6), 141–56; M. A. Hitt, B. W. Keats, H. E. Harback, and R. D. Nixon, 1994, Rightsizing: Building and maintaining strategic leadership and long-term competitiveness, *Organizational Dynamics,* 23: 18–32; R. L. Priem and D. A. Harrison, 1994, Exploring strategic judgment: Methods for testing the

assumptions of prescriptive contingency theories, *Strategic Management Journal*, 15: 311–24.

65  M. J. Waller, G. P. Huber, and W. H. Glick, 1995, Functional background as a determinant of executives' selective perception, *Academy of Management Journal*, 38: 943–74; N. Rajagopalan, A. M. Rasheed, and D. K. Datta, 1993, Strategic decision processes: Critical review and future directions, *Journal of Management*, 19: 349–84.

66  Finkelstein and Hambrick, *Strategic Leadership*, 26–34; D. C. Hambrick and E. Abrahamson, 1995, Assessing managerial discretion across industries: A multimethod approach, *Academy of Management Journal*, 38: 1427–41; D. C. Hambrick and S. Finkelstein, 1987, Managerial discretion: A bridge between polar views of organizational outcomes, in B. Staw and L. L. Cummings (eds.), *Research in Organizational Behavior* (Greenwich, CT: JAI Press), 369–406.

67  R. C. Mayer, J. H. Davis, and F. D. Schoorman, 1995, An integrative model of organizational trust, *Academy of Management Review*, 20: 709–34.

68  N. Rajagopalan and D. K. Datta, 1996, CEO characteristics: Does industry matter? *Academy of Management Journal*, 39: 197–215.

69  L. M. Fisher, 1997, Novell selects Internet guru to lead company, *The New York Times on the Web*, http://www.nytimes.com, March 19.

70  A. C. Amason, 1996, Distinguishing the effects of functional and dysfunctional conflict on strategic decision making: Resolving a paradox for top management teams, *Academy of Management Journal*, 39: 123–48; Priem and Harrison, Exploring strategic judgment, 311.

71  P. Newman, 1995, Red Wilson's trial by competitive fire, *Maclean's*, 108 (35), 34.

72  R. E. Stross, 1997, Mr. Gates builds his brain trust, *Fortune*, December 8, 84–98.

73  Magna Mania, 1995, *Financial Post*, 89(32), August 12/14, 12; University of Michigan Business School, 1999, Magna International Chairman Stronach Wins 1998 Entrepreneur Award, http://www.bus.umich.edu/news/magna.html.

74  H.A. Krishnan, 1997, Diversification and top management team complementarity: Is performance improved by merging similar or dissimilar teams? *Strategic Management Journal*, 18: 361–74; J. G. Michel and D. C. Hambrick, 1992, Diversification posture and top management team characteristics, *Academy of Management Journal*, 35: 9–37.

75  A. L. Iaquito and J. W. Fredrickson, 1997, Top management team agreement about the strategic decision process: A test of some of its determinants and consequences, *Strategic Management Journal*, 18: 63–75; K. G. Smith, D. A. Smith, J. D. Olian, H. P. Sims, Jr., D. P. O'Bannon, and J. A. Scully, 1994, Top management

team demography and process: The role of social integration and communication, *Administrative Science Quarterly*, 39: 412–38.

76  Amason, Distinguishing the effects, 127.

77  D. C. Hambrick, T. S. Cho, and M. J. Chen, 1996, The influence of top management team heterogeneity on firms' competitive moves, *Administrative Science Quarterly*, 41: 659–84.

78  J. J. Keller, 1997, AT&T's board faces many twists and turns in search for new CEO, *Wall Street Journal*, October 13, A1, A6.

79  Finkelstein and Hambrick, *Strategic Leadership*, 148.

80  C. C. Miller, L. M. Burke, and W. H. Glick, 1998, Cognitive diversity among upper-echelon executives: Implications for strategic decision processes, *Strategic Management Journal*, 19: 39–58.

81  D. K. Datta and J. P. Guthrie, 1994, Executive succession: Organizational antecedents of CEO characteristics, *Strategic Management Journal*, 15: 569–77; M. A. Hitt and R. D. Ireland, 1986, Relationships among corporate-level distinctive competencies, diversification strategy, corporate structure, and performance, *Journal of Management Studies*, 23: 401–16; M. A. Hitt and R. D. Ireland, 1985, Corporate distinctive competence, strategy, industry, and performance, *Strategic Management Journal*, 6: 273–93.

82  W. Boeker, 1997, Strategic change: The influence of managerial characteristics and organizational growth, *Academy of Management Journal*, 40: 152–70; W. Boeker, 1997, Executive migration and strategic change: The effect of top manager movement on product-market entry, *Administrative Science Quarterly*, 42: 213–36.

83  M. E. Wiersema and K. Bantel, 1992, Top management team demography and corporate strategic change, *Academy of Management Journal* 35: 91–121; K. Bantel and S. Jackson, 1989, Top management and innovations in banking: Does the composition of the top team make a difference? *Strategic Management Journal*, 10: 107–24.

84  J. Gillies, 1992, *Boardroom Renaissance: Power, Morality and Performance in the Modern Corporation* (Toronto: McGraw-Hill Ryerson Limited); W. Q. Judge, Jr. and C. P. Zeithaml, 1992, Institutional and strategic choice perspectives on board involvement in the strategic decision process, *Academy of Management Journal*, 35: 766–94; J. A. Pearce II and S. A. Zahra, 1991, The relative power of CEOs and boards of directors: Associations with corporate performance, *Strategic Management Journal*, 12: 135–54.

85  S. Chase, 1999, Alliance Pipeline dumps CEO at critical point, *The Globe and Mail*, October 14, B4.

86  J. D. Westphal and E. J. Zajac, 1995, Who shall govern? CEO/board power, demographic similarity,

and new director selection, *Administrative Science Quarterly,* 40, 60.

87  Ibid., 66; E. J. Zajac and J. D. Westphal, 1995, Accounting for the explanations of CEO compensation: Substance and symbolism, *Administrative Science Quarterly,* 40: 283–308.

88  B. K. Boyd, 1995, CEO duality and firm performance: A contingency model, *Strategic Management Journal,* 16: 301.

89  C. M. Daily and D. R. Dalton, 1995, CEO and director turnover in failing firms: An illusion of change? *Strategic Management Journal,* 16: 393–400.

90  R. Albanese, M. T. Dacin, and I. C. Harris, 1997, Agents as stewards, *Academy of Management Review,* 22: 609–611; J. H. Davis, F. D. Schoorman, and L. Donaldson, 1997, Toward a stewardship theory of management, *Academy of Management Review,* 22: 20–47.

91  B. R. Baliga and R. C. Moyer, 1996, CEO duality and firm performance: What's the fuss? *Strategic Management Journal,* 17: 41–53.

92  J. D. Westphal and E. J. Zajac, 1997, Defections from the inner circle: Social exchange, reciprocity and diffusion of board independence in U.S. corporations, *Administrative Science Quarterly,* 161–83; A. K. Buchholtz and B. A. Ribbens, 1994, Role of chief executive officers in takeover resistance: Effects of CEO incentives and individual characteristics, *Academy of Management Journal,* 37: 554–79.

93  Rajagopalan and Datta, CEO characteristics, 201.

94  R. A. Johnson, R. E. Hoskisson, and M. A. Hitt, 1993, Board involvement in restructuring: The effect of board versus managerial controls and characteristics, *Strategic Management Journal,* 14 (Special Summer Issue): 33–50.

95  B. K. Boyd, 1995, CEO duality and firm performance: A contingency model, *Strategic Management Journal,* 16: 301–12.

96  J. E. Ettlie, 1996, Review of the perpetual enterprise machine: Seven keys to corporate renewal through successful product and process development, E. Bowman (ed.), (New York: Oxford University Press), *Academy of Management Review,* 21: 294–98; Hitt et al., Rightsizing, 20.

97  J. C. Collins and J. I. Porras, 1996, Building your company's vision, *Harvard Business Review,* 74, (5): 65–77.

98  V. L. Young, 1998, Presentation to MBA Strategic Management students, Memorial University of Newfoundland, April 7.

99  C. M. Falbe, M. P. Kriger, and P. Miesing, 1995, Structure and meaning of organizational vision, *Academy of Management Journal,* 39: 740–69.

100  B. Wysocki, Jr., 1995, As firms downsize, business economists find jobs dwindling, *Wall Street Journal,* October 9, A1, A8.

101  W. L. Gardner and B. J. Avolio, 1998, The charismatic relationship: A dramaturgical perspective, *Academy of Management Review,* 23: 32–58.

102  Finkelstein and Hambrick, 1996, *Strategic Leadership,* 69–72; P. Sellers, 1996, What exactly is charisma? *Fortune,* January 15, 68–75.

103  T. Smart, 1996, Jack Welch's encore, *Business Week,* October 28, 154–60.

104  P. R. Nayyar and K. A. Bantel, 1994, Competitive agility: A source of competitive advantage based on speed and variety, in P. Shrivastava, A. Huff, and J. Dutton (eds.), *Advances in Strategic Management,* 10A, (Greenwich, CT: JAI Press), 193–222.

105  Fishery Products International, *Annual Reports,* 1993–98.

106  R. F. Maruca, 1994, The right way to go global: An interview with Whirlpool CEO David Whitwam, *Harvard Business Review,* 72 (2): 136.

107  Lei, Hitt, and Bettis, Dynamic core competencies, 547–67.

108  B. Nussbaum, 1988, Needed: Human capital, *Business Week,* September 19, 100–02.

109  S. A. Snell and M. A. Youndt, 1995, Human resource management and firm performance: Testing a contingency model of executive controls, *Journal of Management,* 21: 711–37.

110  D. Ulrich, 1998, A new mandate for human resources, *Harvard Business Review,* 76, no. 1: 124–34.

111  Snell and Youndt, Human resource, 711; K. Chilton, 1994, The global challenge of American manufacturers (St. Louis, MO: Washington University, Center for the Study of American Business); J. Pfeffer, 1994, *Competitive Advantage through People* (Cambridge, MA: Harvard Business School Press), 4.

112  H. W. Jenkins, Jr., 1996, What price job security? *Wall Street Journal,* March 26, A19.

113  J. S. Lublin, 1996, An overseas stint can be a ticket to the top, *Wall Street Journal,* January 29, B1, B2.

114  M. G. Harvey and M. R. Buckley, 1997, Managing inpatriates: Building a global core competency, *Journal of World Business,* 32, (1): 35–52.

115  T. Stewart, 1998, Why leadership matters, *Fortune,* March 2, 70–82.

116  L. Grant, 1995, GE: The envelope, please, *Fortune,* June 26, 89–90.

117  B. Morris, 1997, If women ran the world it would look a lot like Avon, *Fortune,* July 21, 74–79.

118  J. Nocera, 1996, Living with layoffs, *Fortune,* April 1, 69–71.

119  F. R. Bleakley, 1997, New round of layoffs may be beginning, *Wall Street Journal,* November 13, A2.

120 M. A. Hitt, R. E. Hoskisson, J. S. Harrison, and B. Summers, 1994, Human capital and strategic competitiveness in the 1990s, *Journal of Management Development,* 13 (1): 35–46; C. R. Greer and T. C. Ireland, 1992, Organizational and financial correlates of a contrarian human resource investment strategy, *Academy of Management Journal,* 35: 956–84.

121 C. L. Martin, C. K. Parsons, and N. Bennett, 1995, The influence of employee involvement program membership during downsizing: Attitudes toward the employer and the union, *Journal of Management,* 21: 879–90.

122 C. M. Fiol, 1991, Managing culture as a competitive resource: An identity-based view of sustainable competitive advantage, *Journal of Management,* 17: 191–211; J. B. Barney, 1986, Organizational culture: Can it be a source of sustained competitive advantage? *Academy of Management Review,* 11: 656–65.

123 S. Ghoshal and C. A. Bartlett, 1994, Linking organizational context and managerial action: The dimensions of quality of management, *Strategic Management Journal,* 15: 91–112.

124 J. Kotter, 1997, Matsushita: The world's greatest entrepreneur? *Fortune,* March 31, 105–11.

125 Sherman, How tomorrow's best, 102.

126 P. Burrows and P. Elstrom, 1999, The boss, *BusinessWeek,* 76, August 2.

127 How can big companies keep the entrepreneurial spirit alive? 1995, *Harvard Business Review,* 73, 6, 183–92; S. G. Scott and R. A. Bruce, 1994, Determinants of innovative behavior: A path model of individual innovation in the workplace, *Academy of Management Journal,* 37: 580–607.

128 C. A. Bartlett and S. Goshal, 1997, The myth of the generic manager: New personal competencies for new managerial roles, *California Management Review,* 40, (1): 92–116.

129 J. Webber, W. Zellner, and G. Smith, 1998, Loud noises at Bombardier, *BusinessWeek,* January 26, 94–5.

130 G. T. Lumpkin and G. G. Dess, 1996, Clarifying the entrepreneurial orientation construct and linking it to performance, *Academy of Management Review,* 21: 135–72.

131 Ibid., 142.

132 Ibid., 137.

133 Ireland and Hitt, Achieving and maintaining strategic competitiveness in the 21st century, 43–57.

134 J. E. Dutton, S. J. Ashford, R. M. O'Neill, E. Hayes, and E. E. Wierba, 1997, Reading the wind: How middle managers assess the context for selling issues to top managers, *Strategic Management Journal,* 18: 407–25.

135 S. Sherman, 1995, Wanted: Company change agents, *Fortune,* December 11, 197–98.

136 A. E. Serwer, 1997, Michael Dell turns the PC world inside out, *Fortune,* September 8, 76–86.

137 R. Jacob, 1995, The resurrection of Michael Dell, *Fortune,* September 18, 117.

138 D. J. Brass, K. D. Butterfield, and B. C. Skaggs, 1998, Relationships and unethical behaviour: A social network perspective, *Academy of Management Review,* 23: 14–31.

139 J. M. Lozano, 1996, Ethics and management: A controversial issue, *Journal of Business Ethics,* 15: 227–36; J. Mitchell, 1996, Professor leads attack on big business, *Dallas Morning News,* March 17, H6; J. Milton-Smith, 1995, Ethics as excellence: A strategic management perspective, *Journal of Business Ethics,* 14: 683–93.

140 C. W. L. Hill, 1990, Cooperation, opportunism, and the invisible hand: Implications for transaction cost theory, *Academy of Management Review,* 15: 500–13.

141 M. Zey, 1993, *Banking on Fraud* (New York: Aldine De Gruyter).

142 D. Blalock, 1996, Study shows many execs are quick to write off ethics, *Wall Street Journal,* March 26, Cl, C3; A. P. Brief, J. M. Dukerich, P. R. Brown, and J. F. Brett, 1996, What's wrong with the Treadway Commission Report? *Journal of Business Ethics,* 15: 183–98; G. Miles, 1993, In search of ethical profits: Insights from strategic management, *Journal of Business Ethics,* 12: 219–25.

143 Zajac and Westphal, Accounting for the explanations of CEO compensation, 283–308.

144 S. R. Premeaux and R. W. Mondy, 1993, Linking management behaviour to ethical philosophy, *Journal of Business Ethics,* 12: 219–25.

145 Brief et al., What's wrong?, 183–98.

146 B. K. Burton and J. P. Near, 1995, Estimating the incidence of wrongdoing and whistle-blowing: Results of a study using randomized response technique, *Journal of Business Ethics,* 14: 17–30.

147 Milton-Smith, Ethics as excellence, 685.

148 Brief et al., What's wrong? 194; P. E. Murphy, 1995, Corporate ethics statements: Current status and future prospects, *Journal of Business Ethics,* 14: 727–40.

149 L. J. Kirsch, 1996, The management of complex tasks in organizations: Controlling the systems development process, *Organization Science,* 7: 1–21.

150 R. Simons, 1994, How new top managers use control systems as levers of strategic renewal, *Strategic Management Journal,* 15: 170–71.

151 K. J. Laverty, 1996, Economic "short-termism": The debate, the unresolved issues, and the implications for management practice and research, *Academy of Management Review,* 21: 825–60.

152 M.A. Hitt, R.E. Hoskisson, and R.D. Ireland, 1990, Mergers and acquisitions and managerial commit-

ment to Innovation in M form firms, *Strategic Management Journal,* 11 (Special Summer Issue): 29–47.

153  R. A. Johnson, Antecedents and outcomes of corporate refocusing, *Journal of Management,* 22: 437–81; R. E. Hoskisson and M. A. Hitt, 1994, *Downscoping: How to Tame the Diversified Firm* (New York: Oxford University Press).

154  Ireland and Hitt, Achieving and maintaining strategic competitiveness in the 21st century, 43–57.

155  W. G. Rowe and P. M. Wright, 1997, Related and unrelated diversification and their effect on human resource management controls, *Strategic Management Journal,* 18 (4), 329–38.

# Chapter Fourteen

## Corporate Entrepreneurship and Innovation

## LEARNING OBJECTIVES

*After reading this chapter, you should be able to:*

1. Define and describe the importance of innovation, entrepreneurship, corporate entrepreneurship, and entrepreneurs.
2. Discuss the three stages of the innovation process.
3. Discuss the two forms of internal corporate venturing: autonomous strategic behaviour and induced strategic behaviour.
4. Discuss how the capability to manage cross-functional teams facilitates the implementation of internal corporate ventures.
5. Explain how strategic alliances are used to produce innovation.
6. Discuss how a firm creates value by acquiring another company to gain access to that company's innovations or innovative capabilities.
7. Explain how large firms use venture capital to increase the effectiveness of their innovation efforts.
8. Describe the resources, capabilities, and core competencies of small versus large firms in producing and managing innovation.

## A Very Small Look at 21st Century Technology

The biggest thing in the 21st century is likely to be the smallest: nanotechnology. Nanotechnology is the ability to work—atom by atom—to create structures more than 100 times thinner than a human hair that exhibit novel and greatly improved physical, chemical, and biological properties. Can you picture shrinking the contents of the world's largest library into a device the size of a sugar cube? Imagine the development of materials ten times stronger than steel at a fraction of the weight, to create highly fuel-efficient land, sea, air, and space vehicles. Visualize improving the computer speed and efficiency of minuscule transistors and memory chips by factors of millions—improvements that would make today's gigahertz speeds seem slow. How about using atomic-sized devices to detect and remove cancerous cells, or using microscopic machines to remove the finest contaminants to create cheap, safe drinking water. These are all possible nanotech devices.

Canadians lead the nanotech revolution in materials nanotechnology. As the millennium began, the University of Toronto was the only institution in the world to have found success in mass-producing large quantities of nanotubes, each having the same dimensions. Nanotubes are a form of carbon only a few hundred atoms in circumference that can be pieced together to form a seamless structure. Nanotubes can be electrical conductors, semiconductors, or even insulators, depending on how they are pieced together. They are also among the most robust and mechanically stable materials known. They could be used in the electronics industry for rugged integrated circuits, thin film-display laptop monitors, photo sensing, infrared emissions and imaging, or as a data-storage medium.

Yet nano-engineered products might be very difficult to construct in large quantities. One of nanotechnology's goals is to develop programmable self-replicating and self-repairing materials. In other words, one could throw a pinch

http://nanozine.com/
http://www.utoronto.ca/~ecan

of molecular-sized nanomachines into a pile of scrap steel, come back the next day and find the scrap turned into a pile of precision gears, tools, machine parts, or whatever else the nanomachines had been programmed to make. These creations could be exact shapes created without machining; instead, the construction of component or replacement parts becomes one of software design. With the right software, programmable nanomachines, and basic raw materials, building anything becomes as simple as starting a program on a computer.

Application of nanotechnology in computers could include nanostructured microprocessors that consume less energy. Small mass storage devices with terabits of capacity would also be possible with University of Toronto nanotubes. Nanotechnology would allow for ten times more bandwidth on optical transmissions. The combination of all these factors allows for fairly cheap virtual reality.

The use of materials with dimensions measuring in the billionths of a metre is not entirely the stuff of the future. MCM-41, a material produced by the oil industry, with pore sizes of 10–100 nanometres, is now used widely in the removal of ultra-fine contaminants The replacing of carbon black in tires by nanometer-scale particles of inorganic clays and polymers is leading to the production of environmentally friendly, wear-resistant tires.

Although the list of possibilities for nanotechnology is endless, the most intriguing possibilities occur in the area of nanobiotechnology. The uses of nanofabricated devices and systems may allow for better diagnostics and therapeutics by efficient genome sequencing and basic studies of cell biology and pathology. Potential nanobiotechnology uses include a number of new applications, including new routes for drug delivery that target new types of medicine to previously inaccessible sites in the body. As well, more durable rejection-resistant artificial tissues and organs could be constructed. Finally, though the list here is hardly all-inclusive, sensor systems that detect emerging disease in the body that would allow for very early disease detection and treatment are possible through nanotechnology. In theory, nanoengineered devices could detect and destroy single cancer cells, clean clogged arteries, and stop the common cold before it starts.

Companies that can apply the basic research in these advancements are likely to have a lead over a wide range of applications. Although the devices being developed may be small, the potential for financial returns is huge. The use of crystalline materials to produce 1 nanometre pore-sized catalysts is the basis for a $40 billion per year industry. Using the giant magneto resistance (GMR) effect in nanostructured magnetic multi-layers (1 to 3 nanometres), sensors were developed using the effect for magnetic disk-read heads within ten years. Such heads are the key component in a market worth almost $50 billion per year. Aurora, Ontario's Magna International and Dow Chemical have a joint program to develop high-performance, low-weight "nanocomposite" materials in automobiles. Successful product development will result in fuel savings of at least 15 billion litres of gasoline in North America alone. As well, materials applications in this field go far beyond the auto industry.

When it comes to nanotechnology, put simply, and literally, "You ain't seen nothing yet."

Sources: National Technology Initiative, 2000, *NSF home page,* http://www.nsf.gov/home/crssprgm/nano/nni.pdf (Retrieved October 2); C. Talbot, 1999, U of T team makes designer material breakthrough: Nanotubes can be sewn together to become metals, insulators or semiconductors, *Silicon Valley North,* November, 19.

The Opening Case suggests that innovation could feed rapid development. Firms that employ their core competence to take advantage of such innovations gain strategic competitiveness and an ability to earn above-average returns. In addition, as a corporate capability, innovation can be a vital source of competitive advantage as firms seek to compete in the arenas created by the global economy.[1]

Producing and managing innovation is a capability that is vital to a firm's efforts to successfully implement its strategies. For example, DaimlerChrysler links its innovations to two business-level strategies: product innovations are linked with the successful use of the product differentiation strategy, and process innovations are linked to the effective use of the cost leadership strategy. In addition to the role they play in strategy implementation, innovations developed by a firm in the course of using its strategies may affect its choice of future strategies. This possibility is shown by the feedback loop in Figure 1.1. Moreover, innovation has a strong effect on an industry's competitive dynamics.[2]

To describe how firms produce and manage innovation, we examine several topics in this chapter. To set the stage, we speak about innovation in general; then we define terms that are central to the chapter: innovation, entrepreneurship, corporate entrepreneurship, and entrepreneurs. In defining these terms, we examine their importance and link to a firm's strategic competitiveness. Next, we discuss international entrepreneurship, a phenomenon reflecting the increased use of entrepreneurship in countries throughout the world. Internally, firms innovate through either autonomous or induced strategic behaviour. After our descriptions of these internal corporate venturing activities, we discuss actions firms take to implement the innovations resulting from those two types of strategic behaviour. In addition to innovating through internal activities, firms can gain access to other companies' innovations or innovative capabilities through strategic alliances and acquisitions. Following our discussion of these topics is a description of entrepreneurship in start-up ventures and smaller firms.

# INNOVATION, ENTREPRENEURSHIP, CORPORATE ENTREPRENEURSHIP, AND ENTREPRENEURS

Peter Drucker argues that "innovation is the specific function of entrepreneurship, whether in an existing business, a public service institution, or a new venture started by a lone individual in the family kitchen." Moreover, Drucker suggests that innovation is "the means by which the entrepreneur either creates new wealth-producing resources or endows existing resources with enhanced potential for creating wealth."[3] Thus, entrepreneurship and the innovation resulting from it are important for large and small firms, as well as start-up ventures, as they compete in the 21st-century competitive landscape. In the words of researchers, "Entrepreneurship and innovation are central to the creative process in the economy and to promoting growth, increasing productivity and creating jobs."[4]

Innovation is as vital to the development of competitive advantages in the service sector as it is in the manufacturing sector. Telecommunications is one of a number of service areas that are growing in size and in which firms are able to develop competitive advantages through innovation (see the list in Table 14.1).[5] Telecommunications giant Deutsche Telekom suggests that innovation is the firm's competitive advantage:

"Innovation—we use it to our advantage. Today, our innovation pipeline is full. From 50-megabit transfers in the telephone network, to applications for the intelligent home, to our pioneering work in wireless/Internet integration, innovation is at the heart of our competitive strategy."[6]

| ■ ■ TABLE 14.1 | Growing Service Areas Where Firms Can Build Advantage Via Innovation[7] | |
|---|---|---|
| **Service Area** | **Canadian Innovators & Innovations** | |
| Data-processing | **Sierra Systems:** | Management consulting and systems integration |
| Health care | **Medicomp:** | Secure transfer of medical information over the Internet |
| Transportation | **Bombardier:** | Making 50–70 seat jets when no one thought there was market demand |
| Financial-planning | **TD Bank:** | TD Capital Trust Securities (TD CaTS): equity securities taxed as interest |
| Telecommunications | **PMC Sierra:** | Microchip designs and applications |

Source: D. Lu-Hovasse, 2000, E-medicine software solutions made at home: Canada's contribution, *National Post*, August 8, E5; A. Toulin, 2000, WTO tells Brazil to cool jets: Canada victorious in dogfight over aircraft subsidies, *National Post*, July 22, D1, D2; B. Critchley, 2000, BMO trades on Harris name: bank brings wealth management under one roof, *National Post*, May 31, D3; M. H. Meyer & A. DeTore, 1999, Product development for services, *Academy of Management Executive*, 13 (3): 64–76.

Although certainly important today, innovation has long been recognized as vital to competitive success. For example, Henry Ford, founder of Ford Motor Company, observed

*Competition whose motive is merely to compete, to drive some other fellow out, never carries very far. The competitor to be feared is one who never bothers about you at all, but goes on making his own business better all the time. Businesses that grow by development and improvement do not die. But when a business ceases to be creative, when it believes it has reached perfection and needs to do nothing but produce—no improvement, no development—it is done.*[8]

Partly because it is intended to disrupt the status quo, entrepreneurship is not risk free.[9] Yet, the characteristics of the 21st-century competitive landscape (see Chapters 1 and 3) generate significant risks that firms cannot avoid while competing in the global economy. In fact, not seeking to innovate through entrepreneurship may be riskier than taking actions to match a firm's capabilities and core competencies with its external environmental opportunities in order to innovate. In one sense, decisions some auto manufacturers make about the Formula One racing season demonstrate the risk of innovating and competing on the basis of that innovation with the risks of not innovating. According to companies involved with Formula One racing, developing a losing car can actually damage a brand. To avoid this outcome, companies sometimes spend "a fortune trying to give their entries a technological edge." In describing this matter, the head of Ford's Premier Auto Group states, "This sport is about perfection. Formula One is the No. 1 communication tool if you have the right brand. But it can backfire if you show that you tried to do something and failed."[10]

Thus, in the rapidly changing global economy, firms simultaneously encounter risk and opportunity in terms of innovation. The Internet is an instructive example of these twin conditions. Dell Computer's chairman Michael Dell suggests that, for almost all firms, the Internet will be their business. Describing the risk the Internet creates for many businesses, Dell observes that "if your business isn't enabled by information, if your business isn't enabled by customers and suppliers having more information and being able to use it, you're probably already in trouble." Moreover, Dell believes that "the Internet is like a weapon sitting on a table ready to be picked up by either you or your competitors."[11] However, for the agile and responsive firm that is committed to innovation and the change that it brings, the Internet is an incredible source of opportunity and competitive advantage. In this book's first 13 chapters, we have offered numerous examples of firms that are innovating through the Internet's capabilities and moving toward competitive success as a result.

## Innovation

As noted earlier, innovation is a key outcome firms seek through entrepreneurship and is often the source of competitive success for firms competing in the global economy. In Rosabeth Moss Kanter's words, "Winning in business today demands innovation. Companies that innovate reap all the advantages of a first mover."[12] Thus, innovation is intended to enhance a firm's strategic competitiveness and financial performance.[13] Academic studies also highlight innovation's importance. For example, research results show that firms competing in global industries that invest more in innovation also achieve the highest returns.[14] In fact, investors often react positively to the introduction of a new product, thereby increasing the price of a firm's stock. Innovation, then, is an essential feature of high-performance firms.[15] The fact that firms differ in their propensity to produce value-creating innovations, as well as in their ability to protect innovations from imitation by competitors, is an another indicator of innovation's ability to be a source of competitive advantage.[16] In other words, because "innovation is relatively rare in organizations, compared to normal administrative routines," the firm that is able to innovate consistently and effectively is well positioned to rely on its innovative skill as a competitive advantage.[17]

In his classic work, Joseph Schumpeter argued that firms engage in three types of innovative activity.[18] **Invention** is the act of creating or developing a new product or process. **Innovation** is the process of creating a commercial product from an invention. In the 21st-century competitive landscape, "innovation may be required to maintain or achieve competitive parity, much less a competitive advantage in many global markets."[19] Moreover, innovation success is influenced by a firm's ability to absorb and evaluate external environmental information.[20] Because they typically are built by integrating knowledge and skills from multiple sources, every innovation creates opportunities for additional innovations.[21] Thus, an invention brings something new into

**Invention** is the act of creating or developing a new product or process. **Innovation** is the process of creating a commercial product from an invention.

being, and an innovation brings something new into use. Accordingly, technical criteria are used to determine the success of an invention, whereas commercial criteria are used to determine the success of an innovation.[22] Waterloo, Ontario's Open Text developed one of the early Internet search engines. The commercial success of the innovation allowed the firm to later become the market leader in knowledge management software for companies.[23] Finally, **imitation** is the adoption of an innovation by similar firms. Imitation usually leads to product or process standardization, and products based on imitation often are offered at lower prices, but without as many differentiated features.

An example of the process is what happened with scooters (see Figure 14.1). In 1996, Gino Tsai asked designers at his Taiwanese bicycle firm—J.D. Corporation— to build a small scooter to help him get around the huge factory. The designers invented a compact, lightweight, collapsible scooter that Mr. Tsai found so useful that he took it to trade shows to allow him to get around expansive convention centres. The invention caught the eye of the CEO at Sharper Image, and his upscale company wanted to buy the product—turning the invention into an innovation. The product now makes up 90 percent of J.D. Corporation's sales—in spite of numerous imitators.[24]

**Imitation** is the adoption of an innovation by similar firms.

■ ■ **FIGURE 14.1**

*The Process of Invention, Innovation, and Imitation*

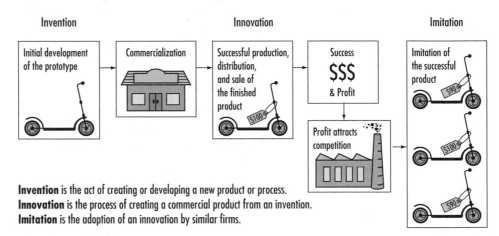

**Invention** is the act of creating or developing a new product or process.
**Innovation** is the process of creating a commercial product from an invention.
**Imitation** is the adoption of an innovation by similar firms.

# Entrepreneurship

Schumpeter viewed entrepreneurship as a process of "creative destruction," through which existing products or methods of production are destroyed and replaced with new ones.[25] Thus, entrepreneurship is "concerned with the discovery and exploitation of profitable opportunities."[26] Formerly, entrepreneurship was defined as, "any attempt at new business or new venture creation, such as self-employment, a new business organization, or the expansion of an existing business, by an individual, a team of individuals, or an established business."[27] As this definition suggests, entrepreneurship is an important mechanism for creating changes, as well as for helping firms adapt to changes created by others.[28] Firms that encourage entrepreneurship are risk-takers, are committed to innovation, and act proactively[29] (i.e., they try to create opportunities rather than waiting to respond to those created by others).

## Corporate Entrepreneurship

**Corporate entrepreneurship** is a process whereby an individual or a group in an existing organization creates a new venture or develops an innovation.

**Corporate entrepreneurship,** which is critical to a firm's survival and performance, is a process whereby an individual or a group in an existing organization creates a new venture or develops an innovation.[30] Corporate entrepreneurship can also be regarded as the sum of a firm's innovation, renewal, and venturing efforts.[31] Evidence suggests that corporate entrepreneurship practices are facilitated through the firm's effective use of a strategic management process.[32] When a firm uses the strategic management process to facilitate corporate entrepreneurship, it must determine how to harness its employees' ingenuity and reward them while retaining some of the rewards of the entrepreneurial efforts for the shareholders.[33]

## Entrepreneurs

**Entrepreneurs** are individuals, acting independently or as part of an organization, who create a new venture or develop an innovation and take risks entering them into the marketplace.

Evidence shows that entrepreneurs are primary agents of economic growth, introducing new products, new production methods, and other innovations that stimulate economic activity.[34] Seeking to create the future, organizational entrepreneurs, engaging in corporate entrepreneurship, take risks and act aggressively and proactively in their firms.[35] Moreover, entrepreneurs sense opportunities before others do and take risks in the face of uncertainty to establish new markets, develop new products, or form innovative production processes or service delivery mechanisms.[36] These characteristics and evidence suggest that **entrepreneurs** are individuals, acting independently or as part of an organization, who create a new venture or develop an innovation and—as noted in the Strategic Focus—take risks entering them into the marketplace.[37]

## STRATEGIC FOCUS

### How Did They Think of That? Entrepreneurs and the Start of the Business

What do dust-collecting watches, broken guitars and a broken promise, an unwanted business, and manic depression have in common? They are all the bases for Canadian business start-ups.

When a Vancouver supermarket wanted to unload watches that were collecting dust in a display case, they asked Aviva Jamensky to lure customers to purchase the watches for $9.98. After selling 300 watches in two hours, Ms. Jamensky had the beginnings of the idea for Tickers. She believed that if watches were not buried with other merchandise so that customers could focus on the purchase, and the product were sold cheaply enough, she might have a successful business. Three years later Tickers' kiosks sell more watches than any other retailer in Canada. At about Can$10 per watch, profit margins are thin. Yet with a volume of about a million watches, Jamensky, still in her 20s, feels the business is strong enough to enter the U.S. market.

As a teenager in St. John's, Newfoundland, Chris Griffiths went to work in a music store. After packing up a number of broken guitars to be shipped to

*continued*

Ontario, Mr. Griffiths realized that there could be a future in guitar repair. Griffiths made a deal with his boss: Griffiths would, at his own expense, train in guitar repair in Michigan, and the boss would hire him to do repairs upon his return. The teenager kept his end of the deal, but his boss didn't. With help from the Youth Ventures Loan Program, Griffiths created a business plan, scraped together working capital from a number of loan programs, and opened Griffiths Guitar Works. Now the largest custom building and repair shop in the Atlantic Provinces, he employs eight craftspeople and builds and repairs 3000 instruments per year. He also operates a summer rock and roll music camp for kids, a real estate venture, and is contemplating going into mass production of guitars. This last venture may be up and running before he turns 30—in 2003.

For over a decade, Wayne Albo provided consulting services on the evaluation and brokering of businesses. Owners who needed evaluations done for tax purposes or divorce settlements later turned to Mr. Albo for help in selling their companies. The business was lucrative, and as Mr. Albo approached 40 he began to look for a place to invest. In 1993, one of his many business contacts informed him that the young owner of a chain of 13 record stores located in small towns had died and left the profitable chain to his parents. His parents had no interest in the business and wanted to sell. Albo bought the chain and immersed himself in the business. As he did, he began to see the advantages stemming from the lack of competition in secondary markets where his stores were located. To expand initially in this market, he picked up a dozen locations from the bankrupt A&A chain. When Winnipeg's National-Record stores became available, Albo obtained their 35 stores, a warehouse, and a wholesale operation. Purchase of the 17 stores of Edmonton's Top Forty chain and the 80 stores of North Bay's Rock Entertainment followed. After three years in the business, Albo knew that the future must lie with the Internet. Although he did not know much about the Web, he knew the owners of the small CDPlus chain did. Albo brought its owners onboard and acquired the chain. With use of the new catchier CDPlus name, and Web experts, the chain now dominates the secondary market with 150 stores and over $150 million in sales.

In 1995, Anthony Stephan's family was falling apart. His wife had committed suicide and two of his children (ages 15 and 24) were diagnosed with manic depression. When he talked to his friend David Hardy about his children, Mr. Hardy thought their symptoms sounded like a nervous disorder in hogs—ear-and-tail biting syndrome. Hogs with ear-and-tail biting syndrome become so irritable they could kill each other. Farmers cure the syndrome with a nutritional pill. A desperate Mr. Stephan tried the pills on his children with astounding results. Since then, hundreds of people have tried the pill—called E.M.Power. The 34 natural ingredients and 2 antioxidants in the pill create dramatic results—sometimes after only four days of use. Stephan and Hardy have formed Synergy Group of Canada to help give the product more clinical trials. Long-term side effects of the pill in humans are yet unknown. Still, E.M. Power user Steve Morton notes that relief of his own manic depression is worth the risk: "If I feel like running around and flopping in a big mud patch once in a while, I suppose that's one of the things I have to put up with."

http://www.truehope.com

Sources: Synergy Group of Canada, 2000, *Truehope home page,* http://www.truehope.com (Retrieved October 11); B. Evenson, 2000, Pill that calms pigs may help humans: E.M. Power being tested, *National Post,* October 5, A7; D. Moulton, 1999, Four companies in a chord: Business harmony, *National Post,* October 20, E1; D. Menzies, 1999, When the big hand points up: Watching sales rise, *National Post,* October 20, E2; T. Belford, 1999, Note-by-note progression creates musical chain: Recording sales, *National Post,* October 20, E6.

Entrepreneurs surface at any organizational level. Thus, top-level managers, middle- and first-level managers, staff personnel, and those producing the company's goods or services can all be entrepreneurs. The following opinion expressed by a corporate executive suggests the importance of each person in a firm acting as an entrepreneur: "In the future—the not-too-distant future—only two groups of people will be in the world of work: entrepreneurs and those who think like entrepreneurs."[38]

Although all members of a firm can be entrepreneurs, expectations of their entrepreneurship vary by organizational level. Top-level managers, for example, should try to establish an entrepreneurial culture that inspires individuals and groups to engage in corporate entrepreneurship.[39] Apple Computer's Steve Jobs is committed to this effort, believing one of his key responsibilities is to help Apple become "more entrepreneurial and start-up like."[40] Top-level executives at 3M have emphasized innovation through entrepreneurship for years. Speaking about this, George Allen, retired vice-president of research and development at 3M, states, "3M innovates for the same reason that cows eat grass. It is a part of our DNA to do so."[41] Middle- and first-level managers are promoters and caretakers of organizational efficiency. Their work is especially important once an idea for a product has been commercialized and the organization necessary to support and promote the product has been formed.[42] Because of their close contacts with customers, suppliers, and other sources of external information, first-level managers are vital to efforts to absorb and evaluate information from outside the firm that signals insights about potentially successful innovations. Because they work with procedures, staff personnel have the knowledge required to develop innovative processes that can increase organizational efficiency. Similarly, those producing a good or service have the experience necessary to propose process innovations, as well as the knowledge of customers' needs required to facilitate a firm's efforts to design and produce product innovations.

Accordingly, innovation, entrepreneurship, corporate entrepreneurship (as one form of entrepreneurship), and the work of entrepreneurs affect a firm's efforts to achieve strategic competitiveness and earn above-average returns. As we shall see in the next section, entrepreneurship and corporate entrepreneurship are being practised more commonly in countries throughout the global economy.

## INTERNATIONAL ENTREPRENEURSHIP

Entrepreneurship is at the top of public policy agendas in many of the world's countries, including Finland, Germany, Israel, Ireland, and France, among others. In Northern Ireland, for example, the minister for enterprise, trade, and investment told businesspeople that their current and future commercial success would be affected by the degree to which they decided to emphasize R&D and innovation (critical components of entrepreneurship).[43]

According to some researchers who study economies throughout the world, virtually all industrial nations "are experiencing some form of transformation in their economies, from the dramatic move from centrally planned to market economies in East-central Europe ... to the efforts by Asian countries to return to their recent high growth levels."[44] Entrepreneurship and corporate entrepreneurship can play central roles in those transformations, in that they have strong potential to fuel economic growth, create employment, and generate prosperity for citizens.[45] For example, in a comprehensive study in which entrepreneurial activity was assessed in 10 countries (Canada, Denmark, Finland,

France, Germany, Israel, Italy, Japan, the United Kingdom, and the United States), researchers discovered that "variation in rates of entrepreneurship may account for as much as one-third of the variation [in countries'] economic growth."[46]

A society's cultural characteristics influence a nation's rate and practice of entrepreneurship. In the late 1970s, for example, Chinese economic reforms facilitated the use of market forces as an important, but not exclusive, driver of economic activity. With increased economic freedom, some businesspeople used entrepreneurship as the foundation to initiate and then operate start-up ventures. In other cases, corporate entrepreneurship was introduced into existing companies to improve their performance.[47]

However, tension surfaced among Chinese workers regarding the need for some degree of individualism to promote entrepreneurship and the more traditional Chinese cultural characteristic of collectivism. It is important to correctly handle the tension between individualism and collectivism (as defined in Figure 14.2) because research shows that entrepreneurship declines as collectivism is emphasized. Simultaneously, however, research results suggest that exceptionally high levels of individualism might be dysfunctional for entrepreneurship since entrepreneurs still need to enlist the aid of others to get their businesses established. Viewed collectively, these results appear to call for a balance to be established between individual initiative and the spirit of cooperation and group ownership of innovation. For firms to achieve corporate entrepreneurship, they must provide appropriate autonomy and incentives for individual initiative to surface but also promote cooperation and group ownership of an innovation if it is to be implemented successfully. Thus, corporate entrepreneurship often requires teams of people with unique skills and resources, especially perhaps in corporate cultures in which collectivism is a valued historical norm.[48]

■ ■ **FIGURE 14.2**

*Individualism and Collectivism*

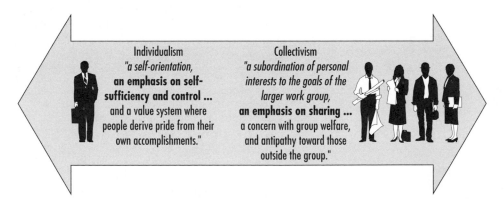

Source: Adapted from M. H. Morris, 1998, Entrepreneurial Intensity: Sustainable Advantages for Individuals, Organizations, and Societies (Westport, CT: Quorum Books), 85–86.

The importance of balancing individualism and collectivism for entrepreneurship is exemplified by the success of Asian entrepreneurs in North America. Some have argued that the success of people of Chinese and Korean origin here is due to their industriousness, perseverance, frugality, and emphasis on family. Research shows, however, that other traits also promote their success. In North America, these individuals are allowed the autonomy necessary for creativity and entrepreneurial behaviour. In addition, the emphasis on collectivism afforded by their cultural background helps them promote cooperation and group ownership of innovation.[49]

Interestingly, Chinese entrepreneurs operating in China have several character traits that are similar to those of Western entrepreneurs, including ambitiousness, independence, and self-determination. But the two sets of entrepreneurs also have different characteristics, particularly those most influenced by Confucian social philosophy.[50] Entrepreneurs of Chinese and Korean descent who operate in North America exhibit differences from all other North American entrepreneurs. For example, Chinese and Korean entrepreneurs conducting business in North America invest more equity, obtain more capital from family and friends, and receive fewer loans from financial institutions. Furthermore, they achieve higher profits than their nonAsian counterparts.[51] In contrast, a study of Israeli women showed that industry experience, business skills, and achievement were related to their performance, much the same as with other entrepreneurs in the West. But, unlike those other entrepreneurs, Israeli women entrepreneurs could attribute their success to their affiliation with a network for support and advice. When they were affiliated with multiple networks, by contrast, their performance suffered, possibly because of too much and potentially conflicting advice.[52]

## INTERNAL CORPORATE VENTURING

**Internal corporate venturing** is the set of activities used to create inventions and innovations through internal means.

**Internal corporate venturing** is the set of activities used to create inventions and innovations through internal means.[53] As noted in the Strategic Focus below, firms such as Nortel may gather R&D knowledge through acquisitions or strategic alliances (both of these are discussed later in this chapter). On the other hand, not all firms have the budget that Nortel does to acquire R&D or buy into an R&D alliance. However, almost all firms employ some degree of internal R&D endeavours—if for no other reason than they would be unable to invent or innovate without such efforts.

### STRATEGIC FOCUS

#### The Three Faces of Innovation at Nortel: Acquisitions, Alliances, and Intrapreneurship

Not discussing Nortel in a review of innovation would be to ignore a world-class leader in the area. Although Nortel gains a great deal of its innovations from acquisitions—and these are discussed below—the firm is also surprisingly adept at innovation through alliances and internal start-ups.

Nortel's innovation acquisitions are extensive. From early 1998 through mid–2000, Nortel purchased over $25 billion worth of other companies. In 1998, Nortel spent over $16 billion to buy Winnipeg's Broadband Networks, Ontario's Cambrian Systems, Massachusett-based Aptis Communications, and California's Bay Networks. In 1999, California's Shasta Networks, England's X-CEL Communications, and New York's Periphonics were scooped up for about $1 billion. In the first half of 2000, Nortel spent about $9 billion for U.S.-based firms Qtera, Clarify, and Promatory Communications and Australia's Photonic Technologies.

*continued*

Why all the activity? Nortel's CEO, John Roth, moved the company in this direction. But why would someone with 30 years experience in traditional telecommunications push Nortel toward the Internet? Simply, Roth saw the power of the Internet while restoring an old car; he used the Web to find a glovebox lining for a 1966 Jaguar he was restoring. "I sat there afterward, thinking, 'This is powerful. How could I have found this supplier if the Web didn't exist? This is so powerful that a garage in London [England] can carry out a real-time business transaction with a guy north of Toronto.'" At a time when more traditional telecom firms were puzzling over what Nortel was doing, Roth was remaking the company with billions in purchases. Although his battles inside the company and investment community were sometimes lonely, he would not be alone in his ability to see the power of the Internet, and Roth has the alliance partners to prove it.

To speed intranet applications, Nortel has been part of the Gigabit Ethernet Alliance since 1996. The alliance—designed to provide a standard for high-speed intranet protocols—includes 3Com, Cisco, Sun, and Intel. In Internet time, 1996 is ancient history, though. Although some of Nortel's future lies with hardwired connections—and they are one of the leaders in the fibre optics area—most of the excitement surrounds wireless communication. Nortel is one of the few firms that have the ability to handle both fibre and wireless. Its recent alliance with Waterloo, Ontario's Research In Motion (RIM)— a firm that makes wireless pagers that can handle two-way e-mail—will also help propel both firms forward. One analyst put it this way: "British Telecom is ordering $700-million to $2-billion worth of infrastructure from Nortel for delivery of next generation wireless stuff ... How difficult would it be for them to order $100 million worth of [RIM] devices to run on that network? It'll be like, 'Do you want fries with that?'"

Nortel is unlikely to be selling fries at any point. They may, however, rent you a video game, or more precisely, their 44 percent–owned spin-off, Channelware, will lease you software. Since 1997, Nortel has had what it calls a Business Ventures Group. The Nortel Business Ventures Group hears an idea from an employee (or intrapreneur) and will help develop a plan if the proposal is still in the idea stage. The plan can then be pitched to the Group again in a more developed form. Although the Nortel intrapreneur may end up with less of the company than an independent entrepreneur, he or she may be able get the company up and running faster and with less difficulty. As Jeff Dodge, Channelware's CEO, notes, "Our largest customer told us that if we weren't a Nortel Networks venture, it never would have done business with us." Nortel also looks after time-consuming tasks that draw time away from entrepreneurial tasks (e.g., legal concerns, leasing office space, etc.). Thus, Nortel's intrapreneurship efforts allow its employees to get in to the customers and out of the more mundane tasks.

Sources: D. Olive, 2000, A new world in his hands, *National Post Business*, August, 38–44; M. Anderson, 2000, High wireless act: Two guys from Waterloo have created the world's best wireless e-mail device, *National Post Business*, July, 48–53; R Lieber, 2000, Startups: The inside story, *Fast Company*, March, 284–95.

Whereas an important goal of R&D may be to create knowledge, the most successful R&D outputs (e.g., new product ideas) may lead to the development of an internal corporate venture.[54] Internal corporate ventures are often formed for radically new products, those that may not be marketed and distributed effectively by an existing business within the current corporate umbrella.[55] Also, corporate ventures emphasize different resources than independent new ventures. For example, corporate ventures emphasize internal capital, development of proprietary knowledge, and building marketing expertise. Alternately, independent ventures primarily emphasize external capital, building technical expertise, and development of brand identification. Most corporate ventures can use the corporate reputation, and, therefore, brand name will be less important. Furthermore, the technical expertise exists, flowing from the larger corporate entity.[56] An example of the importance of the larger corporate entity in the development of internal new ventures was noted in the previous Strategic Focus.

To reiterate, firms will simply be unable to invent or innovate without some form of significant R&D investment. As one observer of R&D trends noted, "Companies are looking at where they need to be in five to 10 years to remain competitive. They have to spend the money now to get there."[57] As shown in Figure 14.3, there are two courses firms can take internally to get there, given that not all firms have the budget that Nortel does to acquire R&D or buy into an alliance. These two forms of internal corporate venturing are autonomous strategic behaviour and induced strategic behaviour. We discuss each form separately.

## Autonomous Strategic Behaviour

**Autonomous strategic behaviour** is a bottom-up process in which product champions pursue new ideas, often through a political process, through which they develop and coordinate the commercialization of a new good or service until it achieves success in the marketplace. **A product champion** is an organizational member with an entrepreneurial vision of a new good or service who seeks to create support for its commercialization. Evidence suggests that product champions play critical roles in moving innovations forward.[58] Autonomous strategic behaviour is based on a firm's wellsprings of knowledge and resources that are the sources of the firm's innovation. Thus, a firm's capabilities and competencies are the basis for new products and processes.[59]

GE is a firm in which autonomous strategic behaviour occurs regularly. Essentially, "the search for marketable services can start in any of GE's myriad businesses. [For example], an operating unit seeks out appropriate technology to better do what it already does. Having mastered the technology, it then incorporates it into a service it can sell to others."[60] In response to frequent crisis calls and requests from customers, GE's Industrial Systems division developed a program that uses artificial intelligence to help assign field engineers to customer sites. The sophisticated program handles thousands of constraints when making assignments. The division's customer relationship manager was a champion for this product. The manager observed that the program "reduced the average time to dispatch an engineer from 18 hours to 4 hours."[61] In addition to facilitating the operations of one of GE's units, the program is being sold as a marketable item that developed through autonomous strategic behaviour.

**Autonomous strategic behaviour** is a bottom-up process in which product champions pursue new ideas, often through a political process, through which they develop and coordinate the commercialization of a new good or service until it achieves success in the marketplace.

**A product champion** is an organizational member with an entrepreneurial vision of a new good or service who seeks to create support for its commercialization.

■ ■ **FIGURE 14.3**

*Model of Internal Corporate Venturing*

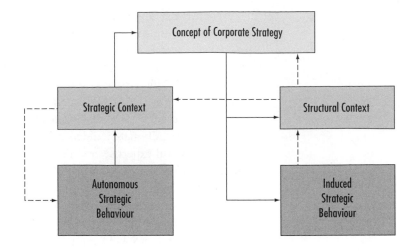

Source: R. A. Burgelman, 1983, A model of the interaction of strategic behaviour, corporate context, and the concept of strategy, *Academy of Management Review,* 8: 65.

Changing the concept of corporate-level strategy through autonomous strategic behaviour results when a product is championed within strategic and structural contexts (see Figure 14.3). The strategic context is the process used to arrive at strategic decisions (often requiring political processes to gain acceptance). The best firms keep changing their strategic context and strategies because of the continuous changes in the 21st-century competitive landscape (see Chapter 1). Thus, some believe that the most competitively successful firms reinvent their industry or develop a completely new one across time as they engage in competition with current and future rivals.[62]

## Induced Strategic Behaviour

**Induced strategic behaviour** is a top-down process whereby the firm's current strategy and structure foster product innovations that are associated closely with that strategy and structure.

The second of the two forms of internal corporate venturing, **induced strategic behaviour,** is a top-down process whereby the firm's current strategy and structure foster product innovations that are associated closely with that strategy and structure. In this situation, the strategy in place is filtered through a matching structural hierarchy.

An example of induced strategic behaviour is shown by Sony's current strategy and structure through which the PlayStation 2 came into being. Introduced into Japan in March 2000 and into Europe and North America in the fall of that year, the PlayStation 2 was viewed by Sony officials "as a sort of Trojan horse that will enter the house as a videogame player and then become a secret weapon to access the Internet, play movies and download music, rivalling the PC as the hub of entertainment in the home."[63] The PlayStation 2's introduction into Japan was nothing short of sensational, with 980 000 initial units sold in record time. Ken Kutaragi, CEO of Sony Computer Entertainment, the video-game unit of Sony, stimulated the innovation of the PlayStation. This strategic leader's objective was to use the firm's current strategy and structure to develop a product that would move Sony to a position of being able to dominate a new wave of Internet gadgets and services. Thus, Sony views its PlayStation 2 as a viable entertainment platform for the home. Interestingly, Sony is currently the world's only company that offers consumers all three devices—the PC, television, and video-game machine—around which homes could be wired with networks of digital products. Moreover, the firm's penetration in markets around the world through these three products is impressive. In North America, for example, one of every five households owns a PlayStation.[64]

Although Sony has the vision and technical experience to accomplish its goals, large firms often encounter difficulties when striving to pursue internal corporate ventures effectively. The induced processes can dominate and create strategic and structural contexts that become barriers to change. Effective internal corporate venturing processes are established only when both internal political processes and strategic and structural contexts allow a new strategic mission to emerge.

Developing and implementing an entrepreneurial strategy is a highly complex task, partly because of the significant uncertainty in the environment.[65] Such a strategy requires firms to decide and deploy corporate resources to develop new technology and then decide which innovative ideas to pursue and bring to the market, often rapidly. Some researchers have argued that there are strategic windows of opportunity of which firms must take advantage. The windows may be open only for a short period of time; thus, it may not be possible to delay decisions to act.[66]

## IMPLEMENTING INTERNAL CORPORATE VENTURES

Innovation is a necessary, but insufficient, condition for competitive success. Having processes and structures in place through which a firm can successfully implement the outcomes of internal corporate ventures is as vital as the innovations themselves. The successful introduction of innovations into the marketplace reflects implementation effectiveness. In the context of internal corporate ventures, processes are the "patterns of interaction, coordination, communication, and decision making employees use"[67] to convert the innovations resulting from either autonomous or induced strategic behaviours into successful market entries. Organizational structures are the sets of formal relationships supporting organizational processes.

To facilitate the implementation of product innovations and to identify opportunities to engage in still more innovation that can create value for customers, IBM is creating a network of innovation centres. Devoted to IBM's e-commerce services, these centres are locales "where business customers can visit with Web designers, software engineers, business strategists and marketing people under the same roof." The purpose of the centres is to foster collaborative relationships among IBM personnel, technologists, business experts, and customers to develop and implement product innovations.[68]

Effective integration among the various functions involved with either autonomous or induced strategic innovation behaviour processes—from engineering to manufacturing and, ultimately, market distribution—is required to implement (i.e., to effectively use) the innovations that result from internal corporate ventures. Increasingly, product development teams are being used as a means of integrating activities associated with different corporate functions. The outcome sought by using product development teams is commonly called cross-functional integration—a concept concerned with coordinating and applying the knowledge and skills of different functional areas in order to maximize innovation.[69]

# Using Product Development Teams to Achieve Cross-Functional Integration

Cross-functional integration's importance has been recognized for some time.[70] **Cross-functional teams** facilitate efforts to integrate activities associated with different organizational functions, such as design, manufacturing, and marketing. Cross-functional integration that results from the work of such teams may help a firm to learn better how to mass-produce a successful new product.[71] In addition, new-product development processes can be completed more quickly when cross-functional teams work effectively.[72] Through the work of cross-functional teams, product development stages are grouped into parallel or overlapping processes. Doing this allows the firm to tailor its product development efforts to its unique core competencies and to the needs of the market.

For example, when Med-Eng of Ottawa rejected a takeover bid 10 years ago, its would-be parent bought out the company's strategic partner. At the time, Med-Eng was selling $1 million of helmets designed specifically for use with its partner's bomb disposal suit. Without a suit supply, Med-Eng had to go it alone. The company not only quickly assembled a team to develop a suit but also took the resulting prototype on a three-month tour to potential customers in 45 countries. Integrating the marketing of the suit by including potential customers' ideas into the design and production of the product allowed Med-Eng to create a less-cumbersome, more protective suit and helmet combination with two-way radio technology. It also created an immediate "buy-in" among the consulting organizations, most of which ordered the new suits. Med-Eng now sells $7 million per year of the improved suits.[73]

Horizontal organizational structures support the use of cross-functional teams in their efforts to integrate innovation-based activities across organizational functions. In a horizontal organization, managing changes in organizational processes across functional units is more critical than managing up and down functional hierarchies.[74] Therefore, instead of being built around vertical hierarchical functions or departments, the organization is built around core horizontal processes that are used to produce and manage innovations. As noted earlier, processes are the patterns of interaction, coordination, communication, and decisionmaking personnel use to transform resources into outputs (e.g., product innovations). Some of the core horizontal processes that are critical to innovation efforts are formal—defined and documented as procedures and practices. More commonly though, these processes are informal: "They are routines or ways of working that evolve over time."[75] Often invisible, informal processes are critical to successful product innovations and are supported properly through horizontal organizational structures more so than through vertical organizational structures.

As we discuss next, barriers sometimes exist that must be overcome for a firm to use cross-functional teams as a means of integrating organizational functions.

## Barriers to Integration

The two primary barriers that may prevent the successful use of cross-functional teams as a means of integrating organizational functions are independent frames of reference of team members and organizational politics.[76]

Personnel working within a distinct specialization (i.e., a particular organizational function) typically have common backgrounds and experiences. Because of these similarities, people within individual organizational functions tend to view situations simi-

**Cross-functional teams** facilitate efforts to integrate activities associated with different organizational functions, such as design, manufacturing, and marketing. Effective cross-functional teams also expedite new-product development processes.

larly and are likely to use the same decision criteria to evaluate issues such as those having to do with product development efforts. In fact, research results suggest that departments around which organizational functions are framed vary along four dimensions (as noted in Figure 14.4): time orientation, interpersonal orientation, goal orientation, and formality of structure.[77] Thus, individuals from different functional departments that have different orientations on these dimensions can be expected to understand aspects of product development in different ways. Accordingly, they place emphasis on different design characteristics and issues.

■ ■ **FIGURE 14.4**

*Barriers to Integration: Orientations and Structures*

For example, a design engineer may consider the characteristics that make a product functional and workable to be the most important of the product's characteristics. Alternatively, a person from the marketing function may hold characteristics that satisfy customer needs most important. These different orientations can create barriers to effective communication across functions.[78] Although functional specialization may be damaging to the horizontal relationships necessary to successfully implement innovations produced from internal corporate venturing efforts, such specialization has an important purpose in creating an efficient organization. Therefore, eliminating functional specialization to overcome barriers to cross-functional integration may do more harm than good to the organization.

Organizational politics is the second potential barrier to the effective integration of organizational functions through use of cross-functional teams. In some organizations, considerable political activity may centre on allocating resources to different functions. Interunit conflict may result from aggressive competition for resources among those representing different organizational functions. Of course, dysfunctional conflict between functions creates a barrier to their integration.[79] Methods must be found through which cross-functional integration can be promoted without excessive concurrent political conflict and without simultaneously changing the basic structural characteristics necessary for task specialization and efficiency.

## Facilitating Integration

Organizations use four methods to achieve cross-functional integration: shared values, leadership, goals and budgets, and an effective communication system. *Shared values* are the first method firms use to achieve effective cross-functional integration.[80] Highly effective shared values are framed around the qualities that make the firm unique compared to its rivals.[81] Moreover, when linked clearly with a firm's strategic intent and mission, shared values reduce political conflict and become the glue that promotes coupling among functional units. Hewlett-Packard, for example, has remained an accomplished technological leader because it has established the "HP way." In essence, the HP way refers to the firm's esteemed organizational culture, which promotes unity and internal innovation.

*Leadership* is a second method of achieving cross-functional integration. Effective strategic leaders remind organizational members continuously of the value of product innovations. In the most desirable situations, this value-creating potential becomes the basis for the integration and management of functional department activities. During his tenure as GE's CEO, Jack Welch has frequently highlighted the importance of integrated work among business units and different functions. To frame this message consistently, Welch helped to establish a management-training centre that focuses on relationships among all levels of the company's management structure.

A third method of achieving cross-functional integration is concerned with *goals and budgets*. This method calls for firms to formulate goals and allocate the budgetary resources necessary to accomplish them. Effective horizontal organizations—those in which accomplishments are expected in terms of processes as well as outcomes such as product innovations—reinforce the importance of integrating activities across organizational functions.

An effective *communication system* is a fourth method used to facilitate cross-functional integration. As shown in Figure 14.5, an effective communication system is shaped by shared values and leadership, and supported by goals and budgets. Some key beneficial outcomes of effective communication are increased motivation, more and better information, and the sharing of knowledge among cross-functional team members.[82] Free-flowing communications between those working within different organizational functions is important, but effective communication within cross-functional teams is critical to the successful implementation of a new product. Without such communication, members of a cross-functional team would find it difficult to integrate their individual function's activities in ways that create synergy. As noted earlier, shared values and leadership practices shape the communication systems that are developed to support the work of cross-functional product development teams (see Figure 14.5).

**■ ■ FIGURE 14.5**

*Facilitating Integration*

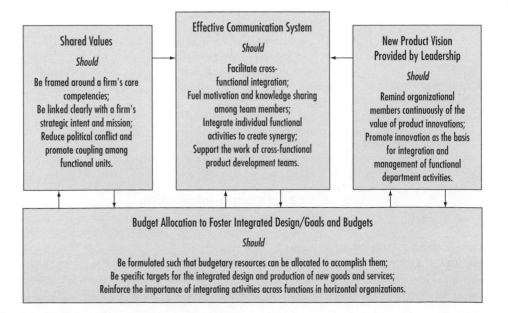

# Appropriating Value from Innovation

Internal corporate-venturing implementation efforts are designed to help a company gain competitive benefits from its product innovations. In other words, implementation efforts are used to help a firm appropriate or gain value from activities undertaken to innovate (i.e., commercialize) inventions.

Figure 14.6 shows how value can be appropriated, or gained, from internal corporate-venturing processes. As mentioned earlier, cross-functional integration is required for innovation's value to be tapped fully. Cross-functional teams increase the likelihood of cross-functional integration, in that their effective use helps to overcome barriers to integration. Also helping a firm's efforts to overcome these barriers are four facilitators of integration: shared values, visionary leadership, supportive budgets and allocations, and effective communication systems.

The model highlights three desirable outcomes of achieving cross-functional integration: time to market, product quality, and the creation of customer value. In several earlier chapters, we described the competitive value of the rapid entry of a product into the marketplace; we highlighted evidence that suggests that a firm can gain a competitive advantage when it is able to develop innovative goods or services and transfer them to the marketplace faster than competitors can.[83] In fact, some argue that developing products rapidly in the global economy has a strong and positive effect on a firm's profitability.[84] But product quality is also important.[85] Although shorter time-to-market cycles that result from the rapid entry of a product into a marketplace have the potential to help a firm appropriate value from its innovations, unacceptably low levels of product quality may contribute to expensive recalls, product performances that fail to meet customers' expectations, and exposure to product liability charges. In the final analysis, customer value is created when product innovations with acceptable levels of quality are introduced rapidly into the marketplace. Thus, as our discussion of the model in Figure 14.6 suggests, internal corporate ventures must be effectively managed to facilitate cross-functional integration so that a firm will be able to appropriate maximum value from its product design and commercialization efforts.[86]

■ ■ **FIGURE 14.6**

*Appropriating Value from Internal Firm Innovation*

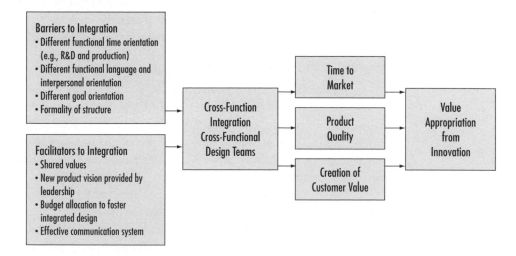

Sources: Adapted from M. A. Hitt, R. E. Hoskisson, and R. D. Nixon, 1993, A mid-range theory of interfunctional integration, its antecedents and outcomes, *Journal of Engineering and Technology Management,* 10: 161–85.

For example, Juergen Puetter used those elements of new product vision leadership and effective communication to develop Hydroxyl Systems of Sydney, B.C. As well, being a millionaire many times over, he was able to invest sufficient funds to allow for a development budget that would permit Hydroxyl to quickly develop its water purification systems. Having both staff and boss share a green environmental orientation created shared values in the organization. Hydroxyl's product's time to market was sufficiently fast, and Puetter's timing was good, as well. When Alaska Governor Tony Knowles announced in late 2000 that cruise ships would no longer be allowed to dump their wastes—which can average a million litres per day—into Alaska's waters, industry participants scrambled for a solution. Now required to treat their wastes, cruise lines beat a path to Hydroxyl's door because its product had value: the method Hydroxyl uses is one of the best for creating clean water with the least offensive odour, and is the most economical to buy and run. Finally, Hydroxyl's product quality is so good that the plant it built in Langford BC to treat waste water for the 400 000 residents of southern Vancouver Island has a $1000 per day no-smell guarantee. In 18 months of operation, the company hasn't needed to pay.[87]

## STRATEGIC ALLIANCES: COOPERATING TO PRODUCE AND MANAGE INNOVATION

It is difficult for a firm to possess all the knowledge required to compete successfully in its product areas over the long term. Complicating this matter is the fact that the knowledge base confronting today's organizations is not only vast but also increasingly specialized. As such, the knowledge needed to commercialize inventions is frequently embedded within different corporations located in various parts of the global economy.

In Chapter 10, we discussed why and how firms use strategic alliances (partnerships between firms whereby resources, capabilities, and core competencies are combined to pursue common interests and goals)[88] to gain either competitive parity or competitive advantage relative to rivals. Used with increasing frequency,[89] alliances are often formed to produce or manage innovations. To innovate through a cooperative relationship such as a strategic alliance, firms share their knowledge and skills.[90] Forming alliances for this purpose is appropriate, in that value is created through the effective formation and use of an alliance.[91]

Porsche AG and Volkswagen AG recently formed an alliance to develop an innovative sport-utility vehicle (SUV) that was to appear as a year-2002 model. Because of a conviction that their product had to be unique compared to existing SUVs, both firms committed significant resources to R&D activities. Although some components (e.g., a core platform) were to be shared, the partners also were seeking to produce their own individualized versions of the jointly developed product. For example, a Porsche executive noted that his firm was "going to great lengths to differentiate the two versions and [to] guard Porsche's brand image." The historically cooperative relationship between the two companies was expected to enhance the probability of the alliance's success.[92]

As noted earlier in the chapter, the rapid introduction of product innovations into the marketplace helps firms appropriate, or gain, value from their innovations. The late entry of the Porsche and Volkswagen alliance into the SUV market thus puts Porsche and Volkswagen at a disadvantage for such gains relative to those competitors already in that market. Yet, the cooperative relationship between Porsche and Volkswagen may eventually help both firms create value for their customers.

However, alliances formed for the purpose of innovation are not without risks. An important risk is that a partner will appropriate a firm's technology or knowledge and use it to enhance its own competitive abilities. To prevent or at least minimize this risk, a firm—particularly a start-up venture—needs to select its partner carefully.[93] The ideal partnership is one in which the firms have complementary skills, as well as compatible goals and strategic orientations.[94] Two other risks include a firm's becoming dependent on its partner for the development of core competencies and the loss of skills that can result when they are not used regularly to produce or manage innovations.

In sum, building successful strategic alliances to produce and manage innovation requires focusing on knowledge, identifying core competencies, and developing strong human resources to manage those core competencies. Expecting to gain financial benefits in the short run may lead to unintended consequences in the long run. Also, firms may view their collaboration with other companies as an indirect form of competition for knowledge.[95]

## ACQUISITIONS AND VENTURE CAPITAL: BUYING INNOVATION

In this section, we focus on acquisitions and venture capital, the third approach firms use to produce and manage innovation.

### Acquisitions

Though we have mentioned the company a number of times, we cannot think of a better example of a company that has innovated through acquisitions than Nortel, as discussed in the previous Strategic Focus. Nortel uses not only acquisitions and internal new ventures but also alliances (e.g., with Microsoft and Hewlett-Packard) to appropriate what it hopes will be full value from its innovation activities.[96] Similar to internal corporate venturing and strategic alliances, acquisitions are not a risk-free approach to producing and managing innovations. A key risk of acquisitions is that a firm may substitute an ability to buy innovations for an ability to produce innovations internally. As discussed next, research results suggest that this substitution may not be in the firm's best interests.[97]

Figure 14.7 shows that firms gaining access to innovations through acquisitions risk reductions in both R&D inputs (as measured by investments in R&D) and R&D outputs (as measured by the number of patents received). The curves indicate that the R&D-to-sales ratio drops after acquisitions have been completed and that the patent-to-sales ratio drops significantly after companies have been involved with large acquisitions. Additional research shows that firms engaging in acquisitions introduce fewer new products into the market.[98] Thus, firms appear to substitute acquisitions for internal corporate-venturing processes. This substitution may take place because firms lose strategic control and emphasize financial control of original, and especially of acquired, business units.[99] Although reduced innovation may not always result, managers of firms seeking to make acquisitions should be aware of this potential outcome.

■ ■ **FIGURE 14.7**

*Evidence of R&D Inputs (Expenditures) and Outputs (Number of Patents) per Dollar of Sales Before and After Large Acquisitions*

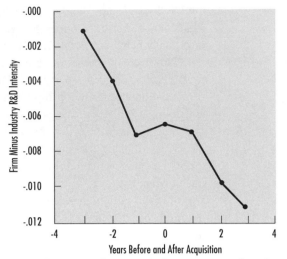

Difference between pre- and post-acquisition observations is statistically significant at $p < .01$.

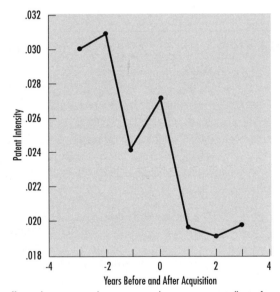

Difference between pre- and post-acquisition observations is statistically significant at $p < .01$.

Source: Adapted from M. A. Hitt, R. E. Hoskisson, R. D. Ireland, & J.S. Harrison, 1991, Are acquisition a poison pill for innovation?, *Academy of Management Executive,* 5 (4): 24–25.

## Venture Capital

Venture capital is a resource typically allocated to entrepreneurs who are involved in a project with high growth potential. The intent of venture capitalists is to help achieve a high rate of return on the funds they invest.[100] Increasingly, venture capital is being used to facilitate the earning of high rates of return by supporting the acquisition of capabilities that might yield a competitive advantage. In other instances, a firm might decide to serve as an internal source of capital for innovative product ideas that can be spun off as independent or affiliated firms. New enterprises that are backed by venture capital provide an important source of innovation, new technology, wealth creation, and employment.[101]

Historically, the venture capital business has been associated primarily with independent venture capital firms, but both domestic and foreign corporations have discovered that investing in venture capital adds a new dimension to their corporate development strategies and can produce an attractive return on their investments.[102] A major strategic benefit to a corporation is the ability to invest early and observe what happens to the new venture. This may lead to subsequent acquisitions, the licensing of technology, product marketing rights, and, possibly, the development of international opportunities. Large firms often view venture capital as a window on future technological development. Participation by corporations can take many forms, but usually begins with investment in several venture capital funds as a limited partner and evolves into direct investments in new business ventures. Many firms begin this strategy by forming a venture development division.

The disdain of large corporations by outside entrepreneurs can be a potential pitfall. Entrepreneurs may be wary of large corporations that seek to dominate fledgling companies. The syndication of venture funds to reduce risk may also be a factor limiting potential gains from venture capital investments. Other large firms may become part of the syndication and reduce the potential returns for the large corporate partner (through the sharing of knowledge).[103] Nevertheless, with corporate restructuring and downsizing continuing, executives seem willing to try more entrepreneurial ventures. Apparently, venture capital is one way to participate, and it may be less risky than internal development.[104]

Our focus has been on corporate entrepreneurship. But entrepreneurship may be practised successfully in small firms as well, especially those that are entrepreneurial ventures. In fact, both company experiences and research results suggest that small businesses and entrepreneurial ventures may have superior product innovation skills, although larger corporations may have superior innovation management skills (i.e., the skills required to maximize the marketplace return of product innovations).

## ENTREPRENEURSHIP IN SMALL BUSINESSES AND ENTREPRENEURIAL VENTURES

Although 80 percent of the world's R&D activity in developed nations is concentrated in firms with 10 000 or more employees, by some accounts, these large firms account for under half of the world's technological activity.[105] Thus, while large firms are important for technological advances, small businesses, entrepreneurial ventures, and individual entrepreneurs account for a significant share of today's innovative activity and the technological progress resulting from it. Concurrently, smaller nations are contributing meaningfully to the global economy's innovative activity. One business writer observed recently that, "Many of the most important innovations in cell-phone technology have come from some of the smallest economies in the developed world, in Scandinavia. Even though a pharmaceutical company may spend billions shepherding a new product through the regulatory process, the spark of innovation behind new drugs comes increasingly from college labs and biotech start-ups."[106]

Among the factors accounting for the growth of job creation and economic productivity in small businesses and entrepreneurial ventures are the greater amounts of flexibility, resourcefulness, and agility that these enterprises have, compared to large organizations. Partly because of those desirable job attributes, a substantial shift toward self-employment and entrepreneurial ventures is occurring. This has been observed particularly in Canada, Israel, and the United States.[107]

Executives and women are two categories of workers who are changing their employment venue in large numbers. Evidence suggests, for example, that, "Executives leaving large companies are taking jobs with smaller firms, including Internet start-ups. The latest figures ... show that seven out of 10 job-switching executives and managers are signing on with smaller firms."[108] Moreover, at least in developed countries, "the greatest and most rapid gain in firm start-ups will be achieved by increasing the participation of women in the entrepreneurial process."[109] Thus, data suggest that small businesses and entrepreneurial ventures are rapidly becoming an important part of the mainstream economy and business activity, most certainly in developed countries.[110]

One reason that small businesses and entrepreneurial ventures tend to outperform large organizations in terms of producing innovations is that entrepreneurs have been found to be more innovative than managers of large firms. The increased level of innovative capability that entrepreneurs possess is at least partly a function of their tendency to use more heuristics in making decisions than those managing large organizations do.[111] However, successfully managing innovations is more difficult for small firms and entrepreneurial ventures than it is for large established firms. Integrating and coordinating the work required to fund the introduction of an innovation to the marketplace (work that includes writing a strategic plan and a marketing plan and establishing effective production and distribution systems) typically challenges what are often constrained resources in small and entrepreneurial firms. These disadvantages notwithstanding, small and entrepreneurial ventures are proving vital to the growth of several industries, such as semiconductors, communications, biotechnology, and the entire Internet phenomenon, among others.[112] In these industry settings and others, some small businesses and entrepreneurial ventures seem to be demonstrating their capacity to excel in terms of producing and managing innovation. Hydroxyl, mentioned above, is one such enterprise, as are a number of the businesses mentioned in the first Strategic Focus in this chapter.

## Producing More Innovation in Large Organizations

Full value from innovation is achieved when a firm is able to produce and manage innovation effectively. As we have mentioned, large organizations are less effective than small and entrepreneurial ventures in producing innovations. Given their deficiency relative to smaller and more entrepreneurial ventures, what can large firms do to act small and improve their ability to produce innovations?

Several actions can be taken. First, greater levels of individual autonomy can be created through the restructuring of a firm into smaller, more manageable units (see Chapter 8). The additional amounts of creativity and innovation that tend to be witnessed among those granted more autonomy stimulates autonomous strategic behaviour when a firm pursues innovation through internal corporate ventures.[113] Simultaneously, a firm can reengineer its operations to develop more efficient work-related processes and to form channels through which customers' interests can be expressed with greater clarity and intensity.[114] The cross-functional work teams described earlier also provide opportunities for personnel to think and act creatively. Handled effectively, even downsizing (see Chapter 8) can create arrangements through which a firm is able to better focus its efforts on key tasks, such as those required to produce innovations.[115] Other actions a firm can take to stimulate the production of innovations are allocating significant levels of resources to R&D and using cooperative arrangements effectively.

Thus, both large and small firms can innovate. Until the skills required to both produce and manage innovation are mastered by either large organizations or small businesses and entrepreneurial ventures, cooperative arrangements will be an attractive option. Through effective collaborations, the small partner has an opportunity to concentrate on producing an innovation that the large partner can manage to marketplace success.[116] As the Strategic Focus shows, regardless of the approach used to produce and manage innovations, a firm may be able to appropriate or gain the greatest amount of value when its innovations create exceptional value for customers.

## STRATEGIC FOCUS

### Innovation as a Key Source of Value Creation

In Chapter 5, we discussed the relationship between value creation and strategic competitiveness. As noted there, value consists of the performance characteristics and attributes that a company offers in the form of a good or service for which customers are willing to pay. Thus, the ability to create value is at the core of a firm's competitive success. In this chapter, the importance of innovation to a firm's success in the global economy has been emphasized. In fact, innovation, which is the process of creating a commercial good or service from an invention, is critical to competitive success for today's firms.

Combining value with innovation yields an interesting term called value innovation. According to researchers Kim and Mauborgne, "Value innovation makes the competition irrelevant by offering fundamentally new and superior value in existing markets and by enabling a quantum leap in buyer value to create new markets." Through value innovation, a firm seeks to commercialize each invention so that a new good or service is able to offer performance characteristics to customers that exceed their expectations or that actually create a new market through the use of unique product characteristics or attributes. Thus, effective value innovation creates radically different or greater value for customers, rather than producing incremental value enhancements. To make this possible, a firm must learn consistently and effectively and must be able to convert what is learned into knowledge that can become the foundation for developing new core competencies.

The actions of firms in numerous industries have resulted and will continue to result in value innovation. In the newest wave of wireless Internet applications, we will note the activities of two Toronto companies: Classwave Wireless and MobileQ.com.

Classwave Wireless makes servers for routing applications to and from wireless devices and the Internet. Its technology relies on the Bluetooth industry standard. As noted in the Chapter 10 opening case, Bluetooth will allow phones to wirelessly talk to computers and printers. Classwave servers improve Bluetooth by extending its range and allow for the routing of vast amounts of information wirelessly to points on the Internet. Yet the technologies that

*continued*

are involved have all been around for a number of years—telephones, radio, computers, etc. Getting these technologies to work together is not only Classwave's challenge but also its innovation.

While Classwave's products are designed to help hardware work better together, MobileQ.com's product is aimed at the software end. MobileQ.com's main product is the XMLEdge software platform. Since wireless products use a number of programming languages and protocols, writing applications to work across different devices has been troublesome. XMLEdge allows wireless applications to work across phones, dedicated dispatch services, interactive mobile TV, etc.

Other companies recognized for their value innovations include Wal-Mart in discount retailing, West Jet Airlines in short-haul air travel, and IKEA in the retailing of home furnishings. Product development teams can be instrumental in helping a firm appropriate or gain maximum value from its value innovations. In the final analysis, value innovation challenges firms to develop their knowledge-generating capabilities. With knowledge as the foundation for the shaping and nurturing of core competencies, a firm has the capacity to produce and manage innovations that have the potential to create new markets or significantly expand current ones.

Sources: A. Wahl, 2000, 5 guys, no wires: Want to know who's leading the next communications wave? In the wireless future, Canadians rule, *Canadian Business,* June 12, 63–79; M. A. Hitt, R. D. Nixon, R. E. Hoskisson, & R. Kochhar, 1999, Corporate entrepreneurship and cross-functional fertilization: Activation, process and disintegration of a new product design team, *Entrepreneurship: Theory and Practice,* 23 (3): 147–67; W. C. Kim & R. Mauborgne, 1999, Strategy, value innovation, and the knowledge economy, *Sloan Management Review,* 40 (3): 41–44; S. A. Zahra, A. P. Nielsen, & W. C. Bogner, 1999, Corporate entrepreneurship, knowledge, and competence development, *Entrepreneurship: Theory and Practice,* 23 (3): 169–89.

# SUMMARY

- Firms engage in three types of innovative activity. Invention is the act of creating and developing an idea for a new product or process. Innovation is the process of commercializing the products or processes that surfaced through invention. Imitation is the adoption of an innovation by others, often the firm's competitors. Imitation usually leads to product or process standardization and market acceptance.

- Increasingly, entrepreneurship and corporate entrepreneurship are being practised in many countries. Entrepreneurship and corporate entrepreneurship are strongly related to a nation's economic growth. This relationship is a primary reason for the increasing use of entrepreneurship and corporate entrepreneurship in countries throughout the global economy.

- Three basic approaches are used to produce and manage innovation: internal corporate venturing, strategic alliances, and acquisitions. Autonomous strategic behaviour and induced strategic behaviour are the two processes of internal corporate venturing. Autonomous strategic behaviour is a bottom-up process through which a product champion facilitates the commercialization of an innovative good or service. Induced strategic behaviour is a top-down process in which a firm's current strategy and structure facilitate product or process innovations that are associated with them. Thus, induced strategic behaviour is driven by the organization's current corporate strategy, structure, and reward and control systems.

- Increasingly, cross-functional integration is vital to a firm's efforts to appropriate or gain value from its internal corporate venturing efforts. Facilitated by cross-functional teams, cross-functional integration can reduce the time a firm needs to introduce innovative products into the marketplace. Cross-functional integration also can improve product quality and, ultimately, create value for customers.

- In the complex global economy, it is difficult for an individual firm to possess all the knowledge needed to innovate consistently and effectively. To gain access to the kind of specialized knowledge that often is required to innovate, firms may form a cooperative relationship such as a strategic alliance with others—sometimes even with competitors.

- Acquisitions are the third basic approach firms use to produce and manage innovation. Innovation can be acquired either through direct acquisition or through indirect investment. Examples of indirect investment are the formation of a wholly owned venture capital division and the use of private placement of venture capital. Buying innovation, however, comes with the risk of reducing a firm's internal invention and innovative capabilities.

- Small firms are particularly well suited for fostering innovations that do not require large amounts of capital. Small firms have therefore become a vibrant part of industrialized nations, accounting for more job creation than large firms during the last decade.

- Large firms are needed to foster innovation due to capital requirements. Small firms are often found to be better at creating specialty products and diffusing the innovation through spinoffs from large corporations. Thus, collaborations between large and small firms often lead to successful product innovation processes.

## REVIEW QUESTIONS

1. What is innovation? What is entrepreneurship? What is corporate entrepreneurship? Who are entrepreneurs? What is the importance of these terms for firms competing in the global economy?

2. What are the three stages of the innovation process, and why are the differences among them important?

3. What is autonomous strategic behaviour? What is induced strategic behaviour?

4. Some believe that, when managed successfully, cross-functional teams facilitate the implementa-

tion of internal corporate ventures and a firm's innovation efforts. How should cross-functional teams be managed to achieve these desirable outcomes?

5. How do firms use strategic alliances to help them produce innovation?

6. How can a firm create value when it acquires another company to gain access to its innovations or its ability to produce innovations?

7. How do large firms use venture capital to produce innovations and to identify new product opportunities?

8. What are the differences in the resources, capabilities, and core competencies of large and small firms to produce and manage innovation?

## DISCUSSION QUESTIONS

1. During the 1980s and 1990s, the number of acquisitions grew, as did the amount of money available as venture capital. Is there a relationship between the wave of acquisitions and the increase in available venture capital?

2. In your opinion, is the term "corporate entrepreneurship" an oxymoron? In other words, can corporations—especially large ones—be innovative?

3. Have you observed a product champion supporting an innovation in a corporation? If so, what were the results of the champion's efforts?

4. The economies of countries such as Russia and China have for 80 and 50 years, respectively, been operated through centralized bureaucracies. What can be done to infuse such economies with a commitment to corporate entrepreneurship and the innovation resulting from it?

5. Use the Internet to find an example of two corporate innovations—one brought about through autonomous strategic behaviour and one developed through induced strategic behaviour. Which innovation do you believe holds the most promise for commercial success and why?

6. Are strategic alliances a way to enhance a firm's technological capacity, or are they used more commonly to maintain pace with technological developments in a company's industry? In other words, are strategic alliances a tool of firms that have a technological advantage, or are they a tool of technologically disadvantaged companies?

# ETHICS QUESTIONS

1. Is it ethical for a company to purchase another firm to gain ownership of its product innovations and innovative capabilities? Why or why not?

2. Do firms encounter ethical issues when they use internal corporate venturing processes to produce and manage innovation? If so, what are these issues?

3. Firms that are partners in a strategic alliance may legitimately seek to gain knowledge from each other. At what point does it become unethical for a firm to gain additional and competitively relevant knowledge from its partner? Is this point different when a firm partners with a domestic firm as opposed to a foreign firm? If so, why?

4. Small firms often have innovative products. When is it appropriate for a large firm to buy a small firm for its product innovations and new product ideas?

# INTERNET EXERCISE

North America's most successful pizza delivery chains have long relied on phone orders. How can the Internet's capabilities be integrated into their business? Weighing the pros and cons of ordering pizza on-line, make a list of 10 management concerns and techniques that you would need to consider to successfully promote, develop, and run an on-line business in this lucrative market. Start your search with Richmond B.C.'s Boston Pizza, Moncton, N.B's Pizza Delight, or the U.S. chains: Dominos or Pizza Hut.

http://www.bostonpizza.com

http://www.pizzadelight.com

http://www.pizzahut.com

http://www.dominos.com

# STRATEGIC SURFING

The World Wide Web has made it both possible and necessary for many traditional businesses to market and sell their goods and services on-line. Consumer goods and services such as banking, clothing, vacations, and grocery items can be ordered through the Internet. Creating new, safe, and reliable methods to access, pay for, and deliver goods and services via the Web has added to the list of innovations and management strategies that corporate entrepreneurs need to explore to be successful. To find out more about entrepreneurship and innovation, explore the following Web sites:

Association of Collegiate Entrepreneurs:
http://www.acecanada.ca
Canadian Youth Business Foundation:
http://www.cybf.ca
The Kauffman Foundation's EntreWorld at
http://www.entreworld.org
Babson College's Center for Entrepreneurial Studies at http://www.babson.edu/entrep
EGOPHER, a site produced by St. Louis University at http://www.slu.edu.eweb/egopher.html

# NOTES

1 M. A. Hitt, R. D. Nixon, P. G. Clifford, & K. P. Coyne, 1999, The development and use of strategic resources, in M. A. Hitt, P. G. Clifford, R. D. Nixon, & K. P. Coyne (eds.), *Dynamic Strategic Resources: Development, Diffusion and Integration* (Chichester: John Wiley & Sons), 1–14.

2 H. Lee, K. G. Smith, C. M. Grimm, & A. Schomburg, 2000, Timing, order and durability of new product advantages with imitation, *Strategic Management Journal,* 21: 23–30.

3 P. F. Drucker, 1998, The discipline of innovation, *Harvard Business Review,* 76 (6): 149–57.

4 P. D. Reynolds, M. Hay, & S. M. Camp, 1999, *Global Entrepreneurship Monitor, 1999 Executive Report* (Babson Park, MA.: Babson College).

5 M. H. Meyer & A. DeTore, 1999, Product development for services, *Academy of Management Executive,* 13 (3): 64–76.

6 Deutsche Telekom, 2000, The new millennium with a capital "T," *Forbes,* January 24, 81.

7 D. Lu-Hovasse, 2000, E-medicine software solutions made at home: Canada's contribution, *National Post,* August 8, E5; A. Toulin, 2000, WTO tells Brazil to cool jets: Canada victorious in dogfight over aircraft subsidies, *National Post,* July 22, D1, D2; B. Critchley, 2000, BMO trades on Harris name: Bank brings wealth management under one roof, *National Post,* May 31, D3; M. H. Meyer & A. DeTore, 1999, Product development for services, *Academy of Management Executive,* 13 (3): 64–76.

8 H. Ford, 2000, Noteworthy quotes, *Strategy & Business,* 18: 154.

9 S. A. Zahra, D. F. Kuratko, & D. F. Jennings, 1999, Guest editorial: Entrepreneurship and the acquisition

of dynamic organizational capabilities, *Entrepreneurship: Theory and Practice,* 23 (3): 5–10.

10   S. Miller, 2000, Formula One racing gets riskier—for its sponsors, *Wall Street Journal,* February 25, B1, B4.

11   D. Roth, 1999, Dell's big new act, *Fortune,* December 6, 152–55.

12   R. M. Kanter, 1999, From spare change to real change: The social sector as Beta site for business innovation, *Harvard Business Review,* 77 (3): 122–32.

13   M. A. Mone, W. McKinley, & V. L. Barker, III, 1998, Organizational decline and innovation: A contingency framework, *Academy of Management Review,* 23: 115–32.

14   R. Price, 1996, Technology and strategic advantage, *California Management Review,* 38 (3): 38–56; L. G. Franko, 1989, Global corporate competition: Who's winning, who's losing and the R&D factor as one reason why, *Strategic Management Journal,* 10: 449–74.

15   G. T. Lumpkin & G. G. Dess, 1996, Clarifying the entrepreneurial orientation construct and linking it to performance, *Academy of Management Review,* 21: 135–72; K. M. Kelm, V. K. Narayanan, & G. E. Pinches, 1995, Shareholder value creation during R&D innovation and commercialization stages, *Academy of Management Journal,* 38: 770–86.

16   P. W. Roberts, 1999, Product innovation, product-market competition and persistent profitability in the U.S. pharmaceutical industry, *Strategic Management Journal,* 20: 655–70.

17   Mone, McKinley, & Barker, *Organizational Decline,* 117.

18   J. Schumpeter, 1934, *The Theory of Economic Development* (Cambridge, MA: Harvard University Press).

19   M. A. Hitt, R. D. Nixon, R. E. Hoskisson, & R. Kochhar, 1999, Corporate entrepreneurship and cross-functional fertilization: Activation, process and disintegration of a new product design team, *Entrepreneurship: Theory and Practice,* 23 (3): 145–67.

20   D. L. Deeds, D. DeCarolis, & J. Coombs, 2000, Dynamic capabilities and new product development in high technology ventures: An empirical analysis of new biotechnology firms, *Journal of Business Venturing,* 15: 211–29.

21   T. Petzinger, Jr., 2000, So long, supply and demand, *Wall Street Journal,* January 1, R31.

22   P. Sharma & J. L. Chrisman, 1999, Toward a reconciliation of the definitional issues in the field of corporate entrepreneurship, *Entrepreneurship: Theory and Practice,* 23 (3): 11–27; R. A. Burgelman & L. R. Sayles, 1986, *Inside Corporate Innovation: Strategy,* Structure, and Managerial Skills (New York: Free Press).

23   How to succeed in the U.S. market by really really trying, 1999, *National Post,* June 3, 76.

24   B. Hannon, 2000, Riding high on little wheels, *BusinessWeek,* September 4, 123.

25   Schumpeter, *The Theory of Economic Development.*

26   S. Shane & S. Venkataraman, 2000, The promise of entrepreneurship as a field of research, *Academy of Management Review,* 25: 217–26.

27   Reynolds, Hay, & Camp, *Global Entrepreneurship Monitor,* 3.

28   A. Zacharakis, P. D. Reynolds, & W. D. Bygrave, 1999, *Global Entrepreneurship Monitor, National Entrepreneurship Assessment, United States of America* (Babson Park, MA.: Babson College).

29   B. R. Barringer & A. C. Bluedorn, 1999, The relationship between corporate entrepreneurship and strategic management, *Strategic Management Journal,* 20: 421–44.

30   Sharma & Chrisman, Toward a reconciliation, 18.

31   S. A. Zahra, 1995, Corporate entrepreneurship and financial performance: The case of management leveraged buyouts, *Journal of Business Venturing,* 10: 225–47.

32   Barringer & Bluedorn, The relationship between corporate entrepreneurship and strategic management, 421.

33   S. D. Sarasvathy, 2000, Seminar on research perspectives in entrepreneurship (1997), *Journal of Business Venturing,* 15: 1–57.

34   Barringer & Bluedorn, The relationship between corporate entrepreneurship and strategic management, 422; R. W. Smilor, 1997, Entrepreneurship: Reflections on a subversive activity, *Journal of Business Venturing,* 12: 341–46.

35   Lumpkin and Dess, Clarifying the entrepreneurial orientation construct.

36   Reynolds, Hay, & Camp, *Global Entrepreneurship Monitor,* 7.

37   Sharma & Chrisman, Toward a reconciliation, 17.

38   Fast Company, 2000, *Fast Pack 2000,* www.fastcompany.com (Retrieved March 8).

39   J. Birkinshaw, 1999, The determinants and consequences of subsidiary initiative in multinational corporations, *Entrepreneurship: Theory and Practice,* 24 (1): 9–36.

40   B. Schlender, 2000, Jobs' Apple, *Fortune,* January 24, 66–76.

41   J. Bowles, 1997, Best practices: Driving growth through innovation, alliances, and stakeholder symbiosis, *Fortune,* November 14, S3–S24.

42   S. W. Floyd & B. Wooldridge, 1999, Knowledge creation and social networks in corporate entrepreneurship: The renewal of organizational capability,

Entrepreneurship: *Theory and Practice*, 23 (3): 123–43; J. P. Kotter, 1990, *A Force for Change* (New York: The Free Press).

43 Staff reporter, 2000, Business innovation urged, *Irish Times*, 23.

44 J. E. Jackson, J. Klich, & V. Kontorovich, 1999, Firm creation and economic transitions, *Journal of Business Venturing*, 14: 427–50.

45 Reynolds, Hay, & Camp, *Global Entrepreneurship Monitor*, 7.

46 Ibid., 3.

47 F. N. Pieke, 1995, Bureaucracy, friends and money: The growth of capital socialism in China, *Comparative Studies in Society and History*, 37: 494–518.

48 Ibid; M. H. Morris, D. L. Davis, & J. W. Allen, 1994, Fostering corporate entrepreneurship: Cross-cultural comparisons of the importance of individualism versus collectivism, *Journal of International Business Studies*, 25: 65–89.

49 P. S. Li, 1993, Chinese investment and business in Canada: Ethnic entrepreneurship reconsidered, *Pacific Affairs*, 66: 219–43.

50 D. H. Holt, 1997, A comparative study of values among Chinese and U.S. entrepreneurs: Pragmatic convergence between contrasting cultures, *Journal of Business Venturing*, 12: 483–505.

51 T. Bates, 1997, Financing small business creation: The case of Chinese and Korean immigrant entrepreneurs, *Journal of Business Venturing*, 12: 109–24.

52 M. Lerner, C. Brush, & R. Hisrich, 1997, Israeli women entrepreneurs: An examination of factors affecting performance, *Journal of Business Venturing*, 12: 315–39.

53 R. A. Burgelman, 1983, A model of the interaction of strategic behavior, corporate context, and the concept of strategy, *Academy of Management Review*, 8: 61–70.

54 D. M. A. Rogers, 1996, The challenge of fifth generation R&D, *Research-Technology Management*, July–August: 33–41.

55 B. L. David, 1994, How internal venture groups innovate, *Research-Technology Management*, March–April: 38–43.

56 R. C. Shrader and M. Simon, 1997, Corporate versus independent new ventures: Resource, strategy, and performance differences, *Journal of Business Venturing*, 12: 47–66.

57 M. Guidera, 2000, Report: Research funds to surge, *Waco Tribune-Herald*, January 2, B4.

58 R. Leifer & M. Rice, 1999, Unnatural acts: Building the mature firm's capability for breakthrough innovation, in M. A. Hitt, P. G. Clifford, R. D. Nixon, & K. P. Coyne (eds.), *Dynamic Strategic Resources:*

*Development, Diffusion and Integration* (Chichester: John Wiley & Sons), 433–53.

59 M. A. Hitt, R. D. Ireland, & H. Lee, 2000, Technological learning, knowledge management, firm growth and performance, *Journal of Engineering and Technology Management*, September–December, 17 (3, 7): 321; D. Leonard-Barton, 1995, *Wellsprings of Knowledge: Building and Sustaining the Sources of Innovation* (Cambridge, MA: Harvard Business School Press).

60 S. S. Rao, 2000, General Electric, software vendor, *Forbes*, January 24, 144–46.

61 Ibid.

62 G. Hamel, 1997, Killer strategies that make shareholders rich, *Fortune*, June 23: 70–88.

63 R. A. Guth, 2000, Inside Sony's Trojan horse, *Wall Street Journal*, February 25, B1, B4;

64 C. Taylor, 2000, Game wars, *Time*, March 20, 44–45; *Sony home page*, 2000, www.sony.com (Retrieved March 13).

65 G. G. Dess, G. T. Lumpkin, and J. G. Covin, 1997, Entrepreneurial strategy and firm performance: Tests of contingency and configurational models, *Strategic Management Journal*, 18: 677–95.

66 L. C. Wright and R. W. Wright, 1997, Developing and deploying corporate resources in the technological race to market in H. Thomas, D. O'Neal, and M. Ghertman (eds.), *Strategy, Structure and Style* (Chichester, GB: John Wiley & Sons), 114–35.

67 C. M. Christensen & M. Overdorf, 2000, Meeting the challenge of disruptive change, *Harvard Business Review*, 78 (2): 66–77.

68 A. Goldstein, 1999, IBM plans e-commerce network, *Dallas Morning News*, November 16, D1, D11.

69 P. S. Adler, 1995, Interdepartmental interdependence and coordination: The case of the design/manufacturing interface, *Organization Science*, 6: 147–67.

70 B. L. Kirkman & B. Rosen, 1999, Beyond self-management: Antecedents and consequences of team empowerment, *Academy of Management Journal*, 42: 58–74.

71 Hitt, Nixon, Hoskisson, & Kochhar, Corporate entrepreneurship, 146.

72 A. R. Jassawalla & H. C. Sashittal, 1999, Building collaborative cross-functional new product teams, *Academy of Management Executive*, 13 (3): 50–63.

73 B. Livesey, 1998, Great moments in marketing, *Profit: The Magazine for Canadian Entrepreneurs*, February–March, 34–40.

74 J. A. Byrne, 1993, The horizontal corporation: It's about managing across, not up and down, *BusinessWeek*, December 20, 76–81.

75 Christensen & Overdorf, Meeting the challenge, 68.

76 Hitt, Nixon, Hoskisson, & Kochhar, Corporate entrepreneurship, 149–50.

77  A. C. Amason, 1996, Distinguishing the effects of functional and dysfunctional conflict on strategic decision making: Resolving a paradox for top management teams, *Academy of Management Journal,* 39: 123–48; P. R. Lawrence & J. W. Lorsch, 1969, *Organization and Environment* (Homewood, IL: Richard D. Irwin).

78  D. Dougherty, L. Borrelli, K. Muncir, & A. O'Sullivan, 2000, Systems of organizational sensemaking for sustained product innovation, *Journal of Engineering and Technology Management,* September–December, 17 (3, 4): 321; D. Dougherty, 1992, Interpretive barriers to successful product innovation in large firms, *Organization Science,* 3: 179–202; D. Dougherty, 1990, Understanding new markets for new products, *Strategic Management Journal,* 11 (Special Summer Issue), 59–78.

79  Hitt, Nixon, Hoskisson, & Kochhar, Corporate entrepreneurship, 150.

80  E. C. Wenger & W. M. Snyder, 2000, Communities of practice: The organizational frontier, *Harvard Business Review,* 78 (1): 139–44; J. D. Orton & K. E. Weick, 1990, Loosely coupled systems: A reconsideration, *Academy of Management Review,* 15: 203–23.

81  J. Champy, 2000, Only a few sea turtles survive, *Forbes,* February 21, 96.

82  G. Rifkin, 1998, Competing through innovation: The case of Broderbund, Strategy & Business, 11: 48–58.

83  K. M. Eisenhardt, 1999, Strategy as strategic decision making, *Sloan Management Review,* 40 (3): 65–72.

84  B. B. Flynn & E. J. Flynn, 2000, Fast product development, *Newswise,* March 23http://www.newswise.com/articles/1999/11/TIP1199.BSM.html (Retrieved May 6).

85  S. A. Zahra & W. C. Bogner, 2001, Technology strategy and software new ventures' performance: Exploring the moderating effect of the competitive environment, *Journal of Business Venturing,* 15: 135–73.

86  S. W. Fowler, A. W. King, S. J. Marsh, & B. Victor, 2000, Beyond products: New strategic imperatives for developing competencies in dynamic environments, *Journal of Engineering and Technology Management,* September–December, 17 (3, 4): 357.

87  E. Nickson, 2001, Meet the hydroxyl radical, *National Post,* February 24, B1, B5–B6.

88  P. Kale, H. Singh, & H. Perlmutter, 2000, Learning and protection of proprietary assets in strategic alliances: Building relational capital, *Strategic Management Journal,* 21: 217–37.

89  R. Gulati, N. Nohria, & A. Zaheer, 2000, Strategic networks, *Strategic Management Journal,* 21 (Special Issue): 203–15.

90  Hitt, Ireland, & Lee, Technological learning.

91  B. N. Anand & T. Khanna, 2000, Do firms learn to create value? The case of alliances, *Strategic Management Journal,* 21 (Special Issue): 295–315.

92  S. Miller, 1999, Porsche profits may leave the fast lane, *Wall Street Journal,* December 9, A21.

93  J. A. C. Baum, T. Calabrese, & B. S. Silverman, 2000, Don't go it alone: Alliance network composition and startups' performance in Canadian biotechnology, *Strategic Management Journal,* 21 (Special Issue): 267–94.

94  M. T. Dacin, M. A. Hitt, & E. Levitas, 1997, Selecting partners for successful international alliances: Examination of U.S. and Korean firms, *Journal of World Business,* 32 (1): 3–16; M. A. Hitt, M. T. Dacin, B. B. Tyler, & D. Park, 1997, Understanding the differences in Korean and U.S. executive's strategic orientations, *Strategic Management Journal,* 18: 159–67.

95  G. Hamel, 1991, Competition for competence and interpartner learning within international strategic alliances, *Strategic Management Journal,* 12: 83–103.

96  D. Olive, 2000, A new world in his hands [Excerpt from No Guts, No Glory: How Canada's Greatest CEOs Built Their Empires], *National Post Business,* August, 38–44.

97  M. A. Hitt, R. E. Hoskisson, R. A. Johnson, & D. D. Moesel, 1996, The market for corporate control and firm innovation, *Academy of Management Journal,* 39: 1084–1119; M. A. Hitt, R. E. Hoskisson, R. D. Ireland, & J. S. Harrison, 1991, Effects of acquisitions on R&D inputs and outputs, *Academy of Management Journal,* 34: 693–706.

98  Hitt et al., The market for corporate control.

99  M. A. Hitt, J. S. Harrison, & R. D. Ireland, 2001, *Creating Value through Mergers and Acquisitions: A Complete Guide to Successful M&As* (New York: Oxford University Press); M. A. Hitt, J. S. Harrison, R. D. Ireland, & A. Best, 1998, Attributes of successful and unsuccessful acquisitions of U.S. firms, *British Journal of Management,* 9: 91–114.

100  J. A. Timmons, 1999, *New Venture Creation: Entrepreneurship for the 21st Century* (5th ed.) (New York: Irwin/McGraw-Hill), 440.

101  D. S. Cable & S. Shane, 1997, A prisoner's dilemma approach to entrepreneur-venture capitalist relationships, *Academy of Management Review,* 22: 142–76.

102  T. E. Winters & D. L. Murfin, 1988, Venture capital investing for corporate development objectives, *Journal of Business Venturing,* 3: 207–22.

103  G. F. Hardymon, M. J. DeNino, & M. S. Salter, 1983, When corporate venture capital doesn't work, *Harvard Business Review,* 61 (3): 114–20.

104 U. Gupta, 1993, Venture capital investment soars, reversing four-year slide, *Wall Street Journal*, June 1, B2.

105 As measured by U.S. patents awarded; A. Paul, 1999, Made in Japan, *Fortune*, December 6, 190–200.

106 Petzinger, Jr., So long, R31.

107 Reynolds, Hay, & Camp, *Global Entrepreneurship Monitor*, 7.

108 R. Poe & C. L. Courter, 2000, Small is beautiful again, *Across the Board*, January, 9.

109 Reynolds, Hay, & Camp, *Global Entrepreneurship Monitor*, 4.

110 A. L. Anna, G. N. Chandler, E. Jansen, & N. P. Mero, 2000, Women business owners in traditional and non-traditional industries, *Journal of Business Venturing*, 15: 279–303.

111 L. W. Busenitz, 1997, Differences between entrepreneurs and managers in large organizations: Biases and heuristics in strategic decision making, *Journal of Business Venturing*, 12: 9–30.

112 A. Goldstein, 2000, Culture of money, *Dallas Morning News*, January 30, H1, H2.

113 R. A. Melcher, 1993, How Goliaths can act like Davids, *BusinessWeek* (Special Bonus Issue): 192–201.

114 Champy, Only a few, 96.

115 M. A. Hitt, B. W. Keats, H. F. Harback, & R. D. Nixon, 1994, Rightsizing: Building and maintaining strategic leadership and long-term competitiveness, *Organizational Dynamics*, 23 (2): 18–32.

116 M. A. Hitt, B. W. Keats, & S. M. DeMarie, 1998, Navigating in the new competitive landscape, *Academy of Management Executive*, 12 (4): 22–42.

# NAME INDEX

# COMPANY INDEX

# SUBJECT INDEX

# PHOTO CREDITS